AMDUAT
The Great Awakening

Diana Kreikamp

Mandrake

Copyright © 2021 by Diana Kreikamp, First edition
Second impression 2022

All rights reserved. No part of this Work may be reproduced, distributed, transmitted or utilised in any form or by any means, electronically or mechanically, including xerography, photocopying, microfilm and recording, or via any information storage or retrieval system without the prior written permission of the Publisher. For permission requests, write to the publisher at the address below. Any person who does any unauthorised act in relation to this publication may be liable for criminal prosecution and civil claims of damages.

The Moral Rights of the Authors have been asserted.

Disclaimer
This book is designed to provide information, based on the knowledge and personal experience of the Author, to our readers. It is hoped the reader will find this information useful to apply in their own lives, but this is entirely at their own risk and responsibility. The information in this book should not be used as a substitute for professional advice. Neither the Publisher nor the Author shall be liable for any loss, claim or damage arising out of the use, or misuse of the suggestions made, failure to take professional advice or for any material on third party websites.

Every reasonable effort has been made to acknowledge all copyright holders. Any errors or omissions that have occurred are inadvertent, and anyone with any copyright queries is invited to write to the Publisher, so that full acknowledgement may be included in any reprints and future editions of the Work.

A CIP catalogue record of this book is available from the British Library

Cover Illustration Copyright © 2021 by Diana Kreikamp
Translated by Marly Mosterd

Mandrake, PO Box 250, OXFORD, OX1 1AP, UK

ISBN 978-1-914153-04-4 casebound
ISBN 978-1-914153-05-1 Softcover mono
ISBN 978-1-914153-06-8 Softcover

This book is dedicated to

ANUBIS
Lord of the Secluded Land
He who is over the Secrets

And to

THE ANCIENT ONES
WHO LIVE FOREVER

Contents

ACKNOWLEDGMENTS 8
AUTHOR'S NOTE 9
FOREWORD
By Dolores Ashcroft Nowicki 10
PREFACE 12

PART ONE
INTRODUCTION

The Amduat;
The Book of the Hidden Chamber 16
The Sungod Râ 19
The Mystical journey of the Sungod Râ 21
The Realm of the Duat 23
Osiris, Lord of the Duat 26
The group of Elite Priests 28
Netjeru; the Gods of the ancient Egyptians 32
The Sacredness of the Amduat 35
The Ba, the Ka and the Akh 37
The Ba 38
The Ka 39
The Akh 40
Consciousness; Know Thy Self 42
True Mastery 44
The Great Awakening;
The Way of the Heart 47
A true remedy to a person on earth 52
The Secrecy 53
Symbolism; the language of the
subconsciousness 55
How to descend in the Duat 58
To know; The title of the Amduat 62
The power of the Name 64
Magical Names in the Duat 67
The Amduat in our lives 68
The healing aspect of duality 69
The influence of the Sacred River
during the inundation 71
The Sun barque and its crew 72
Wepwawet "The Opener of the Ways" 74
Sia "Percipience" 77
Nebet wia "Lady of the Barque" 78
Iuf "Flesh (of the Sungod)" 79
Heru Hekenu "Horus of Fragrance" 81
Ka Maât "Bull of Maât 83
Nehes "Wakeful One" 86
Hu "Utterance" 86
Kherep wia "Guide of the barque" 88

PART TWO
THE TWELVE HOURS OF THE NIGHT

THE FIRST HOUR
"Water of Râ" 90
The Entrance to the Duat 91
Introduction 94
The Duatians on the left riverbank
(upper section) 96
The Duatians of The Sacred River
(middle section – upper part) 99
The Duatians of the Sacred River
(middle section – lower part) 104
The Duatians on the right riverbank
(lower section) 110
Closing text 115
Manifestation of the First Hour
in daily life 116

THE SECOND HOUR
"Wernes" 122
Introduction 124
The Duatians on the left riverbank
(upper section) 127
The Duatians of the Sacred River

(middle section) 132
The Duatians on the right riverbank
(lower section) 140
Closing text 144
The manifestation of the Second Hour
in daily life 145

THE THIRD HOUR
"Water of the Unique Lord,
which brings forth nourishment" 150
Introduction 152
The Duatians on the left riverbank
(Upper section) 153
The Duatians of the Sacred River
(middle section) 165
The Duatians on the right riverbank
(lower section) 170
Closing text 174
The manifestation of the Third Hour
in daily life 177

THE FOURTH HOUR
"With Living Manifestations" 182
Introduction 184
The Duatians on the left riverbank
(upper section) 188
The Duatians of the Sacred River
(middle section) 193
The Duatians on the right riverbank
(lower section) 200
The manifestation of the Fourth Hour
in daily life 202

THE FIFTH HOUR
"West" 206
Introduction 208
The route of the Sungod 210
The Duatians on the left riverbank
(upper section) 211
The Duatians of the Sacred River
(middle section) 216
The Duatians on the right riverbank
(lower section) 220
The manifestation of the Fifth Hour
in daily life 225

THE SIXTH HOUR
"Deep Waters, Lady of the Duatians" 230
Introduction 232
The Duatians on the left riverbank
(upper section) 233
The Duatians of the Sacred River
(middle section) 243
The Duatians on the right riverbank
(lower section) 247
The manifestation of the Sixth Hour
in daily life 252

THE SEVENTH HOUR
"Mysterious Cavern" 258
Introduction 260
The Duatians on the left riverbank
(Upper section) 261
The Duatians of the Sacred River
(Middle section) 268
The Duatians of the right riverbank 275
(lower section) 275
The manifestation of the Seventh Hour
in daily life 279
Heka or Magic, the creative force 283

THE EIGHTH HOUR
"Sarcophagus of her Gods" 286
Introduction 288
The Duatians on the left riverbank
(upper section) 291
The Duatians of the Sacred River
(middle section) 297
The Duatians on the right riverbank
(lower section) 300
The Manifestation of the Eighth Hour
in daily life 302

THE NINTH HOUR
"Flowing forth of images, with living manifestations" 308
Introduction 310
The Duatians on the left riverbank (upper section) 312
The Duatians of the Sacred River (middle section) 316
The Duatians on the right riverbank (lower section) 319
The manifestation of the Ninth Hour in daily life 323

THE TENTH HOUR
"Deep water and high banks" 328
Introduction 330
The Duatians on the left riverbank (Upper section) 331
The Duatians of the Sacred River (middle section) 338
The Duatians on the right riverbank (lower section) 343
The manifestation of the Tenth Hour in daily life 345

THE ELEVENTH HOUR
"Opening of the cavern which examines the corpses" 350
Introduction 352
The Duatians on the left riverbank (upper section) 354
The Duatians of the Sacred River (middle section) 361
The Duatians on the right riverbank (lower section) 365
The manifestation of the Eleventh Hour in daily life 369

THE TWELFTH HOUR
"With emerging darkness and appearing births" 376
Introduction 378
The Duatians on the left riverbank (upper section) 379
The Duatians of the Sacred River (middle section) 383
The Duatians on the right riverbank (lower section) 390
The manifestation of the Twelfth Hour in daily life 396

NOTES 404
BIBLIOGRAPHY 417
ILLUSTRATION CREDITS 423
INDEX 424

ACKNOWLEDGMENTS

I wish to express my profound gratitude to both my daughter Marly and to Dolores Ashcroft-Nowicki. Dolores stimulated me to finally pick up my writer's quill and to start writing this book. I wish to thank Dolores for her support and the trust she had in me from the very beginning.

My gratitude also goes to my daughter Marly who skillfully translated the text without losing sight of the essence. She was an indispensable support and companion during the whole process, sacrificing her free time to work with me.

I am most grateful to Theodor Abt who granted me permission to use the texts and pictures in the following two books;

* *The Egyptian Amduat; The Book of the Hidden Chamber* by Erik Hornung and Theodor Abt.

* *Knowledge for the Afterlife; The Egyptian Amduat – A quest for Immortality* by Theodor Abt and Erik Hornung.

It goes without saying that I am indebted to both Erik Hornung and Theodor Abt for their work on the subject of the Amduat.

Furthermore, I am grateful to all the Egyptologists and scholars who have lifted the veil of the amazing world of ancient Egypt for us over the past two hundred years. Their knowledge and understanding of the culture and the language of the ancient Egyptians was invaluable. All of them were a great source of inspiration to me.

My deep appreciation goes to all the artists and scribes of ancient Egypt. I feel great respect, awe and admiration for their work and extraordinary skills. They are the ones who made Egypt grand and eternal.

I am very thankful to Herbie Brennan for sharing his experience and insights about publishing. His support to find a home for my book was invaluable.

I want to say a heartfelt thank you to my publisher Mogg Morgan who edited and gave my book a home.

Last but not least, I would like to thank my husband, for his patience and understanding during all the times where I was busy writing and studying.

AUTHOR'S NOTE

The guide used to write this book is *The Egyptian Amduat, The Book of the Hidden Chamber*, written by Erik Hornung and Theodor Abt. Their book made use of the texts in the tomb of Amenhotep II (KV 35) and of Tuthmosis III (KV 34) in the Valley of the Kings. The schematics of the twelve Hours of the Amduat are, with some exceptions, based on the drawings of the hours as seen in the tomb of Amenhotep II. These drawings display the Deities very clear and in a structured manner. Unlike the tomb of Tuthmosis III, in which several Deities are depicted closely behind each other. Therefore, they are not clearly visible.

In this book the names of the twelve Hours of the night, the Hour Goddesses, Gates, the Guardians and the numbered Deities (No. 1 – 908) originate from *The Egyptian Amduat, The Book of the Hidden Chamber* by Erik Hornung and Theodore Abt. However, I made modifications and alterations to some of these names. These alterations are based on my own knowledge of hieroglyphs and insights unless stated otherwise.

The photographs used in this book are my own and legally taken in Egypt in January 2018 with the use of photo tickets. The exceptions to this are the photographs of objects in the National Museum of Antiquities Leiden in the Netherlands that are owned and provided by the museum. The museum granted permission to use them, for which I am very grateful.

FOREWORD by Dolores Ashcroft-Nowicki

The Last Great Adventure is how my much loved teacher Ernest Butler described Death. This adventure comes to all of us, some dread it, some welcome it. It can come quietly or sadly, it can come violently, but come it will. Over the long centuries of human existence it has remained a mystery not of itself... but of what lies beyond it. Every belief system offers its own idea, its own promise, its own threat, but still the mystery remains.

Books have been written about it ever since writing was invented, each offering explanations and ways of coping with its aftermath. Two of the best known are The Tibetan Book of the Dead, and the Egyptian Book of the Dead. Over time both of them have been translated, explained, talked about, and in some cases re-written to fit in with modern ways of thinking.

What you hold in your hands is an Egyptian Book of the Afterlife as it would have been known thousands of years ago. But with a difference... The author has given many years of her life to its study and she has actually undertaken the journey herself. She did this through meditation and via a series of what is known as Pathworking, or Imaginative Mental Experiences on a high level.

Each part of the journey to the Halls of Osiris has been studied. She has undergone each gateway, prayer, utterance, emotion and visual event with the intent of making the process of passing understandable, as free from dread as possible and accessible during life.

During this journey the author detected within the Amduat something rarely understood. That the Journey, as described in the Amduat, is not just a way to pass over into the Fields of Osiris.... But also a journey into life, an awakening into the full awareness of the Higher Self, its powers, its ability to recognise and use the hidden side of that Self. It has a dual function where it teaches you to die during life to renew your consciousness and prepares you for the departure into Death at the end of your life at the same time.

The Egyptians saw Death as something they looked forward to undergoing. The following is part of a poem written thousands of years ago.

> I have a beloved.
> Each night I hasten towards her.
> I long to stay with her,
> but she sends me away.
> But one day she will enfold me in her arms.
> Do you know the name of my beloved?
> Her name is Death.

This book is unique for it does not glorify Death or preach its supposed horror. It accepts it as another part of the Life experience. Its writer does not say, "This is really what happens." She simply offers what was written by an unknown author in ancient times and says to you, "This is the way they viewed Death and rebirth back then." Each part of the experience can be seen, understood, and experienced as something deeply personal.

The language, the images, the emotions and feelings can be interpreted by the one undergoing the journey. Of course it's a journey…what else can it be? You are going from here… to there. It is a process which takes time and brings you many insights and experiences. Along the way your life will be seen, looked at, examined, undergone in retrospect and remembered with regret, joy, laughter, or despair.

At this moment in life, I am 91 years of age and already, through this book, I have made part of the journey and will go on to complete it… because that is the meaning and the reason for it. This book enables you to undergo the experience while you are still able to change, increase, regret, enjoy, relive, the life you have lived until now. That is the genius of this book. You can experience the adventure before actually taking it. You can undergo all it sets out and by re-experiencing each event of your life, you can know the joy, the excitement, and the pleasure, or regret of what was done. Then you can seek to lessen the impact, if not in deed then by understanding its effect at the time, and offer your sadness while acknowledging your fault.

In effect the Journey is a way of facing the questions of the 42 Assessors and in doing so, clearing the way into the Halls of Osiris.

The detail and the way in which the author has presented each stage in the journey is in fact an entire Lifetime lived as it was meant to be. This is not hellfire and brimstone and an eternity of agony as promised by the overzealous early Christian priesthood. This is saying…. This is what you chose; and this is the result.

To fully understand the journey, you will need to have a grasp of Egyptian imagery, symbolism and mythology. It is not a book for those seeking a gentle read. It will demand your attention, challenge your knowledge and often bring you to despair as your true self is revealed. I have spent most of my life in this kind of work, and have read my way through thousands of books. This has challenged me to retrace my life here and now and to prepare to make the journey when the time comes myself.

The skill, understanding, compassion, and dedication of the author is remarkable. I have seen it through all its many stages and applaud her dedication.

Read it and learn, read it and experience, read it and understand its message.

Dolores Ashcroft-Nowicki
Jersey 2021

PREFACE

Most people are curious about what happens after we make our departure into the Afterlife. The most pressing question usually entails the finality of it all. Is death truly the end of life, the end of our being? Or is death merely the transition to a new place where we can continue our life in a different form? Unfortunately, no person living on earth is able to provide a definitive answer to this mystery. The Egyptian Amduat, "Book of the Hidden Chamber", however, provides a solution to this riddle as it clearly describes the entire journey after death through texts and illustrations. According to the Amduat, it was a journey which lasted twelve hours starting at dusk and ending at dawn.

Without any shadow of a doubt, the ancient Egyptians believed that after death one was reborn into a new life. The Amduat, therefore, provides the encouraging promise that every human being, who embarks on this journey, will renew himself to eventually rise from the dead.

Never before have I found a description of the journey after death as captivating and clearly defined as in the Amduat. It touched me deeply as if a memory, I had previously forgotten, was suddenly awakened deep within. An amazing experience, but also one that raised some questions. Is this journey solely for those who have passed away? Or is it accessible for those still living on earth as well? This voyage centres on the renewal of consciousness wherein the old consciousness dies. In life, we continuously strife to grow and develop our being to renew ourselves. Through our experiences in life and the road towards adulthood, our old concepts and convictions are steadily being replaced by new insights. In other words, life itself is a continuous process of death and rebirth wherein the old is left behind to develop into something new. Therefore, it ought to be possible to embark on such a voyage during the earthly life as well.

To obtain a better insight in this mystery, I began studying the Amduat to decipher it to the best of my abilities. Furthermore, I also studied the complex concepts and convictions of the ancient Egyptians themselves who had created this intriguing book of the Amduat. In doing so, I had created the first opening into the amazing world of the Duat. However, in order to delve deeper into the wisdom of the Amduat, the knowledge of the rational thinking alone is not enough. The heritage of the ancient Egyptians is one that stretches far beyond the plane of the rational thinking into that of magic and spiritual practice. It was a world that consisted of the worship of Gods, rituals, ceremonies, dedication and prayer. This culture connected the earthly visible life to the deeper invisible dimension that lies hidden beneath it. Thus, the wisdom of the Amduat is found in the profound layers far beyond the physical realm. Although it is a realm beyond the horizon, it still lies parallel to the earthly life.

To the living on earth, this invisible dimension is accessible only after leaving the reasoning mind behind. Meditation is one of the techniques to achieve this, which is what I began to do during my mission to explore. I meditated daily using the Amduat, while focussing on the texts and the corresponding Deities of the various hours. During this time, I made three rounds through the twelve hours of this nocturnal world. Each round brought new insights and experiences. It was a truly remarkable and amazing journey of transformation that resulted in the gain of wisdom and in the renewal of my inner and outer world. Missing links and pieces of the puzzle that had been lost before suddenly fell into place, making it a journey of remembrance, the raising of awareness and healing.

Every day I wrote down all of my findings and realisations in a journal. After completing the third and final round, following a decade of practice, I had filled nine voluminous journals with my experiences and accomplishments. As I started to work through these diaries, I realised it had not been a mere spontaneous or coincidental voyage at all. It became clear that the Amduat is actually an ingenious system comprised of a consistent pattern with a clear goal; to awaken and to become aware. Through achieving a connection with the deep dimension of the Amduat by means of meditation, I became a part of this pattern. I started resonating with it, which created an inner communication that provided me with answers, realisations and inspiration. I received inner lessons during which the wisdom given to me began to slowly embed itself in me and into my daily life.

As I made three rounds through the entire Duat, I was able to compare them. Every hour contains specific topics and subjects. During each round, these subjects resulted in similar experiences and realisations in my life. However, during each subsequent round these experiences and realisations became more and more profound as I entered a deeper plane of understanding. The intensity of these experiences forced me to wake up and to look beyond the obvious to see what lies underneath. It opened my eyes and allowed me to transform my perspective of myself and my environment. This cleared and opened the way to develop my talents further and to renew my relation with the world I was living in. In other words, the more I focused on this inner world, more and more doors opened for me. Each one on a deeper level.

The voyage described in the Amduat is, therefore, a journey that can be completed during life as well as after death. It is a journey of awareness that allows us to awaken from the slumber of ignorance. Many people live their lives and simply do what they have to do without being aware of the Greater Plan that lies hidden behind it all. Due to this missing piece of consciousness, these people can only partly comprehend themselves and the world they are living in, or not at all. In this state, they are not aware of the many talents and gifts that lie dormant within them. These slumbering potentials are not activated and cannot be expressed in life. This is very unfortunate since these potentials are a gift that can supply the person with enrichment and fulfilment for themselves as well as for the world.

The Amduat is a timeless and proven system that has been provided for us by the ancient Egyptians. Despite its age, it is not bound to an era, so every spiritual seeker during any time can always use it. It is as applicable in our modern world as it was thousands of years ago. Thus, it is very important that the Amduat is not lost simply because no one is aware of its existence.

Currently, we have experienced thousands of years of evolution during which humankind developed itself and became more aware. The time is ripe to bring the Amduat back into the picture.

It is a road that teaches true Wisdom and Knowledge from the inner dimensions. This allows for our inner world to be mapped. The Duat is a world that centres on memories, dreams, inner thoughts and feelings. However, should you focus only on this psychological content, you will not be able to embark on this journey. Simply following your feelings is not enough. To truly comprehend this inner wisdom and to embed it in life itself, you need some basic knowledge as well. Therefore, this book provides the essential knowledge to prepare for the Great Journey. The journey that prepares you not only for death, but also teaches you to live your life to its full potential and to become a self-aware and awakened human being.

Diana Kreikamp
January 2021

PART ONE

INTRODUCTION

The Amduat;
The Book of the Hidden Chamber

The Amduat was an important funerary text in the New Kingdom of ancient Egypt. It tells of the fascinating story of the journey of the Sungod Râ (r^c) through the twelve hours of the night. The journey commences in the evening as the Sungod Râ dies and he (the sun) sets behind the Western horizon. Râ then embarks on his Night Sun barque to start his twelve-hour-long journey through the nocturnal world of the Duat. The Duat is the realm where the souls of people went after death. Eventually, after the twelve hour journey, the Sungod is resurrected from the dead and is reborn in the East in his new form as Khepri.

The original title of the Amduat is *sesh n ât iment* (*sš n ʿt imn.t*) that translates as "Book of the Hidden Chamber". Another title of the Amduat, from a later period, is *ta medjat imy duat* (*t3 mdj.t imy-dw3.t*), "Book of What is in the Duat". This demonstrates that the word "Amduat" is derived from the hieroglyphic word *imy duat* (*imy dw3.t*), which means "What is in the Duat". The word "duat" (*dw3.t*) is a derivative of the verb *dua* (*dw3*) which means "praise, worship or rise early".

The world of the Duat is divided into twelve different regions. Each region represents a specific hour of the night and has its own landscape and inhabitants. The Book of the Amduat consists of twelve chapters in which each hour of the night is described. Every chapter begins with an introduction text that contains some general information about the progress of the Sungod through that particular hour. The First, Second and the Third Hour end with a closing text as well. The remaining hours do not have such a text. Aside from the accompanying texts, the nocturnal journey is displayed with beautiful illustrations.

Though mythical or legendary this journey may seem, it was an actual voyage performed after death by the Pharaohs, who were considered Gods themselves. During this journey, the Pharaoh followed the example of his father, the Sungod Râ, with the aim to ultimately unify with him. In this unification, the Pharaoh would obtain

Fig. 1. The hieroglyphic word for Duat (*dw3.t*)

immortality, which was the highest goal of the journey. The knowledge of the Amduat was meant for the Pharaoh alone for he represented all of the deceased.

In the New Kingdom, from the 18th to the 21st dynasty, the Amduat text was found exclusively carved and painted on the walls of the tombs of the privileged Pharaohs. A rare exception of a non-royal tomb with the Amduat decoration was the tomb of Useramun (TT 61), who was the vizier of Tuthmosis III and Hatshepsut. The oldest complete version of the Amduat can be found in the tomb of Tuthmosis III (KV 34). Although very beautiful, this version is skilfully painted in a plain style.

As mentioned in the author's note, the guide for this book is *The Egyptian Amduat* written by Erik Hornung and Theodor Abt. Their book, like this book, uses the texts in the tombs of Amenhotep II and Tuthmosis III. Furthermore, the schemata of the hours, with some exceptions, are based on the drawings as seen in the tomb of Amenhotep II. Following is a description of these two tombs.

Tuthmosis III was the sixth Pharaoh in the 18th dynasty of the New Kingdom; ca. 1479 – 1425 B.C. His tomb, KV 34, is situated in a narrow cleft in the Southern end of the Valley of the Kings. The royal necropolis of the Valley of the Kings is located on the West Bank of the Nile, opposite of Thebes, modern Luxor. The entrance of the tomb is cut high in the mountain approximately 98 feet (thirty meters) above the ground. It is an extraordinary tomb decorated with several unusual scenes. For example, the pillared hall contains a special decoration found only in this tomb. On the wall 741 Deities of the Amduat are depicted and described. The Amduat contains a total of 908 Deities including the repeating crew in every hour. The short catalogue on the wall in this hall, however, counts the crew only once and it does not include the punished and the damned.[1] Naturally, the Pharaoh wanted to portray these depraved souls as little as possible. Therefore, these damned and punished souls are depicted only in the Amduat within his burial chamber.

In the left corner of the pillared hall a few steps descend into the burial chamber. The burial chamber is absolutely stunning. It has an ellipse shape, similar to the Cavern of Sokar in the Fifth Hour, and its blue ceiling is decorated with Duat stars. Two pillars, decorated with the "Little Litany" of Râ, which is the "Book of Adoring Râ in the West", support the chamber. In this book 74 (of the 75, the Great Litany) Divine names and forms of Râ are described. These are the forms that he embodies every day. In the back of the burial chamber, a beautiful large red cartouche shaped quartzite sarcophagus can be found. The complete version of the Amduat unfolds on the four walls around the sarcophagus. This results in the King lying literally in the middle of the Duat. The ellipse shape of the chamber divides the Duat in four cardinal directions; North, East, South and West. The head of the sarcophagus is facing North, so the feet point towards the South. In this position the King gazes upon the Fifth and the Twelfth Hour that are depicted next to each other. This is a very befitting position for the King since these two hours signify the beginning of the transformation process and the final rebirth.

The route of the Sungod through the twelve hours is quite interesting since every hour takes place in a specific cardinal direction. The text of the Amduat clearly explains in which specific cardinal direction an hour has to be depicted on the wall in the hidden chamber (i.e. burial chamber). These instructions can be found in the introductory text of each hour. Due to these instructions, the hours do not seem to be depicted in a chronological order on the walls. However, since the Sungod jumps from one cardinal direction to another, he does travel through the hours in a chronological order.

The version in the tomb of Tuthmosis III follows these instructions carefully where the hours are depicted on the wall in the indicated cardinal direction. In the tomb of Amenhotep II the hours are depicted in a chronological order, from the First to the Twelfth, over the four walls

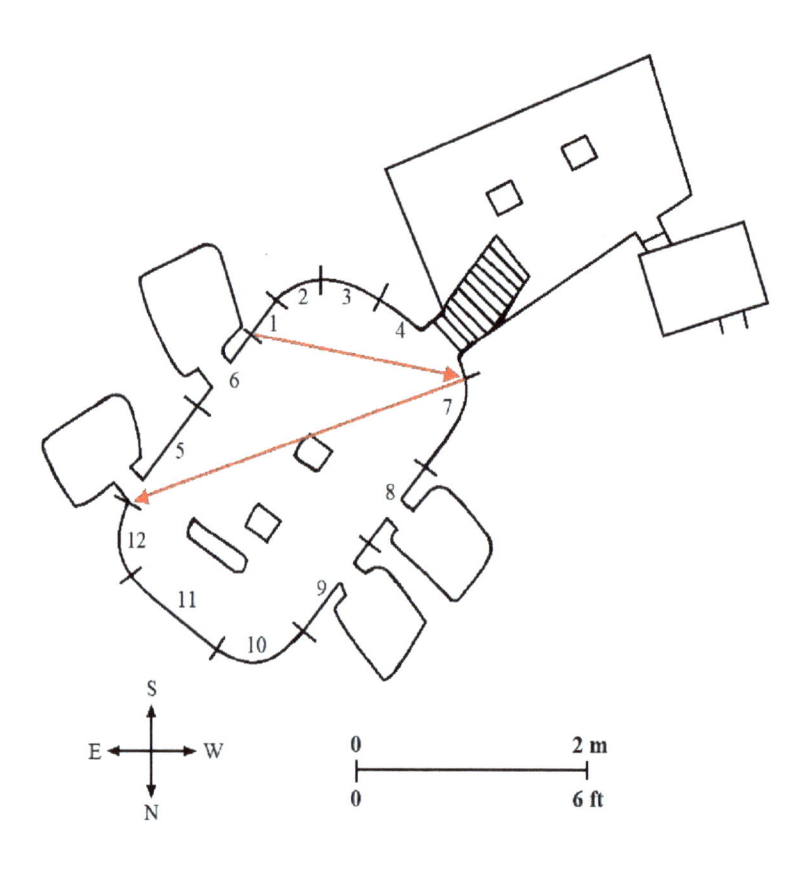

Fig. 2. The arrangement of the twelve hours in the burial chamber of Tuthmosis III.

without interruptions. Consequently, this tomb does not follow the instructed route according the text of the Amduat.

Normally, when the sun sets in the West, the sun travels through the North and rises again in the East, thus skipping South. According to the instructions of the text of the Amduat however, Râ takes a defined route that allows him to travel through all four cardinal directions (fig. 2.). The journey commences on the West wall, the quarter of the setting sun, where the route through the first four hours is performed. After the Fourth Hour the Sun barque turns to the South, making a diagonal jump to the Fifth Hour. The Fifth and Sixth Hour are both depicted on the South wall. After completing the Sixth Hour, the Sun barque turns again, jumping to the North in a straight line. On the North wall the Sun barque travels through the Seventh and Eighth Hour before it turns to the final wall in the East. Here, Râ travels from the Ninth up to and including the Twelfth Hour where he rises as Khepri, the newborn sun.

In ancient Egypt nothing was done without reason since everything was always in line with the world of the Divine. This also applies to the unusual route of the Sungod. The importance of this route will be explained in further detail in the chapter; The Fifth Hour "West", where the Sungod makes his first jump.

Amenhotep II is the son of Tuthmosis III. He is the seventh Pharaoh in the 18th Dynasty of the New Kingdom (1427 – 1397 BC.). The tomb of Amenhotep II, KV 35, has a design similar to that of his father. It is one of the most beautiful graves from the 18th Dynasty. The burial chamber is comprised of two sections and has a rectangular shape instead of an ellipse. The antechamber is supported by six pillars. The quartzite sarcophagus is located in the lower back part that is accessible via a stepladder. Like Tuthmosis III, the burial chamber of Amenhotep II is completely decorated with the Amduat. It is a splendid version that portrays the journey of the Sungod in an orderly and comprehensible fashion.

The Sungod Râ

The Sungod Râ is one of the creator Gods of ancient Egypt dating back to the second dynasty. His name, Râ (*r*ˁ), means "sun". It has also been suggested that *râ* can be translated as "operative or creative power" as well.[2] According to one of the creation myths Râ arose from the primeval waters at the beginning of time. Thus, he was regarded as the supreme creator of the sky, the earth and the Netherworld and of all the beings living there. As the first King, he reigned on earth in accordance with the Divine Law of Order, Truth and Justice or *Maât*. This made him the embodiment of Divine Kingship. When Râ was getting too old, he ascended to the sky where he continued his Divine rulership as the King and God of the heavens. Each following Pharaoh was seen as the descendant and son of Râ.

Râ's cult centre was in the Nile delta, in a city known in ancient Egypt as *Iunu* (*iwnw*). The Greeks renamed the city and referred to it as

Heliopolis, "the City of the Sun" while the Hebrews called it Ôn. Râ can be found in various forms and shapes like a hawk- or ram-headed man who is wearing a solar disk encircled by the Uraeus-serpent on his head. He usually holds the *Ankh*, the sign of eternal Life, in his right hand and in his left hand the *Was*-sceptre, the sign of dominion and power. He can also be found in the form of a radiating sun disk.

In ancient Egypt the sun disk in the sky was the symbol of the body or the Eye of the Sungod Râ. This made him visible to the public from the moment he rose in the morning to the point where he set in the evening, making him a very tangible God to the people. Due to his realistic presence in everyday life, Râ, like various other cosmic Deities, did not have a sanctuary. This was unneeded since he was visible each and every day as he radiated his energy, warmth and light from up high in the sky for everyone to see. His beaming light gave life and colour to the world. This made him a very powerful creator God of the universe. However, his power changed during the day. At noon Râ reached the highest point in the sky where his light was at its strongest and brightest. When Râ continued his journey through the day, the intensity of his light diminished until it vanished completely beyond the horizon of the West at the end of the day.

In other words, the Sungod Râ aged during the day until he finally disappeared in the evening behind the horizon in the West, leaving only a reddish colour in the sky. The ancient Egyptians believed this colour represented the blood shed by the old sun as it was dying. Once the sun had set completely, this colour disappeared and darkness fell over the country. Râ had disappeared and with him the light. His death was symbolised by the setting of the sun. However, twelve hours later, the sun would miraculously rise again, fully regenerated, to fill the sky with his newborn light. This event repeated itself every single day. It was something the people could rely on.

This became the basis of an interesting notion for it seemed death was not irrevocable

The Sungod Râ,
KV 14 Tausert/Setnakht (Valley of the Kings)

after all. Something in the Netherworld could bring the dead back to life. If the Sungod could regenerate and be reborn, would it be possible for other living beings to be resurrected from the dead and live forever as well? What was happening down there in the darkness, hidden from earthly life? Was it possible to unveil this hidden secret? The Amduat suggests it is, presenting us with the key to the hidden knowledge.

The Mystical journey of the Sungod Râ

The story of the Amduat begins the moment the burned out Râ disappears behind the horizon of the West. Râ then transforms into a *Ba*-soul and takes the shape of a ram-headed God. The world is then shrouded in darkness, which is necessary for the earth to assimilate the sunlight of the day. This is the time for the day world to rest, nurtured by the darkness, as long as it does not last longer than twelve hours. This means the sun has to go down and rise again at the right moment. If this does not happen, it would mean the end of all life since both twelve hours of light as well as twelve hours of darkness are essential for life itself. If one of these elements is missing, chaos will rise resulting in death. So the dying Râ now has twelve hours to restore his drained Vital Life Force with the aim to ultimately get his light to shine again to its optimal ability. Osiris, who dwells deep within the Duat, is the embodiment of the Vital Life Force, known as the *Ka*. Râ has to descend behind the horizon of the West, where the entrance of the Duat lies, to find Osiris.

Once in the Duat Râ embarks on his Night Sun barque accompanied by his crew of eight to escort him on his journey. Then he travels through the different hours on his quest to search for Osiris. It is a dangerous journey full of tests and challenges. This world is inhabited by Deities who support and protect Râ, but it houses creatures and demons who want to destroy Râ as well. Every hour contains new threats as well as new supporting powers.

In the deepest part of the night, the Fifth and Sixth Hour, Râ finds Osiris and has a secret meeting with him. This is where the great Mystery, the transformation of death into life, takes place, far away from everyday life. Osiris embraces Râ his *Ba*-soul to transmit his own *Ka* or Vital Life Force to Râ. Râ is infused with this new life force which enables him to transform his extinguished sunlight into the first spark of light.

The unification is followed by six more challenging hours. This is an essential part of the journey since Râ still needs to face the forces of darkness and chaos. It are these confrontations and his struggle against them that transform his vulnerable spark of light into a powerful and radiant sun. The most dangerous opponent during these hours is the horrendous serpent Apophis. He is also known as Apep or Apepi (*ꜥ3pp*) and is the personification of absolute evil. Apophis, the "Lord of Chaos", is on a mission to destroy Râ's light. In doing so, the serpent makes every effort to stop Râ's rebirth to cause death and chaos. Fortunately, Râ does not have to fight this battle between darkness and light alone, for he is supported by several Deities.

And then finally, at dawn, Râ has accomplished his nocturnal journey. During the night Râ has travelled through death starting as the dying light in the First Hour. At the end of the Twelfth Hour Râ emerges rejuvenated and revitalised in the East. Râ is not the same anymore for he has transformed into his new form of Khepri. Khepri is the symbol of the transfigured soul, the *Akh*. Recharged with strength and power he illuminates the world with his new born light.

This journey, and the resulting process, repeats itself day after day in a never ending circle of creation.

> Hymn to the Sungod:
> Hail to you, Râ,
> perfect each day,
> who rises at dawn without failing,
> Khepri who wearies himself with toil!
> Your rays are on the face, yet unknown,
> fine gold does not match your splendour;
> Self-made you fashioned your body,
> creator uncreated.
> Sole one, unique one,
> who traverses eternity,
> remote one, with millions under his care;

The scarab God Khepri, Temple of Horus at Edfu

your splendour is like heaven's splendour,
your colour brighter than its hues.
When you cross the sky all faces see you,
when you set you are hidden
from their sight;
daily you give yourself at dawn,
safe is your sailing under your majesty.
In a brief day you race a course,
hundred thousands, millions of miles;
a moment is each day to you,
it has passed when you go down,
you also complete the hours of night,
you order it without pause in your labour.
Through you do all eyes see,
they lack aim when your majesty sets.
When you stir to rise at dawn,
your brightness opens the eyes of the herds;
when you set in the Western mountain,
they sleep as in the state of death.[3]

The Realm of the Duat

Several funerary texts have described where the realm of the Duat is situated. However, these perspectives differ from one another. This is not surprising since the texts were written by ancient Egyptians who were still very much alive on earth and had not yet actually passed on to this realm. Most commonly, the Duat is explained as the "underworld" for it seemed to be situated beneath the horizon. After all, it tells the story of the setting sun. This indicates it is a place deep below the earth. On the other hand, it could also be seen as a realm in the starry heavens like a celestial sphere where departed souls ascend to.

In actuality, the Duat is not a place deep below the earth like a hellish demon realm in the underworld. Neither is it a place situated somewhere high above earthly life. The Duat is the representation of the Netherworld. The Netherworld in this context refers to the other world *beyond* the world of the living. It is a secret and hidden realm like a parallel dimension where the Gods, spirits and other beings dwell. The Pyramid Texts emphasises this point of view as it describes the Duat as a mystical place, beyond our earthly world. It is the unseen and invisible world that is connected to the Higher realms as symbolised by the celestial body of the Goddess of the sky, Nut.

The Goddess Nut (*nw.t*) is the personification of the heavenly sky. In early times she was seen as the nightly sky adorned with the constellations of the stars. In later times she was identified as the sky during the night as well as the day. She is usually depicted as a nude woman in a bent over body posture while standing on the tips of her toes and fingers. In this way the sky was formed by her enormous body that arched over the entire earth. Her hands, as well as her feet, were positioned close to each other. Somehow each hand and each foot rested upon a cardinal point. Nut was also depicted as a celestial cow with a starry belly.

Her father is Shu, the God of air and her mother is Tefnut, the Goddess of moisture. Geb, the God of the earth, is her brother and also her husband. Nut and Geb loved each other intensely and embraced each other so tight that the earth and the sky formed a single unit. There was no room for any form of life on earth or in the sky. Their father Shu had had enough of their behaviour and separated Nut and Geb from each other. Now there was plenty of space for existence and Nut herself gave birth to five children; Osiris, Isis, Seth, Nephthys and Horus the Elder.

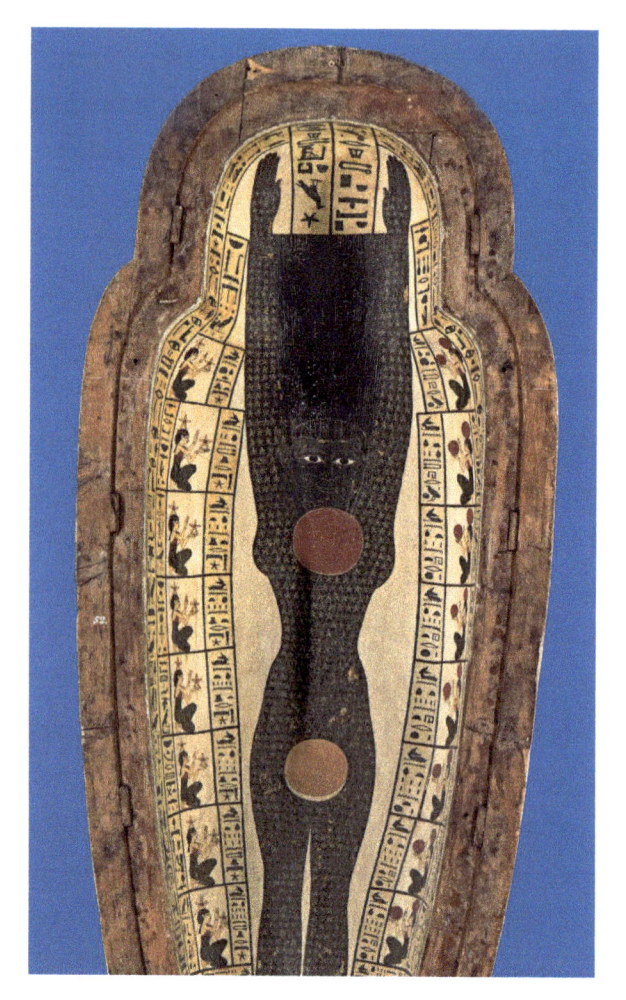

The Sungod Râ travels through the heavenly body of the Goddess Nut. The coffin of Peftjauneith (AMM 5-e); Late period; 26th dynasty c. 650 BC, Dutch National Museum of Antiquities Leiden

Nut has a special relationship with the Sungod Râ. According to one myth Nut, as the celestial cow, lifted the Sungod up between her horns into the sky. She is always there to help him on his journey through the vast expanse of her sky. During the day, Nut's heavenly body supports Râ from the Eastern horizon to the Western horizon. During the night she keeps the vulnerable Râ safe inside her body.

Nut's name is probably derived from the word for water or flood, *nuy* (nwy) or the word for primordial waters or Nun *nunu* (nnw). This is emphasised by her symbol which is a water pot that she sometimes carries on top of her head. The nocturnal world of the Duat that is located in Nut's body is infused with these primordial waters of Nun. When Râ departs as the setting sun, he descends into the Nun. The Nun represents the limitless waters of the primeval flood and symbolises the state before creation; the nonexistence. This is the unrealised potential, predating creation. The ancient Egyptians envisioned the Nun as a watery chaos that surrounded the earth. These waters stretched out far above the sky and deep below in the abyss of the underworld. Consequently, Nun was often referred to as "The Abyss".

The God Nun was the personification of these primeval waters. He was often depicted as a male Deity with the head of a frog or in frog form. With his female counterpart, Nunet, he formed the first pair of the eight oldest Gods, the Ogdoad. This gave him the epithet, the

"Father of the Gods".

> I am Nu, the Sole One who has no equal,
> and I came into being yonder on the great occasion of my flood,
> when I came into being.
> I am he who flew up, whose shape is (that of) *dbnn* who is in his egg;
> I am he who originated in the Abyss,
> and see,
> the Chaos God came out to me;
> see, I am hale.
> I brought my body into being through my power;
> I am one who made myself,
> and I formed myself at my will according to my desire.[4]

– Coffin Texts, Spell 714

The quality of water comes closest to the abstract concept of the Nun. Water is formless, transparent and does not assume a shape of its own. It is infinite, making all directions, dimensions, boundaries and measurements irrelevant. Even though the primeval waters is the nonexistence, this does not mean that it does not exist. In fact, it is very real, though not on the physical layer since it existed prior to the manifestation of the world. The water of Nun is the basic substance from which all living things are created. It forms the foundation and source of life. Every living being needs this "water of life". In fact, creation emerged from the Nun since all life begins in water.

Water is a reservoir of possibilities that precedes every form. The contact with water results in the decomposition or disintegration of every form. This enables regeneration and eventually rebirth. Thus, the island rising from the water is the symbol of creation. Inversely, the submersion in water represents the return to the amorphous state of non-existence. Thus, the cosmic ocean, Nun, is the symbol for life, death and rebirth.

In ancient Egypt, after a period of drought and bareness, the Valley of the Nile was submerged in the primeval waters during the annual inundation in the season called *akhet*. Once the water returned to the riverbed, it left behind a deposit of rich black silt that made the land fertile again. The primeval waters had brought back strength and fertility to the land. Life was purified and vivified as it re-emerged from the life-giving waters of Nun, to begin a new cycle of creation.

Every day, at sunset, the Sungod Râ descends into the world of the Duat. Then he is swallowed by the starry heavens of the Goddess Nut and he immerses himself into the waters of Nun. First, this submersion causes his decay as seen in the Third Hour of the Amduat where he has disappeared completely. These regenerative waters of Nun purify, cleanse and rejuvenate. At sunrise Ra ascends from the nocturnal world of the Duat. Then Nut gives birth to Râ, who re-emerges as Khepri from the waters of Nun in a reborn state of perfection.

Osiris, Lord of the Duat

Osiris, *asir* (*3sir*) or *wsir* (*wsir*), stays behind when Râ leaves the Duat after twelve hours. His place is not in the land of the living like Râ, but in the world of the dead as Lord of the Duat. Here he has a very important task to fulfil where he transforms death through the transmittance of his Vital Life Force. This allows the new life to ascend. Without the Vital Life Force of this Lord of Life, life would simply be impossible and be doomed to disappear.

At some point, Osiris himself was alive on earth as the very first Pharaoh, until his brother Seth killed him through trickery and slashed his body into fourteen pieces. Isis, his wife and sister, gathered the pieces of his dismembered body in her despair. With the help of the God Thoth she rejoined the fragments using her magical powers. Thanks to this miracle, Osiris was resurrected and returned from dead. Despite the victory over death, it was no longer possible for Osiris to return to the earth, which is why he remained in the realm of the dead for the rest of eternity.

Once the body of Osiris was restored to life, Isis became pregnant via magical ways with their son Horus. Hence, Osiris was the first to complete the transformation of life, death and resurrection. As such, he is regarded as the embodiment of the growth cycle of the plants. His germinating power lies deep within the earth and transforms death into life since Osiris is able to reproduce even within the Kingdom of the dead. From within the Duat, Osiris provides for all life with his *Ka* or Vital Life Force to help it fulfil its potential. His Vital Life Force makes the seeds, ensouled by Râ, sprout. The seedlings then grow above the ground and blossom in the earthly life.

Osiris was also known as Wenennefer or Wennefer (*wnn-nfrw*) which means "the Lasting or Completed one". The hieroglyphic word *wenen* (*wnn*) means "to be, to exist or to live". The hieroglyphic word *nefer* (*nfr*) has several meanings including "beautiful, goodness, happiness, perfect or good fortune". The beautiful Osiris has fulfilled the goal of every living being, which is to conquer death. Thus, he is the symbol of perfection and eternal Life. This is why Osiris does not need to die and be reborn like the Sungod Râ. He is the embodiment of the indestructible Vital Life Force that remains for all eternity. Hence, Osiris is passive while Râ is active for the latter embarks on the voyage eternally throughout the day and the night to keep the cycle of life, death and rebirth in motion.

Osiris and Râ thus each symbolise two different concepts of time. Osiris stands for the *djet* (*dt*) time while Râ represents the *neheh* (*nḥḥ*) time. Although both *djet* and *neheh* mean "eternity", they each show a very different side of the movement of time. *Neheh* represents the cycle of life, death and rebirth wherein time keeps moving in circles. *Djet*, on the other hand, shows the completed perfection that moves in a straight line. Despite the fact that the *djet* time does no longer need to change, it does not stand still either for stagnation would mean death. This is inevitable, even for the eternal perfection of the *djet* time. The ancient Egyptians believed that everything that is in existence needs to be renewed. It does not matter whether it is perfect since even the Gods themselves are subjected to this process of regeneration and renewal.

Fig. 3. Neheh time.

Fig. 4. Djet time.

Osiris too participates in this eternal development and continues to move and renew himself. Every single night, he meets the Sungod Râ in secret during the latter's travels through the darkness of the night to become part of the process of regeneration. This daily cycle does not resume each time at the exact beginning point of the previous cycle. Although the sun always rises from the Eastern horizon, it still signifies the beginning on the next level of the renewed cycle. Just like in spring, when the plants and the trees continue their growth from the point where they left off in the winter. Should the growth of nature start from the beginning each time again, plants would return to seeds that still need to sprout. In other words, the development during each cycle would be destroyed as soon as it finished. Obviously, this does not happen since life evolves on and on in a vast upward spiral. To do this, each cycle continues where the previous one left off.

The evolution of life is dependent on the cooperation between Osiris and Râ. Râ can only draw from Osiris his Vital Life Force if Osiris joins in his process of renewal. Osiris is the foundation Râ needs and from which Râ is able to ascend at the end of the Duat. Should the supportive foundation of Osiris stay too far behind in the depths during this uplifting process, it would be impossible for Râ to rise up above the horizon. Thus, Osiris rises together with Râ in the Duat without rising above the horizon himself since he remains in the Duat.

To establish this ascension, Osiris, in turn, requires the ensoulment of the Sungod Râ. Without this daily ensoulment within the deepest point of the Duat, his Vital Life Force loses its power. Therefore, Osiris and Râ have a mutual dependency and are bound together forever. In their relationship they pull each other up even though they both remain moving in their own specific way to renew. In doing so, Osiris rises straight up while Râ spirals around him in his ascent. The light of the Sungod envelops the corpse of Osiris with illuminating wrappings. Osiris then literally and figuratively becomes the central point of life and keeps the evolution of creation in motion together with Râ.

Hail to you, Osiris, Lord of eternity,
King of Gods,
of many names, of holy forms,
of secret rites in temples!
Noble of *Ka* he presides in Djedu,
he is rich in sustenance in Sekhem,
Lord of acclaim in Andjty,
Foremost in Offerings in Ôn.
Lord of remembrance in the Hall of Justice,
secret *Ba* of the Lord of the cavern,
holy in White-Wall, *Ba* of Râ, his very body.
Who reposes in Hnes,
who is worshipped in the *naret*-tree,
that grew up to bear his *Ba*.
Lord of the palace in Khnum,
much revered in Shashotep.
Eternal Lord who presides in Abydos,
who dwells in the graveyard,
whose name endures in peoples' mouth.
Oldest in the joined Two Lands,
nourisher before the Nine Gods,
potent spirit among spirits.
Nun has given him his waters,
North wind journeys south to him,
sky makes wind before his nose,
that his heart be satisfied.
Plants sprout by his wish,
Earth grows its food for him.
Sky and its stars obey him,
the great portals open for him
Lord of acclaim in the Southern sky,
sanctified in the Northern sky,
the imperishable stars are under his rule,
the unwearying stars are his abode.
One offers to him by Geb's command,
the Nine Gods adore him,
those in *dat* kiss the ground,
those on high bow down.
the ancestors rejoice to see him,
those yonder are in awe of him.[5]

– A section of the Great Hymn to Osiris

Figure 5: The Sungod (neheh time) spirals around Osiris (djet time).

The group of Elite Priests

In the early days the Pharaoh was not only the King but also the High Priest of Egypt. As mediator between his people and the Gods, he occupied a position with political as well as religious authority. In his role as "Lord of the Two Lands" he was the ruler of Upper and Lower Egypt. The term "Lower" and "Upper" is based on the direction of the Nile from South to North, where it flows from Northeastern Africa into the Mediterranean Sea. Lower Egypt was the Northern region, including the Cairo region and where the Nile branches out into the Nile Delta. Upper Egypt was the Southern region from Thebes (Luxor) to Aswan. The Pharaoh was in possession of this land and defended Egypt against intruders as leader of the army. All the inhabitants of Egypt were indebted to pay taxes to him. He wrote the laws and brought Order, Justice and Truth, or *Maât*, upon the land.

The concept of *Maât* was a central theme in ancient Egypt. The Goddess Maât is the embodiment of this concept of the cosmic order and harmony. The German Egyptologist, Siegfried Morenz, has defined this complex concept very clearly.

> *Maât* is right order in nature and society, as established by the act of creation, and hence means, according to the context what is right, what is correct, law, order, justice and truth. This state of righteousness needs to be preserved or established, in great matters as in small. *Maât* is, therefore, not only right order but also the object of human activity. *Maât* is both the task which man sets himself and also, as righteousness, the promise and reward which await him on fulfilling it.[6]

– Siegfried Morenz

The Gods created and established the Divine order or *Maât*. Since the Pharaoh was seen as the living God on earth, it is understandable that the maintenance of *Maât* was his primary task. In his leading role he used human actions to serve the Gods and to bring the army against chaos and destruction. As soon as there was order in the world of the humans, there would also be order in the world of the Gods, which would then allow for contact with them.

Another title and task of the Pharaoh was "High Priest of Every Temple". It was his responsibility to see to the needs of the Gods in order to assure their good will or to appease their ill will. In doing so, he guaranteed creation, and therefore life itself, continued. He had to perform the sacred rituals every day in the sanctuary of all temples scattered throughout Egypt to serve the Gods. The sanctuary, or Holy of Holies, was the resting place of the God and the Pharaoh was the only person allowed to enter this sacred area of great spiritual power. Due to the vast amount of temples in Egypt this task was, of course, an impossible one. For this reason, the Pharaoh appointed men and women from the priests who served in the temples. This selected group received the title of "High Priests" and performed the sacred rituals in the name of the Pharaoh.

As mentioned, the Pharaoh was seen as the embodiment of a living God on earth and was privileged, after death, to accompany the Sungod

Râ on his journey through the twelve hours of the night. In doing so, he represented all of the people in Egypt, since the journey of rejuvenation was inaccessible to the common citizens. The Pharaoh was the guiding example, guarding the cycle of regeneration and rebirth so creation could continue.

However, this journey was comprised of far more than what the common people were able to perceive. First of all, the Pharaoh was actually not the only person to undergo this journey of renewal. Secondly, the journey was not exclusively made after death as it was possible to venture through the Duat during life as well. That being said, the undertaking of the voyage took many years of training and preparation and was, therefore, accessible only for an elite group of priests who had the means and training to do so.

This group of elite priests dedicated their lives as servants of the Gods, spending a lifetime in service of the temple. Their intensive training was performed in complete secrecy and consisted of various exercises like meditation, visualisation, dream work, the study of the sacred texts, the performance of rituals, rites and ceremonies.

When the required level of development was finally reached after many years of training, the candidate would undertake the journey through the twelve hours of the night. This was regarded as the highest level of initiation, known as the

Seti I offers a small figure of the Goddess Maât, the symbol of Order, Justice and Truth, during an important ritual "the Presentation of Maât", Temple of Seti I at Abydos

Great Awakening. The intensity and extraordinary exertion needed to complete this final step was achievable for a select few only. The initiation was performed inside a sarcophagus, which symbolised the hidden realm of the Duat. The candidate had to remain inside for three days and nights. However, even a lifetime of intense training and preparation was not always enough to prepare the candidate for this last trial, ultimately resulting in the death of the latter. Nevertheless, if the candidate was able to overcome the last test, he would rise from the sarcophagus having transformed death into a new life.

The resulting intense transformation gave the initiate the opportunity to experience death during their life, preparing for death as well as for the rebirth thereafter. The most important reason for the journey, however, was to create an intimate inner connection between the different layers of consciousness, the *Ba* and the *Ka*, within oneself. This re-connection would lead to the awakening of the Divine Spark, the *Akh*, within, transforming the candidate into a transfigured soul. The state of inner illumination was accomplished without freeing oneself from the physical body, as in death.

Henceforth, the connection with the Divine Spark gave the initiate unrestricted access to the Duat, enabling him to descend and emerge upon his own free will. The initiate was, therefore, also known as "The walker between the worlds". After the intense transformation, the initiate was granted the title of "Winged One". The Divine Spark now radiated through the Higher Self in the heightened consciousness of the initiate. This caused a subtle radiance around the initiate that resembled wings. Subsequently, this transformation led to a connection and communication with the Gods or *Netjeru* and the spirit world.

> Opening the Netherworld
> and going in and out from it.
> The Sole One shines,
> and I go forth among his multitudes;
> I walk side by side with (?) them,
> namely those who are in the sunshine;
> I have opened the Netherworld.[7]
> – Coffin Texts; Spell 108

It was very important to undertake this journey of regeneration to transform the consciousness of the candidate to a higher level. It was an act of devotion to offer life to the Sacred. When making something sacred, you are required to manifest it by touching it and living it, here and now, in everyday life. The initiates acted as servants and mediators of the Gods for the benefits of others, helping and teaching other people to raise their consciousness as well.

By no means were the initiates allowed to seclude themselves from their earthly lives. In fact, the initiation was never intended to liberate the candidate from his earthly tasks. On the contrary, the purpose of life is to obey the Law of the Gods and signify the manifestation of

Order, Justice and Truth, *Maât*, in life itself. Therefore, these priests were required to occupy an exemplary function to the general folk and live their lives in accordance with *Maât* through the obtained Inner Wisdom.

> Forget "elites" and recognise the true Elite. It is formed of individuals who have already gone beyond Nature. To be of the Elite is to want to give and to be able to give; it is to know how to draw on the inexhaustible source and give this food to those who are hungry and thirsty in the form which is suited to them.[8]
>
> – R. Schwaller de Lubicz

Although the Amduat is known as a funerary text, the above-mentioned text implies it was not. The Pharaoh and the group of elite priests used the text to become initiates and they were most certainly still alive. When studying and experiencing the Amduat, you will get to understand its true meaning and intention. It is the road to initiation for those who are alive on earth and wish to heighten their consciousness. The text with the corresponding images serves as a guide, showing us the way to our goal step by step. It is a proven system which has been used for thousands of years and is still applicable today. Thus, it holds an enormous value for the modern human being as well.

As mentioned in the Preface, the best method for working with this proven system is by means of meditation. The exact technique of how to do this will be explained in further detail in chapter "How to descend in the Duat".

Netjeru, the Gods of the ancient Egyptians

The ancient Egyptian word for God is *Netjer* (n̲tr). The hieroglyph for *Netjer* is a pole with a pennant on top. The pennant consists of strips of bandages, similar to the wrappings of a mummy, and both the top and the bottom are slanted. *Netjeru*, in its plural form, means "Gods". The hieroglyph for *Netjeru* is depicted as three flags, or one flag with three vertical stripes next to it;

or.

A flag or pennant is the symbol for a country, a state, residence or an organisation, and should be treated with dignity and respect. The flag of the hieroglyph *Netjer* symbolises the realm of the Gods. The bandages forming the flag symbolise the wrappings used to bandage the deceased during the mummification process, "That which is placed in the coffin". This protected the deceased from decomposition to enable the transformation of death into life. The *Netjeru* went through this transformation, leaving the perishable body behind in order for the soul to ascend as the Divine Spark, the *Akh*. The *Netjeru* are "out of their wrappings", revealing their true

Divine nature.

In the final phase of the Egyptian language, the Coptic language was formed. This was a mix of Egyptian with an adaptation of the Greek alphabet. The Coptic word *nutar*, meaning "sustaining power" or "Divine force", possibly is a remnant of the Egyptian word *Netjer*. *Nutar* is phonetically related to other terms with the same meaning, such as "nature" in English and "natura" in Latin. *Nature* is a term usually used to refer to the natural world, geology and wildlife. The Latin term *natura* refers to the qualities or capacities of a person, but in ancient times it meant "birth". In a sense, both terms refer to creation as nature is generally perceived as the mother of creation, and birth in itself is of course a form of creation. Furthermore, the qualities and capacities of a person are tools to enable creativity or creation. *Netjer*, as the possible origin of both words, is also a principle of creation. Every *Netjer* represents a specific force and energy found in nature. These *Netjeru* helped the ancient Egyptians to understand the energies and forces in nature and, therefore, the many aspects of the Divine.

The God Osiris had been a living King on earth before he died and became a God. This is why the earliest Pharaohs were regarded as living Gods. Therefore, the Divine was the central focus of the ancient Egyptians, as they knew they were of direct Divine origin. Divinity was in their blood and part of their being. The ancient Egyptians did not experience the *Netjeru* as abstract or remote, but rather as a presence all around them visible in nature and signifying their ancestors. The *Netjer* was a Divine substance, present in every aspect of the physical world. There was no separation between the physical world and the world of the Divine. As above so below. As within so without.

> The *Netjer* is the active power which produces and creates things in regular recurrence; which bestows new life upon them and gives back to them their youthful vigour.
> – Dr. Heinrich Karl Brugsch

Since every force and energy was perceived as a Divine influence, the *Netjeru* played an important role in everyday life. Most of them had temples dedicated to them. Even though the temples were an essential part of the community, they did not serve as public religious centres, as do the churches today. Ordinary people were allowed only in the outer court of the temple. During sacred celebrations, festivals and processions the people took part in the festivities as an audience in the ceremonies, but still only in the outer court.

The temple was known as the "House of God" and considered the physical residence of the specific *Netjer* it was dedicated to. The concerning *Netjer* ensouled the temple to make it a holy place. The priests honoured the *Netjeru* by means of daily rituals, offerings, prayers, singing of hymns, recitation of sacred words, and so on. The *Netjeru* in turn would then maintain the Divine order of life itself. Aside from performing the daily ceremonies and rituals it was required for the priests to pass through different stages of initiation to prepare them for an eternal union with the *Netjeru*. In doing, so they would become a *Netjer* themselves which was the ultimate goal of every novice.

There were several different kinds of *Netjeru* that varied in importance. The state *Netjeru* were the most important ones and well-known all over Egypt. Their temples were scattered throughout the country and the festivals in their honour were national celebrations. The priesthoods were appointed by the Pharaoh or vizier and were responsible for the care and worship of the *Netjeru*. There were also *Netjeru* who were worshipped only in specific areas or locations and had their own festivals and ceremonies. The people built the shrines themselves for their local *Netjer* and appointed priests from their own community. Lastly, the least important *Netjeru* were the ones who took residence on the private altar of the people at home, the household Deities. This allowed the common people to have a connection with the Divine through prayers and placing offerings in front of the statue. Thus, Egypt was a very religious nation wherein all layers of the population took part, from the beginning until the end of their history.

Around the 19th Dynasty there were about 1200 Gods, a huge number. It was not surprising specific characteristics of certain Gods became mixed up. In time, the Gods changed wherein some Gods merged as one or a God adopted the function of another, changing their position entirely. This intricate cosmological system complicates the process to define the Gods. This explains why it is impossible to categorise every *Netjer* in order to comprehend their nature. The *Netjeru* extend beyond and across all borders of the perception of the human mind.

Some say the Egyptian Gods were viewed as immanent, due to their so called physicality they were present in everyday life. In contrast to most Gods from other religions that are often transcendental and seen as a higher power, invisible and untouchable. However, this concept of the Egyptian Gods is not entirely correct. The world of the *Netjeru* represents the macrocosm, or omnipresence. The particular Divine principles of this world are reflected in the nature of the microcosm, which signifies our own personal existence. From the human point of view, which lies in the microcosm, it is extremely difficult, if not impossible, to grasp the concept of the vast macrocosm. Because of this, the abstract concept of the Divine was divided into several concrete Gods. In doing so, these Gods were more comprehensible and real for human beings and this helped them to understand the omnipresence of the Divine. It allowed mankind to identify the Divine and acknowledge its presence within themselves. Judging from the enormous amount of Gods worshiped in the various temples, this principle was well understood among the ancient Egyptians.

The Gods can take various forms: that of a

human, animal, a combination of a human with an animal head or even combinations of several animals. Many different Gods are present in the Amduat although they are not always easily recognisable since they sometimes adopt a different form and name than customary. These alterations originate from the specific principle the *Netjer* embodies that can have different consequences depending on the situation. The Goddess Isis, for example, has many names and forms. In the Second Hour she appears in two forms as she is a cobra (No. 150) on the Sun barque of Râ as well as an investigator (No. 149) with a knife on the left riverbank. In the Fifth Hour, her name is "Flesh of Isis who is upon the sand of the Land of Sokar" (No.374), a form in which she covers the oval of Sokar to protect it. In that same hour she is also depicted in the form of a wailing bird (No. 345). In the Sixth Hour she makes another appearance, this time in the form of Isis-Tait (No. 421).

The Sacredness of the Amduat

During the Old Kingdom (5th and 6th Dynasty) magical and ritual spells were carved on the walls of the corridors and burial chambers of the pyramids at Saqqara. The oldest texts have been dated between ca. 2353 – 2107 B.C. These texts were called the "Pyramid Texts". They were comprised of spells meant to guide the deceased Pharaoh and enabled him to ascend into the Afterlife safely. These spells ensured that the Pharaoh would regain his freedom of movement in the Afterlife and provided him with water and food. Naturally, there were also many spells intended to protect the Pharaoh from various kinds of evil that would confront him on the way. Some of the spells refer to the Duat without detailed descriptions of the twelve hours of the night.

However, the twelve hour journey through the Duat had been performed by every Pharaoh since ancient times, long before any sign of such rituals were inscribed on walls, papyri and coffins. The lack of physical evidence of this journey confirms the sacredness of the knowledge. In the beginning of the ancient Egyptian history, the knowledge was conveyed exclusively through oral transmission and only to the few chosen ones. These chosen ones, the elite priests, became the initiates and were thus able to fully comprehend the value of the wisdom bestowed upon them. In keeping the knowledge secret, they prevented its desecration as would happen if given to the common people who did not understand its value, or so called "casting pearls before swine". The Greek philosopher Plato acknowledged this way of teaching in one of his letters as he believed knowledge should be obtained without writing it down. Oral transmission would prevent the knowledge from reaching the ignorant for they could interpret the wisdom incorrectly and desecrate it in the process.

Be especially careful that you need

never be sorry for having allowed these things to fall into unworthy hands. The best precaution is not to write but to learn, since it is impossible for what has been written not to be lost.[10]

– Plato

It was not until the 18th dynasty that the walls of the tombs of the Pharaohs were decorated with the Amduat. The use of the sacred text had changed as it was now visibly registered in the tombs. In spite of this change, the text was coded and thus still inaccessible to the ignorant. However, something interesting had occurred as the conveyance of the knowledge had been transferred from the "audible" realm to the written and painted "visual" realm. This made the knowledge more tangible, more real. In other words, the knowledge came into being. This is the next step in creation, a very powerful thing and obviously an act of applied Magic.

The entire journey was now manifested on the walls of the tombs, from the beginning of the First to the end of the Twelfth Hour. The journey had taken root in the present, every hour, all the Deities and beings and all the forces, visible and tangible on the walls. This is how it connected past, present and future, bridging the time aspect in a timeless dimension. This immemorial journey had, therefore, already taken place and been completed as proven by the inscriptions on the walls. Naturally, the Pharaoh was still required to complete the transformation through the twelve hours himself, but fortunately he could make use of the guidance of the visual representation and the text of the Amduat. Now he was assured of a good ending wherein the goal, "Rebirth and thus eternal Life", was guaranteed.

Since the Amduat had now manifested in the present, not only the Pharaoh and the elite priests, but also a few workmen who were excavating and decorating the beautiful tombs in the Valley of the Kings exclusively for the Pharaoh, became acquainted with the knowledge. The full title of these workmen was "servants in the Beautiful Place of the mighty King". They lived in the village hidden from the outside world called Deir el-Medina, situated near the Valley of the Kings. It was also known as *Set Maât*, "Place of Truth", and according to some papyri this was another name for the Netherworld.

These artists did not simply copy the texts and images without having any knowledge of the exact contents. When you take a closer look at the versions of the Amduat in the tombs, especially the tomb of Seti I, you will notice it is so much more than just a copy. The artists knew exactly what they were painting and carving on those walls, grasping the deeper meaning behind every image. Even after thousands of years, the knowledge and understanding is still shining through those beautiful and refined pieces of art, charged by the artists with magical power.

At the end of the New Kingdom the Amduat was further manifested through writings on papyri. It was no longer a privilege for the King alone. Now even non-initiates could decorate their coffins with it. This change in the use of the Amduat, however, did lead to the modification of its meaning. Now having certain knowledge of its existence did not make you a "Winged One" since you would still lack the deep wisdom and understanding of the Amduat that still required training and practice.

The *Ba*, the *Ka* and the *Akh*

The ancient Egyptian view of the body was that it existed of nine different principles. The *Khat* (the physical body), *Khaibit* (shadow), *ib* (the heart), *Sekhem* (power), *Ren* (the name or words of power), *Ba* (the soul), *Ka* (the Vital Life force), *Akh* (transfigured soul or Divine Spark) and *Sâhu* (spiritual body). Although all of these principles have a part in the journey throughout the Duat, it are the *Ba*, the *Ka* and the *Akh* that fulfil the most important roles.

As mentioned, the Sungod Râ represents the *Ba*. Osiris, as the embodiment of the Vital Life Force, represents the *Ka*. And Khepri, the form of the newborn sun, is the *Akh*. These principles, that are part of the unseen realm, are not easy to grasp for the reasoning mind. They cannot be categorised for it is impossible to give these concepts a black-and-white explanation. These concepts consist of different layers where each layer has its own energy. This is especially true for the *Ba* and the *Ka* that cannot be seen separate

Deir el-Medina "Place of Truth"

from each other. There is a strong interaction between these two concepts where they interchange their active and passive roles with one another. Moreover, the interaction between the principles of the *Ba*, the *Ka* and the *Akh* is essential in the process of regeneration and rebirth. It is, therefore, obligatory to gain more insight in these concepts.

The *Ba*

Fig. 6. The Ba.

The *Ba* (*b3*), known as the "Breath of Life", gives us life. The word *Ba* is similar to the hieroglyph for the word "ram" which represents power and strength. The Sungod Râ transforms into a *Ba*-soul as he descends into the Duat. Then he changes from his usual sun form into a Deity with a ram's head.

The *Ba* is the non-physical essence, the soul, represented by a bird with a human head and a ceremonial Divine beard. Its wings signify the fact that it is able to move between heaven and earth. The *Ba* is not bound to the physical body since it originated from the higher planes. Still, it is in close contact with the person whom it animates as it functions as a guide during life. It is similar to the Higher Self in man, the link between the spirit world and our day consciousness, which inspires us through insights and dreams.

> The uniform darkness, fount of the Gods,
> the place from which birds come: […]
> How these birds exist is
> with their faces as people
> and their nature as birds,
> one of them speaking to the other
> with the speech of crying.
> After they come to eat plants
> and to get nourished in the Black Land,
> alighting under the brightness of the sky,
> then they change into their nature of birds.[11]

– From the ceiling of the Cenotaph of Seti I at Abydos

After death, the *Ba* travels to the *Ka* to melt together and transform into the *Akh*, the Divine Spark. Due to the Divine nature of the *Ba* it will return to the Great Consciousness when the final breath escapes the body.

Although the *Ba* is impersonal and universal, it is conditioned by its connection with the *Ka*. Since the *Ka* is linked to our destiny, which is determined at birth, the *Ba* is connected to this as well.[12] In other words, the *Ba* and the *Ka* form a pair so to speak. The *Ba* animates the *Ka* whereas the *Ka* provides for the stability the formless *Ba* needs to manifest. Due to its freedom of movement, the *Ba* is also capable of connecting with the *Akh*, the Divine Spark.

On a cosmic level, the *Ba* is the cosmic soul who gives life to the universe as the spirit of fire. In the beginning there is the *Ba*, in the end there is the *Ba* and between these two extreme concepts the *Ba* resides in everything.[13]

Hence, the Divine *Ba* was considered omnipresent and was therefore also known as the World-Soul. It is the soul of the universe, the soul of nature and, at the same time, the soul of the Gods and men. In addition, the Divine statues of the Gods were seen as the residence of the *Ba* to enable men to communicate with the Gods. As the Gods possessed several *Ba's*, they were able to manifest their presence in various different shrines or temples at the same time. This emphasises the omnipresent nature of the *Ba*.

As the representative of the Divine Law of Order, Truth and Justice or *Maât* the *Ba* is our True inner Voice. Thus, when the person is in contact with his *Ba*, the *Ba* resides in his heart and the person will live his life just and true. After death the person travels to the Hall of Judgement where his heart is weighed in the balance against the feather of Truth. The heart, as the residence of the *Ba*, will be as light as a feather and the person will be permitted to stand before Osiris.

The *Ka*

Fig. 7. The Ka

The *Ka* (*k3*) is depicted with two extended upraised arms from a horizontal base to show the muscles of the breast. The *Ka* was never well defined in the texts of ancient Egypt and is thus difficult to grasp, especially from Western concepts. In general, the *Ka* is a transmitter of the Vital Life Force on different levels and prevents the decay of the body. The symbol of the *Ka* seems to be a gesture of protection and love. By embracing someone, the transmission of the Vital Life Force takes place.

On an individual level, the *Ka* contains the unique characteristics and potential of a person, like an imprint. The *Ka* is the inner protector of our unique talents and embraces us with our potential to help us to manifest our qualities in life as our own unique signature. Hence, it is linked to ones destiny in life.

There is not one English term to describe the complete essence of the *Ka*, though the Power-self in the subconscious realm is comparable with it. This will be further explained in the chapter "True Mastery".

When the *Ka* leaves the body, the person no longer belongs to the world of the living for he has died. The ancient Egyptians believed that the *Ka* of the deceased needed food and drink and would come back to the tomb to obtain these offerings. The offerings consisted of all sorts of food, flowers and a bowl of water which were used to perform the offering ritual. The offerings were placed on an offering table that stood in front of the false door situated in the West wall of the tomb. This door was a gate, a divine entrance, between the world of the living and the world of the dead. The *Ka* of the deceased used this portal to ascend into the sky and to come and go when needed to acquire the offerings. It was the embodiment of the vitalising quality presented in the food and drink. Therefore, it did not feed itself with the physical food, but with the Vital Life Force within it.

On a cosmic level, the *Ka* represents the power of life. It is the bearer of all the powers of manifestation that realise the continuation of creation.[13] The *Ka* is a principle of attraction and fixation and its power attracts, stabilises and transforms the transparent and formless animating principle, the *Ba*.[12] The creator was the one who transmitted the *Ka* to the human beings and the Gods. Although humankind possessed a single *Ka*, the Gods could have several *Ka's*.

The *Ka* also symbolised the powerful and virile bull, which was associated with the Pharaoh. Usually, following the first thirty years of reign of the Pharaoh, his vital force or *Ka*-force was tested during the Sed festival *(Heb Sed)*. The festival was also known as the Feast of the Tail, referring to the King's ceremonial garment with a tail attached to the backside. It is possible that this feast was related to the jackal God Sed *(sd)* whose name means "(bulls) tail". Sed was an important protector of the King and also a protector of justice. Allegedly, he was associated with the concept of *Maât* and possibly with the Goddess Maât herself. Usually, he is depicted as a jackal standing on a standard. This standard, which is also associated with Wepwawet, was often carried up front to open the way for the King during the ceremonies of the festival.[14]

The *Heb Sed* was a sacred feast during which the Pharaoh reaffirmed his dedication to the Gods. Naturally, devotion and offerings were paramount here. Another purpose of the Sed feast was the renewal of the Kingship of the ageing Pharaoh. It reaffirmed his possession of the vital power needed to rule the country. During one of the ceremonies, the Pharaoh was required to demonstrate his vitality and strength by running a ritual race at full speed around a fixed course. This reanimated the force of the *Ka* and increased and renewed his royal power. Additionally, the Pharaoh, as the representative of his country, would also rejuvenate the *Ka*, the Vital Life Force, of Egypt itself. Hereafter, the subsequent Sed festivals were held every three to four years.

The *Akh*

Fig. 8. The Akh.

The *Akh* (*3ḫ*) is the blessed or transfigured soul of a person after death. To become an *Akh*, the *Ba* and the *Ka* must be reunited. In the Pyramid Texts the *Akh* is often mentioned as "Shining

One" or "Effective One" and depicted with the hieroglyph of the crested ibis. The verb *akh* (*3ḥ*) denotes both the process of becoming an *Akh* and the quality of becoming or being "effective". The *Akh* never changed or perished and was believed to remain the same forever. It is the unchangeable spark of life, the Divine Spark, found in every human being and the symbol for immortality.

In the Amduat, the *Akh* is represented by the God Khepri, the form of the Sungod Râ after his rebirth, as the new dawning sun. Due to his shining appearance, the Pyramid Texts sometimes addresses him as the "Shining One". He is a God with the head of a scarab or dung beetle. The Egyptian dung beetle is typically seen rolling balls of dung over the ground, which he uses as a food source, but also to lay eggs inside. The ancient Egyptians thought the newborn beetles would then spontaneously emerge from the dung ball. Therefore, the dung beetle was seen as the personification of Khepri, the creator God. The rolling of the ball was the representation of the movement of the sun across the sky. The name of Khepri (*ḥpri*) means "the Becoming One" or "He who is coming into being" and refers to this movement and development. The name Khepri is derived from the verb *kheper* (*ḥpr*) which translates as "come in to being, to become, be effective, to create, to develop".

The ancient Egyptians saw the *Akh* as the stellar body that radiated for eternity. The *Akh* was powered by the stars and, thus, consisted of stardust. Every human would eventually return to the original source of the stars and become a star in the sky. Therefore, the ancient Egyptians already knew that the body of a human is actually structured from the same materials as the stars, stardust, since matter never truly disappears.

Stardust is formed by the solar system and is part of the makeup of everything that exists in our solar system. The atoms forming our bodies have been part of some star before, so ultimately everyone is made up of stardust. We are part of the cosmic evolution that has lasted for billions of years and we all originate from the same source of existence. We are truly stars on earth and will eventually return to the Great Source.

Interestingly, the dung beetles are particularly well suited to represent the essence of the *Akh* since they are the only known insects able to navigate using the Milky Way. Two of its four eyes are always pointed upwards as they focus on the galaxy. The shining lights of the stars guide it as it tries to find its way. These stars can be perceived as the Divine upon which the dung beetle navigates when it looks up. Hence, possibly, the ancient Egyptians knew this fact as they envisioned the dung beetle as the perfect personification of the *Akh*. Like the beetle, to unite the *Ba* and the *Ka*, one should let himself be guided by the Divine. Only then, from this unity, will the *Akh* be born.

When an Egyptian was born he was believed to possess a physical body (*Khat*) and an immaterial Double (*Ka*), which lived inside the body and was associated closely with the *Ba*, which dwelt in the heart, and which appears to have been connected with the Shadow of the physical body. Somewhere in the body lived the *Khu* (*Akh*) or Spirit-soul, the nature of which was unchangeable, incorruptible, and immortal. When the body died there could be raised from it by means of words, holy or magical, and ceremonies performed by the priests, a Spirit-body called *Sâhu*, which the *Khu* (*Akh* or Spirit-soul) could inhabit at pleasure. The *Ka*, *Ba*, or Heart-soul, and Shadow dwelt in the tomb with the body, or wandered about outside it and away from it, when they desired to do so.[15]

– Sir E.A. Wallis Budge

Consciousness; Know Thy Self

The journey through the twelve hours of the night symbolises the journey we make time after time through our own inner world to become conscious of who we truly are. Having said that, what does consciousness signify exactly? Consciousness is a state of awareness. Being conscious enables us to perceive the impressions of the outside world.

However, this is not limited to the outside world as one can also be aware of the perceptions of the inner being. The awareness outside of ourselves is the result of the observations we make of the world around us. This gives us a frame of reference to compare ourselves to and to make us aware of the position we hold in the world. Therefore, being conscious can arise only when there is separation, duality. Two objects, that attract and repel each other, are required to function as a mirror for one another. Duality is the first step to consciousness in order to eventually return to the source, to unity.

The ancient solar God of the city of Heliopolis, Atum, demonstrates the necessity of duality. In the myth of creation, Atum, the "Complete One", made the first creation out of his flesh. At first, Atum created himself through his Divine thoughts and will. He then emerged from the primeval waters called Nun. His next action, after conceiving himself, was to create the first mound or primordial hill out of the waters of Nun to provide for a place for him to stand on. This became the beginning of time called *Zep Tepi*, the "First Occasion".

Atum was all alone in the world. There was nothing in the world to compare himself with and he was, therefore, unable to become conscious of himself. To solve this problem, he needed an object outside of himself. However, since Atum was not able to reproduce by himself, he had to make this creation out of his own being, meaning his *Ka*. Thus, he spit out moisture to create the Goddess Tefnut and named her "Righteousness". Then Atum sneezed air to create the God Shu and named him "Living One". This first duality became the first awakening of consciousness. It refers to the fact that creation, just like consciousness, is only able to expand through the act of duality.

> [... while I was alone with Nun in lassitude,
> and I could find no place on which to stand or sit,
> when Ôn had not yet been founded
> that I might dwell in it,
> when my throne(?) had not yet been put together that I might sit on it;
> before I had made Nut
> that she might be above me,
> before the first generation had been born,
> before the Primeval Ennead
> had come into being
> that they might dwell with me.[16]
> – Coffin texts; Spell 80

Duality and the resulting expansion of consciousness are reflected in the Duat. The whole journey through the Duat revolves around the renewal of light. Râ, as the day light, is the polar opposite of Osiris, who is the night light. Râ needs Osiris to ignite his burned-out light. Light is the symbol for consciousness. In other words Râ's consciousness is outdated and has to be renewed. To achieve this, Râ has to look at his own mirror image, which is the reflective shadow of Osiris. This reflective confrontation is necessary to generate the new light or consciousness on a higher level and enable Râ to be born as the new dawning sun, Khepri.

In our inner being, renewal is a continuous process that takes place between the different layers of our consciousness. Our journey through life is a journey to become conscious of ourselves, of who we truly are. To Know Thy Self. "To know", in this case, does not refer to intellectual knowledge acquired by education. It refers to the inner process of becoming aware of our inner being. Thus, "to Know" is a state of identification. Through this identification we can identify ourselves, "to become one", with who we truly are.

In ancient times "Know Thy Self" was written above the temple gate. It was the purpose of all the novices and priests to Know Thy Self, to know the Divine within and to become one with it. We are all driven by this deep memory of our Divine origin to which we want to return, to come Home.

> Man, know thyself, and thou shalt know the Universe and God.
> – Pythagoras

The Amduat reveals in a beautiful symbolic way how to return to our origin. Then we are able to renew ourselves again and again to gain a higher plane of consciousness. The Amduat functions as a detailed roadmap. It shows us the way and makes us aware of the different layers of consciousness, the Higher Self (*Ba*), the Powerself (*Ka*) and the Divine Spark (*Akh*), within ourselves to achieve the Inner Wisdom of our inner world. It is precisely this Knowledge that ensures these separate layers of consciousness are joined to form a unity. This state of oneness forms the feeding ground from where the heightened consciousness, the *Akh*, can arise.

True Mastery

The *Akh*, or the Divine Spark, is the part of us that is directly linked to the Divine. It contains everything we have ever been and that what we truly are, Divine, transcending time and space. We all originate from the Divine. Once we become completely conscious of ourselves, we return to the Divine and free ourselves from the physical incarnation. Due to its direct link with the Divine, the Divine Spark has a very subtle vibration that makes it impossible to connect directly with our present personality. Therefore, it needs a messenger to translate the inspirations to the coarser layer of the physique.

The Higher Self, or True Self, is the one who transmits these messages. In the Amduat the Sungod Râ is the representation of the Higher Self as the *Ba*-soul. The Higher Self, like the Sungod Râ, resides high above the day world where he illuminates the earthly life, or day consciousness, from higher spheres. He is also able to descend into the hidden night world, the subconscious realm. In doing so, he acts like a Messenger between the different worlds. Therefore, the Higher Self is the one who translates the inspiration of the Divine Spark to the day consciousness, which is the personality. The Higher Self functions as our Guide and Guardian, adjusting the courses we take in life as our True inner Voice. The True inner Voice expresses itself through intuition and speaks with the voice of the conscience that is located in the heart. In addition, it stimulates the unexplained tendency to perform the correct action, often without understanding the how and why of this sudden impulse. The only sure thing is the need to follow this gut feeling. The personality is usually unaware of the True inner Voice as he is too noisy to notice the subtle remarks of the latter. He is the king in his own universe and keen to wave his sceptre.

The impulses from the day world are transmitted to the night world. The night world symbolises the hidden inner world of our being. In this book the night world is referred to as the subconscious. It is a vast realm, consisting of several layers, that stretches out beneath the threshold of the wakening consciousness of the personality, beyond our physical world. In a sense, the night world is the reflection of the day world. Nevertheless, the two differ from one another as well.

Although this subconscious realm is usually referred to as the unconscious, in this book I deliberately chose the term subconscious. Being conscious or unconscious are states of mind for you can be aware of something or not. These states of mind can both exist in the day world and likewise in the night world or the subconscious realm. The subconscious realm is like a library, containing information that you can be conscious of or not. It contains books you have read after pulling them up into the day world.

There also are books you have not read, or books you did not even know existed. The once read contents can also be forgotten. In other words, the subconscious realm contains many layers of awareness or consciousness. It contains knowledge you are conscious of, but also things that are obscured in the unconscious. The Amduat, however, strives to raise the consciousness, or awareness, so more and more 'books' are read and remembered.

During life, each person develops their own subconscious or night world. Everything contained within this dark world, no matter how strange or incomprehensible, is the product of everyone's own mind. It is, therefore, a memory bank containing the mental information concerning the personal experiences. Every repeating thought and conviction of the personality will eventually be stored here as the truth. The repeating characteristic of the information, coloured by emotions and feelings, eventually results in deep grooves in the subconscious layer. Thus, this mental information is far from lost. In fact, it starts to lead a life of its own by means of helpful forces as well as inner saboteurs. It sends automatic impulses to the personality without restraint. The personality reacts on these impulses without being aware of the how and why. With this in mind, the night world almost seems to be an unpredictable and mysterious world. However, it is also a miraculous world full of treasures and highlights. These highlights are represented by the stars that lighten this dark night.

The stars are visible high in the night sky. They symbolise the Gods and Inner Plane Beings who reside in the Higher realms. Due to our physicality we are unable to reach the Higher realms directly from our day consciousness. However, when descending into the subconscious world, it is possible to reach these realms. Therefore, the paradox is that the contact with the Higher world lies within our inner underworld. This applies to the contact with the Higher Self as well. We need to dive deep to connect ourselves with this higher part of our being.

The Higher Self will take the personality under his wing when the personality decides to start his descent to explore his inner world. Under the supervision of the Higher Self he starts mapping his inner night world. The Higher Self teaches him where the pitfalls and dangers lie and where to find the power and treasures. During his journey it is of the utmost importance for the personality to purify his mental and energetic system. This serves and assists him as it affects his journey through life in a constructive way. The personality absolutely needs the guidance of the Higher Self to acknowledge all the aspects of himself from a higher point of view. The personality is unable to obtain this overview on his own due to his restricted vision when on the layer of the day consciousness.

Clearing the old emotional debris opens a doorway to descend deeper within. During this descent, the personality gradually surrenders to the inner Sungod, the Higher Self. The further he descends, the more he is able to identify himself with this inner light. The resulting connection illuminates the way further down.

Here, in the depth of the night world dwells Osiris, the Lord of the Duat. Osiris is the embodiment of the Vital Life Force, the *Ka*. The *Ka* represents the powerful force within our being that wants to survive and express itself. In the context of this book the *Ka* is called the Powerself. The Powerself contains a unique imprint that distinguishes us from other people, making each individual unique. Thus, this part of our being contains our true potential, the force behind our purpose of life. Here lies the opportunity to discover our gifts and talents and to implement them in the physical world to show who we truly are. All the power we will ever need to create something from ourselves is already here. We just need to reach for it in our night world or subconscious and learn to deal with it.

If you have the courage to make contact with this powerful aspect of yourself, the Powerself will awaken. The interconnection of the personality with the Higher Self and the Powerself forms a channel between the above and the below. The Higher Self functions as the mediator between the Divine Spark and the personality to establish an indirect link between the two. The Divine Spark, or *Akh*, is now able to use this channel. He radiates via the Higher Self into the personality, which causes a state of inner illumination. The personality, in turn, functions on the earthly layer in the body while being inspired from the higher world and guided by the Higher Self.

Now, the Powerself empowers the personality with the Vital Life Force to manifest these higher insights from the Higher Self in life itself. This gives rise to the gifts and talents of the personality and grants the ability to create his own unique life. The Higher Self, in turn, makes the personality conscious of this creation. This perception provides for the opportunity to fulfil his purpose to the best of his abilities.

Since the person has learned to "Know Thy Self", he is able to connect with the Great "Know Thy Self", the Source to which we are all connected. Creation in this heightened conscious state is the true Mastery. The personality has become aware of the fact that his earlier reign was an illusion guided by the self-centred desires.

The entire process is an eternal spiralling cycle to manifest every newborn consciousness on a higher level. Though repetitive, each new cycle continues where the previous one left off on a higher level, increasing the Self-awareness of ones divinity.

> The Height must penetrate the Depth, if you wish the Depth to become as the Height, "to accomplish the miracle of the One Thing" as says the Emerald Table. But since there are Depth and Height, neither can be moved without the other, and they depend upon each other. And the light (of the world) shineth in darkness.[17]
>
> – Isha Schwaller de Lubicz

The Great Awakening; The Way of the Heart

The interaction and connection between the three different layers of the consciousness, the Higher Self (*Ba*), the Powerself (*Ka*) and the Divine Spark (*Akh*), represents the Great Awakening. The newly awakened consciousness enables the opening of the True Heart. However, this heart is not the organ pumping blood through the body. Neither is it guided by the personal desires and emotions, or the outside world. This heart is about the True Heart that speaks with the True Voice of *Maât*, "Order, Truth and Justice". It is the seat of the Divine Knowledge and Wisdom as it is inspired by the world of the Divine.

> May your *ib*-heart be with you
> in the right way,
> And your *ḥȝty*-heart of your existence
> on earth,
> you being restored to your previous form,
> as on the day when you were born.[18]
> – Stela text from early Dynasty 18
>   (ca. 1500 B.C.E.)

In ancient Egypt, the heart was a very important organ as it was seen as the residence of all consciousness, righteousness and wisdom. Therefore, they left it inside the body to allow the heart to travel with the deceased to the Afterlife where it would be weighed in the Judgement Hall. The heart needed to be judged first before the resurrection could begin.

Fig. 9. Hieroglyphic sign for heart.

When a person did not act in accordance with the Divine Law of *Maât*, he could not connect with his True Heart. The True Heart would be unable to recognise the heart of the person and plead against him during the weighing process. The resulting false heart became weighed down and out of balance with the feather of *Maât*. The scales then tilted towards the heart and lowered it to the ground where it was within reach of the monstrous Goddess Âmmut or Âmmit (ʿm mwt). Immediately, she would seize the opportunity to eat the heavy heart of the damned soul. Âmmut her name translates as the "swallower of the weight or the dead". She has the head of a crocodile, the upper body of a lion and the lower body of a hippopotamus. Obviously, nobody wanted to be devoured by this fearsome creature and be wiped out of existence for eternity.

To prevent this gruesome death, the ancient Egyptians placed an amulet depicting a scarab on the heart. The scarab God Khepri was an important symbol of rebirth for every deceased as they longed to be reborn in the Afterlife. Hence, the scarab amulet was intended as a stand-in for the heart. Spell 30 B from the Book of the Dead was engraved on the back of the amulet. This spell ensured that the heart would not plead against the deceased in the Hall of Judgement and that it helped the deceased to enter the Afterlife.

> O my heart which I had from my mother!
> O my heart which I had from my mother!
> O my heart of my different ages!
> Do not stand up as a witness against me,
> do not be opposed to me in the tribunal,
> do not be hostile to me in the presence of the Keeper of the Balance,
> for you are my *Ka* which was in my body,
> the protector who made my members hale.
> Go forth to the happy place whereto we speed;
> do not make my name stink to the Entourage who make men.
> Do not tell lies about me in the presence of the God;
> it is indeed well that you should hear! [19]
> – Book of the Dead; Spell 30 B

The True Heart acts like a gateway through which the heightened consciousness, symbolised by Khepri, is expressed. This heart is connected to the true insights originating from the inner Higher world via the Higher Self, who in turn is inspired by the Divine Spark. The True Heart is the heart of the transfigured soul that has become aware, resulting in the awakening of the "Inner Wisdom and Knowledge". The Inner Wisdom and Knowledge, as mentioned here, are not the same as the knowledge of the reasoning mind. It is about a way of knowing reality from within, which goes beyond space and time.

Thoth, or Djehuty (*dhwty*), who is the God of Divine Wisdom and Truth, is the representation of this Wisdom of the Heart. One of his many names is *Ib-n-Râ* (*ib-n-rˁ*), which translates as "Heart of Râ". This means that Thoth came forth from the heart of Râ. At the same time, it is Thoth who embodies the Heart and the source of all Wisdom for the Sungod Râ. This aspect of Thoth clearly explains the meaning and energy of the True Heart as it is ensouled with "the Mind and Will of the Divine".

Moreover, Thoth is sometimes referred to as *tekh* (*th*), which means "a weight or plummet of balance". The determinative of this word is the hieroglyph of the "heart". The determinative is a sign behind a word that gives an indication of the meaning of the word. Sometimes the word "heart" was also written with an ibis, the bird sacred to Thoth.[20] This demonstrates that Thoth is the personification of the True Heart that is in balance with the feather of Divine Truth.

Naturally, Thoth is also the expert in the knowledge of the heart of every human being. He has the Divine ability to look right through the body, through every identity-concealing mask for he knows exactly what is hidden deep inside each heart. Understandably, Thoth is the mediator and messenger between the Divine and the humans, effectively bridging the gap between both worlds.

Thoth is, therefore, the designated God to provide you with important instructions during your voyage through the Duat. His insights and knowledge help you to truly embrace the rebirth process of the new consciousness to ultimately open the True Heart. This consciousness is symbolically represented in the form of eyes. Hence, it should come as no surprise that one of the names of Thoth is "Bringer back of the Eye". These eyes, the organs granting sight, absorb the light from the environment and convert it to images to enable us to see. This ability to "see" symbolises awareness and thus the consciousness.

The God Thoth "Djehuti" seated on a throne, Temple of Seti I at Abydos

The hieroglyphic word for eye is *iret* (*ir.t*). It is a derivation of the verb *iri*, which has multiple meanings like "to create, to make, to construct or to beget". The development of consciousness is a creative process that results in the expansion of vision or awareness. This is why the eyes are a focal point in the Amduat. Through their changing appearance, they let us see the development of the consciousness along the journey. The eyes, as the mirrors of the soul, can be found depicted in several hours.

The God Anubis also plays a significant role during the Great Awakening when the True Heart is opened. Anubis's name, *Inpu* (*inp.w*), means "Royal child". He is one of the oldest Gods and he, therefore, has many names and appearances. He can be found depicted as a jackal-headed God, as a black jackal (laying down, standing, seated, passant or mummified) or in human form. Sometimes he can also be found in the form of a couchant jackal on a shrine with a feather on his back. This emphasises his association with *Maât* and his role as the Weigher of Hearts in the Hall of Judgement.

Anubis, as the God of the Dead, functions as the guide, messenger and protector of the death into life process. He alone knows the way and has access to the Forbidden Land where the Initiation takes place. It is in this Sacred Place where death is cured and the True Heart is opened to enable it to beat with renewed life once more. All these special skills of Anubis make him the perfect God of Initiation and the "Opener of

Hearts". He, like no other God, possesses the knowledge and competence to guide the deceased through their transformation process to become a justified soul. However, Anubis also guides the travellers who are still alive and have embarked on the journey through the Duat to become aware.

> O Thoth, go and proclaim to the Western Gods and their spirits;
> This King comes indeed,
> an imperishable spirit,
> adorned with Anubis on the neck,
> who presides over the Western Height.
> He claims hearts, he has power over hearts.
> whom he wishes to live will live;
> whom he wishes to die will die.[21]
> – Pyramid Texts; Utterance 217

During this journey your unfaithful heart will perish, which results in the unravelling of the old consciousness. To prevent you from truly dying, Anubis wraps and conceals you tenderly like a mummy. This protects and ultimately mends the inner-tearing process. You are then engulfed in the safe protection of a cocoon in which you change like a caterpillar. Everything that burdened or clouded your heart is scraped off, layer by layer, to eventually free you from these falsehoods. Now you are able to descend into the core of your being and make a connection with the Higher Self who resides here. As you are in tune with your inner Sungod once more, the bandages are unwrapped, freeing you from your cocoon. These unifying bandages are no longer needed for your inner world has healed.

Your heart is then exposed to the tests to determine whether it can withstand the light. Anubis, in his role as "Guardian of the Scales", guides you to the scales, under the watchful eye of Thoth, and takes your transformed heart in his hands. He then places your renewed heart with great care on the scale to determine whether it is in balance with the feather of *Maât*. If so, the beam of the scales remains exactly horizontal and proves that your heart has become the seat of the renewed consciousness. Then it is deemed as light as a feather, embodying the Truth.

The jackal God Anubis, Temple of Seti I at Abydos

Thus says Thoth
(after the weighing of the heart):
Hear this word of every truth.
I have judged the heart of the deceased,
and his soul stands as a witness for him.
His deeds are righteous in the great balance,
and no sin has been found in him.
He did not diminish the offerings
in the temples,
he did not destroy what had been made,
he did not go about with deceitful speech
while he was on earth.[22]
– Book of the Dead; Spell 30B

Now, the Divine Spark has gained access to the True Heart. This gives you the opportunity to spread your wings and become a "Winged One". However, this does not mean you can fly away, for the road of awakening always goes through the depths of the earth. Your wings are useful only as long as you remain connected to the earth. The ground provides you with a foundation that you can utilise to reach out to the Divine. In addition, the Powerself resides in the profound depths of the earth and needs to be heard as well, which is possible only when you are grounded. This indicates that you have to embody the power of this Self to be able to express your potential. You are the representative on the earth plane. Realise that this very important task lies within your hands.

The scales of Maât in the Hall of Judgement. The temple of Hathor, Chapel of Amun-Râ-Osiris, Deir el-Medina

The entire process of awakening the heightened consciousness, which opens the True Heart along the way, has to be connected to life itself. Everyday life is the training ground where you get tested. In other words, it is your actions in life that demonstrate whether your renewed consciousness is true and viable.

The Great Awakening is a beautiful voyage that allows us to awaken with a renewed consciousness on a higher level. However, there is one key element that can make or break the journey. This element is Love. Love is the fuel and the most important force required during our travels. Without Love, the True Heart cannot be opened and come to life. The sister Goddesses Isis and Nephthys remind us of the importance of Love in the myth about the murder of Osiris. It was their cries of profound grief and, above all, unconditional Love that allowed their beloved husband and brother Osiris to come back to life. Therefore, here within the Duat Nephthys and especially Isis play an important part in the Great Awakening. They are present during several hours to grant their support and eternal Love to the process of renewal for both Osiris and Râ, and for you as well. It is this power of Love that conquers decay and death. Thus, it ensures that the renewed life awakens and rises.

A true remedy to a person on earth

The Sacred Texts of ancient Egypt always refer to the process of dying in order to become an *Akh*. Dying is the transformation process to a different state of consciousness. Since the physical body is left behind, the true transformation into an *Akh* can take place. However, as we now know, it is not the physical death alone that gives the opportunity to make the transformation. On a deeper level, the transformation process is accessible during life as well. This is what the

The Goddesses Isis and Nephthys,
KV 14 Tausert/Setnakt

training of the group of elite priests was all about; the initiation of death into life. The transformation could be experienced multiple times in a lifetime, increasing the illumination of the *Akh* within. Eventually the physical body then becomes the vessel of this inner light source as it emits its light from within.

The Amduat is clear proof this transformation can take place during life as well. The text emphasises multiple times that the journey is not exclusively for the deceased, but accessible to the living humans on earth as well. We do not have to wait until we are dead to make this journey to raise our consciousness. We can experience the transformation right now at this very moment while still being alive on earth.

> It is efficient for a man on earth,
> a true remedy, (proven) a million times.[23]

> It is beneficial for whoever knows it,
> on earth, in heaven and in the earth.[24]

The initiation text of the Amduat is a treasure for all of us to bring more consciousness in the world of the living. It provides us with a map that can lead us through the secret paths and gateways of our own inner being. It helps us to connect with our inner Sungod, the Higher Self, who is our guiding light to know our true Self. Self with the capital S. The aim is to explore those inner realms inside of us and to encounter all those demons and Deities that are reflections of the aspects of ourselves. In the deepest hour of the night we surrender to Râ, our inner Sungod, and connect with Osiris, our Powerself, and likewise awaken the light and power within ourselves.

And yes, it is a journey through death, but for the living this does not literally mean dying. It means death of the old self to allow the new self to be born into a higher plane of consciousness. It means death in life, which is an initiation. It is a rite of passage into a new self and thus a true remedy to and for a person on earth.

This journey was recorded and documented by the ancient Egyptians in a unique and very complex manner. Other traditions describe this journey as well. Although they all use different names and images, the journey is essentially the same. An example is the Tibetan book of the Dead. It describes a similar journey of the human soul to become conscious of all the aspects of the inner world. Or, as the ancient Egyptians describe it, the unification of the Higher Self (*Ba*), and the Powerself (*Ka*) to become a Divine Spark (*Akh*). Yes, in a sense, we are unique, but we are also all equal and derived from the same source.

The Secrecy

The Amduat seems inaccessible to the modern human. It uses strange names and references in the text from a different timeframe as it is based on the myths and ideas of the ancient Egyptians. Still everyone has access to the world of the Duat as it symbolises the journey that every human being undertakes through life and after death. In the Duat, the images of regeneration, renewal and rebirth are accessible to all who want to know.

The Amduat is written in hieroglyphs, the language of the ancient Egyptians. It is a pictorial writing system with a huge number of characters. These characters are based on the many different elements in the physical world. This complex writing system blends symbolic images and the written word in a multifunctional way that has never been surpassed by any other writing system. Therefore, it has a far deeper meaning than any language that consists of letters alone could hope to achieve.

The "sacred writing" of the hieroglyphs consists of many different kinds of symbols, like logograms, phonograms and determinatives. A logogram represents an entire word. For example, the hieroglyph for "house" is an image of a house. A phonogram is a written character that represents a word or a letter, like an alphabet. Every single hieroglyph is an image and thus has a specific meaning. As mentioned earlier, the determinative is a sign behind a word that gives an indication of the meaning of the word.

The hieroglyphs were written in a flexible script and either placed in columns or in rows. The upper symbols are to be read before the lower symbols. The hieroglyphs can be read from right to left and from left to right. The reading direction is indicated by the direction the human and animal figures are facing. These hieroglyphs are always looking at the beginning of the sentence, so against the reading direction. Since all symbols in the Amduat text are looking to the right, one could assume it has to be read from right to left. Surprisingly, however, this text is read in the opposite direction from left to right. This conversion of reading direction is called "retrograde" writing and signifies the secrecy of the text.

The ancient Egyptians referred to the hieroglyphs as *Medu Netjer* (*mdw ntr*) meaning the "Divine Words". The hieroglyphs were seen as a gift from the Gods and were said to have been created by the God of Divine Knowledge and Wisdom, Thoth. Furthermore, since the writing of hieroglyphs was a system of drawing images, the meaning of *Medu Netjeru* applied to the drawing of art as well. The Amduat, as a sacred text, was written in those Divine words that could be interpreted by the priests alone who had been initiated in the Sacred Knowledge. Even the scribes, who were educated in the Divine words, did not comprehend the hidden meaning behind the enigmatic words and images of the Amduat since they were no Initiates themselves.

The text refers several times to "the secrecy of the Duat" (*imnt nt dw3.t*). The hieroglyphic word for secrecy, *iment* (*imnt*), is a derivative of the word *imen or imun* (*imn*) which means "secret, hidden or conceal". Another translation is "to create". This emphasises the double meaning of the secret of the Duat. It concerns the secret of the mystery of creation that takes place deep within the concealment of the Duat out of sight from the ignorant. In a way, it tells of a mystery shrouded in secrecy. Furthermore, the text uses the word *seshta* (sšt3) several times which means "make secret, make mysterious or make inaccessible".

At first glance, it seems obvious what these words are implying. It is hidden and secret, therefore, out of the range of the non-initiates who are not allowed to know. The initiate did not speak of it, which protected the hidden nature of the Knowledge. This Knowledge was transferred through oral transmission only to those who were in training to become initiates themselves.

However, the concept of the word "secret", as used here, has a more complex meaning. It refers specifically to the not understanding of the Knowledge to keep it hidden. Even though a non-initiate could see and maybe read the text, they would not gain access to the meaning behind these images and symbols. Similar to reading a book in a language you are not familiar with, it is impossible to comprehend its context. You can see the words, turn all the pages while holding the book, but the story remains inaccessible. Or, when you read the book but are unable to truly understand it as the subject is too complex and exceeds your level of comprehension.

Therefore, knowledge has a certain layering to it. The more you know, the greater the access to the underlying wisdom becomes. This enables you to unveil the layers step by step to understand the "secret" within. This applies to the secrecy of the Duat as well. The texts of the Amduat contain secret layers, conveyed through symbolic images and hieroglyphs. The first layer tells about the journey of the Sungod Râ through the twelve hours of the night. Looking at the images of all the hours, you can follow him from his death in the evening until his rebirth and rise in the morning. The next layer tells about your own journey through the depths of your inner world to become conscious of who you are and what your purpose in life is. It is a journey you will make over and over again to expand your consciousness and to get to know your true Self. Every time you descend, guided by the Sungod Râ, you unveil a new secret that grants you greater access to your inner Wisdom. Therefore, the "secrecy of the Amduat" contains the key to unlock the secrets of your own inner world.

Symbolism; the language of the subconsciousness

Everything you encounter and experience in the Duat is a reflection of the depth of your own subconsciousness. This inner world communicates with you through the language of symbolism. The symbolic language is a very different kind of communication compared to the everyday language that is composed of words and gestures. Symbols reveal the deepest aspects of reality on a more intense level. The symbols are the language of intuition that supersedes rational thought and allows you to connect with your inner being. It is a form of expression that is universal and timeless, offering recognition, insight and understanding. Hence, one well-defined symbol provides more clarity and reaches far deeper than words ever could. The understanding of these symbols provides you with the answers for your own rebirth to reconnect with your inner being. Healing, just like unification, is always there. We only have to be aware of our inner world and learn to listen to the True inner Voice within, the Higher Self, our inner Sungod.

> In our modern languages there is no word that designates the exact meaning of Symbol, as it was conceived by the Ancients. This is why I should like to replace the word symbol with the word *Medu Netjer*, which conveys the "signs that bear the Netjeru".[25]
> – R.A. Schwaller de Lubicz

This symbolical language can be found in our dreams. Dreams are an expression of our subconsciousness. However, the day consciousness does not always understand the meaning of the dreams. Or it does not remember them completely and labels them as illusions. Nevertheless, dreams can tell us a lot since they contain our inner truth. The illusion simply arises from the incorrect interpretation of these inner images by the day consciousness. Dreams have a clear voice, calling you with the intention to awaken the day consciousness.

Our reasoning mind has a restrictive character since its focus is directed at the material world. Thus, concepts like the Divine nature of the Higher Self and the Divine Spark are difficult to grasp for the personality. These concepts are invisible, untouchable and, therefore, incomprehensible. To enter this unseen world, or to descend into the Duat, you need to let go of the reasoning mind. As long as rational thinking is active, the gate to the Duat remains closed. This explains why the deceased are able to descend through this gate since they leave the restrictions of the body and the reasoning mind behind.

Nevertheless, every living human being is able to get access to the Duat, as the text emphasises numerous times, "A true remedy for a person on earth". The entrance, however, is on a different level of awareness where rational thinking does not have the lead. Thinking is linked to the day consciousness while the Duat takes place in the subconsciousness, the night- or inner world. The day and night worlds are mirror images of each other. The perspective has to be reversed to be able to enter. The text of the Amduat addresses this fact as the hieroglyphs are written in a "retrograde" fashion and have to be read in the "opposite" direction.

The reversal of the perspective is the reason why the texts and the images of the Amduat seem strange and incomprehensible to the day consciousness since you have to view them from an upside down angle, so to speak. Hence, it is impossible to become master of the Inner Knowledge from the layer of the day consciousness. You have to focus inward through connecting with the inner feelings and images.

Only then the door to the inner world will open to you.

Once the door has been opened, the subconsciousness starts to speak to you in the symbolic language. This language expresses itself differently compared to our conscious language in the material world where we trust our senses. In daily life everything has a place and seems predictable. What you see is what you get. At least, we think it is. It is ruled by the personality, who is guided by the outside world and his self-centred desires. The outside world is based on dogmas, conditioning, fears and emotions. Here, the truth of the environment is usually more important than the inner truth. The world of the day consciousness, therefore, carries many uncertainties. It is precisely here where the great unknown can be found, as opposed to the dark world of the subconsciousness.

Though, in a sense, fear for daily life seems more appropriate than fear for the inner life inside of us. In fact, as you learn to navigate through the inner world, you will experience the reliability of this world. Here you navigate on the inner images that the Higher Self makes you cognizant of. Clear, honest and truthful, thus anything but unpredictable. This emphasises that the inner truth is especially attainable in this underworld.

Moreover, when the focus is primarily on the outside world, the process of renewal usually proceeds unconsciously. As a result of this, the acquired new consciousness is not retained. This leads to the regression in old ingrained patterns anchored deep within the subconsciousness after the moment of renewal. The rebirth of the new consciousness is communicated through the symbolic language. Since the personality is unable to comprehend these symbols, the obtained knowledge is lost and the personality relapses in the old consciousness.

Consequently, it is crucial for you to be able to comprehend the language of the subconsciousness. You are the representative in the physical world, the one who is able to manifest on earth. You are the vessel of the Higher Self and the Powerself. You are the one to fulfil the potential in the present as you are the channel through which the Divine Spark can shine. Without you the new consciousness cannot be expressed and is unable to sanctify the earth. It goes without saying that you are equally sacred as are the other layers of consciousness within yourself. Like the other layers, you originate from the Divine as well. Albeit your energy is coarser as you are made of flesh and blood. This enables you to function in the physical layer. The more you can comprehend the inner language, the better you are able to manifest your Divine origin. On a larger scale, it is you who ensure the evolution of mankind. Therefore, listening to the right inner language does not just serve you, but also all of humanity.

How to descend in the Duat

Meditation is the best method to actively and consciously work with the Amduat and to gain access to the centuries old knowledge. The meditation should be performed in a quiet room without interruptions for approximately half an hour a day. During the meditation you need to sit on a chair with a straightened posture, hands on your upper legs and feet next to each other on the ground. You could also use a footstool to facilitate a better posture. Numerous images and statues can be found of Pharaohs adopting this posture. This position allows you to concentrate without falling asleep.

It is preferable to meditate daily around the same time as a part of your daily activities. This will allow you to make it a habit and to properly build a relationship with your inner world. Although, daily meditation is not feasible for everyone, you could still work with the Amduat. Simply try to create a pattern to, for example, meditate on a few fixed days during the week. Try to find a rhythm that works for you. Similar to studying, you will benefit depending on how much you invest. The same rule applies to the Amduat.

If you have no experience with meditation, it might take some getting used to before you can find a rhythm. However, if you follow through and are able to make it a habit, it will come naturally like brushing your teeth or combing your hair. At some point, if you are not able to meditate due to illness or other reasons, it might even feel like you have forgotten to do something important. Meditation is an engagement with your subconscious world. If you do not show up on the agreed upon time, your subconsciousness will make you aware of that.

Then there is the meditation itself. When you meditate, it is essential that it has a clear starting and ending point. In doing so, you will ensure that

Queen Hatshepsut; 18th dynasty, 1473 – 1458 B.C. Dutch National Museum of Antiquities Leiden

both worlds, the day consciousness and the subconsciousness, have a clearly defined place. Although these worlds are connected to one another, you have to be aware of when you are in which world. In doing so, you prevent them from flowing into each other. Therefore, each meditation has to have the same beginning and ending regardless of the specific hour of the Amduat you are working with. Always start by visualizing the setting sun. When you follow the sun, you will descend into your inner world. To end the meditation, visualise a rising sun. Your focus on this rising light will ensure your ascend from the subconscious world and allow you to reconnect with your daily life.

As an addition, you could think of a practical gesture to mark the beginning and the end of your meditation as well. You could, for example, light a candle at the beginning which you extinguish at the end. There are numerous other alternatives to think of that can do the job just as well. The only demand is that the sign is very clear and that you use it every time. In doing so, you will create a defined meditation within which you can work safely.

Now get comfortable and close your eyes. Follow your natural breath and notice how your body moves while you inhale and exhale. The next step is to make the effort to control your breathing. Inhale deeply and feel the expanding of your belly. Hold your breath for a moment. Then exhale slowly while your belly returns to normal. Hold your breath again for a moment. Repeat this a few times. When you feel that your mind and body are relaxed, it is time to enter the Duat.

To actually descend into the Duat, it is important to know where the entrance lies. The Sungod Râ is your guide to this entrance, functioning as the example to follow. You can see him disappear behind the horizon of the West, the position where the Duat opens in the First Hour. The image of the setting sun is the image to focus on when you start your meditation. This area is called the twilight zone, when the light slowly extinguishes just before the darkness sets in.

Here, on the threshold between waking and sleeping, is the ideal moment to enter the Duat. It is important to balance between these two layers for as soon as the day consciousness gains the upper hand, the information concerning the Duat is viewed from the perspective of the reasoning mind. From this angle the Duat, the subconsciousness, is inaccessible and the inner knowledge will remain a "secret". On the other hand, when you fall asleep, you enter the world of the Duat. However, in this state it is impossible to use the acquired knowledge on a conscious level since it will remain in the subconsciousness once you wake up.

The moment the day consciousness stays silent in the background during the stage where you dwell on the edge of sleep yet still awake, is when the Duat opens on a conscious level. This is the moment when the perspective starts to turn from the outside world into your inner world. Images and inspirations emerge as the inner world starts to communicate with you. You are then able to look in your inner mirror and become conscious of yourself, like Râ who looks in the mirror that is Osiris.

The images of fig. 10. (day consciousness) and fig. 11. (subconsciousness) show us how this conversion works. Fig. 10. is the representation of the waking consciousness. Here, the earth God Geb is awake and the Sungod Râ, in his form of Khepri, travels through the twelve hours of the day. Râ is visible in the sky and sails, in his Day Sun barque, from East to West. During this journey Râ ages and ultimately dies as the setting sun in the West.

Fig. 11. shows the moment the conversion has taken place. The day consciousness is asleep as symbolised by the earth God Geb. The sky Goddess Nut is visible in the sky as the stars illuminate our subconsciousness. Here, the Sungod Râ sails on his Night Sun barque through the twelve hours of the night. This time his course is set from West to East. From the perspective of the day consciousness (fig. 10.) it would seem like the night journey takes place in the opposite

Fig. 10. Day consciousness

Fig. 11. Subconsciousness.

direction. However, this would imply Râ returns to his starting point every day. If that were true, Râ would obviously never progress nor would a renewed consciousness be able to arise. The old consciousness would merely be reset, cancelling the developments made during the last round. Râ would then need to start anew every day, repeating the same round indefinitely.

Obviously, the perspective of the day consciousness is mistaken as it gets confused when gazing into the night. After all, the perspective needs to be turned around when looking at the night world. As shown in fig. 11. Râ does not travel back in time at all. He clearly proceeds forward through death to be born anew. Along the way he rejuvenates and transforms his old form into his new shape as Khepri. The moment he rises as Khepri, signifies the beginning of the next cycle that proceeds on a higher level. This cycle allows life to continue developing and evolving over time.

As indicated by these two images, Râ sails day and night through the sky that is also the celestial body of the Goddess Nut. Her beautiful shining stars give shape to the constellations of the world of the Gods and symbolise the higher consciousness. Although the stars of Nut surround the earth day and night, they are visible only in the sky during the night. This means that only the journey through the night world, the subconsciousness, links us to these stars. In other words, this is when we can connect with the Divine world in ourselves.

The Duat is a dimension, parallel to our own world, but mirrored. Though invisible from the physical world, the Duat is absolutely a genuine existing world. Just like the stars of Nut that are invisible during the day, even though they are most certainly still present. The landscape of the Duat appears to be quite similar to the day world. The Sacred River, as the life line of the Duat, dominates the landscape. It is situated in a valley in between two chains of mountains. In this valley there are also fields, deserts, lakes and caverns. One of its regions is known as Wernes. This is a fertile place and the land of agriculture. This is quite remarkable since the Duat is a dark place.

Aside from this recognisable landscape, the Duat also holds features unparalleled in the day world. Beings like snakes with multiple heads, legs and wings, Deities with peculiar heads and demons with horrible names can be found. Also pits with fire, strange mountains, a region of turquoise, a lake of fire, mysterious paths and caverns, and so on.

Once you enter this world, you get to know all the beings living here that are the reflections of your own inner being. Each chapter, describing an hour, names and explains all of the beings and Deities found within that specific hour (See Part Two; The twelve hours of the night). Your journey starts in the First Hour from where you work through all the hours in sequence. During your meditations you concentrate on a Deity or a group of Deities in that specific hour. You are going to study them from all angles, look them in the eyes and ask them questions. This inquiry is very important for in doing so, your subconsciousness will provide you with answers.

When the time has come to return to the daily life, you may close the meditation. As mentioned above, visualise the rising sun and follow the light. As the sun slowly climbs up from the Duat, so will you return to everyday life. Reconnect with your body through alternately contracting and relaxing your muscles. Feel the chair you are sitting on. Once you have returned to the here and now, you may open your eyes. Then, slowly stretch yourself before you stand up.

As soon as you have finished your meditation, it is important to write down your discoveries. Dedicate a diary to write down your observations and findings in the Duat. Try to do this immediately after ending your meditation, otherwise you will forget the pearls of wisdom due to the rush of everyday life. When you write them down, you will embed them in your day consciousness. This stimulates the process of becoming aware of your subconscious world. Try to write down everything, even the things you might not understand or which might not seem important. There is always the chance that these things actually are important but you might need some time to get the message.

Aside from logging your adventures during meditation, it is also important to write down the insights that inspire you in the form of realisations during the waking hours of the day. This also applies to documenting your dreams. These insights might answer questions you have asked during your meditations. They could also be affirmations of things you have experienced in your meditations. These will help clear up whether an experience or insight you think you have gained is actually true. When you write them down, you learn to be sharp and vigilant in your everyday life. Soon, you will learn that there is no such thing as coincidence. Life follows a certain pattern and you are going to learn to recognise it.

Furthermore, it is possible that the events you encounter in daily life refer to the events you have already come across in your inner world. At the end of each hour, in the chapter "The manifestation into daily life", the experience you may expect during your journey is described. Thus, the world of the Duat is neither far away nor "invisible". It is a world very much alive that manifests itself in your daily life, making the unconscious conscious and the invisible visible.

To know; The title of the Amduat

The Amduat begins with an extraordinary long title that contains a summary of all the different beings you will encounter during your travels through the hours. These beings consist mainly of *Ba*-souls, Gods, shadows, visible appearances, *Akh*-spirits, the honoured and the damned. It also briefly refers to the beginning and the end of the journey. Finally, it summarises a list of everything you are supposed to know.

> Treatise of the hidden region,
> the positions of the *Ba*-souls, the Gods,
> the shadows, the *Akh*-spirits
> and what is done.
> The beginning is the Horn of the West,
> the gate of the Western horizon,
> the end is the Unified Darkness,
> the gate of the Western horizon,
> to know the *Ba*'s of the Duat,
> to know what is done,
> to know their transfigurations for Râ,
> to know the secret *Ba*-souls,
> to know what is in the Hours
> and their Gods,
> to know what he calls to them,
> to know the gates
> and the ways upon which
> the Great God passes,
> to know the courses of the Hours
> and their Gods,
> to know the flourishing
> and the annihilated.[26]

To emphasise the necessity of this knowledge, the hieroglyphic word *rekh* (*rḫ*) is used nine times. *Rekh* can be translated as "to know, to learn, be aware of, to inquire or knowledge". As you might have realised, repeating this word nine times is no coincidence. Numbers were of great importance in ancient Egypt. To understand the number nine, one should first understand the symbolism of the number three. Number three represents plurality and is written with three stripes. When placed behind a word, these stripes indicate the plurality of the concerning word. Number nine, as the multiplication of three times three, the plural of plurals, is the representation of the concept of a great number; a lot and an indeterminate number.

An example of the importance of the number nine is the Ennead, a group of nine Deities, *pesdjet* (*psḏt*), meaning "nine". One such company was the Ennead of Heliopolis, known as the Great Ennead, and associated with the creation myth of Heliopolis. These Gods and Goddesses are Atum, Shu and Tefnut, Geb and Nut, Osiris and Isis, Seth and Nephthys. Their number of nine alludes to the fact that these very important Deities represent every God and Goddess in creation.

Using the word "to know" nine times in the title emphasises the importance of having "a lot" of knowledge about everything you are going to encounter in the Duat. The long list with subjects you are required to know seems hard to understand at first glance. You need to know the *Ba*-souls, the hours and their Gods, and all the other beings. However, "to know" in this context is about an experience beyond the reasoning mind in the depth of the subconscious realm. In fact, you cannot know these beings before you enter the Duat.

Even though, the elite priests of ancient Egypt needed years and years, or even a life time, of training and education to prepare for the journey through the Duat, the moment they were finally ready to descend into the Duat, they liberated themselves from all the intellectual knowledge. Only through leaving the thinking mind behind, it was possible to submerge into the Secret Knowledge of the Duat to become a Winged One.

You too have to liberate yourself from the important intellectual knowledge that you simultaneously also need to prepare for the journey. When you let go of the reasoning mind, the gate of the Duat will open itself to you. Once you have entered this inner realm, you are ready to find and meet these beings in order to get to know them. Therefore, to "know" means that you have to recognise and identify all of these subjects in your own inner being. Only through this identification will you become conscious of the subject, its meaning and contents. You will have discovered the "true name" of the beings and become familiar with the attributes you encountered along the way. It simultaneously provides you with knowledge of your own inner world, about who you are, to Know Thy Self. Then, you have uncovered your own "true name".

The power of the Name

In ancient Egypt a name, *ren* (*rn*), was a representation of the power and, thus, the identity of a person. Therefore, it was chosen with great care. The hieroglyph of the *Ka* was sometimes also used for the word "name". This indicates that the name symbolises the Vital Life Force of a person. To the ancient Egyptians the name was regarded as an essential part of the person, just like the body, soul and the *Ka*. Therefore, coming into being as a human on earth was possible only if the name had been pronounced by the Gods.

Knowing someone's name, and thus their identity, gave someone power and dominion over that person. Aside from knowing the name, the pronunciation of the right name in the correct manner was important as well. A prayer or recitation of sacred words spoken with the right tone of voice and in the correct manner creates a connection between the one speaking the name and the evoked name. When evoking the Gods in such a way, this would strengthen the connection between men and the Gods. This explains the importance of the recitation of the sacred names of the Gods, which was an ongoing process in the temples.

A name consisted of several hieroglyphs and each of these symbols represented a specific meaning and power. Every symbol referred to a specific aspect of the character of the subject in question. Thus, the meaning and power of a name was not just in the name, but in the symbols as well. Consequently, writing a name down was a very powerful way to take control of the concerning person, animal or demon. This explains the practice of smashing pottery, with the names of dangerous animals or enemies written on them, to pieces on the ground. In doing so, the evil had been symbolically killed and it would frighten away the enemies. Numerous pieces of those so called "execration texts" have been discovered near burial grounds.

So in short, the name was very important, gave you mastery over the person or animal and was to be used with great care. In spite of this, the Pharaoh, who was obviously very important to the ancient Egyptians, had only one name during the late pre-dynastic period. In later times, the name used for the Pharaoh was changed to befit his statues since the name of a person was very powerful. Ever since the beginning of the Middle Kingdom, the Pharaoh had five names to signify his power and his complex identity. Each name was a representation of the special connection between the Pharaoh and the Gods.

His first name is the Horus or *Heru* name (*ḥr*) " ", making him of equal standing with Horus, the son and heir of Osiris. It is written within a rectangular frame or *serekh* as the representation of a palace façade. The second name is the *Nebty* name (*nb.ty*), which means the "Two Ladies" " ". This refers to the Goddesses Nekhbet and Wadjet, the protectors of Upper and Lower Egypt respectively. The third name is the Golden Horus or the *Heru nebu* name (*ḥr nbw*) " ". The specific meaning of this name is unknown. The fourth name (the first cartouche-name or praenomen) is the name which the Pharaoh received during his coronation, *Nysut bity (n(y)-sw.t bi.ty)* " ". It means "The King of Upper and Lower Egypt" and expresses the sovereignty of the King as the supreme ruler of both lands. The fifth name (the second cartouche-name or nomen) is the Son of Râ name, or *Sa Râ (s3 rˤ)* " ". This makes the King the son of the Sungod Râ and his heir on earth. It is the birth name of the Pharaoh and also the name to refer to the Pharaoh.

These five names reveal the complexity and importance of the identity of the Pharaoh and emphasise his great power since he was a God on earth. Hence, knowing him and obtaining power over him was no easy task.

To manifest his power as the ruler and protector of Egypt, the names of the Pharaoh were carved in the temples and buildings that were constructed upon his orders. However, if there had been a conflict and a new Pharaoh ascended the throne, it could occur that the names of the previous Pharaoh were hammered out. This effectively destroyed the previous Pharaoh, leaving him forgotten and making his power disappear.

Removal of a name was equal to erasing a person from existence on earth as well as in the Afterlife. Being buried without a proper ceremony, without mummification or names carved on the sarcophagus, was the ultimate form of punishment. Without a name the deceased could not be identified in the Hall of Judgement since the Gods would be unable to utter the name. So the person was dead in every sense of the word, forgotten, powerless, never to live again. The possession of his name alone, however, was not enough for the deceased to continue his journey towards the Afterlife. He was required to know other very important names as well to gain access to the realm of the blessed dead.

In the Hall of Judgement, or Hall of *Maât*, the deceased was confronted with the forty-two judges, lined up in two rows of twenty-one. Each judge asked a particular question about a certain sin. The deceased had to deny these sins, known as the "Negative Confession". Afterwards, the heart of the deceased was weighed on the scales of *Maât*. However, even if the deceased was able to deny all sins and his heart was as light as a feather, he was still not allowed passage into the region of the blessed dead. To enter, the deceased was required to know the magical names of the different parts of the door that granted access to this realm. Only when the deceased was able to utter the right names, the door opened up for him. Then he was led before Osiris who in turn welcomed him into his realm. This demonstrates that the deceased needed a certain spiritual level to get access. Only the inner knowledge, obtained in life, could open this door.

The power of the name can also be found in the myth "The secret name of Râ". Râ's name contained the secret of his power. Isis longed for this power and thought of a trick to figure out his name. She made sure Râ was injured and then she would heal him only if he gave her his secret name. As Isis was the only one able to deliver him from his pain, Râ finally gave up his name to be released from the unbearable suffering. This act transferred his power to Isis which she used to cure him. Ever since, Isis has been able to use the secret name of Râ in her Magic.

> As for any spirit who knows
> the name of the Shining Sun,
> he knows his (own) name;
> the gate […] in the twilight.
> Come (…). As for him who knows
> the names of those paths of his,
> it is he who will go in to the Coiled One.
> As for him who knows this Spell,
> he will never perish.
> He will live on what Râ lives (on)
> in the seat of the Shining Sun
> which guards these gates
> in myriad after myriad (of years).[27]
> – Coffin Texts; Spell 760

The journey through the Duat is all about knowing the true names of the beings and the subjects you encounter on your way. The character of each being or subject contains many aspects. In connecting with these different aspects or layers you will begin to understand the true power of the being or subject. This knowledge reveals the true power of the name. It enables you to name the power, to evoke and to confront it. This gives you control over a being or subject. As mentioned before, the beings in the Duat are all reflections of your own inner world. Therefore, knowing their true names gives you mastery of your own inner world and, thus, over yourself.

Magical Names in the Duat

Similar to the Hall of *Maât*, you need several names to gain access to the Duat and its different hours. Every time you complete an hour, you encounter a gate that opens only if you know the specific names of the hour. These names have to be pronounced in a correct manner with the right tone of voice. In other words, it is all about the underlying intention and emotion in your heart the moment you utter the name. This desire shapes the words and enables you to speak up truthfully, which is the key to opening the gate.

Maâ Kheru (*m3ꜥ ḥrw*), meaning "be justified or vindicated", is the term used to refer to this speaking from the heart with the "True of Voice". This title was appointed to the deceased if his heart, after the weighing ceremony in the Hall of Judgement, was judged to be as light as a feather. His pure heart with its true intentions provided him with great power. This enabled him to use his voice in such a way that every door opened to him. Furthermore, he acquired the power enabling him to know the names of all the beings in the Netherworld. Once he then uttered their names with the "True of Voice", they became helpers and friends on his way.

Sometimes, *Maâ Kheru* was used as an epithet for a living person.[28] When used in such a manner, the term contained a different meaning. It served more as an honorary title and was meant as a kind of blessing.

To be allowed entrance to an hour in the Duat, you need to know four names that are different for each hour. The first name you need to know is the name of the hour. This name tells you something about the specific energy of the hour.

The second name is the name of the gate. Every hour has a gate at the entrance. This gate has an important function as it separates the hours from each other. Every hour contains a special kind of energy and capacity that should not be mixed with the specific energy of another hour. An hour is a hidden space where special activities and events take place to activate the development of consciousness. It needs to be a protected place to build up the power you need on your journey without the disturbances of the outside world or the energy of other hours. The gates guard the order and harmony of the hours.

The knowledge of the name of the gate indicates you possess sufficient inner wisdom to discover the secret world that lies hidden behind it. This automatically makes you part of that world and grants you the permission to enter. Without this inner knowledge the gate remains closed. During your travels through the Duat you are going to develop this specific knowledge that allows for more and more doors to open for you.

The third name is the name of the Hour Goddess. This Goddess is the appointed guide for the Sungod Râ, and for you as well, through a particular hour. As she knows the way, she is a great support to you during your journey. The name of the Hour Goddess reveals her power and must be pronounced with great respect. In the First Hour, at the end of the upper sections, all twelve Hour Goddesses can be seen together.

The fourth name is the name of the Guardian. The function of the Guardian is to protect the process of transformation in a particular hour. However, not every hour has a Guardian and there also are hours that contain several Guardians. Usually the Guardian is standing while facing the opposite direction from the other Deities at the end of the hour in the lower section. In this position, standing with his back to the gate of the next hour, he has the overview of the entire hour. Like the Hour Goddesses, the Guardians must be treated with great respect.

The Amduat in our lives

Presently, in the 21st century, the wisdom of the Amduat has become available to everyone. Books, containing the knowledge of the Amduat, can be bought freely and everyone can visit the decorated tombs in Egypt. Through thousands of years, the human consciousness has grown considerably and it is in fact developing still. The Amduat remains a valuable tool, a gift for anyone who wants to become conscious and who wants to "Know". After thousands of years, the knowledge is still alive and true. The Amduat contains eternal Wisdom for humanity that is applicable in every era.

When you learn to work with the Amduat, you will become aware of the fact that your whole life is a journey through the Duat. Commencing from birth and ending the moment you leave the earth after death; the big cycle of life and death. However, the Duat can work in smaller cycles as well that can take as long as a few years, a year or even a few months or days in your life.

All of life, on every layer, is involved in this journey of regeneration and rebirth. It takes place on a personal level in your own life, on the level of all humanity and even on the level of the cosmos. All these cycles are intertwined and influence each other. It is the grand journey of awakening that involves every living being and has taken place for millions of years. Every day, with the rise of the sun, our awakening increases a little further as well, expanding our consciousness.

So you can ask yourself, how coincidental is life really? Does life happen accidentally, or is there a road to travel upon? The Amduat shows us life consists of cycles that follow a certain rhythm. This is reflected in the seasons in nature, the hours of the day and the night, the alignment of the stars and the planets, the orbit of the sun around the centre of the Milky Way, and so on. Once we recognise this rhythm in our own lives, we can learn to navigate upon the great stream. This enables us to make better choices for optimal use of this flood. In other words, there is a ground plan we can use to give direction to our own lives.

However, it is up to us whether we use it and choose to proceed forward, or to stay put.

When travelling the ancient Road of the Duat, you become aware of the inner guidance of your inner light, your inner Sungod. Following his orders will give another meaning to experiences in life like pain and sorrow, as well as happiness and victory. The inner Sungod enables you to develop a helicopter view, to rise above your own limited vision and learn to see the bigger picture. This expanded vision allows you to become conscious of your Self and of what your responsibilities in life are. Your life is your own creation and there is nobody else to blame for it but yourself. You are the creator of your own universe, which makes you a co-creator of creation. Realise that you are a god on earth, a fact the ancient Egyptians already knew well. Thus, the Amduat encourages you to be honest to yourself. Make choices between what is right and what is wrong. Stand for who you are, manifest your talents and gifts in your life and reach your highest potential. The purpose of life was, and still is, to obey the Law of the *Netjeru*, to manifest *Maât*, "Order, Truth and Justice", into your life and to become a *Netjer* in the end.

The healing aspect of duality

The Amduat teaches us to embrace both darkness and light within ourselves and in our lives, as both aspects are equally important. They are two parts of one concept, forming a pair. They complement each other and are both needed to exist. If separated, neither will be able to survive. Without the darkness of the Duat the light of the Sungod Râ is unable to regenerate and shine again. Likewise, Osiris, who needs the shelter of the darkness, cannot renew his Vital Life Force without Râ's light to ensoul it.

A power can never exist on its own considering that it adopts its identity through the interplay with another object. Without the other object there will be no force at all, no movement, no progress and thus no life. There is no light without darkness, no good without evil, no silence without sound as both sides are needed to experience one of them. It is the tension between different forces that supplies the energy to keep the flow of life in motion. Hence, duality is fundamental to maintain creation.

When accepting the different influences into your life, you will learn to navigate through the various cycles in life to enable your consciousness to expand. The descent into your inner darkness is just as much a challenge as is to openly and honestly stand in the light to show who you truly are. The Amduat makes us aware that we need both sides in our nature to heal, regenerate and be born again.

In fact, darkness and light are both essential for our spiritual and biological welfare. We need the rhythm of day and night to nourish ourselves with the life provided for us by the light of the sun as well as by the darkness of the night. Too much light, similar to too much darkness, eventually leads to destruction. Therefore, the inclusion and balancing of all opposite forces is essential to continue creation.

The Duat, like the physical world, assures us opposite forces need to exist side by side. Both are essential and play a role in the development of the consciousness without judgement. We too possess these opposing forces within our own nature where they coexist. Hence, the Duat is no judgemental world of good and evil, right or wrong. It is simply a world of experiences that allows us to grow into awareness. This world does not aim to give punishments or rewards depending on our actions in real life. It is our own ignorance and incomprehension that leads us to judge and condemn ourselves, for the Gods themselves would never denounce us like that.

> I open up the obstacles,
> I split open the Netherworld,
> I go out among the retinue of the Lord of ......,
> he makes me into one who goes to and fro,
> and it means that I am he
> who opened the obstacles
> and split open the Netherworld,
> having power in my feet,
> who broke open the firmament
> and lightened the darkness.
> I go to and fro in contentment,
> I am strong,
> and my mark of distinction is on my head.[29]
> – Coffin texts; Spell 643

It is important to face these opposite forces in life for every confrontation around you is a reflection of your inner battle. Look at it as a challenge and take it up like an adventure. This allows you to gain mastery over yourself and your life instead of being lived. After all, the struggles with your demons are actually a reflection of the opposites within your own nature.

When in the Duat, you will meet these inner demons. Although, not every demon has something to say to you, you will be able to recognise the ones that do soon enough. They resonate or irritate something within you, begging your attention. Do not walk away from these demons for you will only walk away from yourself. Engage in these meetings. However, you are not required to destroy the confronting demon for when destroyed, you have gained nothing. Then you only have denied and rejected a part of yourself. In no time, a new similar demon makes its appearance and challenges you yet again. Therefore, the lesson for you is to learn how to deal with the opposites of your own nature and how to gain control over them. Only then, this inner force will cease to attack you and become a loyal servant instead. You will have overcome the duality and have integrated the opposites within yourself that make you come closer to becoming a whole. This acquired unity does not fall apart as long as you remain conscious of it. When you lose awareness, however, the unity disintegrates resulting in renewed confrontations. These confrontations prepare you for yet another constructive process until you have become conscious once more.

The influence of the Sacred River during the inundation

The hours in the Amduat are structured in a fixed order and further divided into three sections. The middle section forms the centre of the hour that represents the Sacred River flowing through the Duat. This river does not always contain water, as it is dried-up in some of the hours. During those times it is filled with sand only. This river is the source from which all life arises and it forms the origin of the Nile in the physical world. The upper and lower sections represent the left and right riverbanks respectively on either side of the Sacred River. This is the landscape through which the Sungod Râ, like you, will sail.

The middle section always begins with the sailing Sun barque with its crew on the Sacred River. The First Hour is the only hour partitioned into four sections instead of three. The middle section of this Hour, which is the Sacred River, consists of two sections instead of one.

The area of the first three hours is where the inundation takes place; the great flood from the primeval ocean of Nun. This is the time during which the Sacred River bursts its banks and becomes much broader than it usually is in the process. The entire area on both sides of the river becomes completely flooded, effectively putting an end to the drought. The life-giving water then initiates movement and life once again.

The tomb of Tuthmosis III displays this widening of the river in the Second and the Third Hour clearly on the walls. Both hours contain four sections instead of three, similar to the First Hour. As a result the middle register, which depicts the Sacred River, is doubled in size and consists of two parts. At first glance the reason for this division seems to be the shortage of space since the wall is too narrow to depict three long sections. However, if the designer really wanted to, he could have simply altered the distribution of the hours over the walls. The hieroglyphic text on the left side could have easily been written above the Second and Third hour to leave more room for the three sections. Instead the designer deliberately chose to use four sections for precisely these two hours to emphasise the specific energy of these two hours.

The rise of the water during these hours has a double meaning. On one hand, it signifies the water world that symbolises the subconsciousness. On the other hand, it is the vast amount of water that is necessary to cleanse the inner world and wash the inner garbage away. Therefore, these hours have a significant impact on the traveller. They give the impression everything comes down on you all at once like a ton of bricks, or like an ocean of water. The power of the inundation acts like a wake-up call for the subconsciousness, reviving it. This causes an inner turmoil, which is crucial to soak and loosen the mental debris. The inner system is cleansed in the process, granting serenity to the personality. The inner inundation makes the personality aware of the events taking place in his own inner world and of the leading role of the inner Sungod, the Higher Self. These important hours are used to build trust and grant insight to enable the descent into the Fourth Hour with complete and utter submission.

In the Fourth Hour, the flow of the stream comes to an end. Here it transitions into a small zigzag sand path that leads into the abyss. After the inner clean up, the personality surrenders the control of the helm to the Higher Self. This is emphasised by the absence of the steersman on the barque. The message is clear: when you embrace the guidance and release your inner control, you will be able to descend further.

It is essential to understand the underlying symbolism of these first three hours since it explains why it is actually very fitting to divide them in four instead of three sections, as can be seen in the tomb of Tuthmosis III. This allows for the Sacred River to be broader, granting it an additional emphasis compared to the use of only three sections. As will be clear by now, the Sacred River plays a very prominent role in these hours.

The Sun barque and its crew

Before we make our descent into the Duat, it is important to know more about the vessel, the Sun barque, we are going to use to make this journey. There was an important reason why Râ needed to travel inside a barque. Râ's being, as the radiating sun, was considered to be composed of fire. The sky, on the other hand, was believed to be a vast mass of water. If Râ would travel through this watery world his fiery being would be extinguished. Consequently, the world would be left in complete darkness. To avoid this catastrophe, Râ travels using a barque to evade the touch of water.

The Sungod Râ sails in two different Sun barques during the cycle of one natural day. During the twelve hours of a day, he crosses the sky above the earth in the Day Sun barque called *Mândjet* (*mꜥnḏ.t*), meaning "becoming strong". As soon as the sun sets and the Sungod descends into the Duat, he exchanges his Day Sun barque for the Night Sun barque. The Night Sun barque is an important vessel for Râ to navigate safely through the primordial waters of Nun without drowning or straying and, most importantly, without extinguishing. The name of the Night Sun barque is *Mesktet* (*msktt*), meaning "becoming weak". Another variant of this word is *meskt* (*mskt*) meaning "Milky Way". The Milky Way looks like a band of light in the night sky, or as the celestial body of the Goddess Nut. It consists of countless stars that illuminate the sky at night. As mentioned earlier, the name of the Goddess Nut (*nw.t*) is most likely derived from the word for water, *nuy* (*nwy*) or from the primordial waters of Nun *nunu* (*nnw*). This underlines the belief that the sky was seen as a watery place with boats sailing and creatures floating around. Râ travels each night in his Night Sun barque through the heavenly body of Nut where he is surrounded by all her stars.

> O Nut, spread yourself over me
> when you enfold me with the life
> which belongs to you;
> may you fold your arms over this seat of mine,
> for I am a languid Great One.
> Open to me, for I am Osiris;
> do not close your doors against me,
> so that I may cross the firmament
> and be joined to the dawn,
> and that I may expel what Râ detests from his barque.[30]
> – Coffin Texts; Spell 644

The Night Sun barque is also known as "The Barque of Millions of Years", referring to the vast amount of deceased who have sailed with it and created the route before us. This journey has been performed for millions of years since it began at the beginning of time. From this early start countless predecessors, our ancestors, have sailed the waters before us. Their memories and experiences have built this Night Sun barque to make it seaworthy.

This barque allows us to benefit from the experiences and knowledge from which it was built, aiding us on our journey. This is a journey for all souls to transform into a renewed consciousness. The Night Sun barque with its crew and the Sungod Râ, our Higher Self, functions as the example of this journey of renewal.

From this point onwards, the Night Sun barque of Râ is simply referred to as Sun barque since this book tells the story of the night journey. Should the journey through the day be mentioned, the barque will be referred to as Day Sun barque.

During the descent, the conversion takes place that causes the barque to sail at the back instead of in front of the row of the Gods. The barque appears to be sailing backwards, making things confusing to the reasoning mind. This feeling of a disturbed orientation will disappear as soon as you have descended and adjusted to this "retrograde" world.

On the riverbanks, to the left and the right of the Sacred River, all sorts of Deities are waiting for Râ to pass them by. They are the inhabitants of the Duat, known as the Duatians. The moment Râ arrives in an hour, all Duatians come to life, for they are revitalised by Râ himself. Symbolically, this means the Higher Self sheds light on certain aspects of the subconsciousness, awakening it and making it conscious for you. This means that the moment you arrive in an hour, the Deities who reside there awaken and come to life. These Deities are inhabitants of your subconsciousness and thus, reflections of your inner being.

Altogether, there are nine Gods, including Râ, present on the Sun barque. They form the fixed crew aside from a few small alterations in certain hours. As explained before, the number nine symbolises an uncountable number and, according to the Coffin Texts; Spell 1126, the exact number of crewmembers of Râ is hence unknown.[31] In a sense, this indicates that all Gods and Goddesses are involved in the process of rejuvenation during the nocturnal journey.

The crewmembers play an important part in the transformation and rebirth of Râ. Without the crewmembers, it would be impossible for Râ to sail through the Duat. Now is the time to become acquainted with these Deities since they will be your helpers and guides on your way.

Wepwawet "The Opener of the Ways"

Wepwawet stands, in human form, at the prow of the Sun barque. His name *Wepwawet (wp-w3wt)* is derived from the word *wepi (wpi)*, which means "separate, divide, open or judge". He is the "Controller of the Two Lands" and opens the way for the traveller in the world of the living as well as in the Afterlife. In the Duat he opens the way for the Sungod Râ to allow the Sungod to travel through the night. The word *wepwety (wpwty)* means "messenger". Wepwawet is a walker between the worlds and is able to travel in both the day and night world. This allows him to function as a messenger and psychopomp.

He is usually depicted as a black or greyish white jackal-headed God, or a standing jackal on a standard. The jackal on the standard is often depicted with a Uraeus-serpent and a mysterious object as a protuberance in front of him. The mysterious object as shown is the *shedshed (šdšd)* and it is unclear what it represents. It could be a schematic version of a location in the Netherworld as a symbol of the place where the Pharaoh was reborn. It could also be a placenta.[32]

The placenta is the symbol of life and death since it nurtures new life and dies at the moment of birth. Wepwawet as a funerary Deity is the Lord of life and death and the protector of the process of rebirth. The Uraeus-serpent on the standard indicates that it concerns the royal placenta of the King. Thus, Wepwawet supports the King in his transformation process of death into eternal Life. He opens a path by separating the earth from the sky enabling the King to ascend and be reborn in the Afterlife.

Wepwawet was also the protector of the King on earth and guaranteed the safety of all the paths used by the King. If the King set out to wage a war, there was always a standard with Wepwawet on it carried in front of the convoy. Therefore, he was seen as the warrior God who defeats all the enemies of the King.

During the annual performance of the mysteries of Osiris in Abydos, Wepwawet occupied the significant role of the "Opener of the Ways" and the "Divine Herald". The festival started with a parade, named the "Procession of Wepwawet" which was open to the general public. During this procession the standard with the jackal Deity was carried up front. Wepwawet could then open the way to ensure the safe journey of Osiris to his supposed tomb at Umm el-Qa'ab, "Mother of pots". The ancient name of this necropolis was Poker. During this procession, as Wepwawet opened the ways, the enemies of Osiris were defeated during brawls that were staged for the public.

Once the roads were deemed safe, the "Great Procession of Osiris" commenced with Osiris in his form of Khenty-Imentyu, "The Foremost of the Westerns". The cult statue of Osiris was removed from his temple and transported over the cemetery. Subsequently, "the God's barque journey to Poker" took place during which Osiris, the dead King, was placed upon the sacred boat, the *Neshmet* (*nšmt*) barque. The priests carried the *Neshmet* barque through the desert on their shoulders towards Osiris's grave in Poker. This was the undisclosed part and off limits to the general public. Once there, the sacred rites were performed by priests wherein the suffering and death of Osiris were staged. During the night wake the perished Osiris became completely rejuvenated and transformed into his new form as Wenennefer, "the One who continues to be perfect". The next day the entire group, including Osiris, returned to Abydos. The reborn Osiris, or Wenennefer, was then given a warm and joyful welcome by the general public before he was returned to his temple.[33]

Wepwawet in his function as Opener of the Ways, as seen in the mysteries of Osiris, also performs other tasks. For example, he also opened the ways through the opening or splitting of the Mouth with his *Seb Ur* or *adze*. The opening of the mouth was part of the eponymous ceremony, known as Opening (or splitting) the Mouth, during which he personally assisted. This is also a task of the God Anubis. During this ritual the eyes, ears and the mouth of the deceased were opened symbolically with several magical instruments including the *adze*. This would grant the departed the use of all senses in the Afterlife and subsequently for life to open up to him and be reborn.

> Your mouth is in good order,
> for I split open your mouth for you,
> I split open your eyes for you.
> O King, I open your mouth for you
> with the *adze* of Wepwawet,
> I split open your mouth for you
> with the adze of iron
> which split open the mouths of the Gods.[34]
> – Pyramid Texts; Utterance 21

In the Old Kingdom, Wepwawet was the patron God of an area near Abydos known as Shen-Hor and venerated as the "Lord of Shen-Hor". During the 12th Dynasty Wepwawet was no longer worshiped as he was replaced by Khenty-Imentyu. Eventually Khenty-Imentyu was absorbed by the God Osiris. Upon later times the cult centre of Wepwawet was relocated to the capital of the Lycopolitan nome, Asyut. Anubis was also venerated in Lycopolis. He was connected to the Netherworld as the protector of the deceased while Wepwawet was usually connected to the world of the living as the protector of the Pharaoh on earth.

In the Pyramid Texts; Utterance 210 Wepwawet is described as "the Wepwawet-jackal which emerged from the tamarisk".[35] The ever green tamarisk tree has slender branches and forms dense thickets. This provides for the perfect hiding place for jackals in the barren terrain of the desert.

Wepwawet has several titles like "Lord of Asyut", "Controller of the Two Lands", "Who is on his standard", "Governor of the Bows" and "Lord of the Secluded Land".[36] This last title is also an epithet of Anubis since he adopted many tasks of Wepwawet after Wepwawet was absorbed in Osiris upon later times. Even so, Wepwawet continued to exist as a separate entity. He and Anubis are usually identified as being independent Gods who each have their own specific tasks aside from many shared roles.

However, when viewed from a different perspective, these two jackal Deities could actually indeed be seen as two different sides of one and the same God. The nature of this God they both embody, contains many contradicting sides. This duality is also reflected in the two very different worlds where he lives; the Netherworld and the world of the living. Hence, he can easily walk through the veils that separate the worlds and switch his appearance, role and tasks in the process.

In the Duat Wepwawet and Anubis both have the task of guiding the Sungod Râ through the twelve hours of the night. Anubis opens the Secret paths within the Fourth Hour and guides Râ through this Forbidden land. In the Fifth Hour he is the Guardian and the Opener of the chest "Darkness" (No. 344), which forms the entrance to the Cavern of Sokar. In those two Hours Anubis is the protector of the Sungod. Anubis is also present in the First, Third and Tenth Hour to support Râ during his transformation process. Although Wepwawet also acts as the Opener of the Ways and as a Guide, he does it differently. He stands up front on the Sun barque to ensure Râ has a safe passage from one hour to the next. It is Wepwawet who opens the way for Râ, after

Wepwawet, Temple of Seti I at Abydos

the twelve hour journey, to enable Râ to ascend into the sky. Furthermore, Anubis, like Wepwawet, has an active role in the ascension of the King and the deceased.

> Anubis is upon you as your protection,
> Wepwawet has opened up fair paths
> for you.[37]
> – Coffin Texts; Spell 24

Sia "Percipience"

Sia (*si3*) is a Divine being in human form who is the personification of the sense of touch. The exact meaning of the concept of touch does not imply the act of touching something or someone physically. This form of touch signifies intelligence. It refers to the ability to grasp an idea through inner knowledge and understanding. The Intelligence of Sia, though, is not the intelligence of the reasoning mind, but represents the process of identification beyond the personality. Therefore, Sia personifies the Inner Wisdom conceived through Intuition or Divine Insight.

Sia appears to be regarded as the Divine Eye of Râ. Since Râ gazes through this eye, he sees everything from the Divine insight of Sia. This allows Râ to know and understand the things he sees since he is able to comprehend the Wisdom that lies underneath. Thus, with the percipience of Sia, the Sungod is able to plan the Divine work.

According to myth Sia was created, together with Hu, from the blood that dripped from Râ's phallus after he cut himself.

> It means the blood which fell
> from the phallus of Râ
> when he took to cutting himself.
> Then there came into being the Gods
> who are in the presence of Râ,
> who are Authority and Intelligence,
> while I followed after my father Atum
> daily.[38]
> – Book of the Dead; Spell 17

The act of Râ cutting himself might be a reference to circumcision. Circumcision was customary in Ancient Egypt, in particular among the priests in furtherance of cleanliness. Other purposes of circumcision were the sacrifice for spiritual reasons and as a rite of passage into adulthood. Spell 17 possibly states that Râ made a sacrifice as well as a rite of passage to transform into Divine Wisdom (Divine insight of Sia) and the Authority of the Divine word (creative utterance of Hu).

Via this action, Sia and Hu were bound together as well as to the Sungod. They were regarded as two Divine aspects, the Divine insight and creative utterance. Both of these are aspects that every Pharaoh needed to rule in accordance with the Divine Law of *Maât*. Furthermore, Sia and Hu are also mentioned in the text of the creation myth, "the Memphite Theology", in which they are the heart and the tongue of the God Ptah.

Sia and Hu can both be found on the Sun barque where they are part of the loyal crew and stand by Râ's side. Aside from them, the creator

God Heka is also indispensable to Râ. He is the personification of Magic that is the Divine creative force to ensure the manifestation of something. Hence, Sia, Hu and Heka are the three special forces who help the Sungod to realise the Divine Will. Heka is also present on the Sun barque in his form as the crewmember Kherep wia.

In the Pyramid Texts, Utterance 250, Sia is described as the "Bearer of the Divine Book". He stands at the right hand of Râ and is in charge of all Wisdom. The Divine Book is the great book of the government of Râ in which every detail of his empire and administration was noted. Thoth, as "Râ's scribe of *Maât*", was unmistakably the scribe of this Divine Book.[39]

It should come as no surprise that Sia, as the personification of Inner Wisdom, was seen as a form of Thoth and even as a variant of the name Thoth upon later times. Another important task of Sia was to be a Divine spokesman and mediator. He was, therefore, the one who announced the Pharaoh to the Gods. In the Book of the Gates, Sia as one of the members of the Sun barque, is the spokesman of Râ.[40] There he gives orders to all sorts of Deities on behalf of the Sungod. In the Amduat, however, he stands in silence next to Wepwawet, at the prow of the Sun barque, during the nocturnal journey.

> This is the King who is over the spirits,
> who unites hearts
> so says he who is in charge of wisdom, being great,
> and who bears the God's book,
> (even) Sia who is at the right hand of Râ.[41]
> – Pyramid Texts; Utterance 250

Nebet wia
"Lady of the Barque"

Nebet wia (*nb.t wi3*) is an aspect of the Goddess Hathor. Hathor is a very complex Goddess who is depicted in numerous forms. She is the Goddess of joy, love, sexuality, dance, ecstasy, drunkenness and the abundance and pleasures of life. In the temples dedicated to Hathor, she was honoured with music, singing and dancing. As the symbol of the Female Soul, She was the Goddess of women, motherhood, fertility and childbirth. In her role as the great cosmic Mother of mothers, she was seen as the Great Wet Nurse, which refers to her form as a cow. In the Duat she is the "Mistress of the West", a roll shared with Isis, where she welcomes all the deceased when they enter the Duat. Being the "Lady of offerings" and the Great Provider, she gives them celestial food and refreshing water. These offerings of spiritual food and drink are essential to facilitate the intense transformation process the deceased go through to become reborn in the Afterlife.

Her relationship with Râ is a very complex one considering she is his daughter but also his mother. As his daughter she is the embodiment of the Eye of Râ, the sun disk. This "all seeing Eye" signifies Wisdom and thus consciousness. She is also the protector of Râ's Eye, which symbolises the Sungod his light. When her beloved Râ is threatened by enemies, she transforms in a bloodthirsty and vengeful Goddess and destroys them all. This reveals a completely different side to her positive nature.

Every day, Hathor accompanies the Sungod in the Day Sun barque on his journey through the day. In her form as Nebet wia she travels with Râ through the dark world of the night. Every night, she welcomes the dying Râ in the Duat and takes her position right in front of the shrine of the Sungod. During the twelve nocturnal hours she protects and nurtures the Sungod with food and refreshing water. As the Lady of the barque, in her role of Divine mother, she supports Râ's transformation by carrying the sun disk "the Eye" on her head, between her horns. The exceptions are the Third and Fourth Hour where the sun disk has disappeared. In the Third Hour her horns are gone as well. In spite of these changes in her appearance, as his loving and caring mother, she does not leave Râ's side until he is completely rejuvenated and reborn in the morning. However, in the Seventh Hour only she entrusts the responsibility to protect and care for the Sungod to the skilled hands of Isis.

Iuf "Flesh (of the Sungod)"

Iuf (*iwf*) means "flesh or body". In this case it refers to the flesh or body of Râ. Once Râ has descended through the gate of the West, he has passed away. Râ then transforms into a *Ba*-soul and takes the appearance of a ram-headed God. His body, which is now a corpse, is referred to as "flesh". His journey of transformation serves as an exemplary one where he, as the Great *Ba*-soul, represents all *Ba*-souls during his journey of renewal. Furthermore, when traveling through the night the Great God Râ grants life to all *Ba*-souls, *Akh*-spirits, Gods and those dwelling in the Duat.

The ancient Egyptians did not make a distinction between the body, soul and spirit. Hence, they believed the ascended *Ba*-soul remained bound to the body. Consequently, the physical body continued to play a vital role even after death. This is reflected in the amount of time and care spent on the mummification process of the body of the deceased. During this process the organs, except for the heart, were removed from the body and the body itself was dehydrated with the use of natron. Afterwards, the body was carefully wrapped in bandages. The entire process took approximately seventy days to complete before the mummy could be placed inside the tomb. Once in the tomb, the necessary rituals and ceremonies were performed to enable the deceased to descend into the Netherworld.

It is often thought the ancient Egyptians believed that the corpse would come back to life after death and that this was the reason for their meticulousness in preserving the body. However, this is a misperception for the physical body was a necessary vessel through which the spiritual body could take shape. In a way, it served as a gateway to enable the transformation into the new spiritual body. This new body was known as the *Sâhu* (s‛ḥw). This body, however, is not comprised of physical matter for it is a spiritual body and made of intangible spiritual substances. It served as a nutrient medium from which the new consciousness and thus new life could sprout. Obviously, the ancient Egyptians knew the mummified body did not revive, but was merely used as a means to an end.

> *Sâhu* or spiritual body was the ethereal, intangible, transparent and translucent body, which was supposed, in dynastic times at all events, to grow from the dead body, the form of which it preserved.[42]
>
> – Sir E.A. Wallis Budge

The *Ba*-soul, though still linked to the physical body, joined in this transformation process. This soul, in turn, needed to renew itself through the connection with the *Ka* deep within the earth. From this unity a new life would arise which was viable only if the *Ba*-soul was still connected to the corpse in the transformed shape of the *Sâhu*. Without this spiritual body, the creation of a new life or a new consciousness was impossible.

The *Sâhu* was also regarded as the body of Nun. The body of Nun, which is the primeval waters, contains the waters from which everything is born and to which everything eventually returns. Death is no different from

(From left) Ka Maât, Heru Hekenu, Râ and Nebet wia, KV 14 Tausert/Setnakht

returning to one's origin to be born again in a new life wherein the body serves as a vessel. Thus, it is essential for Râ to transform his body or corpse in the *Sâhu* for this allows him to be reborn in his new form as the *Akh*, or Khepri.

Furthermore, the body of Nun has stored everything, since *Zep Tepi*, concerning humanity in his spiritual body. All wisdom and knowledge and every experience, culture and so on is saved in here. It thus serves as a huge library of consciousness for us to submerge ourselves in during our journey through the Duat. The journey of Râ, as a corpse, is a representation of the reconnection with this great source of Knowledge and Wisdom. To get to this point, we need to experience death, just like Râ, to ensure the decay of our old consciousness. Only after total disintegration will our new consciousness be able to rise. This explains why the texts continuously mention the corpse as being subjected to the process of decay.

The process Râ experiences during his journey needs to be protected, for he is very vulnerable in his *Ba*-soul form. Therefore, Râ resides in his shrine on the Sun barque. The shrine protects his *Ba*-soul since his body has died and is no longer able to keep the soul from harm. This protection is also reflected in the custom of the ancient Egyptians to place statues of the Gods inside a shrine. The shrine itself was placed in the sanctuary of the temple, the Holy of Holies, which was located at the rear of the temple. This would keep the statues safe and protect them from desecration. For Râ, the shrine enables him to safely undergo the transformation process. This is reflected throughout the hours as his form starts to change.

Heru Hekenu "Horus of Fragrance"

Heru Hekenu (ḥrw-ḥknw) is a form of the God Horus. He is a singing and praying God in the barque of Iuf or Râ. The meaning of the hieroglyphic word *hekenu* (ḥknw) is "praise or thanks giving". This God stands behind the shrine of Râ during the entire voyage as he worships and honours Râ. He shows us the importance of

Heru Hekenu stands behind the shrine worshiping and honouring Râ, KV 8 Merenptah

the worship of Râ. Through adoration, you connect yourself with the Divine. In this case this indicates the connection, between yourself and the inner Sungod, the Higher Self. Worship is a way of surrendering yourself to create an opening through which the Divine becomes visible. In essence, you then tune into the correct frequency that enables you to hear the True inner Voice of the Higher Self.

In ancient Egypt, the act of worship and adoration of the Gods was very important. Each day the priests performed all kinds of rituals and ceremonies to glorify and praise the Gods. After all, the *Netjeru* were the ones who ensured that the Divine order, or *Maât*, was maintained.

Therefore, Heru Hekenu is present here while singing his sacred prayers to the Sungod Râ. Through this worship, Râ is given courage and strength, which he in turn uses to continue the cycle of creation in line with the Divine Law of *Maât*. The actions of Heru Hekenu are not entirely selfless for he, like any other living being, benefits from the continuation of creation as well.

Furthermore, Hekenu is the name of the adoration oil that is part of the seven sacred oils. These oils were used in the Opening of the Mouth ceremony to anoint the mouth and the eyes of the deceased. The Pyramid texts; Utterance 72 – 78 describe the anointing while using each of these oils.

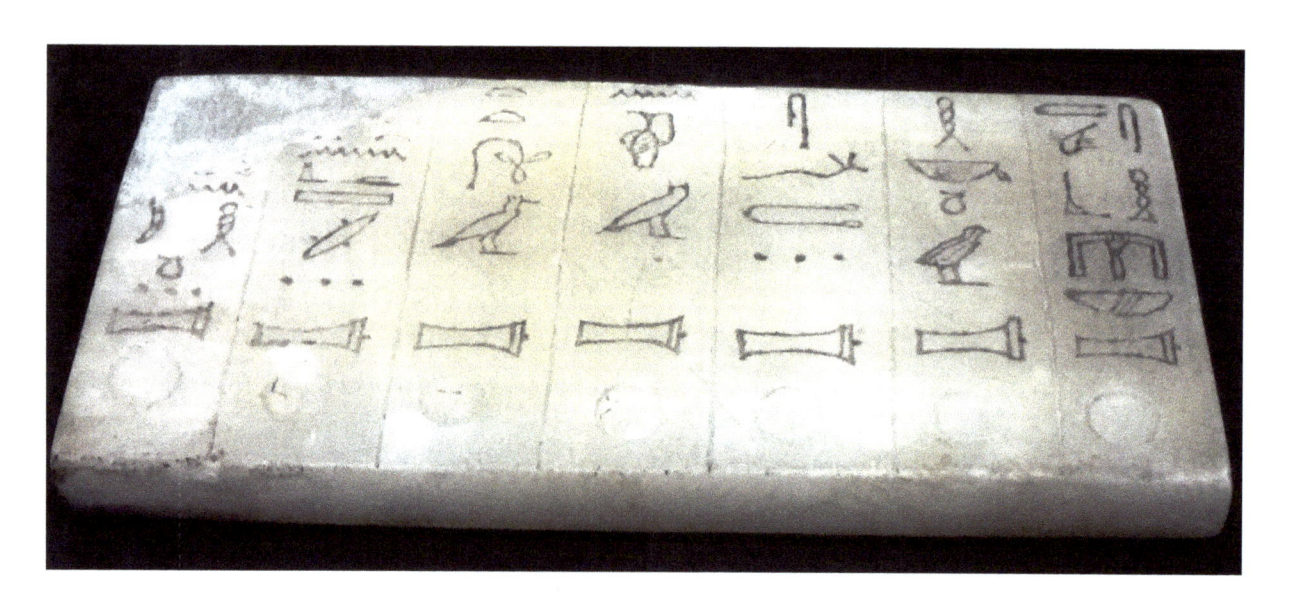

Alabaster ointment slab (F 1954/4.4) inscribed with the names of the seven holy oils. Dutch National Museum of Antiquities Leiden. (From right) Setj(i)-heb (*st(i)-ḥb*) festival oil; Hekenu (*ḥknw*) adoration oil; Sefetj (*sft*) oil used during the Sed festival; Nekhemen (*nḥmn*) unknown; Tua (wet) (*tw3(wt)*) unknown; Hâtet âsh (*ḥꜥt.t ꜥš*) oil of pine, cedar wood or conifer and Tjehenu (*tḥnw*) high quality oil from Libya

Recite four times:
O Osiris the King,
I have filled your Eye for you
(with) the ointment - festival perfume.
O Osiris the King,
take the ferment which is in his face
- ḥknw-oil.
O Osiris the King, take the Eye of Horus
on account of which he suffered - sfṯ-oil.
O Osiris the King, take the Eye of Horus,
which he has protected
- nḫmn- oil
O Osiris the King, take the Eye of Horus,
wherewith he has brought and
supported the Gods - tw3wt-oil.
Ointment, ointment, where are you?
O you who should be on the brow
of Horus,
where are you?
If you are on the brow of Horus,
I will put you on the brow of this King,
that you may give pleasure to him
who has you,
that you may make a spirit of him
who has you,
that you may cause him to have power
in his body,
and that you may put the dread of him
in the eyes of all the spirits
who shall look at him
and everyone who shall hear his name
- first quality pine-oil.
O Osiris the King,

I bring to you the Eye of Horus,
which he has taken to your brow -
first quality Libyan-oil.[43]
– Pyramid Texts; Utterance 72 – 78

Ka Maât "Bull of *Maât*

Ka Maât (*k3 m3ᶜt*) stands on the left side at the stern of the Sun barque. This crewmember has a very interesting name. The two hieroglyphic signs in his name are two upraised arms and a feather. The two upraised arms represent *"Ka"* or "bull". The meaning of the feather is *"Maât"*, which is also used as the sign for the God Shu. Due to these diverse meanings, Ka Maât can be referred to with several names. Sir. E.A. Wallis Budge translated this name as Ka Shu, meaning "double of Shu" (*k3 shu*).[44] Professor Hornung, on the other hand, translated it as Ka Maât, meaning "Bull of *Maât*" (*k3 m3ᶜt*).[45] Either way, the nature of this God is obviously complex as reflected in the various overlapping forms of manifestation.

Ka Maât is a form of Thoth, or Djehuti, the God of Divine Wisdom and Truth. Thoth and the Goddess Maât stood together on the barque of Râ when it rose up from the primeval waters of Nun for the very first time. Therefore, Thoth has been a crewmember aboard the barque since the beginning. The myth telling of the time when the child Horus was stung by a scorpion, also provides evidence of Thoth's presence on the Sun barque. After Horus was stung, Isis cried out to the heavens for help. When Râ heard her cries, he stopped the Sun barque. However, it was

Thoth who departed the barque and came down to resuscitate Horus with his Divine words of power.

Thoth has many qualities, which makes his nature very complex. He is the "Lord of *Maât*" and the "Lord of the Divine words". In the Hall of Judgement he was the scribe who weighed the words in accordance with the Divine Law of *Maât*, the ultimate ordeal for the deceased. In the Coffin Texts, he is also referred to as the "Bull of Justice", Ka Maât, and linked to the Tribunal.

> I am the Bull of Justice;
> men respect my voice
> and dread my fierceness.
> I am the confidant of the Palace
> in the presence of the Bull of Justice.
> May your souls be quiet,
> be quiet for me, for I am Thoth.[46]
> – Coffin Texts; Spell 277

Thoth is a self created or self begotten God since no other God gave birth to him. He keeps heaven and earth in equilibrium using his Divine will. He manifested the Divine Law of *Maât*, using celestial mathematics, to provide a foundation for the universe. As a moon God, he is connected to the measurement of time and the seasons. Consequently, he was also regarded as the "Lord of Time", giving him the power to grant long reigning periods to the Pharaohs.

Thoth says:
"I write for thee years without number,
and hundreds of thousands
of *Heb Sed* feasts".[47]
– Temple of Ramses II at Abydos

Thus, his power was even greater than the power of Osiris or Râ himself. In fact, his mightiness seems to supersede the power of any of the other Gods. As mentioned earlier, one of Thoth's names is "Heart of Râ", *Ib-n-Râ* (*ib-n-rꜥ*), for he is the source of all wisdom for the Sungod Râ. His eternal Wisdom was viewed upon as "the Mind and Will of the Divine".

The position of Ka Maât on the barque is related to the concept of *Maât*. Every journey through the Duat has to follow the Divine Law of *Maât*. Ka Maât can be regarded as the Vital Life Force of *Maât* that forms the foundation needed to maintain creation. He is, therefore, extremely important to the progress of the cycle of the Sungod.

Ka Maât also has a deeper meaning related to the God Shu. Shu was viewed upon as an early form of the God Thoth. This explains why the name of this crewmember can be translated in two different ways, Ka Maât and Ka Shu.

Shu is the God of air, but also of life, light, space and the atmosphere. The meaning of the word *Shu* (*šw*) is "be empty, ascend, light or dryness". This refers to his task where he holds up the sky with his two hands, to create space for the sun disk between heaven and earth. One hand supports the sky at the place of sunrise and his other hand at the place of sunset. The atmosphere created in this space, which was now filled with light and air, enabled earthly life. Therefore, Shu was seen as the breath of Râ. Moreover, the atmosphere created by Shu prevents the waters of Nun from flooding the material world and destroying earthly life.

As he is one of the Gods of the Great Ennead, Shu was created first by the creator God, Atum, together with his counterpart, Tefnut. The Pyramid Texts; Utterance 600 tells us the story of the creator God Atum who rose from the primordial hill while spitting out Shu and sneezing out Tefnut. Atum extended his arms in the *Ka*-posture around them in order for his *Ka*-force to enter Shu and Tefnut.

> O Atum-Khoprer,
> you became high on the height,
> your rose up as the bnbn-stone
> in the Mansion of the 'Phoenix' in Ôn,
> you spat out Shu, you expectorated Tefenet,
> and you set your arms about them
> as the arms of a *Ka*-symbol,
> that your essence might be in them.[48]
> – Pyramid Texts; Utterance 600

In the Duat, Shu uses this *Ka*-force to continue the next generation of creation. At the end of the Twelfth Hour he lifts the new dawning sun Khepri in the *Ka*-posture to start a new day and commence a new creation. Then, the sun rises from the waters of Nun and takes his first breath in the atmosphere created for him by Shu.

Shu is a very complex God with many characteristics. He already existed in the Abyss or primeval waters of Nun before the oldest Gods, known as the Ogdoad and also as the eight Heh or Chaos Gods, had taken shape. This is very remarkable since Shu was not created by Atum until after these Gods, came into being. Even so, Shu already existed in "darkness and in gloom" and is even referred to as the father of the eight Chaos Gods.

Thoth is also connected to these eight Chaos Gods for he is seen as their leader. According to some priesthoods, Thoth is the spirit and soul of the primeval waters, or the abyss, wherefrom these eight Gods arose. Therefore, these Gods are also known as the "Souls of Thoth".

Furthermore, Shu, like Thoth, was seen as an important member of the crew of the Sungod. However, since Shu primarily supports the ascension to the sky, he is usually depicted as a crewmember on the Day Sun barque. According to Spell 662 of the Coffin Texts, Shu is the navigator of the Day Sun barque.[49]

This is also reflected in the Book of the Gates wherein the Sungod switches his Night Sun barque after his nocturnal voyage for the Day Sun barque. On the Day Sun barque the crew is comprised of the Doorkeepers, Nebet wia, Isis, Geb, Shu, Heka, Hu and Sia. Thus, Shu actually is a crewmember during the voyage through the day. However, the natures of both Shu and Thoth are essential aspects that provide a great support to Râ during his travels through the night. Shu knows the way in the abyssal waters of Nun where the Night Sun barque sails like no other. And Thoth has been a crewmember aboard the

Sungod's barque since the beginning. Hence, both Gods are integrated into this special crewmember, Ka Maât.

> [...] Shu and Thoth, whom he loves and who are united behind the Great God [...] [50]
>
> – Coffin Texts; Spell 610

Nehes "Wakeful One"

Nehes (*nhs*) is a form of Seth and stands at the stern of the Sun barque, between Ka Maât and Hu. The hieroglyphic meaning of the word Nehes is "hippopotamus". The hippopotamus is a very dangerous and destructive animal in the water as well as on the land. It is, therefore, the perfect embodiment of Seth for he wields his enormous power in the waters and on the sandy ground of the Duat to protect Râ. In the Duat he plays a key role in the defeat of the malicious snake Apophis. Apophis is the embodiment of absolute evil and on a mission to kill the Sungod Râ. If left to his devices, this would eventually lead to a state of non-existence. Seth, with his destructive nature, is well acquainted with evil and subsequently able to triumph over pure evil.

The *Netjer* Seth is a force of nature and generally judged as being evil from a certain point of view. He embodies the evil needed to balance the cosmos. He binds life to physical existence and enables the incarnation of celestial substances, but he stagnates their development on the other hand as well. However, his "evilness" and destructive behaviour is of great importance in order to separate the unified. We need duality to develop our consciousness and to manifest our potential in life. In spite of these interesting qualities, you should not worship Seth. Instead, you have to fight him with all your strength in order to find your own power. This battle prevents you from faltering and stagnating into the matter, which is the purpose of this God of boundaries and confusion. During your journey, you will get to know other forms of Seth as well.

The reason for Seth's unconventional form on the barque is due to the fact that Râ had once banished him from the Sun barque, for Seth's behaviour left a lot to be desired. He would boast continuously about being the bravest God of them all for he was able to defeat Apophis. Therefore, Seth demanded to be treated with the utmost respect by everyone else. He even insisted that Râ payed him respect for he would use his storm against Râ otherwise. Râ became fed up with his insolent behaviour and ultimately expelled him from the Sun barque. However, as Seth is still a necessary force during the journey, he was allowed to return to the Sun barque, but only when adopting this new form as Nehes.

Hu "Utterance"

Hu (*ḥw*) is a Divine being who is depicted either as a ram-headed man, in falcon or in human form. In the Duat, he can be found in human shape at the stern of the barque, between Nehes and

Kherep wia. According to one myth the first word uttered by Atum, while creating the Great Ennead by means of masturbation, was "Hu". So Hu is the embodiment of the very first word of creation and he, therefore, symbolises the creative utterance and the voice of Authority. In the Pyramid Texts Hu is also mentioned as the companion of the deceased King.

As mentioned before, Hu is one of the three special forces that support the process of creation. Hu is the second step in creation for he is the Divine word that comes forth from the sacred Insight or Idea of Sia. Hu is not just merely the utterance of the Divine Word for he is the utterance in accordance with the Divine Law of *Maât*, "Order, Truth and Justice". Through Hu, the powerless Sungod Râ maintains his Authority of utterance in the Duat. Subsequently, Hu is of great importance to Râ.

> To me belongs authoritative utterance;
> what I say is good, my utterance is good,
> and what I say is done accordingly.
> I am Hu, Lord of authoritative utterance.[51]
> – Coffin Texts; Spell 325

Kherep wia
"Guide of the barque"

Kherep wia (*ḥrp wiꜣ*) is the helmsman who stands to the right at the stern of the barque. The hieroglyphic word *kherep* (*ḥrp*) means "to govern, to control, to lead, to guide, to direct". In the Book of the Gates the helmsman of the barque is the God Heka. We could assume Kherep wia is a form of the God Heka and thus one of the three special forces that always accompany Râ on his nocturnal journey. Heka is the third step in creation. The Divine idea or Insight of Sia is uttered in Divine Words by Hu and realised through the creative force of *Heka* by Kherep wia. The Sungod needs all three of these capacities to continue the first creation, *Zep Tepi*, every day.

Heka is generally translated as Magic. Magic in this context has nothing to do with sorcery. It is an invisible though potent energy preceding creation. It ensures that the intention, uttered in words by the *Netjeru*, is manifested. Magic is, therefore, the creative force that ensures the "Words of power" come into existence. The Creator God used Magic to create the world. Without this creative force, physical existence would be impossible.

It is vital that this Divine power is applied in accordance with the Law of the Divine. If not, this same power is regarded as black magic in service of evil. Magic is a neutral force adopting the "colour", black or white, depending on the way it is used and the way it transforms the world. Magic is generally, though incorrectly, seen as a supernatural power. However, it actually is a creative force that manifests itself in accordance with *Maât*. If you do not comprehend this Law of creation, "Magic" can be mistaken for the supernatural.

The invisible power of Magic has been captured in certain images in the art of the ancient

Egyptians. These images depict Deities holding a net filled with invisible energy. This net can be found in the Tenth Hour of the Book of the Gates. It emphasises, in a symbolic way, the fact that Magic is an energetic forcefield.

Coming back to Kherep wia, or "guide of the barque", who is a very important crewmember. It is his intention to support, guide and lead Râ during his voyage which is reflected in the meaning of the word *kherep*. He is the steersman of the barque of Râ and maintains or adjusts the course when needed. The *Kherep* is also a sceptre used to consecrate objects by tapping on them. The helm used to steer the barque resembles this sceptre. Hence, it can be regarded as the sceptre used to sanctify and manifest the journey in accordance with the Will of the Divine, *Maât*. During the journey the posture of the guide, where he does or does not hold the helm, changes. In the Fourth Hour the guide has disappeared as the Sun barque descends on its own following the unapproachable paths of *Imhet* in the Forbidden Land of Sokar.

Deities holding a magical net, Tenth Hour of the Book of the Gates, KV 9 Ramses V and VI

PART TWO

THE TWELVE HOURS OF THE NIGHT

THE FIRST HOUR
"Water of Râ"

The Gate: (no name mentioned)
The Hour Goddess: "She who smashes the foreheads of the enemies of Râ"
The Guardian: "Keeper of the Two Flames"

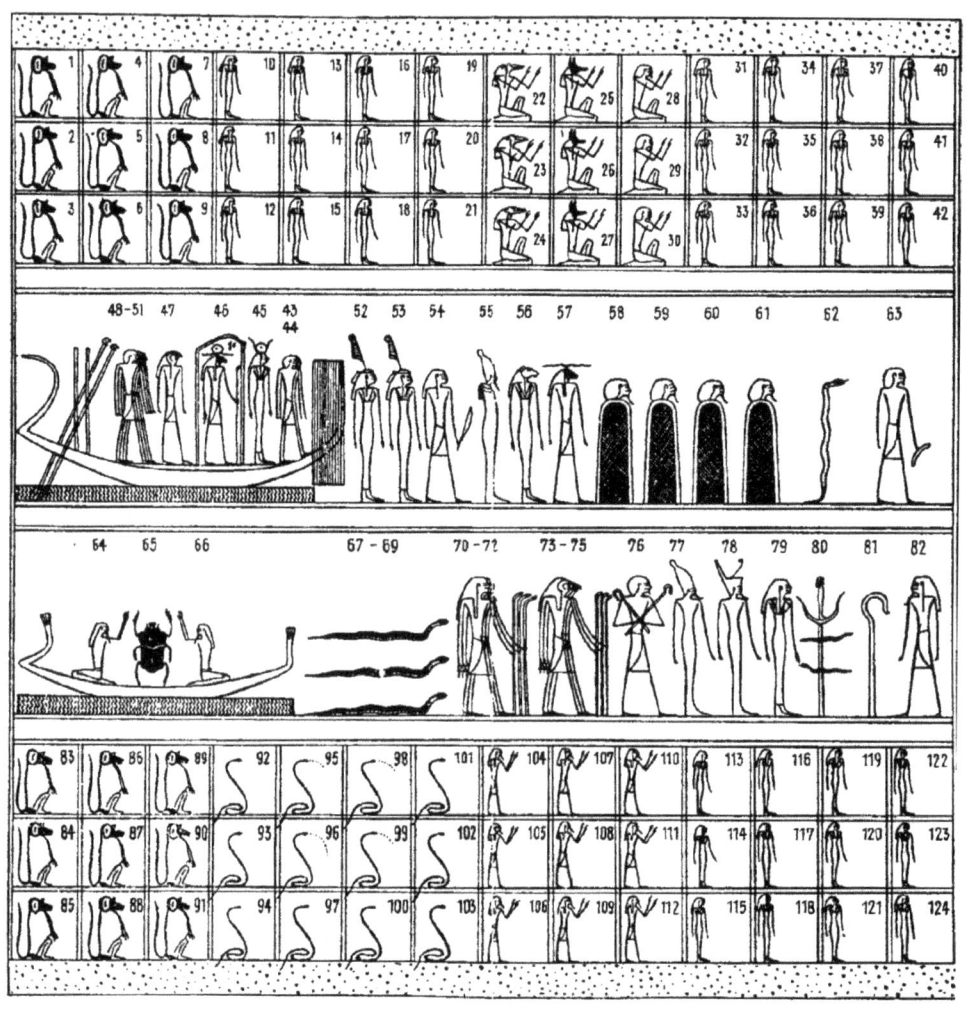

Figure 12: the First Hour

The Entrance to the Duat

The First Hour is the twilight zone during which the light of the sun slowly extinguishes from dusk to darkness. It forms a borderline between the world of the living and the world of the dead. It is a fleeting area that functions as a portal or a gateway. It opens only briefly to grant passage to the deceased. Afterwards it closes as if it was never there.

There are two different types of gates mentioned in the Amduat. The first is called *âryt* (*ʿryt*), which means "forecourt or portal". For example, a forecourt of a temple grants access to the temple without the need to pass through a physical gate. It is an open area accessible to every visitor of the temple. An *âryt* is, therefore, not a physical door.[1]

There are two *âryt* gates in the Duat. The first *âryt* gateway forms the antechamber of the Duat, the First Hour. It is a transitional area that separates the Duat from the world of the living. It is located at the horizon in the West where it opens for the setting sun in the evening. The second *âryt* gateway marks the exit of the Duat at the end of the Twelfth Hour. It lies in the horizon of the East where it opens to the rising sun in the morning. Like the First Hour, this area is a transitional zone between the two different worlds.

The second type of gate is called *seba* (*sbȝ*), which means "door or gate". This type is an actual physical gateway or door.[1]

The first real *seba* gate in the realm of the Duat does not appear until the end of the First Hour where it grants access to the Second Hour. Every hour, with exception of the first, opens with a *seba* gate. And yet there is another *seba* gate that is situated before the first *âryt* gateway. This gate is mentioned only in the title of the Amduat as shown in the text below.

> The beginning is the Horn of the West,
> the gate (*seba*) of the Western horizon,
> the end is Unified Darkness
> the gate (*seba*) of the Western Horizon.[2]

This gate is called "the Horn of the West". It is a real "door" to the far Western horizon where the sun sets. The Horn, or Peak, is the very entrance. It forms the opening to the first *âryt* gate which grants access to the Duat. This means there are two gates that need to be passed before one can enter the realm of the Duat. The Horn of the West differs from the *seba* gates between the various hours in the Duat since it does not belong to the "unseen" world of the Duat. It is visible and tangible in the world of the living and an actual peak with the appearance of a pyramid-shaped mountain overlooking the Valley of the Kings in Egypt. In Arabic it is called El-Qurn and it is the highest point of the Theban hills on the Western bank of the Nile. The ancient name was *Ta Dehent*, which means "The Peak". The royal necropolis can be found below this pyramidal peak in the Valley of the Kings. The pyramid symbolises the primordial mound that emerged from the waters of Nun in the beginning of time. Thus it was seen as a place of rebirth from which new life arose. It is possible *Ta Dehent* was chosen because of this peak, as the sun truly disappears behind it which makes the area below, where the royal necropolis can be found, a symbolical place of resurrection in the world of the dead.

In the Old Kingdom the gateway to the Duat was located elsewhere, near Abydos. To the West of Abydos there are limestone mountains positioned in the shape of a crescent that surrounds the villages. In the centre of these mountains there is a peculiar gap, which was known as Pega-the-Gap. The Gap was believed to be the direct entrance to the West, the realm of the dead. Unsurprisingly, the royal tombs of the first Pharaohs were built near the gap, leading the Kings directly into the Duat. During the New Kingdom, the Pharaohs began building their "Houses of Eternity" in the Valley of the Kings at the West Bank of Thebes, which is modern Luxor, instead. Therefore, the gateway to the Duat was relocated as well, as it was now represented by the Horn. Since the Duat became written down on the walls during the New Kingdom, it makes sense the gate was now described as the Horn instead of the Gap.

The Guardian of the Horn of the West is the cobra Goddess Meretseger who lives on this peak and was regarded as the personification of the mountain itself. Her epithets are "She who loves Silence" and "She who is on her mountain". She is a Goddess with the head of a Cobra and was often depicted in the shape of a cobra. There must have been numerous living examples of these cobras on the West Bank. Meretseger was the local Goddess of the workmen in the village Deir el-Medina, Place of Truth, who excavated and decorated the royal tombs. She was considered very dangerous as she spat venom at anyone who tried to desecrate the tombs. However, the cobra Goddess was merciful to anyone who showed repentance and promised to obey her. Several small shrines were dedicated to Meretseger in the hope of receiving her blessing. These shrines and a large rock sanctuary are located near the narrow path leading from the workmen's village to the Queen's Valley.

Neferabu was a draftsman who lived in Deir el-Medina. He wrote several hymns including one in honour of the Goddess Meretseger. In this hymn he warns his fellow workmen of the power of this Goddess. He clearly describes, from his own experience, what the Goddess is capable of when treated with disrespect. However, he also describes another side of her that arises when she is treated with the respect she deserves.

> Giving praise to the Peak of the West,
> kissing the ground to her *Ka*.
> I give praise, hear (my) call,
> I was a truthful man on earth!
> Made by the servant in the
> Place-of-Truth, Neferabu, Justified.
>
> (I was) an ignorant man and foolish,
> who knew not good from evil;

I did the transgression against the Peak,
and she taught a lesson to me.
I was in her hand by night as by day,
I sat on bricks like the woman in labor,
I called to the wind, it came not to me,
I libated to the Peak of the West,
great of strength,
and to every God and Goddess.
Behold, I will say to the great and small,
who are in the troop:
Beware of the Peak!
For there is a lion within her!
The Peak strikes with the stroke
of a savage lion,
she is after him who offends her!

I called upon my Mistress,
I found her coming to me as sweet breeze;
She was merciful to me,
having made me see her hand.
She returned to me appeased,
She made my malady forgotten;
for the Peak of the West is appeased,
if one calls upon her.
So says Neferabu, Justified.
He says: Behold, let hear every ear,

El-Qurn, Horn of the West, West Bank of Luxor

that lives upon earth:
beware the Peak of the West! [3]

– Hymn to Merteseger of Neferabu,
Deir el-Medina

Introduction

This God enters through the Western gateway of the horizon.
Seth stands at the river-bank.
120 *iteru* is the journey
through this gateway
before the barque reaches the Duatians.
He passes the water after it to Wernes.[4]

The First Hour starts with the short introduction, above, wherein Râ enters the hour through the Western gateway of the horizon. Since the realm of the First Hour is filled with water, known as the "Water of Râ", the Sun barque can easily sail through this hour. Râ is swallowed by the Goddess Nut and disappears from sight of the world of the living. Consequently, he is assumed to be dead. In ancient Egypt, the setting sun was, therefore, the symbol of death. After Râ enters the realm of the dead, he emerges as a *Ba*-soul. This transforms him in his new shape as a ram-headed God. In this form his name is changed to "flesh", a reference to his body that is now a corpse.

The First Hour is quite unlike any other hour. It is the transitional area, known as the antechamber of the Duat. Interestingly, the real Duat does not actually begin until the Second Hour, after the 120 *iteru* long journey through the First Hour. The hieroglyphic word *iteru* (*itrw*) means "measure of length or schoenus".[5]

The schoenus was an ancient measurement of length that was based on a knotted rope. The rope was fitted with knots on fixed distances to make it suitable as a measuring tape. The *iteru* is an earthly unit of measurement. However, since it is also used in the Duat, the *iteru* here is regarded to be Divine in nature.

Another meaning of *iteru* is "river". Since the First Hour is 120 *iteru* long and the entire journey here takes place exclusively on the Sacred River, this indicates that the Sacred River itself is 120 *iteru* long in the First Hour. Interestingly, the Nile that flows through Egypt has approximately the same length. Both rivers are flowing next to each other for they are each other's mirror image. Nevertheless, the Nile finds its way in the land of the living while the Sacred River flows through the Duat. These two completely different worlds exist here next to one another and are separated only by a very thin line or veil.

After Râ passes through the Horn of the West, Seth is standing at the riverbank where he quietly observes everyone who embarks on the Sun barque. Seth is an ill-tempered God who symbolises chaos, violence and destruction. He is the embodiment of the opposite force and will do everything possible to knock the Divine order of *Maât* off balance. He does this, for example, through drought, creating storms or foul weather to destroy the fertile lands. It is hardly surprising that it was Seth who killed his brother Osiris, the Pharaoh of Egypt. After this dreadful event Egypt, which was in harmony and in accordance with *Maât* before, was immediately submerged in chaos. Thus, the land needed a new King to lead the country and restore the balance and harmony. This resulted in the battle between Seth and his other brother, Horus the Elder, Heru ur, where they fought for the throne. Eventually, they both gained a part of the rulership of Egypt. Seth became King of the Red land, the deserts and borders of Egypt as well as the region of the dead. He became known as "He who is below". Horus the Elder became the King of the Black land, Upper and Lower Egypt, and became known as "He who is above".

Together, Horus and Seth restored balance as they merged their opposite forces in a new united country. Obviously, there remained a certain rivalry and friction between these two completely different Kings. However, through the conflicts in life, and in this case in Egypt, life is continuously challenged to renew and develop itself. This battle also takes place in the Duat where life, or light, fight with the darkness, or death. This is a necessary battle to realise renewal and regeneration. Seth is always the one to initiate these conflicts, which is why he is standing at the border between the world of the living and the Duat. He reminds Râ of the fact that harmony is disrupted the moment Râ enters the Duat. The old life, which no longer functions, has to dissolve first before a new life can be born. The moment Râ leaves his Day Sun barque to board the Night Sun barque, Seth himself is present as well in his form of Nehes. Seth is the most suited Deity capable of recognising evil and he is more than willing to aid Râ with this. It might come as a surprise, however, that total destruction is not what Seth wants. It was never his intention to wipe everything out. The only thing he wants is to create resistance and defiance to enable the old to keep renewing itself. Hence, Seth, as the God of confusion and chaos, does not only oppose the old established order, but also the all-consuming pure evil that is symbolised by the serpent Apophis. He welcomes Râ and everyone else who has been granted access in the Duat to fight this battle with him.

The First Hour is a summary of the entire Duat. The Sacred River in the middle section is divided in two parts, as mentioned before in the chapter "The influence of the Sacred River during the inundation" (page 72). The upper part of the Sacred River, represents the barque of the aged Sungod Râ at the beginning of his journey. The lower part of the Sacred River, represents the resurrected Sungod Râ. Here, he can be seen in his new form as the scarab Khepri, who is worshiped by two praising figures of Osiris. At this point he has arrived at the end of his journey. The two Sun barques, as depicted in the First Hour, sail next to each other and represent the eternal cycle of regeneration. Every ending contains a beginning of a new cycle. A fact that has been occurring since the beginning of time, *Zep Tepi*.

The two riverbanks at the left and right side of the Sacred River represent harmony and balance. This is emphasised by the clear division of the Gods, Goddesses, and cobras at each side of the riverbank. There are nine baboons, twelve Goddesses, nine kneeling Gods and twelve Goddesses on the left riverbank. On the right riverbank there are nine baboons, twelve cobras, nine praising Gods and twelve Goddesses.

The number nine symbolises the concept of a great number, the plural of the plural. Twelve is the number of completeness. For example, a year contains twelve months, there are twelve hours during the day and twelve hours in the night, twelve signs of the zodiac and so on. Here, it refers to the twelve hours of the night and to the completion of a cycle. The entire journey is a continuous cycle of twelve hours that are repeated indefinitely, as symbolised by the number nine. Similar to the sun, who travels through the sky during the day, sets at dusk and travels through the night to rise again in a new day. The everlasting cycle enables creation to continue.

The First Hour provides a clear picture of the reliable structure and order in the Duat. This overview offers the essential feeling of trust and confidence and provides Râ with the courage to make the descent into the world of the unknown. No matter what happens along the way, the Sungod can be assured of a successful outcome.

The Duatians on the left riverbank (upper section)

On the riverbank at the left side of the Sacred River, Râ is greeted by nine baboons the moment he sails into the Duat. They have opened the gates for their beloved Sungod while glorifying him. Râ is the light in their lives and as true adorers the baboons bow to and pray for him.

(No. 1) "Baboon"
(No. 2) "Acclaiming One"
(No. 3) "Djehdjeh"
(No. 4) "Heart of the earth"
(No. 5) "Favourite of the earth"
(No. 6) "Praising One"
(No. 7) "Opener of the earth"
(No. 8) "*Ba*-soul of the earth"
(No. 9) "Whom Râ sees"

In ancient Egypt baboons were kept as pets. They were seen as intelligent animals that could be trained to do things like picking fruit from the trees and catching criminals. Because of their cleverness they became the sacred animal of Thoth, the God of wisdom and communication. Through the identification with Thoth, who is also a God of Magic, the baboons were regarded as animals with supernatural powers and the representation of wisdom and communication. Their number of nine (the plural of the plural) refers to the infinite wisdom and communication that can be found in this dark world.

Baboons bark very loudly when the sun sets in the evening and rises in the morning. Therefore, the moment Râ descends as the setting sun in the First Hour of the night, the baboons bark to greet and welcome Râ as they open the gates for him. Râ does not perceive their greeting as merely barking. He truly understands them for he is able to comprehend their language.

The baboons are followed by the twelve standing Goddesses (No. 10 – 21).

(No. 10) "She of the throat"
(No. 11) "Maiden"
(No. 12) "Mistress of Life"
(No. 13) "She who praises through her *Ba*-soul"
(No. 14) "She who is elevated through her *Akh*-spirit"
(No. 15) "She who overpowers her foes"
(No. 16) "Great Hidden One"
(No. 17) "Honoured One"
(No. 18) "She of the fetters"
(No. 19) "She with the uplifted arm"
(No. 20) "Mistress of protection"
(No. 21) "Deaf One"

The Goddesses are here to praise and adore "the One within the earth", which is Râ. The weary Râ receives a warm welcome from them. He is no longer on the earth, *tep ta (tp-t3)*, which is the world of the living, for he has entered inside the earth, *imy ta (imy-t3)*, the Duat.

Names of the Goddesses who lead the Great God in the West.
May they lead Osiris N to every place which he desires like Râ.
May they cause that He live in his barque.[6]

Next are nine adoring Gods (No. 22 – 30) in a kneeling posture with upraised hands. The first three are crocodile-headed Gods who represent great strength and power.

(No. 22) "Who traverses the Duat"
(No. 23) "Who screams"
(No. 24) "Powerful of face"

The following three Gods are jackal-headed and represent the different forms of Anubis.

(No. 25) "Lord of the Sacred Land".
This is one of the titles of Anubis.
(No. 26) "Who keeps apart the Two Lands"
(No. 27) "Who keeps apart the two powers".
This name, like the previous name, is a reference to another title of Anubis, "Controller of the Two Lands" (*shm-t3.wy*).

Hence, these three Gods are a salute to Anubis. Their presence here is not surprising since jackals are animals who feel particularly at home in the borderland as they live on the edge of the desert. They can usually be seen at sunset when they start their hunt. Here, in the First Hour on the border of day and night, they are present to worship Râ.

The last three Gods have a human head.

(No. 28) "Whose arm is shining"

(No. 29) "Whose arm is seen"
(No. 30) "Whose arm is praising"

> Name of the Gods who praise Râ,
> May they adore the Osiris N
> before the Lords of the Duat,
> like those who are within the Earth.[7]

The final Goddesses, at the end of the left riverbank, are the twelve important Hour Goddesses. Here, at the beginning of the Duat, they welcome the Sungod as a reception committee. The Hour Goddesses represent different aspects of the Goddess Hathor. They are the local Goddesses who correspond with a specific hour of the night. Due to their protective, helpful and powerful nature, they are the eminently suited guides to support Râ through their respective hours of the night. Each Hour Goddess is familiar with the correct sailing route over the Sacred River in her own district. She knows what difficulties are ahead. However, this does not mean that she helps Râ to bypass these obstacles. In fact, she leads Râ straight towards them since gaining control over these opposing forces is especially important. This strengthens Râ and supports him in his transformation process. The names of the Hour Goddesses refer to their specific function within their respective hours. Confusing enough, the names as mentioned in the introduction text of each hour, may deviate from the names used during the actual hour. For clarity, these alternative names for each Hour Goddess can be found in parenthesis in the list below.

(No. 31) First Hour;
"She who smashes the brows of her foes"
("She who smashes the foreheads
of the enemies of Râ")
(No. 32) Second Hour;
"Wise One who protects her master"
(No. 33) Third Hour;
"She who cuts *Ba*-souls"
(No. 34) Fourth Hour;
"Great One in the Duat"
("She who is great in her power")
(No. 35) Fifth Hour;
"She who is in the midst of her barque"
("She who guides in the midst of her
barque")
(No. 36) Sixth Hour; "She who arrives"
("Arrival who gives the right (way)"
or "True Sanctuary")
(No. 37) Seventh Hour;
"She who repels the gangs of Seth"
("Repelling the "Evil One"
and beheading "Neha-her")
(No. 38) Eight Hour; "She of the midnight"
("Mistress of Deep Night")
(No. 39) Ninth Hour;
"Protectress of her eye"
("She who adores and protects her Lord")
(No. 40) Tenth Hour; "She who rages"
("The Furious One who slaughters
Him with crooked heart")
(No. 41) Eleventh Hour;
"Starry One"
("Starry One, Lady of the barque,

who repels the enemy when he appears")
(No. 42) Twelfth Hour;
"She who beholds the perfection
of her Lord"
("Beholding the perfection of Râ")

The Duatians of The Sacred River (middle section – upper part)

The two Maât Goddesses tow this God in the Night barque,
passing through the gateway of this region.
120 *iteru* it is that he passes after it to Wernes, whose length is 300 *iteru*,
assigning land to them (to) the Gods who are behind him.
"Water of Râ" is the name of this field.
"Keeper of the Two Flames"
is the name of its Guardian.
This God begins to give orders
and to take care for those
who are in the Duat at this field.[8]

The upper part of the Sacred River begins with the Sun barque of the aged Sungod Râ and his crew. "Wepwawet" (No. 43) and "Sia" (No. 44) are standing at the prow of the barque. Wepwawet is standing to the left and he has already opened the way for Râ to grant the Sungod and his Sun barque safe passage. Sia is standing to the right, on the right side of Râ, to enable the Sungod to watch through his eyes and gaze upon the world with Divine insight. Behind them, and in front of the Sungod, stands the Lady of the Barque, "Nebet wia" (No. 45). After Râ enters through the gate, she welcomes the aged Sungod with open arms. Her heart-warming welcome smoothes the transition of Râ from the day into the night world and makes it more bearable. She will remain standing here, in front of Râ's shrine, with the exception of the Seventh Hour, and feeds him with her spiritual nourishment.

In the middle of the barque the Sungod Râ, or "Iuf or Flesh" (No. 46), himself is standing in a shrine as the ram-headed *Ba*-soul. He holds a Serpent-sceptre, a symbol of absolute power, in one hand and the *Ankh* in the other. He carries the solar disk between his ram horns. Though Râ has not arrived in the real Duat, since it does not begin until the Second Hour, his transformation from the day into the night sun has already begun.

The *Ankh* (ʿnḫ) in Râ's hand is a hieroglyphic sign which looks like a loop with a t-shape attached to it. Its meaning is "living or life". It is carried in the right hand by Divine Beings, Gods and Goddesses. In many images these *Netjeru* can be seen gifting the *Ankh* to the Pharaoh. The origin and exact meaning of the sign is unknown. It may be a reference to the Breath of Life, which is the source of life itself. However, it is clear the symbolical meaning of this sign is not restricted to life alone. It is far more than that. The *Ankh* is the symbol of the indestructible nature of eternal Life that will never perish. Only the Gods know the secrets of everlasting life, which is why they are the only ones able to grant this gift to humanity through the Pharaoh.

Fig. 13. The hieroglyphic sign Ankh

Naturally, the Sungod himself is carrying this sign of eternal Life as well. The continuation of the entire creation is literally in his hands and depends on whether he succeeds during his nightly voyage. Along his journey he ensouls every Duatian he encounters as he grants them the Breath of Life. This action allows the Duatians to come back to life. However, as soon as Râ leaves, their life leaves with him. Nevertheless, these Duatians do not truly die for they lie waiting for his return during the next night. At that point Râ once again fills them with the Breath of Life. The Duatians, in turn, simultaneously exhale and fill Râ himself with strength and life. This interaction provides for everlasting breathing and thus eternal Life, for Râ as well as for the Duatians.

"Heru Hekenu" (No. 47) is standing directly behind the shrine. Right after the Sungod embarks, Heru Hekenu begins worshipping Râ through his beautiful prayers. At the stern of the barque the last four crewmembers are standing next to each other. The first at the left is the wise Lord of *Maât*, "Ka Maât" (No. 48). No matter what happens along the way, he guarantees that the entire journey from start to finish proceeds in accordance with the Divine Law of *Maât*. Next is the powerful and wilful God Seth in his form as "Nehes" (No. 49). Following is the Divine being "Hu" (No. 50) who ensures the severely weakened Sungod maintains his Divine Authority within the Duat. The final crewmember at the right is the guide of the barque, "Kherep wia" (No. 51), who is standing at the helm. Whenever needed he adjusts the course to keep the Sun barque under control. With the helm in his hands, he guarantees a blessed journey.

In front of the prow of the barque is a kind of veil that symbolises the still veiled nature of this first area. This is still the antechamber that is designed for Râ to adjust to the dimming light and the structure of this area. The actual Duat is not unveiled until the Sungod has passed through the *seba* gate of the Second Hour. Until that time, the clear division functions as a protective layer for this hidden world.

The veil also has other meanings. It is the magical net which gathers Magic, or *Heka*, to form a field of energy and projects it forth. This is necessary to make it possible for the barque to descend into the Duat. The veil is also a weapon used by Râ in the darkness of the Duat to gain mastery over his opponents.

There are two Maât Goddesses, or Maâty (No. 52 and 53), standing in front of the barque.

They tow the Sun barque of Râ through the First Hour and, according to the closing text of this hour, they are the two daughters of Râ.

Maât is the Goddess of Order, Truth and Justice and wears an ostrich feather fastened to her headdress. The ostrich feather is the symbol of that which is straight, righteous and true, or *Maât*. It refers to the feather in one of the scales used to balance against the heart of the deceased in the Hall of Judgement.

> The Goddess Maât was, then, the personification of physical and moral law, and order and truth. In connexion with the Sungod Râ she indicated the regularity with which he rose and set in the sky, and the course which he followed daily from East to West.[9]

– Sir E.A. Wallis Budge

The dual Maât, or Maâty, is a term for the two Maât Goddesses who participate in the judgment of the deceased as they sit on either side in the Hall of Judgement. Thus, the Hall is also known as *weskht net Maâty*, which translates as the Hall of double *Maât*, or Truth. This is where the heart is weighed against the feather of *Maât* to determine the balance of the life of the deceased compared to the Truth. The number two shows us that a concept can be grasped only when compared with its opposite. These two different sides represent the grand scheme of things from which the truth arises. Truth, therefore, is never singular but dual. It can only be weighed with two scales under the watchful eyes of the two Maât Goddesses.

Oftentimes, the two Maât Goddesses are identified as the twin sisters Isis and Nephthys. This seems plausible since these two Goddesses are opposites in their nature. They emphasise the fact Truth has two sides to it and needs to be judged from a dual vision.

The appearance of the two Maât Goddesses right at the beginning of the First Hour, ensures us that even in this unknown dark world, there is still Order, Truth and Justice. On the other hand, however, the two Goddesses also make Râ aware of the upcoming confrontations between opposites. This forthcoming friction is necessary to eventually reach completion or Truth and to guarantee the continuation of creation.

> Maât is with you every day,
> when you set in the Duat.
> Maât is with you,
> after you have illumined the bodies of the cavern dwellers,
> after you have crossed
> into the Hidden Chamber.[10]

Following the two Maât Goddesses there is a row of Gods;

(No. 54) "Cutter"
a God holding a large knife

(No. 55) "Foremost of the West", Khenty-Iment, who is Osiris in his mummified form. He is wearing the White Crown, known as *Hedjet* (*ḥḏt*), which represents Upper Egypt. The White Crown was an emblem of the vulture Goddess

Nekhbet. She was the patron and tutelary Goddess of Upper Egypt. Her cult centre was located in Nekheb, the ancient capital of the 3rd nome of Upper Egypt (modern El-Kab near Luxor). Some of her epithets are "Lady of the Great House", "Lady of the grassland", "Lady of the inaccessible land", "Lady of the contented ones" and "White One of Nekheb". Usually she is depicted as a vulture or a vulture-headed Goddess. In vulture form she often holds the *shen* ring in her claws which is a symbol of eternity. According to the Pyramid Texts she was a defender and protector of the King. She is also described in Utterance 228 as the mother of the deceased King. In her form as a great wild cow she provided the King with nourishment.

> Your mother is the great wild cow
> in the midst of Nekheb,
> with white headcloth, wide plumages,
> and dangling breasts.
> She will suckle you and not wean you.[11]

As stated in Coffin Texts, Spell 398, Nekhbet was a protector of Horus, 'Nekhbet with her arms about Horus".[12] She also opened her wings in an embracing gesture for Râ to protect and guide him on his course through the sky. "[Her(?) wings] are opened [to(?)] me, and Râ lives thereby every day".[13] The vulture, who is a scavenger, is connected to death, rebirth and purification. It feeds itself with the carcasses of animals and thus keeps the environment clean and free of diseases. Purity was the prerequisite to be reborn into a new life. Hence, according to Spell 863 of the Coffin Texts, the deceased identified himself with Nekhbet to guarantee pure food and drink. "If N be hungry, Nekhbet will be hungry; if N be thirsty, Nekhbet will be thirsty".[14]

Coming back to "Foremost of the West" who asides the White Crown, also wears a necklace called the *menit* or *menat* (*mnit*). This necklace is a symbol of new life, resurrection, potency, fertility, health and happiness. The front of the necklace consists of strings with beads

Two Maât Goddesses, KV 9 Ramses V and VI

that lie on the chest. To counterweight the beads there is a pendant attached at the back. The pendant ensures that the positive forces of this piece of jewellery can flow into the spinal column. The necklace is the emblem of the Goddess Hathor due to her association with birth, abundance and fecundity. However, she is not the only one who wears this for Osiris, Nut, Sekhmet, Isis and Ptah are all wearing it as well. Furthermore, the *menit* was also given to the deceased in the form of an amulet. This was done to ensure that the sexual organs remained active in the Afterlife as well to bring forth new life.

Fig. 14. The menit necklace.

(No. 56) "Sekhmet" is a Goddess depicted as a woman with the head of a lioness. Her name means the Powerful or the Mighty One. She was regarded as the destructive form of the Goddesses Hathor and the Goddess Mut. Despite her ravaging nature she is also a Goddess of healing and the patron of physicians and healers. Hence her title; "The Mistress of Life". It are precisely these two sides of her nature that make her a righteous Goddess who warrants that the Divine Law of *Maât* is complied with. She destroys sickness and falsehood in order to heal the truth and enable it to reach maturity. This transformation requires a lot of fire that is provided by Sekhmet herself. She is usually depicted with the sun disk encircled by the Uraeus cobra on top of her head that symbolises this fire. It is a reference to the heat of the sun as it reaches its highest point during the day, which enlightens or burns the world. This solar disk is obviously the Sungod Râ, or the Eye of Râ, whom she protects. During the Tenth Hour she plays an important part in the protection of this Eye.

(No. 57) "Great illuminator"
a ram-headed God.

Next are four stelea depicted with human heads.

(No. 58) "Decree of Râ"
(No. 59) "Decree of Atum"
(No. 60) "Decree of Khepri"
(No. 61) "Decree of Osiris"

They are the representations of the four forms of the sun. Râ symbolises the day, Atum the setting sun in the evening, Osiris the sun at night and Khepri the rising sun in the morning. Together they form the cycle of the sun and refer to completeness and wholeness.

The next two Deities are;

(No. 62) "Hour" an upraised serpent;
(No. 63) "Traverser of the hours"

a God with a magical knife.

Magical knives were used during childbirth to ward off evil and to protect the vulnerable new life. During labour, women would squat down on the ground while holding this large knife in their hands. After the child was born, the women kept the knife beside them for seven days, to keep the evil spirits away.[15]

Often these knives were made from the ivory of the hippopotamus, which is a reference to the Goddess Taweret. She is the Goddess of childbirth and fertility and is depicted as a hippopotamus with the back of a crocodile.

The God "Traverser of the hours" is the protector of birth. He is walking at the front of the procession of the Sun barque with the magical knife in his hand. With it, he protects the birth canal through which Râ has entered here. The moment Râ dies as the setting sun in the land of the living, he is born here in the realm of the Duat. The transition from one world into the other is not one without danger. Fortunately, "Traverser of the hours" warrants a safe passage for the Sungod.

The text above this section mentions a Guardian, "Keeper of the Two Flames". This Guardian does not partake in the row of Deities in this section. It is unclear who he is. It may be another name for the Guardian "Who Seals the earth" (No. 82) who is standing at the end of the lower part of the middle section of the Sacred River. However, this name could also be a reference to the Guardian of the Second Hour (No. 193) "Two Flames". He may have a double role and watches over the Second as well as the First Hour.

The Duatians of the Sacred River (middle section – lower part)

Right beneath the Sun barque another barque is depicted. In it stands the resurrected Sungod displayed as the scarab "Khepri" (No. 65) who is worshipped by two squatting figures of "Osiris" (No. 64 and 66). Again, the number

Sekhmet the lioness Goddess,
Temple of Horus at Edfu

two refers, similarly to the two Maât Goddesses, to the union of opposites necessary for the rebirth and regeneration of new life. To emphasise the duality, the Night Sun barque *"Mesktet"* of Râ is positioned right next to the Day Sun barque *"Mândjet"* of Khepri. The Day Sun barque reveals the upcoming rebirth at the end of the journey and has an ambiance of jubilation and adoration.

In front of the barque there are three serpents (No. 67 – 69). Their number of three is once again a reference to a large number of serpents.

(No. 67) "Who sweeps the mouth"
(No. 68) "Slicer"
(No. 69) "The Pointed One"

Serpents live in holes beneath the ground and feel at home in dark places. Thus, they are able to make contact with the underworld. This gives them the ability to adopt the power of the dead, Magic and omniscience. The Duat, therefore, is an excellent dwelling place for these creatures. The symbolism of the serpent is a very complex one. Snakes have the ability to shed their skin, which makes them a symbol of the process of transformation, resurrection and regeneration. Its physique is regarded as primitive, as it crawls on the ground. This is why it was seen as the primeval form of all creatures, symbolising the beginning of creation. Due to this connection with the primordial life force, the serpent represents the coiled potential power, lying dormant until it is ready to rise. It has a dual character associated with both negative and positive forces. It is unsurprising that it was the snake in paradise at the beginning of times who caused the duality that resulted in the development of consciousness.

In the underworld, the serpents and snake like Deities are either good or evil by nature. The ones who are good function as guides and guardians. The evil ones do anything within their power to cause death and destruction. Along Râ's journey, he will encounter both the good and evil serpents, who are either giving protection or trying to destroy him.

In front of the three snakes is a procession of all kinds of Gods, Goddesses and two staffs. These Deities guide Râ through the First Hour. The first six Gods are holding a Serpent-sceptre, a symbol of absolute power, in one hand and the *Ankh*, the sign of eternal Life, in the other. The first three take care of the food supply, which is reflected in their names. These Deities are in human shape.

(No. 70) "He of the fields"
(No. 71) "He of the meadows"
(No. 72) "He of the pointed bread"

The other three Deities are falcon-headed.

(No. 73) "Hebenu"
(No. 74) "He of the staff"
(No. 75) "He of the garment"

(No. 76) "He of the plot" carries two shepherd's crooks, or *Heka*-sceptres, crossed over his chest.

This sceptre is an attribute to catch or direct a sheep who has strayed from the herd by hooking the neck or leg. Consequently, the sceptre is a symbol of power and rulership.

(No. 77) "Neith" (*nit* or *nt*) is wearing the White Crown of Upper Egypt. However, she is usually depicted as a Goddess wearing the Red Crown. She is one of the oldest Deities and has a very complex character. During the Early Dynastic Period she was regarded as a creator Goddess and called "the Mother and Father of all things". In one myth she was even seen as the mother of the creator sun God Atum, who she birthed herself. According to a text in the temple of Esna, Neith created all living beings through pronouncing seven magical words. Due to her enormous creative powers she was seen as the personification of the creative potency of the primeval waters. That is why she was also known as the "Great Flood" and "Great Cow". Her identification with the fertile waters gave her the role of mother of all snakes and crocodiles. In particular the role as mother of the crocodile God Sobek.[16]

Neith is represented by a curious symbol that can be explained from different angles. The symbol could represent a click beetle, a shield with two crossed arrows, or a weaving shuttle. The click beetle was usually found near water, such as in the Nile valley. The beetle saved itself from the rising water of the inundation through jumping. This could be the reason for Neith her association with the power of this animal as she is the Great Flood. Furthermore, she is identified as the Goddess of hunting and war. In this specific role she is referred to as "Mistress of the Bow" and "Ruler of Arrows" and depicted while holding a bow and arrows in her hand. She uses the arrows to shoot the enemies of the Sungod Râ, which explains the two crossed arrows. In her other role as the Goddess of weaving, she provides the dead with the clothing (the mummy bandages) and covers the faces of the deceased.[17] The symbol of a weaving shuttle, therefore, applies to her as well.

Additionally, Neith is a funerary Goddess and one of the four protective Goddesses

The Goddess Neith with the weaving shuttle above her head, QV 44 Kha-em-Waset

guarding the coffins, canopic chests and jars. The other Goddesses belonging to this group are Isis, Nephthys and Serket.

Neith sometimes played the part of Anubis during the mummification process where she took care of the provision of unguents and linen.[18] When adopting this function, she oversaw the Divine Pavilion in which the dead were embalmed and wrapped in linen.

Thus, Neith is an important and powerful Goddess affiliated with the continuation of creation and the protection of the Sungod Râ as well as of the deceased.

(No. 78) "The Divine goat" is in mummiform and is wearing the Red Crown of Lower Egypt on his head.

The Red Crown is called the *Desheret* (*dšrt*) and is the representation of Lower Egypt, the North. The image of the Red Crown was also used as the "n" hieroglyph and referred to as the *nt*-crown. Utterances 220 and 221 of the Pyramid Texts provide a good insight into the powers of the crown. It describes the fact that the crown is not just a crown at all. It actually is a mighty serpent. There is no doubt that the Red Crown is the embodiment of the cobra Goddess Wadjet.

The Goddess Wadjet (*w3ḏt*), or Wadjyt (*w3ḏyt*), is the symbol of royal might and power, also known as the Uraeus. In old days she was the local Goddess of Buto (Pe and Dep) located in the Nile Delta of Lower Egypt. Over time she became the patron Goddess of entire Lower Egypt. She is closely related to the Sungod Râ as one of her titles is the "Eye of Râ". *Wadj* has several meanings like green, fortunate, papyrus, healthy, fresh and happy. That is why the healed and uninjured Eye of Horus is referred to as the Eye of Wadjet. Usually, Wadjet is depicted as a rearing cobra with outspread hood, a cobra-headed Goddess or a winged cobra. Other epithets of Wadjet include: "Green One", "She of Buto", "Mistress of all Gods", "Mighty One" and "Mistress of fear and awe".

Clearly, Wadjet is a dangerous cobra who also happens to be in possession of magical and fiery powers. This is why the King showed his fear and respect first before putting the Red Crown of Lower Egypt on top of his head. In a beautiful prayer he would speak to the crown and the crown would reply to his prayer.

> Ho *Nt*-crown! Ho '*Ini*-crown!
> Ho Great Crown!
> Ho Crown great of Magic!
> Ho Fiery Serpent! Grant that the dread
> of me be like the dread of you;
> grant that the fear of me be like
> the fear of you;
> grant that the acclaim of me
> be like the acclaim of you;
> grant that the love of me
> be like the love of you.
> Set my ˁ*b3*-sceptre at the head of the living,
> [set] my [*shm*-sceptre]
> at the head of the spirits,
> and grant that my sword
> prevail over my foes.

Ho *'Ini*-crown!
If you have gone forth from me,
so have I gone forth from you.
If *Ikhet* the Great has borne you,
Ikhet the Serpent has adorned you;
If *Ikhet* the Serpent has borne you,
Ikhet the Great has adorned you,
because you are Horus
encircled with the protection of his Eye.[19]
– Pyramid Texts; Utterance 220 and 221

(No. 79) "Nephthys" is usually depicted as a Goddess wearing the hieroglyphic symbol for her name, a house with a basket on top of it, on her head. Her name *Nebet-hut* (*nbt-ḥwt*) means the "Mistress of the Temple or Mansion". The hieroglyphic word *hut* (*ḥwt*) can also be translated as "funerary chapel". Hence, Nephthys is the protector of the dead and she is one of the four Goddesses who protect the canopic jars that hold the eviscerated organs of the deceased. The sky Goddess Nut is her mother and the earth God Geb is her father. Isis, Osiris, Horus the Elder and Seth are her sister and brothers and Seth is also her husband. Seth was infertile and unable to give Nepthtys any children. However, she had an affair with her brother Osiris that resulted in the birth of their son, the God Anubis.

Nephthys is inseparably associated with her twin sister Isis. They are two opposites forming a whole. Nephthys is the wife of Seth and the Goddess of the unseen world. She is the representation of the darkness, the night, death, decay and the end. Whereas Isis is the wife of Osiris, the Goddess of the visible world and the representation of the day, birth, growth, development and the beginning. Together they assist with the resurrection of Osiris and with the rise of the Sungod Râ. They are also of great support to the deceased as they help them ascend to a new life.

(No. 80) "Who separates the water". This is an extraordinary pole crossed by two serpents, one facing the right and the other left. On top of the pole is a mummy standing in the hieroglyphic sign for "open or separate". Here, at the end of the First Hour, is where the division occurs between the day and the night world. The pole symbolises the vertical opening between above and below, whereas the two serpents refer to the horizontal opening. These two different openings together are forming a passageway through the infinite waters of Nun. The pole marks the beginning of the descent on the path where the process of regeneration and rebirth unfolds. The mummy on top of the pole refers to the upcoming process of the transformation of death into life. His gaze is focused on the gate, where he faces his own required death before he is able to unwrap his own Divinity. The serpents are symbols of transformation. They are referring to this process of rejuvenation that takes place in the depths of the earth, which is their dwelling place.

(No. 81) "Staff" is a very large shepherd's crook.

(No. 82) "Who seals the earth" is standing at the end of the First Hour facing the opposite direction. Although the Guardian of this hour is "Keeper of the Two Flames", the God "Who seals the earth" also has a protective role. As his name suggests, it is his task to seal the earth after Râ passes through the gate to the Second Hour. This concealment of the secret world of the Duat is extremely important as it guarantees a clear separation of this antechamber from the night world. The antechamber still allows one to return to the day world, whereas the actual Duat does not. Sealing the antechamber ensures that the energies of the different worlds remain separated from each other. The night world should not be permitted to penetrate the day world and vice versa. The transformation that takes place during the night should be safe and sheltered from interference of the day world. Intrusions can be disruptive and confusing and result in the shattering of the energy. The power needed to create a new light, or consciousness, will then be insufficient. The necessary unification, to regenerate new life, can be

The Goddess Nephthys, Temple of Hathor, Chapel of Amun-Sokar-Osiris at Deir el-Medina

The Goddess Isis Temple of Hathor, Chapel of Amun-Sokar-Osiris at Deir el-Medina

established only in the secured depths of the darkness. Any small beam of light will destroy this process.

As soon as the Sungod Râ passes "Who seals the earth", the Deity bends his arm in a gesture of respect and adoration. It is, after all, an honour to serve the Sungod Râ. Subsequently, he locks the door behind the Sun barque and its crew the moment it disappears through the gate. Afterwards he immediately resumes his position where he stands with his back facing the door. No one is allowed to pass this gate without his permission.

Strong be your gate,
firm your doors,
sealed your bolts.[20]

The Duatians on the right riverbank (lower section)

On the riverbank to the right of the Sacred River there are once again nine baboons.

(No. 83) "Baboon"
(No. 84) "Shrieker"
(No. 85) "The Flaming One"
(No. 86) "Who praises with his flame"
(No. 87) "Dancer"
(No. 88) no name mentioned
(No. 89) "He in the shrine"
(No. 90) "Foremost of his land"
(No. 91) "He of the phallus"

This time the baboons are making music while dancing, singing and shouting. In doing so, they create a joyful atmosphere that strengthens Râ and supports his journey through the Duat.

Next there are twelve Goddesses in their forms of upraised cobras spitting fire. The spitting of fire is reflected in some of the names of the Goddesses.

(No. 92) "The Flaming One"
(No. 93) "The Burning One"
(No. 94) "Wadjyt"
(No. 95) "She with the hurtful flame"

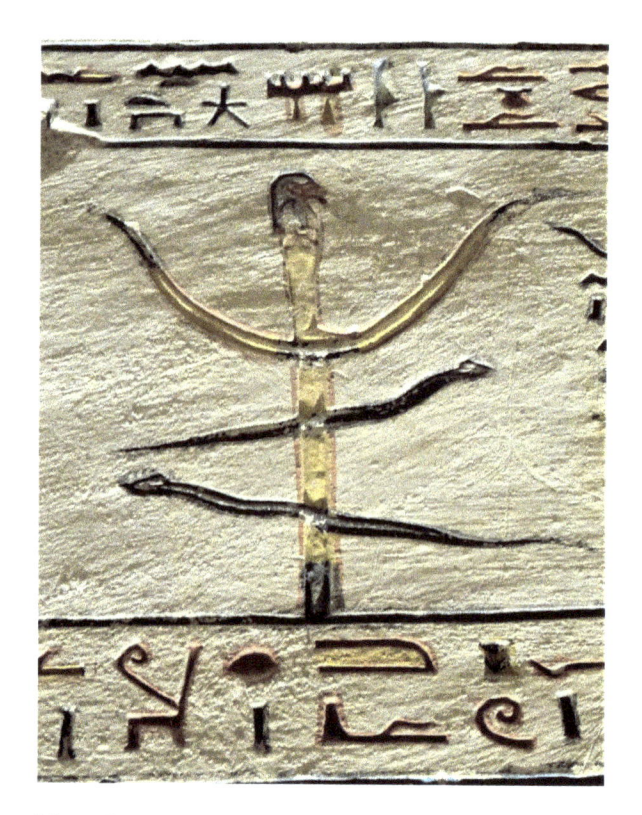

The pole "Who separates the water",
KV 9 Ramses V and VI

(No. 96) "She who cuts"
(No. 97) "The Radiant One"
(No. 98) "Protectress of the lands"
(No. 99) "Executioner of her enemies"
(No. 100) "She with the beautiful appearance"
(No. 101) "The Fiery One"
(No. 102) "The Peaceful One"
(No. 103) no name mentioned

They are powerful and deadly cobras and are to be treated with great respect. Their fire illuminates the way for Râ through the darkness. The spitting of fire also protects him from harm while executing and incinerating his enemies.

The following nine Gods are standing with their hands raised in the posture of adoration and praying. They worship the Sungod Râ as he is the one who takes away the night and brings the day. After all, it is Râ who traverses the hours to guarantee that the world keeps turning and that life proceeds.

(No. 104) "He of the Duat"
(No. 105) "Praiser of Râ"
(No. 106) "Adorer"
(No. 107) "He of the right river-banks"
(No. 108) "He who bellows"
(No. 109) "Bull of forms"
(No. 110) "Bull of the Duat"
(No. 111) "Fitted with heart"
(No. 112) "Guardian"

The section ends with twelve standing Goddesses (No. 113 – 124). Though they do not have any special attributes, they are very special Goddesses.

(No. 113) "She of the realm".

(No. 114) "Iment" or "West". This is the Goddess Imentet who is the personification of the West. The West, in this context, indicates the realm of the dead and refers to the necropolis at the West side of the Nile. Her name, Imentet (*imnt.t*), means "She of the West". The hieroglyphic word *Imentet* is a derivative of the words *iment* (*imnt*), "West", and *imen* (*imn*), which means "hidden, secret, conceal". Usually Imentet is depicted with the hieroglyphic sign for "West" on her head. She is closely related to the Goddess Hathor and Isis and was seen as a form of those two Goddesses. The God Aken, the ferryman of the dead, is her consort.

Fig. 15. The hieroglyphic signs for "West".

Her region, thus, is the hidden and secret realm of the West, the Duat. In her role as the Goddess of the dead, she receives each soul who descends in the Duat. She welcomes these newly arrived souls with food and water to refresh and revitalise them in preparation of their impending dangerous voyage through the Netherworld. Hence, she always keeps a watchful eye on the gates of the Duat from the tree that is her home. This tree is located right on the edge of the desert where the division between the world of the living and the world of the dead is situated. Even though Imentet may not be a mighty Goddess, she does play a very important role in the Afterlife. After all, she is the one who protects and supports every deceased during their process of rebirth.

Here, in the First Hour she stands at the entry of the Duat to welcome and embrace Râ. During his journey through the hours he will encounter her again under different names like "the Beautiful West" in the Second Hour and "the Concealing One" in the Sixth Hour.

Among the twelve Goddesses there are three who are part of the Great Ennead, "Isis" (No. 115), "Nephthys" (No. 116) and "Tefnut" (No. 118). Nephthys (No. 79) was also mentioned as one of the Deities in the procession in front of the Sun barque.

The Goddess Isis, or *Aset* (*3st*), is one of the most important Goddesses who was worshipped throughout ancient Egypt. She is the sister and wife of Osiris, the mother of Horus and the twin sister of Nephthys. Usually, she is depicted as a woman wearing the solar disk between a pair of cow horns or a throne on her head. Her benevolence reaches from heaven down to earth and into the realm of the dead. With her love and magical powers, she protects and nourishes all life.

In her role as the fertility Goddess, she restores death to rise up in a new life. All of these aspects are reflected in her desperate search for her murdered husband Osiris. Her love and dedication eventually enables her to find Osiris, with the help of her sister Nephthys, and bring him back to life. As she is also the Goddess of motherhood, she protects her son Horus from the evil influences of his uncle Seth. Furthermore, she also cured her son from a deadly scorpion sting.

Her greatness is reflected by her many titles

Imentet, Goddess of the West,
TT 219 Nebenmaat, Deir el-Medina

like "Great Mother", "The Great Enchantress", "Queen of Heaven", "Goddess with ten thousand Names", "The Divine One" and "The Queen of all Gods".

In the Duat her immense power and diversity is clearly demonstrated. She appears in many forms. For example, she appears as one of the *Netjeru* of the Great Ennead, as a powerful magician, as a dangerous fire spitting head to safeguard the Sacred Mystery, as an Investigator with a knife, as a wailing bird to protect the chest that gives access to the secret Cavern of Sokar, twice in the form of a cobra and as the Goddess of the West and of Isis of *Imhet*, the Sacred Land of Sokar. In these different forms she uses fire, magical power, life giving tears, wings, cobra power, Love and empathy, the power of mourning and grief, worship and praise, Knowledge and Wisdom, Authority and Might.

Her emblem is the *tit* (*tit*) or *tyet*, which is also known as "knot or blood of Isis". The sign looks like an *Ankh* were it not for the fact that the arms are bent down. It was seen as a symbol of the genital organs of Isis and would, thus, bring the virtue of her blood; welfare and eternal Life.[21] Therefore, it had a red colour, which is why this sign was usually made with red materials like red glass, wood, porcelain, sand or red carnelian, agate, jasper or porphyry. Pregnant women used the *tit* with the accompanying Magic spell to protect their unborn child. Additionally, it was also used as a funerary amulet and placed on the neck of the deceased. This provided the deceased with protection during his journey in the Afterlife. Isis was a great magician and her emblem diffused the Magic used against the deceased in the Afterlife. In contrast, the Magic used by the deceased themselves, was actually enhanced by this amulet.

> Chapter for a knot-amulet of red jasper
> You have your blood, O Isis,
> you have your power, O Isis,
> you have your Magic, O Isis.
> The amulet is a protection
> for this Great One
> which will drive away whoever
> would commit a crime against him.
> (To be said over a knot-amulet of red jasper moistened with juice of the "Life-is-in-it" fruit and embellished with sycamore-bast and placed on the neck of the deceased on the day of interment. As for him for whom this is done, the power of Isis will be the protection of his body, and Horus son of Isis will rejoice over him when he sees him; no path will be hidden from him, and one side of him will be towards the sky and the other towards the earth. A true matter; you shall not let anyone see it in your hand, for there is nothing equal to it).[22]
>
> – Book of the Dead; Spell 156

Fig. 16. The Tit symbol.

The Goddess Tefnut is usually depicted as a woman with a lion head or as a lioness who wears a solar disk upon her head encircled by the Uraeus cobra. She is the Goddess of moisture and the counterpart of Shu. According to the Pyramid Texts, Tefnut is supposed to carry away the thirst and Shu the hunger from the deceased.[23]

Furthermore, she seems to be connected to the weighing of the heart since she is mentioned in the Pyramid Texts of Unas together with the two Maât Goddesses. As we now know, these two Goddesses are present during the mentioned ceremony.

> Tefen and Tefnet have weighed Unas,
> and the Maât Goddesses have hearkened,
> and Shu hath borne witness.[24]

The remaining seven Goddesses are;

(No. 117) "The Double-Faced One"
(No. 119) "She of the water"
(No. 120) "Who is equipped with a mouth"

(No. 121) "Iabet" or "East" This is the Goddess Iabet *(i3bt)* who is the personification of the East. One of her epithets is Khentet-Iabet which means "Foremost of the East". Thus, her realm is the land of the East, with in particular, the Eastern desert. She is the Goddess of renewal, rebirth and fertility. Due to her close affinity with Hathor, Isis and Nephthys she was seen as a form of those Goddesses. Her cult centre was in Khent-Min "Shrine of Min", the capital of the ninth Nome of Upper Egypt. The ancient Greeks named it Panapolis, modern Akhmim in the Sohag Governorate. Together with Isis and the lioness Goddess Repyt, Iabet was the consort of the God Min.

Iabet is quite unknown compared to her counterpart, Imentet, the Goddess of the West. Both Goddesses are connected to the Sungod Râ, acting as his protectors in the Land of the living as well as in the realm of the dead. Every day, Iabet welcomes the new born Sungod in her realm, the East, at dawn. And at the end of the day Imentet, welcomes the aged Sungod into her realm, the West. Iabet and Imentet were called "Beautiful East" and "Beautiful West" respectively, because they were beautiful in appearance.

(No. 122) "Beholder of her God"
(No. 123) "Belonging to her God"
(No. 124) "The Praising One"

The Goddesses are all gathered here to show Râ the way out while encouraging and praising him. This is the final part of the antechamber. The antechamber is a place of great power in preparation for the upcoming journey. The festive parade of music, prayer, worship and gratitude supports Râ with his descent into the real Duat. All of the Gods and Goddesses have come to magnify and glorify Râ, providing him with the energy to fulfil his journey. It is a trustful ambience with the great conviction and unshakable belief that the journey will end well. However, they know that, despite Râ's continuous triumph every night, it still is a dangerous venture. The feast is, therefore, necessary to encourage Râ to take this challenging voyage every time again, since it is a matter of life and death. The very moment Râ disappears through the gate of the Second Hour, he has truly descended into the Duat.

Closing text

The First Hour ends with a very long closing text that describes the communication between Râ and the Gods and Goddesses of this hour. Râ begins with assigning orders to those living in this hour. He asks them to open the gates for him widely and to light the way through the hour. Then he tells them they have all come forth from him. It is pretty obvious everyone here owes their existence to the Sungod. At the same time, Râ lets the Deities know how much he needs them as well.

> Open your gates for me!
> Open wide your gateways for me!
> Illuminate for me what I have made!
> Guide me, ye who came forth
> from my limbs!

> Indeed, I commended you to my corpse!
> I made you for my *Ba*-soul.
> I created you for my Magic power.[25]

The Gods and Goddesses recognise this important interaction between them and Râ. It is quite clear they are dependent upon each other to exist. Then the extraordinary moment arrives where the Deities open the doors for the Sungod to allow for his passages into the Greatest City, the Duat.[26]

Even though the Sungod visits them every single night, it still is a special event. The moment they gaze upon the Sungod, their beings are filled with happiness and new life. They immediately start to worship their beloved Sungod and speak words of great praise and adoration. Joy and bliss radiates from their bodies, which enables them to illuminate the way for Râ.

> Opened for you is the hidden
> which contains the secret images,
> wide open for you are the doors
> of the Greatest City.
> Illuminated for you is the darkened,
> that you let breathe the place of
> destruction,
> that you approach in your name of Râ
> to the place where Osiris is,
> Foremost of the Westerners.[27]

Râ, in turn, is not deaf to their exclamations for he requests them to stay strong and remain firm in their places. It is extremely important that the Deities never leave their places. Every night, Râ needs them to open up the gate of the Duat for him. If the doors are locked the moment Râ needs to proceed, he is doomed to die. Then, as Râ passes and leaves them behind, the Gods and Goddesses wail, knowing that they have to wait until the next night for Râ to resurrect them again.

Next, the text emphasises the voyage is not just beneficial to those living in the Duat, but to the ones alive on earth as well. The text concludes with the mention of the Hour Goddess, "She who smashes the foreheads of the enemies of Râ".

The name of the Hour Goddess refers to the destructive power as symbolised by the Uraeus-serpent. The Pharaoh wore the Uraeus-serpent, as a stylised upraised cobra attached to his crown, on his forehead. This upraised cobra makes an appearance in one of the myths of the Sungod Atum as well. In this particular story the serpent first embodied the Eye of Atum. Atum had ripped out this eye and ordered it to find his lost children, Shu and Tefnut. A new eye regenerated in its place. When the first eye returned, Atum burst into tears of joy and happiness. The moment his tears fell on the earth, they transformed into the first human beings. The first eye, however, was not pleased at all. It became furious when it saw its place had been taken by a new eye. To appease the angry eye, Atum provided it with a new place on his forehead. Once settled there, "The Fiery Eye" transformed in an upraised cobra and served as the third eye of the Sungod. From its renewed position, it became the protector of Atum. It spat fire and poison at his enemies, which consequently led to it becoming the symbol of Divine Authority and rulership. Each Pharaoh wore the Uraeus on his forehead as a token of his legitimate lordship.

Hence, to smash the forehead of an opponent is a reference to destroying the power and the rulership of an enemy. This is why the Hour Goddess truly embodies the destruction of anyone obstructing the safe passage of Râ, as her name clearly indicates. She is a very

Seti I with the uraeus on his crown,
From Temple of Seti I at Abydos

dangerous and powerful guide to aid Râ along the route in this hour.

Manifestation of the First Hour in daily life

The First Hour of the Duat embodies the beginning of the twelve hour journey. The light starts to shimmer and the colours fade as the day gradually transitions into the night. Râ's shining solar disk has changed into a red globe, slowly descending behind the Horn of the West. Although you do not need to know the name of this first gate, you are required to know where to find it. Fortunately, the Horn of the West exists on the earth plane as a rocky point at the West Bank of Luxor. This facilitates the finding and envisioning of the entrance and assists with making the transition into the Duat. Râ helps you as your guide and shows you the way. Follow him in silence as you pay respect to the Guardian at the entrance, the Goddess Meretseger. As you bow in silence before her, she unlocks the gate for you. This gate opens the way towards the Unified Darkness, to the forecourt, the *ârryt* of the First Hour. Before you join Râ in his descent into the Duat, during your meditation, you first need to pronounce the name of the region, "Water of Râ". Only then the doors of the "Greatest City" are opened for you.

On the other side of the gate you meet the Hour Goddess "She who smashes the foreheads of the enemies of Râ". You bow to her while pronouncing her name with the right tone of voice in the correct manner.

Now you have entered the antechamber of the Duat, the twilight zone. This area helps you to adjust slowly to the dimming light before the darkness falls. It helps you prepare before you descend into the real darkness. It is a time of transition, to explore this strange place. This invisible night world is parallel to our manifested day world. It is a mysterious intermediate dimension that makes you feel like you are somewhere between reality and fantasy. Are you awake, or are you dreaming? The extraordinary fact, though, is that you are neither. You are floating between the two realms, that of the visible and the invisible world.

As soon as you sink deep into meditation you are experiencing the conversion of the day into the night world, which makes everything reversed. Once you have adjusted, you discover it is no topsy-turvy world at all. You know exactly what is below and above, what is left and right, and what is behind and in front of you, for you have reversed your perspective. Even the landscape might seem familiar, similar to the normal earth world. You see a broad waterway with a Sun barque sailing in the middle, riverbanks on both sides and mountains in the distance. The stars of Nut are surrounding you. Her sparkling lights are giving you a comfortable and sheltered feeling.

The contrast between light and darkness is casting shadows. These are your first encounter with your inner world. These shades are projections of images that are intended to make you aware of what is going on inside you. They are the reproductions of your own inner truth, although usually shown in deformed images. The First Hour gives you the space to look these deformed versions of your own truth in the eye. The dual Maât Goddesses, in front of the Sun barque, help you to face the truth from a greater perspective. Additionally, the orderly and reliable structure of this hour supports you in this process as well.

Seth is waiting at the riverbank. He is the God of chaos and confusion and is the patron of the military. Seth is Great of Strength and the first to confront you. Nevertheless, you have to stand your ground and be willing to face the duality in yourself. This is the moment where you become aware of the journey you are about to begin and what choices to make. You can choose to go onboard the Sun barque of Râ. However, you are also allowed to postpone the voyage for another time. You have to balance doubt and insecurity with the sense of adventure and courage. You know and you do not know, swinging back and forth between curiosity and fear. Feelings and convictions about yourself that you were certain of before, suddenly look very different. This can be reflected in your normal day life where you might encounter situations during which you are not sure of things either. The daily rhythm you were used to might seem disturbed, making way for insecurity and doubt.

When choosing to board the barque, the first step on this vessel results in some undulation that gives you a wobbly feeling. Suddenly the ground beneath your feet has disappeared, for you are now being carried by the waters of Nun. This changes your feeling and experience of the world completely. In this retrograde world the reasoning mind does not have access, which makes it essential for you to switch to your inner feelings and intuition. You have to ease yourself down in the water, the world of the intuition, and surrender to it.

This opens the connection with your inner Sungod, the Higher Self, who now function as your guide. Right from the First Hour, the process of identifying yourself with your inner light, the Higher Self, begins. The Higher Self, or Râ, serves as the example for your own transformation process towards self-awareness. Once you descend into this hour, the first step is made to let go of old patterns and ideas you were used to. This is the beginning of the passing of the old self, since Râ died and transformed into a corpse as well. Everything that made sense before is completely different in this world and makes it loose its values. It is important not to rush. Take your time in this process of dying as the Higher Self leads you. Trust the Higher Self. He ensures the process is going to feel natural and fluent, while the waters of Nun cleanse you.

Within this new relationship, you learn to consciously listen to the True inner Voice of the Higher Self that reaches you through your intuition. This is the voice in your heart that comes to you like a soft breeze. You are barely able to catch it for it disappears again just as swiftly. It holds the intelligence of the heart and of pure inspirations that come straight out of the soul. However, these insights are not to be confused with your personal feelings that are subjective in nature. Therefore, it is very important to learn to differentiate between both influences. Only then you can learn to comprehend the inner secret language of symbols of your true Self, step by step.

However, the input of the Higher Self is not exclusive to your descended state into the Duat. He speaks to you outside of the Duat during meditation, in your normal earth life as well. He might reach out to you in dreams or through other people when you communicate with them. You might read or see something or have a sudden realisation or idea. As you start to listen, you realise that the Higher Self has tried to reach out to you all along. The symbolical communications then become more rule than exception. Still, you continue to perceive them as miracles that fill you with joy.

When you focus your attention on the subconscious, you establish an interaction. As you nourish your night world, this inner world nourishes you in return. The inner connection becomes visible and tangible and you realise the Duat is not as far off or unreachable as you might have previously thought. It is no mere unseen road far away in a dream world. It actually runs parallel to the physical world and sometimes penetrates clearly into the daily life.

The dancing, shouting and singing of the baboons, in the upper and lower section, is a reference to this inner communication. They open their arms for the Sungod Râ, just as you are opening your arms for the Higher Self. This inner wake-up call makes you aware of the weal and the woe inside of you.

An opening has formed for you to begin comprehending the deeper meaning of all aspects of yourself. Things you could never have understood from your view in the day world. In the depths you can acquaint yourself with these aspects and knowingly 'flip the switch' to enable these insights to flow into the day consciousness as well. Here, in the depths, you will find the inner Wisdom.

This inner Wisdom is referred to in the closing text as the "secret images". The hieroglyphic words *shetat iru (št3t irw)* and *sefeg iru (sfg irw)*, that are translated here as "secret images", can also be interpreted as "the secret or the hidden of visible forms". Additionally, these important images are described throughout the Amduat using several different hieroglyphic words. A common hieroglyphic word is *seshmu (sšmw)*, which can be translated as "image" but also as "portrait or counterpart". Another common word is *senty (snty)*, which can be interpreted as "likeness". It is quite clear that these mysterious images function as doorways to the inner knowledge and understanding of who you truly are. They help you to identify your inner world step by step.

During the First Hour, these images are no more than vague shadows due to the shimmering light. When trying to analyse these images on an intellectual level, the door to the wisdom of the inner night world slams in your face. You then hit a wall, unable to continue. However, when approaching these images on the level of the intuition, the door opens and vivifies the images to allow them to speak to you.

Furthermore, all of the Deities and attributes you encounter in this hour are here to tell you something about your inner world as well. They reflect certain characteristics of yourself and form the key to opening the inner gates. In doing so, they stimulate and proceed in powering the coming to life of the secret images. When you walk past them, you breathe new life into them and they, in turn, revitalise your inner world. Some of these Deities have a more significant impact on you than the others. Observe them all and ask them questions in order to get to know them.

> One has made these like this image
> in the secrecy of the Duat.
> He who makes these images (likeness)
> is like the Great God Himself.
> It is beneficial to him on earth,
> a very true remedy,
> corresponding to their secret images
> that are painted.[25]

The crewmembers of the Sun barque are the foremost helping forces and join you on your voyage. This group consists of different Gods, or *Netjeru*. Each one symbolises a different aspect of nature. They exist inside as well as outside of you. The macro cosmos in the micro cosmos. Getting to know the nature of each God on the Sun barque is like getting to know a Divine aspect of your own nature. Therefore, they all embody a specific function in their quest to help and support you during the process of becoming self-aware. Their influence changes between the different hours where it is prominently present in one hour and more to the background in another. During the First Hour, they are the reception committee to give you a comfortable feeling for your upcoming journey. Do not be afraid to talk to them and ask them questions, for they have so much to show and teach you.

The barque itself also aids you to adjust to the new experiences as you sail through the waters. The reliable and solid structure of the Barque of Millions of Years carries and protects you. It enables you to tune into the thousands of years of ancient knowledge that is built upon the heritage of your ancestors.

Even though you boarded the Sun barque and are already sailing on the water, the antechamber still allows you the choice to turn back and leave the barque. This area is very accessible since the entrance gate is still a tangible door in the physical world. This is also the area where people can have a near death experience and still be able to return to the world of the living. This accessibility changes as soon as you pass the first real gate that grants you access to the Second Hour. The gate has the appropriate name of "He who swallows all". In front of the gate stands the Guardian "Who seals the earth". You have to bow before him and pronounce his name with the right tone of voice in the correct manner. Then, the Guardian opens the gate for you and the time has come for you to descend into the real Duat. As soon as you have passed through the gate, the Guardian shuts it behind you and seals the earth in the process. Everything that is not yours remains outside. Everything that does belong to you, will be encountered along your journey. The gate also protects the world of the subconsciousness and inner images from the interference of the reasoning mind.

As mentioned before, the gate at the end, which opens the Second Hour, is a *seba* gate. The word *seba* can also be written with the determinative or meaning-sign for star at the end and then it translates as star. This five-pointed star represents the stars in the constellations. This symbol is based on the image of the starfish that lives in the ocean. Starfish were regarded as reflections of the stars in the sky. Therefore, the ancient Egyptians knew that the visible world was the counterpart of the invisible world of the Divine. As above so below. As within so without.

The starfish has remarkable regenerative powers as it is able to grow new arms after damage. Hence, the star is a fitting representation of the Duat. Another meaning of the hieroglyphic word *seba*, is "learning or teaching". Each of these definitions of the word *seba* is intertwined with one another. The Duat is the world of the stars. Once you are prepared to submerge yourself in this night world and learn its teachings, knowledge and wisdom, the gates to your own regeneration and rebirth will open to you.

THE SECOND HOUR
"Wernes"

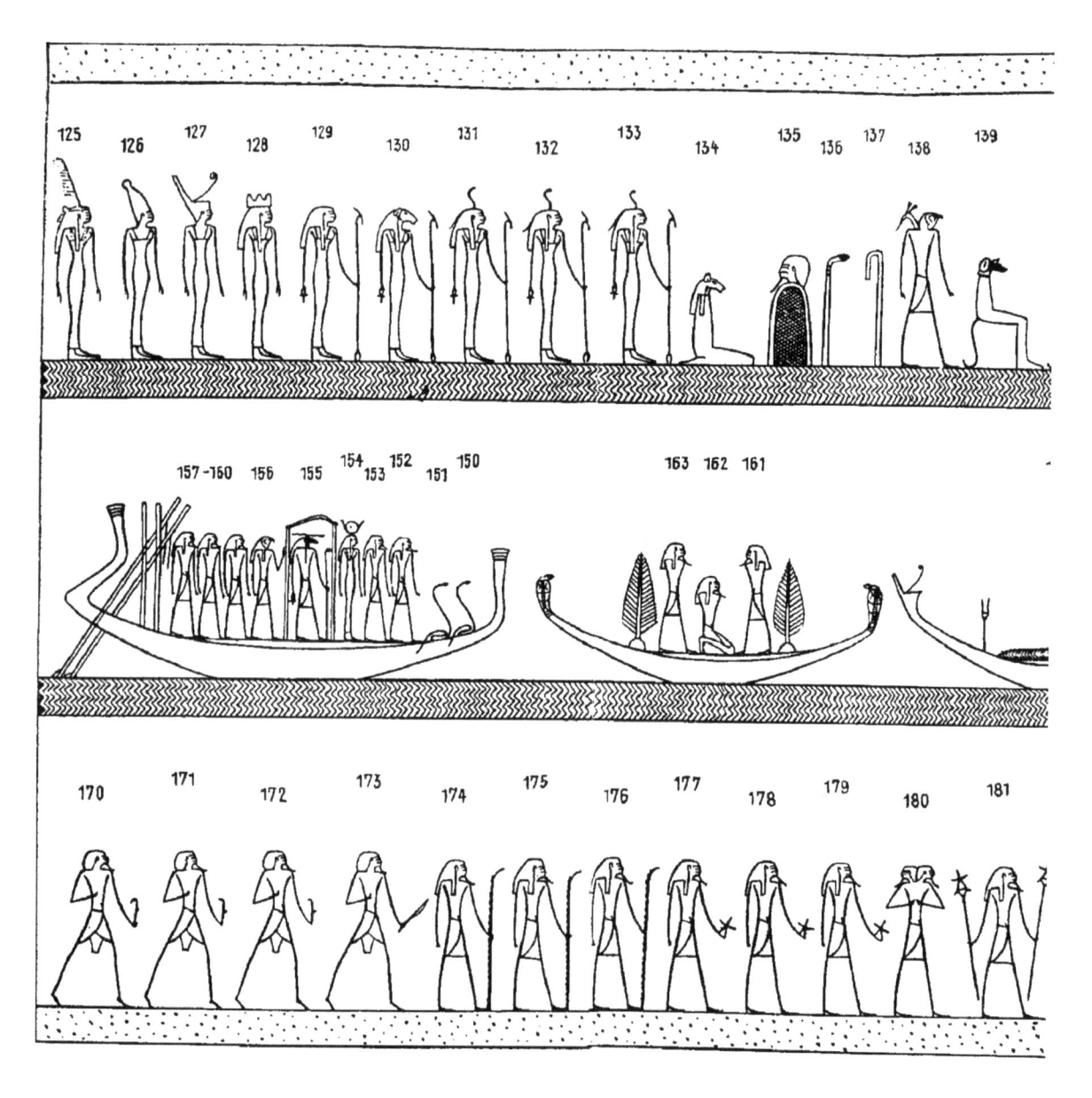

Figure 17: The Second Hour

The Gate : "He who swallows all
The Hour Goddess: "Wise One who protects her master"
The Guardian: "Two flames"

Introduction

Setting in Wernes by the person
of this God,
rowing *Iaru* in the waters of Râ.[1]
309 *iteru* is the length of this field;
120 *sekhu* is its breadth.
This Great God assigns plots to the Gods
at this region.
The name of the Hour of the night
guiding this Great God is
"Wise One who protects her master".
The name of the Gate of this region is
"He who swallows all".
This Great God assigns fields
to the Gods of the Duat,
he takes care of them at this region.
Know those of the Duat!
He who knows their names
will be among them.
This Great God will assign fields to him
at their place of the fields of Wernes.
He will stand at the positions
of the *Ba*-soul (i.e. the Sungod)
and he will proceed after this Great God.
He will enter the earth and open the Duat,
will unbraid the locks of the braided ones.
He will pass by the "Donkey-swallower"
after the *Maât* of the plot.
Always will he eat bread
at the barque of the earth,
and will be given the prow-rope
of the Sun barque.
These drawings of the *Ba*-souls of the Duat
are painted like that form
in the secrecy of the Duat,
the beginning of the writing
towards the West.
Offerings are made for them upon earth
in their names.
It is efficient for a man on earth,
a true remedy, (proven) a million times.[2]

The Second Hour starts with a long introduction text that summarises the events of the Second Hour. We are still sailing in the region of the West and have arrived in an area called Wernes. This area is 309 *iteru* long and 120 *sekhu* wide.

The Sacred River, which has run its course closely to the surface next to the Nile in the previous hour, is now diving further into the depth of the Duat. The name of the *seba* gate, "He who swallows all", emphasises the descent into the abyss. This is the real entrance into the Duat, also known as the secret gate. Once Râ has passed through this gate, he gets swallowed whole in the world of the Duat. He now distances himself from the land of the living, for the Guardian of the First Hour, "Who seals the earth", has closed the way back to earth indefinitely. Both worlds have become isolated from one another, so there is no turning back. A division has been made between the Sacred and the profane.

It is here where the great transformation process commences. The introduction text refers to this as "unbraid the locks of the braided ones".³ This is a reference to the fashion in which the children of ancient Egypt used to wear their hair. Both boys and girls shaved their heads except for a single long braided lock at the side of their heads, "the sidelock of youth". The plait, like the snake, is a symbol of new life, regeneration, resurrection and rebirth. Every child adopted this hairstyle until puberty. Once puberty was reached, the boys shaved off the lock whereas the girls grew out their hair. In other words, the journey through the Duat is a process with the aim to reach spiritual adulthood. However, the paradox here is that to reach spiritual maturity, old age must be transformed in rejuvenation and rebirth.

The Second Hour is also known as the region of turquoise. The turquoise region is mainly located within the Eastern horizon. Two turquoise sycamores are growing there, which is also the location from where the Sungod emerges at dawn. The name turquoise originates from the blue green mineral turquoise, a copper and aluminium hydrated phosphate. Thousands of years ago the ancient Egyptians mined this

The Iwn-mut-ef priest with the sidelock of youth, Temple of Seti I at Abydos

mineral in the Sinai Peninsula. It was a precious gemstone worn by the Pharaohs and royalty and used in jewellery, amulets and artefacts. The greenish shade was associated with fresh new life, green vegetation, resurrection and fertility. The blueish shade symbolised the heavenly sky, divinity and rebirth. Thus, the colour turquoise is very befitting the Second Hour at the beginning of the real Duat.

The Sungod passed away in the horizon of the West to begin his journey of rejuvenation. In the present hour he is born in a backwards way to regain his shining life force. The beginning of the rebirth process is reflected in the fecundity of the landscape, since it is a fertile wetland with the appearance of a true paradise. It has fields filled with crops and seedlings that grant it a fresh green appeal.

The Sacred River is overflowing with the running waters of Nun. The inundation makes the river broader than it usually is. The water is used to irrigate the crops and enables an abundance of life and vegetation. The seasons in this region are similar to the ones on earth with *Akhet*, the flooding season, *Peret*, the sowing season, and *Shemu*, the harvesting season. The three seasons, flooding, sowing and harvesting, are mirrors of the continuous process of creation according to the Divine Law of *Maât*. The Goddess Maât, who is standing at the beginning of the riverbank at the left side of the Sacred River, emphasises this aspect.

Râ feels like he has entered a paradise, for the water grants life that results in the birth of wealth and fertility. It is an oasis of abundance and happiness. To enter and maintain this heavenly place opposite sides are required. Hence, throughout the hour opposite forces, seemingly misplaced, can be found. These are for example tribunals, double-headed Gods, several knives and so on. Things you would not usually associate with a paradise. However, it is this train of thought of the 'perfect' paradise that is the real illusion. Everything is always revolving around the balance between opposites from which the unity, the paradise, can arise. In fact, it are the opposite forces that are essential to maintain the idyllic spirit. The overgrowth has to be pruned to prevent the oasis from turning into a vast jungle. As paradise needs maintenance, so does the person within this unity. Râ must remain alert and aware in this state of harmony, cutting down any vine threatening to overgrow, for the struggle between light and darkness is a continuous process. Aside from the negative forces, the forces perceived as positive have to be kept within certain limits as well. For too much sunshine causes drought followed by death.

The presence of the God "Donkey-swallower" (No. 185) ensures the establishment and preservation of this state of righteousness. As his role is a very important one, the God is mentioned straight away at the beginning in the introduction text.

The Hour Goddess underlines the importance of the opposite forces as she guides Râ through the hour. Her name is "Wise One who protects her master". She understands better than anyone that Râ needs to be confronted with these contradictory aspects. Only then he is capable of truly understanding these forces to gain mastery over them. It is this knowledge that Râ requires to be able to sail past all the discrepancies.

Furthermore, he has to identify himself with every single Deity he meets on his way. In so doing, he gets to know their names and understand their true identities, which grants him power over them. Râ himself is the one who draws the attention of the traveller towards this important fact. Knowing these names enables the traveller to become a blessed dead. This grants the traveller a spot on the Sun barque as a *Ba*-soul to join Râ on his travels. The Sungod, in turn, always provides the traveller with food to warrant life. In addition, the traveller is given the prow-rope of the Sun barque. These conditions do not just apply to the dead living and travelling in the Duat, but also to the ones undertaking the journey while still alive and living on earth. "It is a true remedy".

The Duatians on the left riverbank (upper section)

As Râ sails through the hour, the Deities on the left side of the riverbank call upon him. When Râ hears their call for attention, he lets himself be guided by their voices. Once he reaches them, the Gods and Goddesses line up in utter worship and cry about his earthly death. They also cry for joy, since Râ has finally returned to them. The Sungod acknowledges their vocalisations and gives them assignments. It is the task of these Deities to function as the mediators for those living on earth. They ensure the words of the earthly inhabitants reach Râ since he is the representative of the Ba-souls. In doing so, these Deities assist the Ba-souls in their transition from the day into the night world. In the day world "those of the earth" seemingly fall asleep, enabling their Ba-souls to leave their bodies and enter the Duat. As soon as they awake in their new form as a Ba-soul, their souls are capable of travelling throughout this realm. The term "sleep" indicates the state of consciousness needed to enter the Duat. The day consciousness disappears or fades into the background to awaken the night consciousness. This may refer to death, however, it can also indicate the state of consciousness during sleep or, for example, meditation or trance.

To achieve this state of "sleep", utter darkness is required. The Deities, therefore, see to it that the onset of the profound darkness of the night continues. As guardians of the darkness, they aim to keep the blackness of the night separate from the light of the day. Only within total darkness can the marvel of rebirth, "to go forth by day", take place.

It is they who guard the day and bring the night, till this Great God has come

out from the Unified Darkness, to settle in the gateway of the Eastern horizon of the sky".[4]

The Goddess Maât, with the feather of Truth on her head, can be found at the beginning of the left riverbank, "Maât at the head of the wadi" (No. 125). Her presence here warrants that the Divine Law of *Maât* is abided by within the Duat as well. In the absence of the principle of *Maât*, rebirth is impossible. This would cause creation to be halted and be replaced by the chaos of non-existence. *Maât* is, therefore, a crucial support for the Sungod as she stands behind him according to the Pyramid Texts. This implies she does not just physically stand behind him, for she provides for mental assistance as well.

> May you shine as Râ; repress wrongdoing,
> cause Maât to stand behind Râ,
> shine every day for him
> who is in the horizon of the sky.
> Open the gates which are in the Abyss.[5]
> – Pyramid Texts; Utterance 586

In front of the Goddess Maât are eight Goddesses. The first three of these Goddesses are;

(No. 126) "White Crown at the head of the wadi", is wearing the White Crown of Upper Egypt.
(No. 127) "Red Crown at the head of the wadi", is wearing the Red Crown of Lower Egypt.
(No. 128) "Beautiful West", is the Goddess of the West and is wearing the hieroglyph of "desert" on her head. The Goddess has already made an appearance before during the First Hour to welcome Râ and every deceased into the antechamber of the Duat. In the present hour her presence is required since this is the moment during which the true transition from one world into the next is made. Thus, she is needed to greet, and from now on, escort Râ and the deceased throughout the Afterlife.

The following five Goddesses are each holding a *Was*-sceptre in one hand and the *Ankh* in the other.

(No. 129) "She who swallows all"
(No. 130) "Sekhmet of the *Was*-sceptre", who is the lion goddess Sekhmet.

The remaining three Goddesses are human-headed. The upraised cobras on top of their heads are a symbol of transformation and resurrection. The Goddesses, therefore, provide for a great support in the rejuvenation process of Râ and the deceased.

(No. 131) "She presides those of the Duat"
(No. 132) "She who swallows the dead"
(No. 133) "She who gives birth to herself"

The *Was*-sceptre, known as the "Key of the Nile", is a long staff with an animal head on top and a forked tip at the other end. It symbolises dominion and the power that controls death and darkness. It is usually carried by the *Netjeru* or Gods to ensure the wellbeing of both the living and the deceased. Hence, the staff is often recovered from graves. There are many theories as to what the head on the staff represents. Some suggest it to be the head of Seth, others are more inclined to think of Anubis. On the other hand, it could also represent an Ibis, a fox or the Bennu bird. As to its real identity, it will probably remain a mystery. The staff can be found in many illustrations where it serves as a supporting pole of heaven while standing on the earth.

The final Goddess has a lion head and is kneeling, "She who imposes respect to the *Akh-spirits*" (No. 134). She sits across from a stela with a human head who faces her, "Commands of Osiris" (No. 135). The stela refers to "Decree of Osiris" (No. 61) in the First Hour. It represents the sun at night, as one of the four parts of the cycle of the sun. The stela is the sign that twilight has been replaced with the night. Râ has now truly entered the Kingdom of Osiris. This is the land where the Lord of the Duat rules, which is indicated by the two different staffs, "Snake-staff of Osiris" (No. 136) and "Shepherd's crook of Osiris" (No. 137). Both sceptres are signs of power and dominion.

Right in the middle of the riverbank a God with two heads can be found, "His two faces" (No. 138). One head represents Horus who looks to the right. The other is in the image of Seth, who looks to the left. "His two faces" shows us two different aspects of the power of nature represented by Horus and Seth; order and chaos, fertility and barrenness, life and death, light and darkness, above and below, and so on. Together, the opposite forces of these two *Netjeru* form a unity, as is made apparent by the body they share.

There is a myth describing the interaction between the different powers of these two Gods. In this myth the floor of heaven was described

Horus with the Was-sceptre and the Ankh in his hands
Temple of Seti I at Abydos

as a square iron plate that was held up by four pillars that stood on the edges of the earth. To reach heaven, the deceased had to climb a ladder. Horus held the top and Seth the bottom of the ladder, joining their forces to secure a safe passage for the deceased to rise into a new life in heaven.

> Hail to you, Ladder of the God!
> Hail to you, Ladder of Seth!
> Stand up Ladder of the God!
> Stand up, Ladder of Seth!
> Stand up, Ladder of Horus,
> which was made for Osiris
> that he might ascend on it to the sky
> and escort Râ! [6]
> – Pyramid Texts; Utterance 478

The two-headed God is, therefore, the representation of the healing aspects of duality. To emphasise this aspect, another two-headed God (No. 180) can be found on the opposite side of the Sacred River on the right riverbank.

Next to the two-headed God are two sitting baboons wrapped like mummies "Wailing baboon" (No. 139) and "Baboon" (No. 140).

Following is "He who causes to fall, who beheads shadows" (No. 141). His fighting stance shows that he will attack all of the enemies of Râ with his knife. He will not stop with just causing bodily harm for he decapitates the shadows of the enemies as well. This effectively extinguishes the hostiles completely from existence.

The shadow or *khaibit* (*šwyt*) is the mirror image of a body. It is an essential part of a person that is always connected with the body and the soul. Hence, it is impossible to exist without a shadow as the absence of a shadow indicates one does not possess a soul and, thus, no life. The possession of a shadow is not just a requirement in the world of the living, for it is essential in the world of the dead as well.

> A path is opened for my soul,
> my spirit, my Magic and my shade,
> and it will enter to Râ within his shrine,
> it will see the Great God in his true shape,
> and it will repeat the words of Osiris
> to those whose places are secret,
> who are in charge of the members of Osiris.
> O you who watch over all souls
> and constrain the shades
> of all who are dead,
> may you not have power to constrain me
> or to watch over
> my soul, my shade, my spirit or my Magic.
> It possesses the ritual
> which is for bringing Right to Râ,
> and it has asked that it may live
> by means of it.
> Go, go, my soul, my spirit,
> my Magic and my shade,
> open the shutters of the sky-windows,
> throw open the Great Mansion,
> so that you may go to and fro
> and have power in your legs;
> you shall not be restrained by those

who are in charge
of the members of Osiris,
who watch over all souls and who constrain
the shades of all the dead.
Go, go, my soul, my spirit,
my Magic and my shade,
so that you may have power in your legs
and that you may bring Right to Râ.[7]
– Coffin Texts; Spell 491

Next are two more Gods.

(No. 142) "Horus of the Duat" is a hawk-headed God with a serpent on his head.

(No. 143) "Whose arm is powerful, smiter of his foes" is a human-headed God holding a sceptre in his hand. The sceptre can be a *Sekhem*, *Kherep*- or *Âba*-sceptre as these are rather similar looking sceptres and difficult to distinguish. Each of these sceptres is a symbol of royal and Divine Authority, used by the Gods and the Pharaohs to endorse power. They resemble a flat paddle on a papyrus handle. The *Sekhem*-sceptre refers to "to be mighty and powerful". The *Kherep*-sceptre to "that which guides or directs" and the *Âba*-sceptre to "that which commands".

Fig. 18. Sekhem-, Kherep- or *Âba*-sceptre

The final Gods on the left riverbank are six judges in mummified form who are sitting on their thrones, each with a knife in their lap (No. 144 – 149). These judges form the tribunal to guarantee the Divine Law of *Maât* is complied with, for this Law have to be obeyed in the Duat as well as on earth. When the judges give a death sentence, this indicates a second death for the convict. This was the only true death that the ancient Egyptians absolutely feared. Once the sentence passed was executed, it permanently and completely wiped that person from existence. Never again would he be able to awaken and renew himself. He would disappear into non-existence for eternity. The judges, therefore, show us another side of paradise that is essential to maintain its divinity. Their knives refer to the Law of *Maât* as it balances on the razor's edge. It requires great vigilance to be constantly aware of ones actions.

> I will not die a second time,
> and the dwellers in the Netherworld
> have no power over me.
> I will not eat their fish,
> their fowl shall not scream over me,
> for I am Horus, son of Osiris.
> *NOT TO DIE A SECOND TIME
> IN THE REALM OF THE DEAD.*[8]
> – Coffin texts; Spell 458

The first judge is a lion-headed Goddess, "She of the fireplace who cuts up *Ba*-souls" (No. 144). The Goddess shows us stringent measures are taken against anyone who disobeys the Law of *Maât*. She uses the element of fire to punish the *Ba*-souls who violate the Divine Law, which gives the offender the sensation of being chopped to pieces. The *Ba*-soul is the soul, otherwise known as the identity, of a person living in his heart. Thus, the destruction of this *Ba*-soul leads to irrevocable death and completely obliterates the existence of the person. This is the harsh but honest reality.

The following judges are;

(No. 145) "Flesh on its throne",
a baboon-headed God.
(No. 146) "Djehuty on his throne",
the ibis-headed God Thoth.

(No. 147) "Khnum of the court", the long-horned ram-headed God Khnum. He is the God of water, creation and rebirth. With his power he is able to control the amount of water of the annual inundation. Hence, he will be present in the Third Hour, where the inundation continues, as well.

(No. 148) "Geb of the court", the earth God Geb. Geb is the son of Shu and Tefnut and both the brother and husband of Nut. His body is the earth, which is why the earth is called "the House of Geb". He is usually depicted with a goose on his head, which is his sacred animal. As the personification of the earth, Geb's body is covered with trees and vegetation. His authority, however, is not limited to the world above the ground, for it reaches beneath the earth into the Netherworld as well. The tombs holding the bodies of the departed are also under his reign. This connects him to the deceased. He assists at the weighing of the heart ceremony, trapping the heavy hearted within his body, which is the earth. Hence, Geb is a very important judge.

The final judge is the Goddess Isis, "Isis the investigator" (No. 149).

The six judges at the end of the left riverbank (No. 144 – 149) KV 9 Ramses V and VI

The Duatians of the Sacred River (middle section)

The Sacred River begins with the Sun barque of Râ. The River is overflowing with water due to the inundation. This has broadened the stream and increased the current. The Sungod, "Iuf" (No. 155), is standing within the shrine and holds the serpent staff in one hand and the *Ankh*, in the other. He has ram horns on top of his head, but no solar disk. He has become weary from his journey through the day sky to the point where he no longer has the power to illuminate the darkness with his light. This results in his light becoming completely engulfed by the Unified Darkness of the Duat. In front of the Sungod stands the Lady of the barque, "Nebet wia" (No. 154). Fortunately, she does still carry the sun disk between her cow horns instead of the old and weakened Râ.

The usual crew of the barque in the present hour has increased with two extra members who are lying at the prow. These two are "Isis" (No. 150) and "Nephthys" (No. 151), both in the shape of an upraised cobra. These important Goddesses protect and assist Râ during his process of rebirth. In their supportive task they simultaneously aid the deceased in this process as well. Although they are twin sisters, they form polar opposites within this hour of contrast, emphasising the importance of contradicting forces. Two different sides are needed to create wholeness, just like day and night together form the twenty-four hours of a natural day. Isis and Nephthys are also forming a whole by joining their different forces. Only through this unity are they capable of supporting Râ and Osiris in the process of rejuvenation. Their cobra shape refers to this process where death is transformed into new life. The resulting rise into a new light or consciousness is reflected in their upraised snake bodies.

(No. 150) "Isis"
(No. 151) "Nephthys"
(No. 152) "Wepwawet"
(No. 153) "Sia"
(No. 154) "Nebet wia"
(No. 155) "Iuf"
(No. 156) "Heru Hekenu"
(No. 157) "Ka Maât"
(No. 158) "Nehes"
(No. 159) "Hu"
(No. 160) "Kherep wia"

The Sun barque is followed by four other barques that belong to the entourage of the Sungod. Each of the barques is constructed slightly different and carries a varied content. All of the varying cargo possesses a specific symbolical meaning that contributes to the transformation process of the Sungod.

The first barque has a cobra head at the prow and the stern. It is called "Rowing through the flood", which refers to the vast amount of water. The barque carries two ears of grain. Between the ears there are three figures without arms. A God without a name is kneeling in the middle of the barque (No. 162). At his left stands the God "Barley staff" (No. 163) and to his right side is the God "Neper" (No. 161). The name Neper, or Nepri, means "grain" for he is the God of grain and equated with Osiris. He represents the life sustaining power incorporated within the grain. The Coffin Texts, Spell 330 to become Neper, clearly states the nature of this God.

> I live and I die, I am Osiris,
> I have gone in and out by means of you,
> I have grown fat through you,
> I flourish through you,
> I have fallen through you.
> I have fallen on my side,
> the Gods live on me.
> I live and grow as Neper
> whom the honoured ones cherish,
> one whom Geb hides,
> I live and I die, for I am emmer (wheat),
> and I will not perish.[9]

The seed of grain, which sprouts deep within the earth, eventually grows into an ear of wheat that in turn contains new seeds of grain. Once the ear of wheat reaches adulthood, its grains are harvested, which causes the death of the former. A portion of the grains is used as food while the remaining share will be sown to provide for the new ears of wheat. The life force of these grains remains dormant until they are sowed during spring in the earth. This sets the next cycle of life, death and rebirth in motion.

Grain is the symbol for eternal Life. It will always flourish no matter how long it has been kept in proper storage, as if it has returned from the dead. Therefore, grain can be identified with the resurrection of Osiris.

Grain was the main source of wealth in ancient Egypt. Aside from its practical applications to bake bread and brew beer, it was also used as a currency. Well stocked grain storages could be compared to the present banks. However, grain was very important not only for the physical but also for the spiritual wellbeing of the ancient Egyptians. Moreover, its products, bread and beer, were the two main offerings for the Gods and the deceased as a reference to "all good things".

> An offering given by the King to Osiris,
> Lord of Djedu, Great God,
> Lord of Abydos.
> So that he may give a voice-offering
> of bread and beer, ox and fowl,
> alabaster and linen,
> and everything good and pure
> on which a God lives.
> For the Ka of the revered one,
> overseer of the chamber Amenemhat,
> True of Voice (maâ kheru), justified.[10]
> – Offering formula from the funerary monument of Amenemhat, the overseer of the chamber

The importance of grain is also reflected in the various offering lists. An example is the offering list of Spell 936 of the Coffin texts. It

THE GREAT AWAKENING 135

gives a detailed summery of offering goods among which various kinds of grain, bread, cakes and beer are mentioned.

A fresh *p3t*-cake; A *p3t*-cake spread into two halves; A bowl of *mnw*-stone containing beer; A sack of bread; bread, two loaves; *ith*-bread; Four *idtt*-loaves; Three *prsn*-loaves; An *imy-t3*-loaf; Four *ḥnfw*-loaves; Four *iḥbnnt*-loaves; Four *p3wt*-loaves; Four toasted loaves; Four *ḳmḥw*-loaves; A *syf*-loaf; Four *msyt*-cakes; Three bowls of milky ale; Three bowls of strong ale; Two bowls of beer; Green *sḫt*-grain; White *sḫt*-grain; Two portions of scorched wheat; Scorched barley; *ḥnms*-beer; A jar of *šns*-loaves; Two *ḥrt*-loaves; Two *nḥrw*-loaves; Four *dptt*-loaves.[11]

The ears of grain on the barque thus symbolise the importance of the concept of offering. Although the Gods do not need food or substance themselves, it is of the utmost importance for their existence to be acknowledged on earth as well as in the Duat. The offerings and devotions are proof of their presence and the position they have in the lives of mankind. Through man, the Gods are able to manifest on earth and in the Afterlife.

An offering of bread, The Temple of Seti I at Abydos

Without mankind, they are simply unable to come into being.

Man, in turn, needs the Gods to grasp and understand the essence of the underlying power of life itself. The Gods show us our heritage and provide us with a purpose, an objective to return to. Hence, offerings are essential to unite the lives of man with those of the Gods. It bridges the gap between both worlds, enabling the equilibrium of creation. This principal is not just crucial for those living on earth, but for the deceased living in the Duat as well. For, as you may well know by now, life continuous after death.

The ancient Egyptian word for offering is *hotep* (*ḥtp*). The offering formula was called *hotep di nesu* (*ḥtp di nsw*), which means "an offering which the King gives".

The offering formula is a kind of prayer comprised of a fixed combination of words. It ensured that the deceased participated in the offerings that were presented to the Gods. Even after death the deceased needed food and drink to be able to continue to live in the Afterlife.

Hotep holds various other meanings that are all part of the process of offering like; "altar, be pleased, be peaceful, become calm, be happy, be gracious or satisfy". *Hotep* is also one of the many aspects of the earth God Geb. He provides us with food as the fundamental source of life.

Both Râ and Neper command the Duatians in this hour to take possession of the fields. Thus, it is the task of the Duatians to grow grain in Wernes. The grain enables the Duatians to feed themselves. In return, they offer a part of their harvest to the Gods, feeding them as well.

For all the above reasons, grain obviously holds a deep and complex meaning that bridges the gap between the profane and the sacred. Even though this connection is not clearly visible or tangible, its presence is evident. Furthermore, the symbolical meaning of grain holds the big secret of life, for it will always conquer death. This, in itself, is a great mystery and its knowledge is a puzzle or a secret to every living soul. The three Gods on the barque, "Rowing through the flood", are part of this Mystery. They have hidden their arms to prevent anyone from seeing the secret they are carrying with them.

This act of hiding is also reflected in mummies. Mummies hide their entire bodies beneath their wrappings to conceal the mysterious transformation of death into new life. The hidden and the out of sight are the only ways to keep this big secret safe. The initiates, like the three Gods in the barque, will never ever reveal this secret.

The name of the second barque is "Barque which the *Netjeru* row". The stern of the barque is shaped like the Red Crown of Lower Egypt, and the prow as the White Crown of Upper Egypt. The barque contains a crocodile, "Image which is in it" (No. 164), lying in between two sceptres. In this context it is irrelevant whether these sceptres are *Kherep-*, *Âba-* or *Sekhem-* sceptres as they are all symbols of royal and Divine power. The crocodile is the embodiment of these sceptres for he is a controller, a commander, and very powerful.

The crocodile is a mighty animal on land as well as in the water. This animal symbolises the connection between the physical world and the Duat, allowing for the transition from one world into the other. The unification of both worlds provides for true rulership. This is accentuated by the White Crown of Upper Egypt and the Red Crown of Lower Egypt that together give shape to the barque.

In the Amduat, as depicted in the tomb of Tuthmosis III, it is unclear what the crocodile carries on his back. The Amduat in the tomb of Seti I (KV 17) and Ramesses VI (KV 9), however, shows us the crocodile bears a White Crown and a head on his back. These two objects refer to Osiris.

The crocodile in the barque could be the crocodile God Sobek. Sobek has a double nature. On one hand he is an aggressive and violent creature. On the other hand he is associated with the art of healing and protection. In one of the Osirian myths, Sobek demonstrates his good nature by presenting himself as the protector of Osiris. After Osiris was murdered by Seth, Sobek searched for the mutilated body of Osiris. When he found it, he carried him on his back. The crocodile in the barque indicates that Osiris,

Second barque "Barque which the Netjeru row" KV 9 Ramses V and VI

as the Lord of the Duat, is well protected by the immense power of Sobek as the ruler of the watery world. This also applies to the vulnerable Sungod Râ, since Osiris and Râ are connected. The God Sobek is addressed in further detail in the Third Hour.

However, this crocodile could also be the creator God Khenty-Khety. He is usually depicted in the form of a crocodile or as a man with a crocodile or falcon head. His cult centre was located at Khem-Wer, modern Tell Atrib, in Lower Egypt. He had a protective nature and was associated with the safeguarding and healing of the heart. Due to these characteristics he was connected to the weighing of the heart ceremony in the Hall of Judgement. Khenty-Khety was identified with Sobek and upon later times with Horus as Horus-Khenty-Khety. He was also often associated with Osiris. In this context, the crocodile in the barque shows that Osiris is the powerful and mighty Ruler, Judge and Lord of the watery world of the Duat. Naturally, Osiris protects Râ during his journey through Osiris's Kingdom.

In both cases, Râ can count on the mighty power of a crocodile on his side during his nocturnal journey. This is also reflected in the fact that the barque belongs to the entourage of Râ. Therefore, the great power it carries is meant to benefit the Sungod.

The name of the third barque is "Carried by Wernes". The stern of the barques is shaped like a human head with a divine beard and on top of its head the Two Feathers Crown. This crown is the symbol of light and the Divine Law of *Maât*. The two feathers emphasise the fact that Truth will be established from the assessment between two different concepts. Only then, the Truth can be as "light" as a feather. Consequently, the Two Feathers *"shuty"* (šw.ty) Crown is also a symbol of light, *"shu"* (šw). It is usually worn by Amun, a self-created God, who is perceived as the King of the Gods. His name means "Hidden", which refers to the hidden mystery taking place when the sun sets.

The prow of the barque is missing. A scarab is placed on the edge instead as a reference to the process of regeneration and rebirth. The scarab is the personification of Khepri who emerges from the primeval waters of Nun as the new born sun. This glimpse, of what is to come in the future, fills Râ with hope and courage on his way.

In the middle of the barque is a huge sistrum (No. 166), which is an attribute of the Goddess Hathor. The sistrum is a musical instrument used by the ancient Egyptians. It was a sacred instrument made of wood, clay, bronze or brass. The instrument looks like a U-shaped frame attached to a handle. Often, the handle is shaped like the face of the Goddess Hathor with the frame resembling a shrine. The frame is pierced with horizontally placed movable crossbars with small rings. When shaken, it produces a jingling noise similar to the sound the wind makes when it passes through the papyrus reeds or the sound of flowing water. The sound guarantees divine blessing, renewal and protection. It was used during dances, celebrations and sacred ceremonies to worship the Goddess Hathor. Shaking the instrument generates energy to intensify the ceremonies. Furthermore, it was also used to moderate the overwhelming inundation of the Nile.

The sistrum plays an important part in the present hour. Its rattling sound ensures the onset of the inundation that makes the waters overflow the riverbanks. The water fertilises the lands, enabling the farmers of Wernes to plant their seeds deep within the black earth after the inundation. The sistrum controls the amount of water overflowing the lands, as too much will make the seeds rot, whereas too little will make them dry out. The right amount of water facilitates the sprouting of the seeds to grow into lovely crops that serve as food. Therefore, the barque represents the life-giving water and the food that will be grown for the deceased.

Furthermore, the sistrum refers to the Goddess Hathor herself who was perceived as the right Eye of Râ. This eye is the healthy Eye of the Sungod and the symbol of his optimally shining light as well as wholeness and perfection. The sistrum is surrounded by two Goddesses (No. 165 and 167), without a name, who are standing on either side of the object. These two Goddesses could potentially be Isis and Nephthys. They are the protectors of the process of regeneration and assist Râ in his rebirthing process.

The last barque is named the "Ship of the Duatians". The stern of the barque is shaped in the form of a human head with a divine beard. The prow of the barque is missing as well. In the middle of the barque the full moon, with the crescent moon underneath it, can be found. Both celestial bodies are supported by a stand (No. 168).

The moon is the symbol of regeneration, healing and eternal Life as well as death and decay. Every month the moon undergoes a complete transformation as it shape-shifts from a full moon into a new moon and back again. The different phases demonstrate the cycle of life, death and rebirth in a relatively short space of time. Osiris was regarded as the moon God for he is the representation of the cycle of creation. He is the sun of the night world, or in other words, the moon. As opposed to Râ who is the sun of the day world.

The ancient Egyptians acknowledged the power of the moon since it influences the tides, the seasons and the growing cycle of the plants. Therefore, they took into account the various phases of the moon as they began sowing and harvesting their crops. In consequence, the moon within this hour is the focal point for "the peasants of Wernes". Once the moon reaches the appropriate phase, the peasants begin to take possession of the fields appointed to them by Râ and Neper to start sowing their crops.

The moon was generally perceived as the left Eye, whereas the sun was regarded as the right Eye. The left Eye is also the injured eye as is mentioned in the myth of Horus and Seth. This myth tells the story of the conflict between Horus and Seth as they fought over the inheritance left by Osiris. During the fight, Seth managed to damage Horus's left Eye, which was later healed by Thoth. The story connects the left Eye to healing, rejuvenation and regeneration. Therefore, the left Eye also symbolises the damaged light of the Sungod that is in the process of healing and regeneration. It is still incomplete and needs to develop completely during the journey. In the Fourth Hour, the healing of the Eye will be addressed in further detail.

Back to the barque, to the left of the crescent and the full moon, a God is kneeling "Who supports *Maât*" (No. 169). He is holding an ostrich feather with both his hands. The God assists the feather and, therefore, the Divine Law of *Maât*. He can be regarded as Thoth, "Lord of *Maât*", who ensures compliance with the Divine Law of *Maât*. However, the figure could also be the traveller as he upholds Truth and Order along his journey through the Duat. The barque shows that the process of renewal and rebirth is continued as long as the Law of *Maât* is adhered. At this time, it is still only the beginning of the transformation process, as made apparent by the crescent moon. Eventually, the transformation will be completed, as indicated by the full moon.

As mentioned before, the last two barques are missing their prows, which make them incomplete. The third barque with the sistrum shows the inundation has only just begun. The fourth barque displays a crescent moon at the beginning of its growth process. In other words, both barques show the beginning of a process that has yet to be finished.

The Duatians on the right riverbank (lower section)

The farmers of Wernes can be found on the right riverbank. They call upon Râ with adorations as soon as the Sungod reaches them. Râ, for his part, grants them vitality through his voice, which enables them to live. In doing so, Râ resurrects them with the Breath of Life. Then the Sungod provides them with plants that they can use to cultivate the fields according to the seasons. Once the crops are fully grown, they can be harvested and are in turn offered as a gift to Râ. Like this, an exchange of Divine energy between the peasants of Wernes and Râ is accomplished.

The peasants also offer water to the *Akh*-spirits living in the Duat, in order to protect these spirits. Although these spirits do not require food or drink they do need water. Only within the deep waters of Nun can the unification of the *Ba* and the *Ka* be achieved, to give rise to the *Akh*. Therefore, water is an essential element for the birth of the *Akh*. The protective nature of water for the *Akh* is made apparent in an old practice in Egypt. If someone stumbled hard to the ground, the earth was immediately sprayed with water. This prevented damage to the unfortunate *Akh's* who might have been present at that exact moment the person stumbled on them.

However, the protecting role of the Duatians is not limited to the *Akh*-spirits, for they protect Râ himself as well. They do so by stoking the fire used to burn Râ's enemies. The hearts of those rebels are tossed in the fire, wiping them from existence completely.

The right riverbank begins with four Gods in a running position. The first three Gods are holding the hieroglyphic sign *ter (tr)*, which means "season or time", in their hands.

(No. 170) "He who keeps apart the seasons"
(No. 171) "Guardian of the seasons"
(No. 172) "Bearer"

These Gods are responsible for the safekeeping of the three seasons. Every season is important and needs to be followed by the next one in chronological order to allow for the land to be cultivated. This is an essential concept to maintain the natural rhythm in the Duat, just like on earth. The sign *ter* is also a reference to the perfect moment, or time. Although the concept of time has a different meaning in the Afterlife, the *ter*-sign shows that the deceased are provided with time or the perfect moment to continue their lives for eternity.

The fourth running God, "Bearing arm" (No. 173), is holding a knife in his hands. He too is a protector of the rhythm of the seasons and guarantees the beginning of a new cycle after the harvest.

The subsequent three Gods are holding a palm branch in their hands. The staff like plant is the hieroglyphic sign *renep (rnp)*, which means "year or young". The palm branch symbolises long life and the notches in it represent the years. In temples, the time was ritually recorded using these palm branches. The three Gods are here to take care of the continuation of the years. This grants the deceased eternal Life and in addition provides them with fresh food supplies.

(No. 174) "He of the year"
(No. 175) "Who belongs to the grain bundle"
(No. 176) "Petitioner"

Following are three different Gods who are each holding a five-pointed star in their hands.

(No. 177) "He of the light"
(No. 178) "Great youth"
(No. 179) "The Great Shining One"

These stars are hieroglyphic signs, referring to "star, hour, night or decan". The ancient Egyptians divided the stars in thirty-six groups to form small constellations known as decans. Each decan is visible in the night sky during ten days. The beginning of the decan is marked with the heliacal rise of a new decanic star group just before sunrise. During ten days these stars travel through the night sky due to the earth rotation. At the end of the ten days, the next decan star group arises that also represents the beginning of a new week. The ancient Egyptians divided the year in ten day weeks, with three weeks to a month, twelve months to a year and an extra five days at the end to amount for a year of 365 days. Each decan star group rose at a specific period during the year and concurrently marked for a certain event. For example, the heliacal rise of Sirius marked the beginning of annual flooding of the Nile. The stars were, therefore, used as a celestial star clock.

However, aside from their astronomical significance, the stars also embody the movement of the Sun barque of Râ. As the stars of every decan travel through the sky, marking the hours, so does the Sun barque continue its travels as it sails through the twelve hours of the night. Therefore, the Gods holding the stars guarantee the continuation of this journey in the right order and time.

The next God is a double-headed Deity with his hands before his chest "He whose two faces and two arms are within him" (No. 180). He symbolises the joining of opposite forces to become whole, similar to the Deity "His two faces" (No. 138) who is on the other side of the Sacred River.

The God "The Radiant One" (No. 181) is holding two papyrus sceptres in both hands with a five-pointed star on top. The two sceptres refer to duality since opposite forces are needed to ensure the birth of the Shining One, which is Khepri. The stars on top of the sceptres indicate the process of resurrection as it starts unfolding within the Second Hour of the Duat. And, as always, the fact the sceptres are made of papyrus is not a coincidence. The papyrus is a fresh green plant that grows in shallow water. Due to its fresh green colour it is regarded as the symbol of youth, vigour, life and eternity. The plant was used for many purposes. The flowers of the plant bore edible fruits that could be used as a food source. The plant itself was used, for example, to create writing paper, sandals, rope and even

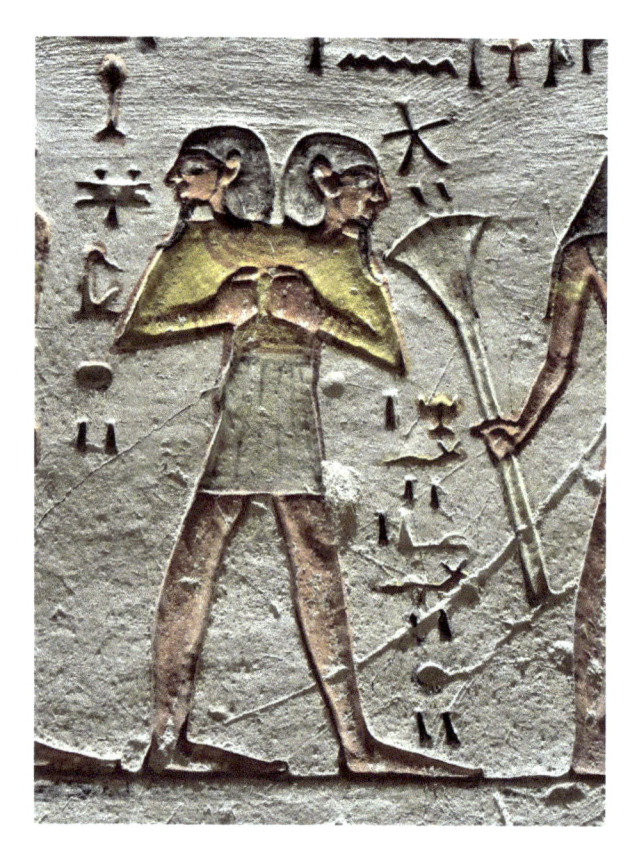

The God," He whose two faces and two arms are within him" KV9 Ramses V and VI

boats. It was also utilised to make amulets in the form of an *Ankh* to be used as offerings for the Gods. The papyrus was, therefore, a very important plant in this society.

The "Field of Reeds", or *Sekhet Iaru* (sḫt i3rw), was comprised of papyrus reeds. The "Field of Reeds or Offerings" was known as the Afterlife, the Netherworldly land of milk and honey. It is a wetland consisting of several islands covered with fields of reeds. It was viewed upon as the reflexion of the fertile Nile Valley with an idyllic touch to it. Before reaching this region, the deceased had to complete a dangerous journey full of obstacles. To brave these hardships, the deceased was equipped with various spells and amulets.

The papyrus shaped sceptre was also an important attribute to the deceased along his journey. On the day of the funeral the departed was provided with this sceptre in the form of an amulet hung around his neck. It bestowed upon the person the vitality and vigour needed to begin the journey through the Netherworld. Furthermore, it gave protection against dark forces along the way, ensuring rebirth to take place.

> Chapter for a papyrus-column
> of green feldspar
> to be placed on the throat of the deceased.
> O you who have come forth today
> from the God's house,
> she whose voice is loud goes round about
> from the door of the Two Houses,
> she has assumed the power of her father,
> who is ennobled
> as Bull of the Nursing Goddess,
> and she accepts those of her followers
> who do great deeds to her.
> To be spoken over a papyrus-column
> of green feldspar
> with this spell inscribed on it;
> It is to be set on the throat
> of the deceased.[12]
>
> – Book of the Dead; Spell 159

The God "Osiris, Wenennefer" (No. 182) is the mummified Osiris. His name means "The Perfect Being or Completed One", which is a reference to his resurrection from death. Osiris, as we know, once was a King on earth until he met his demise in a gruesome way and was killed by the evil powers of his brother Seth. After suffering through a great ordeal, he was finally able to overcome death and to be resurrected as the King of the Netherworld. Additionally, he became the Judge of the dead as his experience made him suited, unlike any other, to judge over good and evil. Hence, his function was an exemplary one. Everyone wanted to conquer death and rise as a Perfect Being, just as Osiris had done.

On this side of the Sacred River there is a tribunal of three mummified Gods sitting on their thrones.

The first God, "Lord of the Sacred Land" (No. 183), is a jackal-headed God with a five-pointed star in his lap. He is a form of Anubis and functions as Guide and Guardian for the deceased. The second God, "Akhebit" (No. 184), has a human head with a five-pointed star in his lap as well. His name means "Swallower".

The last God, "Donkey-swallower" (No. 185), is a bull-headed God with a knife in his lap, as mentioned in the introduction text. The donkey is one of the forms of Seth and symbolises evil. The purpose of "Donkey-swallower" is to swallow evil. It is required for the Sungod, as well as for every traveller, to be pure of heart in order to gain passage. If the heart is filled with evil deeds, it is tossed into the fire to be destroyed.

The following seven Gods are also peasants of Wernes (No. 186 – 192). They are taking care of the food provision for the deceased. The first one holds a knife in his hands, "He who belongs to the Divine place" (No. 186). The next three are holding an ear of grain in their hands.

(No. 187) "Grain"
(No. 188) "*Âba*-sceptre"
(No. 189) "Whose arm shines"

The last three Gods are carrying two ears of grain on their heads.

(No. 190) "Who belongs to the head"
(No. 191) "Neper", the grain God.
(No. 192) "Protection"

The final figure at the end of the riverbank is the Guardian of this hour, "Two Flames" (No. 193). He is facing the opposite direction, as he stands with his back to the door of the Third Hour. The two flames on top of his head refer to the two different sides of fire. It can enlighten and give warmth, but it can also burn and destroy. "Two Flames" is the Guardian of duality that is needed to cultivate the process of awareness.

Closing text

As Râ finally arrives in his form as "flesh", he is greeted by all the Deities within the hour; "O! Appear, great *Ba*-soul!"[13] They rejoice and cheer, listing all the protective and combative skills of Râ to encourage him. Furthermore, they ask the Sungod to light up the hour and defeat the darkness, for he is the Great Illuminator. The Uraeus on his brow then begins to shine, a sign of rulership and power, enabling the renewal and revival of all life. In appreciation, the Deities open the double-door entrance of the earth to allow Râ to descend deep into the Duat. The darkness of this world forms a protective layer around Râ and Osiris, with the latter in anticipation of Râ's arrival.

All Duatians have complete faith in Râ and applaud him not just for his arrival, but for his upcoming renewed ascent in the morning as well. Then he will have defeated his enemies. Râ acknowledges their praise and asks them to open the secret gates for him. Subsequently, he gives a speech, to inform them of his many contributions to them. He bestows upon them his breath; the Breath of Life. He nourishes them as he gifts them the seedlings of barley and emmer wheat needed to bake bread. Additionally this bread is used by the Duatians as an offering for the Gods, feeding both sides in the process. Furthermore, he protects their bodies from desiccation and decay, enabling them to remove their wrappings. This grants them more range of motion in order for them to take large steps forward once more, "stride far". The statement of Râ to stride far is a reference to the way Osiris has risen from death and ascended to the sky in his form as Orion. Râ orders the Duatians to raise themselves just like Osiris.

> Your wrappings are undone,
> your feet may stretch,
> that you may walk on them,
> that you may stride far.[14]

That is still not all. Râ also rejuvenates their *Ba*-souls, enabling them to speak their Magic spells. This grants them the power to gain mastery over the enemies of Osiris. To do this, they make use of their sharp knives. Consequently, the seasons will last, the years will endure, and food will be produced with the promise of eternal Life. Thus, Râ's vast power guarantees these Duatians will live. The Duatians in turn also help Râ by protecting him from Apophis. They are dependent on one another and therefore take care of each other. Due to this mutual dependency it is of great importance that each Deity remains in their protected places. If they leave their places, no one will open the secret gates to let Râ in the Duat. Râ will then be unable to proceed and will die a second death. However, if they are in their designated positions, the process of eternal renewal can be carried out to continue life. This is not just in the interest of Râ alone, but for the continuation of the entire creation. After these encouraging and inspiring words, Râ is prepared to leave and travel to the next hour. The Duatians of this hour weep and wail as he moves past them. They have to wait until the next night for Râ to enter the hour and resurrect them again.

The manifestation of the Second Hour in daily life

The Second Hour opens with the *seba* gate "Who swallows all". As mentioned in the First Hour, the hieroglyphic word *seba* means "door or teaching". However, it also holds another meaning, which is "pupil". You are now in front of this gate that constitutes the division between the forecourt and the inner court of the temple. Behind the door lies the teaching of the sacred Wisdom and Knowledge of the Amduat. Therefore, this is the moment to think about whether you truly wish to commit yourself to this path of Initiation. When you decide to proceed, the door will open itself for you. The moment you enter the next realm, you have become a pupil of the secret teachings. The gate "Who swallows all" then closes itself behind you to protect the enlightened Knowledge of the night world from the influences of the day world.

During the First Hour you became acquainted with the transition of the day into the night world. However, this was only the first dip into the waters of the subconsciousness without becoming completely submerged. Presently, you have to make the leap of faith and dive into these waters, leaving the day world behind completely. This hour contains an abundance of water as the inundation has now truly begun. The riverbanks have flooded, making the river twice as broad and doubling the reflective surface of the water. In other words, an enormous mirror is held up in front of you that requests your attention. There is no escape, for water is all around you. Here, the first real confrontation with your inner realm takes place. You will discover things about yourself that you never even knew existed. These can be surprising aspects, but also things that might frighten you or things you would rather ignore.

This inner duality is very important. It allows you to get to know all aspects of yourself, which you have hidden somewhere in the dark corners of your consciousness. There are probably numerous reasons to think of why you hid these aspects. They are the hidden side of yourself that you are ashamed of or that you might find too powerful. These do not fit the personality type you have, or that others perceive you as. You do not wish to be confronted with these features, nor be identified with them. Unfortunately, there is no escaping the giant mirror in front of you.

Try to be neutral and do not judge yourself. It does not matter what you think or feel about it. It is about confronting yourself. But fret not, Râ the Higher Self, is there to assist. Step outside of your tiny, little world and look through the Eyes of your inner Sungod. This heightened perspective improves your overview and expands your awareness. It grants you an overall picture of all characteristics you could never have discovered from your own little corner of the universe. As it raises your awareness, it provides you with the tools to work with these features. You should think of this part of yourself as a power that can be yielded to work with or against you. It all depends on your own decision of how to deal with it.

This inner duality is triggered by the many opposite forces in this hour. The Gods "His two faces" (No. 138) and "He whose two faces and two arms are within him" (No. 180) can be of great assistance. They are, like no other, able to resuscitate these discrepancies within yourself and make you conscious of them. Furthermore, they possess the knowledge to help you integrate these inner conflicts to create a unity within yourself.

In addition, you will be confronted with two tribunals. The first one can be found on the riverbank on the left side of the Sacred River (No. 144 – 149). The six judges, forming the first tribunal, all carry a knife in their laps and direct your attention to your inner discernment. They aim the focus towards the seat of your consciousness, your heart and to that what is happening inside. There are features that make your heart as light as a feather. However, there also are aspects that weigh you down and burden your heart. The question is; what is pure and true and what is falsehood and deceitful. The judges press a knife in your hand to sharpen your discernment. As you well know, *Maât* is on the razor's edge.

The second tribunal is on the right riverbank of the Sacred River (No. 183 – 185). The three Gods who are part of this tribunal are here to make you conscious of your actions. Specifically "Donkey-swallower" (No. 185) merits your attention. The donkey is a very stubborn animal and not easy to direct. However, if you are able to control his temper, he will prove to be a very helpful force. Then he relieves you of your burdens and carries the weight instead of you. Thus, the donkey refers to the part of yourself that is unwilling to comply with the Higher Self. It pursues its own course guided by personal desires and emotions. This part must be "swallowed" to redirect the focus back to the Higher Self. Still, swallowing does not mean to destroy these adversarial aspects. It is about transformation, to make the stubborn head lower

The tribunal of three mummified Gods seated on thrones, KV 9 Ramses V and VI

itself and become in service of the Higher Self.

This is the hour to clear-out your mental state as indicated by the immense amount of water. Your actions, the person you are, may become just as transparent as this clear water. The haze is washed away, allowing you to see what lies beneath. The force of the water pushes certain aspects of yourself upwards. Characteristics that lay dormant at the bottom before. This is all part of the process of the raising of the inner awareness, which has now started to fully flow.

The water can be quit overwhelming for it comes down on you like an enormous avalanche. Once you try to resist, you are swept away with the dynamic current. You are submerged and come up for air only every so often. Digging your heels into the sand is useless as the feeling of chaos does not submit to control. There is no steady ground, no comfort. Fighting against the current only leads to the waste of precious energy and strengthens the feeling of insecurity. So go along with the flow, and begin your first quest as you dive to find the hidden treasures in your inner paradise.

Your ascent into the subconsciousness makes your own paradise blossom. You are the one, after a long period of draught, who turns on the faucet with the life-granting water. Your inner focus feeds this world. The sub-consciousness, in turn, provides you with secret images. These images, which had been just faint shadows in the previous hour, are now visible more clearly as the gates to the day world have been shut tight. The way in which this process manifests itself is a very personal experience. It all depends on the way easiest for you to become familiar with this information. One person might be very visual, while the other is more perceptive to audible or kinaesthetic input. The information can present itself to you by means of dreams or memories. Or it might try to catch your attention in daily life, leaving precious gems when or where you least expect it. When this happens, you recognise it immediately for what it is; a response from your inner world.

Either way, you always have to take the first step yourself. For only when you ask clear questions or take specific actions, you are provided with a response. Your freedom and free will are respected at all times. This allows for the inner communication to take place and for the building of confidence and trust between you and your Higher Self. The Higher Self is the one who guides you safely through the vast amount of water.

The importance of the connection between you and your Higher Self, your inner Sungod, is emphasized by the presence of the Maât Goddess right at the beginning of this hour. The lightness of her feather reminds us that if we stay connected to our inner Sungod, we are capable of transcending the gravity of falsehood. It is the prerequisite to remain in balance with *Maât*. Her presence guarantees a reliable order and structure, just like in the First Hour.

Everything, that takes place, is in harmony with this Law. It is important to be aware of this since not every experience on your way seems to abide Truth or *Maât*. Nevertheless, this Law is most definitely the norm. Only when you are able to view everything from a greater perspective through your connection with the Sungod Râ, will you realise this. All you need is a bird's eye view to see it.

The four barques mentioned in this hour carry important symbols with them that are requesting your attention. The Gods in the first barque, "Rowing through the flood", are missing their arms, a reference to the principal of offering. The offering in this context does not refer to the physical offering of bread and beer, but the spiritual offering. It is the offering during which you offer yourself to the Divine or the Higher Self. You symbolically offer your arms to the inner Sungod to enable him to work through you. Hence, you are putting yourself in the hands of the Divine.

The second barque, "Barque which the *Netjeru* row", symbolises the enormous amount of power made available once you commit yourself to the Divine. The sceptres of royal and Divine power are handled on behalf of you as you identify yourself with the Higher Self.

The third barque, "Carried by Wernes", symbolises the abundance within your hidden realm. The rattling sound of the sistrum is a wake-up call for you to become alert. Thus, it sets your inner world into motion. Naturally, you are not supposed to drown in the overwhelming amount of water. The sistrum acts as a balance to maintain the equilibrium of the life-giving waters. Not too much and not too little. This submerges and cleanses your inner world and enables it to start bearing fruit.

The last barque, "Ship of the Duatians", represents the eternal process of renewal in accordance with the Divine Law of *Maât*. The inner development and raising of your consciousness is an ongoing process. It is never too late to become aware of this process and to participate in it.

All four barques are filled with precious gifts for you. However, it is up to you whether you receive them and realise them in your daily life. These are not the only gifts bestowed upon you within this hour. The most important gift is that you have given your inner world the right to exist. It is allowed to come into being once more through the attention you are giving it. This is symbolised by Râ as he and the grain god Neper assign the fields to the Duatians. The Duatians have been granted a place to live and to grow their crops to feed themselves, just like you.

THE THIRD HOUR
"Water of the Unique Lord, which brings forth nourishment"

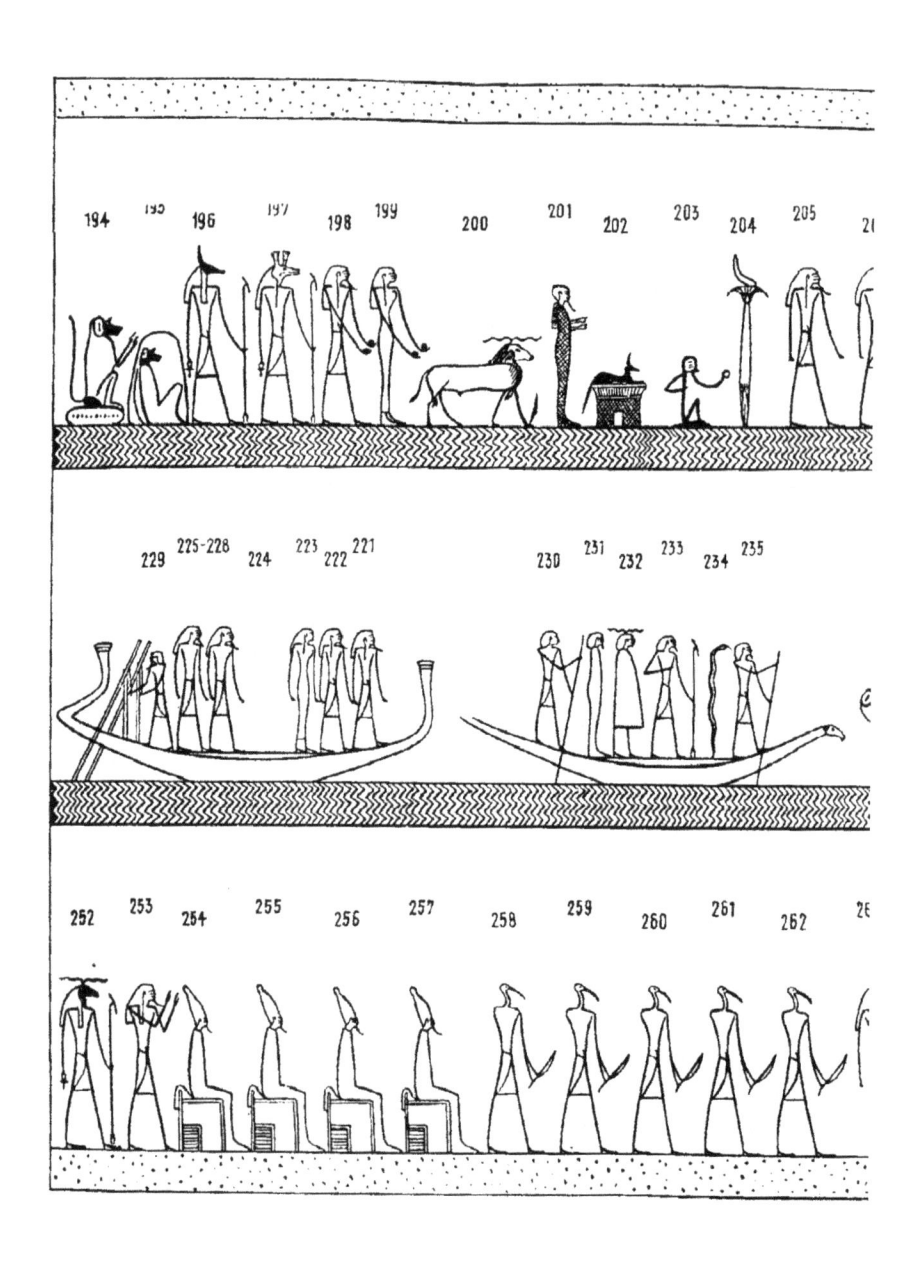

Figure 19: The Third Hour

The Gate:	"Robber"
The Hour Goddess:	"She who cuts *Ba*-souls"
The Guardian:	"Khetery (ichneumon)"

Introduction

Setting into the region of the shore-dwellers
by the person of this Great God.
Rowing on the water of Osiris – 309 *iteru*
is the length of this region.
Then this Great God gives orders
to the *Akh*-spirits
who are in the following of Osiris
at this region.
The name of the Hour of the night
guiding this Great God is
"She who cuts *Ba*-souls".
The name of the Gate of this region
is "Robber".
This Great God cares for the Gods
in the following of Osiris,
he assigns plots to them at this region.
Know the mysterious *Ba*-souls!
He who knows their names [on earth]
will approach
to the place where Osiris is.
Water is given to him at this his region.
"Water of the Unique Lord,
which brings forth nourishment"
is the name of this region.
These images of the mysterious Ba-souls
have been made
like that form which is painted
in the secrecy of the Duat.
The beginning of the writing (belongs)
towards the West.
It is efficient for a man on earth,
(and) in the necropolis, a true remedy.[1]

Once Râ passes the gate "Robber", he enters the Third Hour. Here he is welcomed by the Hour Goddess, "She who cuts *Ba*-souls", who is going to guide Râ through this realm. Her name indicates that she completely destroys the *Ba*-souls of the enemies of the Sungod in order to protect him.

This region is 309 *iteru* long and still oriented in the West. It is called "Water of the Unique Lord, which brings forth nourishment". The Unique Lord is none other than Osiris himself. These wetlands are under the banner of this God who will make several appearances in different forms.

The inundation is now present at full power, which makes the river wider than usual. The flooded riverbanks absorb the life-giving waters and are transformed into fertile seedbeds.

During his travels through this hour, Râ is still allocating plots of land to the Duatians. These Duatians are in the following of Osiris and use the land to grow their crops. The abundance of fertility is now utilised to grow a rich harvest. It is in Râ's best interest that the Duatians are well taken care of and provided with the proper nutrition. Râ needs them as much as they need him in order to live. They are interdependent. Therefore, Râ does not just grant them his help unconditionally, for he also expects something in return. He does this by means of instructions. As he is weak and vulnerable, he needs the guiding and protecting powers of the

Duatians now more than ever. Without their help, he will not be able to renew himself, which would halt his regeneration process. Hence, this mutual dependency is not just in both of their interests, but also for the continuation of creation itself.

Râ sails past all Duatians present in this hour. Every single one of them receives his undivided attention. Râ, in turn, connects himself with the mysteries that these Duatians represent. Through this identification he gets to know the name of each of these mysterious *Ba*-souls. Only with this knowledge will he be able to descend further down into the depths of the Duat to meet with Osiris himself. This does not just apply to Râ, for every traveller sailing through this hour must connect and identify himself with these *Ba*-souls.

The Duatians on the left riverbank (Upper section)

The Duatians on the left riverbank have once again formed a procession consisting of several Gods. They undergo the same transformation process as Râ. They too are bound to their bodies that are necessary vessels from which the spiritual body, the *Sâhu*, is formed. Their first transformation is already complete, which allowed for their *Ba*-souls to descend into the Duat. Here they have a new life that is made evident by the fact that they possess a shadow.

Râ commences his communication with them by calling upon them. This rejuvenates them and enables them to speak. As soon as they are revived, they connect themselves with the Divinity of the Sungod through their adoration. This grants them life and nutrition. It is, therefore, understandable that the departure of Râ leaves them wailing as they are not allowed to join Râ on his Sun barque. They are required to stay behind and accomplish the important tasks given to them by Râ.

They dutifully comply with his demands, granting Râ safe passage as they "grind the enemy". Furthermore, they see to it that the waters of Nun emerge and manifest into the inundation. The deluge, which already started in the Second Hour, reaches its peak in this hour. To ensure the continuous flow of the water, the Duatians provide plenty of wind. The paradise-like ambience from the previous hour has changed into a grim menace. The water now forms huge waves as it is empowered by the raging storm. This massive outburst of energy creates a forcefield that enables Râ to take the next step in his transformation process. Fortunately, the Duatians possess the knowledge and wisdom needed to guide Râ through. Their collaboration with Râ is essential for the process to succeed. Râ, in turn, is required to know the names and identities of every one of these Duatians, for only then he is able to utilise their power. Without this knowledge, the journey will not end well. When ignorant, the Duatians roar and see to the demise of the unknowing passer-by as they fall into the pits and perish. This applies to an ignorant Râ as well. Râ might be a God, but he too is expected to abide by the rules of these Duatians and familiarise himself with the required knowledge.

The procession on the left riverbank starts with two baboons sitting in the front. The first one, "He on his sand" (No. 194), sits on an ellipse of sand in an adoring pose with upraised arms. The ellipse of sand refers to the entire Duat and is also a specific reference to the oval shaped Cavern of Sokar at the bottom of the Fifth Hour. Within this mysterious enclosure, the first contact between Râ and Osiris commences causing the rekindling of the very first spark of light. The baboon is the sacred animal of the God of Wisdom, Thoth. Therefore, "He on his sand" is already referring to the importance of Wisdom and Knowledge that are the keys to manifesting the journey of renewal and regeneration.

The second baboon, "Djeby Netjer" (No. 195), is mummified and holed up within the protection of a burial chest. He sits here with his attention turned inward. The burial chest itself is a reference to the chest in the Fifth Hour, "Darkness" (No. 344). The chest marks the entrance to the secret Cavern of Sokar. From this chest, the scarab Khepri will appear as the symbol of rebirth.

The wise baboons both know intuitively that despite the ferocious water mass, the regeneration of Râ's light is at hand. Therefore, they take their respective spots with great confidence right at the front. This is a leading statement at the opening of the Third Hour.

Following the baboons, the jackal-headed God, "Inpu" (No. 196), is walking with the *Was*-sceptre in one hand and the *Ankh* in the other. Inpu, or Anubis, is the Protector of the deceased and the Healer of the dead. He is the Divine Surgeon and the Patron of the chief physician.

> His majesty says to the chief physician
> Ni-ankh-Sakhmit:
> Health to your nose.
> Everything which comes forth
> from your mouth
> will come into effect for me,
> because the God Anubis
> has made him (you)
> accomplished in medical matters...
> He will be beloved of Anubis,
> (the one who makes) offerings for him (you)
> on the day of the New Year...[2]

With great precision, he takes care of the mummification process. He tenderly balms the corpse and wraps it in bandages. Due to his extraordinary ability, the corpse will never be subjected to decay.

After the funerary ceremonies, Anubis, or Inpu, guides the deceased through the Netherworld. During the travels the deceased experiences the transformation of death and comes back to life in the Afterlife. The renewal

THE GREAT AWAKENING ଓ 155

of life takes place in the depth of the Duat. It is Inpu himself who is the protector of this hidden realm. He is also present here, on the left riverbank, in this particular protective form. His name is "Inpu of the *Was*-sceptre" (No. 202) and he lies as a couchant jackal on top of a ritual shrine. The shrine underneath him symbolises the Duat and the burial chamber with the Mysteries that take place within. He protects this sacred place to ensure safety during the rejuvenation of the body and soul. No one knows the exact course of this enigmatic process as it is part of one of the greatest mysteries of creation. With the exception of Inpu, who is the Guardian and Keeper of this secret. Hence, one of Inpu's names is "He who is over the secret" *hery seshta* (ḥry-sštȝ). In this form, Inpu can be seen on the left riverbank in the Tenth Hour (No. 713).

Following Inpu is a walking crocodile-headed God, "Neha Kheru" (No. 197), with an *Ankh* and *Was*-sceptre in his hands. His name means the "Terrible of voice". It is possible that this Deity is the powerful crocodile God Sobek

Anubis prepares funeral rituals, TT 218 Amennakht, Deir el-Medina

who is also known as the "Raging One". Like the Nile crocodile, he has a very aggressive and all-consuming nature that led to him being worshipped with the greatest respect. However, aside from the destructive aspects, Sobek also possesses a salutary side due to his connection with the life-giving waters in which he resides. Since the crocodiles popped up from the Nile in large numbers during the annual inundation, Sobek was associated with the inundation and therefore with the creation of new life that resulted from this flood. After all, the moment when Sobek made an appearance, the dry land was hydrated by the water and the riverbanks became green and fertile. On one end, Sobek is a true water God, which is also indicated with other epithets like "Lord of the Winding Waterway" and "Lord of the Nile". On the other end, he is a God of the fertile land, which gave him the name "Lord of the river-banks".

His mother was the Goddess Neith who was regarded as a creator Goddess and associated with the primeval waters. Sobek himself is a creator God as well who, according to myth, was the first to appear from the waters of Nun to create the world afterwards. He did this through laying his eggs on the riverbank of the waters of Nun. He was also seen as the creator of the Nile that he made out of his sweat. It is evident that Sobek is an essential force who allows for the life-giving waters of Nun to come into existence.

To become Sobek
I am the seed which issued
from the encircling wrapping.
I am he who broke the teeth of him
who cut away the iron.
I am the Lord of strength and might
who took crocodile-shape.
I am the Lord of wrong who lives on woe.
I am that crocodile
whose tongue was cut out
because of the mutilation of Osiris.
I am he who puts fear [into...] whom
the Ennead fear.
I am Lord of the Nile [...].
I am that God who rises in the East
and sets in the West,
to whom the Niles are given.
I am he who rises, who has no weakness
because of the Gods of the nomes.
I am that God whom the eight row.
I am Sobek, the rebel who is among you,
[you Gods];
You cannot do anything against me,
you spirits or you dead,
for I have taken possession of the sky
and have taken possession of the earth.
I am a possessor of worship [...]
to whom are given his *smwt* women
and their hair.[3]
I am [...] a multitude.
I am Sobek, Lord of strife,
who lingers [...].
I am Sobek, Lord of the river-banks [...]

his blood.
I am he who impregnates *smwt*-women.
I am he who has recourse to robbery.
I am [the Great Fish]
giving to the region of the Bull.
I am a possessor of strength in Khem.[4]
– Coffin texts; Spell 991

The next two Deities are the God "He who brings" (No. 198) and the Goddess "She who brings" (No. 199). They both hold their hands stretched forward to display the eyes they are holding. The eyes are the Divine Eyes of Râ and are a reference to his light or consciousness. These Eyes are a central theme and will change along the course of the journey.

(No. 200) "Slayer of his foes" is a ram holding a knife in his forefoot. His name clearly implies his intentions, for he will attack any of Râ's foes with this knife.

(No. 201) "Standing Bow" is a mummified God with a divine beard and an artisan's skull cap. He is wearing the *menit* necklace which is a symbol of potency, fertility, new life, resurrection, health and happiness. "Standing Bow" resembles the God Ptah and is therefore a reference to this important creator God. Normally, Ptah is holding a *Was*-sceptre, "dominion", in his hands combined with the *Ankh*, "eternal Life", and the *Djed*, "stability". He is then standing on a pedestal shaped like the hieroglyphic sign of *Maât*. Here, though, this sceptre and pedestal are missing.

Ptah is the Lord of Life, the patron of craftsmanship and the God of intelligence and Creative Utterance. He has been worshiped since the earliest times in the dynastic period. His name means "create". Additionally, his name also bears resemblance with the Semitic word *pâthakh*, meaning "opener". In fact, Ptah was seen as the Opener of the day as he represents the moment the sun rises. Therefore, he was usually regarded as a form of the Sungod. However, the definition of "open" does not just mean "to open something". It also refers to "to engrave, to carve or to chisel". His abilities of sculpting and engraving made Ptah the head God

The God Ptah, TT 219 Nebenmaat, Deir el-Medina

of all craftsmen, especially the workers in metal and stone.⁵ Consequently, he was linked to the Opening of the Mouth ceremony. In his role as the Divine sculptor and the God of Creative Utterance, he carved or opened the mouth of the cult statues he had fashioned. In fact, Ptah was considered the creator of the ceremony of the Opening of the Mouth.

Furthermore, Ptah's omnipotence made him the creator of all the Gods and all else "through his heart and through his tongue". This means he intentionally envisaged creation through his thoughts and speech. He was also involved in the rebirth of the departed souls and created new bodies for them. This new vessel enabled the deceased to continue their existence in the Afterlife. His association with the Afterlife and the first creation resulted in the merging of Ptah with the earth God Tatenen into the God Ptah-Tatenen. Together with Sokar and Osiris, Ptah is also part of the triple God Ptah-Sokar-Osiris. These three Gods portray the entire cycle of regeneration. Within this conjunction, Ptah symbolises creation, Sokar death and Osiris resurrection.⁶

Ptah is a multifaceted God. To support this fact, he is not just a masculine God for he possesses both female and male elements within himself. His female side is connected to the sky and his male side to the earth and he thus effectively forms a bridge between both worlds.⁷

It is clear Ptah possesses many features that can be traced back to his epithets; "The Beautiful Face", "Lord of Truth and Justice", "Ptah the Great", "Who listens to prayers", "Master of Ceremonies", "Sculptor of the Earth" and "Lord of Eternity". These features make him a God of great importance to Râ. Thus, the Deity "Standing Bow" is present here, at the beginning of the Third Hour, to remind Râ of all of this.

In front of "Standing Bow" lies "Inpu of the *Was*-sceptre" (No. 202) in his protective form as a couchant jackal on top of a ritual shrine. Following this hour the descent into the actual Duat will begin. Therefore, Râ needs the guidance and protection of both forms of Inpu for this God is the only one who knows the way.

Following "Inpu of the *Was*-sceptre" is a squatting God with an eye held up in his outstretched hand "He who brings the Eye and satisfies the Gods (with it)" (No. 203). This gesture is a reference to the ongoing process of the rejuvenation of the light of Râ, which is symbolised by the eye. On this side of the Sacred River the signs of the renewal and regeneration are present in abundance. These aspects are emphasised by the stylised papyrus stem or *Wadj*-sceptre "Great of Magic" (No. 204). The fresh green papyrus plant is the symbol of fertility, vitality, youth, rebirth and life after death. It was associated with an abundance of vegetation. The *Wadj*-sceptre is, therefore, an important support for the rebirth of Râ. The name of the *Wadj*-sceptre, "Great of Magic", is a reference to the fact that creation emerges from the creative force of Magic. Without Magic, physical existence is impossible.

The *Wadj*-sceptre within this context has a magical knife on top. As mentioned in the First Hour, magical knives were used during childbirth to ward of evil and protect the vulnerable new life. It may come as no surprise a magical knife is the only object able to protect the magical act of creation.

The next four Gods are walking without any attributes. They too stand for helpful and strong powers.

(No. 205) "He with noble heart"
(No. 206) "The Strong One"
(No. 207) "Who rejuvenates the mummies"
(No. 208) "Who seizes by night"

They are followed by a group of four mummified Gods of whom the last three are wearing various attributes on top of their heads.

(No. 209) "The Attired One"
(No. 210) "The Robber", a God with a double tailed serpent on his head.
(No. 211) "Bull of forms", a God
with the small horns of a bull on his head.
(No. 212) "That *Ba*-soul", a God
with the large horns of a bull on his head.

Following is a group of four Goddesses, three of whom are wailing and weeping.

(No. 213) "She who weeps"
(No. 214) "She who praises"
(No. 215) "She who mourns"
(No. 216) "She who wails"

The sorrowful bewailing of the dead was an important part of the funeral ceremony. Consequently, in ancient Egypt, women were hired to weep and moan as part in the funeral procession. The professional mourners expressed their intense grief dramatically. They held their hands on their head, threw dust in their hair and face, beat their exposed breasts and raised their arms. Their uncontrollable wailing was loud while tears were running down their cheeks. The lamentation was thought to be beneficial to the soul of the deceased. The crying would wake the deceased from his slumbering death and enable him to move forward.

A mummified hawk, "Henu" (No. 217), can be seen sitting on a standard in front of the four wailing Goddesses. *Henu* is also the name of the barque of Sokar. Since Sokar is usually depicted as a hawk-headed mummy, we can assume this hawk is a reference to this God.

Sokar is the God of the dead and resides in the deepest regions of the Netherworld. As the representative of the darkness and the night sun he was strongly linked with Osiris. Moreover, after Osiris had been put to death by Seth, his name was changed into Sokar. As mentioned above, together with Ptah and Osiris, Sokar is part of the triple God Ptah-Sokar-Osiris.

Memphis was the primary cult centre of Sokar with in particular the cemeteries. Sokar's realm is located deep within the earth where the transformation of death into life takes place.

Sokar is the one who takes care of the regeneration process. When the earth needed to be ploughed and chopped to sow for the crops, or to build a tomb, one was required to ask for Sokar's blessing first.

Sokar was the chief Deity of the workmen who built the tombs in the necropolis and also of the metal workers who forged the tomb artefacts and ritual tools and objects needed for the mummification and the funeral.

The sacred *Henu* barque of Sokar was used during the festival of Sokar, *"heb sokar"* (ḥb skr). The prow was shaped like the head of some kind of antelope. In the middle of the barque was a chapel in the shape of a mound with a falcon head on top. The chapel, or coffin, contained the symbolical body of Sokar in his form as Osiris. The festival was one of the most important celebrations that took place in every temple at the end of the flooding season, *Akhet*. It marked the beginning of the next season, *Peret*, or the sowing season. Since the earth was now soaked with an abundance of life-giving water, it had now become fertile again. This was the perfect time to work the soil and sow the seeds for the new crops. Hence, the resurrection of

Wailing women, TT 219 Nebenmaat, Deir el-Medina

life from death, as symbolised by Osiris, was the central theme of the festival. Moreover, this was also the moment when the rulership of the Pharaoh was reaffirmed and renewed.

The first eight days of the festival were dedicated to embalming and the performance of magical funerary ceremonies. To do this, they used "grain mummies" that symbolised the dead and mummified Osiris. The dolls were made of wood and were hollow inside. The cavity was filled with soil and the seeds of barley. The grain mummies were watered daily. On the ninth day the dried seeds germinated into living green sprouts after which the complete ritual of the Opening of the Mouth, *"wepet ra"* (*wpt-r3*), was performed on the mummies. After completing the ritual, the grain mummies were then buried in the earth. This act was also performed during a ritual called the "Great hacking of the earth". The ceremony was carried out by the Pharaoh himself as he was the personification of the God Horus on earth. Horus, who is the heir to the throne of his "father" Osiris, symbolises the renewed life after death. Therefore, the Pharaoh acted as the mediator between the Gods and men for his actions alone would grant the fertility

The Henu barque, Temple of Hathor, chapel of Amun-Râ-Osiris, Deir el-Medina

to return to the earth and allow for the growth of lush crops. The God Sokar, in the form of a statue, was removed from the temple to assist the Pharaoh and to give the King his blessing. The earth was hacked up for the sowing. The act of sowing the grain was mourned since it was placed beneath the ground like a corpse. Therefore, it was bewailed as if it was the slain Osiris himself who they buried.[8]

This period was followed by a wake, Night of the Divine, *"gereh netjeryt"* (grḥ nṯry.t), that was performed before the procession with the *Henu* barque the next day. The wake revolved around the connection between Horus, the symbol of the renewal of light or life, and Sokar, the symbol of death. The life, and thus the light, was now soon to return and conquer death. The wake was held in the temples and also in the tombs. The tombs were opened during the festival to support the owner of the tomb during his process of resurrection in the Afterlife. The Night of the Divine was also known as "the Day of tying onions" for the participants made garlands out of onions during the wake and wore them around their neck. There were also onions offered to the God Sokar and to the deceased.[9]

> What is carried out during the nṯry.t-night,
> in the dreadful night,
> that night of going away
> and becoming distant,
> that night of the going forth of the voice,
> that night of lonely sleep,
> that night of great defensive Magic,
> that night of hacking the earth in tears,
> that night of loneliness,
> that night of mourning,
> that night of hacking the earth,
> when the whole land gazes upon Sokar,
> Upper and Lower Egypt are in silence,
> and the entrance to the closed place
> remains at rest.[10]

The hieroglyphic word for onion is *hedju* (ḥdw). It is related to the word *hedj* (ḥd) meaning "white, bright, set forth at dawn". The onion is a bulbous plant that has a white colour beneath the outer dry and brittle scale. The colour of the outer scale in the common modern unions can vary from yellow, brown/red or red/purple. However, the exact origin of the onion is unknown and it has been cultivated over the millenia. It will remain a mystery as to what colour or kind of onion the ancient Egyptians used. Either way, it did have the typical spherical shape with the white glassy concentric rings inside. It was regarded the perfect symbol for the process of regeneration and the renewal of life as the onion has the ability to sprout new runners long after it has been harvested.

During the festival of Sokar, which marked the beginning of *Peret*, the crops obviously had yet to be sown. Consequently, there were no fresh crops available to serve as an offering. Nevertheless, the onion, if stored in a proper manner, can still produce green leaves. It is not inconceivable to think that the ancient

Egyptians used this characteristic to store the onions appropriately and allow them to sprout leaves for the festival. The green leaves then made a perfect gift for the Gods and the deceased to celebrate and promote the return of life.

The next day, the statue of Sokar was placed on the *Henu* barque during an elaborate morning ritual. The barque was then placed on top of a sledge. At the moment of sunrise, the barque was initially ceremonially dragged by the Pharaoh. However, upon later times, this role of the Pharaoh was adopted by the priests instead. They lifted the barque and carried it around. The procession was called "Going around the wall" since it originally took place around the white walls of Memphis.[11] Everybody took part in this important event during which death (Sokar) was transformed into the resurrection of life (Osiris).

During the final day, the festival was concluded with one last big ceremony during which the *Djed*-pillar was upraised and would remain standing for ten days. The pillar looked like a spine. Hence, it was regarded as the backbone of Osiris and, thus, the symbol of stability and duration. "The raising of the *Djed*" portrayed the resurrection of Osiris in the Netherworld. It stands for the triumph over death and the renewal of the annual cycle.

The name "Sokar" can also be spelled as *sek-er* (*sk-r*), which means "to wipe out the mouth". Unsurprisingly, Sokar himself plays an important role in "the Opening of the Mouth" ceremony. He is the Lord of the forbidden realm in the Netherworld, Ro-Setjau, in which death is transformed into a new life. The entrance, or the mouth, of Ro-Setjau falls under his jurisdiction. The process of rebirth is possible only if Sokar opens his realm and provides access for the deceased. In addition, he was the Divine creator of the ritualistic instruments that were used in the Opening of the Mouth ceremony. The tools were forged by the metal workers on his behalf.

The Opening of the Mouth ceremony was a significant ritual for the deceased as it allowed

Isis and Seti I set up the sacred Djed-pillar, Temple of Seti I (First Osiris Hall, west wall) at Abydos

him to be reborn into the Afterlife. The ceremony was performed after the completion of the embalming and mummification process, which was after seventy days. Subsequently, the mummy was hauled in a procession towards the tomb where the ceremony was performed in the forecourt. There the mummy was taken out the coffin and put upright, from the supine position of death, as a reference to the "raising of the *Djed*". The upright mummy was turned with his face towards the South. This enabled the deceased to gaze upon the highest light, the light of the Sungod Râ, which supported him along his journey towards his own resurrection and rebirth into a new life.

> The day of burial,
> striding freely to his tomb.
> Performing the Opening of the Mouth at the [...]
> in the House of Gold,
> set upright on the desert soil,
> its face turned to the South,
> bathed in light on earth
> on the day of being clothed.[12]

The ceremony was a very complex one consisting of approximately thirty individual rituals. Several ritual instruments and tools were used to recreate the body. One of these tools was the *Seb Ur* or *adze*. This instrument was made of meteoric iron that was found in the desert and called the iron of the sky. It was also known as *meskhtyu* (*msḫtyw*), which is a reference to the constellation of the Great Bear, "Ursa Major". The mouth and eyes were touched with the *adze* in order to restore the senses. It allowed the deceased to regain his abilities of speech, sight, hearing and taste in the Afterlife. Aside from the opening of the senses, the rest of the body was healed as well. Death had broken the unity that was restored during the ceremony. The same goes for the shadow, or *Khaibit*, which is an essential part of the body. The restoration of this mirror image re-established the unity, making the body infused with life once more. The deceased was now effectively reborn, able to move with every sensory organ at his disposal. Once again, he could ingest food and drink to nourish his *Ka*.

> The iron is broken by Anubis
> in the sky. Ho,
> iron which opened up the West!
> This is the iron which is on my mouth,
> which Sokar spiritualized in Õn,
> which makes the water of my mouth to rise,
> the iron is washed, and it is sharp and strong.
> This is the iron which Sokar raised on high
> in the name of the Great One in it in Õn,
> the iron which raises me up,
> which lifts me up so that I may
> open the land of the West (in)
> which I dwelt ...].[13]
> – Coffin Texts; spell 816

Here, nearly at the end of the Third Hour, Sokar can be seen in the form of "Henu", a mummified hawk. This is a reference to the end of the inundation. He is the herald for the coming resurrection where death is prevailed. During the Fourth and Fifth Hour, we will get to know the God Sokar as "He who is upon his sand" and "He of Ro-Setjau". Throughout these hours Râ, like Sokar, will be pulled along on his barque, which has transformed into a serpent-like sledge.

The left riverbank concludes with three walking Gods each with an *Ankh* and a *Was*-sceptre in their hands.

(No. 218) "Horus of the terrace"
(No. 219) "Most perfect of the Gods"
(No. 220) "He who completes *Maât*"

The Duatians of the Sacred River (middle section)

The Sacred River opens with the Sun barque. Isis and Nephthys have disappeared from the barque resulting in it being manned once again

The ritual instruments and tools used in the Opening of the Mouth ceremony,
The temple of Seti I, West Bank of Luxor

with the regular crew. A small version of the guide of the barque, Kherep wia, is depicted at the stern of the barque. He only has a small task during the journey in this hour. The water runs profusely as it carries the Sun barque along with the flow. Kherep wia is present only to adjust their course slightly every so often with the helm.

(No. 221) "Wepwawet"
(No. 222) "Sia"
(No. 223) "Nebet wia"
(No. 224) "Iuf" is missing
(No. 225) "Heru Hekenu"
(No. 226) "Ka Maât"
(No. 227) "Nehes"
(No. 228) "Hu"
(No. 229) "Kherep wia"

The Sun barque is on course and crosses the "Water of the Unique Lord". Nonetheless, an essential part of the dynamic journey is missing. This element being the Sungod Râ himself. During this hour he is the most notable absentee for even his shrine is missing. He is no longer visible, leaving an empty space on the Sun barque. Even Nebet wia, the Lady of the barque, does not wear a sun disc with horns on top of her head. Every memory of the light has completely disappeared, leaving behind total darkness. Meanwhile, Râ experiences an intense transformation process. For this he takes all the time he needs. "This Great God pauses a while in this region".[14]

The empty spot on the Sun barque emphasises the total absence of Râ, or Iuf, his presence. His existence has been obscured, as if he has been wrapped like a mummy. Thus, he is both present as well as absent since, according to the text, he no longer sails with the Sun barque for 'He is rowed in the barques which are in the earth" instead.[15]

So Râ has vanished completely and has been dismembered into four parts. These parts have been mysteriously divided over the four barques as they sail on the Sacred River. The Sungod can be regarded as a mummy, his body prepared with the organs put away in four canopic jars. The old state, or body, has to be dismantled first before a new one can be build up. This process of decomposition is very intense yet necessary to get to the foundation that is already present underneath. Dividing the body in four parts is an essential aspect since the number four refers to totality, perfection and completeness.

Decomposition always precedes renewal. This also explains the name of the gate "Robber". It implies the soul of Râ has been stolen, dissolved into nothingness. Therefore, his light has been extinguished or stolen, enabling the darkness to take the upper hand.

This hour, "Water of the Unique Lord, which brings forth nourishment", offers the much needed nutrition for the transformation process. It ensures the mysterious barques, carrying the four parts of Râ, are supported and propelled on their journey to wholeness. The Unique Lord himself is none other than Osiris. He is part of the division that is made evident by his many shapes throughout this hour. It is precisely this mauling of Râ and Osiris which enables them to merge within the life-giving water.

In front of the Sun barque there are three mysterious barques sailing that are manned by equally mysterious crewmembers. These members are all part of the hidden secret that takes place within the darkness of this hour. The first of the three barques is called "Pakhet". It is incomplete as it is missing the stern. The prow is shaped like the head of a lioness, which is a reference to the lioness Goddess Pakhet, a form of the Goddess Sekhmet. Pakhet is the Goddess of "the Mouth of the Wadi". A wadi is a watery area at the border of the desert. One of Pakhet her titles is "She who opens the Ways of the stormy rains". The barque, as the personification of Pakhet, contributes to the amount of water. It also strengthens the movement of the flow as it borders to the desert of the Fourth Hour. Furthermore, in her role as the guardian of the royal residence, she protects the vulnerable and ravaged Râ for she invites him to her barque.

> I have appeared as Pakhet the Great,
> whose eyes are keen (?)
> and whose claws are sharp,
> the lioness who sees and catches by night.[16]
> – Coffin texts; spell 470
> "Spell for reaching Orion"

The barque is under the control of two rowers, one positioned at the stern, "Rower" (No. 230), and the other, without a name (No. 235), at the prow. In between them are a mummy, "He in the earth" (No. 231), a God wrapped in a short cloak with ram horns on top of his head, "He of honour" (No. 232), and a God who has one hand placed on top of his chest while holding a *Was*-sceptre in his other hand, "Lord of the *Was*-sceptre" (No. 233).

Behind the front rower is an upraised serpent, "He who burns with his eye" (No. 234). This serpent is the symbol of transformation and protects the process Râ experiences. In its role as protector the serpent is at the head of the barque as are the other serpents on the following barques.

The short robe worn by the third Deity, "He of honour", is a garment usually worn by the King during one of the ceremonies of the Sed festival (*heb sed*). The Pharaoh was seen as the embodiment of the Sungod on earth. During the ceremony the Pharaoh was required to make a rite of passage through the Duat in the Night Sun barque of Râ. This is depicted in Theban Tomb 192 in the necropolis of El-Assasif that belongs to the high official Kheruef. It contains a scene of the Sed festival on the wall of the West portico, South of doorway, upper registers. In this scene the Pharaoh, Amenhotep III, is dressed in the distinctive short tunic of the Sed festival while standing in the Night Sun barque of Râ. A net is hanging from the prow of the

Sun barque, which indicates the fact that the King has just begun his spiritual journey in the First Hour of the night.[17]

The King had to travel through the twelve hours of the night to identify himself with his father Râ. In doing so, like Râ, he would experience the intense process of dying and the reconnection with the *Ka*-force of Osiris. After finishing the nocturnal journey, the King was reborn and completely rejuvenated through the Vital Life Force of Osiris and the ensoulment of Râ. He had renewed his role as the living Sungod on earth and subsequently reaffirmed his position as the "Son of Râ" in the invisible realm of the Divine.

The prow and stern of the second barque are shaped like the head of a baboon. It is befitted with the appropriate name "Baboon-barque". The rowers of the barque have names, unlike the rowers in the previous barque. Their names are "He who cuts with his face" (No. 236) and "He who rows without tiring" (No. 241). In front the rower at the stern is a headless God who has adopted a bending pose, "The Radiant One" (No. 237). Therefore, the barque too shows us a defect that emphasises the disintegration of the Sungod. Next are two Gods, without names, in mummy (No. 238) and human form (No. 239). The God in human form is holding the *Ankh* in his hand. An upraised serpent can be seen behind the rower at the prow, "He who burns with his face" (No. 240).

The third barque is shaped like a common papyrus barque and is named the "Equipped barque". There are two rowers, "Flaming face" (No. 242) on the stern and one without a name (No. 247), who are moving the barque forward. Behind the rower at the prow is another upraised serpent, "Torchface" (No. 246). In front of the rower at the stern stands a God with a hawk head on top of a serpent. He holds a *Was*-sceptre and an *Ankh* in his hands and is called "Attendant and follower of Horus" (No. 243). He is standing on the back of a serpent. The serpent is the symbol of transformation and rebirth. In doing so, he shows that death has been prevailed and life is triumphant. The posture of "Attendant and follower of Horus", as he stands on the serpent, is an indirect reference to the regeneration process that is about to begin in the Cavern of Sokar in the Fifth Hour.

Furthermore, this God belongs to the group of mysterious beings, known as the "Followers of Horus". The identity of these Followers of Horus, or *Shemsu Hor* (*šmsw ḥr*), is shrouded in mystery. They could be the earliest Divine Kings on earth. This would indicate that they were not just merely the followers of Horus, but actually his direct successors. According to the Pyramid texts the "Followers of Horus" were Gods themselves. They formed the welcoming party in the Afterlife to accommodate the Pharaohs who just passed away. As the representatives of Horus they supported the deceased King as they helped him clean, bathe and dry off. Following this purification ceremony, the Pharaoh was then able to ascend to the sky.

> The Followers of Horus cleanse me,
> they bathe me, they dry me,
> they recite for me
> "The Spell for Him who is on the Right Way", they recite for me
> "The Spell of Him who ascends",
> and I ascend to the sky.
> I will go aboard this bark of Râ,
> it is I who will command on my own account those
> Gods who row him.
> Every God will rejoice at meeting me
> just as they rejoice
> at meeting Râ,
> when he ascends from the Eastern side of the sky in peace, in peace.[18]
> – Pyramid texts; Utterance 471

Each Pharaoh, while alive, was considered the heir and embodiment of Horus as a living King on earth. After death, however, the Pharaoh was instead affiliated with Osiris. Due to this identification, the deceased Kings would resurrect and live for eternity in the Afterlife, just like Osiris.

Following are two kite-headed Deities facing each other. They have crossed their arms in front of their chests in a gesture of lamentation, (No. 244 and 245). They both share the name "Kite". It is highly likely these two Deities are the Goddesses Isis and Nephthys. The two sisters occasionally transformed themselves both into a kite, *djeryt* (*drt*), to watch over the dead body of Osiris.

> [... the Two Kites,
> who are Isis and Nephthys,
> scream for you,
> striking for you on two gongs
> in the presence of the Gods.[19]
> – Coffin texts; Spell 24

The kite is a bird of prey from the same family as the hawk. It is known for its piercing scream that is similar to shrieks of grief. When Isis and Nephthys are in their kite forms they are grieving for the dead Osiris. They can then be found standing near the lion couch where Osiris's body is laid out, to express their lament. Isis is standing before Osiris, at his feet while looking him in the eyes. Nephthys is standing behind Osiris, at his head and out of sight. During their bewail, they call upon the soul of Osiris to return to life. They put their hands over their hearts to express their sorrow and love for the loss of their beloved husband and brother. The flexed arms symbolise the flapping of wings to protect Osiris. This movement also results in the creation of wind that is used to give Osiris the Breath of Life.

> Glorify his soul! Establish his dead body!
> Praise his spirit! Give breath to his nostrils and to his parched throat!
> Give gladness unto the heart of Isis and to that of Nephthys;
> Place Horus upon the throne of his Father

Give life, stability
and power to Osiris Thentirti.[20]
– Berlin papyrus 1425

Isis and Nephthys, or "the two mourning birds", show us that the process of bereavement is essential for the deceased to be resurrected from death. The combination of their lamentation and the love they feel within their hearts empowers Osiris and guarantees his awakening into a new life. These two Goddesses are standing here on the last barque and support Osiris, as well as Râ, during the regeneration process.

This is a process that continuous to repeat itself for all eternity. Therefore, after these mysterious barques have traversed this hour, they return to the shore. There they wait at the gate "The Robber" until Râ returns for his next transformation.

At the end of the row of barques there are four Gods. They all have their arms crossed in front of their chests. As acting guardians, they are standing in the opposite direction from where they can watch the process of transformation. They guarantee that the land is flooded with the life-giving waters of Nun during the inundation. They manage the flood and make sure it stays within certain bounds. Their supervision keeps the water in check and makes it a blessing for the land instead of a raging destroyer.

(No. 248) "Lord of the water"
(No. 249) "Moorer of the earth"
(No. 250) "He who sets the limits"
(No. 251) "He who sees the limits"

The Duatians on the right riverbank (lower section)

The Gods on the right riverbank come to life instantly when Râ calls upon them. He breaths life into them, enabling them to seize their identities and grasp their existence. "They receive their heads through the breath of (Râ) his mouth".[21]

In addition, the Sungod grants them the life-giving water, which is an essential element to continue their existence. His care for them is very important as their presence is critical to carry out the tasks instructed to them by Râ.

What they have to do in the West is:
Doing the roasting
and cutting up of the *Ba*-souls,
imprisoning the shadows
and putting an end to those
who do not exist,
who are at the place of destruction.
They kindle the flame
and let burn the enemies
through the (flames)
on top of their knives".[22]

It is evident that destructive forces are right around the corner trying to halt Râ on his journey. The Gods on this riverbank, however, are ready to assist and act as his guardians where they make every effort to destroy the enemies.

The right riverbank begins with the God "Khnum" (No. 252) who has the head of a flat-horned ram. As mentioned in the Second Hour he is the God of water, creation and rebirth. The meaning of his name is "to unite, to join or to build". He was viewed as the God of the origin of the Nile who had this sacred river under his command. His residence was the Island of Elephantine, which was considered the source of the Nile. Here the waters from the depths of the Netherworld arose and passed into the Nile on earth. Elephantine was also de location where the leg of the dismembered body of Osiris was found. According to myth, the annual inundation resulted from a wound on this leg. Therefore, Khnum, as God of the source and controller of the Nile, is associated with the annual inundation that transforms the dry lands into wetlands. As soon as the water returned from the land to the normal stream, fertile silt and clay were left behind. This resulted in the perfect seedbed for the new crops. Khnum, as the "Divine Potter", utilised the residual clay to sculpt the Gods and humankind on his potter's wheel.

> God of the potter's wheel,
> who settled the land by his handiwork;
> who joins in secret, who builds soundly,
> who nourishes the nestlings
> by the breath of his mouth;
> who drenches this land with Nun,
> while round sea and great ocean surrounds him.
> He has fashioned Gods and men,
> he has formed flocks and herds;
> he made birds as well as fishes,
> he created bulls, engendered cows.
> he knotted the flow of blood to the bones,
> formed in his workshop as his handiwork,
> so the Breath of Life is within everything,
> blood bound with semen in the bones,
> to knit the bones from the start.[23]

–A section of the Great Hymn to Khnum

Furthermore, the astronomical meaning of his name refers to the conjunction of the sun and the moon during specified seasons of the year.[24] This demonstrates the paramount importance of Khnum's presence here. He provides for the water during the inundation from which all life arises. During this hour, he stands along the Sacred River of the Duat, which is also the original source of the Nile. Within this life-giving water Râ, as the Sun, and Osiris, as the Moon, soon merge together. Then they are gifted the fertile ground from which their new bodies can be build.

Following is a God with his hands raised upright in a posture of adoration. His name, "Guardian of the earth" (No. 253), refers to his function as a guardian. He nearly touches the White Crown of the seated Osiris in front of him. He does not only bless the four forms of Osiris, but also the entire process of renewal. The four forms of Osiris in front of the Guardian are all seated on a throne in their mummified form with the White Crown of Upper Egypt on their heads. Each of these forms confirms that Osiris participates in the process of decomposition. He too, like Râ, is divided in four parts to make room for the new foundation.

(No. 254) "Osiris, Lord of the West"
(No. 255) "Osiris, Foremost of the West"
(No. 256) "Osiris of the place"
(No. 257) "Osiris who seizes millions"

The next five Gods all have an ibis-shaped head and are holding a knife with both hands.

(No. 258) "Horrible of face"
(No. 259) "Their flood"
(No. 260) without a name
(No. 261) "Destroyer"
(No. 262) "Roarer"

The Ibis is the symbol of the God Thoth and refers to wisdom. These Gods take part in the process of fragmentation. For this purpose they use their powers of discernment and their razor sharp intellect. This process draws on many disciplines that require the Gods to handle the knife with both hands. Here is where falsehood and ignorance are destroyed to make room for the new birth.

These Gods stand directly behind the Goddess of birth "Meskhenet" (No. 263). The meaning of her name is "birthing brick". This name makes sense once you look into the birthing process in ancient Egypt. It was normal for the women to give birth while assuming a squatting posture on top of two birthing bricks.

The stones were intended to assist and to see to it that the women remained in the correct posture. The bricks were beautifully decorated with all kinds of magical images and symbols. These images were meant to call upon the goodwill of the Gods in order to protect mother and child and grant them health. The Goddess Meskhenet is the Divine midwife of the Birthing Place and supports the rebirth of Râ and all of the other deceased travellers. She breaths the *Ka*, Vital Life Force, into a person at the moment of birth. As mentioned before, the *Ka* contains the unique characteristics and potentials of a person and is, therefore, linked to ones destiny in life. Thus, Meskhenet was seen as the Goddess of fate.

The next God is also holding a knife with both hands "Who guards the slaughter" (No. 264). He too, like the five ibis-headed Gods, guides the process of division.

The following two Deities, the Goddess "She over her flame" (No. 265) and the God "Who belongs to the hidden" (No. 266), are holding each other's hand. This too is a reference to the opposite forces, female and male, that form a unit together. In front of them are again four forms of Osiris, but this time they are wearing the Red Crown of Lower Egypt on their heads. The prominent attendance of Osiris shows us he is not dead. This strengthens the believe that life will prevail over death. The four forms of Osiris are each bearing a powerful name to support this vision.

(No. 267) "Osiris, Bull of the West"
(No. 268) "Osiris on his throne"
(No. 269) "Osiris with the Red Crown"
(No. 270) "Osiris most powerful of the Gods"

Following are two Gods, "Sah" (*s3ḥ*) (No. 271) and "Âhâu" (*ꜥḥꜥw*) (No. 272). They are standing while gazing in the opposite direction with their knees bent and are each holding a *Was-sceptre* with both hands. Sah symbolises the soul of Osiris and is frequently referred to in the Pyramid texts as "Father of the Gods". In the Pyramid and Coffin Texts Sah is identified as Orion. This implies that the constellation of Orion is the very soul of Osiris.

> Look, he is come as Orion,
> Look, Osiris is come as Orion.[25]
> – Pyramid texts; Utterance 38

After death, Osiris returned to the original source of the stars and became a star in the sky. The constellation of Orion, however, consists of several stars. It is highly doubtful that the soul of Osiris was divided between the stars of this constellation. The Pyramid texts mention Sah as a singular form, not plural. Therefore, Sah refers to one star in the constellation of Orion. This particular star is the star Rigel. The hieroglyphic meaning of Sah is "toe", which refers to one of the feet of the constellation of Orion. The star Rigel (Beta Orionis) forms one foot and Saiph (Kappa Orionis) the other.[26]

> Thy shalt tiptoe heaven like *s3ḥ* (the toe-star).[27]
> – Pyramid texts, Utterance 412

Rigel is the brightest star of the constellation of Orion and one of the most important navigational stars. Its bright light in the night sky is the perfect symbol for the shining soul of Osiris. Additionally, this star was a tangible orientation point for the Pharaoh to rise towards the heavens after death. This star helped the Pharaoh to identify himself with Osiris and to become a star himself. The Pyramid Texts even describe how the Pharaoh could ascend to the sky, like Osiris, in his form as the toe-star "long of leg and lengthy of stride".[28]

The name of the other God, "Âhâu", means "attendant, stand-by or helper". From this we can conclude Âhâu is here beside Sah to support him. Consequently, Âhâu is the other foot of the constellation of Orion, the star Saiph (Kappa Orionis). The two stars sustain and balance each other.

The text of the lower section of the Third Hour gives an indirect mention of these two feet; "He who knows them is an Akh-spirit, who masters his two feet".[29] This is a reference to the resurrection of the deceased as an Osiris. For this process, the mummy is upraised, "raising the *Djed*", from the supine position of death. This enables the mummy to stand on both feet, just as Osiris stands on both feet in the heavens as an *Akh*-spirit.

The following three Gods are supporting themselves with their hands for they are incapable of standing upright. Their bodily deficiencies make moving forward difficult, which they are forced to do in a bent and crawling manner.

(No. 273) "The Bent One"
(No. 274) "The Creeping One"
(No. 275) "He with difficult going"

Standing in the opposite direction is a Goddess, "She of the Eastern Mountain" (No. 276), who holds a pair of eyes in her outstretched hands. Her back is facing the West as she demonstrates the eyes that are a reference to the light, or consciousness, of the Sungod. Her gaze is turned towards the East, expressing the need to keep ones focus on the enlightened horizon. She knows at dawn the renewed Eyes, or the light of the Sungod, will rise as the newborn sun.

Behind her stands the Guardian "Khetery" (No. 277) who also faces the opposite direction. He is named after, and identified with, the Egyptian mongoose or Pharaoh rat (Ichneumon). In one of the myths, the Sungod Râ transformed himself in a giant Ichneumon to fight the serpent Apophis. The transformation into this form is an understandable one since the Ichneumon is a very capable snake killer who is immune to snake poison. The creature is a catlike carnivore with a long slender and flexible body. This species are very agile and incredibly fast with their attacks, just like snakes. They can even dig out holes to catch pray that lives underground. Another talent of the Ichneumon was his keen sight. The Guardian Khetery possesses these skills as well, which makes him the perfect guardian for the gate. He repels Apophis and any other evil to make sure the process within this hour is not disturbed.

Closing text

The Third Hour closes with a beautiful lengthy closing text. It opens with the words of the Duatians, who are called the mysterious Gods. They are the mysterious *Ba*-souls who are in the following of Osiris. It was Râ himself who made them mysterious by hiding their souls. They invite Râ to come to them and call him the "Lord of Breath", as he breathes life into them. To accentuate their gratefulness, they describe him in a wonderful tribute. They name Râ the mediator of the Duat as he connects the earth with the sky. This refers to his union with Osiris during which the night and day world become connected. The connection between the above and the below gives rise to the Uraeus-serpent "the Unique One". This cobra symbolises the link between both worlds and is referred to as Divine Authority and rulership.

Furthermore, they declare that the two Maât Goddesses will accompany Râ and show him the way through the darkness. The journey is therefore under the banner of the Divine Law of *Maât*. This ensures Râ's victory over the darkness and enables him to strike down all his enemies as "Lord of the Sun disk". While the threats are eliminated, the Sun barque does not stall for the jackals take the prow-rope. They are the guardians and the nocturnal haulers of the Sun barque. We will get to know them during the Fourth Hour.

> Come to us,
> you whose flesh is being rowed,
> and who is guided to his own body,
> Interpreter of the Duat, Lord of Breath,
> whose body speaks,
> who provides for his life!
> Your *Ba*-soul appears
> and your power flourishes.
> Your two *Maât* Goddesses guide you
> on the way of darkness.
> The sky belongs to your *Ba*-soul,
> the earth to your corpse.
> The Unique One (Uraeus-serpent) rises up
> for you,
> alone at the tow-rope
> which the Jackals moor.[30]

The Duatians do not speak just for themselves, but on behalf of all Westerners living in the Duat as well. All receive Râ with open arms as he departs beyond the Western Horizon in his form as an "Old Man". They are satisfied as soon as Râ's voice reaches them and his radiant *Ba*-soul enlightens their existence. They gratefully praise him as "Gold Khepri", seed of the Gods!

As Râ answers them, he asks them to come close to him. The purpose of these souls is not just for the punishment of his enemies. They are here to meet Osiris, the "Foremost of the Westerners", to act in his best interest and to safeguard his corpse. The Westerners are part of the entourage of Osiris and will destroy everything and anything that binds Osiris.

Thereafter, Râ appoints them as the *Akh*-spirits of Osiris, who are in their blessed state. Râ bestows upon them the Breath of Life and grants them light so their eyes can see. He also opens their ears so their ears can hear. Their beings are completely renewed and are no longer in need of the protective mummy wrappings.

> Your forms are enduring,
> Blessed state to your illuminations!
> May your noses breathe air,
> May your faces see,
> and may your ears hear!
> Uncovering for your covers,
> Release for your wrappings![31]

Similarly to the Opening of the Mouth ceremony, their senses are opened as they are brought back to life. This enables them to eat, drink and move once more. Râ provides them with offerings and water from the divine riverbank. They are also given fields to grow their crops. The Sungod takes great care to make them comfortable and provide for all their needs. All of the four elements, air, light (fire), water and earth, support these Duatians in their existence. Râ also guarantees them that their *Ba*-

souls will not fall and their corpses will not be turned upside down.

Being upside down was a harsh punishment for the damned souls. As mentioned before, the mummy needs to be upraised to be able to become resurrected. Therefore, there is a spell in the Book of the Dead to prevent this dreadful sentence. Spell 189; "Chapter for preventing a man from going upside down and from eating faeces".[32] The details of this punishment and the spell will be extensively addressed in the Eleventh Hour. These Duatians, however, do not need to use the spell as they are the blessed *Akh*-spirits of Osiris. Their doors are always open to allow Râ to enter. His light will shine in their caverns. The precondition for this to happen is that they remain in their individual places once Râ arrives.

Their presence in the right place at the right time is essential for Râ to be able to meet Osiris. Râ has to witness his own reflection in the perfect image, which is Osiris. As Râ speaks with Osiris, he tells him in a secretive manner that they are both part of a whole. Since Râ is able

Seti I receives the Breath of Life, Temple of Seti I at Abydos

to travel through the day as well as the night world, unlike Osiris, it is possible for him to meet Osiris and to merge with him.

> Your *Ba*-soul belongs to the sky, Osiris,
> your corpse belongs to the earth,
> Foremost of *Igeret*![33]
> Your Gods are behind you,
> your *Akh*-spirits before you,
> your images are transformed
> in which you are.
> Lo, blessed state for your *Akh*-spirit Osiris,
> and blessed state to your *Akh*-spirits,
> who are in the following of Osiris.
> When I approach the earth, day behind me.
> I pass the night that my *Ba*-soul may rest.
> Your forms belong to the day,
> but your *Akh*-spirits
> I have made for the night.
> I created your *Ba*-souls for myself,
> after me, when you had (already)
> been made.
> You have not fallen
> into the place of destruction.[34]

The manifestation of the Third Hour in daily life

The inundation is still present in full swing and submerges you deep within the subconsciousness. This inner world comes to the foreground even more in this hour as it is pushed up by the ferocious waves and the storm. This means a considerable stir is incited deep within your being. More and more hidden aspects of yourself surface and wash over you. They have suddenly washed up on your inner beach and are begging for your attention. They lay there, visible at your feet in the shape of emotions and feelings, as well as character traits and specific conducts. Everything bubbles up in order to give you a wake-up call to make you aware of yourself. You have to look at them with a fresh pair of eyes. Never before have you viewed these features of yourself in such a way. It is like your eyes are slightly opening themselves for the first time.

Four Gods help you with the transformation of the old consciousness. "He who brings" (No. 198), "She who brings" (No. 199), "He who brings the Eye and satisfies the Gods (with it) (No. 203)" and "She of the Eastern Mountain" (No. 276). Their number of four refers to the creation of a new foundation. First, you have to take a closer look at your outdated views and beliefs. Everything that has become worn and frayed is dissolved. This provides for room to establish the four cardinal pillars of your new world, the world with the refreshed and rejuvenated vision. You experience the inner clean up with mixed feelings. On one hand, it is soothing like a warm bath. On the other hand, however, it feels like a cold shower. Both sides are needed to stay alert and to keep moving.

Suddenly there is chaos in your life as the old familiar ways, you were so used to, have been dissolved. The Guide of the Barque, Kherep wia (No. 229), shows you it is best to accept these changes and to go with the flow. He makes you aware of your incapability to take control at this point. He himself takes the helm, but only to keep the barque within the flow. Your sole requirement is to stay in line with the preceding barques in front of you. Only then you are able to take part in the necessary purification process. Counter-steering is counter productive and does not incite renewal. Have trust in the necessity of the events and try to just ride the wave.

The old stiff-necked patterns need to be cleared out first before the new ones can arise. However, when you are caught in the middle, this is hard to imagine. You think at the very least that the submersion is surely making you drown. These intense emotions are also part of the process and ensure that you experience everything thoroughly. Nevertheless, know this, after the vast flood, the tide will go out again. That is the way the cycle of life works.

This is the inner death process that always precedes a new beginning. You have to let go of the life that no longer befits and now restricts you. This aspect is reflected in the three disabled (No. 273 – 275). They move forward with great difficulty as they are no longer able to stand up. Their disabilities and restrictions refer to the old beliefs like narrow-minded ideas, rusty patterns and entrenched images. All these things may now perish to allow for room for the fresh youthfulness of new life.

Wash everything away with your tears and take the time to mourn. Tears are salutary and wipe you clean. Through crying you connect with your true emotions and feelings, which enables you to further descend into your inner world. Now you can clear the decks and work through whatever needs your attention. Crying invigorates you and brings you back into life. It illuminates your heart and gives you room to breath. Bottling these feelings and emotions up inside leads to a suffocating gloom that weighs down on you heavily. It squeezes the life out of you, hindering the rebirth process. Therefore, it is important to give these emotions free rein and pay them the attention they deserve. The ancient Egyptians understood the significance of this process. Therefore they used the professional wailing women. These women were hired to show their grief during a funeral. Their lamentation made sure that the deceased was reborn into the Afterlife. The departed was then able to breathe again. The kite form of Isis and Nephthys (No. 244 – 245) also shows us the importance of the expression of grief.

Here we are talking about the old part of yourself, which has become superfluous and may perish. Do not be afraid, for you do not truly die. Your Higher Self makes sure of that. Just as Râ provides the Duatians with life through gifts of nourishment and water, so too does the Higher Self care for you and feed you. He has once more taken a step in your direction as you have entered this hour. His Voice has become louder as you opened yourself up to him.

Still, it may be that you do not experience this connection and communication at all times. There are times during which the Higher Self lets his presence be known as he speaks to you loud and clear through your inner link. However, during other times, inner stir and chaos makes you hear the storm and fierce waves only. During such moments the inner canal is clouded and the Higher Self is the notable absentee. Worry not, this is all part of the process of decomposition and purification. Besides, the Higher Self is always at your side. There simply are times during which you need to take a few steps on your own. During these times it might feel like you are left alone to fend for yourself. Nevertheless know this; the Higher Self is the first to catch you should you fall.

Furthermore, this hour is filled with stunning Gods who are all reaching out to you in order to give additional support during this intense process. They show you during the painful periods that you are not alone. This fills you with an inspiring and beautiful experience. As you are opening up to the flood, you are able to dive for true treasures, which would have remained hidden from you otherwise. Only after flushing down the trash you are able to perceive what lies underneath.

Osiris is the leading presence during this hour as you encounter him in several different forms (No. 254 -257 and 267 – 270). He knows the pain of dying and of being broken down better than anyone. It is, therefore, very important to focus on each of these forms of Osiris, for they provide you with a better understanding of your own death process. That is why, like Râ, he stands by your side. He knows how to die as well as how to ascend as an enlightened soul. In his form as the shining star "Sah" (No. 271), supported by "Âhau" (No. 272), he demonstrates this magnificent future.

Osiris, as the symbol of the Powerself, clearly shows himself throughout this hour. This indicates you have already created a connection with the deeper layers within yourself since the old emotional garbage is slowly clearing out. The clean up and the inner fragmentation are the results of the death process and allow you to get your first glimpse of the potential and the power buried deep within you.

"Meskhenet" (No. 263), the Goddess of Birth, affirms this image of innovation. Though the birth itself is nowhere near ready to happen, the first signs of the renewed life are already starting to show. The Goddess observes and gives assistance during the process as a wise midwife. She confirms that a new life will arise from death for she would not be here otherwise. Her presence inspires the traveller with courage and hope.

It is made clear that dying and birth are two aspects of the same creation process that go hand in hand. Both aspects come forth strongly within this hour. On one end, your old self dies. At the same time, though, the first signs of a renewed consciousness and the new you appear. The renewal after death is also made apparent during the Opening of the Mouth ceremony wherein the deceased is gifted with a new life.

Ptah, in his form as "Standing Bow" (No. 201), is one of the Gods who plays an important part during this ceremony. As the "Lord of Truth and Justice and the God of Creative Utterance", he encourages you to open your mouth and speak from the heart with the true voice of *Maât*, or *Maâ Kheru*. Hence, be faithful to yourself, the True Self, that has surfaced by means of the water flood of this hour. This truth is the foundation upon which you can build your new world with the skills of a craftsman. Your connection with Ptah makes you aware of the fact that it is your thoughts and the expression thereof that create your own universe. You, and you alone, are responsible for your own life. Be aware of the tremendous power lurking behind your thoughts. Follow the example of Ptah, the Divine Artist, who consciously utters the words that shape the world into being.

> Ptah hath opened thy mouth,
> Sokar hath opened thy mouth,
> with the instrument made of iron
> wherewith he opened the mouth
> of the Gods.
> Thou speakest in the presence of
> all the Gods of Pe (Buto),
> and thou hearest when thou art called
> in Tepu (Buto).
> Hail thou Osiris,
> thy mouth hath been opened.
> I am Ptah, I have split open thy mouth.
> I am Henu,
> and I have given unto thee thy two arms.
> I am Thoth. Receive thou the water
> wherewith thy mouth was opened.
> I have brought unto thee thy son,
> whom thou seest
> renewing this youth through Seb.
> Thy mouth is opened, thy heart is to thee
> and thy heart-sack is to thee.
> Thou hast thy food with the Gods
> who are in heaven,
> and no distinction can be made between
> thee and one of them.
> Pure, pure is the Osiris.
> Pure, pure is the Osiris.
> Pure, pure is the Osiris.
> Pure, pure is the Osiris.[35]
> – From the tomb of Seti I,
>   KV 17, Valley of the Kings

Sokar, in the form of "Henu" (No. 217), takes part in the opening of the renewed awareness as well. Sokar is the one who provides for the foundation during the Opening of the Mouth Ceremony. This is the ceremony from which the new life arises. In the Fourth Hour you are granted access to Sokar's sacred realm known as the Land of Sokar-upon-his-sand. He then opens the consecrated earth to allow you to descend. Since this descent is very deep, you will not experience the first renewal until you have reached the bottom of the Fifth Hour.

Therefore, the Opening of the Mouth is a ceremony during which the deceased is symbolically brought to life in the forecourt of his tomb. After the ceremony, the mummy was returned to his coffin. Then the coffin was dragged into the depth toward the burial chamber and placed inside the sarcophagus. From that point onward, the process of rejuvenation could truly unfold. During the upcoming hours you will undergo this process as well, just like the mummy. Henu, the Divine herald, is announcing this upcoming event.

During this hour you participate in a magnificent and powerful transformation process. Everything accelerates, giving you the feeling that the world is made up of swirling water. Therefore, here too, you should trust in the Higher Self. He speaks to you in the shape of the inner Sungod:

Your *Ba*-souls do not fall,
your corpses are not turned upside down."
Opening be for your gates,
light to your caverns.
May you stand at your places! [36]

You will not go down as long as you are not afraid to connect with the Secrets revealed to you. They provide you with Self-knowledge and teach you to get back on your feet.

It is made similar in the secrecy of the Duat.
He who knows these will be
a spiritual *Ba*-soul,
mastering his two feet,
without entering
the place of destruction.[37]

At the end of this hour you are ready to make the profound descent into the following hour where you will eventually reach the bottom. At long last, you will experience the firm soil beneath your feet once more.

THE FOURTH HOUR
"With Living Manifestations"

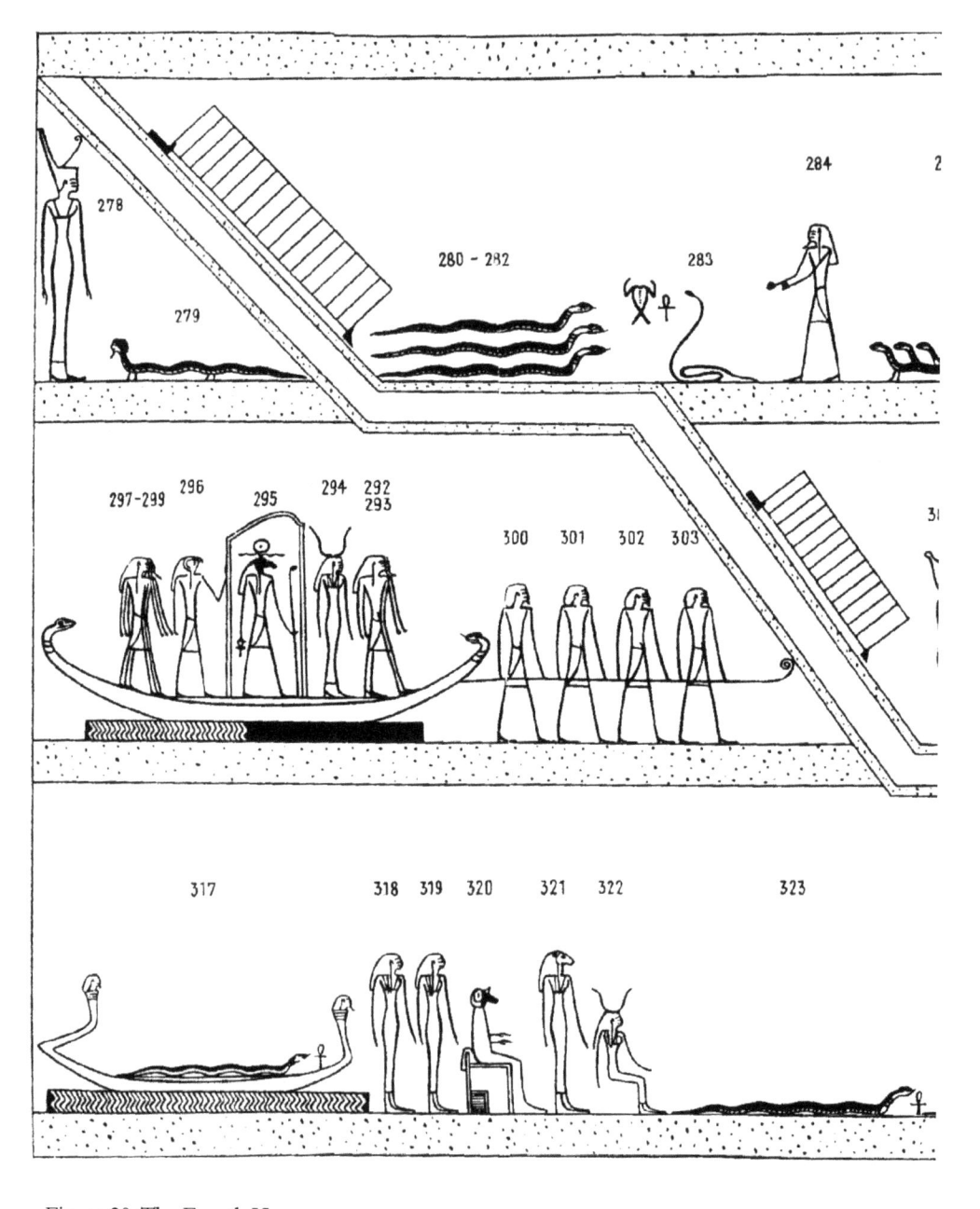

Figure 20: The Fourth Hour

The Gate:	"Which hides the towing"
The Hour Goddess:	"She who is great in her power"
The Guardian:	(there are several guardians in this hour)

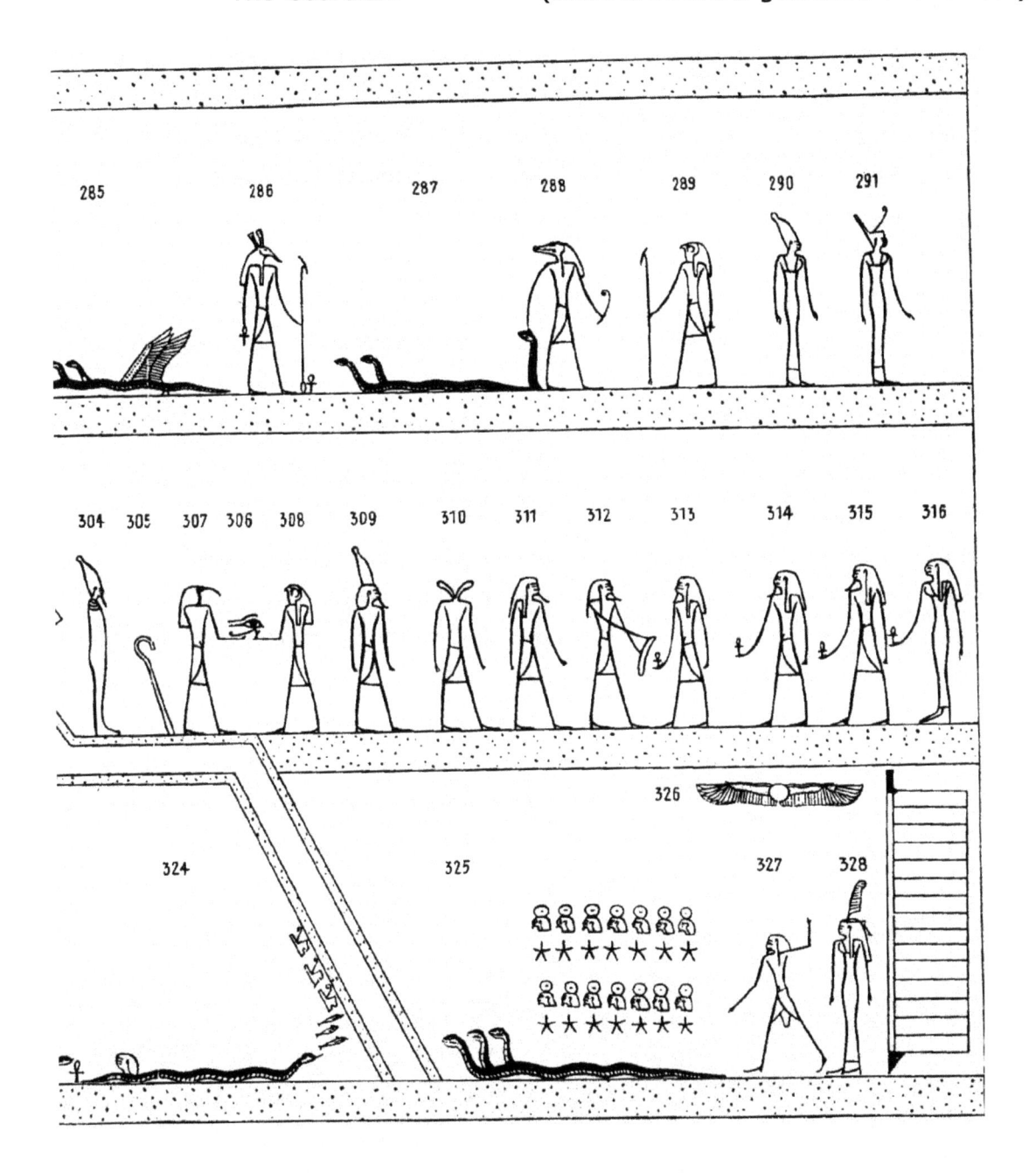

Introduction

Pausing in being towed by the person
of this Great God
in the mysterious cavern of the West
"With protected forms".
Taking care of those who are in it
with his voice,
without his seeing them.
"With Living Manifestations"
is the name of this Cavern.
The name of the Gate of this cavern
is "Which hides the towing".
The name of the Hour of the night
guiding this Great God is
"She who is great in her power".
He who knows this image
is one who eats bread
beside the living in the temple of Atum.
The mysterious ways of Ro-Setjau,
the unapproachable paths of *Imhet*,
the hidden gates in the Land
of Sokar-upon-his-sand.
This image is made, in paint,
in the secrecy of the Duat,
on the Western side of
the Hidden Chamber.
Whoever knows it is one with right paths,
treading the ways of Ro-Setjau,
beholding the image of *Imhet*.[1]

After the stormy voyage through the Third Hour, Râ enters through the gate "Which hides the towing". This is the last hour located in the Western region. In this hour the vast amount of water, which was present in the Third Hour, has magically disappeared. Hence, Râ arrives in his Sun barque in a barren desert. Everything is dry and infertile. No trace of the life-giving water can be found. In the common life on earth the drought precedes the inundation. In the Duat, however, the drought comes after the inundation. A deviation from the mundane life on earth. As mentioned before, the Duat is a reflection of life on earth, although everything here is reversed.

This hour, like the upcoming Fifth Hour, is very different from the other hours. Together, these two hours form the deepest region of the Duat called *Imhet*. *Imhet* means "The Filled One" and is a reference to the fact that these two hours are filled with sand. The sand and lack of water prevents the Sun barque from sailing on its own. The resulting stagnation is a serious issue as the progression of the creation is dependent on the advance of the Sungod Râ. The continuous movement of the Sun barque is therefore of the highest priority. The impending problem is solved as the barque is hauled through this hour. To facilitate the transport over sand, the usual form of the Sun barque is transformed into a serpent. A rope is tied at the prow of the Sun barque and used by four Gods to tow the barque through the hour.

As soon as Râ enters the gate and the door is shut behind him, he is welcomed by the Hour Goddess "She who is great in her power". Râ makes good use of her immense power as this hour is not an easy one to cross. Fortunately, the Goddess remains by his side from the beginning to the end. She, like no other, knows the way and ensures Râ gets through all of the blockades. Her assistance is much appreciated since this hour is filled with barriers and gates. The usual pattern, as seen in the other hours, has been overthrown for the path now follows a zigzag course. As the path descends, it is characterised by three very steep drops. These desert paths are described in a short text;

I   The One belonging to Ro-Setjau

II   Secret paths of Ro-Setjau. The Divine Gate. He cannot pass them, but it is (only) his voice which they hear.

III   Path entered by the corpse of Sokar-upon-his-sand. Secret image which can neither be seen nor beheld.

IV   Secret path entered by Anubis to conceal the corpse of Osiris.

V   Secret path of the entrance of *Imhet*.[2]

Additionally, there are two gates downhill that are called "Knives". These knives cut through the fixed structure, or rhythm, and are secured by serpents. The third knife can be found at the end of the hour as it stands in front of the gate of the Fifth Hour. It means this hour has doubled the surveillance at the exit. It is, therefore, much easier to enter this hour than it is to leave. Râ is forced to go through every element of this difficult hour to be able to leave again. He is not at liberty to skip anything. He has to know the hidden paths and the Duatians living here. He has to identify himself with everything that goes on in this hour. Only through the integration of the knowledge and its application will he be able to continue his journey. The knife at the end of this hour opens only for those who are in possession of this wisdom.

However, this will prove to be quite challenging as everything is hidden and mysterious. Nothing is taken for granted. Even the paths Râ needs to descend are proving to be impassable. These sloping sand ways are known as the mysterious ways of Ro-Setjau. Ro-Setjau means "Place or Gate of towing". On the earthly plane this is the name of the necropolis of Giza or Memphis. In the land of the dead it is the name of the realm of the God Sokar. So Râ is about to enter the depth of the earth where the God Sokar dwells.

Sokar plays an essential supportive role within this hour and the next. His desert land is where the sacred foundation is created upon which new life can develop. Another name for Sokar is "He who is upon his sand". The name is an indirect reference to the Opening of the Mouth ceremony. In the first ritual of the ceremony the earth was consecrated. This was done by heaping up sand to create a mound. The mound was then used as the sacred foundation upon which the mummy was placed while facing South.

[...] Sokar of Rostau is my steward,
and he has reckoned up the property in it;
he has brought good things,
and he has heaped up the altar-chambers for this mansion of mine.³

– Coffin texts, Spell 571

The consecration of the earth was also done when a new temple was built. During this ritual sand was scattered across the designated area for the future temple in order to sanctify the ground beneath. The holy sand helped consolidate the ground and allowed for a sturdy and consecrated base for the foundation of the temple.⁴

The mound of sand that was created during the first ritual symbolised the primordial hill, as the symbol of the first creation. This hill was also the sacred foundation from which the deceased would be symbolically reborn. It showed an image of the future and preceded the actual funeral itself. Therefore, it comes as no surprise that the Opening of the Mouth ceremony was quite a lengthy one. Following several rituals a very powerful intention was created through which the deceased was symbolically brought back to life. This created a very accurate ideal image that would then become a reality in the Afterlife as a logical consequence. For that is the way Magic works.

Afterwards the deceased was buried to become truly reborn, since this process could only take place within the utter darkness of the earth, in the realm of Sokar. Similar to a seed that needs to be buried before it can sprout. This was also reflected in the festival of Sokar. After the completion of the Opening of the Mouth ritual on the grain mummies, the "Great hacking of the earth" took place during which these mummies were buried.

The God Amun-Sokar-Osiris, Temple of Hathor, Deir el-Medina

When the Opening of the Mouth ceremony was completed for the deceased, he was towed along a long sloping passageway into the burial chamber and placed inside the sarcophagus. The descent led into the mountain westwards and symbolised the passage from the world of the living into the world of the dead. The tomb itself was, therefore, off-limits to the living. After the burial into the tomb was completed, it was bricked up to seal it. Afterwards the shaft, leading up to the tomb, was filled with broken stones.

Râ is also dragged deep into the earth across the zigzag paths. This is the forbidden area, the sacred Land of Sokar, which is sealed with the gates in the form of knives. Sokar "He of Ro-Setjau" welcomes Râ in his desert land where he has opened the earth with his sharp and strong *adze*. In doing so, Sokar consecrates the earth to form a foundation for the upcoming rebirth. The sandy soil has a completely different purpose with respect to the water in the previous hours. Water flows, supports life and has cleansing properties. On the flip side, though, it also facilitates putrefaction and decay. Sand, on the other hand, dehydrates and creates barrenness which makes it hard for life to emerge. It acts as a preservative and is able to halt decay. In its own right, sand has cleansing properties as well.

On the other hand, sand also decreases the speed of the Sun barque and reduces its progression. However, this is actually an essential part of the process. If Râ were to proceed with the pace acquired on the water, he would speed down the zigzag paths and be crushed by the knives. For that reason he proceeds slowly while the old life gradually desiccates and withers away. This transformation process takes time as the old lifeblood needs to dry out to prevent decay. It is a delicate process that has to be completed with care since putrefaction at this stage would mean total and utter destruction of the body. The body, in itself, is the fundamental feeding ground from which the renewed life can sprout. That is why the absence of water is crucial at this point.

But be warned, it is crawling with serpents here, huge and fearsome ones. Some look like common snakes while others have legs, wings or several heads. This hour is their dwelling place for serpents prefer to live within holes deep underneath the ground. They enjoy the dark, especially the pitch black of this hour.

Râ is not able to see through the dense darkness. Additionally, the hour is characterised by the absolute silence. The sound of the roaring waves of the previous hour has disappeared, as has the water. The Fourth Hour is the domain of the sand which absorbs all light and sound as well as all life. Here, Râ is unable to communicate with the Duatians. His voice can reach only the four Gods towing the Sun barque as they are close enough to detect the sound. This subtle sign of life ensures that these Gods continue the towing of the Sun barque.

The Duatians on the left riverbank (upper section)

The first Duatian on the left riverbank is a very tall Goddess, "She is at the rising" (No. 278). She wears the Red Crown of Lower Egypt on her head. She shines at the beginning of this hour in all her magnificence. Her focus is directed towards the East, which is where the ultimate goal of the journey lies. It is the Eastern horizon that opens up at the end of the night to make way for the rising sun. Her presence provides Râ with the courage to begin his descent. No matter how tough the upcoming journey across the impassable secret paths may be, the promise of the forthcoming light is already stipulated.

In front of her a serpent, "He with the head who guards the way" (no. 279), can be seen. He is shaped like a snake on legs with a bearded head and is one of the many serpents present within this hour. His tail points to the first zigzag path, "Path belonging to Ro-Setjau". His backward posture indicates that he is the guardian of the first knife, "Knife of the mooring place". The knife functions as the barricade for the first path. The serpent never leaves his important post since he performs his duty for all of eternity.

Beyond the knife begins the "Secret paths of Ro-Setjau. The Divine Gate". Here three serpents can be found lying on the ground, "Those on their bellies" (No. 280 – 282). Their number of three refers to a plurality of serpents since, as mentioned before, this hour accommodates a vast amount of serpents. These three serpents too remain in their respective places with commitment.

Following is a scorpion with an *Ankh* and an upraised cobra facing the opposite direction. The cobra is the scorpion Goddess "Serket" (Selkis or Selket) (No. 283). She is one of the four protective Goddesses. Together with Isis, Nephthys and Neith she guards the coffins, canopic chests and jars. She had a protective role during the funeral and is sometimes called "Mistress of the Beautiful House". The

The Goddess Serket, QV 44 Kha-em-Waset

Beautiful House is a reference to the embalming pavilion where the mummification process took place.[5]

Hence, she is associated with the West, the realm of death and rebirth. She is usually depicted with a scorpion with its tail curved forward over its back, on top of her head. This refers to her power over scorpions and venomous snakes. She has a double nature for she has the capacity to heal, but conversely she is a dangerous Goddess as well. Her power can cure a person from a venomous sting or bite. But she can also kill a person when she sends snakes and scorpions after them. Her name, Serket (*srkt*), means "She who causes the throat to breathe". This is a derivative of the verb *serk* (*srḳ*) which means "inhale or permit to breathe". The effect of the poison of a scorpion or snake can be so painful that it takes ones breath away quite literally. On the other hand, Serket is also capable of returning the breath, and thus life, known as the "Breath of Life". The physicians who treated the scorpion sting were named after the Goddess and known as *Serket Hetu*, "He who let the throat breathe".

> […] my cavern is (that of) Selket,
> the snake is in my hand and cannot bite me
> […][6]
> – Coffin Texts; Spell 885

Serket is an important Goddess who assists Râ during the battle against the dangerous serpent Apophis. During the Seventh Hour she will be present once more. In the present hour, she can be found at the beginning of the first zigzag path. In front of her there is a scorpion. The scorpion was a powerful symbol and was given, in the shape of a talisman, to the Pharaoh in his grave at his funeral. It was meant to protect him from evil and danger. For this reason the symbol of the scorpion is evident at the beginning of the zigzag path as it provides for protection during the perilous way down.

Serket also fulfils the duty as the mother Goddess. In this role she is called "Serket the Great or the Divine Mother". According to Egyptian mythology, she herself was regarded as the mother of the serpent God Neheb Kau who is also present here himself on the left riverbank.[7]

The following God faces the opposite direction as well and holds two eyes, "He who separates the Two Gods" (No. 284). With the eyes he is holding in his hands he refers to the light of Râ that is rejuvenating along the way through the hours. The accompanying text tells us the God is an image of Horus himself, similar to various other Gods within this hour.

The God Horus or Heru (*ḥr*) is a very complex Deity with many different appearances. Originally, he was a God of the sky, "He who is above", depicted either as a falcon or in humanoid form with the head of a falcon. The falcon was a sacred animal to the ancient Egyptians and the personification of the highest cosmic powers. It was regarded as a celestial bird whose right eye was the sun and his left eye the moon. Its speckled breast was believed to be the stars and its wings the sky.[8]

Horus is the embodiment of all of these aspects for he is the spirit of the heights of heaven. The ancient Egyptians considered him a solar God, similar to the Sungod Râ. In his form of Horakhty, "Horus of the two horizons", which is a form of the Sungod, he represents the daily course of the sun through the sky from dawn until dusk. Horus as Heru semau (Harsomptus) embodies the features of a reigning King. In this form he is the son of Horus the elder and the Goddess Hathor. He unites Upper and Lower Egypt and rules over the whole of Egypt, as "Horus the Unifier of the South and North".

The two main appearances of Horus are "Horus the great" or "Horus the elder" (Heru wer or Haroeris) as the son of the earth God Geb and the sky Goddess Nut. The other form is Horus as "Horus son of Isis" where he is the personification of the East as well as the newborn sun.

Heru pa khered (Harpocrates) is the young form of "Horus son of Isis" where he is known as "Horus the child". In this form he is depicted as a naked little boy with one plaited sidelock of hair on the side of his shaven head. There are stelae which show Heru pa khered standing on the back of crocodiles while holding snakes, scorpions and other dangerous animals in his outstretched hands. These stelae were believed to have healing and protective powers.

> Hail to you, God, son of a God!
> Hail to you, heir, son of an heir!
> Hail to you, bull, son of a bull,
> whom the Divine cow bore.
> Hail to you, Horus,
> who came forth from Osiris,
> whom the Goddess Isis bore![9]
> – Magical Spell;
>   An adoration of Horus, to glorify Him

After his father's death, the grown Horus was the lawful heir to the throne and thus the living King on earth. Due to this role combined with his falcon aspects, he is seen as the symbol

The God Horus, Temple of Seti I at Abydos

of Divine Kingship. Hence, every Pharaoh indentified himself with Horus to become the befitting mediator between heaven and earth.

However, Horus's presence is not just for the living for he is here for the dead as well. He oversaw the funerary ceremonies of his father and ensured that the proper methods were conducted. The mummification, the method of swathing, placing the amulets and so forth, had to be completed with the utmost care. In addition to his loving care for his father, he helped the other deceased in much the same way. This is highlighted in his function as the mediator between the judge of the Netherworld and the deceased. After the weighing of the heart he guided the deceased to his father.[10]

All of these Divine aspects make Horus the idealised image that every man and woman on and in the earth strive for. In fact, these are features everyone should aspire to, not just the Pharaoh. The God, "He who separates the two Gods" (No. 284) that we got to know on the left riverbank, equates himself to the beautiful future image of renewed life as symbolised by Horus. Once Horus rises to the throne, Osiris has been reborn in his son and life has prevailed over death. Aside from this magnificent image embodied by the God "He who separates the two Gods", his presence is also required to discern the secret image on the unapproachable path. This secret image, which is Osiris, can be found in the depth of the Duat. "He who separates the Two Gods" welcomes Râ and opens the unapproachable path to encourage him to make the descent on his way to meet Osiris.

Next is a three-headed serpent with legs and wings, "The Great God" (No. 285). Beneath his first head you can see the *Ankh*, the sign of eternal Life. By flapping his wings he can generate air which enables him to breath. He has taken position here at the edge of the unapproachable path of Ro-Setjau facing the opposite direction like the God preceding him. With his three heads he monitors anyone who intents to travel down the path.

The next God, "Divider of the Duat" (No. 286), has the head of Seth and is holding the *Was*-sceptre and the *Ankh* in his hands. As mentioned in the First and Second Hour, Seth is the God of chaos and destruction and the twin brother of Horus the elder. His dwelling place is the desert, which explains his presence in this hour. He is a God of immense strength and a real rabble-rouser. His main intention is to disrupt the old established order to make way for new development and growth. As the protector of the Sungod, Seth's destructive energy, is very important to assist Râ in the essential process of dying. The old Râ needs to fall apart first before his light can be healed and rejuvenated.

"Neheb Kau" (No. 287) lies in front of the God "Divider of the Duat" on the ground in the shape of a two-headed serpent. He is the son of the Goddess Serket, but he was also considered the son of the Earth God Geb and the Goddess Renenutet. As a matter of fact, he was even deemed a form of the Sungod himself. His name means "He who unites or appoints the *Ka's*". He is usually depicted as a two-headed serpent with a human body or as a two-headed serpent with at the end of his tail another head.

> Ho N! You are Neheb Kau, son of Geb,
> born of your mother Ernutet (Renenutet);
> you are indeed the double of every God,
> having power in your heart.
> Stand up; Horus has greeted you,
> for he recognizes you as the double
> of all the Gods;
> there is no God who has not his double
> in you.
> You have come into being
> and have become on high
> in company with your father Horus
> who is in the sky,
> the Great One who is among the Gods.[11]
> – Coffin Texts; Spell 762

The spell above indicates Neheb Kau embodies the *Ka* to which every God is connected. Neheb Kau is, therefore, the bearer of the Vital Life Force and carries every life in his hand.

> I am King of the sky, (even) Neheb Kau
> who rules the Two Lands,
> Neheb Kau who grants souls,
> crownings, doubles and beginnings.
> I am Neheb Kau,
> and their lives are at my hand;
> When I wish, I act, and they live.[12]
> – Coffin Texts; Spell 647

Furthermore, Neheb Kau possesses great magical power that he obtained from swallowing seven scorpions.[13] Magic grants him resistance to venomous bites such as those of snakes and scorpions. He is also one of the forty-two assessors in the Hall of *Maât* and occupies a protective role as he offers the deceased Pharaoh food and water. According to the Pyramid Texts he is a benevolent companion of Râ along his voyage through the Duat. He employs his power during the journey to ensure the continuation of creation and, thus, the cosmic order.

Neheb Kau existed long before creation started, a time throughout which he swam in the primeval waters of Nun. The festival in his honour was celebrated on the first or second day of the New Year. During this day the resurrection of Osiris was celebrated along with the onset of the crops. Therefore, it was a festival of rebirth and rejuvenation.

All of these features vouch for the fact that Neheb Kau is an important protector of creation. Hence, he is the protector of life on, as well as deep within, the Earth. In Spell 822 "for not letting corpses perish in the Earth" the deceased identifies himself with the throat of Neheb Kau.[14] This indicates Neheb Kau grants the Breath of Life just like his mother Serket. He does not only offer this to others, for he uses it to sustain himself as well. Thus, Neheb Kau creates his own existence and ensures his own presence.

> He is like this at his place
> of the unapproachable way
> of the path of Ro-Setjau,
> without going to any (other) place any time.
> He lives from the breath of his mouth.[15]

This is of great importance for he is the guardian of the entrance of the Duat and watches over the sacred place Ro-Setjau, the Land of Sokar. In addition, his presence here is essential to the Sungod since Neheb Kau is the one who unites the *Ka's*. Râ now begins with his descent deep into the earth with as ultimate goal to unite with the *Ka* of Osiris.

The final four Deities on the left riverbank are images made by Horus.
(No. 288) "Whose head praises" a God with the head of a crocodile. He is gazing in the opposite direction while holding the head of a serpent, who emerges out of the sand, in one hand. In his other hand he holds a curved staff.
(No. 289) "Who praises the Duat" a God with the head of a falcon. He faces the opposite direction with his entire body and holds a *Was*-sceptre and an *Ankh* in his hands.
(No. 290) "Southern One" a Goddess with the White Crown of Upper Egypt on her head.
(No. 291) "Northern One" a Goddess with the Red Crown of Lower Egypt on her head.

These four Deities are the ones who show the Sungod Râ the way to the mystery that can be found deep within the earth. Since gaining access to a hidden secret is the issue here, the road is not easily accessible. The path shows itself only if the deceased is willing to face his own death. This act of surrender creates an enormous discharge of energy that splits the earth open with a mighty earthquake. For Râ too, an earthquake opens the way for him. However, the four Deities need themselves to be careful to avoid falling in the depths of the created abyss. Therefore, they are guarded to do their task by the "Protector". The exact identity of the "Protector" is unknown. Still, the fact the two Gods and two Goddesses are protected by this mysterious figure, proves the significance of their function.

The Duatians of the Sacred River (middle section)

The Sun barque has taken the shape of a serpent with snakeheads adorning the stern and prow. The barque has now transformed into the perfect vessel to travel through the desert Land of Sokar. It is now called "Piercing the way", a reference to its ability to cross the sloping sand ways. The snakeheads on the prow and stern produce flames from their mouths that guide Râ on these mysterious paths. Although they illuminate the path slightly, Râ is still unable to discern the various Deities of this hour. Unsurprising, since this hour is shrouded in complete and utter darkness.

Râ has returned to his shrine on the Sun barque. He is wearing the solar disk with the ram horns on top of his head once more. Nebet wia "the Lady of the Barque" is again not wearing a solar disk. Her light is absent throughout this hour to enable the nurturing darkness to do its job during the next step in the transformation process. Even without her light she is still present here, together with the six other crew members, to support Râ.

(No. 292) "Wepwawet"
(No. 293) "Sia"
(No. 294) "Nebet wia"
(No. 295) "Iuf"
(No. 296) "Heru Hekenu"
(No. 297) "Ka Maât"
(No. 298) "Nehes"
(No. 299) "Hu"

Remarkably enough, one of the crewmembers is missing. Kherep wia, "the Guide of the barque", is absent from the Sun barque. His helm to steer the Sun barque is missing as well. This demonstrates the fact that within this hour navigation is impossible. Therefore, Râ has to make the descent while letting go of everything and having complete faith. Kherep wia is not allowed to help him during the descent. The control needs to be surrendered completely to the four Gods who walk in front of the Sun barque as they haul it.

The names of these four Gods illustrate their mastery over the rope used to tow the barque.

(No. 300) "He of the secret (rope)"
(No. 301) "He who belongs to the tow-rope"
(No. 302) "He above the rope"
(No. 303) "He who stretches the rope"

The name of the fourth God, "He who stretches the rope", refers to the importance of the ceremony known as "Stretching the Cord". The ritual preceded the construction of a temple, or that of other significant buildings. The rope in the ritual was used to determine the magnitude of the building in order for it to become aligned with the stars. This allowed for the earth to become connected to the heavens, which ultimately indicates that the temple was built on sacred ground.

Furthermore, the rope was used to measure distances. The rope was fitted with knots on fixed intervals allowing it to be used as a measuring tape. "He who stretches the rope" is, therefore, well-informed about the exact distance along which the Sun barque needs to be towed. The path used during the journey is a sacred path that is aligned with the stars or the Gods.

The name of "He who stretches the rope" can also be translated as "He who stretches Maât" (*dwn mȝꜥt*). A fitting name since the unapproachable path used by these four Gods is also in line with the Divine Law of *Maât*.

These four Gods are the only ones able to hear the voice of Râ for they are closest to the Sun barque. Râ is now prepared to further his descent as the four Gods tow him to the next gate, "Knife which renews the earth (Netherworld)". The four Gods symbolise the four jackals that are also known as the Spirits or the Divine Souls of the West. The Jackals are the Divine Haulers of the Sun barque and another form of the God Anubis. With their keen senses they guide the Sungod Râ through the dark and dangerous desert of Ro-Setjau.

Râ comes to rest in the Night barque equipped with the Tireless Ones.
The Jackals are gathered at the prow-rope:
as they tow you
your heart is glad until you rest
at the Western Mountain's horizon.
The Radiant Ones the Spirits of the West
rejoice at your majesty's approach
for they see you when you come in peace
in your nobility
as a spirit in the sky.[16]
– Berlin stela 7306

Ro-Setjau is the sacred dwelling place of the God Sokar. As mentioned in the Third Hour this is the God whose barque was ceremonially

Divine Souls of the West, TT 359 Inherkha, Deir el-Medina

hauled during his festival of the renewal of life and light. The word Ro-Setjau or Ra-Setjau (*r3-st3w*) is related to the word *setja* (*st3*) meaning "dragging or pulling". It was the name of the sloping way upon which the sarcophagus was towed towards the burial chamber. *Setja* is also typically used to refer to the towing Jackals.[17]

Aside from the God Sokar, Anubis himself is also Lord and Master of Ro-Setjau. Hence, one of Anubis's epithets is "Lord of Ro-Setjau". Anubis, in his form as the four Gods or Jackals, is the one hauling the Sun barque of Râ across the sloping sand paths towards the most secret place in the deepest depths of the Duat. These four are the only ones allowed to cross the knives or gates that grant access to the unapproachable zigzag path into the Forbidden Land.

The God "He adorned with the tassel" (No. 304) stands just past the gate, "Knife which renews the earth". Here begins the path "Secret path entered by Anubis to conceal the corpse of Osiris". This path traverses through the structure of the Sacred River. The name of the path refers to one of the titles of Anubis as "He who is in the place of embalming". Anubis is assigned with the task to mummify, wrap and conceal the body of his father Osiris. Thus, protecting the vulnerable body to allow for the transformation process of death into life simultaneously. In other words, "He adorned with the tassel" is Osiris himself wrapped like a mummy with the White Crown on his head.

The tassel, as mentioned in his name, is possibly a reference to the catkins of a willow. The Willow is the sacred tree of Osiris and grows along the riverbanks. According to myth, Seth imprisoned his brother Osiris in a coffin that he tossed into the river. As the coffin was dragged with the current, it eventually washed up on the riverbank of the Nile. There, a willow grew and surrounded the coffin to protect the slain body of Osiris. Furthermore, willows grew at the locations where the parts of the dismembered body of Osiris were buried. This explains why willow branches braided in the shape of a crown were found with several mummies. These crowns symbolise justification and the resurrected Osiris. When the deceased wore them, they were identified with Osiris. Hence, the willow is linked to funerals and death. However, it also signifies rebirth and resurrection as it grows on the riverbank on the border of the world of the living and the world of the dead.

The catkin, or tassel, of a willow appears very early in spring. When the rest of nature still looks lifeless, the willow tassel is the first sign of the victory of life over death. As such, "He adorned with the tassel" holds the promise of resurrection and is thus the perfect name for Osiris.

However, the hieroglyphic word for tassel, *"menkhty"* (*mꜥnḫty*), can also be translated as pendant. In that case the name of the God is translated as "He adorned with the pendant" (No. 304). This could be a reference to the necklace, the *menit* that Osiris sometimes wears.

As mentioned in the First Hour, this piece of jewellery symbolises new life, resurrection, potency, fertility, health and happiness. The pendant at the back of the *menit* ensures that all of these positive forces flow into the backbone. It holds the promise of the upcoming victory of life over death, similar to the catkin. No matter how dark and infertile the atmosphere in this hour is, the supine position of death will ultimately be conquered. Whatever happens, Osiris will be renewed and his spine, or the *Djed*, will be raised. The God "He adorned with the pendant" already heralds this miraculous event.

In front of Osiris, his shepherd's crook can be seen standing on the ground, "Staff of Osiris" (No. 305), which is the symbol of power and rulership. Despite the fact that Osiris is not ready to assume the leadership of the Duat, the crook is already there ready to be used when the time comes. The crook is semi upraised within easy reach.

The following two Gods are Thoth, "The One who lifts" (No. 307), and Sokar, "He with extended arm" (No. 308). Together they carry the Divine Eye, "(Eye of) Sokar" (No. 306). This Divine Eye is the symbol of the moon, or the left Eye. It is the eye that becomes damaged repeatedly to be healed again. Both Gods take responsibility for the Eye in order to protect it from dark forces. The evil that creeps around

Thoth and Sokar lift up the Divine Eye, KV 9 Ramses V and VI

here has stolen the light from the Eye and is the reason for the darkness within this hour. If Thoth and Sokar do not intervene, the light dies, never to shine again. They elevate the Divine Eye and carry it with great care to prevent death from taking control over it.

Thoth is eminently suited as the protector of the Eye as evident from the myth about the battle over the rulership of Egypt between Horus and Seth. During the fight Seth tore out the left Eye of Horus and damaged it in the process. Thoth, as the master physician, was then put to work to restore the Eye.

> I am Thoth who approaches
> the Great Ladies,
> I have come that I may seek out
> the Eye of Horus,
> I have brought and examined it,
> and I have found it complete,
> fully numbered and intact.[18]
> – Coffin Texts; Spell 249

The Eye of Horus is also known as the Wadjet Eye (also spelled Udjat, Uadjet, Wadjet, Wadjyt). Wadjet (*wd3t*) is a derivative of the verb *wadj* (*wd3*), which means "uninjured, salvation or prosperity". The Eye of Horus, or Wadjet, is therefore the symbol of protection and healing. It shows that everything is reversible, even death. That is the reason why some offerings were also called the Eye of Horus for it symbolised the event where the God Thoth offered the healed eye to Horus. Those offerings then possessed healing properties as they could restore what had fallen apart, renew what had been worn, replenish what had been diminished and bring back what had been stolen.[19]

Another myth mentions Thoth as the healer of the Eye of Râ since Seth, in the shape of a black pig, had damaged and blinded it. Here, in the Fourth Hour as well, Thoth takes it upon himself to heal the Eye with his Divine Wisdom and Knowledge.

Sokar, on the other hand, offers the protection and the nurturing safety of his realm, the deepest region of the Duat. The deep dark earth provides for the nourishment essential for the renewal of the Eye. It might sound contradicting, but it is actually the deep darkness that can bring back the light. Every beam of light will undo the process of rebirth at this time. Therefore, the Eye is in good hands with the wise Thoth and the dark Sokar. Together they have the power and the Wisdom to guarantee the proceeding of the process to heal and renew the light or consciousness.

The next four Gods are:
(No. 309) "Whose front is crowned", a God who is wearing the White Crown of Upper Egypt in a very unusual fashion on the top of his head.
(No. 310) "He over his rope"
has two ropes instead of a head.
(No. 311) "He with fresh face"
is a God without any attributes.
(No. 312) "Peaceful One" is a God carrying a magical knife with both hands as he presents it

to a group of three Gods and a Goddess who are facing him. The magical knife protects the vulnerable new life and was present in the First Hour (No. 63) and the Third Hour (No. 204) as well. Presently, the knife warrants the protection of the creative force, or Magic. Only through the force of Magic the Utterance of the Divine will come into existence. Magic always precedes the creation and is, therefore, the foundation for eternal Life. Even though no sign of life can be found in this dry and deathly desert, the God "Peaceful One" indicates that new life is on the verge of emerging from death.

The four Deities facing "Peaceful One" confirm this fact. In their outstretched hands they are presenting the *Ankh*, the sign of eternal Life, to "Peaceful One".

These four Deities are:
(No. 313) The God
"Guide of the *Ankh*-sign"
(No. 314) The God "Onuris or In-hert (He who brings the distant Goddess)" In-hert (*in(i)-ḥrt*) or Onuris is the God of war and hunting. The name In-hert means "Who brings back the face or sight". According to myth, In-hert left Egypt to go hunting in the nearby desert of Nubia. There he caught a lioness that he managed to domesticate and he took her back with him to Egypt. This lioness was regarded as the leonine Goddess "Eye of Râ" who ran away after an argument with her father, the Sungod. In-hert brought the leonine Goddess, or the sight of Râ, back with him, which enabled the light to return to harmony. His task is also reflected in another myth where In-hert returned the damaged Eye of the God Horus.

(No. 315) The God "He who commands"
(No. 316) The Goddess "Mistress of Life"

The four Deities are facing the opposite direction, which enables them not only to look at "Peaceful One", but also upon the Sungod and the traveller following this path. Their gesture is a reassuring sign to the passing traveller while making the difficult journey. Though the Land of Sokar may seem dry and barren, it hides the secret of eternal Life. This secret needs to be guarded well to prevent the entry of unauthorised persons. These four Deities ensure this does not happen.

They can be found at the entry to the hidden realm. It is their task to protect Anubis, for he acts as the Guide for the Forbidden Land. Anubis is the Master of Secrets and he, and he alone, is capable of guiding the traveller into the depths of the Duat. Anubis is the Jackal God, "the Towing One", and is reflected in the four Gods towing the Sun barque. He, like no one else, knows the way through the dark desert. The protection of Anubis is, therefore, of the greatest importance, for without Anubis it is impossible for Râ to continue his voyage.

> I have come to Ro-Setjau in order to know
> the secret of the Netherworld
> into which Anubis is initiated.[20]
> – Coffin Texts; Spell 241

The Duatians on the right riverbank (lower section)

There is a papyrus barque at the beginning of the right riverbank. The stern and prow are shaped like bearded heads that produce sounds. On the barque lies an enormous serpent, "The Smooth One who shines" (No. 317), who lives from these sounds. "He lives from the sound when the heads of his barque speak".[21]

This refers to sound or creative utterance. These are the sounds from which existence emerges. Thus, the serpent shall live forever, a true immortal that is made apparent by the *Ankh* in front of him. He resides here at the beginning of one of the secret paths and acts like the guardian for this part of the Duat, *Imhet*. "The Smooth One who shines" will reappear in the Twelfth Hour as the gigantic serpent "Life of the Gods" or "Smooth". There he will function as the birthing canal to assist the Sungod to smoothly come into being.

Following are five Deities who are standing here on the secret way of *Imhet* and are part of the creation that gradually takes place in the earth.

(No. 318) "She of the road"
a Goddess without attributes.
(No. 319) "She who has claws"
a Goddess also without attributes.
(No. 320) "Baboon" a mummified baboon sitting on a throne.
(No. 321) "She who has teeth"

Anubis leads Nebenmaat before Osiris and the Goddess of the West, TT 219 Nebenmaat, Deir el-Medina

a Goddess with the head of a lion.
(No. 322) "She who raises the horn" a Goddess in a sitting posture with horns on her head.

In front of them a huge serpent, "The Hidden One" (No. 323), lies on the ground with an *Ankh* under his head. He is also part of the secret pathway of *Imhet* and remains in his position at all times. His existence is made possible by the voices of the Deities who belong to this path. He too lives by means of creative utterance. Thus, within this part of *Imhet*, the silence is somewhat disturbed. However, the silence is broken only by these sounds, for not a single word is spoken. The sounds do not reach Râ, which is why there is no communication between the Sungod and these Gods.

Before the last gate lies another huge serpent with two heads, "She who adores" (No. 324). From the backside of her long body a human head has emerged that is facing the opposite direction. She is the guardian of this path and lies in front of the last part of the secret desert path. With her two heads she praises the Sungod using a magical chant.

This final stretch of road is called "Waters of the corpses" as indicated by the hieroglyphs that are written next to it. This is the 'Secret path of the edge of *Imhet*'. Hence, we have reached the edge of this hour, the end of the sloping zigzag path. The time has almost come for the Sungod Râ to enter the secret Cavern of Sokar.

Beyond the final path lies another huge serpent, "The One who moves" (No. 325). It is quite clear that the right riverbank is crawling with snakes. This serpent, however, is by far the biggest among them. It faces the opposite direction with its three large impressive heads. With his faces he ensures that there is light here on a daily basis. It probably means he spits fire from his mouths to illuminate the darkness until the moment Râ is reborn as the new rising sun Khepri.

> Light is in it daily until the birth of Khepri who goes forth
> from the faces of the "He who moves" serpent.[22]

Khepri himself can be seen here as the winged solar disk "Khepri" (No. 326). This shape is the form he uses when he rises at the Eastern horizon. At that moment life will once again be illuminated, ending the darkness. All colours will return as a sign of life. Hence, Khepri is described as a "God of coloured feathers".[22]

Above the body of "The One who moves" are two rows of seven bearded human heads. They all wear a solar disk on top of their heads. Below each head a five-pointed star can be seen. The exact significance of this image is unclear for there is no accompanying text. The presentation could be a reference to the mauled body of Osiris that was chopped into fourteen pieces.

Osiris, who embodies the *Ka*, is now divided into fourteen *Ka's*. As we know, Osiris is the *Ka* of Râ. Thus, the Sungod himself is also comprised of fourteen *Ka*'s. Each one of these *Ka*'s symbolises a part of his essence in the form of a different virtue. Together these virtues stand for the basis of the foundation of life itself, which are: Magical power (*ḥk3*), Strength (*nḫt*), Splendour (*3ḫ*), Might (*wsr*), Vigour (*w3ḏ*), Abundance (*df3*), Wealth (*šps*), Invocation (*snm*), Provision (*spd*), Stability (*dd*), Sight (*m33*), Hearing (*sḏm*), Percipience (*si3*) and Authority of utterance (*ḥw*).[23]

During the following hours the Sungod and Osiris will be united. This, in turn, also leads to the integration of each of these individual divided pieces into a single body. However, there is a lot more hidden in this mysterious image than meets the eye. This is all part of the secret of the Duat. Therefore, it is of no use to break the silence with words, for these words will never be able to incorporate and express the true meaning of the secret hidden within.

The second to last God of this hour is "Who is in Heaven" (No. 327). He has adopted a combative posture and is facing the opposite direction. There is no doubt he uses this pose to spot and defeat the enemies of Râ. Close behind him stands the Goddess "Maât" (No. 328) with the feather of Truth on her head. She too shows that everything within this hour obeys the Divine Law of *Maât*. Her back is facing the final gate in her watchful pose. She grants passage only to the blessed and justified dead. The final gate, "Knife of Eternity", and the gate of the Fifth Hour, form a double protection. As the name of the knife indicates, this is the way to eternal Life.

The manifestation of the Fourth Hour in daily life

The moment you enter this hour, you become aware of the enormous changes that take place within this realm. The water from the previous hours, that you have grown used to, has completely disappeared. Not a single drop to be found. The feeling of weightlessness, while in the water, has suddenly vanished. You are now pulled into the depths of the earth without mercy.

In an instant you experience the firm ground beneath your body and are confronted with the pulling force of the earth. Though you cannot stand yet, you are symbolically dropped to your feet and have to get used to the weight. You are unable to move at this time as you are being pulled into the oppressive atmosphere.

You have been buried deep beneath the earth, isolated from all sound with nothing but dead silence surrounding you. The silence can be quite disheartening. You want to hear music and voices or perceive any other sign of life. None of these things are now within your reach. You are unable to communicate with anyone and have no one to ask for assistance to free you from your plight. Because that is what it feels like, as if you are stuck, trapped, with nowhere to run. Wrapped like a mummy, placed inside a coffin and pulled on the sledge headed for the burial chamber.

This is the next step for your inner process of dying where you are descending deeper into yourself. This time, however, the descent does not happen due to the force of the water as you have experienced in the previous hours. In those hours the flowing water cleared out the old debris that came to the surface from the depths of your being. The debris came into sight due to the transparency of the water. The desert in the present hour, however, works in quite a different way. It has a pulling power turned inward that makes everything dry out and desiccate. Therefore, the focus now lies inward and isolates you from all external events. You are on your own, for that is all that is left.

There is nowhere to run. You are forced to confront the challenge head-on. Burying your head in the sand or digging your heals is useless. This only results in the delay of the inevitable. There is no escaping it. Instead, take advantage of the surplus of energy at your disposal that is released, for you cannot use it to move. You notice, once you give in, that the need for silence and serenity only grows stronger. You know the answers can be found in the loneliness that connects you to your inner Wisdom.

Apart from the silence, the darkness also has cleansing properties. This realm is pitch-black so you cannot see six inches in front of your face. This can be perceived as frightening and threatening as you cannot see what is coming. It devours your power and makes you feel vulnerable. The more you try to reach out, the more the confining feeling weighs down on you. There is only one way to win this battle and that is to turn inward. Only then you can overcome the darkness and counter the hold it has over you. Consequently, you are finally able to harness this dark power instead of it working against you. It is no longer a threat as it becomes a protective layer supporting you and enabling you to focus all of your attention inward. The concealment from the outside world creates an opening for you to connect with the Higher Self more deeply.

However, here too you will be tested, for the communication with the Higher Self has halted. You feel like the connection you worked so hard to build in the previous hours has suddenly disappeared. You are starting to doubt whether the communication was ever there at all as you are met with dead silence. This gives rise to the feeling of being all alone in the desert as you exclaim towards the sky "God, why hast Thou forsaken me". Your entire concept of God or your image of the Divine is jeopardised as you desperately ask yourself if such things ever existed at all. Everything falls apart, you feel deserted in this lonely desert. All roads outside of yourself have been cut off. The search can go only in one direction since you have to descend deep within yourself. You go through a very intense trial as the connection between you and the Higher Self is re-established. This has a cleansing effect which automatically results in the death of your old self to make room for the new.

Thoth (No. 307) and Sokar (No. 308) are here to make you aware of this. They carry the Eye of consciousness that is starting to transform. This is the Eye that is damaged again and again and repeatedly renewed. Every time you obtain a new consciousness, it is bound to eventually become obsolete as things change all the time. It is a continuous process that occurs over and over again. Thoth grants you wisdom to make you aware and to facilitate the transformation process. Sokar, in turn, offers you the darkness that guards the transformation. It could help you and offer you many insights if you meditate on these two Gods and the Eye they are carrying.

Aside from these Gods several other Gods offer you their support as well. The four Gods, or the four Jackals (No. 300 – 303), are the most essential guides on your way. They symbolise Anubis who is your faithful companion, always by your side along your voyage. He is the Guide and knows the way to ensure you will not get lost in the dark. You can learn a lot from him about the process of dying and you can ask him any question. Try to bond with his keen senses to gain clarity on your own process. Surrender yourself to these Divine Souls of the West. Relax as you are drawn into this process. They guide you to the Holy of Holies where the Higher Self awaits your arrival.

Kherep wia, the guide of the Sun barque, also makes you aware of the surrender that needs to take place. The fact that he is the notable absentee and the helm is missing from the barque, signifies the need for you to surrender your inner steering to the only remaining captain on your boat, the Higher Self. Despite the dead silence and the impossibility to communicate with the Higher Self, he shows you he is still there for you in a subtle way. Like a gentle breeze, he touches you lightly, to disappear again before you have time to process his appearance. These subtle touches make the dark experience slightly more bearable and help you to regain Self-confidence.

These delicate signs are not the only little lights on your way through the darkness for your dreams can help you with the transformation as well. Since the dark depth of this hour is the home to numerous snakes and scorpions, you may meet these animals in your dreams. It is a beautiful sign when these creatures reveal themselves to you in the nightly hours of your sleep. The serpent and the scorpion are both linked to death, which precedes rebirth. They trigger your awareness, telling you to shed the old in order to clear some space for the new. Record these dreams in detail once you wake up. They contain valuable symbols designed to make you aware of what is going on during your transformation.

The scorpion is the symbol for self-preservation. The old self wages war to defend its spot as the new self endeavours to take its place. Thus, the old is required to perish first as it is impossible to manifest your new consciousness otherwise. Serket (No. 283), the scorpion Goddess, is connected to this process of dying. As protector of the deceased, she guards the death process. She cures you from your death state as she grants you the Breath of Life to revive the new self or consciousness. She is the mother of Neheb Kau (No. 287), a God who also guides you in your process of renewal. Neheb Kau, "He who unites the *Ka's*", is the bearer of the Vital Life Force that he now offers to you. This connects you to your true heritage, in other words, a connection with your True Self.

Furthermore, the name of this hour "With living manifestation" reminds you of the fact that although you might experience a feeling of dying, the new life is approaching. Osiris (No. 304) in his form as "He adorned with the tassel or pendant" announces this as well. As you can see, there are many helpful Deities within this hour encouraging you on your way down. Every Deity, whether in human or serpent form, holds a key to unlocking the secret images of your inner world. Since you are shielded by the silence of the darkness, these inner images are much more evident compared to the previous hours. These secret images fill the void that has developed due to the death of the old. The name of this particular part of the Duat, *Imhet* or "the Filled One", is a reference to this process. The space created from the dying of the old is filled with the things that really matter. These new parts are your True Self or the Higher Self, who embody the newly formed consciousness. The road leading to this point is extremely narrow and sharp. It cuts through falsehood and anything that is not essential, clearing the way. Eventually, only the True Self remains as the image of Horus himself. Then the ideal image has manifested itself, bridging the above and the below. The renewed consciousness has been revived. The darkness dissolves, giving way to the light of Khepri as it returns the colours to your world once more.

All of these events are shrouded in a mysterious and secretive atmosphere. The process of inner renewal is therefore a topic that should not be discussed. The truth can only be found in your own inner world as it presents itself to you through symbols. It are these symbols that guide you on your way. One of these very important symbols can be found in the final part of this hour. Above the body of the huge serpent, "The One who moves" (No. 325), there are fourteen heads wearing a solar disk with fourteen five-pointed stars underneath them. These are powerful symbols that open the last knife of this hour once you connect yourself with them. Then the road finally opens up to you, enabling you to descend into the Fifth Hour where the secret Cavern of Sokar, can be found.

THE FIFTH HOUR
"West"

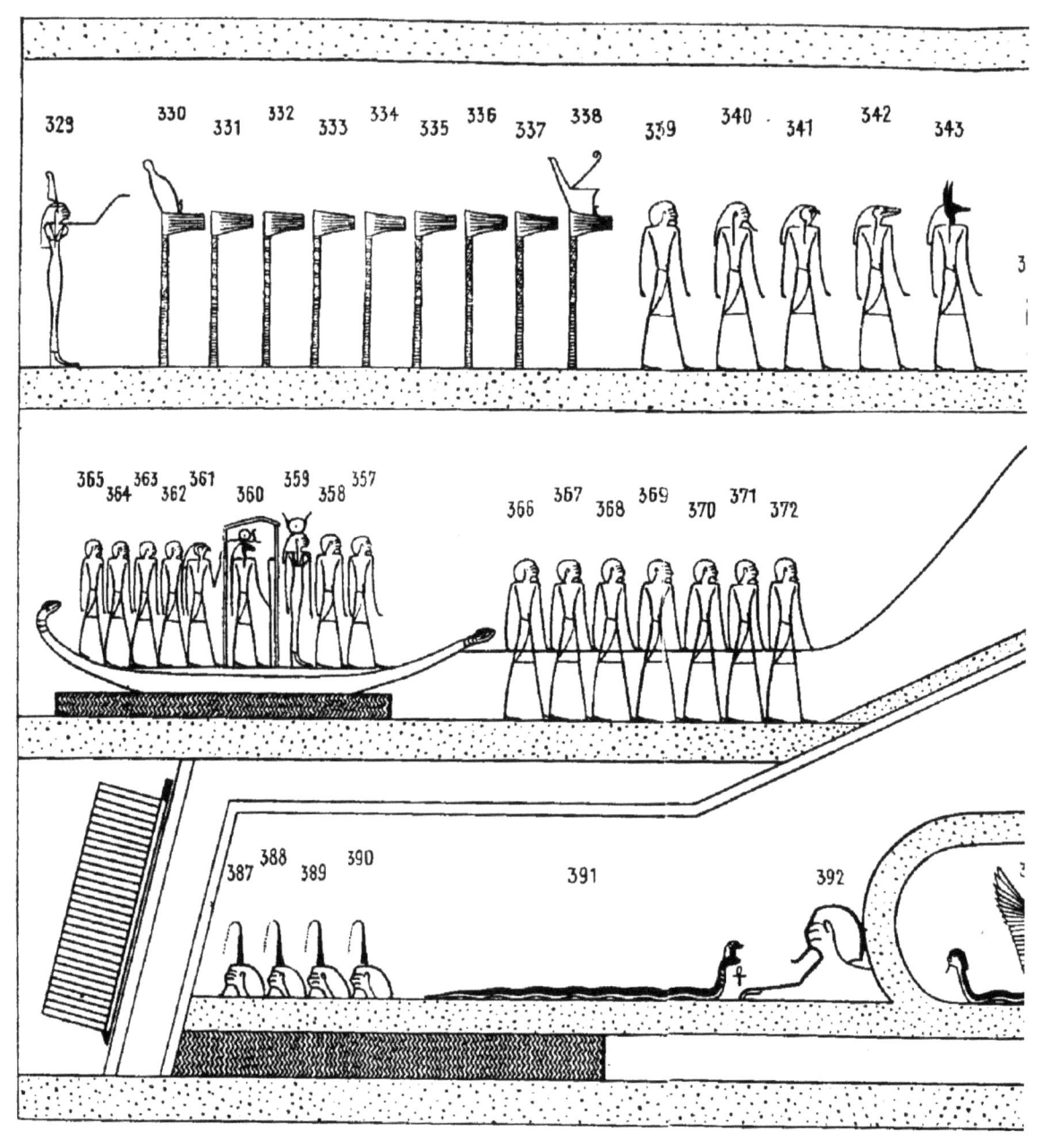

Figure 21: The Fifth Hour

The Gate: "Position of Gods"
The Hour Goddess: "She who guides in the midst of her barque"
The Guardian: "Living God"

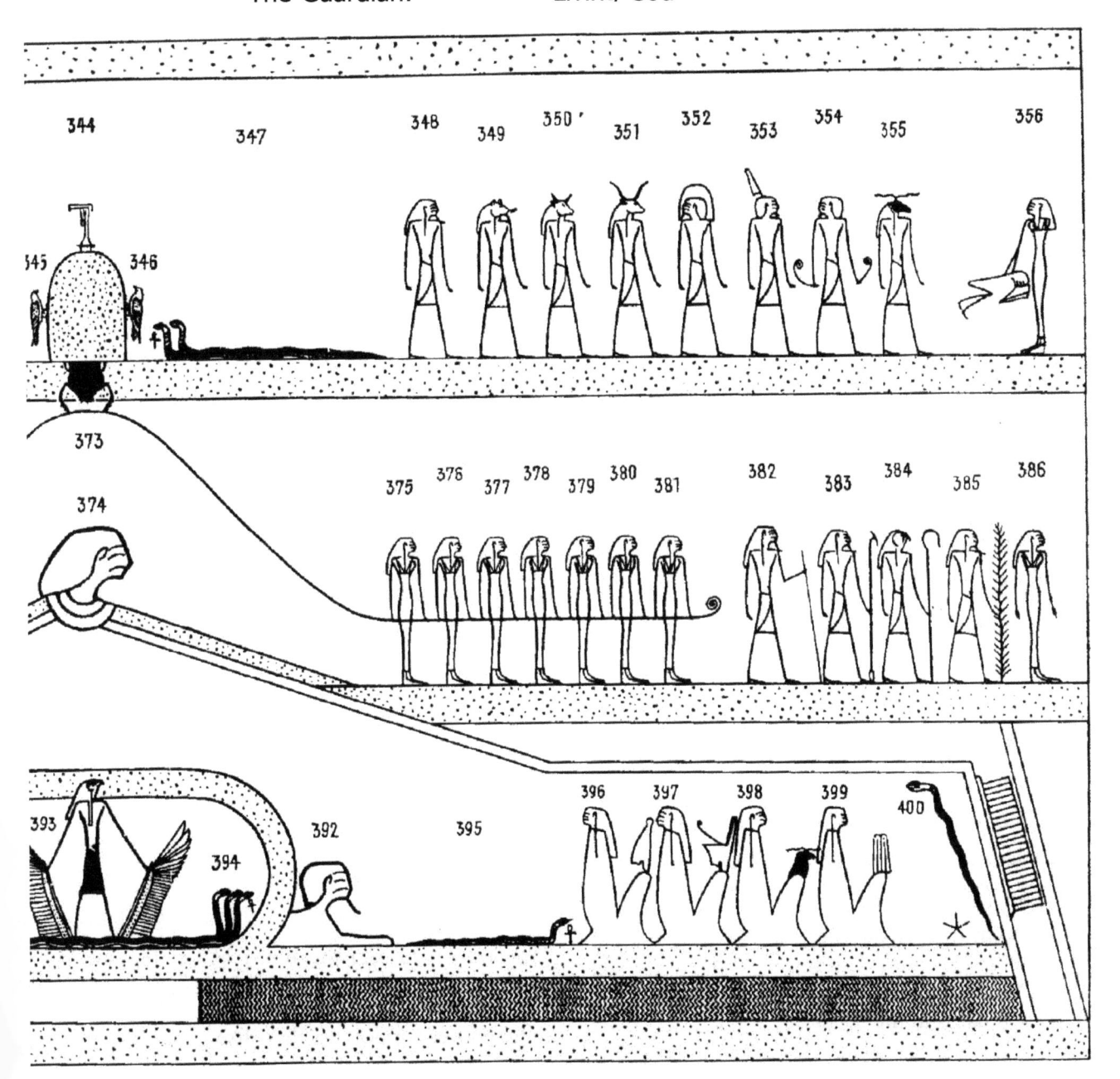

Introduction

This Great God is towed along the proper
ways of the Duat,
in the upper half of the secret Cavern
of Sokar-upon-his-sand.
Invisible and imperceptible
is this secret image
of the land which bears the flesh
of this God.
Those among whom this God is,
they hear the voice of Râ,
when he calls out to the vicinity
of this God.
The name of the Gate of this place
is "Position of Gods".
The name of the Cavern of this God
is "West".
The name of the Hour of the night
guiding this Great God is,
"She who guides
in the midst of her barque".
The secret paths of the West,
gates through which the hidden is entered,
the unapproachable place of the Land
of Sokar,
flesh and body as the first manifestation.
Knowledge of the *Ba*-souls
which are in the Duat,
(and) their functions
according to the (book?)
"What is in the Hours",
with their secret names.

Unknown, unseen, imperceptible
is this image of Horus himself.
This is made like this image which is
painted in the secrecy of the Duat
on the Southern side of the
Hidden Chamber.
He who knows it, his *Ba*-soul is content,
and he is satisfied with the offerings
of Sokar.
Khemyt ("She who overthrows")
cannot cut his corpse.[1]
Offerings are made to them on earth.[2]

The Fifth Hour is still within the region of the Duat called *Imhet*, "The Filled One". This entire hour, like the previous one, is filled with sand. The Sacred River is still dry. Thus, the Sun barque remains in its serpent shape to ease the hauling over the sand. This is the Sacred Land of Sokar hidden deep within the earth, far away from the world of the living. It is completely isolated, accessible only via the secret paths that descent into the depths of the earth. The first descent has taken place in the Fourth Hour across a very dangerous area filled with serpents. However, Râ has managed to overcome all obstacles and challenges thrown his way and he is now ready to enter the Fifth Hour through the gate "Position of Gods".

When Râ enters the hour, the Hour Goddess "She who guides in the midst of her barque" takes him under her protection. Her name suggests her support to Râ is like a safe haven.

Within its security, Râ can make his next descent. Although he has already descended quite a long way across the secret paths in the Fourth Hour, during this hour he is still required to descend even further. The Hour Goddess guides him through the terrifying darkness down the secret paths of the West toward the innermost part of the journey. Here is where the deepest region of the Duat can be found, the place where the entrance to the Hidden lies.

This hour is known as "West", the hidden realm of the dead. The name "West" is unrelated to the cardinal direction of the West. "West" in this context means the hidden and secret place. It refers to the Cavern or Oval of Sokar that can be found in the profound depths. It is a concealed place within a pyramid shaped mound accessible only via a very narrow and dangerous path. The pyramid mound is at the centre of this hour, which alters the usual division of the three sections. As a result, the three sections are all connected to each other. This demonstrates clearly what is about to happen within this hour. Opposite forces are brought face to face. Obviously, this will result in a lot of friction and tension. However, it is precisely this area of tension that is necessary to generate the maximum amount of energy. The climax of this electric force pushes the middle section up in the shape of a pyramid mound. Inside, Osiris and Râ will meet for the first time.

The entry and exit at the bottom of the pyramid are blocked by gates and the upper part is shielded by the head of Isis. Since this is the sacred Land of Sokar, the Sanctuary is heavily guarded from all sides. Here, in this hidden land, the mystery of the first sign of life unfolds itself in secret.

Along the voyage through this hour, Râ is able to speak out again and his voice is heard by the Duatians. He addresses all the Deities of the Sacred River and the Deities on the left riverbank by giving them orders. However, the only ones that answer his call are the towing Gods and Goddesses in front of the Sun barque. Even so, contact between the Deities and Râ has finally returned to some extent within the upper two layers of this hour. Nevertheless, this applies only to the upper and middle section of this hour for within the pyramid mound there is a serene and mysterious silence. It is not allowed to break the silence within this sacred space. Even Râ himself is required to be silent once he enters this area for silence, like darkness, is the precondition for the miracle to happen.

It is quite clear that a complete turnaround is about to happen. To make this possible, the necessary preparations have to be made. All the Duatians living here are involved in this process. They all have to perform their specific tasks to allow for the extraordinary event to unfold within the depths of this hour. Consequently, it is essential that every Duatian takes their respective position. The name of the gate, "Position of the Gods", already emphasises this fact right at the beginning of this hour.

The route of the Sungod

The Fifth Hour, like the Sixth Hour, is a unique hour that is reflected in the route the Sungod Râ follows through the Duat. This route is quite interesting since every hour takes place in a specific cardinal direction as instructed in the text of the Amduat. In order to travel through the hours in chronological order the Sungod has to jump from one cardinal direction to another.

The first four hours of the journey were situated in the cardinal direction of the West. The Fifth Hour, like the Sixth Hour, however, is situated in the South. After finishing the Fourth Hour, the Sun barque with Râ and his crew changes course and makes a diagonal jump from the West to the South. In the land of the living, the South is the quarter where the sun reaches its highest point and shines the brightest. This quarter is, therefore, linked to the element of fire and symbolises transition, transformation, purification and rising up. All of these features represent the events taking place in the Fifth and Sixth Hour. Within these dark hours

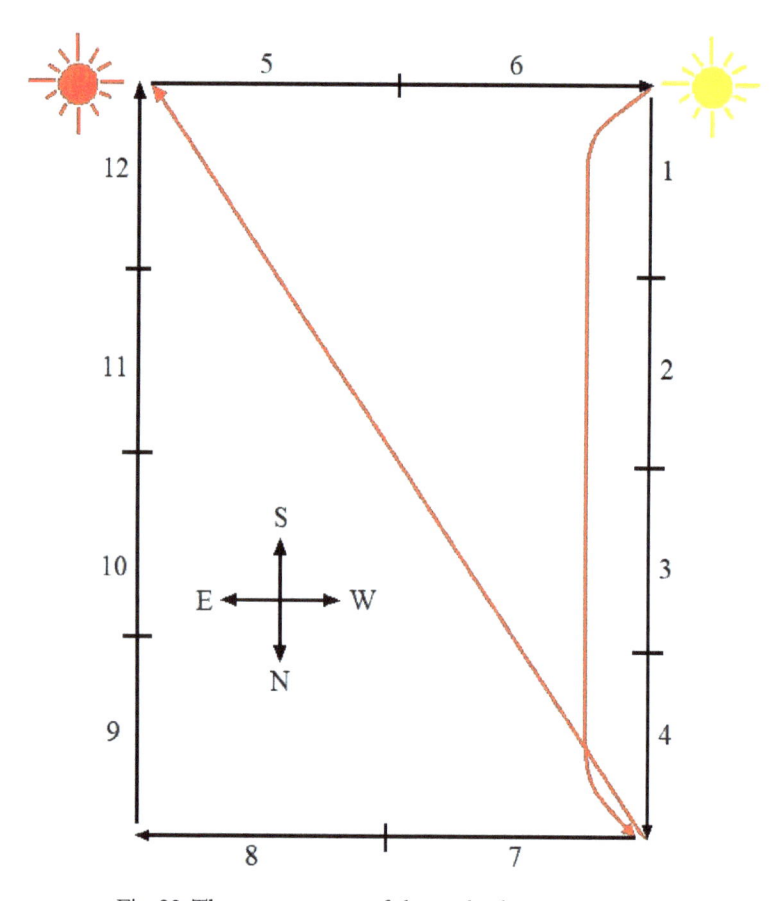

Fig. 22. The arrangement of the twelve hours according to the text of the Amduat.

of the night the highest light is the focal point.

The complete reversal of the Sun barque to head towards the South is a crucial event in the process of transformation. Here the very first contact between Râ and Osiris is conducted. To reach this state of coming together, it is essential to completely let go of the old known order. Only then death can be reversed into life and regenerate both Râ and Osiris in the process.

Within the Fifth and the Sixth Hour, the Hidden Mystery unfolds itself. Together they form a realm shrouded in darkness, completely isolated from everyday life. Hence, these two hours are outside of the scope of the usual itinerary. However, it is preciously this isolation that allows for the Mystery to be protected without disturbances or interferences from the outside world. During this early start of the renewal process of the Sungod Râ, it is very important to protect it at all costs. At the initial beginning, this process is still very frail and delicate. Just like a tiny seed in the black soil, where the soothing darkness helps it to sprout. Once the seed has transformed completely into the beginnings of a plant, it breaks through the surface of the soil towards the light. Before this time, though, a seed can sprout only when hidden in complete darkness. Light would destroy its life vigour.

The turnaround of the Fifth Hour results in it lying adjacent to the Twelfth Hour. In this way the highest and deepest point of the journey are side by side. The profound darkness during the very first meeting between Sokar-Osiris and Râ in the Fifth Hour alongside the promise of the rebirth of the new light in the Twelfth Hour. This vision of the future of the final rebirth gives Râ the hope to go on, not to give up and to keep his faith in spite of the darkness in this process. At the same time, though, even if the promise of rebirth is already there, it is an illusion to think the goal has already been reached. Râ's journey has not ended. Far from it actually, as he is not even half way there yet.

The Duatians on the left riverbank (upper section)

The left riverbank commences with the Goddess "She who is (in) the water of rejuvenation" (No. 329). On top of her head she wears the feather of *Maât* and she has her hands upraised in a consecrating gesture. Râ addresses her as the Goddess of the West. It is unsurprising this Goddess is at the beginning of this hour. She does not just welcome each newly deceased in her realm, for she also watches over the process of rejuvenation. She takes the hand of the deceased and guides them towards their own rebirth. Râ too asks for her guidance during his own transformation of death into new life.

> Words spoken by this Great God:
> "(Goddess of the) West! Give your hand!
> Perfect is the great road which is
> in the earth,
> the way of the tombs,

resting place of my Gods.³

In front of her is a row of nine flags that are hieroglyphic signs for *Netjer*, or God. Their number of nine demonstrates that the signs are the representation of the Great Ennead. Nevertheless, the Ennead represented here is different from the usual Ennead. The first sign, with a White Crown on top, represents Khepri instead of Atum. The last sign, with a Red Crown on top, represents Horus instead of Seth. The switch of these Gods demonstrates the fact that the focus is on the creation myth of the solar cycle. Here Khepri and Horus are the representatives of the new light whereas the original Ennead shows the initial beginning of the creation, *Zep Tepi*.

The Ennead depicted here represents the eternal renewal that has arisen from the first creation. Râ confirms this as he says these Gods come forth from his flesh, not from Atum. They can exist due to the cycle of the Sungod through the day and the night. Râ is aware of the fact that everyone is dependent on him and his voyage. Therefore, he assures them he will protect them. Every time he travels through this hour, he gifts everyone the Breath of Life.

The nine hieroglyphic signs are the following;

(No. 330) "Southern Divine symbol of Khepri"
(No. 331) "Divine symbol of Shu"
(No. 332) "Divine symbol of Tefnut"
(No. 333) "Divine symbol of Geb"
(No. 334) "Divine symbol of Nut"
(No. 335) "Divine symbol of Osiris"
(No. 336) "Divine symbol of Isis"
(No. 337) "Divine symbol of Nephthys"
(No. 338) "Northern Divine symbol of Horus of the Duat"

The subsequent Gods are;
(No. 339) "He who belongs to the water of the drowned" a God in human form.
(No. 340) "Guardian of the riverbanks" a God in human form.
(No. 341) "He with living heart" a God with the head of a hawk.
(No. 342) "The primeval one of the counter-heaven" a God with the head of a crocodile.

These four Gods belong to the waters of the drowned in the Duat. This is noteworthy since there is no water on this side of the Sacred River. In this hour, the only water to be found is in the Lake of Fire. The lake lies within the protection of the pyramid shaped mound on the right riverbank. The water in the lake is combined with the element of fire, granting it cleansing properties. It is not possible to drown here so the Gods mentioned above obviously do not belong to this lake.

The water to which they are connected are the primeval waters of Nun. Every hour of the Duat, whether it contains water or not, is submerged in this regenerative flood. Without this water, the process of the rejuvenation of

Râ would be impossible. Hence, the primal waters of Nun also symbolically imbues the hours without water. Râ remains submerged in this water until he arises from it at the end of the Twelfth Hour.

The four Gods are standing near the life-giving waters of the Nun, which belong to them, to ensure the Nun does not dry out. There are several deceased drifting around here in these waters, known as the Floating Ones. The four Gods provide them with a flood to help them wash towards the shore. The Gods proceed with great caution to not let them drown. This means these deceased are guaranteed that they will be able to go ashore safely in the Afterlife.

The four Gods also guard the riverbanks and make sure the banks remain high to prevent the water from flowing away and to keep it under control. This enables the Sun barque to arrive here every night and float past the Gods in peace while they bow their heads for Râ.

The next God is "Anubis or Inpu of the Chest" (no. 343) in his role as "Lord of the Coffin". He is the Guardian of the transformation process that unfolds itself deep within the earth. Another epithet of this God is "He who is on his mountain", *Tepy Duef (tpy-dw=f)*. This mountain is a reference to the primordial hill that is the source from which all life arises. Anubis keeps watch over the secret Mystery of life and death that takes place deep within the primordial hill. Here, he is standing at the entrance of the pyramid shaped mound that holds the secret Cavern of Sokar within its depths. This concealed realm is where the secret Mystery of the regeneration of Life is conducted.

> Copy of a Spell for Burial in the West.
> O Anubis who inters me at this mighty
> mound among those who are
> foremost among the Silent Ones,
> You know that I am not among
> the Mound-dwellers;
> I am among the first ones of the *smm.tyw*,
> I am the God of reckoning
> in the Garden of the Silent One,
> I am the owner of fields
> in the Great Mound
> through burial in the beautiful West.
> To be spoken over sand
> of the Temple of Anubis,
> it being placed about him.
> This means burial in the West.[4]
> – Coffin Texts; Spell 111

The Chest (No. 344) in front of Anubis is called *keku (kkw)*, which means "Darkness". The hieroglyphic sign for "night or heaven" is fixed on top of it. This sign is the stylised image of the Goddess Nut whose body is comprised of the heavens. The name of the chest is a reference to the necessity of complete darkness before new life can emerge out of death.

The Secret path of Ro-Setjau, that crosses the Fourth Hour in a zigzag fashion, is connected directly to the opening of this Chest. The Chest marks the entranceway to the secret Cavern of Sokar, within which the Sungod Râ is initiated with the Secret Knowledge. Hence, the Chest is the Divine Gate of Knowledge. Anubis, as the "Lord of Ro-Setjau", is the Guardian of this Divine Gate of Knowledge and he acts as its keeper here on the threshold. The mysterious gate opens itself slightly to be shut closed almost immediately after, as if it never opened at all.

> I have come as an equipped
> [and worthy] spirit,
> I heal my members,
> And my (priestly) service is in this house.
> I have come in order to do my duty and
> in order to enter into the Gate
> which is under the care of Anubis.[5]
> – Coffin Texts; Spell 825

The Chest opens the way straight down to the secret Cavern of Sokar. Osiris is inside, in his form as Sokar, the God of death. The Goddesses Isis (No. 345) and Nephthys (No. 346) can be found on either side of the Chest in their shape as wailing birds. Their lamentation and affection contributes to the process of regeneration. Khepri (No. 373), who symbolises rebirth, emerges from under the Chest. Only half of him is visible, which is a reference to the transformation that is presently not even halfway done.

Râ addresses both Goddesses and asks them if they are willing to protect this Chest. It is essential for their lamentation to be loud and clear with the words spoken from a true heart in accordance with *Maât*. The combination of their love bundled with these magical words is

The Goddess Isis,
TT 218 Amennakt, Deir el-Medina

The Goddess Nephthys,
TT 218 Amennakt, Deir el-Medina

a crucial contribution to the process of rejuvenation of Osiris as well as Râ within the Cavern of Sokar. Furthermore, the two Goddesses protect the Chest with their wings, for the Chest holds the only access to this miracle. Therefore, they do not just conceal the physical Chest but, above all, the Secret that is happening within.

> May you guard your Chest.
> May your voice be loud
> and your throats truthful!
> May this image you guard be concealed.
> May you spread your wings
> and do your duties,
> that I may pass by you in peace.[6]

On the other side of the Chest, facing the opposite direction lies a two-headed serpent (No. 347), without a name, on the ground. He protects the burial mound with his two heads and the coils of his body. At all times, he performs this task as he never leaves his place. Therefore, the Chest is well guarded from the right side as well, since the serpent is a very dangerous guardian. He is able to spit fire and shoots his poison, in the form of arrows, at all unauthorised persons. Even Râ himself has to ask permission for him and his entourage to be granted safe passage without the serpent attacking them. The Sungod addresses the serpent in a correct and respectful tone as he calls him *"Djeser"* (*ḏsr*), which means "Sanctified". The serpent is, after all, a sacred creature who protects the Holy of Holies or *Djeser Djeseru* (*ḏsr ḏsr.w*).

Following the serpent is a procession of eight Gods, each with a different head. They are the eight butchers who have been appointed with the task to punish the damned of the Duat. The damned are those who disobey the Divine Law of *Maât*. The eight Gods act like real butchers for they use various disciplinary methods. With hot scorching breath from their mouth they burn the corpses of the damned. They also use slaughtering blocks and sharp knives. They bind their victims tightly while uttering brilliant magical words. With their power they grind the enemies, annihilate the damned and cut their shadows down. The eight butchers are not half-hearted and take their job very seriously as they completely wipe out the damned from existence. This they do for Osiris, the Perfect Being, to guard his wellbeing from the threat of these rebels.

(No. 348) "He who satisfies the Gods"
has a human head.
(No. 349) "Whom the Westerners fear"
with the head of a shrewmouse.
(No. 350) "Staff" with the head of a bull.
(No. 351) "Swallower" with the head
of a cow.
(No. 352) "The Horned One"
with a shadow around his head.
(No. 353) "Bringer of *Maât*"
with the feather of *Maât* on his head.
(No. 354) "Backward facing who catches with the lasso" has a human head and holds a lasso

in each hand. The lasso, or *sephu (sphw)*, was predominantly used to catch cattle. However, this God uses the lasso to catch the damned to prevent their escape.

(No. 355) "That *Ba*-soul who belongs to the damned" with the head of a ram.

The riverbank concludes with a Goddess standing while facing the opposite direction, "The Demolishing One, who cuts the damned to pieces" (No. 356). She holds a damned soul within her grasp as she is about to execute him. It is her job, like the eight butchers, to punish the damned. She does this by molesting the damned and cutting them to pieces as she feasts upon their blood. However, if Râ possesses the Knowledge to identify this Goddess, he may pass her in peace.

The left riverbank clearly shows us that duality can be found throughout the Duat. On the left side of the Chest, the creator Deities and the Gods connected to the life-granting waters and the primal flood, can be found. To the right of the Chest, though, the punishing and destructive Gods can be seen as they perform their tasks. Exactly in the middle of these two different sides there is the Chest, surrounded by protective Deities, that incorporates the process where the opposite forces come together.

The Duatians of the Sacred River (middle section)

The Sun barque is still shaped like an enormous serpent with a serpent head at the prow and the stern. The name of the barque has changed into "With living *Ba*-souls". The entire crew is present since the guide of the Sun barque, Kherep wia, has returned. However, he is not required to steer, for the helm and the oars are missing. He still surrenders the control of the Sun barque while it continuous its dragging process.

(No. 357) "Wepwawet"
(No. 358) "Sia"
(No. 359) "Nebet wia"
(No. 360) "Iuf"
(No. 361) "Heru Hekenu"
(No. 362) "Ka Maât"
(No. 363) "Nehes"
(No. 364) "Hu"
(No. 365) "Kherep wia"

Râ is standing inside the safe enclosure of his shrine as usual. He is wearing a solar disk with ram horns on top of his head. And, for the first time, the Uraeus-serpent is visible on his forehead. This is a good sign for it is the first reference to the returning life force that will restore Râ's power and authority. The Uraeus-serpent can be seen in the Fifth Hour only. Here, his presence is desperately needed to protect Râ during the current transformation process. After Râ has completed this process and leaves this hour, the Uraeus-serpent is absent again. He does not return to Râ's brow until the final hour.

Nebet wia, "the Lady of the barque", is standing in front of Râ. The solar disk has returned on top of her head. It goes without saying that she, like the Uraeus-serpent, will protect Râ.

The crewmembers turn to Râ by means of a litany. Through their songs they describe the various aspects of Râ to show him his might. These words of praise and glory are intended to encourage Râ and to strengthen his power and confidence. Every crewmember is aware of the dangers that lie ahead. Yet, Râ should not be held back by this precarious situation. To further encourage him, they welcome him nine times with the words *im hotep* (*m ḥtp*). The power of the litany and the Magic emerging from repeating it nine times ensures Râ's success as he will reach the Cavern of Sokar no matter what.

> Welcome! Welcome! Lord of Life!
> Welcome! Pacifier of the West!
> Welcome! Opener of the earth!
> Welcome! He who unlocks the earth!
> Welcome! Who is in heaven!
> Welcome! Pacifier of the Counter Heaven!
> Welcome! Triumphant is the Lord
> of the Ennead!
> Welcome! The earth opens her arms for you, the necropolis prepares its ways for you! [7]

The Sun barque is pulled by seven Gods (No. 366 – 372) and seven Goddesses (No. 375 – 381) without names. The seven Gods address the Sungod and they promise to tow him above the Cavern of Sokar. This means Râ is towed between the Chest with Khepri and the Goddess Isis "Flesh of Isis" (No. 374). Only Isis her head is visible upon the top of the pyramid mound. The text refers to her as "Flesh of Isis who is upon the sand of the Land of Sokar".

The path above the cavern is a very narrow and dangerous path as the head of Isis seizes half of it. However, Khepri comes to aid Râ as he lifts the rope to ease the towing process. He does so in a subtle manner without pulling the rope too tight. This way he gives Râ a gentle and loving hand and effectively supports his own rebirth process.

All the while the towing Gods speak encouraging words addressed to both Râ and Khepri. They inspire Râ as they tell him to make contact with Osiris through speaking with him. Osiris is present within the Cavern of Sokar in his form of "Flesh of Sokar-upon-his-sand" (No. 393). Râ needs to speak very clearly in order for his voice to be heard far below inside the depths of the sacred Land of Sokar.

> You speak, Râ, to Osiris!
> You call, Râ, to the Land of Sokar,
> And Horus-upon-his-sand lives. [8]

The towing Gods inspire Khepri to extend his hand in a helping gesture towards Râ to straighten the mysterious way. This enables Râ to continue his voyage from horizon to horizon in his form as Râ-Horakhty and install peace in the heavens.

> Come to Khepri, Râ! Come, Râ, to Khepri!
> The rope which you have brought,
> the rope is raised to Khepri,
> that he extends a hand to Râ, that he paves the mysterious ways for Râ-Horakhty.
> Heaven is in peace, in peace,
> and Râ belongs to the beautiful West! [8]

Directly below Khepri the tip of the pyramid shaped mound can be seen as it is formed by the head of the Goddess Isis. According to myth, she is the one who restored the dismembered body of Osiris through the power of her magical words. Here too, she is involved with the care of Osiris. She ensures the pyramid burial mound protects the Cavern of Sokar where her beloved Osiris, in his form of Sokar, can be found. Furthermore, she fills the pyramid mound with the flames from her mouth. As she fulfils this duty, she is aided by the serpent "Wamemty" (No. 395) who lies on the right side next to the Cavern of Sokar. Together they create a blast of fire. The blast is not meant to illuminate the darkness, but to

The trinity, the bearded Atum, the sundisk Râ and the scarab Khepri, Tempel of Seti I at Abydos

provide for the important fuel needed to ignite the impending transformation process.

Râ is hauled across the pyramid mound until he reaches the top of Isis's head. Then he is right in between Khepri and Sokar-Osiris with Isis, as Queen of Heaven and Earth, bridging between both worlds. Râ is now able to make his first contact with Sokar-Osiris.

> This Great God says over this cavern;
> "May you recognize this your image,
> Sokar, which is hidden and secret.
> I call to you that you be efficient,
> my words belong to you,
> that you may rejoice over them.
> Isis belongs to your image,
> and the greatest God to your corpse,
> so that he may guard it [9]

On the opposite side of the head of Isis, the seven Goddesses (No. 375 – 381) are assisting the seven Gods to tow the Sun barque. Like the crewmembers, they welcome Râ with the words *im hotep* and reassure him the road has been prepared for him. The enemies have been annihilated and driven off. Thus, the continuation of the towing of the Sun barque will succeed without fail and Râ will triumph.

Four Gods are walking in front of the seven Goddesses. They all have a human shape, with the exception of the third Deity, Horus, who has the head of a falcon. Each God carries a different sceptre.

(No. 382) "He above the forms" carries a staff.

(No. 383) "He who brings offerings" carries the *Was*-sceptre which represents power and dominion over death and darkness.

(No. 384) "Horus who belongs to the double *Heka*-sceptre" carries the *Heka*-sceptre which represents power and ruler ship.

(No. 385) "He who commands" carries a large palm branch in his hand.

The powers of these sceptres are supporting these Gods as they are fulfilling the tasks appointed to them by Râ. Their tasks are very important for they are required to distribute the food and bread offerings. The lives of all those dwelling inside the Duat are dependent upon these offerings. Therefore, this task is of vital importance and grants the Gods the title of "Lords of provisions in the West".

The Goddess "Isis of the West" (No. 386) concludes the hour. Isis is sometimes merged with the Goddess of the West. In this particular role she is present here as the guardian of the dead. The nourishment of the dead is one of her responsibilities, a task during which she is aided by the four Gods. The Gods distribute the food offerings with the utmost care, much to Isis her content. Therefore, she trusts these four to take care of the West.

The Duatians on the right riverbank (lower section)

The entire structure of the right riverbank has disappeared and been replaced by the bottom of the pyramid shaped mound. It is a prohibited area that is sealed off at the beginning with a gate, "He who does not open to him, who comes close to his image", and at the end with the gate "The Knife". The route through this area is still the secret way of *Imhet* that started in the Fourth Hour. This way is shrouded in secrecy. Not even the Gods, the blessed nor the dead can pass through it. Râ is the only one who has access to this route and, thus, he is the one responsible for the entire process of creation.

The bottom of the pyramid burial mound is made up of a large lake. It is an extraordinary lake since it is filled with the flames from the mouths of Isis and the serpent Wamemty. The Lake unifies the conflicting elements of fire and water. The encounter of these two very different elements is a fundamental prerequisite to empower the process of renewal. This process is bound to happen in the secret Cavern of Sokar, which is located in the middle of the Lake.

> The water of the fiery pit belongs to Osiris,
> and your refreshment to
> the Foremost of the Duat!
> (But) your blast of fire, your amber, is against the *Ba*-souls who will approach to violate Osiris.[10]
> – The Egyptian Book of Gates
>   Sixth Hour (Lake of Fire)

The Lake of Fire has life-giving as well as destructive properties. It is, therefore, a Lake of purification that serves as a Hall of Judgement. If Râ's heart is pure, the Lake of Fire will provide the Sungod with fresh water to quench his thirst. If the Sungod is a sinner, however, his heart is weighed down and his soul darkened. He will then be engulfed in the flames of this Lake that effectively consume him. The secret Cavern can be reached only if Râ is able to overcome the process of purification. Fortunately, Râ's heart is pure and his intentions are inspired by the Divine Law of *Maât*. For this reason, he remains unharmed by the burning heat of the flames and he is able to quench his thirst. He then safely continues his journey to meet Osiris.

Upon entry through the first gate, four divine heads can be found lying on the ground (No. 387 – 390). These "Heads of torches" carry the hieroglyphic sign of fire on top of their heads. They are lying while facing the opposite direction with their heads positioned towards the gate. They guard this gateway with the fire they use to incinerate the enemies.

Following the "Heads of torches" there lies a huge serpent on the ground in front of the secret Cavern of Sokar, "He with the sanctified head" (No. 391). He has two heads, a conventional serpent head with on top of it the head of a baboon. The serpent travels back and forth between the living on earth and the Great God Râ who is in the earth. In doing so, he acts like a mediator and transmits the concerns of the living to the Sungod. This enables Râ to stay in contact with those living on earth without the need for the living to enter upon the Holy of Holies and desecrate it in the process.

All attention is focused on the secret Cavern of Sokar in the depth of the Duat. The lion "Flesh (of Aker)" (No. 392) guards both sides of this hidden and sacred place. He is the representation of the earth God Aker who guards the gates in the pit of the Netherworld. In his plural form he is known as Akeru and is extremely dangerous. He protects Râ from the assaults of Apophis and he negates the symptoms caused by the poison of snakebites. Furthermore, Aker welcomes the deceased Pharaoh when the latter enters the Netherworld.

The "Akeru" lie back to back with their torsos merged into one body. They are also known as Yesterday, *"sef"* (*sf*) and Tomorrow,

Anubis holds the adze in his hand, TT 219 Nebenmaat, Deir el-Medina

"duau" (dw3w), as one lion is facing forward and the other is facing backward. One of the lions guards the gate of the East where the sun rises, while the other guards the gate of the West where the sun sets. Between the two of them lies the horizon. In this case, however, that would be the oval shaped Cavern of Sokar. Shu and Tefnut are also two lions who are the guardians of the East-West horizon that is formed between them. However, Shu and Tefnut are the guardians of the upper region while the Akeru are the guardians of the lower region. Here, in the depth of the Duat, it are the Akeru who form the horizon where East (Râ) meets West (Osiris).

In the Coffin Texts the sphere between the two lions is referred to as the "House of the Double Lion". Within here the Sacred Eye, the symbol of the Sungod, is being healed. Hence, Yesterday and Tomorrow are dependent on the mystery that is currently in the process of coming into being, in between them.

> Spell for opening a door to the soul.
> Recite: I am Thoth who brings justice, who healed the Sacred Eye
> in the House of the Double Lion.
> Open to me that I may see my corpse, for I am a living soul,
> I have come here into the Island of Fire, and there has been given to me vindication concerning what I used to do in the presence of Osiris, Bull of the West, who grants power and vindication to me.[11]
> – Coffin Texts; Spell 242

The word oval is a derivative of the Latin word *ovum* which means "egg cell". The oval is the primordial form from which all life is born. It is a symbol for the beginning of a new life, fertility, potential, birth and resurrection.

The hieroglyphic word for "oval" is *nut* (*nwt*). The word *nut* can be written with several different hieroglyphs that give it a range of different meanings. For example, it can be translated simply as "Nut", the name of the sky Goddess. It is her celestial body through which Râ travels during the night. The oval shaped Cavern of Sokar is basically her womb where the first spark of Râ's light is rekindled.

Furthermore, the word *nut* can also be translated as *adze*. As mentioned before, the *adze* is a ritualistic tool used during the ceremony of the Opening of the Mouth. Presently the earth has been consecrated and is raised in a pyramid shaped mound. Râ has arrived in the South and the regeneration of new life can now commence as it is "opened" with the *adze*. Additionally, the opening with the *adze* also symbolises the opening of the sacred earth where the oval shaped Cavern of Sokar, the hidden place, can be found. Thus, this oval is the opening or portal that grants access to the Mystery of life.

The shape of the Cavern of Sokar can also be regarded as an ellipse form. The ellipse, like the oval, has a shape similar to an elongated circle that is flattened at two opposing sites.

Therefore, it does not posses a focal point like the circle. For this reason the ellipse is not considered a perfect shape, which is also reflected in the meaning behind the word "ellipse". This word is derived from the ancient Greek word *élleipsis*, meaning "falling short" or "omission".

The ellipse, like the oval, symbolises the primordial form from which all life hatches. Once hatched, everything is still new with ongoing development, far from perfect. However, it is this imperfection that ensures the continuation of creation. Perfection would mean the ultimate goal has been reached without room for improvement. All movement, or life itself, would come to a halt and regress into a chaotic state of non-existence. Even the planets surrounding us in the universe show us the importance of the continuation of creation as they move around the sun in an elliptical orbit.

Within the oval, or ellipse shaped Cavern, Osiris can be found in his form as the hawk-headed God Sokar "Flesh of Sokar-upon-his-sand" (No. 393). He stands on top of a three-headed serpent with a tail shaped like a human head with a Divine beard. From the back of the serpent two wings emerge that Sokar-Osiris is holding with both his hands. This feathered serpent is the representation of the Great God Râ (No. 394).

The winged serpent is an ancient symbol for the enlightened consciousness and also for the primal force of life. The creeping snake on earth has transformed into a flying creature of the heavens. The wings symbolise the above while the body symbolises the below, bridging both worlds. The Sungod Râ, in his serpent shape, demonstrates this connection as he establishes a contact with Sokar-Osiris who resides deep within the earth. Sokar-Osiris emphasises this connection as he stands on top of Râ's body and holds both his wings.

The first touch between them causes an electrical charge. This is so powerful that a thundering sound can be heard within the oval. As mentioned above, the hieroglyphic word for oval is "nut". Another translation of the word *nut* is "to quiver, to tremble, to shake". This definition demonstrates exactly what is happening inside the Oval of Sokar. In the midst of the vibrations and the noise, the two eyes in the head at the extension of the tail of the feathered serpent, are starting to glow. This makes the feet of Sokar-Osiris that are wrapped in the coils of the serpent, shine. The first contact between Sokar-Osiris and the Sungod Râ rekindles the very first spark of light or consciousness and regenerates both in the process. Even so, Râ is still unable to give shape to his own light. To do this, he first needs to establish contact with Khepri. Since Khepri is still separated from Râ and unable to contact him, it is still too early for this process. Therefore, the darkness resumes its presence with the exception of the Cavern of Sokar. Inside this oval the black darkness transforms into colours. Colours are visible only through light and are the first confirmation of life. This is reflected in the feathers of the Great God Râ that are multicoloured and come to life as they spread out.

> The oval belonging to this God (Sokar)
> is illuminated
> by the two eyes of the heads
> of the Great God (the serpent).
> His two feed shine in the coils
> of the Great God
> while he protects his image.[12]

The appearance of the Sungod in his form of a primal winged serpent demonstrates that the transformation of death into life is in an early stage. Additionally, the serpent is a fiery creature and the symbol of transformation. Since Râ is in the middle of this fiery transformation, he has changed into a serpent. He has to adopt this primal form first before he can embody his form as the sun. Regeneration can be established only from a fundamental base. This is also reflected in the pyramid mound that symbolises the primordial hill. This mound rose from the waters of Nun at the beginning of creation. Râ's descent into the core of the pyramid mound underlines the fact that he has to connect with the beginning of time, *Zep Tepi*, as created by Atum. Only through this connection with his origin will the aged Râ be able to transform into new life and light.

This applies to Osiris as well who has taken the form of Sokar. He too has to return to the very first beginning and connect himself with death before he can renew himself. Death simply is the portal from which new life can arise.

The transformation of death into life is a secret, hidden by the Unified Darkness of the Land of Sokar. The oval is illuminated only on the inside, out of the view of everyone. The hieroglyphic word *hedj* (ḥḏ), as used in the text about the oval, stands for "illuminate". *Hedj* has numerous homonyms including "bright, set forth at dawn, white". A play on this word is *hedji* (ḥḏi) which has several meanings, among which is "eclipse". The oval of Sokar functions as a protective layer in the midst of the darkness to allow the first spark to ignite within. This mystery is reflected in nature in the form of the solar eclipse. During the solar eclipse the moon is positioned between the sun and the earth, effectively blocking out the light of the sun. From earth these two celestial bodies seem to become a single entity. The only light still visible is a halo around the contour of the united body that gives it a winged appearance. Here too, Râ, as the sun, lines up with Osiris, the moon, resulting in an eclipse between both heavenly bodies. Within the ensuing complete darkness, the mystery takes place. The enigma that cannot be expressed in words. Nobody knows what is happening between these two bodies. Here, in the Fifth Hour, the eclipse commences its first phase. However, the eclipse is not completed until the end of the Sixth Hour.

As mentioned before, next to the right side of the Cavern of Sokar lies a serpent on the ground "Wamemty" (No. 395) with an *Ankh* beneath its head. He too is a guardian of the secret Cavern and fills this area, like Isis, with a blast of fire. Wamemty is one of the names of Apophis. He is, therefore, a very powerful and dangerous serpent. In his form of Wamemty, however, he actually is a protector of the process of rejuvenation. This, once again, shows that a force has different aspects that can be used for good as well as evil.

In front of Wamemty are four crouching Gods. The first two Gods gaze in the opposite direction whereas the last two are looking forward. They are the protectors of the four different crowns of Râ that they are holding on their knees. Each of these crowns is worn by the Sungod Râ and symbolises a different aspect of his power. Displaying the crowns confirms the growing renewed power of Râ.

(No. 396) is the guardian of the
White Crown of Upper Egypt.
(No. 397) is the guardian of the
Red Crown of Lower Egypt.
(No. 398) is the guardian of the Crown shaped like the head of a flat-horned ram.
(No. 399) is the guardian of the
Double Feathers Crown.

The hour concludes with the serpent who stands upraised on his tail, "Living God" (No. 400). He is the guardian of the final gate, "The Knife", and decides when the door is opened. On the ground in front of him lies a five-pointed star. The star refers to the planet Venus. Venus is an extremely bright planet, also known as the Morningstar. The hieroglyphic word for Morningstar is *Netjer duau* (*nṯr dw3w*) which means "Divine morning or Divine dawn". This radiating "star" appears on the Eastern horizon just before the sun rises. Horus is also known as the Morningstar for he, like Khepri, is the representation of the newborn sun in the morning.

> O Morning Star, Horus of the Netherworld, divine Falcon,
> *w3d3d* bird whom the sky bore [...] [13]
> – Pyramid Texts; Utterance 519

The light of the Morningstar, in the early still dark hours of the morning, heralds the rise of the sun, or the Divine Dawn. The appearance of this star at the end of the Fifth Hour proves that the light of Râ is on the verge of emerging.

The manifestation of the Fifth Hour in daily life

After the intense journey of the previous hour through the desert in the Land of Sokar, you feel exhausted and parched. It feels like all life has slipped away from you, leaving nothing but a suffocating emptiness behind. The zigzag paths have cut away all the falsehoods from you, taking away everything you thought you knew about yourself. You want nothing more but to fill up the dry emptiness with new life as you yearn for water. Whether you may quench your thirst depends on whether you are prepared to descend further into the profound depth.

This final descent pushes you to the breaking point until you hit rock bottom. All the way deep down is where you find the major turnaround. Here you finally find firm ground beneath your feet that provides for the foundation upon which your new Self will stand. Even though everything may still seem far away, you are actually really close to your ultimate goal.

However, as long as you have not yet reached the steady ground, things still feel shaky. Everything is new and unknown. Doubts, insecurities and indecisiveness are all part of the change. These aspects can be perceived as unpleasant or awkward. However, they actually are very meaningful. They keep you on your toes, forcing you every time to regard yourself in life from different angles. Nothing is simply true or should be taken for granted. Everything deserves a thorough examination. These careful self-explorations surprise you with insights you would otherwise have overlooked. It widens your perspective and raises your awareness of the life surrounding you and your place in it all. This provides you with a renewed sense of self and with the determination to make your inner conflict disappear.

This inner division is reflected in the duality of this hour. The Goddess of the West, "She who is (in) the water of rejuvenation" (No. 329), can be found in front of the upper section on the left riverbank. She is the one providing nourishment and she protects life itself. On the opposing side of the riverbank stands the Goddess "The Demolishing One, who cuts the damned to pieces" (No. 356) who is exactly the opposite since she is the destroyer of life. These two contrasting aspects are also emphasised through the Gods who stand in between them on the left and right side. In the middle section, the Sacred River, Râ is being hauled by seven male Gods and seven female Goddesses. This emphasises the need for two opposing forces to continue the journey. The lower section also consists of contradictions. There is the Lake of Fire, where the elements of water and fire come together. The two bodies of Akeru, Yesterday and Tomorrow, that create an oval shape in between them. And finally, the four crown bearers at the end of the section. Two of them look backward while the other two look forward.

The opposite forces, as found in this hour, push the pyramid up. This provides for the enclosure and foundation for new life. Without the joining of opposing forces, like positive and negative, life and death, male and female, black and white and so on, creating a new life is simply impossible. The Fifth Hour demonstrates this beautifully and offers a visual handle. Therefore, when you feel like the inner turmoil makes you lose heart, look at the image of the Fifth Hour.

It shows you the process of creation at a glance. This does not only apply to the macrocosm, the universe, but to the microcosm, your own life, as well. This image offers clarity and trust. It reminds you that it are precisely the contradictions that trigger you to create a new vision.

During this final descent, further down into the darkness, you are overwhelmed by the feeling of dying. The entire journey up until this point suddenly seems like an illusion as there is not a single sign of life. Everything is death, dark and forsaken in this Dark Night of the soul. You no longer know what route to take and wonder if you are lost. This utter despair eliminates the last shred of your life as you surrender to the feeling of dying. This surrender is the only solution for there is no turning back. All of your mental garbage, that blocked the way, has been cleared. Hence, there is nothing left to hold on to. It is useless to try and find acknowledgement outside of yourself as you are now alone with your Self. You have to give up the fight and drop to your knees in front of your inner Sungod.

That is the moment where you finally touch the ground and allow the miracle to take place. You have extended your hand to your inner Sungod, the Higher Self, as you acknowledge that he is the only one you can turn to. He, in turn, has waited for this moment and will now make contact with you at this critical time. This initial genuine touch shakes your inner world. The tension in this area is very strong, which is why the Powerself makes an appearance. You feel this fiery cobra power within yourself.

> A noise is heard from this oval,
> after this Great God has passed by them,
> like the thundering sound of the sky
> in a storm.[14]

If you could, you would spread your wings. However, at the same time, you are aware of the vulnerability and fragility of this initial contact. It is still lacking in solidity and unable to take shape in your daily life. It is the preliminary phase that aligns you with the two different layers of the consciousness, the Higher Self and the Powerself. The resulting friction between these layers ignites the very first spark. Although, it is just a pinprick of light surrounded by darkness, it is the first real sign of life from the depth of your inner world.

Your first meeting with the Powerself and the Higher Self attracts the attention of the Divine Spark. However, he does not yet join these layers of the consciousness. The Divine Spark pulls the strings from the side and adjusts the direction when needed. He is not yet able to form a connection with you through the Higher Self. First of all the connection between you, the Higher Self and the Powerself needs to stabilise as a true unity.

Nonetheless, what is happening here is a real highlight. All attention is focused on this moment. This is reflected by the two lions (No. 392) who guard the Oval of Sokar. In between

"Yesterday" and "Tomorrow" the miracle is conducted that ignites the initial spark of light and life. The past and the present are bridged with, in between, the Present Moment where the new life sprouts. Time, past and future, are an illusion for all power lies within the Present Moment.

Both of the lions point out that the contact with the Higher Self is always in the present time. If you get lost in the make-believe world of yesterday and tomorrow, you lose your connection with your inner Sungod as well as the power to substantiate your potential in your life. It is all about balancing in the middle of the Present Moment, which transcends time. That is the only truth in your life.

> I come today from the House
> of the Double Lion,
> I have come forth from it to the
> House of Isis,
> to the secret mysteries,
> I have been conducted
> to her hidden secrets,
> for she caused me to see the birth
> of the Great God.[15]
> – Coffin Texts; Spell 312

The inner Sungod is seen here as the winged serpent. His winged form reminds you that despite your connection with earth, your consciousness is meant to rise above it all. This gives you a much needed bird's-eye view and helps you understand the events in your life without getting entangled. As long as you are connected to your inner Sungod, he can provide you with this broad perspective in the Present Moment. Furthermore the primal form of the Sungod, as a winged serpent, emphasises that this connection is the origin and the essence of your being.

Everything that happens here is a great secret that needs to stay hidden from everyday life. You are not able to express the events in words. However, this is unnecessary for it is something between you and your inner Sungod within your inner Holy of Holies. Guard this hidden area well and draw a line between the Sacred and the profane.

The very first spark attracts darkness. It is, therefore, of the utmost importance to protect this spark of life in your inner sanctum with the power of the eight butchers (No. 348 – 355) and the demolishing Goddess (No. 356). Keep the doors closed from the enemies who are set out to steal and extinguish this tiny little spark of light and life. The name of the door at the left side of the secret area in the lower section also points this out, "He who does not open to him, who comes close to his image". The name of the door "The Knife" at the right side stresses the need for a razor-sharp discernment to protect the very first indication of life and light.

This hour takes you right to your core, your origin. In the end it grants you the first sign of light after all the battles and darkness you have encountered on your way up until this point. You should be aware that this is a great gift presented to you. However, whether you accept or deny the offer depends on your own ability. It is all about your own attitude with respect to yourself. Is your heart clear of all the falsehoods concerning yourself? Are you truly capable of recognising your true and original core? After all, it takes a lot of courage to be confronted with your own light and your own power. Do you have the heart to acknowledge this inner sun and inner fiery cobra power inside of you? Only once you rise to the challenge, will you be able to quench your thirst. The purification process you have gone through has then been completed at the Present Moment. If you are unable to face the challenge due to the presence of unsolved blockades within yourself, you are required to venture through the cleansing fires of the Lake of Fire ones more.

THE SIXTH HOUR
"Deep Waters, Lady of the Duatians"

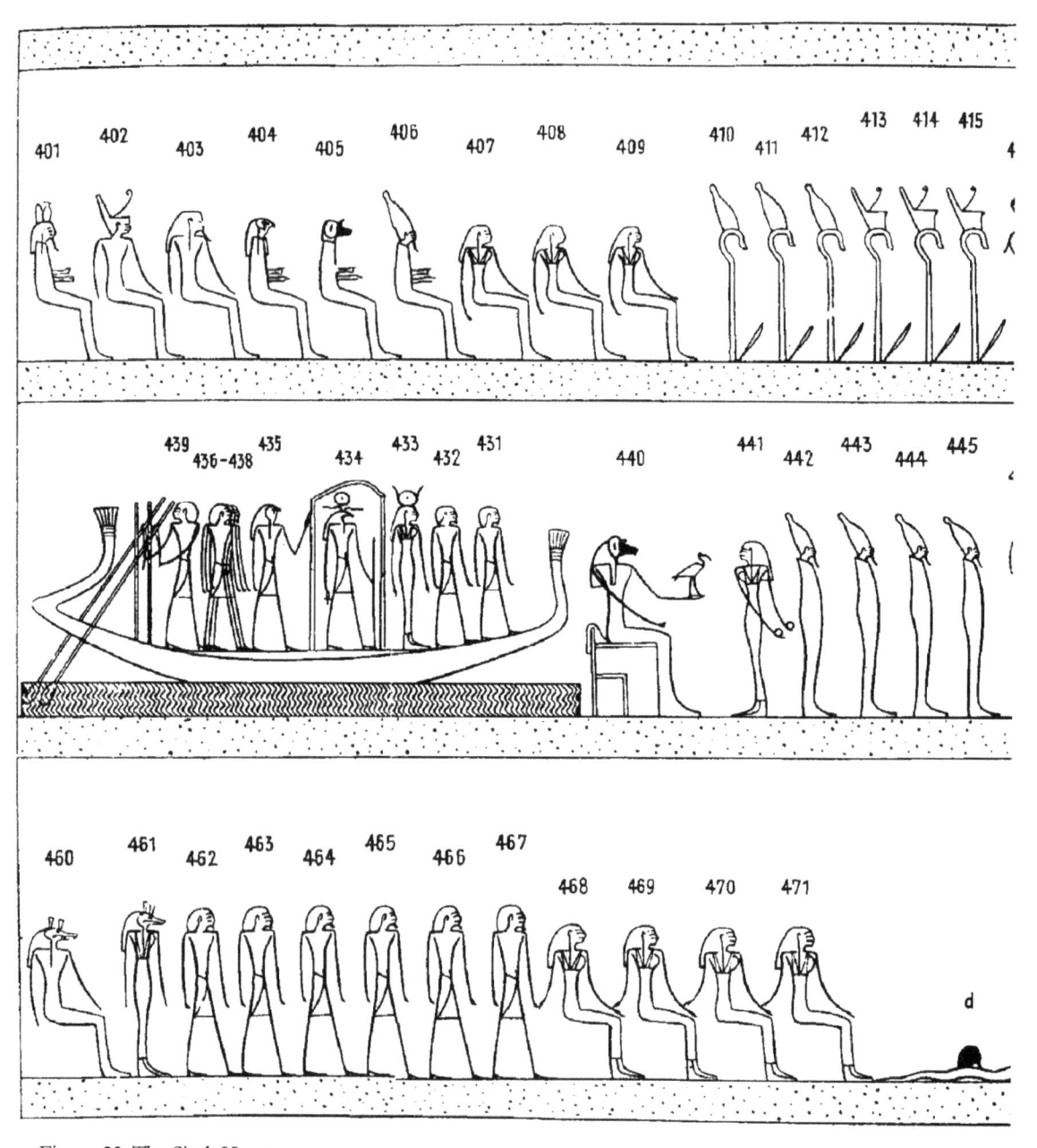

Figure 23: The Sixth Hour

The Gate: "With sharp knives"
The Hour Goddess: "Arrival who gives the right (way)"
"True Sanctuary"
The Guardian: "Nun"

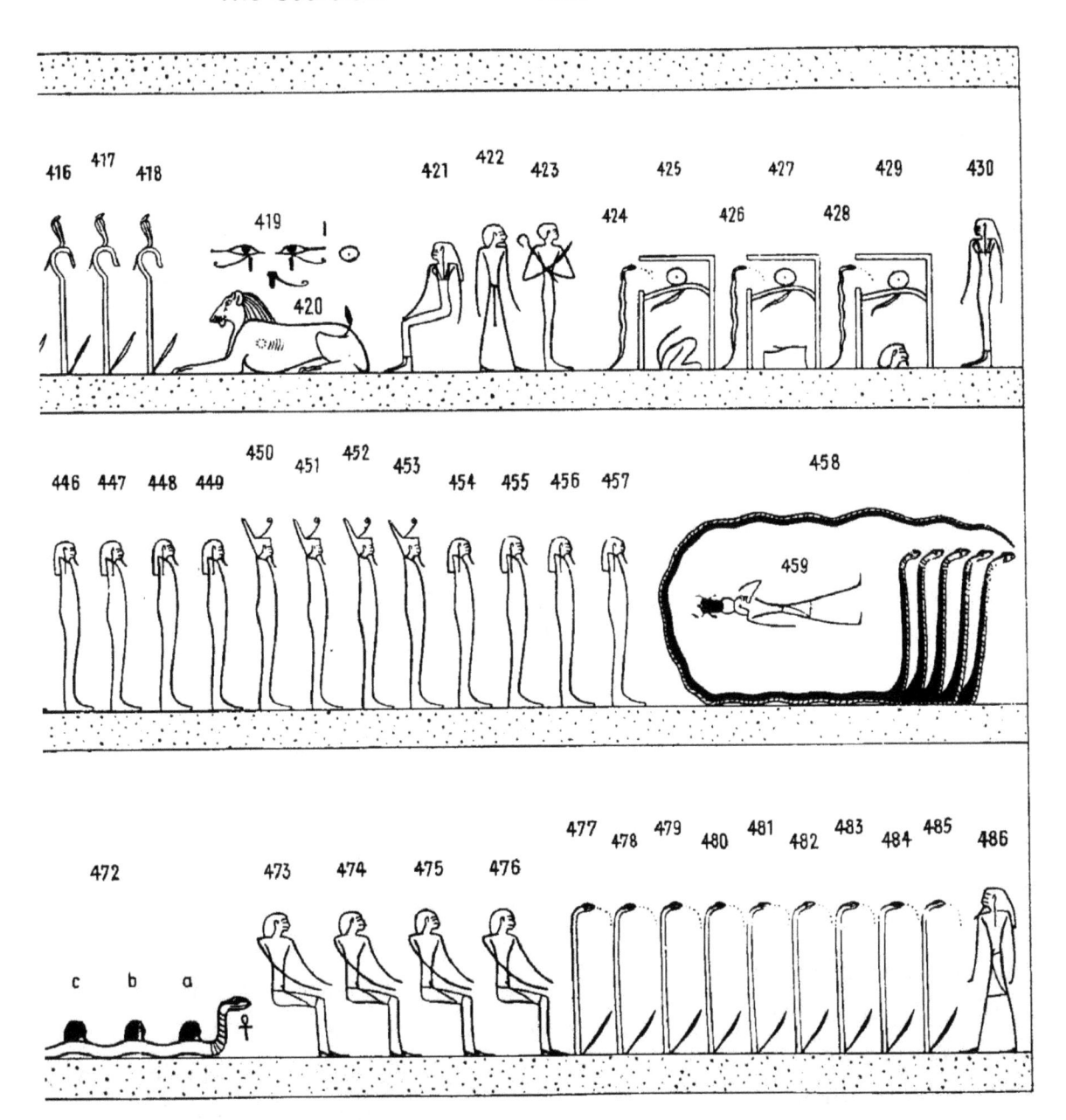

Introduction

Pausing by the person of this Great God in the "Deep Waters, Lady of the Duatians".
This God commands that these Gods take possession
of their Divine offerings at this place.
He proceeds in this [place], equipped with his barque.
And he assigns them their fields for their offerings.
He grants them water from their waterway, when he passes (through) the Duat day after day.
The name of the Gate of this place is "With sharp Knives."
The name of the Hour of the night which guides this Great God is "Arrival who gives the right (way)".
The secret way of the West,
on the water of which this Great God proceeds in his barque,
to care for the needs of those of the Duat.
Pronounced by their names,
known in their bodies,
engraved by their forms are their hours,
mysterious in their essence,
without this secret image of the Duat being known by any human being.
This image is made in paint like this
in the secrecy of the Duat,
on the Southern side
of the Hidden Chamber.

He who knows it will partake of
the offerings in the Duat.
He will be satisfied with the offerings
to the Gods
who are in the following of Osiris.
All he wishes will be offered to him
in the earth.[1]

The Sun barque of Râ has transformed from the serpent shape into its usual form. It is no longer required to haul the barque since the water has returned. It can once again sail on its own. We are still navigating in the region of the South and the name of this hour is "Deep Waters, Lady of the Duatians". The Lady mentioned here is not a reference to a female person. The Lady of the Duatians is the name of the extremely deep water that dominates the present landscape. This landscape is formed by an abyss filled with the primeval waters of Nun. Therefore, this area is no longer called *Imhet*, as were the Fourth and the Fifth Hour, for this region is not filled with sand anymore. The drought and barrenness of the previous two hours has changed into abundance and fertility. Life has returned and the crops are growing along the sides of the Sacred River.

The Sungod Râ gifts all of these crops to the Duatians living here. The Sungod also provides them with water. The Duatians, in turn, take possession of their fields to grow the crops and nourish themselves with the harvest. They share a portion of the yield with Râ, allowing him to benefit from the richness of food.

It has become midnight and Râ is sailing along these fields filled with lush vegetation. This is the peak, or actually more accurately, the deepest point of the night that is shrouded in total darkness. The black darkness is necessary to form a protective enclosure. Since every small ray of light, from outside, will disrupt the ongoing transformation. The hour has come where the Sacred union between Râ and Osiris is going to be realised. Though Râ and Osiris have already met in the Fifth Hour, they are still separate entities. In the present hour the transformation continues as they are about to form a true unity where they share a single body. Khepri is also joining them, though he is not a part of the entity Râ and Osiris are to form.

This process of rejuvenation takes place within the coils of the five-headed serpent "Many-faced". He has replaced the Cavern of Sokar to provide for a secret location. Once again, what is really happening is a great mystery. It is the deepest secret since the beginning of time and hidden so well that the ignorant can only speculate about the actual occurrence. No words can describe the event taking place here. For this reason there is a stillness filled with respect and wonderment.

The mystery, upon which the entire creation depends, has to be well guarded. Therefore, the hour commences with the dangerous gate "With Sharp knives" that does not just simply let you pass into the midnight hour. However, the gate is not the only one with sharp knives. You can see knives on both sides of the Sacred River. Another protection is provided by the royal Ancestors. They stand guard in front of the serpent "Many-faced", ready to destroy the enemies of Râ.

Furthermore, the Hour Goddess herself is a powerful guard as well. Under her guidance Râ is escorted to the core of this hour. The name of the beautiful Goddess is "Arrival who gives the right way" (*mspryt rdyt mȝʿw*). The hieroglyphic word *mesperyt* (*mspryt*) can also be translated as "True Sanctuary". The entire voyage revolves around this sanctuary, "the Holy of Holies", and the Goddess is the one who knows the way.

The Duatians on the left riverbank (upper section)

The left riverbank starts with nine Deities who can be seen in a half upraised position without actually sitting on something (No. 401 – 409). This position refers to the process of regeneration that is now halfway completed. Several Gods in this hour confirm this as they too adopt the half upraised pose.

The first three Gods are;

(No. 401) "Offerer who presides over the Duat". The God wears the symbols for bread and beer on top of his head. These two foods are part of the offerings that are usually given to the Gods. (No. 402) "Isis of *Imhet*". Isis is wearing the Red Crown of Lower Egypt on her head. As mentioned before the word *Imhet* is the name of the special area in the Duat, formed by the Fourth and Fifth Hour. During the Fifth Hour, Isis played an important part in the process of rejuvenation as the Great Mother. In the current hour, she is once again present to continue her protective role.

(No. 403) "Osiris, favourite of the Gods". Osiris himself is present here dressed in normal garments without the White Crown of Upper Egypt on his head. With the assistance of the half upraised Deities he partakes in his own renewal.

The next four Deities are in charge of the fields where the crops are grown that are used for the offerings.

(No. 404) "Horus who presides over his field", Horus is in his mummified form.
(No. 405) "Baboon belonging to his field", a mummy with the head of a baboon.
(No. 406) "Renewed-of-heart presiding over his field", a God who is wearing the White Crown of Upper Egypt. Presumably, he is another form of the God Osiris.
(No. 407) "She of the land-plots", a Goddess without attributes.

The final two Goddesses symbolise the aspects that result from the offerings. Both are without attributes.

(No. 408) "She who unifies"
(No. 409) "She who satisfies the Gods"

Râ addresses the nine Gods and Goddesses as the Seated Ones who are in the Duat. They are the ones who are in charge of the offerings, which they collect in their baskets. Râ too grants them offerings and fields to allow them to provide for all their needs. It is paramount to keep these Deities satisfied for they have been assigned with the significant task to keep Osiris safe from those wishing to oppress and rob him. The offerings presented to the Deities keep them powerful and mighty. This enables them to rise to the challenge and be masters of arms with straight legs. Now they are ready to wield their sceptres to protect Osiris. However, the offerings are not meant for these Gods and Goddesses alone. Râ orders them to give offerings to the other Duatians living here as well. These oblations come into existence the moment the Sungod utters the Divine Words. Clearly, the invisible force of Magic is at work here. These offerings can be created only through this magical power that is generated through the intention with which the Sungod utters the words.

Following are nine *Heka*-sceptres, the symbols of power and rulership. Each sceptre has a knife fixed to the lower end.

The first three are surmounted by White Crowns.

(No. 410) "Shepherd's crook"
(No. 411) "Dew of the earth"
(No. 412) "*Heka*-sceptre of the Duat

The next three are surmounted by Red Crowns.

(No. 413) "*Maât* of the Gods"
(No. 414) "Nurse of the Duatians"
(No. 415) "Waterway of Tatenen"

The last three are surmounted by Uraei.

(No. 416) "She who protects the Gods"
(No. 417) "She who belongs to the heads of the Gods"
(No. 418) "She who belongs to the fields of the Duatians"

The number nine is a reference to a great number. Therefore, these nine sceptres indicate there is a lot of power and authority within this hour. They all belong to the Kings of Upper and Lower Egypt who had at one point reigned the earth and are now residing in the Duat as the blessed dead. They are still wearing their crowns and partake in the offerings. While on earth, each of these Kings obliged the Divine Law of *Maât*. Inside the Duat they enforce this Law as well and protect it with the power of their sceptres. The knives fixed at the lower end of the sceptres indicate that the truth can be found on the cutting edge. They guard Truth and Justice and drive off all the enemies of Râ. As true Kings they still possess tremendous power and support the continuation of creation with all their attributes.

According to the text, the sceptres were also used as staffs, or perches, for the *Ba*-souls of these Kings to land on. As a result, the souls of the Kings are able to connect themselves with the power what these sceptres represent. This provides these souls with a full protection from destructive powers, as these powers now have no control over them. Seth symbolises this force of destruction. One of his names is "He who loves robbery" and he is known as the Robber. He is the one who took away the life of Osiris and dismembered him. He robbed Osiris of all his body parts and scattered them all over Egypt. However, even Seth himself is very much aware of the mighty power of these Kings. He is wary of their lordship and authority and therefore always on his guard.

> Their *Ba*-souls stand in the Duat
> upon their *Heka*-sceptres,
> their (lower) ends are knives.
> The Robber (Seth) is well aware of them.[2]

In the opposite direction lies a lion on the ground "The Bull with roaring voice" (No. 420) (*k3 hmhmt*). This male animal is the King of the animals and symbolises power and kingship. The hieroglyphic word *ka (k3)* means "bull", but can also be translated as "of great vitality, essence of a being, will (of the King) or kingship". The hieroglyphic word *hemhemet (hmhmt)* means "war-shout (of the King)". Thus, the lion represents the mightiness of the Pharaoh as he demonstrates his dominion over the opposite forces.

Above the lion a pair of eyes is visible that

are called "Image of Râ" (No. 419). These two eyes are the Divine Eyes of the Sungod Râ that symbolise the fact that his light is rekindled. This is the prelude for the event that will unfold within the oval shaped body of the serpent "Many-faced" (No. 458). During the Fourth Hour, only the damaged Eye of Râ (No. 306) could be seen while Thoth and Sokar were taking care of it. Currently, in the Sixth Hour, aside from the damaged Eye, another eye has made its appearance. This second Eye is the representation of wholeness and unification. This is the confirmation that the healing of the damaged Eye, or in other words the light of Râ, has begun. However, the healing process is far from complete, which is indicated by a third Eye that has been dismembered into three parts.

The two Divine Eyes of Râ are protected and supported by the lion lying underneath them. The lion embodies the virile life force that can be viewed in various ways. For example, the lion could be the creator God Atum since one of his appearances is a lion. Atum is the creative primal force from which life, at the beginning of time, *Zep Tepi*, emerged. The primary creation of Atum was the first awakening of the consciousness, or the light. The daily cycle of Râ builds upon the foundation of the first awakening and continuous to develop it even further.

The lion is also related to the God of war and hunting, In-hert (*in(i)-ḥrt*) or Onuris, who is occasionally depicted with the head of a lion. He is a very old God from the Old Kingdom and was the local God of the city Thinis near Abydos. It is said that Thinis was the place where the first Pharaohs reigned after Upper and Lower Egypt were united. In-hert was known for his vast amount of power and strength, which was why he was called "Bull of Thinis". Additionally, he also possessed the title of "Son of Râ" and protected the Sungod from enemies. In one of the myths he joined the voyage on the Sun barque to ensure Râ's biggest and darkest opponent, Apophis, was defeated. Eventually In-hert's cult was overthrown by the God Osiris in his form as Khenty-Imentyu. During the Fourth Hour, Onuris (No. 314) was depicted in human form while standing in the desert Land of Sokar. As mentioned, In-hert "Who brings back the face or sight" brought the damaged eye or light back to Râ. In the present hour, the stabilising Vital Life Force, which In-hert embodies, ensures that the light will be restored and that the cosmic order, or *Maât*, eventually returns to a renewed equilibrium.

However, the potent life force that the "Bull with roaring voice" embodies, also symbolises Osiris who is referred to as "Bull of the Duat" himself. Although Osiris was actually seen as a bull and not as a lion per se, the important thing is the symbolical power that the lion, King of the animals, represents. It is Osiris's Vital Life Force, or his *Ka*, that Râ needs to provide for the return of Râ's light and to make it shine to its full potential. As mentioned before, the old Kings of Egypt (No. 410 – 418) are standing in front of the lion in the shape of *Heka*-sceptres. Although they might be the Great Kings, it is Osiris who rules over them. Osiris, like the lion, is the King of Kings here in the Duat.

The Vital Life Force is a powerful primal force, almost as raw and savage as the lion. This force requires to be channelled before it can be put to good use. The Divine Eyes of Râ are necessary to achieve this, to connect the high-powered Vital Life Force with the heightened insight. On the other hand, it is exactly the Vital Life Force that facilitates the opening of the Eyes of the consciousness. It allows for the light to reappear, which attests to the return of the enlightened consciousness. This is reflected in the Sungod Râ as his strength, and thus his light, continuous to grow.

The lion and the Eyes show that the first meeting between Râ and Osiris, in the Fifth Hour, is continued here. Osiris no longer has the appearance of Sokar-upon-his-sand. He has come back to life as a roaring lion radiating power. Râ, in turn, has left his primordial form as the winged serpent and now embodies the Eyes of the heightened consciousness that open themselves here. In their renewed powerful form Osiris and Râ complement each other without forming a true unit at this point.

Behind the lion sits a Goddess in a half

The lion with the two Eyes of Râ above him and the Goddess Isis-Tait sits behind him,
KV 9 Ramses V and VI

upraised posture, "Isis-Tait" (No. 421). The Goddess Tait is a form of the Goddess Neith. However, she is also associated with Isis and Nephthys with regard to their shared funerary tasks. She is present here in her Isis form to protect the light or consciousness during its emergence. She can be found directly behind the lion with the Eyes and safeguards the process of the regeneration of Râ and Osiris. However, this time she offers her protection in a different way as demonstrated by her name.

The meaning of the hieroglyphic word *tait* (*t3yt*) is "shroud". The shroud is a lengthy cloth used to wrap a dead person for the burial. In Ancient Egypt the shroud consisted of the wrappings of the mummy. The shroud or wrappings, like the coffin, were necessary to protect the body from decay and disintegration. The importance of these protective layers are emphasised in the Coffin Texts spell 345;

> Spell for vindication
> in the presence of Thoth,
> the chiefest of the Gods,
> (and for) not taking away a man's shroud
> from him
> or a man's coffin from him
> in the realm of the dead.
> […] Ho N! Anubis the embalmer
> will enwrap you
> with wrappings from the hand of Tait.[3]

Tait is the Goddesses of weaving, a skill she uses to weave the shroud for the deceased. In doing so, she provides the mummy with the protective wrappings to bind all the body parts together. Isis-Tait currently uses this protective shroud to cover the Eyes and the lion to bring, or weave, them together. Like this, she shrouds and conceals the wonder of unity and wholeness that is happening between the *Ba*–soul of Râ and the *Ka*-force of Osiris. This mystery needs a cover and darkness, especially as it takes place outside of a protected place

> Ho N! You are clad in the Eye of Horus
> which belongs to your body.
> Ho! I have given it to you,
> it having appeared
> and having been seen on your flesh
> and having been joined to your flesh
> in this its name of "Red Linen".
> You are clad in it in this its name of "Cloth".
> You are great in it in this its name of "Great One".
> Your face is bright by means of it in this its name of "Bright One".
> It is joined to your flesh in this its name of "Red Linen".
> Here comes Tait. Here comes Taitet.
> Her comes the Eye of Horus
> which issued from the earth.
> Here comes the netting of Isis.
> Here comes the cloth of Nephthys.
> Here comes the plaiting of Neith.
> Here comes the woven stuff of the two Sisterly Companions.
> Here comes what Ptah has worked in.

Here comes what Horus gave to his father Osiris to clothe him in it.
Ho N! Provide yourself with the Eye of Horus which belongs to your body. Provide yourself with
the woven Eye of Horus.[4]
– Coffin Texts; Spell 608

Behind Isis-Tait are two Deities. The first God is naked and represents the new born light, "Shining One" (No. 422). His nudity emphasises the purity and vulnerability of the newborn light. All of the cloaking layers have disappeared allowing for his true soul to be seen. However, Râ points out to this God that the shining light still needs to be protected and hidden.

The other Deity "She whom the Gods respect" (No. 423) looks like a male God. However the verb used in the name of the Deity has a feminine ending. Consequently, this indicates the Deity is female nonetheless. She is mummified and holds a Crook and a knife crossed over her chest. Unlike the God "Shining One" this Deity does protect the Divine light well as she uses her bandages and the attributes in her hands.

In front of these two Deities are three burial chests with an upraised serpent before each of them. Every chest contains a solar disk and a knife in the upper compartment and a mysterious image at the bottom. These images held in the chests are the following;

(No. 425) "Tomb which Seth adores" contains the hind part of a lion.
(No. 427) "Tomb of the towing of Kher-âha" contains the wing of a scarab.
(No. 429) "Tomb that unites Horus" contains a human head.

The middle tomb is called "Tomb of the towing of Kher-âha ($ḥr.y$-$^cḥ3$)". Kher-âha (old Cairo) was an ancient town situated to the south of modern Cairo. It marked the borderland between the Delta of Lower Egypt and the Nile Valley of Upper Egypt. Kher-âha means "The battlefield" and was the location of the battle that was fought to eventually unite the Two Lands to form the renewed united Egypt. Hence, Kher-âha was an important area where wars were fought. According to the myth of Osiris, the battle between Horus and Seth to compete over the kingship, was fought in this area. Furthermore, the enemies of Osiris were also defeated here.

> Get back, great Black One!
> Crawl away into $ḥr$-$^cḥ3$,
> into that place where they (Horus and Seth) crawled! [5]
> – Pyramid Texts; Utterance 550

The patron God of Kher-âha was the God Atum with at his side the Gods of the Great Ennead who he had created himself. Thus, Kher-âha was a region where opposites were joined together to create a new beginning.

> Such is Osiris, King of Gods,
> great power of heaven,

ruler of the living, King of those beyond! Whom thousands bless in Kher-âha, whom mankind extols in Õn.[6]

– A section of a hymn to Osiris

Kher-âha was the cult centre for the worship of the solar corpse of the Sungod. However, it was also the cult centre of the God Sepa or Sep. Sepa was depicted in the shape of a centipede and was believed to be a protector of the Dead. He was identified with Osiris as Sepa-Osiris and sometimes referred to as the "body of the divine Osiris". The corpse of Sepa-Osiris was buried in a tomb at Kher-âha that was known as the "House of Sepa".[7] The "Tomb of the towing of Kher-âha" could be a reference to this tomb.

These three burial chests each contain a solar disk underneath their covers. As we know, it is Osiris who embodies the corpse of the Sungod. Therefore, the chests are the representation of the threefold burial of the solar corpse, which is the dismembered Osiris.

As the genuine renewal is vastly approaching, everything needs to perish and decompose first before Râ can embody the new light. Just like the war that is needed to be fought first to obliterate the old order and allow for the Two Lands to become united. Horus and Seth needed to fight and wound each other first as well before the rightful heir to the throne could take his place as the new ruler.

It is unsurprising that the "Tomb of the towing of Kher-âha" is located exactly between

The three burial chests at the end of the left riverbank, KV 9 Ramses V and VI

the "Tomb which Seth adores" and the "Tomb that unites Horus". Here too it forms a conciliatory border area between the opposite forces, Horus and Seth. From here the new life and light, the healed Osiris and the scarab Khepri, will be resurrected and born respectively.

The number of tombs depicted here has a symbolic meaning for the number three refers to plurality. This emphasises that the process to dismantle and decompose the old is very complex. There are also three serpents aiding to reinforce this process. Serpents are guardians of temples and sacred locations. Here, they are the guardians of the images lying at the bottom of the chests. They rise to stand upraised on their tails to display their imposing posture as they situate themselves in front of the entrance located at the top of the chests. Through the opening they spit fire inside, which symbolises their poison. The poison of a snake leaves a burning sensation that can be utilised to cure or to kill. Administering certain amounts of this poison, however, has the ability to induce an expansion of consciousness. Therefore, these serpents ensure the transformed fires are stirred up high to eliminate the old consciousness and to make way for the healing process and expansion of the new consciousness. The names of these three serpents are;

(No. 424) "Whose eye spits fire"
(No. 426) "Whose tongue spits fire"
(No. 428) "He with high flame"

Directly following the chests, while facing the opposite direction, stands the Goddess "Adoratress belonging to the beginning of the tombs" (No. 430). She supports and ensures that the final piece of the old consciousness of Râ perishes. Her adoration grants Râ the strength needed for this last part of his dying process. Fortunately, this intense process runs smoothly and successfully. According the text it is Râ himself who illuminates the darkness. This means the healing of the Sungod is progressing as he is able to shine again. Also the corpse, which is Osiris, is no longer dismembered since the lost parts are united again.

> Words spoken by this Great God
> in the vicinity of this mysterious image
> of the Duat:
> Illuminated is the darkness in the earth!
> The flesh roars with joy
> and the head speaks,
> after he has united his members.[8]

The Ancient Egyptians believed death to be a process of disintegration and isolation. Life, on the other hand, was seen as a connection, wholeness and unity. They considered the decomposition of life to be reflected in the dying body. The moment when death takes over, the heart stops pumping. Blood, that used to connect all body parts during life, flows through the veins no longer. The body is no unit anymore and falls apart symbolically. Hence, death was always considered to be a violent happening, even if someone passed in a peaceful manner.[9]

During the early days, dismemberment was taken literally as there have been bodies found in prehistoric graves that were chopped into pieces. The heads had been cut off with the hands, feet and legs laid in front of them.[10] Upon later times, this practice disappeared and the body was kept intact after death.

> To say: O, O, raise thyself up, N.;
> Receive thy head, unite thy bones to thee, collect thy limbs,
> shake the earth (dust of the earth)
> from thy flesh.[11]
> – Pyramid Texts, Spell 373

The tearing of the limbs can be found in the myth of Osiris in which Seth cuts the body of his brother Osiris in fourteen pieces. These body parts were later collected by Isis and Nephthys. Using the Wisdom of Thoth and the healing powers of Anubis, the body was then united and healed. Osiris had been renewed and resurrected. Thus, the "uniting" and "collecting" of body members refers to the renewal of life. This was also the theme during the annual celebration in Abydos in the honour of Osiris. According to myth, the head of Osiris was buried in Abydos. During a ceremony, the priests would symbolically reconstruct the body through the raising of the backbone, or *Djed*, and attach the head to it. In this manner Osiris had become whole again and was resurrected from the supine position of death.

Furthermore, the head symbolised the solar disk. It was, therefore, regarded as the solar principle or the *Ba*-soul of a person. The body symbolised the corpse of Osiris and was the representation of the *Ka* or the Vital Life Force. To be more specific, the *Ka* was connected to the body as its double. When a person died, the *Ba* and the *Ka* were both needed for the person to be able to transform into an *Akh*, a blessed soul. When one of these two principles was missing it was impossible to rise from death in the Afterlife. If the head was cut off anyway, it was of vital importance that it remained with the body of the deceased. Without a head the person would simply cease to exist in life as well as in the Afterlife. There are several spells used to protect a person from beheading.

> Not taking a man's head from him.
> I am a Great One, the son of a Great One;
> I am He of the *nsr*-shrine,
> son of Him of the *nsr*-shrine,
> to whom was given his head after it had been cut off.
> His head was not taken from him
> after he was decapitated,
> and my head shall not be taken from me after it has been cut off.[12]
> – Coffin texts; Spell 390

The Duatians of the Sacred River (middle section)

At the beginning of the Sacred River the Sun barque has assumed its usual shape as it sails through the waters of Nun. All crewmembers are present. The Guide of the Barque is at the helm, steering the Sun barque through the waters on the way to the corpse of Osiris.

(No. 431) "Wepwawet"
(No. 432) "Sia"
(No. 433) "Nebet wia"
(No. 434) "Iuf"
(No. 435) "Heru Hekenu"
(No. 436) "Ka Maât"
(No. 437) "Nehes"
(No. 438) "Hu"
(No. 439) "Kherep wia"

The Sungod Râ is standing inside his shrine, wearing the solar disk with the ram horns on top of his head. He holds the Serpent-sceptre in one hand and the *Ankh* in the other. It would seem like the head of the staff is missing in the sketch as well as on the original image of the Sixth Hour. However, this part of the wall has been damaged since the serpent staff is most definitely still intact.

In front of the barque sits Thoth in his baboon-headed form on a throne, "Djehuty who is in front of the "Lady of the Duatians"" (No. 440). As mentioned, the Lady of the Duatians is the name of the abyss that forms the landscape of this Hour. This abyss is filled with the primeval waters of the Nun. In the depth of these waters, the union of Râ and Osiris will be realised. Thoth is sitting in front of these deep waters. He is the God of Divine Wisdom and guards this process of renewal.

Thoth holds an ibis in his uplifted hand that he offers to the Goddess "She who hides her images" (No. 441) in front of him. She, in turn, hides two eyes behind her back. This entire scene is an important part of the Sixth Hour. As Thoth sits on his throne directly in front of the Sun barque, he effectively blocks the way. Râ is unable to continue his voyage as he needs to wait for Thoth to clear the way.

The ibis, which Thoth shows to the Goddess, has multiple meanings. For starters, the ibis is the sacred animal of Thoth and therefore also a form commonly used to depict Thoth. Hence, the ibis is actually the God Thoth himself. Additionally, the ibis is the hieroglyph

Thoth presents the Ibis to the Lady with the Eyes, KV 9 Ramses V and VI

for the *Akh*, the "Shining One". Here it symbolises the unchangeable spark of life or light of Thoth himself. Thoth demonstrates that he surrenders himself unconditionally to the Goddess with the eyes. This is no simple submission for it requires the ultimate sacrifice of the innermost aspect of himself, his true soul.

The eyes, hidden by the Goddess behind her back, are the Eyes of the Sungod Râ. Thoth is unable to see these Eyes and has to entrust his soul blindly to the heightened insight of Râ. At the same time the blind way of submission is the prerequisite since it is all about a complete surrender at the level of the soul. Only then can a connection with the renewed consciousness be made. This attests to "True Faith" and is something completely different from simply "believing". Thoth, as the God of True Wisdom, Knowledge and Understanding, shows this action is an act that demonstrates true Wisdom. After this wise deed the heightened insight of Râ takes the lead and the voyage continues.

Moreover, Thoth shows something else as well. The ibis was used in the creation of the ancient unit of linear measurement, the royal cubit (*mḥ nswt*). This unit was based on the step size of an Ibis. The size of this measurement was about 20.6 inch (52,4 cm), which was further divided into 7 palms or 28 fingers. The meaning of the hieroglyphic word *meh* (*mḥ*) is "make whole, be full of, complete, finish or have faith" and underlines the fact that the cubit was a perfect basic measurement. Another meaning of *meh* is "forearm". Hence, the cubit does not only equal the step of an Ibis, but also the length of the forearm measured from the tip of the middle finger to the bottom of the elbow. It is said that the royal cubit was the exact length of the forearm of Thoth, which is why it is called the "cubit of Thoth".

Thoth, who carries many titles, is also known as "He who reckons in heaven, the counter of stars, the enumerator of the earth and of what is therein, and the measurer of the earth". He is the wise Architect of the universe who used his forearm, the royal cubit, to measure the cosmos and thus Egypt itself. He knows perfect measurements are necessary to establish *Maât*, Order Justice and Truth, for the Divine Law has to be manifested first before the

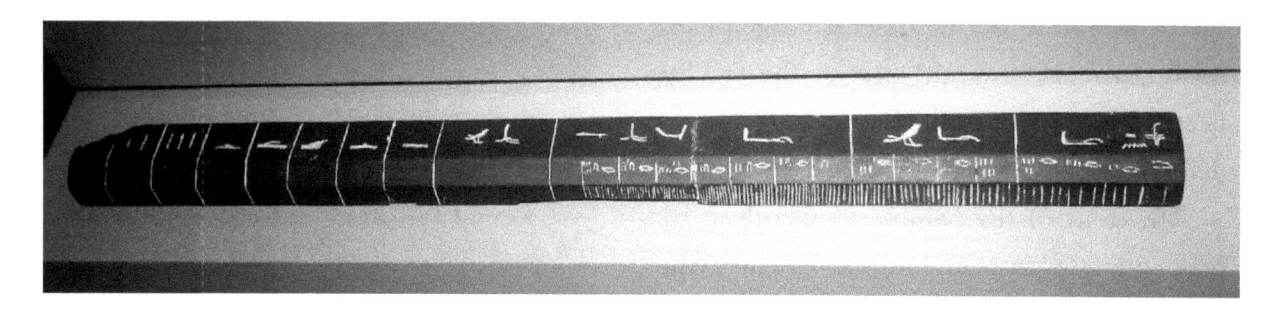

Royal cubit of the chief master builder Ptahmes (AD 54), 18th dynasty of the New Kingdom; Tuthmosis III, 1479-1425 BC, National Museum of Antiquities Leiden, the Netherlands

heightened consciousness of the Sungod can be expressed. This is simply the Law that can never be tampered with and needs to be precise and perfect.

Hence, Thoth is the High priest who is initiated in the sacred art of creation. With his outstretched forearm he conveys this hidden knowledge to the Goddess "She who hides her images". The Goddess, in turn, is not allowed to share this knowledge with anyone. Therefore, she keeps it away from the eyes of the non-initiates. Everything that transpires between the God Thoth and the Goddess "She who hides her images" is a great and hidden secret. Râ refers to her as the "Concealing One" and he emphasises the need to keep the secret she received from Thoth well hidden.

> Concealing One!
> May your arms be hidden, being bare![13]

The art of keeping secrets is something this Goddess is well acquainted with as she is an aspect of the Goddess of the West. The hidden region of the West is her dwelling realm which makes her quite knowledgeable about the secret transformation process taking place here every night. The progression of this mysterious process is depicted through the Eyes of Râ that the Goddess is holding. The Goddess has taken responsibility of these Eyes that simultaneously allows her to provide security for Râ as well. Thus, she is the one who leads the Sungod Râ, during this part of the journey, across the fields.

As the journey continues, following the delay of Thoth, we meet sixteen Gods in their mummiforms.

(No. 442 - 445) "King of Upper Egypt" wearing the White Crown of Upper Egypt.
(No. 446 – 449) "Those provided with offerings" without attributes.
(No. 450 – 453) "King of Lower Egypt" wearing the Red Crown of Lower Egypt.
(No. 454 – 457) "*Akh*-spirit" or the blessed dead, without attributes.

They are the justified souls who have gone through the process of rebirth themselves. Râ addresses each one of these ancestors. They stand faithfully at their respective spots at all times to pay their respects to Râ and listen to his wise words. Through their undying devotion and servitude in the Duat and on earth, Râ rewards them with divine offerings. These offerings are created by means of Magic generated by the divine utterance of the Sungod. Among these ancestors are the impressive Pharaohs who are present to safeguard the upcoming process of renewal. Their sceptres are the symbols of power and rulership and can be found on the left riverbank (No. 410 – 418). Currently, these great Pharaohs themselves are physically present here. Râ recognises them once again as Pharaohs and presents them with their crowns and kingship. The Pharaohs, in turn, are then capable of embodying their full power and kingship to ensure Apophis is punished. As the

Sungod sails along the blessed dead and the Kings, the "Great Ones of Egypt", he acknowledged them for they have developed consciousness throughout the ages. He connects himself with the legacy of eternal wisdom and experience created by these Great Souls. His identification with each one of them functions as the foundation upon which the renewed consciousness of the Sungod can grow.

Subsequently Râ arrives in a secret place once again. This time this place is in the shape of a huge five-headed serpent, "Many-faced" (No. 458). The serpent bends its body with the tail inside his mouth to create an oval shaped space. This posture refers to the ancient symbol of the ouroboros. The word "ouroboros" originates from the Greek words "oura" and "boros", meaning "tail" and "eating" respectively. The tail eating serpent symbolises the beginning and the end of times as an eternal cycle of creation. The cycle of life, death and rebirth refers to immortality and the eternal process of returning to unity. Like this the ouroboros forms an enclosure surrounding the orderly world wherein the eternal renewal takes place. It is this protective circle that keeps the formless disorder and non-existence outside of the world of creation.

The five heads of "Many-faced" represent a complex meaning that refers to the profound symbolism of the hidden space created by his body. The number five represents the four cardinal points of North, East, South and West connected with the Divine, which allows the touch and ensoulment of the physical world. This symbolism is reflected in the shape of a pyramid. The base of a pyramid has four corners on the earth while the tip is connected with the sky. Like this, the two worlds, the above and the below, are connected. In addition, the number five also represents the five-pointed starfish or the Duat star. The Duat stars are the reflection of the stars in the sky and represent the Divine. As mentioned before in the First Hour, the starfish symbolises regenerative power and eternal renewal for it is able to regenerate its arms after damage.

The five heads of the serpent are upraised which refers to alertness and wakefulness. At the same time an opening is formed inside its body to open up life, light and consciousness. During the Fifth Hour the very first spark of light or consciousness was rekindled and at the present time it is getting stronger and taking a new shape. Within the encirclement of the five-headed serpent lies a corpse, "Flesh" (No. 459). On the head of the corpse lies a scarab, which is the representation of the new born light, Khepri. The accompanying text tells us this is the corpse of Khepri. This is the corpse of Khepri as his own flesh [...][14] However, another text explains this is the corpse of Osiris. [...] he rows through this field to the place of the corpse of Osiris.[15]

The word "flesh" is also mentioned as a reference to Râ. Therefore, the corpse does not just belong to only one of these Gods. In fact, it connects them all together. In this case Osiris is the corpse and Râ is the *Ba*-soul within the corpse. Together they now form the first true unit as they share one body. Khepri, in his scarab form, does not partake in this unity. He lies atop of the body and connects himself from his heightened position with the *Ba*-soul of Râ and the *Ka* of Osiris. Through his touch the spiritual body, the *Sâhu*, is now able to germinate from of the corpse. Still, it will take the rest of the journey through the Duat before it is fully grown. Then, in the Twelfth hour, the *Sâhu* will serve as the feeding ground upon which the process of rebirth can take place.

This is the process of reviving Râ and Osiris as demonstrated by the walking pose of the spiritual body. Furthermore, the body is no longer a mummy as it is out of its wrappings. It emphasises the fact that movement and, therefore, life has returned after the sleep of death.

In the previous hour, this first sign of life was generated by the first meeting between Râ, as the primeval winged serpent, and Osiris as Sokar, the God of the Death. Currently, the transformation continues where Râ and Osiris are renewed in their appearances.

The entire focus of this process of renewal is aimed at the scarab on top of the head. The head is the highest point of the body and underlines the fact that it concerns the heightened consciousness. Râ and Osiris are well aware of the renewal of the higher consciousness. They have lifted a hand as they touch the scarab in an effort to create a connection with the higher vision of Khepri, the *Akh*. The scarab, or *Akh* is not part of the body since the intangible and transparent *Akh* does not belong to the physical world. It is the higher consciousness of the Divine. Only through the unity between the *Ba* and the *Ka* is it possible to touch this consciousness. This requires full focus and a deep trust based on True Faith, as previously pointed out by Thoth.

Furthermore, the sharing of a single body of Râ together with Osiris demonstrates that Râ has become an "Osiris". An "Osiris" is a term used to refer to the deceased who is experiencing the process of transformation to become reborn. Each deceased wanted to follow the example of Osiris to become his likeness. This guaranteed the deceased his own resurrection.

The Duatians on the right riverbank (lower section)

The right side of the Sacred River begins with, "Crocodile" (No. 460), sitting in a half upraised pose. The Crocodile is the symbol of strength, power, fertility and creation. Crocodiles build their nests above the flood level. Thus, they were seen as the predictors of the height of the inundation and associated with the regenerative powers that emerge from the waters of Nun.

Furthermore the presence of "Crocodile" here refers to the beginning of creation as he is a primeval creature. His physical form has virtually remained the same over the millions of years after his creation. He demonstrates the never changing primal force of the essence of life that continues to exist.

As a crocodile, he has the ability to live on the land as well as in the water. This makes him a guardian at the boundary between these two different worlds. From the deep waters he supports the renewal of the new life and allows it to eventually manifest in the world. Together with the God "Nun" (No. 486), who stands at the end of the riverbank, "Crocodile" forms a framework within which the process of regeneration can take place.

Next to him stands a crocodile-headed Goddess, "She who is in the great Nun" (No. 461). She too is a personification of the regenerative waters of Nun. She forms a pair with the Deity "Crocodile". Together they vouch for the fertile power of the life-granting water which forms the amniotic fluid in the uterus of the sky Goddess Nut.

In front of the crocodile-headed Goddess stands the child God Ihy (No. 462) who is the son of Hathor and Horus. His name means "Music Priest and Sistrum Player" as he is a God of music and musicians. Usually he is depicted as a young naked boy wearing the sidelock of youth. In this form he holds an index finger to his mouth and carries the sistrum with his right hand. His joy and playfulness show the beauty of childhood that reflects the new life and the beginning of creation. With the rattle of his sistrum he assists the generation of the life-giving waters.

The following five Gods are the children Gods and represent aspects of the God Horus. These young Gods symbolise youthful, vivid and potential powers. They are the next generation and, like Horus, protect the heritage of their father as they too are heirs to the throne.

(No. 463) "He who cries"
(No. 464) "Protector of his father"
(No. 465) "With living face"
(No. 466) "With speaking face"
(No. 467) "Protector"

Next are four Goddesses in a half upraised pose. Their names indicate they are still prevented from standing up straight. The process of renewal is still in the early stages and requires time to manifest completely. These Goddesses therefore indicate that there still lies a long way ahead before the light is ready to rise above the horizon.

(No. 468) "She who is fettered"
(No. 469) "She who is held back"
(No. 470) "She who is turned about"
(No. 471) "She who is burdened"

The Goddesses are all connected as they hold each others hands. The first Goddess also holds the hand of one of the children Gods. The connection with the youthful and potential forces of the children Gods helps the Goddesses overcome the restrictions that are reflected in their names. In doing so they support one another and remain in this half upraised position without further bending their knees. Then again, the holding on to each other also prevents them from rising up too quickly. A new life is vulnerable and needs time to develop slowly to become strong.

Each of the twelve Deities is present here to strengthen the spark of life that is about to renew. Their presence is needed not only to support Râ, Osiris and Khepri, but also to guide all of the *Ba*-souls residing in the Duat. They set the shadows of the *Ba*-souls alight. This means they ignite light that makes the shadows of the bodies visible again. The illumination and subsequent appearance of the shadows demonstrates that these *Ba*-souls have come to life. They have been granted the right to exist, for without a shadow life is simply impossible. Furthermore, they secure the water-supply for the *Akh*-spirits. This water is not meant for consumption as the *Akh*-spirits have no need for water or food. The water-supply mentioned here are the primal waters of Nun. These waters are the foundation and offer protection from which the *Akh*-spirits are born.

In the middle of the right riverbank lies a serpent on the ground, "Swallower of forms" (No. 472). Beneath his head the sign of eternal Life, the *Ankh*, can be seen. It is the task of the serpent to devour the shadows and to erase the stature of the enemies. From his back four heads have emerged who symbolise the four sons of Horus.

(a) "Imset"
(b) "Hapy"
(c) "Duamutef"
(d) "Qebehsenuef"

The four sons of Horus are the protectors of the body of the deceased in the Netherworld. They are connected to the four canopic jars that hold the eviscerated organs of the mummy. The lid of each jar is shaped in the image of the head of the concerning God. Imset, or Imsety, has a human form and protects the liver. Hapy has a baboon form and protects the lungs. Duamutef has a jackal form and protects the stomach, and lastly Qebehsenuef has a hawk form and protects the intestines.

It was the God Anubis who gave the four sons their mummification duties to protect the previously mentioned organs after death. The complete body, including the organs, was needed after death to serve as a nutrient medium from which the new life would emerge. Without a body it was impossible to be resurrected in the Afterlife.

Due to the important tasks of the sons of Horus, the limbs of the deceased were identified with these four Gods. The arms were recognised as Duamutef and Hapy while the legs were associated with Qebehsenuef and Imsety.

Your hands are Hapy and Duamutef.
You demand that you ascend to the sky and you shall ascend.
Your feet are Imsety and Qebehsenuef.
You demand that you descend to the lower sky and you shall descend.[16]
– Pyramid texts; Utterance 215

The very existence in the Afterlife is contingent upon the four Gods. Therefore, for their part, the Gods were protected as well by the powerful "canopic" Goddesses Isis, Nephthys, Neith and Serket. Imsety was protected by Isis, Hapy by Nephthys, Duamutef by Neith and Qebehsenuef by Serket.

The sons of Horus are also the four Gods of the cardinal points. They symbolise the four pillars at the corners of the earth that support the heavens. Imsety represents the South, Hapy the North, Duamatef the East and Qebehsenuef the West. Hence, they connect the heavens with the earth and enable space in between for life to manifest itself. The four canopic Goddesses can be found on the four corners of the sarcophagus that correspond with the specific Gods of the cardinal points. Here, in the Sixth Hour the four sons of Horus ensure that the spiritual and physical become connected. In doing so the first sign of light or life is able to take root in its initial form.

The following four Gods are half upraised.

(No. 473) "He who is constricted"
(No. 474) "Sore foot"
(No. 475) "Footless"
(No. 476) "He who is weary"

Their names indicate each of them exhibits a defect. The text, however, refers to a cure that becomes available as soon as Râ's voice is heard. The Sungod asks them to stand and to stretch out without being weary. They may come forward and conquer their disabilities as *Ba*-souls.

Stand up indeed! Yield not!
Stretch out and be not weary!
May your *Ba*-souls emerge,
and may your shadows rest!
Stretching for your feet,
and straightness for your knees!
May you indeed rest in your flesh,
unbound are your wrappings![17]

Every deceased wanted to be freed from the tight wrappings that constricted the body movements and prevented it from functioning properly. This is very important since immobility and stagnation would mean death. Therefore, it was everyone's explicit wish to be freed and unbound, to be allowed to move in the Afterlife freely. This did not just refer to the use of a physical body, but also the use of the intellect. The four Gods symbolise the restrictions of the freedom of movement from which Râ frees them to be able to function and live fully. Furthermore, they are also freed from their old restrictive convictions that limited their consciousness. The term "unbound are your wrappings", thus, refers to the fact that they embody their Divine nature once more.

Following are nine sceptres in the shape of fire spitting serpents with knives fixed at the lower end. According to the text, the sceptres symbolise the staffs of the male Gods in this region. Râ invokes these Gods as "The Great Ennead". As Gods of the first creation, they are present here during the process of renewal. It is their task to protect Khepri through the consumption, cutting and burning of his enemies. They stand directly below the five-headed serpent where the renewal takes place. The initial life form needs to be protected, as the first threat is already imminent.

The first sceptre represents the God "Tatenen" (No. 477) whose name means "Risen Land" or "exalted earth". He is the personification of the primordial mound, which has risen out of the waters of Nun at the moment of creation. His realm can be found deep within the earth from which all life emerges. Every year he rose from the waters of the inundation as the fertile silt. Subsequently, the new crops could be grown on the enriched ground. Therefore, he is considered the source of food and divine offerings. He is also involved in the future of the deceased for the bodies are buried within his realm in the earth. He welcomes the deceased and assists them on their journey through the Netherworld. Within the Duat he is tasked with the important duty to guard the passage of the Sun barque. With his staff he protects the primordial mound and wards off Apophis. Usually he is depicted in human form with a Divine beard, wearing a tall crown consisted of a pair of long spiral ram's horns surmounted with a solar disk and two feathers on his head.

The second sceptre represents the God "Atum" (No. 478). His name is derived from the word *tem* (*tm*). The meaning of this word depends on the determinative used. It can mean several things like "be complete, everything, the universe, perish or not to be". As mentioned before, he is a self-begotten God who created the first Gods through his saliva or semen. One of his names is "Lord of Totality" since the entire creation is dependent on Atum. Everything was created from his "flesh" and thus every living being and all things contain a fraction of his *Ka*.

Atum, though, has two sides to his nature. On the one hand, he is the creator who completes everything, but on the other hand he is the destroyer who finishes all. If he destroys the world, everything is submerged back into the waters of Nun. Nevertheless, Atum himself would continue to exist in this state of nonexistence in the form of a primeval serpent.

> Atum: You shall be for millions
> on millions of years,
> a lifetime of millions of years.
> I will despatch the Elders
> and destroy all that I have made;
> the earth shall return
> to the Primordial Water,

to the surging flood, as in its original state.
But I will remain with Osiris,
I will transform myself into something else,
namely a serpent, without men knowing
or the Gods seeing.
How good is what I have done for Osiris,
even more than for all the Gods!
I have given him the desert,
and his son Horus is the heir of his throne
which is in the Island of Fire;
I have made what appertains
to his place in the Barque
of Millions of Years,
and Horus is firm on his throne
in order to found his establishments.[18]
– Book of the Dead; Spell 175

The remaining seven sceptres are the representation of the following Gods:

(No. 479) "Khepri"
(No. 480) "Shu"
(No. 481) "Geb"
(No. 482) "Osiris"
(No. 483) "Horus"
(No. 484) "The Judge"
(No. 485) "He of the offerings"

Facing the opposite direction stands the God "Nun" (No. 486) who is the guardian of the present hour. He was already present before the creation took place. Everything came into being from his primal waters. Râ too is renewed within the deep waterhole of Nun that is the foundation of all new life.

The manifestation of the Sixth Hour in daily life

We have now reached the core of the transformation process. The Oval of Sokar has transformed into the living oval shaped enclosure of "Many-faced". This new form emphasises the renewal and the revival of your inner world. Inside this True Sanctuary is where you will form the first true unity with the Higher Self and the Powerself. This integration process is intense and demands sufficient preparation on your part. First, you are subjected to various important themes before this inner unity can take shape.

Therefore, the moment you enter this hour, you are confronted with the central theme upon which the upcoming progress of the journey depends. You might have thought all obstacles had been overcome and that the remainder of the journey would run smoothly. Nothing could be further from the truth for every step you have taken is always tested. Only then you know if you have integrated the knowledge and made it your own. For this reason Thoth (No. 440) is present here to block your path. You need to face whatever he shows you before you can continue your journey.

Thoth (No. 440), together with the Goddess "Lady with the Eyes" (No. 441), demonstrates the surrender to your inner light, the Higher Self. This is a blind and unconditional surrender for you are unable to see what awaits you. It is simply impossible to convey it with words or images given that it is a state of being that you have to experience. For this, you need True Faith. That is your only handhold for you are required to take a leap of faith. You are asked to make a great offering. It is the greatest sacrifice you have ever been required to make for you are offering yourself to your Higher Self. Without this offering you would never be able to complete the process in the hidden space created by the body of "Many-faced" and your inner journey would come to a halt at this stage.

In the Fifth Hour you already got to your knees in front of the Higher Self. Everything had been cut away and you ended up in a profound dark hole where you were faced with death. There was nowhere to run. The only option remaining was to reach out to your inner Sungod and acknowledge his existence. Here, acknowledgement transforms into identification with the Higher Self where you surrender yourself unconditionally. This surrender, as displayed by Thoth, goes much deeper then simple acknowledgement. Oftentimes people are prepared to try to reach the higher dimensions and completely submit to it during times of need or setbacks. We acknowledge we cannot do it on our own and are willing to bend our heads down. However, as soon as the sun begins to shine again and fortune smiles upon us, we once again set our own course. We want to be captain of our own ship and are no longer in need of the guidance of the Higher Self. The surrender required here is not a transient one to be done with whenever you feel like it. It is a total submission for life, for better and for worse, build upon blind faith. Now, your focus shifts towards your inner Sungod, the Higher Self, with whom you identify yourself. You receive another place within yourself and are, therefore, no longer the centre of your universe. Where you used to be lord and master before, you are now no more than a loyal servant.

The identification with the Higher Self is a process which will evolve along your journey throughout the upcoming hours. Step by step you learn to listen to the True inner Voice for he is the one who will navigate you through your life. Slowly but surely your consciousness regarding your actions will grow. Nothing will simply be true for you need to always ask yourself whether your actions are righteous. The perspective of your own little world will steadily but surely shift towards the Grand Design that you are a part of. As you are learning to see through the Eyes of the Higher Self, you will realise the responsibility you have for your own life.

The entire process of becoming aware is starting to take shape and at the initial stage it is solely focused on the realisation of the existence of this process. Deep down in your inner world you are aware of the inner guidance. However, you are not yet able to substantiate it in your daily life. Only when the higher insight anchors itself in your being, can you slowly adjust your actions in accordance with it. This is a lengthy process of trial and error. The old grooves carved during your life do not just disappear. You always need to pay attention, otherwise you could easily end up in these pitfalls.

Thoth also emphasises something else through the ibis in his hand. As mentioned before the word "heart" was sometimes written with an ibis (See chapter The Great Awakening; the Way of the Heart). Therefore, the ibis in his hands can be seen as a heart. However, this is not just any heart for it is the True Heart. The portal through which the higher consciousness is expressed. Thoth points out that only a pure and sincere heart can be the instrument of the Mind and Will of the Divine. Therefore, your heart will be weighed in the upcoming hours on the scales against the feather of Maât. This means you have to investigate whether your heart is the residence of righteousness and Truth. Does your heart speak with the voice of the Higher Self or with your own voice? Here too applies that only the unconditional surrender and identification with your Higher Self can purify your heart from the untrue voice and false insights. The end of your journey will show whether your heart is able to function as the seat of Divine Wisdom and Knowledge as the True Heart.

Following the wise lesson of Thoth, you reach the next theme of this hour, the Lion "Bull with roaring voice" (No. 420) with above it the Eyes "Image of Râ" (No. 419). This is the next step to deepen the inner unity. Here the Eyes are visible that the Goddess, "She who hides her image" (No. 441), is hiding behind her back. The Eyes or "Image of Râ" symbolise the renewal of your consciousness. The lion underneath these eyes is a reference to the Vital Life Force of Osiris that lets itself be heard loud and clear with a roar. The Lion supports the Eyes, just like the power of your Powerself is now going to support your renewed consciousness.

Close behind the Lion three burial chests (No. 425, 427 and 429) can be found. These chests further your preparation before you can gain access to the renewed hidden space in the core of this hour. Once again pieces of your identity are analysed and decomposed if they cannot tolerate the light. This process repeats itself again and again in a never ending cycle for it is an essential part to continue your development and renewal. Everything you renew will eventually become old and in need of replacement.

Each of the three burial chests contains an important theme that you are required to come to terms with before you can enter the hidden space. The first chest, with the hind part of a lion inside, represents "power" (No. 425). Power is one of the biggest challenges to overcome in one's life. How are you going to deal with this power and are you able to handle it in an honourable way with integrity? You are not supposed to abuse this power in any form. On the flip side, though, you are not supposed to dodge and ignore your own power either. It is all about finding the right balance and applying the power accordingly with respect to the Divine Law of *Maât*. The power of the Lion, therefore, needs to be curbed at all times by the higher vision of the Higher Self.

The second chest, with the wing of a scarab inside, contains the theme "Divinity" (No. 427). The *Netjeru*, or Gods, are aspects of nature just like you. You are a god yourself living on earth with the opportunity to express the divinity down here into matter. Are you prepared to embody your divinity and take responsibility for who you truly are? You are the creator of your own life that gives you the opportunity to manifest the Divine Law of *Maât*. If you are prepared to embrace your own divinity, eventually, you become a "Winged One" and will be able to sanctify life.

The final burial chest, with a human head inside, contains the theme "Identification" (No. 429). Know your true Self and be aware of what goes on in your heart and soul. Then you can connect yourself with your true heritage that goes far beyond the life you are currently leading. Each of the lives you have lived is connected, just like the links in a chain. Consequently, you will always return to the beginning. This is your own *Zep Tepi*, a journey towards wholeness that allows you to return to your origins, the Divine Spark.

Everything you go through in this hour eventually brings you to the Holy of Holies. The name of the Hour Goddess, "Arrival who gives the right way", has already pointed you towards this sacred place. The True Sanctuary is the final destination where you can turn everything around. It is also the starting point of the course to sail that the Higher Self has charted for you.

Before you may enter your True Sanctuary, you first need to face the Ancestors (No. 442 – 457). These Justified souls and great Kings have already gone through the transformation of death into life and embody True Knowledge and Wisdom. They have created the path we may use to experience our own renewal. Humanity contributed to this path through combined efforts, creating evolution. Every new group has assisted in building the road to give you the opportunity to walk this path. You are now the next in line to experience the renewal of consciousness and expand the way for the people travelling the road after you. Honour these Great Souls and show your respect. The subsequent travellers after you will then honour you for the building blocks of Wisdom you are going to lay out as well.

The Pharaohs, among the Ancestors, are present here to raise awareness to the fact that you need to remain focused on your True Sanctuary. Furthermore, they stress the need to protect your inner Sanctuary against external influences. In doing so, they refer to the sceptres (No. 410 – 418) that you have to wield to destroy intruders. However, this inner land needs to be protected from within as well by placing an appropriate leader on the throne. Though the Ancestors are majestic Pharaohs and great leaders themselves, they can still be found in front of "Many-faced" where they bow respectfully before the greatest Pharaoh of them all, Osiris. They pay their tribute as servants of the King of the Duat. However, despite the fact that Osiris is the one sitting on the throne, it is Râ who assumes the true leading role. Osiris, though being the King, rules from his Soul, which is the Sungod Râ. Therefore, these great Kings request for you to place your Higher Self, on the throne. Through this true Lordship your own inner land is governed from the "Divine Law of *Maât*". The True inner Voice of the Higher Self expresses itself through your intuition. Moreover, he speaks with the Voice of your conscience that is located in your heart.

Finally, the time has come for you to enter the secret place. This is where you form a unity with the Higher Self for the first time. This unification can be established only if you dare to surrender all control. This is where your old self has to pass away. It is an intense process since you literally have to die. It feels like you assume the death posture while lying under the shroud of the Goddess Isis-Tait. This posture connects you to the corpse of Osiris who, like no-one else, knows what it is like to die. Dying has gifted him eternal Life and enabled him to embody the Vital Life Force. This is the underlying force that transforms death into a new life. It shows death is not the final destination for it actually opens the door to a new form to a new you.

Osiris grants you the strength to die. The moment you experience this strength within yourself is the moment you are connected with the Powerself. From now on, the Powerself participates in the transformation. He offers the Vital Life Force to bring to life the unity with the Higher Self. Now you possess the power to detach the old self and to surrender yourself to the Higher Self. The inner connection with your Higher Self and the Powerself gives the Divine Spark the opportunity to gently touch you through the Higher Self. This subtle touch enables you to view your inner world from a new perspective. Nothing is the same for your perception of this world has clearly changed.

The foundation has been formed from which your spiritual body, the *Sâhu*, can grow. The four sons of Horus, who emerge out of the body of the serpent "Swallower of forms" (No. 472), are supporting this process. Their presence makes you aware of the fact that this spiritual body forms the bridge between your inner world and the higher world of the Divine. In the upcoming hours, this body will gain strength and power. Eventually it will serve as a channel for your indirect connection with the Divine Spark. The soft touch of this Divine Spark will then transform in the inspiration stream which is guided through the Higher Self.

Despite the fact that it is a powerful miracle unfolding here, it still needs an adequate level of protection throughout the upcoming hours. The many knives in this hour and the presence of all the Ancestors and sceptres emphasises this necessity as well. The renewed perspective and experience of being, takes time to fully integrate. When exposed too early, for example through talking about it, you destroy everything you have experienced. It is still unable to withstand the influences of the day world at this time. Every exposure to the world of daily life disrupts it and leads to confusion.

Complete and utter silence is, therefore, the key prerequisite in order for the miracle to take place. The Gods "Crocodile" (No. 460) and "Ihy" (No. 462) are referring to this fact in their own subtle way. The crocodile is a master in the creation of silence. His movements are smooth and silent in his effort to camouflage his presence. When he remains still, he can blend with his surroundings and make you oblivious to the fact he might be in front of you right under your nose. Ihy holds a finger against his mouth. This is the feature of a small child as well as the universal sign for silence. The experience of the inner renewal is an important moment deserving of complete silence and respect. Words only prove to desecrate and negate the miracle.

The God Ihy, Temple of Hathor at Dendera (Mammisi)

THE SEVENTH HOUR
"Mysterious Cavern"

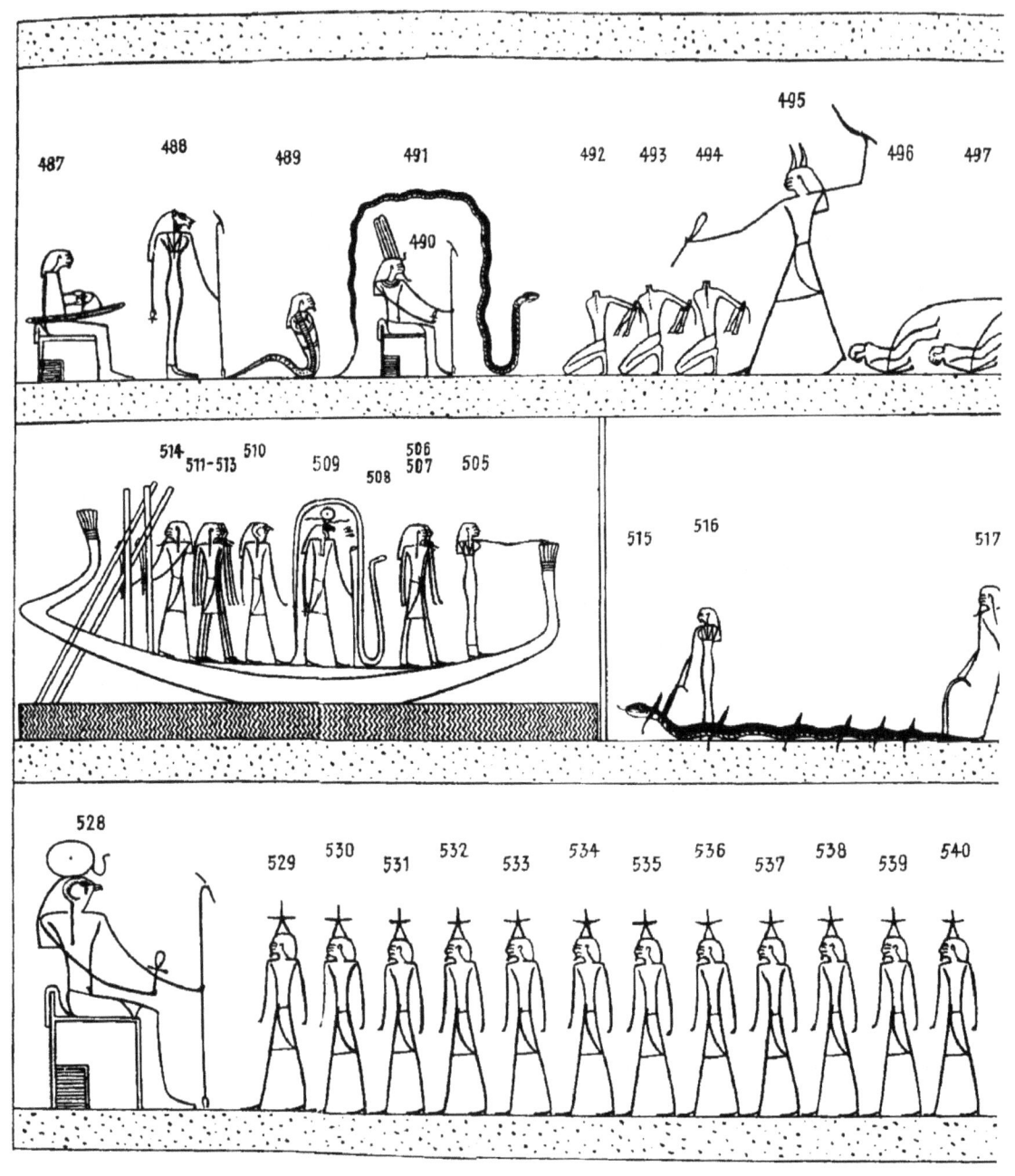

Figure 24: The Seventh Hour

The Gate: "Gate of Osiris"
The Hour Goddess: "Repelling the "Evil One" and beheading "Neha-her""
The Guardian: (no name mentioned)

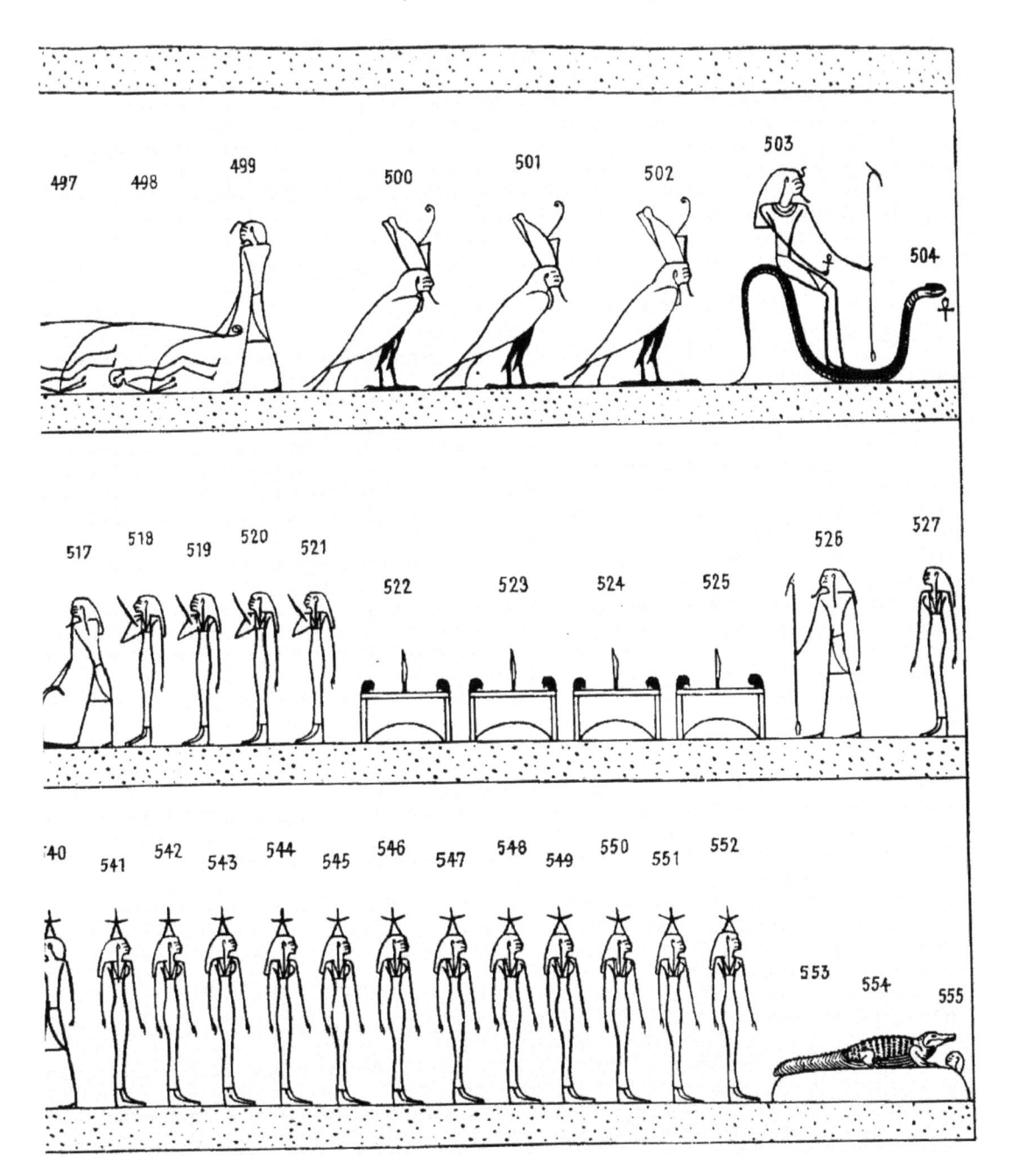

Introduction

Pausing by the person of this Great God
in the cavern of Osiris.
Commands by the person of this Great God
at this cavern
to the Gods who are in it.
This God assumes another form
at this cavern.
He turns away from Apophis
through the Magic of Isis
and the Eldest Magician.
The name of the Gate of this place
through which this God passes is
"Gate of Osiris". The name of this Place
is "Mysterious Cavern".
The name of the Hour of the night
guiding this Great God is
Repelling the "Evil One"
and beheading "Neha-her".
Mysterious way of the West,
upon which the Great God passes
in his protected barque.
He proceeds on this way,
which is without any water,
without (the possibility of) towing.
He sails by the Magic of Isis
and the Eldest Magician,
and by the magical power
which is in the mouth
of this (Great) God himself.
The slaughtering of Apophis
is done in the Duat at this cavern;
his place, however, is in the sky.
This is made like this on the Northern side
of the Hidden Chamber
in the Duat.
It is useful in heaven,
in the earth and on earth.
He who knows it is a *Ba*-soul
of the *Ba*-souls who are with Râ.[1]

Râ has entered the Seventh Hour through the gate referred to as the "Gate of Osiris". The name of this hour is the "Mysterious Cavern" and it contains the hidden residence of the God Osiris. Though Râ and Osiris are still together, they no longer form the true unity as in the previous hour. Both have now taken their own powerful places.

The Sun barque with Râ and his crew has emerged from the profound depth of the Duat. After spending the past two hours within utter darkness, the lowest point of the journey has passed. Although the darkness is less oppressive, it is still dark in the Seventh Hour. To reach this Hour, Râ has once again made a jump, this time from the South to the North. This is the direction where he will remain during his travels in the present and subsequent hour.

The Seventh Hour is next to the Fourth Hour and directly opposite from the Sixth Hour. The Fourth Hour was the hour where all of the water had desiccated and replaced the hot and dry desert of Sokar. This drought returns in the current hour. Hence, the waters, that were abundantly present in the Sixth Hour, have once again completely disappeared. The Seventh Hour is literally and figuratively the opposite of the Sixth Hour.

The absence of water has led to the beaching of the Sun barque on a sandbank. As the barque has become stranded, it is unable to sail and it cannot be towed. The journey is on the verge of stagnation due to this sandbank that is set up by a giant serpent. The name of this serpent is Neha-her, "Horrible of face", better known as Apophis. Being the biggest nemesis of Râ, Apophis poses a serious threat to the process of rebirth. However, this menace is not reserved to Râ alone. It affects Osiris as well for these two Gods are dependent on one another to be able to ascend. In the event of Râ losing the battle, the earth will become shrouded in darkness, suffocating all life. Osiris will then die as well, making it impossible for him to renew his vital life force through the ensoulment of Râ during the night. The entire creation in heaven, in the earth as well as on the earth, will be marked for dead. Then, Apophis will have won and the entire creation will be swallowed whole by a tidal wave originating from the primeval waters of Nun. Creation will crumble and pass into non-existence. Râ's victory over Apophis is therefore vital for the welfare of every living being.

In the fight between existence and non-existence, Râ is aided by the Hour Goddess, "Repelling the 'Evil One' and beheading 'Neha-her'". Her name implies the kind of vicious battle that will be fought. As threatening and intimidating as it might seem, the Sun barque has to continue its journey no matter what. Since it cannot sail through water or by means of towing, it is moved with the aid of magical powers.

Two of the foremost magicians are Isis and the Eldest Magician. Both have taken their respective places on board of the Sun barque. They ensure, through the use of very powerful Magic, that Râ is able to eventually continue his sailing journey. Fortunately, Râ himself is not as weak or vulnerable as was the case during the previous hours. His magical powers have increased to a level that now enables him to face Apophis.

Despite the fact the slaughter of Apophis has yet to take place, the accompanying text is already speaking of a victory. The image of the triumph is very clearly and visibly written down in words. This is an important subsequent stage in the manifestation of this victory. After all, through the power of the intent, the next logical step is to realise the image and make it a reality. That is the way Magic works!

The Duatians on the left riverbank (Upper section)

Râ is aware of his awkward position as he is being confronted by Apophis. Despite his increased magical powers, he recognises the fact that he needs all the help he can get. Therefore, he gives clear instructions to all the Deities on the left riverbank. Being a true born leader, he demonstrates his increased leadership skills. He addresses everyone individually with the "True of Voice" in an unambiguous way. None of the Deities respond to his call with words. All remain silent as they wait for the Sungod's orders after which they can begin their respective assigned tasks. There is no need for words for it are their actions that count.

The left riverbank opens with the God "Noble One" (No. 487) who is seated on a throne. A very special rudder, with the head of Horus fixed on it, is placed in his lap. "Noble One" holds this falcon head firmly with both of his hands. Râ can make good use of this special rudder as the Sun barque is in danger of becoming stranded on the ground. Hence, he requests the help of "Noble One" to enable the Sun barque to keep on sailing. "Noble One" is only too happy to help, for it is Râ's arrival that allowed "Noble One" to emerge from the darkness.

> Words spoken by this Great God:
> Noble One! Give me your hand,
> when Horus goes forth from your rudder![2]

The fact it is the head of the God Horus who is attached to the rudder of "Noble One" is not all that surprising. Horus, being the son of Isis and Osiris, was the rightful heir to the throne after the death of his father. As soon as he ascends the throne, he continues the legacy of his ancestors. This implies that death has been conquered as life goes on, which is a reference to the continuation of creation. "Noble One" gives a helping hand to manifest this future image with his magical oar to row. With his support the Sun barque is rowed through this difficult hour. The continued course of the barque will eventually enable the renewed light to prevail and shine on earth.

"Nobel One" can be found on the same level as "Kherep wia", for this Guide of the barque stands directly below "Noble One" on the Sacred River. Due to the position of "Noble One" the Guide of the Sun barque can rely on his support. Furthermore, "Noble One" is also on the same level with "Horus upon his throne" (No. 528), who can be found sitting upfront on the right riverbank. Horus is a solar God and, like Khepri, he is a symbol of the newborn light. Here, Horus represents the renewed form of the Sungod Râ after his transformation. Horus is sitting on his throne in all his grandeur as he stands above all the rest. The power of the rising light is obviously featured prominently within this hour. This vision is a promise of what the future holds and it can already be felt slightly in the air.

Following "Noble One" is the lion-headed Goddess, "Praising One" (No. 488). She holds a *Was*-sceptre in one hand and an *Ankh* in the other. It is her gift and capacity to bless and worship the Sungod. The act of adoration contains an enormous power and is an expression of the trust in the Divine. Her prayers attest to

Râ's existence and grant him courage and confidence. Râ is very appreciative of her support and can make good use of her aid. Thus, he asks her to use her True and sincere voice loud and clear. Only when uttered with sincere intent will a prayer truly contain the grand power to manifest the sacred words.

> She who adores, let me hear your voice!
> May your throat be truthful! [3]

On the ground in front of her lies an upraised Uraeus-serpent with a human head, "Living One" (No. 489). He symbolises the stylised upraised cobra worn by every ruling Pharaoh on the brow. On the one hand, the Uraeus-serpent illustrates the lordship and authority of the Pharaoh over his Kingdom. On the other hand, it is also this particular serpent who protects this power. The emergence of "Living One" signifies the increase of Râ's power. Nonetheless, it is currently too soon for Râ to shoulder his complete reign. The light of the Sungod is still premature and too weak to effectively rise to the task. Râ is aware of his vulnerability and requests this cobra to envelop him into his protective coils; 'Living One – open your coils!" [3]

In front of this cobra Osiris, "Flesh of Osiris" (No. 490), is seated upon his throne. During the Sixth Hour, Osiris could still be found lying on his back as a reference to him being a corpse. During the present hour, however, his life force and rulership have developed, which enables him to take his seat and sit up straight once more. The Sungod welcomes him and addresses Osiris with "Lord of Life" and "Ruler of the West". Like the light of Râ, the renewed life force of Osiris still needs to grow and rise up even further. Râ encourages him by telling him: 'Life is yours! You live and you are alive!" [4]

The power of the Vital Life Force of Osiris is also essential to Râ, for the more powerful Osiris's Life Force becomes, the brighter Râ's light is able to shine and the higher he can rise. In return, Râ ensouls and illuminates Osiris in their reciprocal ascension. The Sungod is the soul of Osiris and will always be a part of him, even though the both of them go their separate ways after the Twelfth Hour.

Despite the fact the Vital Life Force of Osiris is still evolving, he has already taken his rightful place on the throne like a true ruler crowned with the Two Feathers or *"shuty"* (*šw.ty*). This crown is a symbol of light and represents the Divine Law of *Maât*. Osiris is wearing this crown to emphasise the fact his rulership is in accordance with the Divine Law. The *Ankh*, the sign of eternal Life, is held in his hand as it rests upon his knee. The *Was*-sceptre is held in his other hand to symbolise his control over death and darkness. From his throne he oversees the slaying of his enemies as they are overpowered and fall down before his feet. The Sungod confirms Osiris's increased power as he says:

"May you be exalted over your followers
and may your foes fall to you,
beneath your feet!
You have power over those
who have acted against you".[5]

It would seem like Osiris has assumed total mastery over the Netherworld as the King of the Duat. However, this is an illusion for he still needs to journey through the necessary hours before he can embody the rising life. The renewal of Osiris is still very new, which makes him in need of support and protection. The gigantic serpent "He with living forms" (No. 491) provides Osiris with this safeguard and shelter. This serpent is another form of the snake God "Mehen" (No. 508), who can be found on the Sun barque.

The serpent, that sheds its skin on a regular basis, is the symbol of the process of transformation. Unsurprisingly, it is "He with living forms" who takes on the role of defender and supporter of this particular process of transformation. To do this he wraps his enormous body around Osiris, engulfing this God in his coils like a living shrine. Inside this adaptable skin, Osiris has plenty of room to continue his evolution safely. In doing so, the protective serpent provides for a safe shelter within which Osiris can proceed his development unhindered. This is not the only function of "He with living forms". The serpent also acts as a fierce creature on a mission to keep Osiris safe from the destructive forces of the outside. He spits fire and flames at each enemy who dares to approach Osiris and burns them in the process.

"He with living forms" is not the only one who protects Osiris from enemies. Considering there is a vast amount of enemies trying to harm Osiris, every bit of help is welcome. The fact we are talking about a multitude of enemies is reflected in the three figures, "Enemies of Osiris" (No. 492 – 494), who are kneeling in front of him on the ground. Their number of three is a symbolical reference to plurality. Their kneeling posture displays the fact that their strength and their volition has been taken from them. Their hands are bound behind their backs, effectively incapacitating them. In their restrained state they have been completely oppressed, stripped of all their power. Their heads have been severed and have disappeared, leading to the loss of their identity. Consequently, this eliminates their right to exist, making them doomed for eternity.

The demon Deity with the ears of a cat, "Violent-faced" (No. 495), is the one who defeated each one of these foes. He is holding a knife in one hand and a lasso in the other. In his fighting posture he punishes the "Enemies of Osiris". To do this he restrains these rebels and beheads them with his large knife. Afterwards he spears them on a roasting spit to grill them for himself. "Violent-faced" thus is a very dangerous warrior, not to be messed around with. His impressive appearance has a vibe of authority and dominance as he stands head and shoulders above all the rest by far.

His cat ears are a reference to the "Great Cat", a personification of the Sungod Râ himself. Râ can be seen in this cat form in Spell 17 of the Book of the Dead.[6] The corresponding image of this spell shows Râ in his appearance as the "Great Cat". In his claws he holds a very large knife to chop up his enemy, who has taken the shape of a serpent. Spell 335 of the Coffin Texts also mentions Râ as the "Great Cat".

I am that Great Cat who split the *išd*-tree on its side in Õn,[7]
on that night of making war
and of warding off the rebels,
and on that day on which were destroyed
the foes of the Lord of All.
What is that Great Cat?
He is Râ himself; he was called "Cat"
when Sia spoke about him.
He was cat-like in what he did,
and that is how his name of "Cat"
came into being.[8]
– Coffin Texts; Spell 335

The Great Cat of the Book of the Dead, Spell 17, TT 335 Nakhtamun Deir el-Medina

To be clear, the cat, as mentioned here, is unlike our modern house cat. The Great Cat is actually more similar to the great wild feline species like the lynx. These felines lived in Egypt and hunted small animals and snakes during the night. The wild cats played an important part in the ancient Egyptian mythology. An example is Mafdet, the Goddess of judgment and execution, who is often depicted in a feline form such as a lynx, civet and ocelot. She can also be found in the form of a mongoose. It was her task to battle the offenders of the Divine Law of *Maât* with her claws and teeth that are sharp like knives. One of her titles is "Slayer of serpents" and the "Great Cat".

> Mafdet will jump on the neck of the snake who brings his gift,
> and again on the neck of the snake with sweeping head.
> Which is the one who will remain?
> Unis is the one who will remain.[9]
> – Pyramid Texts; Unis, spell 201

Now, returning to "Violent-faced", he personifies the wild cat and is able to defeat the destructive powers of the serpent Apophis. Following him are more enemies, "Who is bound" (No. 496 – 498), lying down with their backs on the ground. Their hands are bound behind their backs for they have rebelled against Osiris, "the Foremost of the Duat". Here too, their number of three refers to a multitude of enemies.

The Deity "Violent-faced" is assisted in his battle against the foes of Osiris by the Deity "Punisher" (No. 499). This Deity disciplines these rebels who are lying on the ground while Osiris watches from his throne. Though "Punisher" is smaller and less impressive compared to "Violent-faced", he is just as vigorous. He is holding a long rope in his hands that he uses to securely restrain the hostiles. This rope does not just bind their bodies, for their *Ba*-souls and shadows are restrained as well. They are now deprived of all their freedom to ever transform into a transfigured soul. While paying close attention to them, "Punisher" effectively prevents them from ever escaping his watchful eye for all of eternity. This severe punishment seals their fate and results in these enemies being eternally doomed.

The Deity "Punisher" wears a lock of hair flipped in front of his face. The hieroglyphic word for hair lock is *samt* (*s3mt*), which can also be translated as "mourning or grief". Hence, the front lock was regarded as an expression of sorrow. Furthermore, it was compared to the waters of Nun or described as producing fresh air, like the movement of hair that generates a breeze. When mourners wore their hair in this fashion during a funerary ceremony, it would stimulate the life-giving waters and the Breath of Life. Subsequently aiding the reawakening of the deceased from his death slumber.[10]

The lock of hair can also be translated as *nebedet* (*nbdt*) or as *nebed* (*nbd*), which means "plait". Another interesting hieroglyphic word written with the determinative for hair is *nebedj* (*nbd̲*) which means "destructive or the Evil One" as a personification of Apophis, Seth or the demons of darkness. Dishevelled hair stood for chaos and destruction and was associated with the evil and destructive ones that belong to the darkness. The front lock of hair covers the eyes of Punisher as a reference to this darkness that must be defeated.

Following are three birds with human heads.

(No. 500) "The Acclaiming One".
(No. 501) "Who belongs to the images".
(No. 502) "*Ba*-soul of Tatenen".

They are the living *Ba*-souls, wearing the Double Crown on their heads. The Crown is a combination of the White Crown of Upper Egypt and the Red Crown of Lower Egypt. This crown is known as *Sekhemty* (*sḥm.ty*) which means "the Two Powers or the Double Crown".

According to tradition, the King was first crowned with both the Red and the White Crown to represent his power over Upper and Lower Egypt. The coronation ceremony in itself bestowed the divine power upon the King that he required to rule his country in accordance with the Law of Maât. At the same time, the magical power tied to each crown was transmitted to the King on the exact moment of the coronation after both crowns had been placed separately on his head. Then he finally received the Double Crown as the symbol of his lordship over his unified Kingdom of Upper and Lower Egypt.[11]

The living *Ba*-souls are here to protect the body of the Great Creator God Atum, "Flesh of Atum" (No. 503). Hence, they can be found sitting directly behind Atum to ensure that his *Ba*-soul lives. However, they are not the only ones protecting this God. A giant serpent, "He who puts together" (No. 504), has twisted his body in the shape of a throne to offer support to Atum. With his fire this serpent destroys anyone conspiring against Atum.

Atum is holding a *Was*-sceptre and the *Ankh* in his hands. In this context, he represents a form of the Sungod Râ, for he epitomises the solar disk setting in the evening. Atum is therefore, like Râ, in the process of rejuvenation. In fact his name refers to, "flesh of Atum". Both of these Gods are going through a similar transformation process upon which the continuation of the entire creation depends. If Râ succeeds in being reborn, so too will Atum be renewed.

Furthermore, Atum also displays his might and dominion over the entire creation. Every living creature has emerged from his flesh, which is emphasised by his enormous stature. With his mighty power he takes the lead over all the *Ba*-souls who owe their lives to him. The snake he rides, "He who puts together", is the symbolisation of the unification of opposites that is necessary to bring forth new life. Atum guides this unification and provides for the much needed duality to allow for life to develop.

The Duatians of the Sacred River (Middle section)

The Sungod Râ is standing in the middle of the Sun barque while wearing the solar disk and the ram horns on top of his head. The shrine, in which he spent the previous hours, has now transformed into a living enclosure. As Râ has come to life, so too has his shrine come to life in the form of the serpent "Mehen" (No. 508).

Mehen means "Coil or Coiled One". This serpent will remain wrapped around Râ for the remainder of the journey. In doing so, Râ is protected and supported by this snake God during the process of transformation. As mentioned above, the serpent "He with living forms" is another form of Mehen. Therefore, it should come as no surprise that Mehen protects the Sungod in a similar fashion as "He with living forms" does for Osiris.

Mehen's protection is so powerful and alive that it changes the demeanour of the crewmember "Heru Hekenu" (No. 510) from the Seventh Hour onwards. Heru Hekenu is present during every hour of the night to encourage Râ through adoration and worship. He is thus of great support for the Sungod. During the previous hours he had held his hand up in a blessing gesture against the shrine. This posture enabled the power of his prayers to be transferred to the protective shrine. The only exceptions to this scene are found in the First and Third Hour. During the First Hour, which is the transition area of the Duat, the enhanced protection was not needed. In the Third Hour the shrine with Râ was missing, making the scene obviously obsolete. From the present point onward, the Sungod is no longer inside this shrine. He has traded its protection for the sheltering coils of Mehen. This integument is very strong, making the blessing gesture of Heru Hekenu no longer necessary. His adoration, though, does continue as it fills Râ with strength and courage.

The crewmember "Kherep wia" (No. 514) is standing at the stern of the Sun barque, as per usual, while holding the helm securely with both hands. Although he has the Sun barque firmly under his control, his magical helmsmanship is still inadequate for the only passageway is effectively blocked by the horrendous monster Apophis (ʿ3pp) (No. 515), also known as Neha-her, "Horrible of face", who is lying directly in front of the Sun barque. His enormous body is described as *tjes* (*ts*) or "sandbank" and is 440 cubits (756 ft /230.34 mtr) long and 440 cubits wide. To give an idea of the immense size of Apophis, the base of the Pyramid of Khufu, also known as the Great Pyramid of Giza, has exactly the same measurements. Thus, it is quite clear that the body of Apophis forms a massive obstacle that forces the Sun barque to stop. To make matters worse, he has swallowed all of the water of the Sacred River, effectively stranding the barque.

> He (Apophis) is like this at his sandbank
> which is in the Duat.
> "Bringing water" is the name
> of this sandbank,
> it is 440 cubits in length
> and 440 cubits in breadth.[12]

The crew of the Sun barque wishes to help Râ in his fight against Apophis to the best of their abilities. At the same time they realise the usual crew cannot win the upcoming battle. This is why Wepwawet and Nebet wia have left the Sun barque temporarily. "Isis" (No. 505) and the "Eldest Magician" (No. 507) have taken their respective places during this hour instead. Both are great magicians and, therefore, formidable opponents in the battle against the absolute evil embodied by Apophis.

(No. 505) "Isis"
(No. 506) "Sia"
(No. 507) "Eldest Magician"
(No. 508) "Mehen"
(No. 509) "Iuf"
(No. 510) "Heru Hekenu"
(No. 511) "Ka Maât"
(No. 512) "Nehes"
(No. 513) "Hu"
(No. 514) "Kherep wia"

Isis possesses great magical powers, *Heka*, and is known as the "Lady of Enchantment". As previously mentioned, Isis obtained the secret name of Râ using a cunning trick in the myth of "the Name of Râ". This particular name contains Secret Knowledge that allowed Isis to acquire great magical powers. It is precisely this magical power, the power that she acquired through Râ, which simultaneously binds her to him.

> I (the Sungod Râ) will allow myself
> to be searched through by Isis,
> and my name shall come forth
> from my body and go into hers.[13]
> – The legend of Râ and Isis

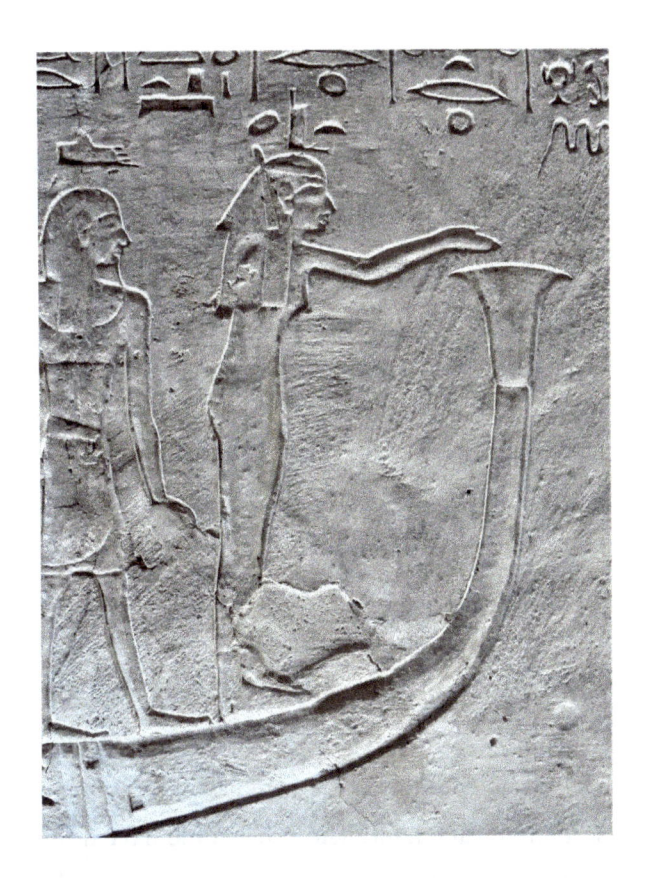

The Goddess Isis stands on the prow of the Sun barque with her hands held in a magical gesture and the "Eldest Magician" stands behind her, KV 14 Tausert/Setnakht

Isis protects Râ from Apophis for she will

lose her magical power in the case of Râ's death. Furthermore, Apophis does not just threaten Râ, but her beloved husband Osiris as well. Consequently, she is closely involved with the rebirth of Râ as well as the renewal of Osiris.

Aside from the use of the magical power of Râ, Isis has also learned the magical formulae of Thoth. These are the magical spells she used to revive the body of Osiris. Thus, she possesses the Secret Knowledge and power to transform death into life. She is familiar with the precise pronunciation of the magical words while using the right tone of voice with a true and genuine intent. In this hour, she is standing up front on the Sun barque with her hands held up in a magical gesture. She projects her power and supremacy as she recites the magical words of power to enchant Apophis.

> (But) Isis came with her Magic power,
> her speech is Breath of Life,
> her utterance removes a suffering,
> her words restore the one
> with an oppressed throat to life.
> She said: 'what is it, my Divine Father? What is the matter?
> A serpent that has brought
> weakness over you?
> One of your children who has raised his head against you?
> Then <I> will slay him with my effective Magic (*ḥk3*),
> I will make him draw back from
> seeing your rays!' [14]

– Magical Spell for warding off poison

Behind Isis stands the Eldest Magician, Heka Semsu (*ḥk3 smsu*), who has replaced Nebet wia. The powers of Nebet wia, the Lady of the barque, are insufficient this time around to protect Râ. It is not entirely clear who the Eldest Magician is exactly. He might be the God of Magic, Heka. However, he could also be Seth, the God of chaos and destruction. There is an argument to be made for both of these Gods as to why they could be the Eldest Magician and, therefore, capable of destroying Apophis.

The God Heka possesses immeasurable magical power which he used to create the world. Heka is a very complex God. He seems to be created by Atum before the God Shu and the Goddess Tefnut came into existence. This would make Heka the eldest son of Atum, instead of Shu. However, he could also be the personification of the creative or magical power of Atum. This suggests that Heka existed at the same time as Atum, before duality had come into being. Or better yet, that Heka, as the potent magical energy, even preceded the creation of Atum himself. Then it was Heka who ensured that Atum was created. From this point of view, this would make Heka the Father of all the Gods and thus, the *eldest* God. This could explain the *Eldest* Magician. However, although Heka was sometimes depicted while holding a serpent in each hand whom he would have done battle with, there are no records that Heka battled with Apophis.

Seth, on the other hand, is a God of chaos and destruction. The only way to defeat the dark evil of Apophis is to fight it with evil, fight fire with fire. From this point of view one could assume that the Eldest Magician is a form of Seth and the designated God to go into battle with this evil. Moreover, it has always been the task of Seth to conquer Apophis. This is reflected in the Book of the Dead. It states that Seth is the Great Magician and capable of defeating this serpent. Seth's destructive powers are then harnessed to save the life of Râ.

> Seth will project a lance of iron
> against him (Apophis) and
> will make him vomit up all that
> he has swallowed.
> Seth will place him before him
> and will say to him with Magic power:
> "Get back at the sharp knife
> which is in my hand!
> I stand before you, navigating aright
> and seeing afar.
> Cover your face, for I ferry across;
> get back because of me, for I am the Male!
> Cover your head, cleanse the palm
> of your hand;
> I am hale and I remain hale,
> for I am the Great Magician, the son of Nut,
> and power against you
> has been granted to me.
> Who is that spirit who goes on his belly,
> his tail and his spine?
> See, I have gone against you,
> and your tail is in my hand,
> for I am one who exhibits strength.
> I have come that I may rescue
> the earth Gods for Râ
> so that he may go to rest for me
> in the evening.
> I go round about the sky,
> but you are in the fetters which
> were decreed for you in the Presence,
> and Râ will go to rest alive in his horizon."[15]
> – Book of the Dead; Spell 108

Finally, between the paws of the Great Sphinx of Giza there is a stela. It is known as the Dream or Sphinx-stela of Tuthmosis IV. The text on it describes a vision of Tuthmosis IV when he was dozing off in the shadow of the Sphinx. In this text the name of Seth is written in combination with the Eldest Magician. It could be translated as Seth, the Eldest Magician.[16]

This could prove that Seth is the Eldest Magician. However, it can also be translated as; Seth *and* the Eldest Magician. This would mean that Seth is not the personification of the Eldest Magician. Then it could be the God of Magic, Heka, the eldest God of all the Gods. It is hard to tell which translation is the correct one.

For now, it seems fitting that it is the boastful Seth who takes all the credits and glory of the destruction of Apophis. To do this in the present hour, Seth does not use the lance of iron as mentioned in the book of the Dead. Instead he utilises the invisible though potent power of

Heka or Magic. This means that the creative magical power, embodied by the God Heka, ensures that Seth's intention, to defeat Apophis, is manifested. Therefore, *Heka* would be the magical force behind the physical power of Seth to defeat Apophis. In a sense, they could both be the Eldest Magician, although Seth is the one who embodies him and manifests the magical force of Heka to defeat Apophis.

Isis and the Eldest Magician are here standing together with joined forces. They use their Magic to repel the evil power of Apophis "Horrible of face". This effectively dispels Apophis, leaving him powerless. Then, Isis and the Eldest Magician elevate Râ to free him from this darkness. The barque can now finally sail across Apophis and resume its voyage.

Apophis was absent in the previous hours, to finally emerge in the Seventh Hour. The fact this embodiment of absolute evil did not make an appearance until now is unsurprising considering the development taking place within this hour. During the Sixth Hour, Râ and Osiris had formed a unit inside of the body of the five-headed serpent "Many-faced", a form of Mehen. This allowed for the *Ba*-soul of the Sungod Râ to become one with the body of Osiris. However, during the present hour this unity changes as they both occupy their own places. Although Râ and Osiris do belong together as body and soul, it is also important for them to experience their own individual development. This is emphasised by the fact that they are both protected by two different serpents. Mehen is the one protecting Râ while his other appearance, "He with living forms", offers protection to Osiris. In a sense, Osiris and Râ are still a unity that is protected by different forms of Mehen to allow the both of them to experience their own respective transformation.

The separation of these two Gods is of the utmost importance for the cosmic cycle to continue. To facilitate the growth of Râ's light, or consciousness, it is vital for him to identify himself with another object. In this case, to reflect himself with Osiris. They both need to take their respective specific places to give shape to this duality.

For this reason, Apophis tries to negate the necessary duality that is reflected in the Seventh Hour with all his evil might. He does everything within his power to realise stagnation, chaos and total utter destruction. It is his job to disrupt harmony. It might sound contradictory, but Râ actually needs this dangerous opponent to become strong himself. The more powerful the foe, the more powerful Râ will become. It is this battle that tests the strength of his early light. Although Râ is surrounded by many combatants willing to aid him, he himself is taking precautions as well. When Apophis calls upon him and comes face to face with him, the Sungod swallows his own Eye, or light. In doing so, the Eye is kept away someplace safe from the destructive powers of Apophis. Furthermore, the swallowing also indicates that Râ identifies himself with his growing light. By swallowing a part of his being, Râ truly embodies this renewed light. This enables him to become more powerful and fierce, which he can use in the battle against Apophis.

It is a battle between life and death we are talking about here, which is why the ancient Egyptians did not want to tempt fate. This was the reason they were very careful about the things they depicted in their images through their various arts. They considered images to be a two dimensional representation of an idea with the purpose of manifesting the idea it portrays. Thus, the drawing or painting of an image was an act of Magic to ensure it would manifest into the three dimensional world of real life. Consequently, the ancient Egyptians would never depict something they would rather not realise into the matter of the real world. This is the reason for the barrier in front of the Sun barque in the image. This wall guarantees that Apophis stays separated from Râ, making the destruction of the Sungod virtually impossible. This barrier could also be a forcefield manifested with the Magic of Isis and the Eldest Magician. After all, both of them are skilled enough to create an impenetrable magical wall to disempower Apophis. Secondly, Apophis is nailed to the ground with six knives, making any attempt to move futile. And lastly, he is also subdued by two Deities, making the victory of Râ practically set in stone.

The first God who subdues Apophis is the scorpion Goddess Serket, "She who lets the throat breathe" (No. 516). As mentioned before, she has power over venomous scorpions and snakes, as well as the gift to return the Breath of Life. However, she is also capable of taking this important Breath of Life away, causing asphyxiation. This is the ability she applies to Apophis as she ties a lasso around his neck. With this lasso she literally takes his Breath of Life away. Not only does this incapacitate his ability to breath, for it also forces the water from the Sacred River he has swallowed out of him. Apophis spits out the liquid, returning the water to the dried up Sacred River. The Coffin Texts describes this skill of Serket as the method to ward off Apophis.

> I am skilled in the craft of
> "Her who permits throats to breathe";
> therefore I will drive off ꜥ3pp (Apophis),
> ferrying across the firmament.[17]
> – Coffin Texts; Spell 752

The other God who overpowers Apophis is "He above his knives" (No. 517). He stands in a bent over posture as he punishes Apophis with all his might. He does this by attaching a rope to the tail of the serpent.

In his effort he is aided by four Goddesses who stand directly behind him. Each Goddess is armed with a large knife to repel the attacks of the enemies of Râ. Naturally, the greatest foe of them all is Apophis. This dangerous serpent is punished by the four Goddesses who cut him to pieces to destroy him.

(No. 518) "She who binds together"

(No. 519) "She who cuts"
(No. 520) "She who punishes"
(No. 521) "She who annihilates"

Following the punishing Goddesses there are four sarcophagi (No. 522 – 525). These sarcophagi are standing all the way at the end of the Sacred River behind the sandbank that is formed by the body of Apophis. This demonstrates the fact that Apophis has seized an impressive part of the Sacred River.

There is a head on every corner of each sarcophagus and large knives are inserted in the lids. These knives are there to safeguard the contents of the sarcophagi that are most precious. They are the Divine forms of the Sungod Râ, buried underneath a mound of sand. These Divine forms are;

(No. 522) "Which contains the image of Atum" represents the setting sun in the evening.
(No. 523) "Which contains the image of Khepri" represents the rising sun in the morning.
(No. 524) "Which contains the image of Râ" represents the day.
(No. 525) "Which contains the image of Osiris" represents the night.

During the First Hour we have already become acquainted with these Gods, or Divine forms, of the Sungod (No. 58 – 61). Each form symbolises a part of the cycle of the sun. Together they refer to completeness and wholeness. Râ passes through each of these different phases during his voyage in the day and the night. Each of these phases of the Sun is important to complete the solar cycle. The fact that these phases or forms are buried in the sarcophagi, demonstrates that death is an essential and indispensable element. It ensures the renewal and continued development of life. Therefore, it is death that guarantees the preservation of eternal Life.

The sarcophagi illustrate the process of dying which, like the process of rebirth, takes place in phases. Each image of the Sungod is required to be subjected to death in order to enable the rise of the next image. Furthermore, these four sarcophagi emphasise the fact that Râ has been dismembered. Each God, or Divine image of Râ, lies here buried individually in a separate sarcophagus, which underlines the fact that the solar cycle cannot be completed. Therefore, Râ travels past them to identify himself with these Divine forms to allow them to become a part of his being once more. As soon as Râ arrives the appearances of these Gods, in the form of heads, come forward to identify themselves with Râ for their part as well. It goes without saying that this venture is a very dangerous one since Apophis is still near. Therefore, each sarcophagus contains a knife that emerges for protection at the exact moment the enchantment of Apophis is audible. Right after the identification process is finished and Râ has resumed his travels, the heads withdraw themselves. Now that they are alone, they once again identify themselves with their own specific being by absorbing their own image. The knives disappear inside the sarcophagus as well, until they are needed again during the next night when Râ makes his appearance.

Behind the sarcophagi there are a God and a Goddess standing while facing the opposite direction. They are the guardians of the precious and mysterious images contained within the four sarcophagi. The God, "Master of the *Was*-sceptre" (No. 526), is holding a *Was*-sceptre in his hand to illustrate his dominion over darkness and death. The Goddess, "She who owns a heart" (No. 527), is standing directly behind him and concludes the procession of the Sacred River. The heart mentioned in her name is the True Heart, the seat of all Consciousness and Wisdom. Hence, her True Heart speaks with the True Voice of *Maât*. Both Gods embody the right qualities to protect the precious contents of the sarcophagi and ward off all evil.

The Duatians of the right riverbank (lower section)

At the front of the right riverbank, the God "Horus upon his throne" (No. 528) is seated on his throne. Horus is wearing a solar disk with an upraised Uraeus on top of his hawk head. In his hands he is holding the *Ankh* and the *Was*-sceptre. Here he is portrayed in a grand manner that emphasises the major influence he has in this area.

Though Osiris is victorious over the enemies on the left riverbank, it is Horus who triumphs on the right riverbank and maintains the cosmic order. He does this by letting the stars rise up in the heavens. Each star takes its position that results in the formation of small constellations, or decans, together with the other stars. As mentioned before, the decans were used as a celestial star clock since their appearance in the sky is linked to the rotation of the earth. The rise of a decan signifies the beginning of a new hour and, therefore, the movement of the Sun barque. As the decans travel through the sky, where they appear and disappear, so too does the Sun barque continue its travels. In other

Horus upon his throne, KV 14 Tausert/Setnakht

words, while these stellar Deities are commanded by Horus, he simultaneously ensures the continued movement of the Sun barque. Their rise guarantees the progression of the journey in the correct order and time.

The first stars set into motion by Horus are a group of twelve male stars, the Star Hour Gods. Each of these Gods is wearing a five-pointed star on top of his head and is facing Horus. Horus requests them to rise up in the sky and to take their respective positions visible in the heavens. These Gods, though, do not belong to Horus alone for they are part of the entourage of Râ of the Horizon. Each night they lighten the road in front of Râ with their beaming starlight.

(No. 529) "With rich supply"
(No. 530) "Master of supply"
(No. 531) "Master of what the earth needs"
(No. 532) "He of the Duat"
(No. 533) "Driver of the stars"
(No. 534) "Driver of the *Akh*-spirits"
(No. 535) "He with raised arm"
(No. 536) "He with protected arm"
(No. 537) "He with strong arm"
(No. 538) "He who cuts with his tongue"
(No. 539) "He who cuts with his eye"
(No. 540) "He who smites heads"

Horus addresses the twelve Star Hour Gods:

May your flesh be in order,
may your forms come into being,
that you may rest in your stars!
You rise indeed before Râ of the horizon
who is in the Duat, day after day.
You are behind him, your stars before him,
until I have passed through
the Beautiful West in peace.
You are the Rising Ones in the earth.
You belong indeed to me,
your stars (however) to him
who is in the heaven,
so that he is satisfied,
the Lord of the horizon.[18]

The subsequent group of stars set in motion

One of the Star Hour Gods, KV 14 Tausert/Setnakht

by Horus is a group of twelve female stars, the Star Hour Goddesses. These Goddesses symbolise the stars and should not be confused with the Hour Goddesses linked to a specific hour of the night. They are not the same. The Star Hour Goddesses are each wearing a five-pointed star on top of their heads with their faces turned away from Horus. Horus asks them to rise up to enable their light to beam. It is their task to protect Râ and to fight for him with their heads held high. They need to guide Râ through the nocturnal world of the Beautiful West. These Star Hour Goddesses, together with the Star Hour Gods, form a protective circle of light around the Sungod as they guide him along his journey through the night.

(No. 541) "She who adores"
(No. 542) "Mistress of the earth"
(No. 543) "Lady of Ladies"
(No. 544) "She of the Duat"
(No. 545) "She who devours"
(No. 546) "She who commands the *Ka*-energies"
(No. 547) "She who brings"
(No. 548) "She who is coloured"
(No. 549) "Tait"
(No. 550) "She who creates brightness"
(No. 551) "She who creates forms"
(No. 552) "She who frees from misfortune"

Horus addresses the twelve Star Hour Goddesses:

O! Hours which have come into being!
O! Star Hours!
O! Hours protecting Râ,
who fight on behalf of him in the horizon!
May you receive your forms,
may you bear your images
and raise your heads,
when you guide this Râ
who is in the horizon
to the Beautiful West, in peace! [19]

These Star Hour Gods and Goddesses are here to emphasise the fact that duality exists in the heavens as well to preserve the cosmic order. Together they highlight the contradictions not

One of the Star Hour Goddesses, KV 14 Tausert/Setnakht

only through their different genders, but also through their positions. The first twelve Star Hour Gods are facing left while the twelve Star Hour Goddesses are facing the right side.

The hour concludes with a crocodile lying on a hill of sand, "Crocodile in the Duat" (No. 553). The crocodile is a creature able to survive on land as well as in the water. The ability to survive in both worlds, on earth and in aquatic environments, accentuates his two sides. On one hand, he is a blessing as he embodies fertility and regeneration. On the other hand, though, he is a terrifying creature known for his gluttony and destructive power.

In the Netherworld he is considered a dangerous opponent who seeks to steal the Magic of the traveller. Without Magic, the journey through this dangerous world is doomed to fail. Fortunately, the Book of the Dead is fitted with two Spells, 31 and 32, used to prevent this robbery by the crocodile. However, the crocodile is also an important protector precisely due to his enormous power. Therefore, the Book of the Dead also contains a spell that transforms the traveller into a crocodile. This enables the traveller to harness these dangerous powers for his own gain.

> I am a crocodile immersed in dread,
> I am a crocodile who takes by robbery,
> I am the great and mighty fish-like being who is in the Bitter Lakes,
> I am the Lord of those who bow down in Letopolis.[20]
> – Book of the Dead; Spell 88

In one of the myths, the crocodile is mentioned as a saviour since he rescued Osiris from drowning by carrying the latter ashore on his back. When Sobek's name (*sbk*) is written in a different manner (*sbk̠*) it translates as "to unite, to collect". This is reflected in another myth where Sobek collected the limbs of the dismembered Osiris in his mouth. In the present hour Osiris is once again protected by the crocodile. The crocodile is depicted on top of the burial mound where the "Head of Osiris" (No. 555) emerges from. This indicates that the regenerative powers and fertility of the once dead and dismembered Osiris are in de process of renewal. A fact that is further reaffirmed by the symbolism of the crocodile who is lying on top of him. This image shows us that the indestructible primal force of life has visibly resurfaced.

Furthermore, the crocodile is also a form of the God Seth. Seth, in his form as the Eldest Magician, does not just protect the Sungod, but Osiris as well. He safeguards the Sungod as he throws his Magic into the battle against Apophis. However, he protects Osiris via completely different means. As mentioned before, the Eye is a symbol of the light of Râ. The Sungod Râ protects this Eye actively as he himself swallows it. In the case of Osiris, it is the crocodile who has taken on the protection of the "Eye of Osiris" (No. 554). This particular Eye is not depicted in the Seventh Hour. This is due to the fact that the crocodile has hidden this Eye inside his spine. In doing so, he has assumed the safeguard of the passive Osiris who does not take action to protect himself like Râ does. These different ways of protecting the Eye highlight the differences in the light between Râ and Osiris. Râ will soon shine his renewed light visibly in the day world, whereas Osiris's light will never be visible. It remains hidden in the dark subconscious realm of the Duat.

> He (crocodile) is like this
> on the sandy shore:
> It is he who guards the image of this place.
> When he hears the voice of the crew
> of the barque of Râ,
> the Eye goes forth from his spine,
> and then the head which
> is in his riverbank appears, too.
> Then he swallows his images again,
> after this Great God has passed him.
> He who knows it is one whose *Ba*-soul the crocodile cannot swallow.[21]

The manifestation of the Seventh Hour in daily life

The second half of the journey has arrived as you enter the Seventh Hour. You have completed the crossing from the transforming South to the stabilising North. The Seventh Hour is directly opposite from the Sixth Hour, which accentuates the differences between these two hours. During the Fifth and Sixth Hour the focus was turned towards the highest light as symbolised by the South. In the Seventh Hour, however, you have arrived in the North. This is the area without sunlight. Although you now travel towards the sunrise, you first have to make it through this dark area in the upcoming two hours.

The beautiful mystery of the unification as accomplished during the Sixth Hour has disappeared in the present hour. You might have had the illusion that you could remain in this little paradise for the rest of eternity. However, the time when you enter the present hour, this illusion is precisely that, an illusion. It bursts like a bubble, making you wonder whether any of it was even real. No need to worry though, for the renewal has most definitely taken place. During the Seventh Hour this newly acquired consciousness is tested. These tests are necessary as the growing consciousness needs to become strong and steadfast during the second half of the journey. To acquire this, you need to take action and work for it. Here you are put firmly to your feet as the confidence in your Higher Self, which you have built up, is put to the test. As are the laws of the universe, the tiny light that is ignited attracts darkness.

The Sun barque has become stranded on a sandbank in the form of Apophis. Therefore, you too are now unable to proceed. You have to get rid of this hampering sandbank first to enable the water to start flowing again. This sandbank is formed by the attacking influences from the outside world. However, it is predominantly produced by reoccurring fearful feelings of the new and the unknown in the form of inner saboteurs. These saboteurs try anything to break the connection with the Higher Self for your submission to your inner Sungod and the resulting renewed vision poses a real threat.

You will experience this in various areas in your life like your work, family and relationships. Suddenly you find yourself in situations during which you are attacked and irritated. The old habits to take charge yourself resurface. In everyday life it is not as simple as it seems to continuously listen to the True inner Voice within. There are many jammers that are interfering with your connection to the Higher Self, which results in static. However, it is most important to be aware of this in order to stay fine-tuned to the correct channel. You are going to learn this ability along the way by trial and error. It is part of the process and something you should not be discouraged by. Reaching spiritual adulthood is not something you achieve overnight.

Your journey results in many transformations that have an impact on your daily life. Things change, especially in the field of your relationships, for you yourself have changed and are gifted with new insights. This puts a new angle on things, making you re-evaluate your relationships and it ultimately leads to modified affiliations. People may disappear from your life as the connection between the both of you might have faded. You have reached a crossroads where everyone goes their own separate way. Alternatively, you also meet new people along the way on this new path. This shift in relationships can result in various confrontations. Letting go and renewal are actions that are usually not without controversy. You might lose people in the initial stages, possibly leading you to doubt yourself. However, be persistent and have True Faith during this phase. It is a necessary step to clear the decks to make space for the new things which do fit you. Everything is a test to see if you are truly ready to choose this development and remain in tune with your inner Sungod.

Your renewed consciousness also requires an increased level of discernment. As your awareness has increased, you are now able and expected to take more responsibility in your life. This includes new and conscious choices and decisions you did not have to make before. After completing the Sixth Hour, you are deemed ready to wield the blade of discernment. This is the blade that you harness in your fight against Apophis to cut his contradicting and aggressive power to pieces.

Furthermore, you need to ensure that your renewed consciousness is protected well enough. It should not be exposed unnecessarily to external influences that you are not able to endure yet. Keep this early consciousness hidden from the outside world, just like Râ who swallowed his Eye. Young trees need a fence surrounding them to prevent them from getting trampled before they have grown tall and straight. Though tempting it may be, do not share your new insights with the outside world. Besides, it is about becoming visible or noticeable through your actions, not your words.

There are many out there who are interested in your progress. They want to destroy what you have worked so hard to build during the previous hours. Apophis symbolises these attacking forces that you will encounter in daily life. However, he especially represents your own inner demons, for we tend to overlook these. Our own way of thinking proves to be our biggest opponent. All our thought patterns and figments of imagination, that make themselves known on a daily basis, fill our minds for the most part with utter nonsense. These are the fears and projections that are hounding us all day long. Fears about a future that will never happen. Frustrations about a past, which have taken root due to a narrow vision. Moreover, the blinders that prevent us from seeing what is truly happening in the Present Moment. They are thoughts polluting our minds and therefore need to be beheaded and bound. You can purify your mentality from these mind games as you become in tune with the True Voice of the Higher Self. At all times you are required to do so as the disruptive thoughts continue to ambush you. Keep on your toes indefinitely for you always need to assess these thoughts in the light of *Maât*.

Fortunately, this hour does not just contain enemy forces compelling you to open battle. There are just as many protective and assisting forces here to support you on your way as well. It is important to be aware of this positive influence. Know there will always be help, you need only ask. The asking part is very important, for your own free will is respected at all times. Communicate with your inner Sungod and ask your questions. You will notice help and answers are always given, though possibly from an angle you might not have expected. That is what makes your battle, even though hard and challenging, an experience rewarded with precious gifts.

The most important supportive force is reflected by Mehen. This serpent has wrapped itself around Râ like a second skin. Mehen symbolises the power and trust that you have built along your voyage. This power and submission to your Higher Self provides you with the protection needed against the destructive forces. It has enabled you to rise and adopt a renewed consciousness. Your old and restricted vision has been cast off, shed like skin that has become too tight. The transformation process has made you flexible, enabling you to move past old rigid patterns. This is the fluidity needed to allow for a process of continuous growth and renewal. The cycle of dying and renewal will eternally keep moving, a fact that is reflected by the four sarcophagi (No. 522 – 525). Each phase of this transformation process is an important step to rise as a renewed light or consciousness.

The snake is an animal that prefers to live underground. This connects him to the world of the subconscious. Mehen represents the intuition that you have connected yourself to during the Sixth Hour. It is the True inner Voice of the Higher Self who has tied this underworld to your day world. This opens the gate for the inner Wisdom and to the powers of our potential that now slowly starts to take shape step by step. Beware of internal as well as external enemies who are waiting to devour this inner stream of intuition. Resign yourself to let the intuition serve as the guardian on the threshold to your own Sanctuary.

Furthermore, the serpent emphasises the contradictions to make you aware of the need for duality to further your development. On one hand, we have the protective forces of Mehen, while on the other hand the destructive powers of Apophis. As always, there are two sides to a story to enable the balance in life. The same thing can be seen with the two Gods Râ and Seth. While Râ embodies the Divine Law of *Maât* and the good and constructive side of creation, Seth is the embodiment of chaos and the evil and destructive side of creation. Only through the cooperation between these two different forces can the destruction of the absolute evil, which is Apophis, be achieved. As long as you keep this train of thought in your mind, the battle in life receives a different meaning. Then you are able to recognise an attack in your personal life as nothing more than an opportunity to restore balance. You might forget this piece of wisdom during the fight. However, your awareness is restored once the battle is over.

Therefore, during the Seventh Hour the unity, which was achieved during the Sixth Hour, falls apart. Râ and Osiris are now separated and no longer share a single body. Each now inhabits his own place. This enables them to mirror each other. Osiris, the Powerself, has once again taken his place upon the throne as Lord of the Duat. He lives in the Underworld and symbolises the power found in our inner life. The power that is increasingly speaking up more clearly. The Powerself has obtained a clear right to exist and addresses us via dreams and feelings. These inner signals do still need to be held up against the light of the inner Sungod. It is the interaction between the sunlight of Râ and the dark night of Osiris that enable us to grow up into a self-conscious human being.

Râ and Osiris each have their own tasks and functions, which they can perform only when separated from each other. Without this separation, the act of creation is impossible. This also applies to you. After the experience during the Sixth Hour you can no longer remain on top of your mountain in meditation. The continuous need to dwell within the Higher planes to experience unity is an illusion. You need to land on earth with both feet firm on the ground. Only then you are able to perform the task entrusted to you. Yet do not worry, for the contact with the Higher Self does not just disappear. You always carry it within you. One day you will return Home completely, but now is not the time. Atum, the ancient Creator God, presents us with the need of diversity before finally returning to unity, our Home.

I am One who becomes Two
I am Two who becomes Four
I am Four who becomes Eight
and then I am One again [22]
– Coffin of Pa-di-Amun

Maybe you are already experiencing homesickness at times and would like nothing more but to return to your true Home. However, aim your gaze upwards and let go of your own little world. Look up at those amazing stars and see the way they are beaming down on you. Remember, your body too is made of stardust. You are therefore a star on earth. Your nature is divine and you exist here on earth to materialise this divinity into matter. This would have been impossible without a body, the vessel for achieving things on earth. It is a privilege to be able to experience your development here. That is why the more you grow spiritually, the more you feel at Home wherever you are.

Heka or Magic, the creative force

Throughout this book of the Amduat the practical use of the creative force, Magic or *Heka*, is implemented. During the previous hours we have seen several ways to put it into practice. For example; by means of breath, magical knives, images, words and formulae. Especially during this hour, the use of Magic is of great importance to defeat the incarnate evil of Apophis.

Magic in ancient Egypt was a fundamental sacred Science necessary to survive and to facilitate life. The earth, the Netherworld and the sky were inhabited by all kinds of visible and invisible beings. Some of which were benevolent and some were malevolent. Through the use of Magic one could come into contact with them and gain control over these contradictive powers.[23]

Furthermore, through the use of Magic, one could embody the power of a certain being in the world of the living as well as in the world of the dead. The person in question could then harness this power to use to his advantage. For example, as mentioned before, Spell 88 from the Book of the Dead is used to transform the user into a crocodile. Anyone who applied the Magic of this spell in the proper manner would become just as great and mighty as the crocodile himself. Thus, he would be able to travel safely through the Netherworld.

Magic was used for almost anything. From healing the ill to fertilising the fields, combating plagues, achieving prosperity, gain protection, prophesying, creating incantations, making contact with the Gods, in rituals and ceremonies, and so on. It was a normal part of daily life and had nothing to do with superstition. Consequently, the question whether you believe in such things was not a question at all. It was actual science taking effect through the Law of nature. You can, for example, compare it with math, physics or chemistry. When you take these courses at school, you do not doubt the credibility of the things you learn. Magic had a similar position to the ancient Egyptians.

The better you were trained in the sacred Science of Magic, the greater the chances were that the things you wished for would actually be realised. To master Magic on a certain level, it was imperative to receive teachings and training. However, these intense and lengthy studies were not accessible to just anyone. Only the Priests and the Wise were allowed to specialise themselves in the Science of Magic. Naturally, the Pharaoh, as the living God on earth, was considered a master in the use of the creative force, or *Heka*.

Magic was connected to the Divine since it was performed using the sacred words of the Gods who had created the world. These sacred words could be found in the religious texts. It was of the utmost importance that these texts were interpreted and understood correctly. To create effective spells, profound knowledge of these texts was a prerequisite. Secondly, it was important to pronounce the words with the right intonations and intention to conjure the desired. Finally, it was essential that this Divine creative power was applied in accordance with the Law of the Divine, or *Maât*.

The Priests and the Wise were educated in the sacred texts and in this Law. Consequently, they were the ones to aid the people who were in need of assistance and not allowed to reach this level of Magic themselves. As you may understand, it was considered a highly respected craft that provided the people with amulets, spells, rituals, medicine, healings, prophecies, images, magical objects, etcetera.

As mentioned before, Magic is an invisible though potent energy preceding the creation. It ensures the intention, uttered in words, is manifested. It is an existing sacred power that abides the Law of nature. Therefore, Magic is still just as much alive and active as it was thousands of years ago. Even in our science controlled society of the 21st century.

The Amduat is a book that aims to help us understand all of these visible and invisible forces that are part of your life. Along your journey through the hours of the night this knowledge will make you more aware of what is happening in your own world. It is precisely this Self Knowledge that provides you with an expanded perception and enables you to make connections with the life surrounding you. You become increasingly involved in the Grand Design instead of being separated from it. Additionally, you also become more aware of the Divine Law of Nature. Your journey through the Duat up until this point has ensured your comprehension of *Maât* and the creative force of Magic, the driving force behind this Law, has increased. Should you choose to truly work with this creative force, you have to follow proper education and an extensive training. Similar to every other science or skill you wish to learn. This was also the case for the Priests and the Wise Ones in ancient times and it still applies to us in the modern age. Magic is a very complex science as it takes many different shapes and forms and can be used for numerous purposes.

A journey through the Duat provides you with just a fraction of the knowledge available and highlights only certain aspects of a specific form of Magic. However, to truly grasp the essence of it and everything the Amduat can teach us, a single trip through the Duat is insufficient. It only marks the beginning of the process in becoming acquainted with and the understanding of Magic. Each subsequent journey through the Duat increases your comprehension and strengthens your own skills in this specific form of Magic. This form is achieved as you start to connect with the Higher Self. Conscious acts from this connection with the Higher Will of the inner Sungod can achieve the things where you alone fall short. Then you have become the canal of the inspired words and thoughts of the Divine, your inner Sungod. This provides you with the ability to manifest this higher intention into the world. The connection with the Higher Self also ensures you are always acting in accordance with the Divine Law of *Maât*. It is the power of this Magic that can conquer and transform contradictive powers, just like Isis and the Eldest Magician could. The Amduat, therefore, teaches you to look behind the veil and allow for the creative force of Magic to shine into your life.

> He who knows it upon earth
> is one whose water "Horrible of face"
> cannot drink.[24]

THE EIGHTH HOUR
"Sarcophagus of her Gods"

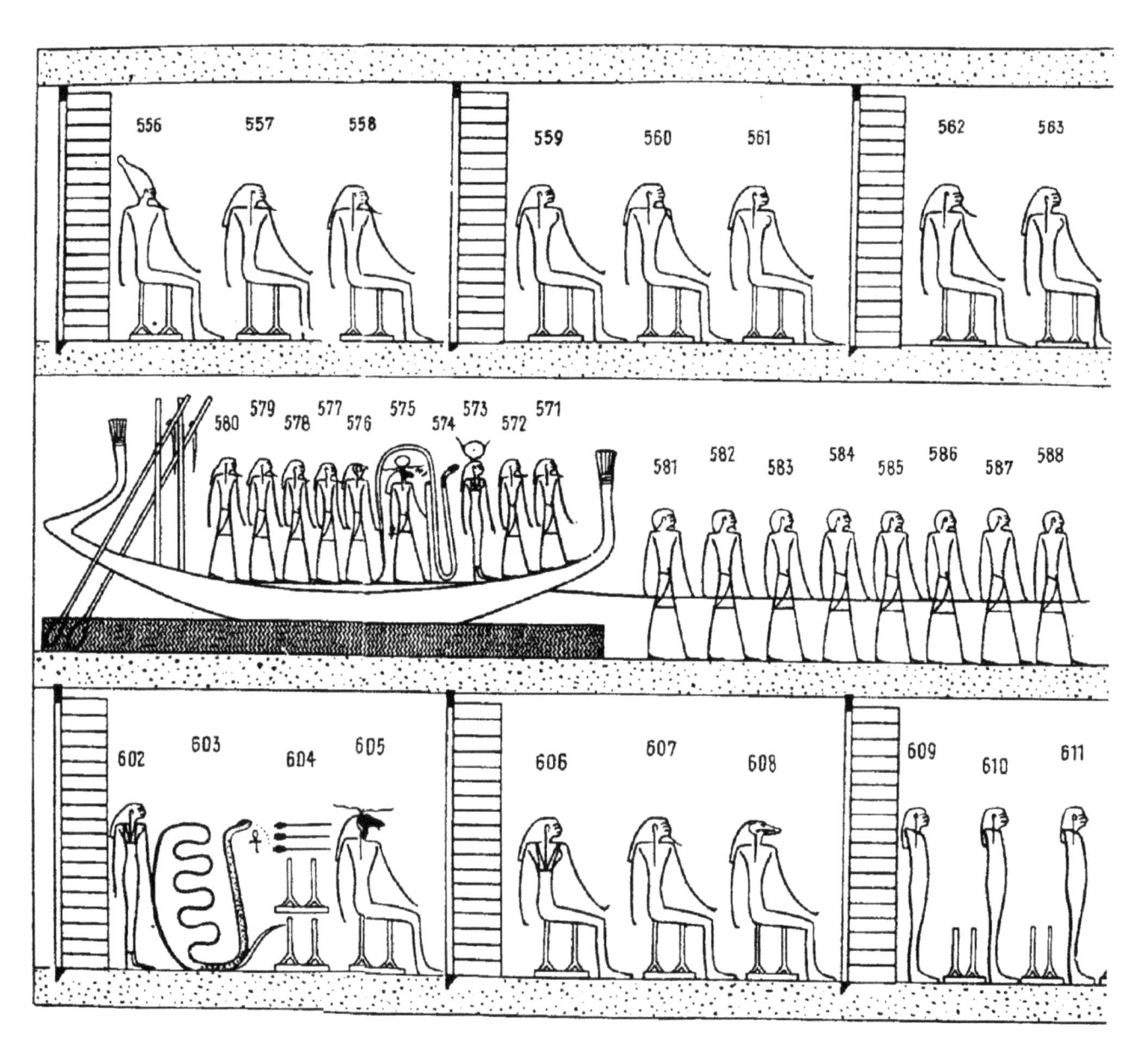

Figure 25: The Eighth Hour

The Gate:	"Which stands without getting tired"
The Hour Goddess:	"Mistress of Deep Night"
The Guardian:	(no name mentioned)

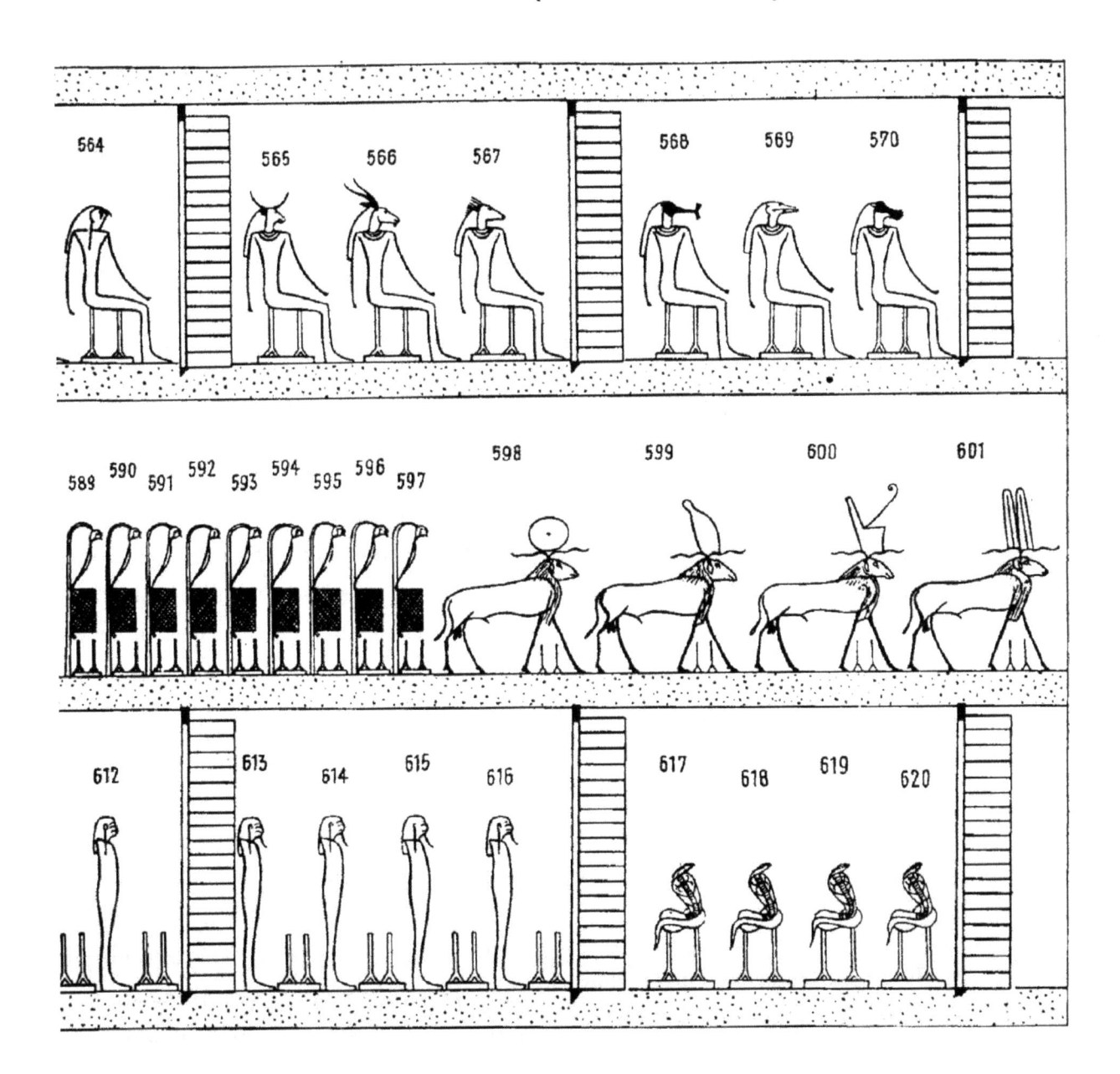

Introduction

Pausing by the person of this Great God
at the caverns of the mysterious Gods
who are upon their sand.
He gives them orders from his barque and
his Gods tow him in this place
in the protected form
of the Mehen-serpent.
The name of the Gate of this place is
"Which stands without getting tired".
The name of this Place is
"Sarcophagus of her Gods".
The name of the Hour of the night guiding
this Great God is
"Mistress of Deep Night".
The mysterious caverns of the West
which this Great God
passes in his barque,
being towed by his Gods
who are in the Duat.
This is done like this image,
on the Northern side
of the Hidden Chamber in the Duat.
He who knows them by their names,
will have clothing in the earth,
without being repelled
from the mysterious gates.
He will be fed at the great tomb.
A true remedy.[1]

During the Eighth Hour the Sungod and his crew are still travelling towards the North. The course of the Sun barque will finally change towards the East after completing this hour. To reinforce the journey towards the light, every God in this hour has turned their gaze forward. The forward facing focus pushes the Sungod in the right direction.

The peace has somewhat settled after the battle against the gigantic serpent Apophis. The dangerous beast has tried everything within his power to prevent the ascension of Râ out of the deepest and darkest point of the night. Despite his best efforts, Apophis failed to succeed in his mission during the fierce fight where he was ultimately defeated by the magical power of Isis (No. 505) and the Eldest Magician (No. 507). The triumph over the absolute evil has replaced chaos with order. The Eighth Hour is therefore characterised by structure and symmetry, similar to the First Hour. This uniformity is reflected in the structure of the hour since the amount of caverns is divided equally over both sides of the riverbank. There are five caverns on the left as well as on the right side. The ten caverns represent every cavern to be found in the Netherworld. Each cavern opens and closes with a gate. The gates are each referred to as "knife". This protection ensures that only authorised persons can gain access to the caverns.

The name of this area is "Sarcophagus of her Gods" (*ḏb3.t nṯr.w=s*). The hieroglyphic word *djebat* (*ḏb3t*) can be translated as "sarcophagus or robing-room". The word *djeba*

($\underline{d}b\beta$) means "cloth, adorn, replace, provide, repay" amongst other things. Hence, the central theme of this hour is all about the supply of clothing. The hieroglyphic sign for clothing can be seen in every cavern. It demonstrates that the Deities within are provided with clothes. This particular sign is composed of two vertical strips of cloth on some kind of standard. The Deities in the caverns are seated upon or standing next to this sign.

Fig. 26. The hieroglyphic sign for clothing.

Clothing was not only an important element in the world of the living, for it was essential in the world of the dead as well. Delicate linen was utilised to create bandages that were used to wind around the deceased during the funerary preparations. The important mummification process and the accompanying rituals ensured the deceased would be prepared sufficiently for the Afterlife. After the preparations the deceased would be able to commence his journey to be born again.

To succeed in this voyage, it was essential for the deceased to receive new clothes in the Afterlife. The tight mummy wrappings had to be removed to make it possible for his renewed being to emerge. The obtained new clothes served as a confirmation that the deceased had truly risen from the dead to be born again. His body was no longer dismembered by death as it was now healed and whole again. He could move once more and enjoy his right to exist in the Afterlife. The gift of clothing, just like offerings, was therefore an essential element to continue ones life in the Afterlife.

Furthermore, the process of putting on new clothes was an important part of the daily temple ritual on behalf of the specific God of a temple. The Deity, represented by a statue, was dressed in a "garment" consisting of a linen shawl or wraparound. The God was tended to during an extensive morning ritual of devotion and offerings. First, the clay seal on the great

Seti changes the garment of Amun,
Temple of Seti I at Abydos

doors of the chapel was broken. This was done by a special priest who was the only one privileged to enter the sanctuary of the temple. Then he cleansed the chapel by burning incense and sprinkled libations of water with natron. Next, he broke the clay seal of the doors of the golden shrine where the statue of the God resided. He opened the doors and knelt down to pray. The sanctuary was also cleaned using incense and water with natron libations. During the subsequent ritual, the crown, ornaments and clothing of the God were removed. Afterwards the God was bathed, dried and anointed with oil.

Once the God was completely clean, he was dressed with fresh new clothes. The old clothing was never used twice, nor was it ever washed. The old garments were gifted to devotees of the God who in turn would use the fabric for their own mummification process after their passing.

Following the clothing ritual, the God was presented with a meal. When the God was fully clothed and fed, the doors of the golden shrine were closed and sealed with a new clay seal.

Offering meal for the Gods, Temple of Seti I at Abydos

Clean sand was poured over the floor of the chapel. Afterwards, the priest would leave the sanctuary while moving backwards and erasing his footsteps with a brush from the sanded floor. The ceremony was concluded with the closing of the great doors of the chapel that would again be secured with a new clay seal.[2]

The dressing and feeding of the God enabled him to literally and metaphorically become incarnated to take his place on earth. The God then left the transparent world of the spirits to become visible and tangible to the people in the world of the living. Through his decent the God was now a living God on earth allowing for the people to come into contact with him more easily.

Clothing is the sign of renewal and life that has become visible. It emphasise the physicality that forms an enclosure for the spirit. The process of dressing is a reflection of the transformation process which Râ himself experiences. After the unification of the Sungod's *Ba*-soul with the body of Osiris in the Sixth Hour, Râ's being has become renewed and reborn. Thus, the *Ba*-soul of the Sungod has been clad in the body of Osiris symbolically. This allows for his light to gain more *Ka*-force and substance which makes it possible to crystallise into the first matter. This next step in his process of renewal is essential for Râ to eventually rise up visibly in the sky.

The Hour Goddess, who accompanies the Sungod along his journey through this hour, is the "Mistress of Deep Night". The darkness still engulfs Râ in the dark North, despite the fact he has started his ascent from the depth of the night. The Hour Goddess is the one who knows the way better than anyone in this region. She, therefore, guides the Sungod through all the dark caverns as soon as he enters through the gate.

The name of the gate "Which stands without getting tired" contains a silent warning for the Sungod. Though, despite the fact that this hour emits much more peace, in contrast to the previous hour, it is still advised to remain vigilant. This is not the time for the Sungod to lose his focus and there certainly is no room for him to become complacent. He needs to stand his ground firmly and continue on his way without becoming weary. There are, after all, twelve knives within this hour, which he needs to cross, that require his attention.

The Duatians on the left riverbank (upper section)

The left riverbank contains five different caverns, each with a specific name. Every cavern is inhabited by three different Deities who are seated on top of the hieroglyphic sign for clothing. They receive their clothes the moment Râ enters their cave. As Râ is now in the process of receiving his own clothes step by step during his journey through the caverns, he is also able to gift clothes to the Deities residing here. The Deities themselves are subjected to the process of death and rebirth as well. They too, like Râ, are in need of the daily renewal. Hence, it is their heartfelt wish to become part of the daily renewal process of the Sungod. Each night when Râ arrives, they are thankful to him, for he grants their wish and offers them a renewed life.

When the Gods and Goddesses hear his voice, they emerge from the sand under which they were buried. Even though the light of the Sungod is still small and in the process of renewal, it illuminates the cavern and brings the inhabiting Deities to life. The shining appearance of Râ awakens the Deities from their slumber of death. They are no longer in need of the constricting mummy wrappings. As the darkening bandages are removed, their faces appear. This opens their eyes and enables them to identify themselves with their beloved Râ. His luminous presence fills their inner beings and restores them as well. To confirm the process and the embodiment of their renewed life, they receive the new clothes. The renewal of life, as the victory over death, is the idealised image that Horus represents. Hence, each Deity on the left and the right riverbank is referred to as "mystery made by Horus".

Through this process of rejuvenation, the life force streams inside and gifts the Deities the Breath of Life. After this initial deep inspiration, the Breath of Life is exhaled. The breath leaving their bodies contains their life cry and symbolises creative utterance. This expression is a confirmation of existence and also a vital one in order to stay alive. The inhalation needs to be exhaled as well to manifest and maintain creation. The sounds uttered here symbolise aspects that give shape to life on earth. It underlines the diversity and complexity of creation and all of its different manifestations.

The diversity is also reflected in the multiple versions of the Amduat that are depicted in the tombs and on the sarcophagi. Some of the versions of the Eighth Hour use different sounds compared to other versions. It does not take a lot of imagination to make some changes and describe other specific sounds that embody aspects of life just as well. The concept remains the same, irrespective of the kind of sound.

These sounds of manifestation are expressed by the Deities the moment the Sungod enters their cavern. Although they might seem like strange and unusual noises, the Sungod is able to comprehend them and grasp their meaning. At first glance, the sounds appear to be ordinary sounds created by nature, humans and animals. However, upon closer inspection, it goes much deeper than that as each sound is coloured by feelings and emotions. The noises can be nice, pleasant and positive, though they can also be penetrating, aggressive, sad and confronting.

It are precisely these contrasting expressions that indicate that the first creation has spread and begun to take shape. Each sound represents a continued development based on the first noise which was heard from the Cavern of Sokar in the Fifth Hour. This noise, the "thundering sound of the sky in a storm", was the first sign of light and life. Since then, Râ has travelled through two more hours and the spread of the different sounds reflects his growing and developing life light.

The Deities in the present hour join in the transformation process of the Sungod. Since they have been granted their new clothes, they are now capable of movement. Unfortunately, their movements are still restricted due to the cavern in which they reside.

> They are like this on their clothing, remaining on their sand as a mystery made by Horus.[3]

Each cavern opens and closes with a gate called "knife". The knives keep the caverns separated from one another. This effectively restricts the movements of the residing Deities. Furthermore, the knives also confine the utterances of the Deities to their own living space where the noises congregate. This means the sounds are centred within the caverns, granting these spaces their power. Therefore, the knives guarantee the power of the caverns due to their separation and seclusion.

Râ voyages through each of these caves and needs to identify himself with the contents. Only once he has acknowledged the contents and connected with it, can he leave the cavern. The newly gained knowledge enables him to utter the right name of the next knife. The gate then grants him access to the next cavern whilst closing the previous one. In doing so, the Sungod continues his transformation, which allows him to connect with the different dimensions of creation.

The fact there are five caverns is significant. The number five symbolises the four physical cardinal points of East, South, West and North linked to the sky. This allows for the physical world to become ensouled and imbued with the Divine. This number illustrates the materialisation of the spirit as it manifests on earth. In the present hour the first step in this process, the crystallisation of the formless Divine into the first matter, will be realised. Thus, the number of caves is an adequate representation of the process that the Sungod himself experiences throughout this hour and allows his light to become more powerful and tangible.

There are a total of ten caverns in this hour. Number ten represents a noteworthy symbolism and emphasises the energy of this hour. Ten contains every elementary number from one up to nine and therefore embodies all potentials and possibilities. When reducing the number ten, going back to basics, it eventually returns to one, symbolising a full circle, completeness and the return to origin. Hence, ten is the perfect number to represent creation, the absolute and the Divine Law of *Maât*, Order, Justice and Truth.

The journey of the Sungod through the ten caves helps him to further realise his ultimate goal to complete a solar cycle in accordance with the Divine Law of *Maât*. Then his beaming spirit will be visible on earth. This final objective is also the start of a new beginning. After all, development never stops.

The first cavern of the left riverbank is called "Mysterious" and opens with the knife "Lord of Sanctify". The cave is inhabited by three Gods in human form who are referred to as the heirs of Osiris. Their bodies are supported by the sign of "clothing", on top of which they have taken their seat.

The first God, "Image of Atum" (No. 556), is wearing the White Crown. This is the Great Creator of the universe Atum, the maker of the first Gods. Everything was created from his flesh. In other words, it was Atum who caused the spirit to take its first real "shape". His support during this phase of the journey is vital to take the next step into the first matter. The following God is Khepri, "Image of Khepri" (No. 557), the symbol of the newborn sun. And the final one is Shu, "Image of Shu" (No. 558), the God of air, life, light and space.

The three Gods are working together to realise the next step in creation. In this process Atum was the first to give shape to the creation as he gave life to Shu and Tefnut. This initial act of creation is a one time deed of Atum. Khepri continuous the first creation of Atum as he transforms it just a little further into manifestation. Khepri however, unlike Atum, remains in this cycle and experiences it over and over again. After each cycle Khepri "comes into being" in his renewed form. This is how life takes form, develops and evolves. Shu plays a key role in the continuation of the creation. He is the one who opens the horizon for Khepri and lifts him up into the sky as the newborn sun. Without the support of Shu, there would be no room for Khepri to rise.

Atum, Khepri and Shu welcome Râ with the sound of the humming of honey bees as he enters their cavern. The honey bee was the symbol of Lower Egypt. This should come as no surprise for this part of Egypt had an abundance of flowering plants in ancient times. The symbol of Upper Egypt, on the other hand, was the Sedge. Together, the two symbols represented the fourth name of the Pharaoh "King of Upper and Lower Egypt", *ny sut bity*. The Pharaoh received this name during his coronation; "He of the Sedge and the Bee". Thus, both the Bee and the Sedge were connected to royalty and power.

The home of the honey bees, the beehive, was seen as the centre of the world from which everything originates. Hence, honey bees were associated with creation, which is also reflected in the myth of "the Tears of Râ". The myth tells of the tears of the Sungod Râ that would transform into honey bees the instant they touched the ground. Like this, his beaming light manifested itself in these insects. The bees in turn produce honey where they transform the transparent sunlight of Râ into the tangible golden liquid. It truly is the nectar of the Gods and was believed to contain great power. Therefore, it had and still has many applications, for example in the art of medicine.

The humming of the honey bees underlines the symbolism mentioned above. The sound is a high resonating tone, which indicates that creation is increasingly expressed into matter. It confirms the growing power of the Sungod and the authority he constantly manages to embody. Nobody can ever truly understand the way the manifestation of the creation works exactly. The name of the cavern itself, which is "Mysterious", also refers to the fact that this is sacred knowledge we are talking about. In other words, this knowledge remains a mystery, never to be disclosed. It is exactly this secret that ensures creation never ends. The knife, "Lord of Sanctify", also assists in the protection of this mystery.

The second cavern is named "Duat" and opens with the knife "Standing One of Tatenen". The three Deities inhabiting the cave are; the Goddess Tefnut "Image of Tefnut" (No. 559), the God Geb "Image of Geb" (No. 560) and the Goddess Nut "Image of Nut" (561). Like Atum and Shu from the first cavern, these three Deities are part of the Great Ennead. Tefnut is the Goddess of moisture, Geb the God of the Earth and Nut the Goddess of the sky. Together they contribute to the manifestation of the first act of creation by Atum. When Râ enters, they emerge from the sand and welcome him with a call right from their souls. The call sounds like the clanging on metal. It is a sound that could be a reference to heaven, since heaven itself was made from an iron plate. However, the sound of their calls could also be described as the sound of striking cymbals.[4] Either way, the divine sound is music to Râ's ears.

The third cavern, the "Tomb of the Gods", opens with the knife "With hovering *Ba*-souls". The three Deities inhabiting the cave are; the God Osiris "Image of Osiris" (No. 562), the Goddess Isis "Image of Isis" (No. 563) and the God Horus "Image of Horus" (564). Isis and Osiris both are Deities who are part of the Great Ennead. Consequently, these first three caverns show us the development of creation step by step that provides the foundation for the entire process. Osiris and Isis continued this process of manifestation as they conceived Horus.

The sound Osiris, Isis and Horus produce once Râ passes them, shows a different power of creation. Their noise is the sound of humans wailing in mourning. Though it is a sad and heartbreaking sound, it is just as much a part of the manifestation as was the cheerful music from the previous cavern. The crying expresses the separation process that takes place between the living and the deceased. It conveys the pain of the disintegration of the unity, as demonstrated by the lifeless body. It also displays the intense desire to restore the unit in a renewed life. Lamentation, therefore, has a beneficial effect on the soul of the deceased who then awakens from his slumbering death. Now he can move forward in the Afterlife into a new life. Additionally, the tears that are being wept are a manifestation of the life-giving waters that are essential to be alive. Thus, the wailing symbolises death and rebirth that are both fundamental aspects of the eternal cycle of creation. Râ too is being nourished by the powerful lamentation. It grants him renewed life force and the energy to move forward.

The fourth cavern, "Mourning", opens with the knife "Belting the Gods". Three Gods, each with the head of an animal, populate the cave. The Gods are;

(No. 565) "Image of the Bull of the West" who has the head of a bull.

(No. 566) "Image of the noblest of the Gods" who has the head of a goat.

(No. 567) "Image of the Weeping One of the Gods" who has the head of a rat.

As soon as Râ enters the cave through the gate, the souls of these Gods express themselves with a loud cry. This is the sound of the bellowing of bulls, or the of bull of bulls being pleased.[5] The sound indicates sexual activity and fertility. It symbolises the renewal of creation.

The fifth and final cavern on the left riverbank is called "Lady of Wind". The knife granting access to the cave is called "Uniting darkness". Inside the cave there are once again

The Gods of the fourth cavern, KV 9 Ramses V and VI

three Gods with the heads of an animal. They are;

(No. 568) "Image of the ichneumon" who has the head of a mongoose.
(No. 569) "Image of the catfish" who has the head of a catfish.
(No. 570) "Image of the one who belongs to his stems" who has the head of hippopotamus.

They welcome Râ as they give voice to a loud wailing cry with great force. As Râ has passed the final cave, he leaves the left riverbank through the closing knife "Shadows of the Duatians". The name of the gate indicates that the Duatians living here possess a shadow or *khaibit*. This means their *Ba*-souls are clothed in a body. The shadow is the mirror image of the body and confirms its physicality. Therefore, the Duatians living here possess a true existence.

During the journey through the first five caves, creation has gotten increasingly "dressed", allowing it to take shape. Each of the Deities on the left riverbank has contributed to this process through the uttering of sounds. As the Sungod furthers his travels and leaves their caves, the Deities return to being corpses. They disappear in the burial mound and are no longer seated on the signs for clothing. As they lie beneath the sand, the darkness engulfs them. Only once the next night arrives, will they renew again through the enlightening presence of Râ.

The Duatians of the Sacred River (middle section)

The Sun barque has begun to move after the delay caused by Apophis. The crew is again comprised of the usual members. Wepwawet, "Opener of the Ways", is standing up front on the barque next to Sia. Behind them stands the Lady of the barque who is wearing the solar disk between her horns on top of her head. She now continues to wear this disk until the end of the journey. Behind Nebet wia is the Sungod Râ himself. He is engulfed in the coils of Mehen. Râ is wearing a solar disk with ram horns on top of his head.

(No. 571) "Wepwawet"
(No. 572) "Sia"
(No. 573) "Nebet wia"
(No. 574) "Mehen"
(No. 575) "Iuf"
(No. 576) "Heru Hekenu"
(No. 577) "Ka Maât"
(No. 578) "Nehes"
(No. 579) "Hu"
(No. 580) "Kherep wia"

Râ's light has grown in power after his battle with Apophis. His voice has become louder as well, giving him the power to address every Deity within this hour. The sounds Râ receives in response to his own shout are a confirmation of the Sungod's own existence. This empowers his light to materialise progressively.

Due to the absence of water, the Sun barque is once again being towed by Eight Gods. The towing Gods (No. 581 – 588) are referred to as "the Gods of the Duat who tow Râ in the "Sarcophagus of her Gods"". When Râ makes his appearance, they invite him in. With a small speech, they tell Râ they are going to tow him through the caverns. Like this, the towing Gods offer Râ the opportunity to identify himself with each of the inhabitants of the caves.

> Come indeed to your images, our God […]
> Come indeed to yourself,
> that you may rest […]⁶

The towing Gods ensure Râ that each of the cave dwellers considers it an honour when the Sungod illuminates their darkness. They conclude their welcome by identifying Râ as the "Lord of Towing". This emphasises the fact that Râ is no longer weak and his authority has increased. Although the eight Gods are the ones towing the Sun barque, it is Râ himself who takes the lead.

In front of the eight towing Gods are nine large signs in the shape of the hieroglyphic sign *shemes* (*šms*), which means "follower" or "attendant". The exact purpose of this sign, though, is not entirely clear. According to the list of hieroglyphic signs of Gardiner, the hieroglyph falls under the category of Warfare, Hunting and Butchery. The hieroglyph also contains a knife in an obliquely turned upward position. The *shemes* sign is also used to indicate the royal ancestors and the followers. These followers symbolise all servants of the reigning Pharaoh who are always there to protect him with their knives.

(No. 589) "Who rests in the earth"
(No. 590) "Hidden One"
(No. 591) "Who makes the *Ba*-souls secret"
(No. 592) "Who brings the shadows to rest"
(No. 593) "Lord of all"
(No. 594) "Offering jar"
(No. 595) "Road-guide"
(No. 596) "Witness"
(No. 597) "Judge"

The nine signs, thus, represent the loyal servants of the Sungod. They are entirely at the service of Râ, there to protect him. The sign of "clothing" can be seen directly in front of each of the servants, indicating that their being will be renewed by Râ. The heads on top of the knives are not part of the original *Shemes* sign. The reason they are added here, is to show the servants come to life when Râ arrives. The instance Râ makes an appearance, their heads emerge, which also makes their identities known. This enables the Sungod to recognise each of these followers. This knowledge, together with their names, grants him power over the dutiful servants. When he calls their names, they immediately come to his aid. As they are Râ's protectors, they instantly stab each enemy who dares to approach Râ using their knives. The moment Râ has left, the servants swallow their own heads and knives. Life leaves them as they lay dormant, patiently awaiting Râ's next arrival the subsequent night, to be brought back to life once again.

> When this Great God calls to them,
> what is in them comes alive,
> and the heads go forth from their images.
> This God, he calls them by their names.
> What they have to do:
> Planting knives into the enemies of Râ
> near this place to which they belong.
> Then they swallow their heads
> and their knives (again),
> After this God has passed by them.[7]

The Sacred River concludes with a procession of four rams. Each ram carries a different crown on top of his horns. The hieroglyphic sign for clothing can be seen between the forelegs of the rams.

(No. 598) "First manifestation, image of Tatenen" is wearing the solar disk.
(No. 599) "Second manifestation, image of Tatenen" is wearing the White Crown.
(No. 600) "Third manifestation, image of Tatenen" is wearing the Red Crown.
(No. 601) "Fourth manifestation, image of Tatenen" is wearing the Two Feathers Crown.

As mentioned, before Tatenen means "Risen Land" or "Exalted Earth". *Ta* means "earth" and *nen* means "inertness". Tatenen is the personification of the primordial mound, which has risen from the waters of original creation. During this particular event, the formless Divine crystallises into the first matter, Prima Materia. The Divine living matter that emerges from this process is still shapeless. It is the potential that is necessary to manifest into real matter on earth. Tatenen embodies this inert, though, Divine living matter and his realm can be found deep within the earth. It is precisely the inertness of the earth that provides for a stable foundation upon which all of life can emerge. Hence, Tatenen also embodies a creating feature, a characteristic sometimes used to depict him. In this form he can be seen seated in front of his potter's wheel while using his hands to create the world egg.

Here, at the end of the Sacred River, we can see four images of Tatenen in the shape of rams. The ram represents dynamics, leadership, action and the power of regeneration. It is the

The servants of the Sungod Râ in the form of shemes-signs, KV 9 Ramses V and VI

symbol of the renewed solar energy in the spring, a reference to fertility and rebirth.

The number four indicates completeness, totality and the order of manifestation. Four symbolises the earth, the foundation from which all life can arise. It are, for example, the four cardinal directions that give shape to the world. Furthermore, the body of the deceased is protected by the four sons of Horus. In other words, the number four indicates the process of the descent further into matter.

The Sungod Râ's light slowly begins to crystallise, which allows his power and authority to increasingly gain strength. A fact that is also reflected in the various crowns worn by the mentioned rams. These crowns are; the Solar disk which is the symbol of Solar regeneration and renewal. The White Crown of Upper Egypt. The Red Crown of Lower Egypt. And lastly, the Two Feathers Crown as a symbol of light and the Divine Law of *Maât*. Râ now embodies each of these different powers once again. To emphasise this fact, each of the four rams receives their respective crown from the Sungod himself. It fills Râ with happiness and delight as he hears their voices. As he enters their cavern, the moment has arrived for him to identify himself with the potent power of these rams. It is a joyful and powerful moment and an accomplishment on its own for his blooming sunlight. The four images of Tatenen become illuminated, which in turn makes them come to life. After Râ has left them, the rams are engulfed in the darkness once more where they lay waiting for the Sungod's next arrival and their subsequent resurrection.

The Duatians on the right riverbank (lower section)

The right riverbank opens with the knife "Half of the earth". The gate grants access to the first cavern called "Satisfying her Lord". When Râ enters the cave, he calls for the Deities living here. They answer his call with the cry of a tomcat. The first inhabitant of the cave is the Goddess "Maiden" (No. 602). The hieroglyphic word maiden, *hewenet* (ḥwn.t), is a derivative from *hewen* (ḥwn) which means "be rejuvenated, be refreshed or youthful vigour". This young maiden is here to nourish the process of renewal with her youthful virginity. Like her name implies, she is a young virgin. She is holding the upraised writhing serpent, "World-encircler" (No. 603), with one hand. This serpent is a form of Mehen and refers to the process of transformation, resurrection and regeneration. Mehen is also the protector of this process. The touch of "Maiden" induces the transformation of old age and death into new life. Hence, death and renewal go hand in hand for they are two different sides of eternal Life. "Maiden" and "World-encircler" are connected to one another and share a single hieroglyphic sign for clothing.

Next is another hieroglyphic sign for

clothing with three arrows lying on top of it, "Arrows of Râ" (No. 604). The three arrows symbolise the multitude of sunrays from the Sungod that are starting to take shape. The final inhabitant of the cavern is the ram-headed God "Lord of the Rekhyt-people" (No. 605). Rekhyt-people refers to ordinary people who belong to the lowest class of society. However, it has also been suggested that they are the people living in Lower Egypt or foreigners who immigrated to Egypt. In any case, this God is the ruler of these people.

The second cavern, "She who annihilates the ignorant", is opened with the knife "Which drives off his enemies". These significant names indicate that the cavern does not provide room for the ignorant or enemies. Râ, on the other hand, is of course allowed to enter. His call is heard and answered by the three Deities living in the cave with the sound of a war-shout of the living. The first Deity is the Goddess "Place" (No. 606). Next is the God "Earth" (No. 607) and lastly a God with the head of a crocodile, "Clever-faced" (No. 608). The moment Râ leaves them and the darkness returns to their cave, the three Deities disappear and become buried underneath the sand.

The third cavern, "She who envelops her images", is opened with the knife "With powerful forms". The cave is inhabited by four Goddesses who rise up instantly when the light of Râ opens the darkness of the sand covering them. They emerge wrapped like mummies to ensure their images stay covered. Despite the cover and them being underneath it, they are still renewed during this hour just like the other Deities. The names of these Goddesses are;

(No. 609) "She who veils"
(No. 610) "The Dark One"
(No. 611) "She who adorns"
(No. 612) "She who puts together"

They answer the call of the Sungod with the sound of the shores falling into the Nun. This is a sound with a double meaning. On the one hand, it is a reference to the inundation and symbolises the new life, which will soon emerge. On the other hand, it alludes to the submergence into the primeval waters of Nun that reverts life back to the shapeless conditions of the non-existence. Therefore, it is a powerful sound that embodies the eternal cycle of life, death and rebirth and ultimately gives shape to the act of creation.

The fourth cavern, "Removing her *Ba*-souls", is opened with the knife "With pointed flames". Inside the cave reside four Gods who, like the previous Goddesses, appear in their mummy shapes. They are four powerful Gods as reflected in their names;

(No. 613) "Darkness"
(No. 614) "Butcher"
(No. 615) "Who keeps off the *Akh*-spirits"
(No. 616) "Hacker of the earth"

They answer Râ's call with the sound of the piercing cry of a Divine hawk. It is a penetrating sound that is associated with the image of the God Horus. In his Divine form of a hawk, Horus rises high up in the sky as a sign the light has been reborn. It is a beautiful vision with the promise of it becoming reality in a few more hours.

The Sungod has now arrived in the fifth and final cavern, "Great of Torches". During his journey through each of the caves, his light has progressively grown further. With his newfound enlightening power, he is qualified to open the second to last knife, "With shining *Akh*-spirits". Here, Râ enters in a fiery atmosphere. With his voice he calls upon the four Uraeus-serpents inhabiting this place;

(No. 617) "Uraeus-serpent"
(No. 618) "The Sinuous One"
(No. 619) "The Flaming One"
(No. 620) "She who is sharp in attack"

They immediately rise out of the sand and respond to the appearance of the Sungod through uttering a cry that sounds like the cry of a nest of young birds. This is a clear sign of the birth of new life. Râ has granted these Uraeus-serpents their new life and he ignites the light within their being. Now, the serpents are capable of illuminating the darkness in their own being. They do so by breathing fire from their mouths. However, the fire is not merely intended for their own illumination as their fiery flames are like fuel to the Sungod as well. It empowers him and pushes him to undergo the final renewal of this hour. Now he has transformed a piece of death into new life once again. However, it is not just the flames of the Uraeus-serpents that contribute to this. Every Deity in this hour has helped to enable the current transformation. Due to the acquired wisdom and renewal, Râ can now open the final knife, "Which consumes the dead through (the serpents) which are in it". As soon as he crosses the gate, it closes behind him. Then the Eighth Hour is engulfed in darkness once more.

The Manifestation of the Eighth Hour in daily life

This is the final hour where you are travelling through the North. The North is connected to the earth element. Therefore, it holds a far more concrete energy compared to the other cardinal directions. After all, the East is linked to the element air, the South to fire and the West to water. The North is thus an area bound to matter, reliability and power. In consequence, it is an area that does not flow, as it is rigid and slow. The earthly energy gives shape to the Eighth and Seventh Hour. During the previous hour, you experienced this inertness through the blockade caused by Apophis. There was an immense amount of power and perseverance needed to break this barricade.

As you have now arrived in the Eighth Hour, the journey has finally picked up some speed. This improvement, however, is relative for several gates are still blocking your way. The gates, or knives, continuously cut you off every time you get on track. Therefore, the journey remains long and difficult during this hour as well. Still, do not be impatient for this slow pace is actually very important. In this hour applies; haste makes waste.

The eight Gods walking in front of the Sun barque are responsible for the towing process. The number eight is a reference to the previous seven hours including the Eighth one. Each God symbolises an hour and the Wisdom you have made your own during your voyage. It are your own insights and achievements that pull the Sun barque forward. Now, your inner Wisdom is going to take a more concrete shape. For this to happen it takes time and you need to genuinely concentrate and focus. Only through this process you can build the initial foundation that is developed further during the upcoming hours. This basic layer will determine the amount of power and strength your continued development will be able to hold. After all, no matter how strong a building may be, the foundation is the essential part that keeps the entire structure from collapsing. This is a fact that applies here as well.

The name of this hour, "Sarcophagus of her Gods", is a reference to this foundation. The sarcophagus is the representation of the body. It forms a tangible and visible housing for the soul into matter. You can think of it as "clothing" for the soul, enabling it to express itself and achieve things in the world.

During the Eighth Hour the first step in the process of crystallisation is going to take place. This means, everything you have experienced from deep within your subconsciousness is going to take root. The experiences from the previous hours are still transparent and fleeting. Now, however, they may crystallise deep within the earth of your inner world. The four manifestations of Tatenen, in the shape of rams (No. 598 – 601), are a reference to this process.

These four dynamic rams symbolise the renewed and reborn sunlight, which has descended into the first matter. This implies your connection with the Higher Self has become stronger and more solid due to the concrete communication between you both. This reciprocal exchange is reflected in the diverse sounds that are audible through the ten caverns. You have now been crowned with His authority and leadership, just like Râ has gifted the crowns to the rams. It allows you to feel the mightiness of the Higher Self and the underlying power of the Powerself flow through you. From your coronation onward, you, in conjunction with your inner Sungod, have to take the lead and the control of your own inner world.

The coronation is the acknowledgement that you are completing an important phase in the present hour. During your journey, the gates to the subconsciousness have steadily started to open up to you. It has increased your inner awareness which allowed you to learn a lot about yourself step by step. The further you develop this inner Knowledge, the greater your spiritual freedom will be. Although, the leeway your heavenly soul has been given through these experiences must always remain within the reach of the base of your inner world. You have to maintain your connection. Once you do this, not only do you inhale life, for you also exhale. The exhalation allows you to express and portray who you truly are.

Hence, this first conclusion is also the start of a new endeavour. "To know", the act that the Amduat continuously refers to, is transformed during this hour in "to understand" and "to do". The knowledge from "to know" has enabled your consciousness to grow. Now, you have to implement your expanded vision in order to see if it holds up. This means you have to act consciously through the heightened vision of the Higher Self. Whether you are capable of remaining loyal to this vision is tested throughout this hour. Only when you succeed, will you know the renewed vision is no illusion.

Are you truthful and faithful enough to allow your inner Sungod to shine through you? Are you genuinely able to express the received coronation in accordance with the Divine Law of *Maât*? The answers to these questions are discovered along your journey through the ten caverns.

Each cavern contains Secret Knowledge meant to make you more conscious and aware of various hidden aspects of yourself. To unveil the secrets, you have to enter these holes below the ground. Judging from the reasoning mind, the caverns may seem rigid, closed off and might even seem rather abstract. The caves, as well as some of the inhabitants, bear symbolical names that do not always tell you much about them. Hence, it is clear the inner caverns do not open up to you on the level of rational thinking. Should you try this, you are immediately met with a stone wall of incomprehension which might seem impenetrable. To truly gain excess, you have to descend into the subconsciousness, like always, for this is where you can turn your perspective around. No book, no person nor any knowledge available in the outer world can help you with this. You are truly on your own for each cave has a different meaning and impact depending on the person. Therefore, you have to trust in your own intuition and imaginary power, for these are the only guides you have along the road.

Thus, simply reading the Amduat alone does not make the Secret Knowledge available to you. You have to actively descend into your own Duat and identify yourself with the hidden aspects within your own being. Only then the Secret Knowledge opens up to you and teaches you the name; "To know the name". Then, those parts are no longer a hidden secret for they become integrated in your consciousness and facilitate the expansion and development to the next level. In this case, this entails that the next knife is opened and that it permits you to proceed to the next cavern. Along your journey you cannot skip things or take shortcuts. Should you still continue your journey without this identification, it would seem like the knives are still opening up to you and allow you to enter. However, this is merely an illusion for you are then confronted with your own incomprehension and the gate to the hidden area within yourself will remain closed. You simply cannot continue your voyage without first identifying yourself with every aspect of your being.

Nevertheless, do not be afraid or expect all kinds of ghosts to emerge from your inner world. Nor fear for the appearance of other foul creatures that represent the darker sides of yourself, the sides you want nothing to do with. They are not to be feared. Instead, open up to this side and to the experiences you have. Be prepared to receive the pearls offered to you. It is these pearls that ensure the inner renewal and healing take place. Therefore, do not take these offerings lightly and see them for what they truly are. A gift. Though you have already become rather familiar with the symbolical language of your inner world, you might still have difficulty to interpret the messages correctly. Be patient and be aware of insights and clarity that can simply emerge during daily life.

The power of this hour is the fact that the first crystallisation takes place to form the renewed foundation of your inner world. As mentioned above, "To know" now becomes clearer for it crystallises in "to understand" and "to do". Thus, the journey throughout the caves triggers parallel events that unfold into your life more than usual. The further you descend, the clearer the response crystallises to take the first form. Soon, you recognise and understand what actions are expected of you. Herein the only thing that matters are your actions. You do not need to explain, defend or discuss it for it is still too early for this. Simply act in accordance with the inner Knowledge.

It goes without saying that the inner transformation attracts enemies who are lurking nearby and are ready to do anything to put a stop to your renewed consciousness. The nine loyal servants of Râ (No. 589 – 597) are here to make you aware of this serious threat.

Furthermore, you have now arrived at a very crucial turning point, something you might not have realised before. At the end of the hour you set course for the East. Therefore, it is very important to continue to be aware of your journey and to stay on track. The moment right before you change your course towards the sunrise is the perfect time for the enemies to try and stop you. Once your course for the East has been definitely set, it is very difficult to make it stop. Therefore, the seeds of doubt are sown in your mind right before your rotation towards the Ninth Hour. Their sole purpose is to confuse you and prevent your continued progress.

The ace up the sleeve of the enemy is simply your insecure position right now. At this point you can hardly imagine for the light to ever return. From the deepest and darkest parts of the night you have risen. However, at this point you still remain engulfed by the darkness. This might make it hard to believe. Will the light truly return at some point? You have not yet received confirmation of this fact, which causes you to continue your sailing based on your own faith. Therefore, this is the perfect moment for the enemies to take advantage of the doubtful situation. You cannot lower your guard at this crucial time. You are required to remain standing with confidence and to stay alert without tiring. The gate "Which stands without getting tired" that gave you access to this hour, already warned you of this situation.

Unfortunately, this is not the only attack. After the seven hour journey you might think you have learned enough. The input of the Higher Self and the power of the Powerself make you feel strong and confident. Maybe you think that you have come far enough by now. To make matters worse, your inner saboteurs do everything in their power to promote this vision. They have regarded the entire voyage as one big threat and believed it to be a terrible idea from the very start. You must understand that these saboteurs will prove to be your biggest opponents on your journey. You are not always able to recognise their sneakiness, as they are part of your own inner world as well. You are used to their ever present comments on everything you do, which makes it difficult to identify them as enemies. Therefore, they actually are extra dangerous due to their cunningness. They use every opportunity to convince you of their superior helmsmanship in an effort to take control of your life.

The change in course at the end of the hour is also a challenge in itself. Do you dare to change your course? Or do you rather continue sailing following the old and familiar route? The choice you make affects your transformation process. If you have doubts about the new direction, it might result in staying too long in the current Hour. On the other hand, it can also result in you trying or forcing proceedings too quickly. This leads to you cutting corners in order to resume your course towards the East as quickly as possible. And, as you well know, without proper roots and understanding, the next part of your journey may prove to be impossible. Therefore, fortitude and a proactive stance need to be balanced.

Additionally, concentration and a sense of purpose are essential during this hour, for loss of focus is yet another enemy to be aware of. The standard and secure structure of the caverns can also become tedious and boring. Loss of focus is tempting, which results in your attention being directed towards earthly business instead of your inner world. You no longer want to strain yourself to make the knowledge of the next cave your own. Naturally, the enemy tries to convince you that this inner descent is not necessary at all. Why make things difficult if the mundane life is so much simpler?

Thus, prepare yourself for the upcoming confrontations for these challenges are here to test the strength of your inner renewal. Your discernment needs to be as sharp as a knife. Everything and anything that blocks or destroys your new vision needs to be torn out, root and branch. The twelve knives within this hour emphasise these actions and assist you by cutting the window dressings and falsehoods away. This is yet another reason for you not to be too hasty. Your journey needs to be slowed down to allow for your discernment to cut away the inaccuracies and to prevent you from missing essential parts. Every aspect, no matter how small or insignificant it might seem, has to be weighed on the scales of *Maât*.

As you might have realised by now, during this hour the inner Sungod, or *Ba*-soul, makes himself heard far more clearly. His powerful presence has resulted from the growing underlying power of the Powerself. It is the *Ka*-force of Osiris that enables the *Ba*-soul of Râ to eventually rise up in the sky of the East. Therefore, it is the Powerself who fixates and stabilises the intention of the Higher Self. Without the *Ka*-force, it is impossible for you to express your divine potential in your life. In such circumstances, these features remain lingering in the incorporeal world like an idea or dream.

However, in spite of the fact your inner world has transformed from a transparent and fleeting area into a clearer and more understandable world, it is still too early to give shape to your divine potential. As the earth God Tatenen shows us, the very first crystallisation of the Divine into the still formless living matter is what happens here. It is the initial stage and the potential of matter that has to develop further first. This then becomes the feeding ground upon which your potential can take root and sprout. In a few more hours, the potential is going to rise up from the dark earth of the Duat and emerge in your daily life. Keep your focus, like the Deities, and maintain facing forward towards the Light. Consequently, your gifts and talents will automatically flourish into your external world the moment they are viable.

When you have finally passed the last knife, "Which consumes the dead through the serpents which are in it", you have completed an important part of your voyage. A renewed foundation has crystallised in the core of your inner world. This Divine living matter has ensured that your renewed consciousness, which is far from completed, has become more tangible. There still are four more hours ahead of you during which you can make the consciousness whole and perfect.

THE NINTH HOUR
"Flowing forth of images, with living manifestations"

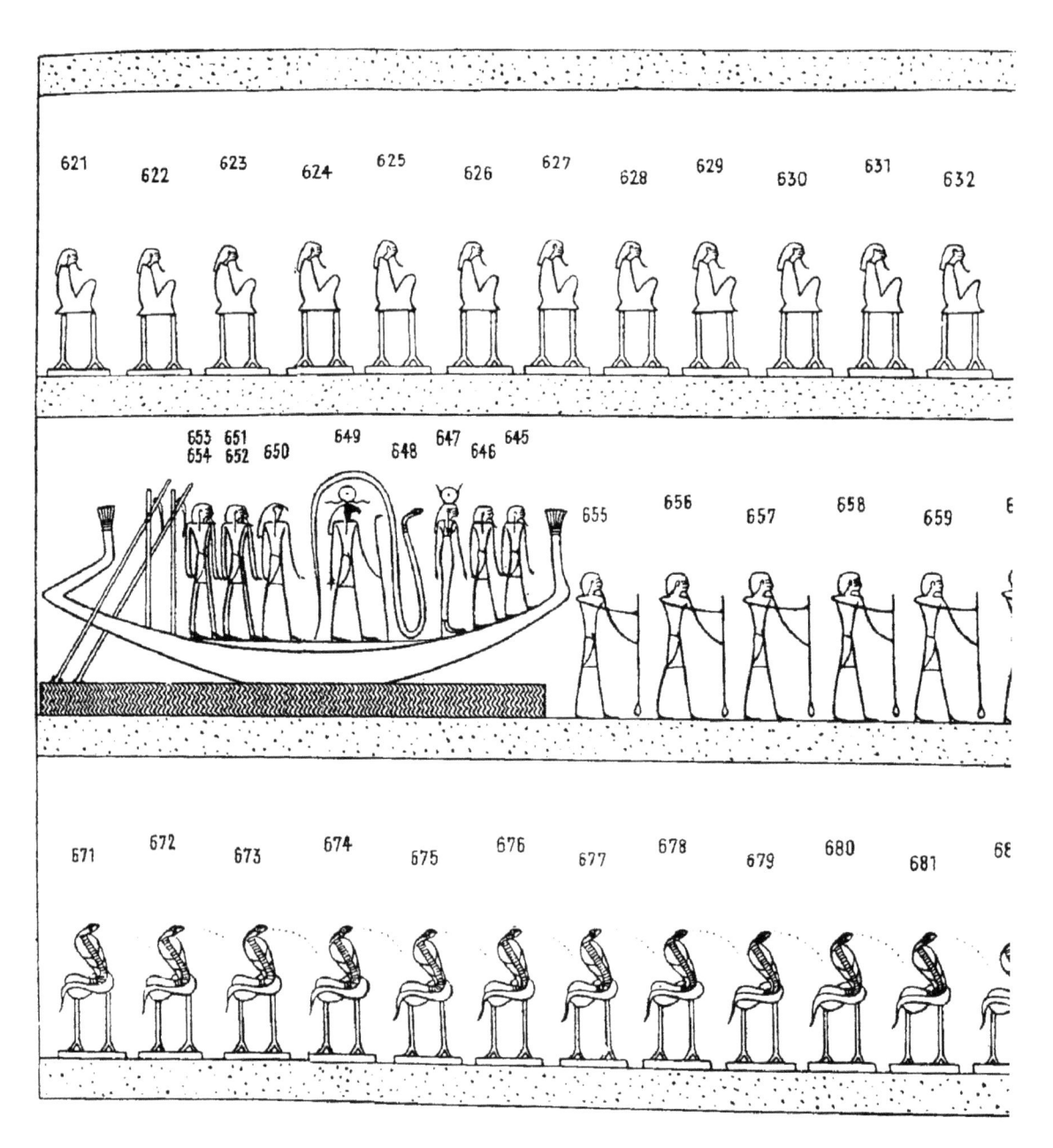

Figure 27: The Ninth Hour

The Gate: "Guardian of the Flood"
The Hour Goddess: "She who adores and protects her Lord"
The Guardian: "Horus above the garden of the Duatians"

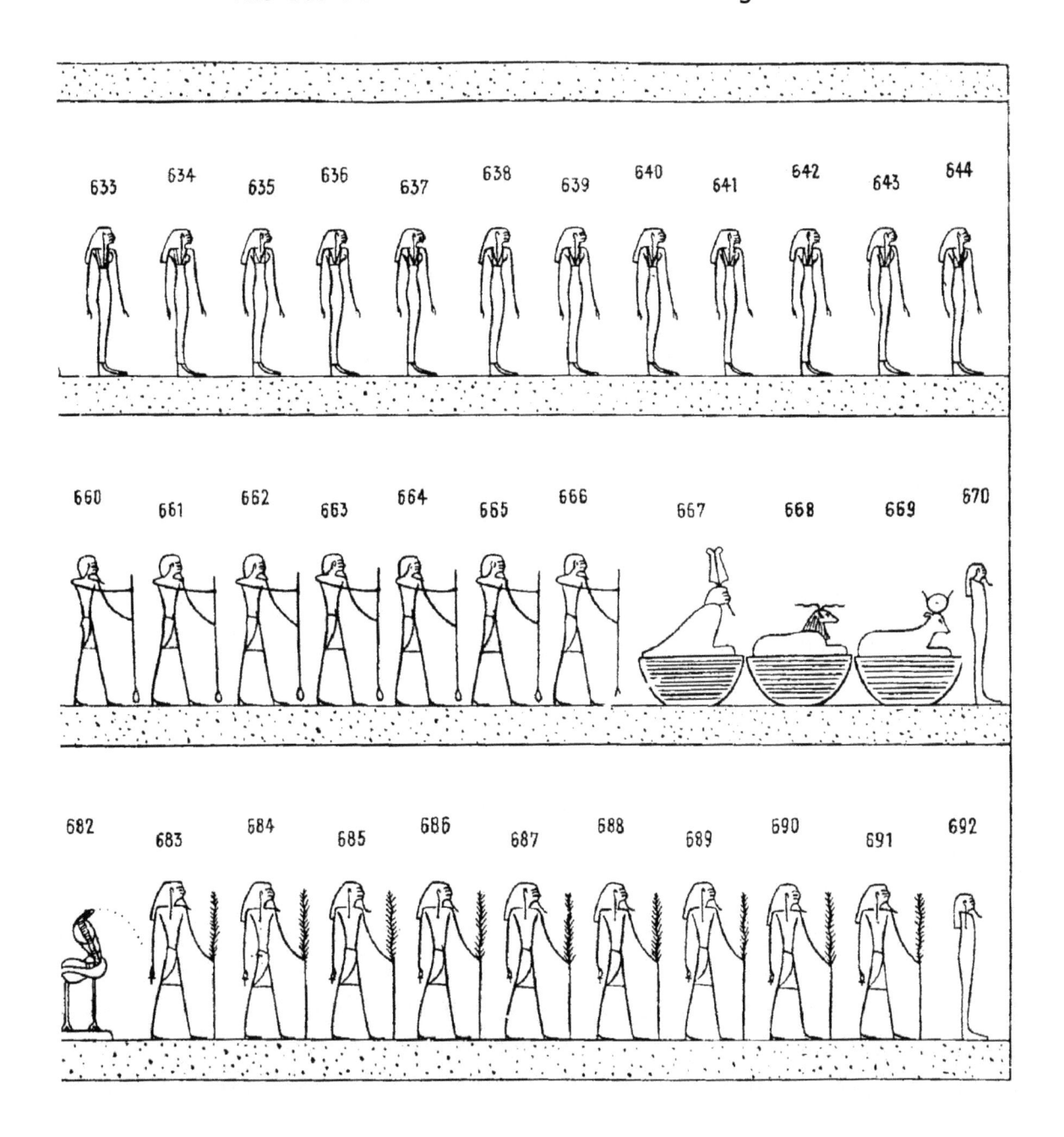

Introduction

Pausing by the person of this Great God
in this cavern.
He gives orders from his barque to the Gods
who are in it.
The crew of the barque of this God (also)
rests at this place.
The name of the Gate of this place,
through which this God enters,
that he rests upon the water
which is in this place,
is "Guardian of the Flood".
The name of this Place is
"Flowing forth of images,
with living manifestations".
The name of the Hour of the night
which guides this Great God
"She who adores and protects her Lord".
The mysterious cavern of the West,
where the Great God
and his crew rest in the Duat.
These are done with their names
like this image which is painted,
on the Eastern side of the Hidden Chamber
of the Duat.
Whoever knows their names on earth
and knows their thrones in the West,
will occupy his throne in the Duat,
standing among the "Lords of provision",
and declared "Justified" by the tribunal on
the day of judgement.
It is useful for him on earth.[1]

When travelling from the Eighth to the Ninth Hour, the Sun barque with Râ and his crew has finally completed its last change in course. It has made a turn, adjusting its course from the North to the East. In the East, Râ will finish the final hours of the journey as the pending sunrise is irrevocably coming closer. Due to the change in course, the landscape has changed as well. The rocky and sandy areas of the previous hour have been replaced with a bountiful water stream. In this hour there are no barriers preventing the sailing of the Sungod. The dynamics here are clearly focused onwards where the future image of the upcoming light pulls like a magnet. From this lively and fluent process, the next stage of renewal unfolds. This is emphasised by the name of this hour, "Flowing forth of images, with living manifestations".

The gate, "Guard of the Flood", at the entrance of this hour guards and protects the flowing process. The gate is standing directly against the concluding knife, "Which consumes the dead through (the serpents) which are in it", at the end of the Eighth Hour. This means the access from the Eighth to the Ninth Hour has a double protection to ensure the caverns in the Eighth Hour do not become flooded with water. Like this, each hour maintains its own landscape for the drought and sand are just as essential as abundance and water. It are precisely these specific features of the different landscapes that assist Râ during his transformation.

As soon as Râ enters through the gate, he

is welcomed by the Hour Goddess "She who adores and protects her Lord". Every single night, she keeps a longing eye out for her beloved Lord Râ. He is the one who enlightens her being and brings her back to life. She expresses her gratitude with praise and joy and bows before Râ in adoration. Her worship wraps Râ in a blanket of protective love and confirms his existence. It fills him with confidence and courage which is exactly what he needs to travel safely through this hour. Therefore, this loyal Goddess does not leave his side as Râ voyages through this stage. From her total and utter dedication towards him, she navigates Râ through the Ninth Hour, allowing for his next renewal stage to stabilise.

During the previous hour, Râ's light has crystallised into the first matter as he identified himself with the ten caverns and their inhabitants. This has given his growing light a more powerful shine. Consequently, it facilitated him to increasingly embody his own Royalty and Divine Authority. To confirm his growing leadership, Râ has crowned the earth God Tatenen with four different crowns. With this act, the Sungod expressed the diversity of his Divine kingship in the Divine living matter for the first time, as symbolised by Tatenen.

This hour is going to demonstrate whether the coronation is waterproof and capable of stabilisation based on the foundation of this first crystallisation. A coronation alone is not enough to express the power of kingship. Râ, therefore, requires a throne to give his bright mightiness a firm and stable seat. This allows for his light to have a solid base and become centred. This stability makes it more difficult for his enemies and the opposite powers to gain power over him.

Naturally, the Sungod's seat of authority is built upon the foundation of the Divine Law of *Maât*. It is the place where judgement is passed in order to manifest Harmony and Truth. The hieroglyphic word for throne, or seat, is *neset* (*nst*). The word *nes* (*ns*) means "tongue or speech". The throne is the place where the reigning monarch let his voice be heard to rule over his land. In this specific case, however, the voice as mentioned here is the True of Voice, *Maâ Kheru*. Thus, the throne is only accessible for those who embody *Maât* and speak from the True Heart. Râ is allowed to take a seat here, just like any of the other deceased who have been declared "Justified" by the tribunal.

The stabilisation of Râ's Divine lordship cannot take place without Osiris. Though Râ and Osiris do no longer share a body, they are still closely connected to one another. Together they continue to experience the various phases of renewal during which they are dependent on each other. The hieroglyphic name of Osiris emphasises this reciprocal connection. His name consists of three hieroglyphs; a throne, an eye and a God. The name can be written in two different ways with the Eye above or below the throne. The Eye symbolises the Heavenly Eye as well as the Eye of Râ. Hence, on one hand the ensoulment of Râ supports the throne of Osiris. On the other hand, it is the throne of

Osiris that provides a seat for the Eye of Râ. In other words, they are inseparably connected to one another as body and soul.

Fig. 28 Two different spellings of the name of Osiris.

During this hour it is Osiris especially who has a prominent task to fulfil in his role as the King of the Duat. His stabilising and fixating *Ka*-forces will become the throne and foundation of Râ's light. Without the grounding Vital Life Force of Osiris, the light of Râ simply cannot be manifested. However, Osiris has to rise up further first before he is able to gift Râ his *Ka*-power. Fortunately, several of the loyal followers of Osiris are present here to assist him and give him strength during the process of his rise.

The Duatians on the left riverbank (upper section)

The left riverbank opens with twelve seated mummies.

(No. 621) "Terrible of the earth"
(No. 622) "Who is adorned"
(No. 623) "Linen-clothed"
(No. 624) "Who belongs to clothes"
(No. 625) "Who is clothed"
(No. 626) "He of the basket"
(No. 627) "Substitute of the God"
(No. 628) "Substitute of the Ennead"
(No. 629) "Who annihilates the *Akh*-spirits"
(No. 630) "Lord of the Elite"
(No. 631) "Who unifies"
(No. 632) "With hidden arm"

Each mummy is seated on the hieroglyphic sign for clothing. As mentioned in the Eighth Hour, this sign is the confirmation of the renewed life that has become visible. The process of renewal becomes further stabilised during the present hour. To establish this it is of vital importance that everything is conducted in accordance with the Divine Law of *Maât*. After all, Order, Truth and Justice are the basic elements of life itself. The compliance with the Divine Law is assessed by these twelve mummies. They are the judges who constitute the tribunal in Osiris's name.

The judges show us that the receipt of clothes is linked to justification. The acquiring of clothes is possible only if the heart is in balance with the feather of *Maât*. Putting on clothes confirms the right to exist and creates the adornment for the truthful being. The judges have completed the process of justification themselves, which has granted them the right to speak from their truthful and righteous heart.

Unsurprisingly, the judges have received their clothes from the hands of Horus himself. Horus has a prominent role in the Hall of

Judgement. He is the mediator between the forty-two tribunal Deities and the deceased. Horus only guides those who are declared "Justified" before his father Osiris. Like this, he protects his father from deceitful enemies. The twelve judges are falling under the responsibility of Horus. Therefore, he is the one who adorns and protects them with new clothes.

Furthermore, Horus is the one who lovingly oversaw the mummification process of his father. It was of vital importance this process was performed correctly. The bandages were meant to protect the vulnerable Osiris and safely hide his body away in the protective embrace of the Duat. Due to this concealment, Osiris is unable to pass judgement himself. Therefore, the judges have appeared to dispense justice on behalf of the King of the Duat. To do this, their mummy wrappings are removed and replaced by new clothes allowing for their faces to be uncovered. Their eyes are opened in order for them to behold the Truth.

> May your heads be uncovered, Gods,
> and may your faces be open,
> that you perform your duties for Osiris,
> that you adore the Lord of the West.[2]

The judges question everyone, in the name

The judges seated on the sign for clothing, KV 9 Ramses V and VI

of Osiris, to assess whether they possess "righteousness of heart". Those who do not meet these requirements are regarded as the enemies of Osiris. Consequently, the judges carry out the sentence to strike these condemned down. Horus, as he is the heir to the throne, has just as much interest in punishing these rebels as does his father Osiris. However, Râ himself also has an interest in the enforcement of the Divine Law of *Maât*. In case Osiris gets killed by these foes, Râ's journey towards transformation comes to a halt as well. Therefore, it is Râ who addresses these judges and highlights the task that befalls to them.

Following these judges is a procession of twelve Goddesses.

(No. 633) "She who goes forth"
(No. 634) "Wanderer of the *Akh*-spirits"
(No. 635) "Mistress of slaughter"
(No. 636) "Mistress of awe"
(No. 637) "Great of plague"
(No. 638) "Mistress of trembling"
(No. 639) "Organizer of her place"
(No. 640) "Mistress of habitations"
(No. 641) "Who protects the valley"
(No. 642) "Great of brilliance"
(No. 643) "Powerful of speech"
(No. 644) "Musician of Râ"

The Sungod calls upon these Goddesses when he arrives at the end of the left riverbank. They are the Followers of Osiris and present here to perform the important task of raising up life and wellbeing. Râ wakes them from their death slumber as he speaks up. It is this loud sound that awakens the Goddesses and gives them the Breath of Life. As they take a deep breath, their being is ensouled with renewed vitality. They get to their feet unwavering and embody the renewed life. Now they have overcome death and become the likeness of Horus.

They are like this in their bodies of the Duat, as images made by Horus.[3]

As these Goddesses have now reached the ideal image, they are ready to take their place and walk in the following of Osiris. However, the presence of these Goddesses here is not only for the benefit of Osiris. They are just as much the representatives of the Sungod for Râ requires the Vital Life Force of Osiris to stabilise his sunlight. Osiris, in turn, has to upraise his own life vigour first before he can give it to Râ. Obviously Râ is unable to help Osiris during this raising of life as he needs the Vital Life Force himself to do this. Therefore, Râ calls upon the supportive forces of these Goddesses to assist Osiris in his stead. These twelve Goddesses then perform a ceremony during which they raise the life force of Osiris step by step. To achieve this they pronounce the correct words in the right tone of voice with a true intention. Consequently, the words they utter are no ordinary words for these are the magical Words of Power.

The accompanying text describes the "raising" of Osiris with the hieroglyphic word *setjesu* (*stsw*). *Setjesu* written with a different determinative means "praises". In a way, the magical words of these Goddesses are a sacred prayer through which they express their adoration for Osiris with all their hearts. Their prayer generates power in such significant quantities that totally and utterly confirm the existence of Osiris. His Vital Life Force has once again become more powerful, enabling him to rise up even further. As Râ follows Osiris in his renewal process, he benefits from this as well. Râ requires stability to give shape to his light.

Confusingly enough, the accompanying text suggests it is the performance of these Goddesses that assures the visible illumination of the Sungod.

> What they have to do in the Duat:
> to perform the raising (*stsw*) of Osiris
> and to let the secret *Ba*-soul alight (*shn*)
> through their words.
> They are those who raise up life
> and dominion
> at the appearance of Him of the Duat,
> when he greets the Duat, day after day.[4]

However, this is not quite correct. They are indeed the ones who facilitate the process of

The procession of the Goddesses, K9 Ramses V and VI

the raising up of life and wellbeing with their magical ceremony. Nevertheless, it is Osiris himself who guarantees that the light of the secret *Ba*-soul, which is Râ, will shine even brighter. The Goddesses merely provide Osiris with the means to do this. The hieroglyphic word *sekheni (shnî)*, which means "alight", can also be translated as *sekhen (shn)*. This means "embrace, occupy a place or bind together". In the ceremony, the Goddesses bind the body of Osiris and the *Ba*-soul of Râ together. Then, Osiris is able to embrace the Sungod and to transmit his Vital Life Force to Râ. This gesture of protection and Love makes Râ's soul become even more radiant and he in turn animates Osiris. This connection between the both of them allows them to truly occupy their places.

The Duatians of the Sacred River (middle section)

The Sun barque continues its sailing course through the waters in the Eastern area of the Duat. On board the barque is the usual combination of crewmembers, who have taken their respective places. Though the presence of these crewmembers is not specifically emphasised, they most definitely play an important part as a quiet power in the background. It is their expertise that enables Râ to find his way through the Duat. Without them, Râ would become completely vulnerable and defenceless against the hungry claws of the darkness.

(No. 645) "Wepwawet"
(No. 646) "Sia"
(No. 647) "Nebet wia"
(No. 648) "Mehen"
(No. 649) "Iuf"
(No. 650) "Heru Hekenu"
(No. 651) "Ka Maât"
(No. 652) "Nehes"
(No. 653) "Hu"
(No. 654) "Kherep wia"

The Sungod Râ himself is standing in the middle of the Sun barque. This also emphasises his role, for he is the centre point of the entire journey. He is wearing a solar disk on his head with ram horns underneath. In his hands he is holding a snake staff. He is still standing within the safe protection of Mehen, the serpent God, who is seen here proudly with his head held high. Kherep wia guides the barque with Râ through the waters of the Ninth Hour. He is using his *Heka* to manifest the Will of the Divine as he has guided the barque through the final turn. Now the course has been permanently set in the direction of the East.

Finally, the Sun barque is sailing towards the morning light. Although there are still several hours of travelling ahead, the oppressive darkness has become slightly enlightened by this image of the future. Râ is determined to continue his travels and is thus difficult to stop. Now that he is sailing here, he knows the light will rise no matter what. Hence, the renewal, which has taken place during the previous hours, can no longer be reversed. However, it is still too early to celebrate. The important question, which has to be answered, is with what intention the light will eventually shine. Will it be a bright sun, empowered to illuminate the entire world to make it come alive with all its gorgeous colours? Or will it be a watery sun that is barely able to illuminate the world and shrouds it in grey hues? The upcoming hours will tell and be decisive in the final development and illuminating power of the sunlight of Râ.

For this reason the pace of the journey, like the transformation process, may not diminish. Even though Râ has come a long way, this is not the time to falter. A delay would be fatal to the expansion of the amount of light necessary to adequately illuminate the world. To prevent this, a group of twelve Divine rowers is added to the usual crew of the barque during the present hour to increase the speed.

(No. 655) "The Rower"
(No. 656) "The Imperishable"
(No. 657) "The Indefatigable"
(No. 658) "Who knows no turning back"
(No. 659) "Who knows no hindrance"
(No. 660) "Who knows no decay"
(No. 661) "Rowing (in) his hour"
(No. 662) "Who crosses his land"
(No. 663) "Who rests (in) the barque"
(No. 664) "The Most Divine"
(No. 665) "Who traverses the Duat"
(No. 666) "Who belongs to the boat"

The names of these sailors emphasises their powerful skills as rowers. After the many delays during the previous two hours, the rowers ensure that the Sun barque can finally pick up pace. Movement means life, so the more movement is generated, the more alive Râ becomes. As Râ has an interest in increasing his illuminating power, it is Râ himself who gives the command to row. As soon as the rowers hear his order, they immediately take action. All at once they take up their oars and start rowing in a smooth motion to move the Sun barque through the waters. This dynamic thrust gives the barque a

The rower "Who crosses his land",
KV 14 Tausert/Setnakht

huge boost forward. As they continue rowing, the oarsmen start to sing a prayer in adoration of Râ as "Lord of the Sun Disc" in unison. These mysterious words of prayer provide Râ with an additional confirmation of his existence. Now, his light starts to develop even further and becomes more visible.

Through these rowing movements, the sailors transmit the life force quality that is embedded in the water, to Râ. However, not only the Sungod is blessed with this life force. When the oarsmen start rowing, their movements make the water splash up. The life-giving water then lands on the riverbanks where the *Akh*-spirits are standing to gaze upon Râ as he sails past them. Like a shower of renewed life it rains down on them like a blessing. In doing so the rowers also quench the *Akh*-spirits thirst for renewal.

Behind the Divine rowers are three Deities in the shape of sphinxes lying on *neb* baskets. The hieroglyphic word *neb* (*nb*), means "Lord or Master". *Neb* with a feminine ending, *nebet*, means "Lady or Mistress". The Gods and Goddesses are often depicted on top of these wicker baskets to emphasise their Godly nature. Therefore, it is quite clear these three Deities possess a Divine status.

(No. 667) "Offerer in front of the Duat" human-headed, crowned with the Two Feathers Crown.

(No. 668) "Kherty in front of the Duat" with the head of a ram. The God Kherty (*ḥrty*) is usually depicted as a ram and occasionally as a bull or lion. His cult centre was located in the ancient town Nezat, which gave him the epithet "Foremost of Nezat". The meaning of his name "He of What is Below" refers to his residence in the Netherworld. There he was a celestial ferryman and the guide and protector of the deceased. According to Utterance 483 of the Pyramid Texts, Kherty was addressed to protect the tomb. *"Go back, be far away! Let Osiris respect me and Kherti protect me"*. However, there was also another side to Kherti's nature. In Utterance 250, Spell for the Spirit's rebirth, of the Pyramid Texts, the deceased asked for protection against Kherty for Kherty lived off of people's hearts.

(No. 669) "Mistress of offerings in front of the Duat" with the head of a cow wearing the sun disk between her horns.

Following these Divine Deities is a standing mummy, "Offerer of the Gods" (No. 670), who closes the Sacred River.

Each of these four Deities (No. 667 – 670) is under orders from Râ to provide everyone with the food offerings of bread and beer. Bread and beer were essential requirements to be able to survive in the Afterlife. The hieroglyphic word shaped like a basket, *neb* (*nb*), also means "all and every". This is reflected in the fact that everyone is being given these food offerings and each and every one of them is confirmed in their eternal existence.

Furthermore, grain symbolises the

resurrected life that has triumphed over death. As we know, grain is the symbol of Osiris. Presently, Osiris himself has taken a subsequent step in his own renewal thanks to the performance of the magical ceremony of the twelve Goddesses (No. 633 - 644). Râ also joins in this rising power of eternal Life.

The Duatians on the right riverbank (lower section)

The right riverbank opens with twelve Uraeus-serpents. Here they are sitting in an upraised posture on top of the hieroglyphic signs for clothing, just like the judges on the other side of the Sacred River. Thus, both riverbanks of the Sacred River commence with Gods who have taken their places on top of this hieroglyphic sign. This underlines the fact that the renewal process is balanced and it supports the rejuvenation of Râ as he sails in between these Gods.

(No. 671) "She with painful flame"
(No. 672) "The Fiery One"
(No. 673) "The Flaming One"
(No. 674) "Who protects the Duat"
(No. 675) "Who repels the tumult"

The Sphinx-Deities seated on baskets, KV 9 Ramses V and VI

(No. 676) "She with bright stars"
(No. 677) "She with living face"
(No. 678) "She with distinguished shape"
(No. 679) "She with perfect appearance"
(No. 680) "She with great form"
(No. 681) "Mistress of Embers"
(No. 682) "Mistress of Heat"

These fire spitting Uraei illuminate the Chamber of Osiris with the flames from their mouths. This Chamber is a reference to the Duat, which is the dwelling place of Osiris. Due to the light from these flames, the darkness is beginning to lose its oppressive vibe and already offers some enlightenment. Osiris, however, is not the only one starting to rise, for the Sungod is coming along in the upraising power as well. This enables Râ too to rise up a bit more. Hence, these helpful Uraei are here to serve both Osiris and Râ.

However, despite their well-intentioned servitude, these fierce creatures are still very dangerous. Anyone trying to enter this part of the Duat without first identifying themselves with the Sungod, is slaughtered by these Uraeus-serpents without mercy. Without this identification these unauthorised ignorant beings do not possess the enlightenment nor the consciousness, which is what the Sungod stands for. This makes these enemies the polar opposite of Râ and a dangerous threat. Due to their dark powers, these foes are perceived as serpents.

The Uraei are without mercy as they slaughter these evil serpents. They do this through beheading them to prevent the poison of these rebels from causing any more harm. During the massacre blood is richly spilled that in turn is used as a food source for the Uraei. Therefore, no one is allowed to enter if they are unaware of the Mystery of the Duat. Only the Initiates, who have participated in the process of Râ's renewal, are given access. The Initiates "Know" these Uraeus-serpents and are capable of facing their flames without getting burned. Since the enlightenment and consciousness of these Initiates have reached the required level, they can now resist the flames. The flames do not blind the eyes of these Wise, nor does it consume their being. In fact, the flames actually serve to increase their inner enlightenment even further and enable them to rise up together with Râ.

Following the Uraeus-serpent there is a group of nine Gods. They are the Gods of the fields who are carrying the *Ankh* in one hand and a stalk of emmer or wheat in the other. Both of the attributes symbolise eternal Life. These Gods are the only Deities on the riverbank who form a group of nine, for the other three groups are comprised of twelve Deities. This imbalance emphasises the fact that growth, which they represent, is still in the middle of development. Thus, it is still imperfect and without complete harmony. Furthermore, their number of nine is a reference to the "plural of plurals" and indicates bountiful vegetation similar to a true paradise.

(No. 683) "Who belongs to the field"
(No. 684) "Who is in his field"
(No. 685) "Who belongs to the bud"
(No. 686) "Who belongs to the *Djâm*-sceptre"
(No. 687) "Lord of the staff"
(No. 688) "*Heka*-sceptre of his Gods"
(No. 689) "Who acts clever"
(No. 690) "Who acts unapproachable"
(No. 691) "The Upraised of the fields"

In addition, these Gods of the fields are also known as the Lords of Life. Their presence here is to ensure that life flourishes eternally and profusely, resulting in the growth of all the plants and trees. The Deities bestow this eternal Life with the *Ankh's* in their hands. Death and darkness are now conquered. This is highlighted by the fact they are holding a plant in their other hand. In actuality, these plants are *Djâm*-sceptres, which is probably an older version of the *Was*-sceptre. The difference between the two sceptres is that the *Djâm*-sceptre is a staff with a coiled shape whereas the *Was*-sceptre has a straight staff.

Fig. 29. Djâm-sceptre   Fig. 30. Was-sceptre

The hieroglyphic meaning of *djâm* (d^cm) is "a sceptre". *Djâm* can also be translated as "be white golden", which is the colour of the body of Osiris. Hence, white gold was considered a very valuable metal, also known as electrum or *djâmu* (d^cmw). Electrum is a mixture of gold and silver that can be found naturally occurring in the wild. It also contains traces of copper and various other metals. The colour can vary from white to amber depending on the gold to silver ratio. It was used to coat important objects like offering tables, mummy masks, the capstone or pyramidion of pyramids, statues etcetera. It was also frequently used to craft jewellery. Consequently, considering the relation between the *Djâm*-sceptre and electrum, this indicates that the *Djâm*-sceptre contains a very valuable and precious power.

As for the reason why the shaft of the *Djâm*-sceptre has a coiled shape, it is still unknown. Perhaps it is a reference to a snake who has wrapped himself around a staff similar to the asklepian. The asklepian is an old Greek symbol for healing and medicine and is still used as the emblem for the physicians. The staff is a memento of Aesculapius, the old Greek half god associated with the medical arts. The exact meaning of the staff can be interpreted in various ways. In all cases, the snake coiling around the staff is a vital element. As this animal sheds its skin on regular basis, it is regarded as a symbol of regeneration and life. The bite of a snake, on the other hand, can cause illness and death. This ambiguity expresses the duality in the nature of the medical arts that deals with poison as well as medicine and with sickness and death as well as healing and life. The asklepian is, therefore, a symbol that reigns over life and death. Hence, the *Djâm*-sceptre could be an early precursor of the asklepian. The sceptre is a symbol of dominion, the raising of life and well-being where death is cured and eternal Life triumphs.

Alternatively, the shaft of the *Djâm*-sceptre could also be interpreted as lightning. Lightning holds an enormous power which emerges from the world of the Gods. During thunderstorms, the Gods would use thunder to demonstrate their power and dominion over the world of mankind. When the lightning strikes the earth the Divine power of the Gods is manifested on earth. This power demands respect and awe as it signifies the mysterious power that reigns over life and death. This indicates that the *Djâm*-sceptre, like the *Was*-sceptre, is an extremely powerful attribute which can be used in the hands of the Gods alone.

The Gods of the fields, who wield these *Djâm*-sceptres, are standing directly across from the twelve Goddesses on the left riverbank. This comes as no surprise since the two groups of Deities complement each others powers perfectly. The Gods of the fields control the power of the *Djâm*-sceptres while the twelve Goddesses perform the ceremony and utter the accompanying words of prayer. Together they guarantee life rises, grows and blossoms.

Râ commissions the nine Gods of the fields to present their staffs to the Duatians living here. However, the Gods of the fields are not just merely displaying their *Djâm*-sceptres. Their true actions go much further than what is simply presented here. In fact they are effectively manifesting the healing powers contained within their mighty *Djâm*-sceptres. Death is now truly cured and provides the residing Duatians here with vitality and well-being. Life is blossoming abundantly, allowing for the plants and trees to grow bountiful. The trees bear fruits and the fields produce crops. Due to this prosperity each of the Duatians living here is properly fed.

> This Great God, he calls to them.
> They are those who present staves
> to the Gods in the Duat at this place
> They are those who cause all the trees
> and all the plants of this place to grow.[5]

This Divine garden is a true paradise. It is none other than Horus himself who is the Guardian of this garden, "Horus above the garden of the Duatians" (No. 692). He is displayed here in his mummy form and he concludes the Ninth Hour. Horus, as the symbol of renewed life, is guarding the budding of life and he is in charge of the Gods of the fields. The garden requires a meticulous care to ensure its continued production of generous food supplies. The ploughing, sowing, watering and harvesting of the plants are all part of the maintenance. However, most of all, the plants and trees require light to live. Horus, in his illuminating appearance, is the bringer and keeper of this light and life.

As seen in the previous hours, the Guardian

who closes the hour is usually facing the opposite direction to watch over all of the Duatians in the hour. However, Horus's gaze is focused on the Eastern horizon away from the Duatians. He does not allow himself to be distracted from his focus on the horizon where the light will soon appear. Nevertheless, it still takes three more hours before the sun finally makes an appearance as it climbs up in the sky. This is why Horus is in his mummy form to emphasise that the sunlight is still in the process of transformation. Despite this continuous development, Horus is already announcing the joyful event that will eventually come to pass. For he knows for certain, the light will always return to the earth.

> I ascend to the sky as the Gods,
> the flood is fostered for me
> and is brought to me;
> abundance is confirmed to me
> and vegetation is planted in this garden
> by this Horus [...] [6]
> – Coffin texts; Spell 696

The manifestation of the Ninth Hour in daily life

The Ninth Hour opens a completely new chapter in your journey. The fact you have been able to reach this point, says a great deal about you. You have shown persistence and a fighting spirit, not so easily beaten in spite of adversities along the way. You have proven to be brave and curious, as you continuously looked in the mirror in front of you. Face to face with yourself you have probably interspersed crying with laughing. As it turns out, you have faith in this voyage of discovery into the realms of your true Self. Willingly, with a spirit of adventure and facing challenges, you bravely and belligerently confronted and transformed your inner enemies. This in itself is invaluable.

As you have reached the Ninth Hour, you have managed to bring about a major reversal within yourself. This reversal is mirrored and confirmed by the change in course that you have performed in this hour for the last time. From this hour onwards, the focus remains directed towards the East up until the final hour. The East, as the cardinal direction of the element of air, has brought about a completely new experience. The air gives you the feeling you can finally take a deep breath again. Suddenly you seem to have more freedom of movement compared to the previous hours. Although it is still night, the darkness seems to have become less oppressive, which already provides you with some enlightenment.

It is a complete relief to be here after the rough and rocky landscapes from the previous hour. The present hour has a soothing air to it that is emphasised by its appearance of an oasis with the bountiful vegetation of beautiful trees and plants. The fresh green is complemented by the first early spring flowers that are erupting everywhere from the ground. It truly has the appearance of a Divine Garden blessed with an abundance of water. The water is streaming plentiful through the landscape, enabling life to be fed and to thrive.

This large amount of water ensures that the inner flow is started up again. It gives you the opportunity to significantly advance forward in your process. Therefore, be mindful to not let your attention be diverted by paddling in the water of this magnificent paradise. This is no time for a holiday. Even though you might think and be convinced you have already reached your ultimate goal. And truth be told, the renewal and expansion of your consciousness truly has come a long way already. As long as you remain aware of this and prevent your attention from faltering, you will retain this extended vision. You can also be sure of the fact that this consciousness becomes truly visible at the end of your journey. However, presently, these jubilant cries of joy are still too early. You have to realise that the renewed vision is still barely viable. It is currently only a faint light that is still lacking in power to truly make you and your talents shine.

Should you decide to continue your journey with determination, you can make sure the development of the consciousness progresses until it is fully grown by the end of the Twelfth Hour. To reach this point, first the harmony between you, the Higher Self and the Powerself must increase. Only when you are able to cooperate with these parts of your being as a unit, you are capable of making your purpose in life visible. Hence, the upcoming hours focus first on creating balance between these different layers of the consciousness.

In the present hour aside from the Sungod, the Higher Self, it is also Osiris, the Powerself, who plays a major role. The Powerself is the one who stabilises the enlightened consciousness symbolised by the Higher Self. The enlightened consciousness is in need of support, a "backbone", to come into being. Hence, it is very important to make a steep dive into the subconscious waters again. The Powerself, like the Higher Self, is found within these inner waters. The only difference is that the Powerself resides in this underworld, whereas the Higher Self belongs to the Higher world. However, this does not mean that the underworld is inferior to the higher one. It only indicates the different layers of the unseen world and should not be judged. By now you have come to realise the Powerself and the Higher Self are both essential parts of your being. They need each other to obtain their right to exist. Obviously, the Higher Self does have the leading position. The Powerself is subjected to him, notwithstanding that the position of the Powerself is just as important. The fact is that Osiris is required to descend deep into the depths of life to germinate the earth with his generative powers. The Sungod, on the other hand, has to ascend and stand above the world to shed his light on the earthly layer.

To understand and to grasp the underlying power of the Powerself, you need to further explore your inner world. Only once you comprehend its functioning properly, you are equipped to harness it yourself and to put it to use. The Powerself, like the Higher Self, communicates with you from the waters of your subconscious world. But there certainly is a difference between the inner calling of the True inner Voice of the Higher Self and the sense of inner strength from the Powerself. During this hour you discover the difference between the both of them. However, this does not necessarily mean you have mastered this skill of discernment perfectly at the end of this hour. It is still only the beginning which requires further development and lots of practice.

The twelve Divine rowers (No. 655 – 666) support you during this hour to strengthen your contact with your Powerself. These rowers, first of all, ensure the inner flow is boosted and sped up. You have to connect yourself with these rowers to facilitate this process. Furthermore, the oarsmen cause waves in the water due to the rowing movements of their oars. Your inner world is now being stirred, causing everything to start moving. Everything that once lay dormant on the bottom now swirls to the surface and becomes visible. Similar to the Third Hour, this is the next step in the clean-up of the inner waters to make them clear again. The subsequent transparency allows you to see what it truly is that is living down there.

Unsurprisingly, you will experience intense and vivid dreams that grant you clarity in the developing events. However, in everyday life the inner turmoil causes developments as well that provide you with lost pieces to your spiritual puzzle. Memories of forgotten or suppressed experiences of the present or past lives suddenly surface. The name of this hour is not "Flowing forth of images with living manifestations" without reason, for this is an hour with eye-opening revelations and clarity. These disclosures can present themselves quite intensely and powerfully, which is typical for the Powerself. This way, the Powerself feeds you with strength and decisiveness and assists you in stabilising your renewed consciousness. The more you learn to understand the power of this Self, the more aware you become of your capabilities. This inner clarity reflects itself in your external world as well where you suddenly perceive relations and events from a new perspective.

Aside from these rowers, other Deities support you during this effervescent process as well. First of all, the twelve judges (No. 621 – 632) are here by your side. Their presence is needed to ensure the Divine Law of *Maât* is a part of the current process. They judge whether your heart remains in balance with the feather of Truth and thus speaks with a clear conscience. Furthermore, the way you perceive truthfulness and sincerity has developed itself further due to the influx of the Higher Self. The concept of *Maât* is now beginning to give a visible shine to your personality. Simultaneously, this Divine Truth entails a larger responsibility. Claiming ignorance is no longer an excuse as the awareness and truth have become an important part of your conscience. Of course you have already come out of this immature behaviour during the previous hours, otherwise you would not be here in the Ninth Hour now. Still, every judge addresses you personally to assess your renewed perspective regarding truth and falsehood. Once again the time has arrived for you to take your power of discernment to the next level.

The twelve Uraeus-serpents on the other side of the Sacred River are working together with these judges. Their collaboration works perfectly since the Uraeus-serpents shed light on the concealing blackness that hides untruthfulness. The judges in turn can exploit the enlightenment for their examinations to pass judgement correctly. The flames of these Uraei illuminate every cavern of your inner world, which is also the habitat of your Powerself. However, be especially wary of the snakes in the grass posing as the Powerself. Shine your light on these vipers for they shy away from it to find solace in dark corners or holes. The power of illumination is essential to expose these snakes for the false gods they are. They are the slippery silent killers who try to poison your renewed vision in order to weaken it and to cause a painful slow death. The only way to exterminate these toxic enemies from your inner world is to resolutely decapitate them to silence them. Do not show mercy under any circumstances and brace yourself for their traps and cunning tricks. Be aware that desperate times require drastic measures.

Hence, subject your conscious self again to the judgement of these Divine judges and the transforming fires of the Uraeus-serpents. Once you have faced the Truth and seen things for what they truly are, you have unravelled a new part of your inner world. The different layers of your consciousness have become more intimately connected with each other through this renewal. It are precisely these underlying connections that form the foundation upon which the renewed consciousness can firmly take root and begin its ascend.

The Uraeus-serpent symbolises this raising of the consciousness that bridges all of the different worlds. The serpent is an animal that creates its home in holes in the ground, slides over the earth and can raise its upper body towards the sky. This animal shows us the connection between the Powerself living in the underworld, the personality who is standing on the earth and the Higher Self who raises himself in the Higher world. All of these worlds need to be balanced and connected to each other. However, herein the earthly and subconscious aspects are just as important as the heavenly dimension. A focus that is unilaterally directed upwards causes your feet to come off the ground and for you to float away. In such a case, you become disconnected from the deep power of your Powerself. Consequently, this causes the light to lose its foundation and to remain an unrealistic dream. This is precisely why it is the Uraeus-serpent that adorns the brow of the

Pharaoh as the sign of Divine rulership.

To proceed with the upraising of your inner power, you are aided by two groups of Deities who are here to lend a hand. The first group consists of the twelve Goddesses (No. 634 – 644) who are standing on the left riverbank. They lovingly worship and protect the Sungod Râ with their magical words of prayer. Out of this Love, Râ draws his right to exist, which simultaneously leads him to grant the gift of life to the Goddesses themselves. This is a two-way interaction making both parties more powerful and more alive. As you realise, it is your own love for your inner Sungod that allows for the light within yourself to visibly shine. This gives you wings, self esteem and the confidence to improve your performances that you never believed possible before. Hence, the inner love is the true and honest unconditional Love. It makes you stronger and adds a shine to who you truly are.

Across from these adoring Goddesses are the Gods of the fields (No. 683 – 691), standing on the right riverbank. These are the healers of death who grant an abundance of eternal Life. They hand the *Djâm*-sceptres, which they are carrying, over to you. You have now transformed your old and latent consciousness in a renewed consciousness where life triumphs over death. This makes you a divine being and a responsible creator of your own blossoming inner world.

You are now ready to take your rightful place as lord and master of your inner land on your throne. Each Pharaoh, who is crowned and takes a seat on the throne, has to make an oath. With this oath he pledges loyalty to his nation, but above all, he promises to serve his people and subjects himself to them. As you are now going to ascend this throne, while wearing the crown you received during the previous hour, you take responsibility for your own inner world as you continue to abide this oath. You are a subject of the inner Sungod, the Higher Self, yourself. The inner Sungod adorns your head like a crown as you are seated on the throne of the Powerself. You are now the living canal between both the Powerself and the Higher Self, while balancing the scales of *Maât* in your hands. The upcoming hours prove the extent to which you are in harmony with power and light as you yourself become the embodiment of the Divine Law of *Maât*.

> The secret cavern of the West.
> Osiris N knows this image upon earth
> and knows their bodies
> within the West
> as one who occupies the bodily form
> in the Duat,
> as one who stands before the possessor
> of necessities,
> as one who is justified in the council
> on the day of reckoning.
> This is effective for him on earth.[7]

THE TENTH HOUR
"Deep water and high banks"

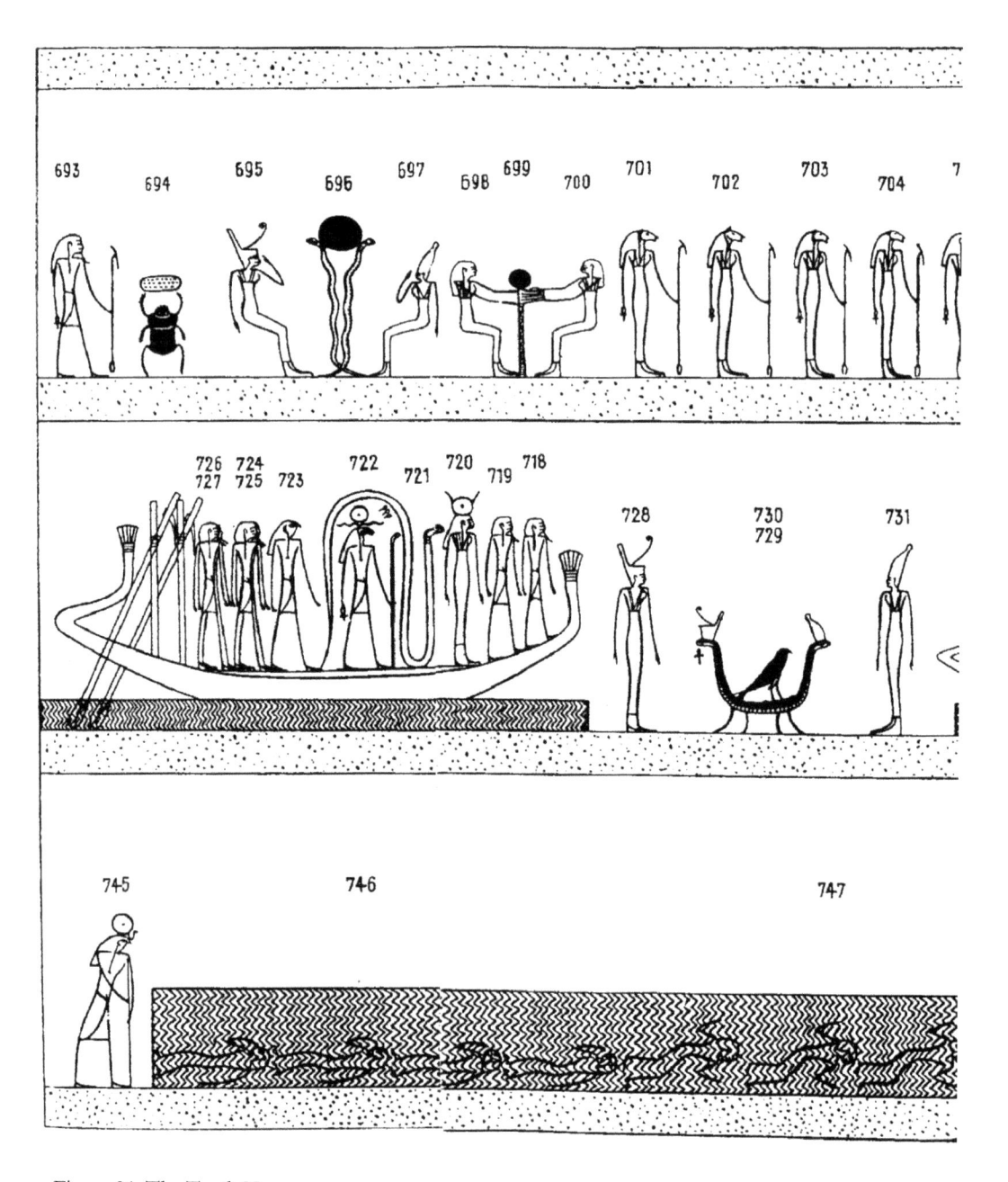

Figure 31: The Tenth Hour

The Gate: "With great manifestations, giving birth to forms"
The Hour Goddess: "The Furious One who slaughters Him with crooked heart"
The Guardian: (no name mentioned)

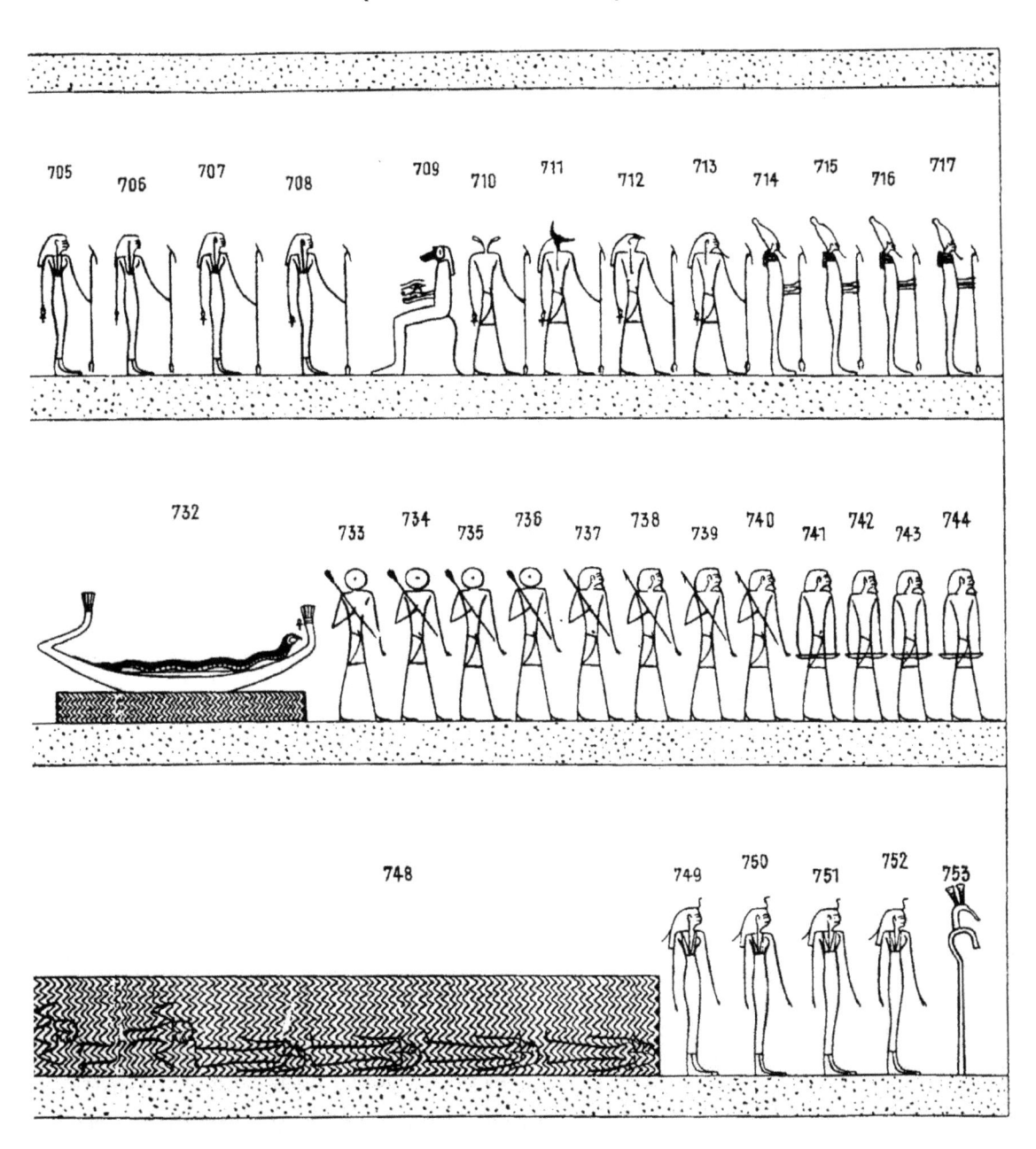

Introduction

Pausing by the person of this Great God
in this cavern.
He gives orders to the Gods who are in it.
The name of the Gate of this place through
which this Great God enters is
"With great manifestations,
giving birth to forms".
The name of this Place is
"Deep water and high banks".
The name of the Hour of the night
which guides this Great God,
to the mysterious paths of this place is
"The Furious One who slaughters Him
with crooked heart".
The mysterious cavern of the West,
where Khepri rests with Râ,
at which Gods, *Akh*-spirits,
and the dead lament
because of the mysterious image of *Igeret*.
This is done like this image
which is painted
on the Eastern side of the Hidden Chamber
of the Duat.
He who knows them,
by their names,
traverses the Duat right to the end,
without being expelled from
the council of Râ.[1]

After a prosperous journey through the Ninth Hour, Râ's power has grown and become further stabilised. He is now ready to enter the Tenth Hour and is standing in front of its gate "With great manifestations, giving birth to forms". This gate is in line with the energy of the previous hour, "Flowing forth of images with living manifestations". The fluent process of regeneration and rebirth continues to move forward at a steady pace. The gate opens itself to Râ to let him enter this hour with his crew. Steadfast and determined he continues his journey in this Eastern area while sailing across the turbulent waters of the Sacred River. The water surface has turned jet black, giving it a mysterious reflection. As the bottom of the Sacred River is now hidden underneath this reflection, it is impossible to triangulate its depth. No wonder, for this hour is called "Deep water and high banks" for a reason.

Once Râ enters this hour, the Hour Goddess "The Furious One who slaughters Him with crooked heart" joins him. This dangerous and powerful Goddess demands everyone's respect for she is a force not to be trifled with. Her impressive fierce lion-like appearance emphasises this fact. She does not hesitate to slaughter every dishonest person, referred to as "him with the crooked heart", without mercy. As a furious and raging Goddess, she does so by beheading each of these deceitful rebels. This is an effective method, which does not only take their lives, but their identities as well. There no longer is any hope for the existence of these foes for they are beyond salvation for the rest of eternity. After all, there simply is no place for the unfaithful, dishonest, insincere and unfair in the Duat. Any sign of these traits is exterminated with an iron fist at all times to let the Divine Law of *Maât* triumph. Only the blessed souls who are in possession of the "True Heart" have admittance here. Their hearts are open to receive the Inner Knowledge that enables them to name each of the Duatians and identify themselves with the wisdom of these beings. It is this Inner Wisdom that provides them with a place on the Sun barque of Râ and allows them to join him on the journey towards rebirth right to the end.

Consequently, the Sungod is surrounded by the Gods, *Akh*-spirits and the dead who participate in the process of renewal. Each of these beings is taking part in the great mystery of "Death into Life" that is unfolding here. Osiris is the symbol of this resurrection that he himself has undergone first. His corpse is the representation of the mysterious image of *Igeret*, the realm of the dead. The moment the Duatians get a view of Osiris's body, they burst into tears. The confrontation reaches deep within their inner souls as they are fully aware what it is they are seeing. On one hand, they begin to lament and give voice to their bereavement over death. On the other hand, tears of joy flow from their eyes to honour the sprouting new life. These deep emotions assist Osiris in his own process of renewal. His being is fed by the life-granting waters of their tears. The sensitive lament of these Duatians sounds like a beautiful prayer drenched with love.

> O Osiris the King,
> You have gone, but you will return,
> You have slept, [but you will awake],
> You have died, but you will live.[2]
> – Pyramid Texts; Utterance 670

Naturally, the transformation of the Sungod Râ is intertwined with Osiris's own process. However, it is Râ, as an active God, who takes a leading position in the process of renewal, unlike the passive Osiris. Thus, the central theme during this hour is the healing of the damaged light of the Sungod Râ, or the "Eye of the West". The recovery of his broken light is of paramount importance to ensure a newly gained balance. Harmony and wholeness are the prerequisite for his light to be able to rise in the morning. To realise this essential healing process, Râ is supported by the Wisdom of the God Thoth and the destroying and healing powers of the Goddess Sekhmet.

The Duatians on the left riverbank (Upper section)

The left riverbank opens with a God, "Who acts clever" (No. 693), who is standing while holding an *Ankh* and a *Was*-sceptre in his hands. It comes as no surprise that it is precisely this God who opens this hour. He can be found here to make a statement. This God is the embodiment of acting upon Wisdom, which is also the essence of this hour. Only the implementation of Wisdom enables the growth of the underdeveloped Eye or light of Râ. Without acting upon inner Wisdom, it is impossible to restore Râ's light. Râ takes this valuable message to heart.

The Sungod still has to undergo quite a transformation before his light can be reborn. Nevertheless, the scarab Khepri, "Living Khepri" (No. 694), has once again made his appearance here to announce the impending rebirth at this early stage. His arrival at this point gives Râ the courage and determination to continue. Khepri is holding a dotted oval, or ellipse, up high with his front legs. The ellipse of sand symbolises the entire Duat and is also a specific reference to the Cavern of Sokar in the Fifth Hour. Inside this hidden area, the process of transforming death into life took place, which is the essence of what the Duat is all about. By now, the transformation has made good progress for the early signs of rebirth have started to become visible. Khepri, as the renewed form of the Sungod, is starting to progressively shine through Râ. The edge of this ellipse is visible at the end of the Twelfth Hour. This is also the place where Râ eventually completes his transfiguration into Khepri. Here, in the Tenth Hour, Khepri himself is aiding the process of "coming into being" as he pushes the ellipse upward in the direction of the Eastern horizon.

[…] I am Râ who issued from the Abyss in this my name of Khepri,
and my soul is a God.[3]
– Coffin Texts; Spell 307

Khepri is followed by a half upraised Goddess, "Red Crown" (No. 695), who is wearing the Red Crown of Lower Egypt. Across from her is another half upraised Goddess, "White Crown" (No. 697), who is wearing the White Crown of Upper Egypt. They are both touching their respective crowns with one hand. This is a gesture that expresses "to carry or burden" and accentuates the two crowns they are wearing.

In between these two Goddesses are two upraised serpents standing on their tails. Together they carry the name "The Double-Coiled" (No. 696). Since the bodies of these serpents are entwined, they provide for a stable support for the disk that can be found on top of their two heads. In the text this disk is addressed as *iabet* (*i3bt*), which means "East" (No. 696). Therefore, this disk refers to the fully grown light or Eye of Râ at the moment he is reborn in the East.

This solar disk is also a reference to the Goddess of the East who, likewise, is known as Iabet. In the First Hour she was already present as one of the Goddesses who praised Râ (No. 121). A derivative of the word *iabet* is *iabety* (*i3bty*) which means "East, Eastern, left side of". Thus, the "Eye of the East" is situated at the left side of the smaller disk (No. 699). However, once you turn this perspective around and gaze upon the solar disk, "East", from within the Duat, you will notice it is actually the right Eye.

The "Eye of the East" is carried between the two heads of the serpents "The Double-Coiled". Each head is looking in a different direction, which provides for a particular stable support for the fully developed Eye. This duality is further emphasised by the dual character of the snake, as it connects both the negative and positive forces. The power of duality is also reflected in the two most important serpents of the Duat. On the one hand, there is Apophis, who has to attack Râ to allow the Sungod to develop his powers. On the other hand, there is Mehen, whose presence is needed to protect the Sungod and help him to safely transform. In other words, opposite forces provide for a steady base upon which the light, or the consciousness, can develop.

In addition, the White and Red Crown of the two Goddesses also emphasise the importance of duality. Upper and Lower Egypt are both essential to give rise to a united Egypt that radiates power. This applies to the Duat as well. Here, the Kingdom of Râ needs to merge with the Kingdom of Osiris to form a unity to restore the light.

Next to the two Goddesses are two other half upraised Goddesses, "She who fetters" (No. 698) and "She who laments (or: embraces) the

The Goddesses "Red Crown" and "White Crown", and the serpent "The Double Coiled".
KV 9 Ramses V and VI

Gods" (No. 700). Together they are holding a staff wrapped in bandages that is standing in between them. This staff is the hieroglyphic sign for God "*Netjer*". On top of the hieroglyph is a second smaller solar disk, or Eye. The Eye is referred to in the text as *iment* (*imnt*), which means "West" (No. 699). Unsurprisingly, this is the "Eye of the West". This Eye is a reference to the aging of the Sungod, who sets in the Western horizon following his journey through the day. As mentioned before, the word *iment* is a derivative of *imen* or *amun* (*imn*), which means "conceal, hide, secret or create". Hence, the Eye is hidden in the secret place of the Duat where it can heal in safety, shrouded in darkness. It is the symbol of the miraculous life that always triumphs over death and it, therefore, carries the secret of creation within.

The solar disk is also a reference to the Goddess of the West, Imentet. In the First Hour she was already present, alongside Iabet, the Goddess of the East, to praise the Sungod as he passed them (No. 114). The word *imen* (*ỉmn*) also means "right side". Thus, the "Eye of the West" is situated at the right side of the "Eye of the East" (No. 696).

However, here too you need to turn the perspective around, for you are in the Duat. As you gaze upon the "Eye of the West" from within the Duat, you notice it is actually the left Eye. This Eye is significantly smaller compared to the fully grown right Eye, the "Eye of the East". The transformation of Râ is completed only once the "Eye of the West" has reached the same size as the "Eye of the East". This development is still in progress, which is reflected by the posture of the four Goddesses (No. 695, 697, 698 and 700). They are only half-upraised for it is too early to stand up straight.

The pole, wrapped in bandages, with the "Eye of the West" on top of it, indicates that Râ is still changing here inside of his wrappings. As soon as this transformation of "Death into Life" is completed, Râ will symbolically emerge from his wrappings as the renewed God Khepri while revealing his true and Divine nature. The two Goddesses on each side of this pole are here to support this process. "She who fetters" also ensures Râ's transformation does not proceed too quickly. It is very important for the Sungod's light to develop slowly to guarantee stability and balance. "She who laments or embraces the Gods" grants her life-giving tears and transmits her life force to the "Eye of the West" through her embrace. Yet this Goddess is not the only one to gift her tears, for the *Ba*-souls living here, present the Eye with their tears as well. Together they sing a song of lament that is not only addressed to the Sungod, but to all of the *Akh*-spirits residing here as well.

The "Eye of the West" can also be regarded as the "Eye of Horus". The Eye of Horus symbolises all that is broken, old, dismembered or even dead. Still, this Eye never truly dies for no matter how broken it is, it can always be cured and become whole again. This shows the resilience, flexibility and regenerative powers of life. Thus, the "Eye of the West" is the representation of Râ in his old and worn state while setting in the West. Instead of dying, the Eye renews itself completely and becomes the mirror image of the "Eye of the East". Both the "Eye of the West" and the "Eye of Horus" underline the unbeatable force that is life. No matter what, life shall always prevail.

Directly behind the immature "Eye of the West" there are eight Goddesses (No. 701 – 708) who are here to assist Râ in the healing of his Eye, or light. The first four Goddesses have the head of a lioness while the other four appear in human form. All of these eight Goddesses are manifestations of the Goddess Sekhmet, "the Mighty One". They are proudly standing tall while holding the *Was*-sceptre in their left and the *Ankh* in their right hand.

(No. 701) "Sekhmet (The Powerful One)"
(No. 702) "Menkeret"
(No. 703) "Maiden"

The Goddesses "She who fetters" and "She who laments (or: embraces) the Gods" hold the hieroglyphic sign "Netjer". KV 9 Ramses V and VI

(No. 704) "She of the *Was*-sceptre"
(No. 705) "Messenger of her Gods"
(No. 706) "Whom Tatenen has made"
(No. 707) "She who is standing"
(No. 708) "She with powerful arm"

Due to her dual nature, the Goddess Sekhmet herself also emphasises the need for duality to reach healing. Being the Goddess of healing and destruction, she shows that two opposing aspects are essential to provide for a healthy growth or development. Everything that has become fully grown eventually needs to be destroyed. Without this destruction, life would stagnate, which ultimately results in death. A tree remains healthy and strong only when it is pruned. This eliminates the wild growth and allows for all of the life force to become available for the development of a strong and healthy tree bearing many fruits.

Sekhmet unites these two different aspects, destruction and healing, which is expressed through the different appearances of the eight Goddesses. The first four Goddesses with the lion heads emphasise the destructive side of nature. The subsequent four Goddesses in human shape emphasise the healing side. Together, they join forces here to protect and heal the "Eye of the West".

Sekhmet has been the protector of Râ since the beginning of times and was regarded as his daughter. Râ gave her the title "Eye of Râ". According to myth, humanity began conspiring against the aging Râ. The Divine Law of *Maât* was no longer abided with, which made the Sungod furious. Therefore, he sent his daughter Sekhmet to punish these rebels. In her shape as the "Lady of terror" she began to destroy almost the entire human race and caused a massive bloodbath to avenge Râ. Eventually, Râ regained his power and the Divine Law of *Maât* was restored.

Naturally, Râ relies upon the protective and healing powers of his daughter Sekhmet. That is the reason why he gives clear orders to the eight Goddesses. Still, the Sungod knows from his own experience that Sekhmet needs to be controlled. To guarantee this, Râ places his "Eye of the West" in the hands of the baboon "Flesh who carries his Eye" (No. 709).

> Power to your forms, you Powerful Ones,
> that you inspect the Eye of Horus for him,
> that you may make firm the Eye of Horus for him,
> that you appease Horus with his image,
> that you give strength to Horus
> with his Eye,
> that you establish for him his prime Eye,
> which is in the arms of
> "Flesh who carries his Eye".[4]

This baboon is Thoth, the God of Divine Wisdom, who takes care of the "Eye of the West". He is standing in a half upraised position right in front of the eight Goddesses, effectively blocking their way. Due to his reversed position, he is able to look each of these Goddesses straight in the eye. He has a very important message that requires the full attention of each of the eight Sekhmets before they can begin healing the Eye. It is essential to realise the healing process is not an isolated act, for it is connected to Divine Wisdom and Knowledge at all times. Only under these conditions, a healthy recovery will be established. The act of healing while using the Divine Wisdom, restores the imbalance and prevents further damage or bloodbath. Therefore, the eight Sekhmets are working together with Thoth to guarantee the "Eye of the West" once again becomes as perfect as the "Eye of the East". Only once this balance has been recreated, the Sungod is able to continue his sailing course with his Sun barque.

Thoth is not just the God of Wisdom for he is also the Master Physician. He was therefore the perfect God to restore the Eye of Horus after it had been damaged when Seth had ripped it out. However, the Eye of Râ itself had been healed by Thoth once before as well after Seth, in the shape of a black pig, had blinded it. Additionally, Thoth is also the Heart of Râ, *Ib-n-Râ*, and the source of all Wisdom and Knowledge for the Sungod. Thus, it is understandable the "Eye of the West" is in highly trusted expert hands with Thoth.

The left riverbank concludes with eight standing Gods who are each holding a *Was-*sceptre in their left hand (No. 710 – 717). The moment the Sungod reaches them, he gives them the Breath of Life with the air which is in his mouth. The life-air ensures these Gods come back to life once more. A magnificent gift that satisfies them and for which they are immensely grateful. Each of the Gods embodies unique powers, which Râ in turn can utilise for his own process of healing and renewal. To gain access to their powers, Râ identifies himself with each one of them by uttering their names.

The presence of these Gods here is also needed to punish the condemned enemies. They do this with a very adequate and efficient method where they rip off the bandages that are wrapped around these rebels. By removing the bandages, their corpses are no longer protected and it inevitably results in the decomposition and decay of their bodies. This effectively excludes the enemies from the transformation into the spiritual body, the *Sâhu*. Thus, the convicted hostiles are doomed to die a "second death" and are denied any possibility of rebirth for eternity.

The first four Gods (No. 710 – 713) are holding the *Ankh* and the *Was*-sceptre in their hands. They each have a unique appearance as they are moving forward together.

(No. 710) "Twin armed" is a God who has two serpents or ropes on top of his shoulders instead of a head.

(No. 711) "Lord of Entry" is the jackal-headed God Anubis. He acts here, similar to the Fifth Hour, as the Guardian on the threshold. Within this borderland, he protects the deceased and assists them with their process of transformation. However, he is also the Protector of the living and assures that the world of the dead remains separated from the world of the living. Furthermore, in his role as a Divine Judge, he is involved with the weighing of the heart and the accompanying judgement that is passed on the deceased. In the present hour his attendance, together with the other seven Gods, is required to put the convicted to death. Furthermore, he is the God of the Divine Pavilion, the place where the bodies were mummified. Thus, Anubis is the expert in the wrapping of bandages around a corpse. However, in his role in the present hour he is doing the exact opposite for he is ripping the bandages off the bodies to ensure the inevitable death of the condemned.

(No. 712) "Who hides the forms" is a hawk-headed God.

(No. 713) "Master of Secrets" *hery shetau* (ḥry št3w) is one of the titles of the God Anubis who is present here in his human shape. He acts as the Guardian and Keeper of the great Mystery of the process of "Death into Life". This transformation will occur only if the deceased has obeyed the Divine Law of *Maât*. Since this is not the case with these enemies, this means "Master of Secrets" withdraws his protection which effectively disintegrates the lives of these rebels.

In ancient Egypt there was a group of priests who went by the title *hery shetau*, "Master of secrets". They were funerary priests who were tasked with the funeral ceremonies and the offerings.[5] Their responsibility consisted of the protection and care taking of the deceased in order to make the transition into the Afterlife possible. The priests were the servants of the God Anubis. They wore jackal masks in the course of their work to impersonate the God. Thus, the Deity "Master of secrets", is either the God Anubis himself or he is one of the funerary priests of Anubis.

The final four Gods are each a different form of the God Osiris which is reflected in their names. Like the Lord of the Duat, they appear in mummified form while wearing a Divine beard and the White Crown. They each have a *menit* necklace around their necks that is the symbol of potency, fertility, new life, resurrection, health and happiness.

(No. 714) "Great sawyer"
(No. 715) "The Great Hidden One"
(No. 716) "Who is before his place"
(No. 717) "Who is before his thighs"

Osiris is connected to the final Judgement that is passed on the deceased. Upon finishing the challenging journey through the Afterlife, the deceased eventually reaches the Hall of Judgement for the final judgement. As mentioned earlier, if the deceased did not pass judgement, his heart was eaten by the monstrous Goddess Âmmut. However, here this punishment alone is not enough. The four Gods mentioned above proceed in stripping the wrappings of the corpses of those convicted to ensure their decay and death. Following all these punishments in this hour, the condemned souls are no longer able to sabotage and endanger the journey of the Sungod and subsequently of Osiris. Moreover, the actions of the four Gods are indirectly also an effective method of self-preservation. They are all forms of Osiris and their actions assure the continued journey of Râ and, therefore, also of Osiris. In other words, Osiris protects his own right to exist.

The Duatians of the Sacred River (middle section)

The Sungod is standing within the safe embrace of Mehen on the Sun barque. He wears the solar disk on top of his head between his ram horns while holding the serpent-sceptre in one hand and the *Ankh* in the other. He is once again surrounded by the usual crew who are working together to assist him to the best of their abilities.

(No. 718) "Wepwawet"
(No. 719) "Sia"
(No. 720) "Nebet wia"
(No. 721) "Mehen"
(No. 722) "Iuf"
(No. 723) "Heru Hekenu"
(No. 724) "Ka Maât"
(No. 725) "Nehes"
(No. 726) "Hu"
(No. 727) "Kherep wia"

Aside from their usual responsibilities, the crewmembers have each been assigned with an additional task. In the previous hour the twelve rowers (No. 655 – 666) ensured that the Sun barque made good progress through their rowing abilities. In the present hour, however, their job has been adopted by the crew members of Râ. With smooth motions, the crew is rowing the Sun barque firmly ahead through the overflowing Sacred River. Their oars are splashed deep in the water. The impact with the water results in the high projection of water droplets upward. The Duatians standing on both sides of the river are showered with the spattering of the life-giving water. This water dip refreshes and renews them. Moreover, they fill their lungs with the Breath of Life through the movement of the rowing oars that generates wind.

In front of the Sun barque are two Goddesses standing across from each other. The Goddess directly in front of the Sun barque is called "Archer" (No. 728) and is wearing the Red Crown of Lower Egypt on top of her head. Her name and her Crown indicate that she is the Goddess Neith. Neith is the "Mistress of the Bow" who uses her arrows to shoot the enemies of Râ. As a creator Goddess she does anything necessary to allow for the process of creation, which takes place every night in the primeval waters of Nun, to continue.

Across from Neith is the Goddess "She who is on the other side" (No. 731) who is wearing the White Crown of Upper Egypt on her head. Between these two Goddesses is the serpent "Uniting faces" (No. 730) who appears here in a very unusual form. This serpent does not crawl for it has two pairs of legs. One set of feet pointing to the left and the other set pointing to the right. Furthermore, he has a head on both sides of his body and he subsequently does not possess a tail. One of his heads gazes upon the Goddess Neith, "Archer". Like her, this head is wearing the Red Crown. The other head is looking towards "She who is on the other side" and like her, it is wearing the White Crown. His body is bent in a U-shape that gives him the appearance of a pair of horns. The snake body has the exact same shape as the two-letter hieroglyphic sign *wep* (*wp*) that is depicted like the horns of an ox.

Fig. 32. The hieroglyphic sign wep.

In the curve of the body of the double-headed serpent stands the black hawk "Foremost of the Sky" (No. 729). He is the *Ba*-soul of Sokar, the God of the dead. Sokar has played a prominent part in several other hours. Within his secret Cavern in the Fifth Hour, the hawk-headed Sokar was standing on a winged serpent. Presently, Sokar is once again standing on top of a snake. This time, however, the snake does not lie on the ground for it has lifted itself up from the earth with its legs. This is a reference to the entire process of regeneration that will be upraised here to the next phase. Râ's renewal has come a very long way and has now reached the point where he is slowly starting to ascend to the moment of rebirth. Sokar plays an important part in this process, for where he opened the way for Râ to descend into the depths of the Duat before, he is now opening the way for Râ to ascend to the Eastern horizon. At that moment the unification of Râ and Osiris will be broken and each will go their separate ways for the following twelve hours.

The serpent "Uniting faces" is already announcing the mandatory separation of Osiris and Râ. The body of this Deity connects the White Crown of Upper Egypt with the Red Crown of Lower Egypt as both of his heads have either crown on top. The unification of the Two Lands is a reference to the merge of the day world of Râ with the night world of Osiris. It shows the highlight resulting from each transformation. However, once this stage has been reached, duality is needed once again to continue development. With his body shape "Uniting faces" is already reminding us of the need for separation. A derivative of the two-letter hieroglyphic sign *wep* (*wp*), that his body mimics, is *wepi* (*wpi*) which means "open, separate or divide".

The Goddess Neith, "Archer", together with the Goddess "She who is on the other side" emphasises the essence of duality. The two Goddesses are the representation of the two opposite aspects, represented by the different Crowns of Upper and Lower Egypt on their head. Together they form a unity that must be broken to open the way for duality. To signify this fact "Uniting faces", in the shape of the hieroglyphic sign for "open or separate", is standing in between them.

Neith has a very special connection with Wepwawet, the "Opener of the Ways". This is seen in a funerary text of the Old Kingdom, were Neith herself is referred to with the title "Opener of the Ways".[6] So, it is understandable that it is Neith who is present here. She is the most suitable Goddess to assist with the Opening of the Way to the crucial duality needed to further creation.

The curved body of "Uniting faces" is also somewhat similar to the *Ka*-posture. In the near future, the God of air, Shu, will assume this exact posture to separate the world of the day from the world of the night. This creates an opening that allows for Khepri to emerge and announce a new day.

Following the Goddess "She who is on the other side" is a barque with the snake "Living One of the earth" (No. 732) lying in it. He is depicted with an *Ankh* above his head. He is the representation of the sacred *Ba*-soul of the Foremost of the Westerners "Khenty-Imentyu", which is Osiris. Instead of a normal snake head, he has the head of a hawk as a reference to Sokar.

In the Fifth Hour Osiris assumed the appearance of "Flesh of Sokar-upon-his-sand" (No. 393) while being in the deepest region of the Duat, the sacred Land of Sokar. Since then, the journey has continued through several hours and Osiris is now preparing himself for the upcoming renewal as well. He is fighting against the Unified Darkness, even though he never leaves this darkness himself for his throne and place is within the Duat. Râ needs this throne as a stepping stone to raise himself above the horizon. Together with Osiris, he travels to the *ârryt* gate, at the end of the Twelfth Hour, which separates the two worlds from each other. At this border, Osiris himself will experience a brief moment of enlightenment. This happens the moment when Râ leaves through this gate to disappear into the day world. Filled with momentum, Osiris, in his serpent form as "Living One of the earth", sets sail for the Eastern Horizon as he is looking forward to this joyful and special moment. "Living One of the earth" assumes a leading role at this point where he positions himself in a protective manner in front of the Sun barque. Like this, he is guiding the Sungod towards the Eastern horizon, which is where the highest point of the nightly voyage is reached.

> He rises against the Unified Darkness
> at the gateway of the Eastern horizon.
> And then he assumes his place (again),
> day after day.
> It is the protecting serpent of the Duat,
> the unapproachable *Ba*-soul
> of Khenty-Imentyu.[7]

In front of the barque with the serpent "Living One of the earth" are twelve armed Gods (No. 733 – 744) walking ahead. They are the personal lifeguards of the Sungod who ensure that Râ reaches the exit of the Duat unharmed. The inescapable notion of threat and danger is always looming over the entire journey through the Duat, from the first, up until the final hour. Even during the very last second before the sun rises, there is still the risk of the Sungod being attacked and killed. At the beginning of the journey, this risk made sense since Râ was still weak and lifeless at that point. However, the voyage has continued through nine hours since then and the force of Râ's sunlight has increased considerably. One might think the dangers during the final stage would be hardly significant. Unfortunately, nothing could be further from the truth. The stronger the light becomes, the more darkness it attracts. This makes the enemies during the final hours stronger due to their dark characters compared to the enemies in the beginning of the journey.

Moreover, there is once again a menace in the air. An evil, the serpent Apophis "Horrible of face", is lurking. Apparently, this hideous monster has managed to survive the massacre in the Seventh Hour and has regained enough power to again make an attempt on the life of the Sungod. Râ recognises the dangers of this situation and has called upon the protection of the twelve brave warriors. From now on, this army remains by Râ's side and guides him towards the Eastern Horizon. Even after the sunrise, when Râ continues his course as Khepri in the Day Sun barque, these soldiers follow him.

To protect Râ to the best of their abilities, the army is divided in three groups of four warriors. Each group is armed with a different weapon to pool their resources and enable cooperation when a battle is fought.

The first group consists of four fighters with a solar disk instead of a head. They are carrying arrows in their hands that are just as intense and piercing as the golden rays of the sun. These beaming warriors are illuminating the darkness that the foes use to hide. Each hideout gets exposed, which blinds the rebels hiding inside and makes them vulnerable to these fierce light arrows. Thus, the arrows are very strong and efficient weapons, which is especially useful in the battle against Apophis. This evil serpent cannot endure any light at all and tries to get away from the mere sight of it.

(No. 733) "Disc-head"
(No. 734) "Arrow-shooter"
(No. 735) "Who stretches out"
(No. 736) "Slinger"

The second group of soldiers are carrying spears in their hands. With immense power these skilled pitchers throw their razor sharp javelins towards the enemies. Their expertise never lets them miss their target and they always pierce through the unfaithful hearts of the rebels. Thus, darkness and chaos do not stand a chance against these warriors who efficiently and thoroughly fight off and destroy the foes.

(No. 737) "Shooter"
(No. 738) "Who hurls"
(No. 739) "Who wards off"
(No. 740) "Who causes pain"

The final group consists of four very capable archers. In ancient Egypt, the bow was a very powerful weapon. The expression, the "Nine Bows", is a reference to the enemies of Egypt, who were killed with the bow. These four archers are trained to keep their bowstrings tightened to the max to enable their arrows to travel with immense speed over great distances. They keep their bows up with a steady hand and aim them at the opponents. Since these archers are such a great distance away, the enemies have no idea of what lies in store for them. All the arrows are send straight through the bodies of the hostiles, taking them by surprise and making them powerless in trying to defend themselves. The enemies are caught off guard and collapse to the earth overwhelmed by death, never to rise again.

(No. 741) "Archer"
(No. 742) "Bowman"
(No. 743) "Who binds together"
(No. 744) "Who shows his arm"

Râ himself is the commander of this powerful and trained army. His personal orders lead to the action of these brave warriors. It is vital that each enemy, who conceals himself in the darkness, is caught and put to death. The most insidious assailant of them all is of course "Horrible of face". This serpent is not to be underestimated at any point.

> Speed to your arrows,
> sharpness to your spears,
> tension to your bows,
> that you punish for me my enemies
> who are in the darkness
> beyond the horizon![8]

The Duatians on the right riverbank (lower section)

In the forefront of the right riverbank stands the God "Horus" (No. 745). On top of his head he wears a solar disk with the Uraeus-serpent on his brow. He has a hunched over posture as he is leaning on a staff. His eyes are focused on the vast water surface that lies stretched out in front of him. This body of water is so large that it covers almost the entire right riverbank.

In the water are twelve drifting bodies of persons who had drowned in the Nile in an unfortunate manner during their lives. Their relatives were unable to find their bodies due to the current of the water. Or maybe their bodies got eaten by one of the Nile inhabitants like the crocodiles or the hippopotamuses. Unfortunately, without the body, the funerary ceremonies and the fundamental process of mummification cannot be performed. Therefore, the bodies of these drowning victims are lost in the water where they eventually decompose and pass into eternal death.

(No. 746) "The Drowned Ones in the Duat"
(No. 747) "The Upturned Ones in the Duat"
(No. 748) "Those who are stretched out in the Duat"

Horus, however, truly cares for the fate of these unlucky ones. Since his father drowned in the Nile as well, he made it his job to ensure the correct rituals would be performed either way. This allowed him to save his father from the drowning death in spite of everything. Hence,

Horus saves the Drowned Ones from an eternal death, KV 9 Ramses V and VI

Osiris was able to become resurrected in the Afterlife. Due to Horus's own experience he knows the tragedy that is the drowning death and, thus, does not wish this upon anyone else. This is why Horus can be found here as he is peering across the water in search of those who are doomed without his help.

To free these unfortunate souls from their position, Horus addresses each of them individually. His words abrogate all of the restrictions that limited those affected in their movements. Their arms, legs and knees are freed, which enables them to swim. No longer are they lying helplessly and powerlessly beneath the water. When their freedom of movement is returned to them, they start to firmly swim upwards until their heads can finally rise above the water surface. Then they immediately start to spit out all of the water that had filled their lungs previously and gasp for air. As they take a deep breath, they fill their being with the Breath of Life. This returns their lives and the right to exist to them. Then they swim to the riverbank where Horus helps them out of the water and welcomes them into the Duat. Due to the rescue mission of Horus, the bodies of these drowned ones do not rot or decay. They are no longer in need of the essential funerary rituals for their bodies are already made eternal.

Subsequently, their bodies are able to

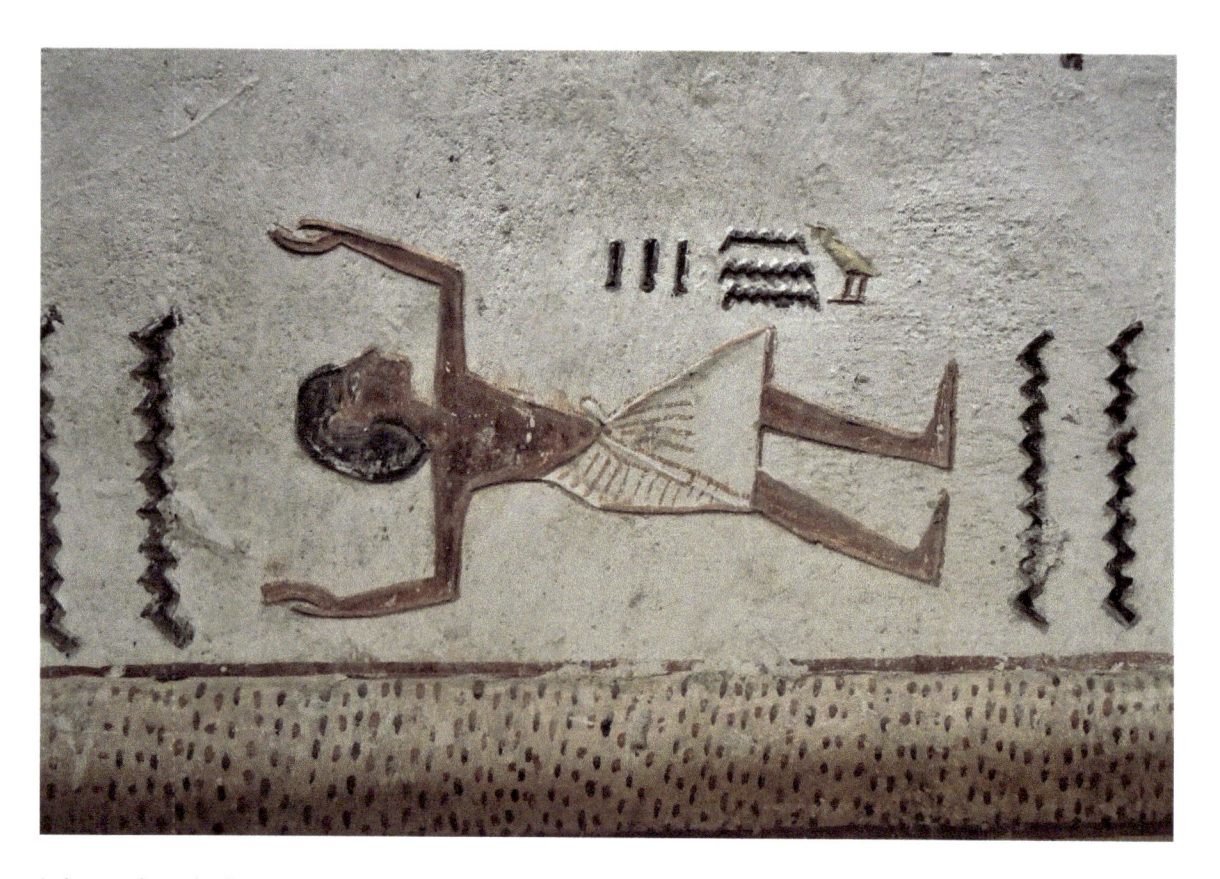

A drowned one in the Duat, KV 9 Ramses V and VI

become unified with their *Ba*-soul. From now on, they are part of the blessed dead and permitted to become an eternal part of the royal entourage of Horus's father, Osiris. This means no one who has ended up under these unfortunate circumstances, is doomed to suffer eternal death. Horus cares for them all and grants everyone hope and faith. This encouraging part of the Duat sheds a light on the darkness.

The four Goddesses who are standing after the water body are present here to support this essential light aspect. Each of them is wearing a Uraeus-serpent on their heads. These fire-spitting serpents illuminate the path before Râ to help him find his way out of the Unified Darkness. This act grants Râ great support for his own sunlight is still not powerful enough to illuminate the darkness on its own.

(No. 749) "She who annihilates"
(No. 750) "She who glows"
(No. 751) "She who pierces"
(No. 752) "Uraeus-serpent"

The hour is concluded with the *Heka*-sceptre that has the head of Seth fixed on top of it, "Crook of Nehes" (No. 753). The shepherd's crook, or *Heka*-sceptre, is a symbol of power and rulership. There are still only two more hours remaining before Râ takes this sceptre into his own hands to rule over the day with his shining light. However, the sceptre depicted here has a special meaning due to the head of Seth that decorates the top. Seth is a God of matter and fixation. This sceptre, therefore, indicates Ra can only take on his true rulership when his *Ba*-soul has connected itself with the matter. He first has to emerge from the dark waters of Nun, out of the not yet manifested, and become visible and tangible in the material world.

This necessary connection between opposites, spirit and matter, is emphasised by Horus and Seth. Horus, the symbol of the spirit, is standing upfront on the right riverbank while Seth, the symbol of matter and fixation, is standing at the end of the left riverbank. Between the both of them are the drowning victims who are re-emerging from their deaths and the Goddesses with the Uraeus-serpents on their heads that breach the darkness. Evidently, it is the presence of duality that creates the crucial feeding ground from which light and life can arise.

The manifestation of the Tenth Hour in daily life

During your journey, which has come a long way by now, you have been submerged in the inner waters multiple times. In some of the hours you might even have experienced the feeling and fear of actually drowning in these waters. However, each time you were able to return to the surface for otherwise you would not have made it to this point. Once again, this hour is characterised by an inner flow that is symbolised by the Sacred

River. However, it is not a small stream we are talking about. It actually is a major water body that takes up all of the space within this hour.

Once you have entered the Tenth Hour through the gate "With great manifestations, giving birth to forms" and it has closed itself behind you, the deluge engulfs you. It is impossible to climb out of this Sacred River onto land since the riverbanks are far too high and too steep. Fortunately, you have left the need to squirm and to resist the Sacred River far behind you. You know how precious this life-giving inner flow is wherein the essential transformation processes take place. The steep riverbanks are here to ensure no water is lost and for it to continue to flow in the right place to do its job. It are precisely these sheer walls that conceal the water from sight to allow you to safely submerge yourself in the water without disturbances.

The resulting trusted space, out of sight from everything and everyone, is something you really need during this hour. This time, you dive really deep into the waters of your inner world. During this unique moment, all of the Deities within this hour support you to truly get through to the core of your inner world. Each God or Goddess has a specific function to give you a wake-up call. When you identify yourself with each one of them, you are provided with surprising insights that shed light on your life from a completely different perspective. These profound revelations are a characteristic feature of the Tenth Hour. Hence, this is the hour to map your entire inner world. You notice this world is still in the process of growth and development and has subsequently not yet reached its equilibrium.

Right at the beginning of this hour you are confronted by this imbalance and you notice your renewed vision has not yet disposed of all of the outdated views. The "Eye of the West" symbolises the old vision that is in the process of regeneration. It is still underdeveloped compared to the all-seeing "Eye of the East", the symbol of rebirth and fully grown light or consciousness. Only when you have the courage to let the old vision go, you can truly heal and renew your inner being. Thus, this hour is an adventurous voyage of discovery during which you track down outdated views. It is quite the expedition where you begin breaking these stagnating patterns and convictions. Previously, these firm believes provided you with a sense of safety. Now, however, they are blocking your way towards the renewal of your consciousness and, thus, to the development of the "Eye of the West". Like the snake, you have outgrown your jacket and are in need of more space and freedom to move.

This is the reason for the tossing around in an effort to rid yourself of this straightjacket and to renew your grip on your life. The inner turmoil emerges in your everyday life as well. A strong breeze begins to air out your life to freshen it up. Needless to say, the consequences of your inner tenacity, to keep the old, have to be straightened up in the external world as well. However, be aware you always need to work from the inner core first to be able to clean house in your external life. When you avoid this essential part, you end up wasting precious energy while you clean the ever-returning side effects. After all, it is the inner Wisdom that you need to take action effectively. The opener of this hour "Who acts clever" emphasises this piece of wisdom.

Before you can effectively start to take action, there is always the process of hemming and hawing between the contradictions. You need to decide which option to choose and what option to reject. What benefits you versus what is destructive. What allows you to grow and develop and what needs to be trimmed. It are these considerations of opposite sides that grant you wisdom and life experience. The two serpents "The Double-Coiled" (No. 696) symbolise this piece of wisdom that arises from contradictions. They show that true Wisdom is a never ending development that rises up from the deepest parts of your own subconscious world. It is not a static or unchangeable aspect. Actually, it is rather dynamic, innovating and creative due to the Higher Inspiration provided by the inner Sungod and the Vital Life Force of the Powerself. Dare to release the old balance as you bow before life. The process of bouncing back in a renewed harmony makes you a more self-conscious and a wiser human being.

The Hour Goddess "The Furious One who slaughters Him with crooked heart" remains by your side during the entire hour to assist you during the renewal of your consciousness. It is her duty to ensure everything that takes place here is consistent with the Feather of *Maât*. She keeps a close eye on you with her fiery eyes, for there is no place here for dishonesty and falsehood, or the "crooked" heart. She wakes you up, loud and clear, to protect you from betraying your True Heart.

Aside from this supportive and determined Goddess, the eight Sekhmet Goddesses (No. 701 – 708) occupy a central role as well. They are at the upper part of this hour precisely in the middle of the left riverbank. Their central position is an allusion to the necessity to mend the no longer properly functioning consciousness. The recovery and healing process can take place only when the old and damaged parts are removed. After all, a wound has to be properly cared for and cleansed of all the dirt first before it can heal. The first four lion-headed Sekhmet Goddesses are confronting you with these outdated visions, patterns and believes and help you to destroy them. With the power of a lioness, they tear up your illusionary views. You are face to face with the untruth that lies hidden in it. This revelation is another wake-up call and enables you to rid yourself of these figments and self-deceptions.

Next, the four Sekhmet Goddesses in human shape step forward to initiate the healing process after the destruction of the old. They make you aware of the appearance of your renewed vision and give you strength to express it firmly and decisively. Thoth (No. 709) keeps a close eye on this intensive process. After all, "Inner Wisdom and Knowledge" can only awaken in the True Heart if destruction and healing are in balance.

As you may understand, you can expect quite some inner enemies who do anything within their power to prevent your recovery. After all, healing means there will be no more room for your foes, which means that they have to move out. So the more you are willing to truly and genuinely look yourself into the eyes, the bigger the counter act is. The eight Gods (No. 710 – 717) support you as they expose these inner contentious traitors who play fast and loose with the truth.

Benefit from all the assistance that is offered to you from all sides. However, keep in mind that you yourself are no longer weak and vulnerable either. The twelve warriors of Râ (No. 733 – 744) draw your attention to this important fact. The weapons they are holding represent your own skills that you have developed during the preceding hours and which you are going to master in the upcoming hours. In this hour, you get these twelve weapons pressed in your hands. Now you are ready to start using them for your own defence and protection. Naturally, you should not become overconfident and assume you have become invincible. You should not underestimate the deceitful abilities of your enemies, which sometimes require extra manpower to overcome. In the present hour it is important to find the right balance between accepting help and taking independent action.

It is now becoming apparent that the renewed life begins to firmly lift itself up inside you. You slowly start to strip away the old dead skin that has become too tight. Just a few more hours remain before you can finally strip away the remainder of the constricting straightjacket, which gives you the freedom to emerge fully awakened. The black hawk "Foremost of the Sky" (No. 729) is present here to announce this memorable moment. He has taken his place on top of the double-headed serpent "Uniting

The God Thoth holds the Eye in his hands, TT 219 Nebenmaat, Deir el-Medina

Faces" to emphasise the fact a new phase of life is about to open up to you.

"Living One of the earth" (No. 732), or Osiris, also confirms this ascension from the depth of your inner being. In the previous hour, your contact with Osiris, the Powerself, has been renewed and become more balanced with the Higher Self. During that particular hour you have already practiced to recognise the difference between the whispered insights of the inner Sungod against the sense of inner strength of the Powerself. The cooperation between the three of you is further balanced during the present hour. The question that remains is, the degree of sincerity and incorruptibility you are displaying while balancing the use of this power with the insights of the Higher Self. Your wish, after all, is to empower the light of your inner Sungod to make a powerful ascension. Too much Power, however, casts shadows on this light, causing you to tumble back into the darkness. Only when you have reached the perfect balance, will your True Heart open and let the magnificent light of Khepri (No. 694) shine brighter with every heartbeat.

> He exists in this fashion in his barque.
> He stands at the uniform darkness at
> this approach to the Eastern horizon.
> Then he occupies his place every day.
> He is the "Stander" of the Duat,
> Holy *Ba* of the Foremost
> of the Westerners.[9]

Hence, the journey through the Tenth Hour is the time where your courage and determination is put to the test. The deeper you dare to descend, the more clarity you will achieve about who you truly are. Do not be scared of drowning in your deep inner waters, for Horus "the Lord of the Sky" would never leave you to fend for yourself. He symbolises the Divine Spark within you, just like Khepri. As he flies high in the sky, he oversees everything that happens here with his sharp hawk eyes, never letting you leave his sight. The moment you are met with unfortunate circumstances during which you are unable to lift yourself out of the deep darkness, he is there for you to save you. He is the essence within you that never perishes nor decays.

Therefore, death is not the end of the line. In fact, it is merely a portal to enter the road towards the manifestation of a new subsequent life. The "Crook of Nehes" or Seth (No. 753) underlines this very important message. Although Seth, with his destructive character, always tries to sever the unity and harmony, this serves only one purpose. This is not to obliterate us into non-existence, for it actually is meant to stabilise us in life itself. This is the way it must be, for we need to be challenged and provoked before we are willing to release the old. Seth stimulates us to make this essential sacrifice whereupon we are capable of taking our place in the new.

THE ELEVENTH HOUR
"Opening of the cavern which examines the corpses"

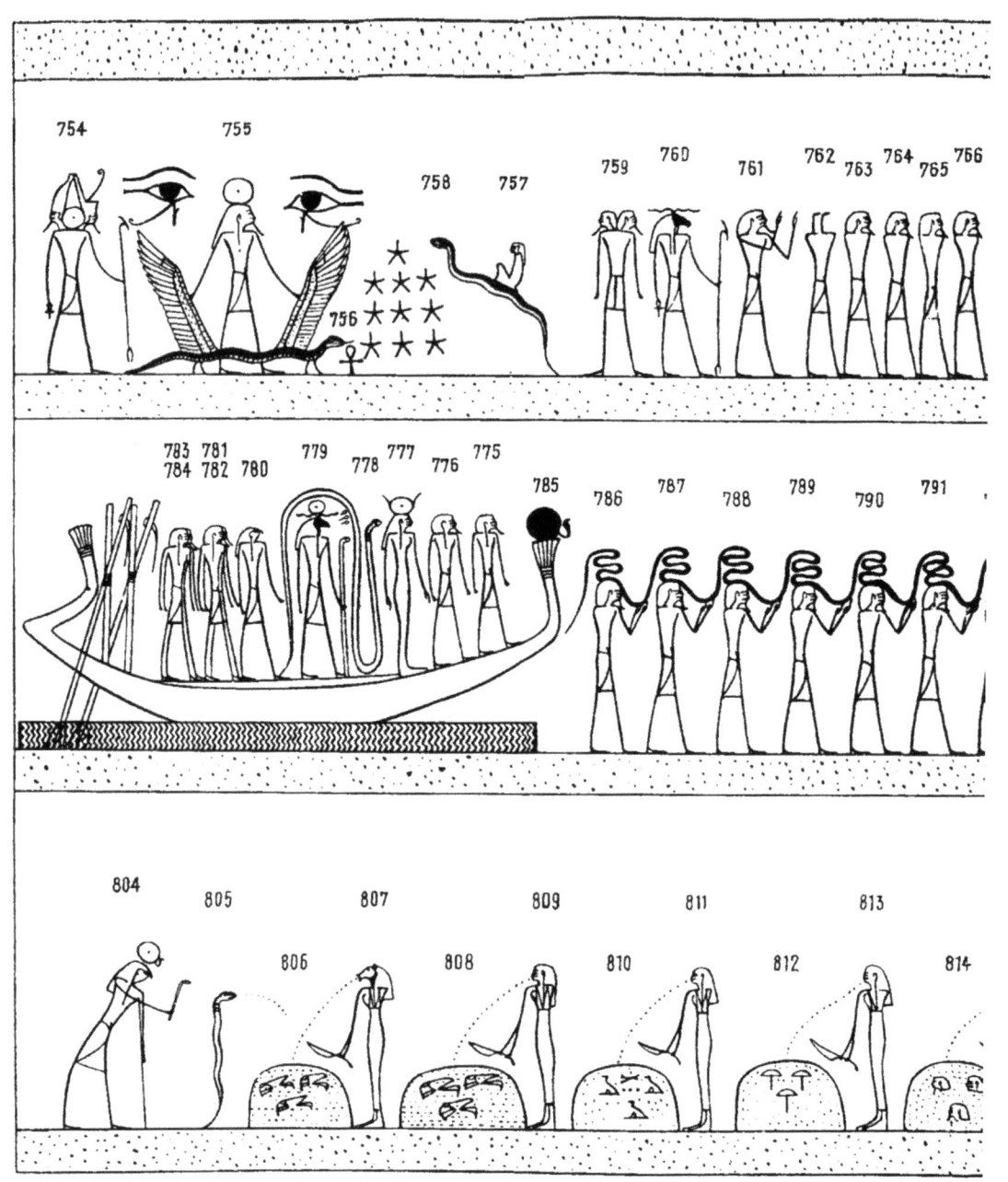

Figure 33: The Eleventh Hour

The Gate: "Resting place of the Duatians"
The Hour Goddess: "Starry One, Lady of the barque, who repels the enemy when he appears"
The Guardian: "He above his kettles"

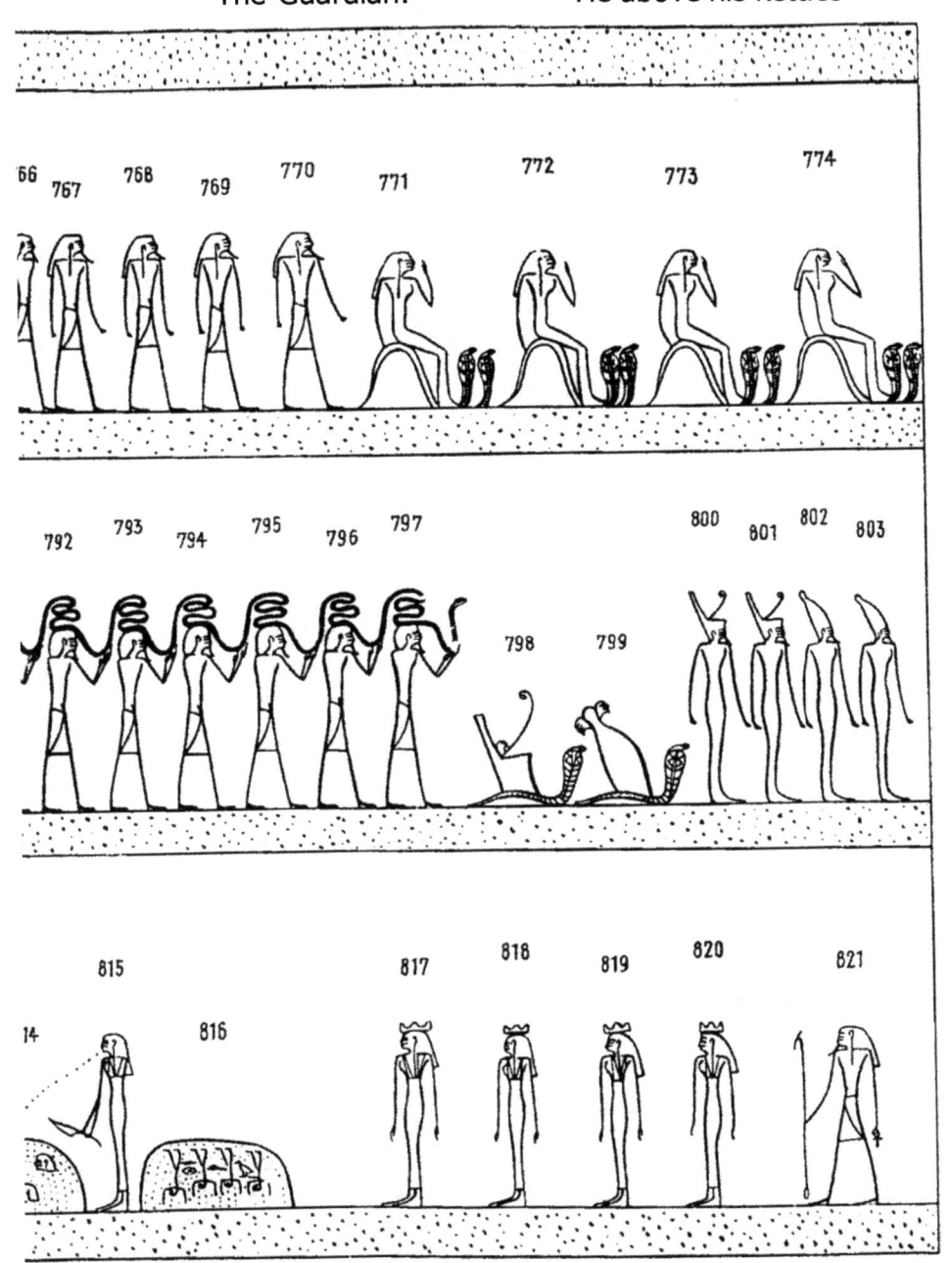

Introduction

Pausing by the person of this Great God
in this cavern.
He gives orders to the Gods who are in it.
The name of the Gate of his place
through which this Great God enters is,
"Resting place of the Duatians".
The name of this Place is
"Opening of the cavern
which examines the corpses".
The name of the Hour of the night
which guides this Great God is,
"Starry One, Lady of the barque,
who repels the enemy when he appears".
The mysterious cavern of the Duat
which this Great God passes
to come out from the Eastern mountain
of the sky.
Eternity swallows her images
in front of the Seer who is in this place,
and returns them afterwards
for the birth of Khepri in the earth.
This is done exactly like this image
which is painted
on the Eastern (side)
of the Hidden Chamber of the Duat.
Whoever knows it participates (in offerings)
as a well-provided *Akh*-spirit,
in heaven and earth. A true remedy.[1]

The second to last hour, known as "Opening of the cavern which examines the corpses", has arrived. Only two more hours, the current and the final one, before the Sungod Râ is able to make his light shine again. The imbalance between the "Eye of the West" and the "Eye of the East" has finally regained its equilibrium. This renewed harmony indicates that Râ's light is no longer damaged for it is on the verge of shining to its optimum ability.

There still remains a lot to be done the moment Râ enters through the gate of this hour, "Resting place of the Duatians", *sekhen duatiu* (*sḫn dw3.tyw*). Interestingly enough, the name of the gate suggests that this is the hour during which Râ can make himself comfortable while floating around. That, however, is an absolute misinterpretation of this name. It is true this hour can be regarded as the waiting area before the real rebirth process commences. Though, during this period, there still are important tasks that need to be completed at exactly the right time. Like in the previous hour, time is an essential factor here. Everything needs to stay in tune with the rhythm of the cosmic order down to the second. In that regard, this hour is indeed a time of waiting for the exact perfect moment to herald the Twelfth Hour. The Sungod is, therefore, not at liberty to dawdle for he might be late otherwise. Alternatively, he cannot leave this hour too early either for he has to properly identify himself with every Deity he encounters on his way. In other words, everything needs to be timed perfectly to ensure Râ is not reborn too early in the next hour, nor too late. Ultimately, both scenarios would have disastrous effects on the continuation of the creation.

In this context the hieroglyphic word *sekhen* means "resting-place". The translation of *sekhen*, as a verb, is "meet, occupy a place, embrace, bind together". All these different meanings allude to the final preparations that need to be made in this very last hour just before sunrise. All the energy and power has to be gathered and all of the Deities ought to occupy their places. It is of the utmost importance that everything is in complete control for the success of the upcoming rebirth of the shining soul of Râ.

Moreover, Râ is about to embrace and embody wholeness and unity once again. He has gathered all of his limbs, which is all of his light in Râ's case, and integrated it to form a living shining unit. This hour is thus a grand meeting place where all of the Duatians residing here are offering their support to Râ during the final phase of the integration process. Due to their helping hand, Râ is soon going to occupy his rightful physical place in the day sky as Khepri.

The Hour Goddess, "Starry One, Lady of the barque, who repels the enemy when he appears", is the perfect guide to escort Râ through this hour. She is connected to the starry sky and knows every movement of every star. After all, when using the position of the stars as reference, it is possible to determine the specific hour. Hence, she, like no one else, knows the course of time and sets the perfect pace for Râ. This makes it possible for the Sungod to reach the gate towards the next hour at exactly the right time.

As the name of this powerful Hour Goddess suggests, she uses her shining appearance in the battle against the darkness where the enemies hide out. As these rebels have become accustomed to their dark hiding places, they get blinded by the shining light of the Goddess. This leaves them completely vulnerable and an easy prey to this "Starry Lady". Hence, Râ stays close to her side to profit from her protection and from her light that shines upon the last spots of darkness.

Either way, this is an hour that revolves around the defeat of the last bit of remaining darkness through the application of light and the element of fire. The Sacred River itself, though, is filled with water to enable the Sun barque to resume its course. The landscape surrounding it is dry and desert-like. A fiery atmosphere with an all-consuming fire is reigning particularly powerful on the right riverbank. This sphere plays an important part in this hour. There are still several things in need of purification and transformation, and fire simply is the perfect tool for the job. In addition, the fire is stirred up even bigger due to a stiff wind. Evidently, the fiery light of the sun needs to be stoked up to its full potential before it can shed a bright light and illuminate the upcoming daybreak. The wind also provides the Sungod with a helping hand that allows the Sun barque to arrive at the gate towards the Twelfth Hour at exactly the right time.

The Duatians on the left riverbank (upper section)

The left riverbank begins with an important God who has two heads that are each gazing in the opposite direction. One of the heads is crowned with the White Crown, while the other head is crowned with the Red Crown. In between the two heads is a solar disk. The God is holding the Ankh in one hand and the Was-sceptre in the other. His name is âper-her neb djet (ꜥpr-ḥr nb ḏt) "He with equipped face, Lord of eternity" (No. 754). He is the creator of time. Time lies within his hands as he guarantees that everything unfolds exactly as planned in the right time. This timing is essential to continue the movement of creation, and thus the continuation of life. This very important forward movement is emphasised by his walking posture.

As mentioned earlier (see chapter; Osiris, Lord of the Duat), the ancient Egyptians applied two different concepts of time, *neheh* and *djet*. *Djet* is the linear time while *neheh* is the continuous cyclic time. *Djet* is symbolised by Osiris, the Lord of the Duat. Osiris has conquered death and lives forevermore in the Duat. The special feature of his life is the fact that it is perfect and eternal. It will never again fall apart or decay for he is the embodiment of the ideal vision of perfection. On earth, there is no place for this eternal perfection. Everything that assumes a form into the matter, in the land of the living, is bound to eventually perish and return to the land of the dead. Therefore, Osiris himself will never resurrect on earth, which is why his son and heir Horus has taken his place on the earthly throne.

Neheh, the continuous cyclic time, is symbolised by the Sungod Râ. Râ travels through the sky of the earthly world and is visible and tangible. Unlike Osiris, Râ is subjected to the earthly laws, for everything on earth is temporary, variable and fleeting. Naturally, these laws apply to the Sungod as well. Consequently, Râ experiences a cycle every day wherein he is born to eventually die again. To that end, it is not intended for Râ to reach the same level of

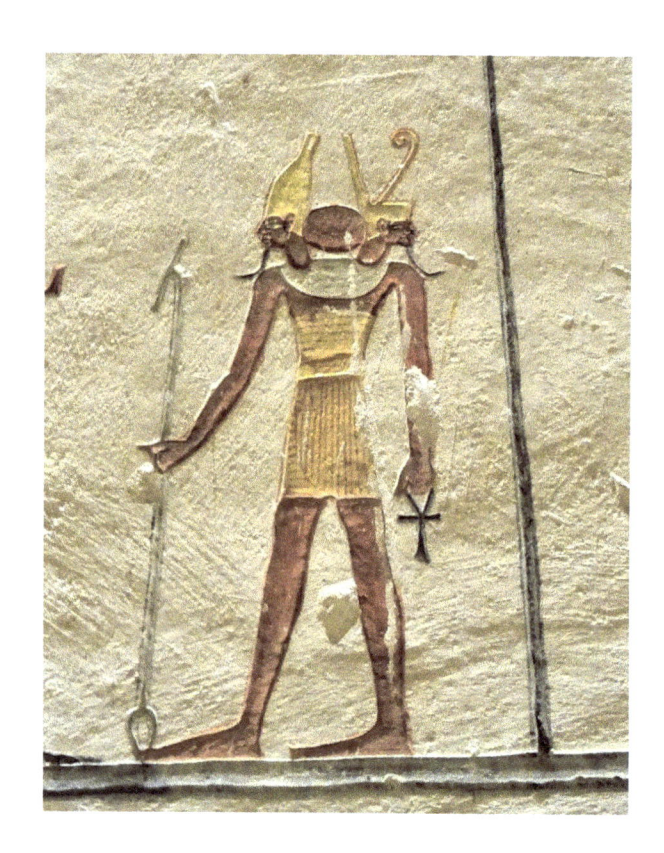

The God "He with equipped face, Lord of eternity", KV 9 Ramses V and VI

perfection as Osiris. His task is to continue his journey through the cycle again and again to reach a higher plane every time a new cycle begins.

Even though these two times, *neheh* and *djet*, each follow an unique course, they are not unrelated. They need each other's movement to keep moving themselves. This mutual dependency is also reflected in the curious head of the God "He with equipped face, Lord of eternity". The two Crowns of Upper and Lower Egypt touch each other at the top and are also connected through the solar disk in between. These two crowns symbolise the two lands. In this case, the day and the night world where Râ, *neheh* time, and Osiris, *djet* time, live respectively. The solar disk represents the Sungod. Since the Sungod is able to move, he can travel through the world of Osiris and provide for the connecting link between both times. Hence, Râ's journey is the bridging factor that guarantees both times can exist next to one another and move in sync.

Alternatively, the solar disk could also symbolise the ancient solar Deity Atum, the "Complete One". He is the creator of all Gods, the world and the first human beings at the beginning of time, *Zep Tepi*. Consequently, all creation, including *neheh* and *djet*, emerged from his flesh, or his *Ka*-force.

The God "He with equipped face, Lord of eternity" *âper-her neb djet*, with his dual nature, emphasises the *djet* time. The underlying power of this *djet* time, which is the Vital Life Force of Osiris, ensures new life can rise from death.

Osiris's time, *djet*, is linear and rises in a vertical fashion. The Sungod Râ, on the other hand, is rising in a circular way. *Djet*, therefore, is the centre of all life that the cyclic time of Râ, *neheh*, revolves around. (see chapter; Osiris, Lord of the Duat, fig. 5.).

Loyally the God "He with equipped face, Lord of eternity" is standing here to guide Râ. Time can absolutely not stand still for this would halt the journey and cause chaos and death. So Râ, like Osiris, must remain moving and does not have the liberty to hesitate or stand still at any point during his travels. Even though this Lord of eternity occupies a fixed position and never leaves the Duat himself, he guarantees that the movement of time continues for all eternity.

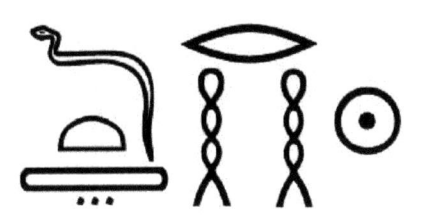

Fig. 34. Continuing and repeating "Djet-r-neheh"

The next Deity is the creator God "Atum" (No. 755) who wears the solar disk on his head. Atum is holding the wings of an enormous serpent. A similar scene was evident in the Fifth Hour where the God of the dead, Sokar (No. 393), held the wings of a serpent. That was the moment during which the very first spark of light in the Sacred Land of Sokar was rekindled. Since then, the renewal of the light has come a long way and is currently at an advanced stage. At this point the creator God Atum replaces Sokar. Now it is Atum who is holding these wings to emphasise the fact that the next solar cycle comes forth from the beginning of time that he has created. Without the support of Atum, the continuation of creation would be impossible to realise. According to the accompanying text of this image, Atum is not standing beside the winged serpent, but has actually come forth from its backbone. This is unsurprising, since Atum is the first born from the very foundation, "the backbone", of life itself.

Every living creature is born from this royal ancestor.

The winged serpent has four legs that elevate his body from the ground. Underneath his head, the *Ankh* can be seen. The name of the winged serpent is "Petry" (No. 756) which means "Seer or Beholder". He is connected to the Eyes of Râ that are depicted above his wings. "Petry" represents the transformation process that the light of Râ has been subjected to during the preceding hours. Râ's damaged light, as symbolised by the "Eye of the West", is now

The God Atum with the two Eyes on either side of his head, holds the wings of the serpent "Petry", KV 9 Ramses V and VI

completely restored and renewed. The Eye has become equally big as the "Eye of the East", which represents wholeness and unity. "Petry or Seer" his name emphasises the fact that the Eye of Râ has regained its "sight". "Petry" has shed his old and worn skin to reveal the renewed winged life underneath that is sprouting from his backbone. Consequently, the time has come near during which Khepri is going to spread his wings.

The solar disk Atum is wearing on top of his head is a reference to this upcoming event. It is a symbol that Atum sometimes wears on his head himself to represent his creative qualities. However, it also represents the perfect solar disk of Râ that would never be able to exist without Atum's support. The solar disk is balancing precisely in between the "Eye of the East" and the "Eye of the West", for creation, like the birth of this solar disk, can be realised only through the friction between opposites.

Atum is very much aware of this fact, which is why he is standing exactly in the middle of these two Eyes. He knows the Law of creation by heart and acts on it. However, he also possesses the knowledge and the ultimate power to eventually destroy everything he has created and return it to a state of non-existence. This would wipe the slate clean after which he himself would revert back to a primeval serpent. All of the gained consciousness and all of the light would then return to the winged serpent "Petry or Seer". He, or actually Râ, would subsequently close his eyes once again.

This conceiving, but also deadly, side of creation is represented in the subsequent serpent *Shedi Wenwet (šdi wn.wt)* as well. His name translates as "He who takes away the hours" (No. 758). A *"wenwety" (wnwty)* was an hour-watcher and astronomer who determined the time while using the position and the ascending and descending paths of the stars.

This serpent is also a quantifier of time. However, in his case he does not do this through the observation of the stars or the hours, for he actively devours them. In front of him, there are ten duat stars that are the representatives of the preceding ten hours. "He who takes away the hours" has ensured each of these previous hours is swallowed. This facilitates the continuation of time and is emphasised through his active upraised posture. However, the hieroglyphic word *shedi (šdi)*, which means "take away or remove", can also be translated as "deliver, rescue or bring". This serpent with his dual nature, therefore, does not only devour the previous hours, but at the same time ensures that the subsequent hour is born at exactly the right time. Each time he consumes an hour, he simultaneously delivers the next hour.

On top of his back is the mummified Goddess *"Djet or eternity"* (No. 757) who represents the eternal *djet* time. She controls the serpent "He who takes away the hours" and supervises the course of the time. She is also the embodiment of the Eleventh Hour and it is her job to be present here every night at the exact right moment to enable Râ to continue his journey. This is an important task for when an hour is missing, the rejuvenation of the Sungod cannot continue, which ultimately results in Râ's death. In addition, the Goddess "Djet" is in need of the shining appearance of Râ herself to continue her own existence. Each time Râ makes his appearance here, she identifies herself with his shining being. When the Sungod leaves again, she resumes her identification with her own being. She does this through swallowing her own image, which means she absorbs her own being. Simultaneously, as she withdraws within herself, she is also devoured by the serpent "He who takes away the hours". Since she is the embodiment of the Eleventh Hour, the serpent swallows the Eleventh Hour in exchange for the Twelfth Hour. In doing so, time continues its course and the journey moves on to the Twelfth Hour. This is how the cosmic clock remains ticking continuously.

Following the serpent "He who takes away the hours" and the Goddess "Djet" there are twelve Gods (No. 759 – 770) who are identified by Râ as the "Secret or Hidden Ones". When the Sungod arrives, he calls each of these Gods by their specific names and simultaneously gifts them the Breath of Life. This enables them to finally resume breathing through their noses. However, this is not the only gift Râ bestows upon the "Secret Ones". On board of his Sun barque he has brought offerings for the *Ba*-souls of these Gods to nourish them. Moreover, Râ also provides them with the life-giving waters originating from the overflow of the Nun. However, the Gods do not keep the water for their own use alone, for they share it with the other Duatians residing here as well. Finally, the "Secret Ones" are declared Justified since they act in accordance with the Divine Law of *Maât*.

With each of these Gifts, Râ ensures the twelve Gods lack absolutely nothing. His care for the Gods is important for Râ himself as well, since they carry the Secret of regeneration with them. They will never reveal the knowledge of this secret and will always hide it within themselves. However, they do support and assist the result and embodiment of this hidden creation process, which is the renewal of the Sungod Râ. Therefore, the Gods are pointing the Sungod in the right direction to enable him to eventually take his sacred place at the Eastern horizon of the day world. Hence, the "Secret Ones" are present here every night to assist Râ in his ascension from the hidden realm of the Duat. They stay close to Râ's side and follow him to the sky.

The first of the twelve Gods has two heads and the very befitting name "He with double head" (No. 759). One of his heads is gazing towards the right while the other one is gazing towards the left. This posture is imitated by his feet where one is pointed towards the right while the other is pointed to the left. This God indicates the return of duality that comes into being the moment Râ and Osiris have separated from each other in the next hour. In addition, "He with double head" watches the past behind him and the future before him. In doing so, he bridges yesterday and tomorrow into the present just like the two lions "Flesh (of Aker)" (No. 392) in the Fifth Hour. "He with double head" emphasises that only in the Present Time, creation is moving forward, resulting in the rebirth of the Sungod.

The following Deity is the ram-headed God Khnum, "Khnum-Renyt" (No. 760). He is holding the *Was*-sceptre in one hand and the *Ankh* in the other. Khnum has made an appearance before in the watery Second and Third Hour due to his association with the inundation and his ability to create new life from the fertile clay. In the present hour, Khnum, the "Divine Potter God", shows himself again to contribute to the upcoming rebirth of the Sungod. Khnum is the one who shapes the body, together with the *Ka*, on his divine potter's wheel. This creation takes place in the heavens and precedes the actual birthing process. Hence, Khnum's presence should come as no surprise in this second to last hour before the physical birth of Khepri is manifested.

> He made hair sprout and tresses grow,
> fastened the skin over the limbs;
> he built the skull, formed the cheeks,
> to furnish shape to the image.
> He opened the eyes, hollowed the ears,
> he made the body inhale air;
> he formed the mouth for eating,
> made the gorge for swallowing.
> He also formed the tongue to speak,
> the jaws to open,
> the gullet to drink,
> the throat to swallow and spit.
> the spine to give support,
> the testicles to move,
> The arm to act with vigor,
> the rear to perform its task.
> the gullet to devour, hands and their fingers to do their work,
> the heart to lead.
> The loins to support the phallus
> in the act of begetting.
> The frontal organs to consume things,
> the rear to aerate the entrails,
> likewise to sit at ease and sustain
> the entrails at night.
> The male member to beget,
> the womb to conceive,
> and increase generations in Egypt.
> The bladder to make water,
> the virile member to inject
> when it swells between the thighs.
> The shins to step, the legs to tread their bones doing their task,
> by the will of his heart.[2]
> – A section of the Great Hymn to Khnum

The subsequent God, "He who guards the earth" (No. 761), is keeping his hands in an upraised position as a posture of adoration and worship. He is the guardian of the sacred earth that forms the cradle wherein the Sungod Râ will soon be born. With his worship, he provides for the much needed support and encourages Râ to ascend to the day world on earth.

Following him there are five Gods who are each missing their arms. The lack of their arms emphasises their association with the hidden mystery of creation that they keep concealed within themselves. The first God has two cobras instead of a head. The other four are all human-headed.

(No. 762) "Whose two arms are in him"
(No. 763) "Judge of the two Lands"
(No. 764) "He who commands his two arms"
(No. 765) "Whose two arms are hidden"
(No. 766) "Who strengthens the flesh"

The final four Gods all have a normal human shape including a head and arms.

(No. 767) "Who adores Horus"
(No. 768) "The Right One"
(No. 769) "Big Dipper" or "Meskhtyu" *(msḫtyw)*
(No. 770) "Who restrains the arm"

The name of the third God "Big Dipper" or "Meskhtyu" is the name of the constellation of the Great Bear, "Ursa Major". This constellation is always present above the horizon and is part of the circumpolar stars that never set. The Big Dipper or "the thigh of the Northern sky" was regarded as the leg of a bull. The bull itself was the symbol of the Vital Life Force of Osiris. The bull's leg was, for example, used during one of the rituals of the ceremony of the Opening of the Mouth to transfer the vital power it possessed to the mummy. As mentioned in the Third Hour *meskhtyu* is also known as the magical instrument the *Seb Ur*, or the *adze*, used to open the mouth. It is quite clear that the God "Meskhtyu" is connected to the birth into new life.

The left riverbank concludes with four Goddesses:

(No. 771) "Lady of the Living"
(No. 772) "Lady of the *Akh*-spirits"
(No. 773) "She who guards the two banks"
(No. 774) "Guardian of the Gods"

These Goddesses are all seated on top of the coils of two-headed cobras with their feet on its back. With one hand, they are firmly holding the coiling body of the moving serpent. Their other hand is held in front of their faces.

Once Râ arrives, he awakens them from their slumber by letting them hear his voice. Simultaneously, his vocal sound generates the Breath of Life. In turn, the four Goddesses are able to take a deep breath after which they immediately start to cry. Tears of mourning, filled with life-giving water, are running down their cheeks. This provides for extra nourishment for the renewed life of Râ. Afterwards they start to blow with great force, which results in a growing strong wind that sounds like the beat of a drum. The blowing wind, just before sunrise, clears out the sky and makes it bright and lucid. The rebels, and other counteracting forces, are unable to keep standing against this explosive force and are blown away.

With their actions, the four Goddesses carry out the preparatory work to provide for a sky that will soon open itself and detach from the Unified Darkness. Hence, the Goddesses conduct a bridging task between the two different realms, the day world and the Duat. The bodies of the cobras they are sitting on are shaped in a bridge like form as well to emphasise this aspect. The feet and hips of the Goddesses are connected with the hidden power stemming from the earth. With their faces they are connected with the sky through the headwind and hurricanes they create. As soon as the separation between the night world of Osiris and the day world of Râ takes place during the sunrise, duality starts again. The double heads of the cobras symbolise this manifestation of opposites. Hence, the weeping of the Goddesses is not just to empower Râ's renewal, for the imminent separation between Râ and Osiris has a sad and painful side to it as well. With their tears of sorrow, they express this striking sadness.

The Duatians of the Sacred River (middle section)

The Sun barque is still being moved by the rowing actions of the personal crew of the Sungod Râ. With unified forces they continue at a strong pace while the Eastern horizon is getting closer and closer.

(No. 775) "Wepwawet"
(No. 776) "Sia"
(No. 777) "Nebet wia"
(No. 778) "Mehen"
(No. 779) "Iuf"
(No. 780) "Heru Hekenu"
(No. 781) "Ka Maât"
(No. 782) "Nehes"
(No. 783) "Hu"
(No. 784) "Kherep wia"

The end of the journey is finally starting to come into view. This progression is vital, for the day world needs to be awakened at exactly the right time with the light of the rejuvenated Râ. Time continues to move and Râ's departure from the day world has already been hours ago. Fortunately, Râ's transformation has progressed exactly according to the schedule.

However, it is still too early for Râ to give shape to the perfect light. Evidently, since Râ is still residing within the celestial body of the sky Goddess Nut. As long as he is sailing in this non-material world, it is impossible to give shape to the renewed sunlight. This is why the beautiful impeccable solar disk "Shining One of the Duat" (*psḏ.t dwȝ.t*) (No. 785) decorated with the upraised Uraeus-serpent, is now lying on the prow of the Sun barque. "Shining One" is a female solar disk. The disk is a reference to the Goddess Hathor since one of her names is "Golden One" or "Shining One". She is connected to the Sungod Râ as his wife or daughter and embodies Râ's Eye. In this form she is the protector of the Sungod and destroys everyone and everything who wants to harm her beloved Râ. Hathor is also associated with birth and plays a part in the process where the dead become reborn in the Afterlife. In her form as a cow she put the Sungod between her horns and lifted him up into the sky.

Here, she has taken the lead with her beautiful shining light and shows Râ the way during the final moments of darkness. As a result, the darkness starts to change and it no longer has the solid impenetrable blackness it had before. During the previous hours the darkness was still referred to as the Unified Darkness, *"keku semau"* (*kkw-sm3w*), while here it is simply identified as darkness, *"keku"* (*kkw*). This indicates that the impregnable darkness is starting to dissolve to make room for the impending dawn.

The hieroglyphic word *pesdj* (*psd̲*) means "to shine", but spelled with a different determinative at the end it translates as "nine". Nine is a reference to the Great Ennead, the company of the nine Deities at the beginning of creation, *Zep Tepi*. The Great Ennead *pesdjet* (*psd̲t*) is a word play on the name of "Shining One" *pesdjet* (*psd̲.t*). The solar disk "Shining One" is the embodiment of the Eye of Râ. Thus, it is the symbol of the eternal renewal that originates from the beginning of all time. This Eye of Râ is named in honour of these ancestors, specifically after the "Father of the Ennead", Atum. Understandably, since the Ennead was created by him. Once again, a subtle allusion is made to the fact that all of life and every God has been created from the flesh of

The Goddess Hathor, Temple of Hathor at Dendera

Atum. Conversely, it is also important to realise that without the rise of the Sungod Râ the creation would revert to the chaotic Unified Darkness. It goes without saying that the creator God Atum himself is also subjected to this eternal renewal process.

There are twelve Gods walking in front of the Sun barque while carrying an enormous coiled serpent on top of their heads.

(No. 786) "Bearer"
(No. 787) "Carrier"
(No. 788) "The Loaded One"
(No. 789) "The One who grasps"
(No. 790) "The One who receives"
(No. 791) "He with firm arm"
(No. 792) "He who takes hold"
(No. 793) "The Pleasant One"
(No. 794) "He who pulls out"
(No. 795) "He who embraces"
(No. 796) "He who conducts the image"
(No. 797) "He who belongs to the Encircler"

The huge coiled serpent is Mehen. He has one final task to perform before Râ's renewal can reach completion. The Sungod still has to ascend a bit further, which is where Mehen can be of assistance. That is why he is not lying on the ground, but is held up by the twelve Gods instead. This way, Mehen, as well as the Sungod Râ, is upraised and carried in the right direction towards the Eastern gateway of the horizon. The twelve Gods are the chosen ones to assume this responsibility. Their names reveal that each and every one of them possesses the perfect skills to empower them to carry Mehen safely high above their heads. Naturally, it is essential they keep an eye on this important protector of Râ on their way to ensure the safe arrival of Râ in the Twelfth Hour. These Gods still have a long way to go and Râ personally encourages them. After all, it is imperative they arrive perfectly on time just before sunrise.

> Do protect your images,
> and raise your heads!
> Strength to your arms,
> endurance to your feet!
> May your proceeding be right,
> may your steps be fast! [3]

By the time they have completed their important task, Râ rewards each of them handsomely with offerings. Afterwards they may take their respective spots, as they are waiting for the next night to carry Mehen once again. The fact these twelve Gods are very important is made evident by their positions after they have completed their tasks. For, according to the text, each of them takes a seat upon a true throne!

Following these twelve Gods there are two cobras lying on the ground, each carrying a crown on their back. The first carries the Red Crown that has a small head on top of it. This cobra is the Goddess Isis, "Image of Isis" (No. 798). The subsequent cobra is carrying the White Crown with two small heads emerging on both sides on the tip of the crown. This cobra is the Goddess Nephthys, "Image of Nephthys" (No. 799). During the Second Hour of the night, Isis and Nephthys have both made an appearance before in the shape of a cobra on the Sun barque. Presently, they once again assume the appearance of a cobra, but this time they are in the procession preceding the Sun barque. Their presence here is needed to assist with the rise of the Sungod Râ and the renewal of Osiris. The crowns they carry the symbolical crowns Râ and Osiris are soon to wear once they take their rightful places in their own worlds. The two lands or worlds will then be separated again to allow for the return of the necessary duality.

Isis and Nephthys are lying here in front of the second gate of the Unified Darkness on the Forbidden Path of Say (s3y), better known as Sais. Sais was the capital city of the fifth Nome, or district, of Lower Egypt. The Goddess Neith, "The Lady of Sais", was the chief Deity of this city. Therefore, the great temple of Sais, known as the "House of the Bee", was dedicated to her. The temple was renowned for its eternally burning fire that was utilised for various purposes. For instance, it was used to purify and bless the weapons of the warriors who were about to go into battle. During the annual feast, "Feast of Lamps" in honour of Neith, the fire was used to light thousands of lights.

According to an old legend, the grave of Osiris was located in Sais.[4] Each night a mystery play was performed by the Sacred Lake located within the walls of the great temple. During the performance the suffering and death of Osiris was re-enacted by initiates. The resurrection into new life was also an essential part of the ceremony. Within these walls and behind closed gates, the mystery of death into life was kept safe far away from daily life. In other words, the mystery play was an initiation path and thus forbidden for the ignorant. Only those who were initiated themselves in the Secret were allowed to see and participate in this ceremony.

Isis and Nephthys are both initiates in the Sacred Mystery and thus authorised to walk the Forbidden Path. They both play an essential part in the resurrection themselves, as we have seen during several hours. Presently, they are at the second gate that provides for access to the final stage of the journey. The ascension is about to be manifested. Hence, Râ is calling on both of the Goddesses for Râ, like Osiris, requires their loving and upraising dedication to ascend.

Naturally, the Goddess Neith herself is present here as well. She concludes the Sacred River in four different forms.

(No. 800) "Male Neith"
(No. 801) "Neith of the Red Crown"
(No. 802) "Neith of the White Crown"
(No. 803) "Neith-Osiris"

The names of these Deities indicate the diverse nature of Neith that is not restricted to the female gender alone. Actually, she is male and female as well as genderless. Furthermore, although Neith does not have a partner, she is still able to give birth. Like the God Atum, she is a self-produced, self-begotten and self-born Deity. Obviously, as she is a creator Goddess, she is an initiate in the Secret of creation and she herself is the protector of the Forbidden Gate of Sais. Beyond this gate is where the great secret takes place, which is unknown, unseen and unperceived.[5]

It was said that Neith, the "Mighty Mother" herself gave birth to the Sungod Râ. She also created Apophis using her saliva that she spat into the Nun. In doing so, she created both sides of creation and provided for the duality needed to continue. In the present hour, her attendance with her fiery character is needed to stir up the light of Râ even further. In her temple it was customary to burn a kind of wax right before sunrise. It is very likely that this wax was produced by honey bees. The delicious scent of this wax would purify the sanctuary, which was the place where Neith as the Deity of the temple would reside during the day on earth. In this hour Neith is present in four different shapes at the front of the procession to sanctify and purify the way herself, before Râ's arrival on earth.

The Duatians on the right riverbank (lower section)

At the beginning of the right riverbank "Horus" (No. 804) is standing with the solar disk encircled with the Uraeus on his head, just like in the Tenth Hour. He is standing here bent forward as he is leaning on a stick while holding a serpent staff in the other hand. He is holding this wand in a menacing gesture in front of him that makes it an extension of his enormous rage. The friendly Horus full of empathy and compassion we became familiar with in the previous hour, has undergone a complete metamorphosis. Presently, an entirely different side of Horus is shown. His presence here is not to save the unfortunate souls, but actually to destroy people. The Sungod Râ personally orders Horus to slaughter anyone who has beaten or wronged Osiris, the father of Horus. Râ gives him a very specific description to define the persons in question:

> Orders given by the person of this God
> to slaughter those
> who beat his father Osiris,
> i.e. the corpses of the enemies,
> the limbs of the dead,
> those who are upside down,
> hindered on going,
> and the shapes of the annihilated.[6]

Horus steps forward in name of his father Osiris to get revenge on these enemies.

> Horus speaks:
> I have come forth from him,
> and now my father strikes back
> after he has been weary! [6]

The word "weary" refers to the physical state

and in particular to the functioning of the heart. As mentioned before, the heart was considered the central organ and the linking factor of the body. Through the pumping of blood it ensured that the separate parts of the body would form a unity. The moment the heart stopped pumping blood, the bodily unit would fall apart and result in death. Hence, death was also referred to as "weariness of the heart". The heart had become aged and fatigued which made it unable to pump the blood around. This then resulted in the falling apart of the body and lead it to perish and decay. Hence, Osiris, who resides in the Duat as the God of the dead, is also known as "weary of heart" (*wrḏ-ib*).[7]

However, another epithet of Osiris is "He who stands and does not become weary" in which he demonstrates the triumph over death as a resurrected God.

As we have arrived in the Eleventh Hour, both Osiris and Râ have almost been completely renewed. Osiris's heart is no longer weary and, considering the return of his power, he would even be able to punish the enemies himself. However, in spite of his revitalised heart, Osiris always remains passive, which is why Horus takes the punishing upon himself. This is the moment where Horus accepts the sceptre of power and dominion from his father and assumes his role of the future King. Horus is now personally guaranteeing that justice prevails and addresses the hostiles with an authoritarian and threatening voice.

Punishment for your corpses
by (the knife) "Punisher",
Annihilation for your *Ba*-souls,
trampling down for your shadows,
severing for your heads!
You have not come into being,
you are upside down!
You will not rise, since you have fallen into your pits!
You cannot escape, you cannot evade! [8]

Horus is reciting here the most horrendous ways to die. Each of these methods is irrevocable and eternal, the so-called "second death", without any hope of life or rebirth. This awful vision was the horror of every soul, which was why people took measurements to protect themselves from this terrible fate. There were several spells that could be used during the travels in the Netherworld to arm oneself against potential threats. Three situations in particular were to be avoided at all costs and were therefore often mentioned together in a single spell. The first two of these specific events were the consummation of faeces and the drinking of urine. Both acts would result in the defiling of your purity. Purity was the prerequisite to be reborn into a new life. It is, therefore, understandable that the preservation of your purity was extremely important.

What I detest, I will not eat.
Faeces is my detestation and I will not eat;
Filth shall not enter into my belly,

I will not go up to it with my hands,
I will not tread on it with my sandals.
I am protected from you
who are bowed down,
I will not walk upside down.
He who serves me is the servant of Horus,
for I am one of you.[9]
– Coffin Texts, Spell 202

The third and also very dangerous situation, which is mentioned in the Third Hour by Râ and now by Horus, is the position where you walk with your head turned downward and the posture of being upside down completely. This awkward position, named *skhedkhed* (*sḫdḫd*), makes it impossible to ascend to the sky and rise into a new life. Being upside down indicates that you are not aware of the fact that you have died and arrived in the land of the dead. Consequently, you are unable to make the reversal to transition into a new consciousness. The world will appear to be upside down. This is very confusing and makes you lose your orientation and sense of direction. It will then be impossible to find your way in this strange world. The road to rebirth to become a blessed dead will be closed to you. Furthermore, everything will feel like it is the other way around, leading to you eating your faeces and drinking your urine instead of secreting it. Thus, the purity essential to become resurrected into a new life, will be lost to you.

Furthermore, this particular train of thought, of being upside down, was probably a result of the experience with breech birth. During such a birth, the baby is positioned upside down and is presenting feet first, if anything at all, instead of the head. Nowadays most of these babies are delivered by caesarean section. In ancient times, however, this position was a very dangerous one since chances were the baby would have died before it could be born and, in the worst-case scenario, taking the mother with him.

Coffin Texts; Spell 205 describes the way the ascension into the sky works beautifully provided that you have both feet firmly on the ground.

Not to walk upside down.
A voice is raised in the Northern sky,
wailing is in the marshland,
because of the voice of the summoning
of the blessed one.
I am raised up to the place where Maât is,
I have flown up to them as a swallow,
like Thoth;
I cackle to them as a goose,
like the Wine-press God;
I fly up as a vulture on this great plateau
that I may stand on it.
I appear as a God,
for he who looks at them will never die.[10]
– Coffin Texts; Spell 205

Horus is here now to ensure the ascension into new life is impossible for the enemies of his father. There are no spells available to save these foes from the clutches of this deadly situation. In front of Horus is a dangerous serpent who is positioned in an upraised pose on his tail, "He who burns millions" (No. 805). Horus assigns him with the task to use his fire against the rebels of his father. The name of this serpent indicates his fire has the power to burn millions. However, the firepower of the serpent alone is insufficient according to Horus, which is why he rallies other dangerous allies to assist in his cause.

In front of the serpent are six steep holes in the earth in which fires are burning. However, since everything is reversed in the Duat, these holes look like hills. These profound pits serve as giant cooking pots. Once you end up in one of these deep holes, it is impossible to escape. Behind every pit, with exception of the last, is a Goddess standing while facing the opposite direction and holding a knife. Horus instructs each of these Goddesses individually to assist with the extermination of the enemies of his father. The destruction is carried out with a most effective and systematic method to guarantee a truly gruesome death for each of the foes.

The first Goddess has the head of a lioness and is called "She above her kettles" (No. 807). It is her pit in which the "Enemies" (No. 806) are thrown first. Using her fiery glow, she ignites the flames within her pit to burn the bodies. The second Goddess is called "She above her pits" (No. 809) and her pit is filled with the corpses of the enemies. She fuels the destruction by shooting at the bodies with flames. By now, these foes are no longer referred to as enemies for they have now been reduced to "Corpses" (No. 808). This name indicates the hostiles have truly died.

However, the amount of destruction is still not enough for Horus as he also sends a third Goddess "She who severs" (No. 811). This Goddess takes the demolition yet again a step further. She severs the unity of the bodies through separating the "*Ba*-souls" (No. 810) from them and tossing these souls in her pit. The death of these foes is starting to become more and more gruesome.

Next is the fourth Goddess, "She above her slaughtering blocks" (No. 813), who adds fuel to the fire with "the embers from her mouth". She continues the dismemberment of the bodies as she separates the "Shadows" (No. 812) from them. The final Goddess, "She above her knives" (No. 815), finishes the job as she severs the "Heads" (No. 814) from the bodies and throws them in her pit. The punishment of these opponents, who have now been completely dismembered, however, is still unsatisfactory to Horus. Therefore, there still is one final pit in which the most horrendous punishment of them all is carried out. This final sanction indefinitely deprives the foes from all hopes of ever being reborn in a new life again. All of the bodies, "Those upside down" (No. 816), are placed upside down in the fire pit "Wadi of those upside down". It is very clear that there is no way out for the rest of eternity. Horus himself is standing here every night in this true hell of fire, to ensure the slaughter of the enemies is decreed, night after night, in name of his father.

Behind the final fire pit are four Goddesses who are facing the opposite direction as well.

(No. 817) "She who boils"
(No. 818) "She who heats"
(No. 819) "She above her sand"
(No. 820) "She who destroys"

On top of their heads they are wearing the hieroglyphic sign for desert, "*khaset*" (*ḫ3st*), to emphasise the fact that now, just before daybreak, we have ended up in the desert. The desert has a purifying nature due to the fiery heat of the burning sun and the abrasive hot sand. It is the perfect place to realise purification through the element of fire. These Goddesses are also associated with the destruction of Osiris's enemies. Although the preceding slaughter has been gruesome, apparently it has still not been enough. By now, it has become quite clear that anyone who opposes Osiris will burn in hell for the rest of eternity. The four desert Goddesses are using their own specific methods, which can be derived from their names, to create a burning heat and establish a bloody punishment. They themselves feed upon the terrible screams and howls of the *Ba*-souls and upon the shadows of the hostiles whom they hurl into the fire pits. All six fire pits are entrusted to the four resolute Goddesses. It is their task to ensure that the enemies of Osiris do not escape but die an eternal death.

The right riverbank concludes with the Guardian "He above his kettles" (No. 821). He has a very important task to perform for he is the guardian of this entire hour. It is essential he oversees the ongoing slaughter in front of him to ensure it is performed as effectively as possible. He inspects each of the fire pits as none of the enemies are allowed to escape since they could slip away into the final hour. This final part of the Eleventh Hour is also the last opportunity to stop and punish the opponents. Every escaped rebel poses a potential serious thread to the ascension of the renewed Râ. Although the slaughter is meant specifically for the enemies of Osiris, obviously these dangerous opposite forces pose just as much a threat to Râ. The Guardian, however, is not to be messed with. One needs to be very cunning to sneak past him without his approval. His ultimate power and dominion is emphasised by the *Was*-sceptre in one of his hands.

The manifestation of the Eleventh Hour in daily life

After the deep submersion in the Tenth Hour, you have now come up from the darkest areas of your inner waters. In the present hour you find yourself just below the surface and the worldly life is gradually coming closer. Thus, be prepared because the pull from daily life tries to draw your attention. Usually this happens in such a subtle way you might fall for it before you even realise it. It is still too early to raise your head above the water surface, for there are still some finishing touches to be made. However, do not worry if you happen to surface, since you can simply dive and return to your transformation process to continue where you have left off. These hold ups are part of the process and no reason to become discouraged.

It is very important to take the appropriate amount of time for this second to last hour. This means you have to stay in the right flow, which is clearly indicated by your Higher Self and is supported by the Powerself. They show you the best course is to stay balancing in the middle, not too fast nor too slow and not too far to the left nor the right. The Sun barque itself is also required to remain perfectly in the middle of the Sacred River to prevent it from running onto the sandy riverbanks on either side. During the previous hour you have learned how to balance and, as always, these skills are now put to the test. Your helmsman-ship is evaluated. However, by now you know you can succeed only if you transfer the helm to your Higher Self.

When you stay in the right flow, you are directly confronted with synchronicity. Synchronicity is the phenomenon where events take place in a perfectly timed fashion and each of these occurrences has a special meaning for you. They get your attention and act as a wake-up call to confirm you are on the right track. These so called uncanny coincidences present themselves in all sorts of ways. For example, you could have dreamt about something that later actually happens in your everyday life. Or you might think of someone right before actually running into this person. Or you are in need of something specific and are suddenly presented with it. These are some examples of the diversity of these unlikely occurrences. All of them are signs that you are properly in tune with your inner world and connected with your inner Sungod.

Although synchronicity revolves around the perfect moment with the right timing, the time mentioned seems to take place in a parallel world outside of our earthly concept of time. All future events are already there, waiting for you, and they make an appearance in your life the moment the door opens at the perfect time. That is why it is of the greatest importance to keep up with the cosmic time. When you are out of synch and arrive too late at such a crucial moment, the door is already closed. On the other hand, should you arrive too early, the door has not opened yet. However, waiting until it does open is not an option either since the sun continues its course, just like time. So you have to move on as well. The God "He with equipped face, Lord of eternity" (No. 754) makes you aware of the importance to learn to go with the flow of the cosmic time. Therefore, like the Goddess "Djet", go along with the right time that is symbolised by the serpent "He who takes away the hours". Then you can walk in the balanced middle and truly see and comprehend the things that are given to you.

Synchronicity is an ever present reality,
for those who have eyes to see.[11]
– Carl Gustav Jung

This true sight is emphasised by the winged

serpent "Seer" (No. 756). He has awoken from the deep slumber of death. With renewed energy he now spreads his wings which results in a bridge between the conscious and subconscious world. His eyes are watching the world, sharp and vigilant, from within the awakened consciousness. These eyes are connected to the Eyes of Râ, the latter of which have now regained their equilibrium and are visible above the wings of "Seer". Right in between the two eyes there is the solar disk on top of the head of the God Atum. This solar disk symbolises the third eye that has opened as a result of the heightened consciousness. Like "Seer", you have now gained enough knowledge to be able to see the truth that is *Maât*. Suddenly you are witnessing truly remarkable and sincere things that were out of sight and hidden deep within the ordinary layers of daily life before. You are the owner of the "Eyes" which indicates that you now view the world through the Eyes of your inner Sungod. The borders of time have evaporated. The past, present and future have blended, since time is only relative.

> I have stood up on the day of eternity
> and the year of everlasting;
> I know it, though none have told it to me.
> Falsehood is of yesterday;
> O Maât, I have attained Truth.[12]
> – Coffin Texts; Spell 624

This is also where it becomes a paradox, for once you have synched and become in tune with the cosmic time, the boundaries of time disappear in a state of timelessness. The clock is ticking on earth alone as time is a phenomenon bound to earth. In between the worlds, the concept of time disappears and changes into the vast state of eternity. Even though the progress of the journey in the Duat is defined using hours, the definition of these hours is not the same compared to our earthly hours. The hours of the Duat are used only to emphasise the fact eternal Life continuous even after death. After all, timelessness is an abstract idea and difficult to grasp or to imagine. As this book of the Amduat is meant for earthly human beings, the concept of the passing of time during the progressing journey is easier to comprehend when defined in hours. Obviously, however, these hours do not take the same amount of time as do the earthly hours.

In one "hour" the birth of your renewed self takes place. You are assisted by the helpful Gods, the "Secret or Hidden Ones" (No. 759 – 770), who aid you in preparing for this occasion. Each of these Gods has something to tell you about your inner power and skills. When you have identified yourself with every single one of these Gods, you are able to recognise these specific skills within yourself. Let these revelations about yourself sink in and give them a place within yourself for you will soon need them to ascend.

The inner process of your becoming is a Sacred Mystery and has no place in the world of the profane. You should cherish it within your hidden Holy inner world, where it is a private revelation between you and your Higher Self. However, the result of this sacred process does need to be made visible and put out there in the world of everyday life. You are the divine creator who uses all his talents and gifts in his inner atelier to create a unique work of art. Once it is finished, you entrust this piece of art to the daylight in order for everyone else, including you, to see and enjoy it. How exactly it came into being is impossible to describe with words, for it is an expression of the sacred creation process. No words can describe the beauty of it and any attempt at this undermines its refinement and leaves a stain on both your art and your soul.

The four Goddesses seated on the double-headed cobras (No. 771 – 774) assist you to prepare the birth canal that will soon be used for the renewed you. Soon, the horizon needs to be opened in order for you to truly make your appearance in the outside world. All of the clouds and opposite forces need to be blown away to let your inner Sungod shine bright through you. However, even though you will soon arise from the Unified darkness, you do have to remain in contact with your inner world. Your feet need to be put firmly on the ground, just like the four Goddesses, meaning that you have to stay connected to your subconscious world. This is the world where your Powerself lives. You need his stabile power to express your potential to the fullest and do it the justice it deserves.

The tears of these four Goddesses are an expression of two opposite aspects: wholeness or dismemberment. On the one hand, their tears are filled with grief, since the Sungod will soon depart from the Duat and leave Osiris behind in this dark world. This separation, or dismemberment, only occurs if you are afraid to truly embody the Powerself in life itself. This also happens should you ignore the inspirational flow from the Higher world of the Divine Spark through the inner Sungod. However, should you decide to truly become a channel for both the Powerself and the Higher Self and give them a clear function in your life, there is no true separation. Although Osiris and Râ are apart, in their respective functions they are a whole as well. Then these Goddesses cry tears filled with joy for the renewed life. You are the medium and the executive force between both worlds. Therefore, the choice between wholeness and dismemberment is entirely up to you.

Should you decide to choose wholeness and unity, then "Shining One of the Duat" (No. 785) lies on the prow of the Sun barque waiting for you. She draws your attention to the shining light of the Divine Spark, who makes your world shine with its perfect light through the Higher Self. This light of consciousness is no longer a tiny speck on the horizon, for it is ready for you. In the last hour, it will become clear how much of this light you will be able to embody. The Higher Self, however, will ensure you get exactly the amount that you can bear.

Through your cooperation with the Higher Self, you have expanded your intuition and trust significantly. This growth process has taken place within the body of the serpent Mehen. As signified by the length of his enormous body, you have already experienced a true evolution. In this hour, this serpent still does not touch the ground for he is carried up high in the air. His body remains full of coils, which provides enough room for you to go through the final ascending developments and transformations. The serpent does not make contact with the earthly dimension until the next hour. Then his flexible body will be drawn out which is the sign of the end of the transformation process. That is the moment where you have to leave his protection. You then have become the flexible channel yourself that opens and closes as guided by the intuition.

The time is drawing near which is why, like the Goddesses Isis and Nephthys, you are standing before the second Gate of Sais. The first gate gave you access to the Sacred Mystery that took place within the hidden world within yourself. You entered as an ignorant several hours ago and now you leave this Forbidden Path as a self-aware human being. However, before the second gate opens, Isis and Nephthys first make you aware of the necessity of the connection between two extremes. Isis embodies the day consciousness, while Nephthys, who lives in the hidden, represents the subconsciousness. Together, they form a unity that creates a magical energy field from which new life arises. This means that you have to maintain the connection between the different worlds within yourself for this generates a magical forcefield that allows for your potential to emerge.

The winged serpent "Seer", the four Goddesses riding on their snakes, Mehen with his long body and finally Isis and Nephthys all underline the importance of this duality. The message is more than clear; keep your inner channel open. View both worlds with open eyes and be aware of what happens in there. Behold, and accept what you see! To do this you need a lot of patience, compassion and self-love. Isis and Nephthys are here to make you aware of this because without this loving power, the inner renewal cannot prevail and rise. Know that being able to love and to accept are both verbs. Therefore, they require you to have an active approach.

The creator Goddess Neith is also present here to support you. She is the guardian of the second Gate of Sais and also the keeper of the sacred flame that burns in her temple. This is the fire that burns with the flame of eternal Love. Only when you have truly ignited this fire within your heart, has the time come to fulfil the Great Awakening. Neith then opens the second gate for you since you are almost ready, as a bearer of your own light, to step forward in the outside world.

Before this time arrives, you are once again confronted with quite some inner opponents. As you have become strong, so too have they gained power. However, they do not show their power in visible offensive behaviour but in a subtle, sneaky and sophisticated way. They are the embodiment of the fundamental saboteurs that have been by your side your entire life. They have made their appearance while adopting several shapes and sizes throughout your life. During your entire life, they have been a common thread interlaced inconspicuously with your being. You need to comb through this thread yourself to learn to discern every sabotaging aspect of yourself.

Interestingly, you may discover that every saboteur possesses a vast amount of power and discipline. Therefore, it would be a waste to simply destroy these inner capacities and erase their existence. This is an unnecessary waste of energy for your saboteurs always re-emerge out of a dark corner somewhere to confront you again. They are simply part of your inner world and a part of who you are. Hence, you should regard them as rogue capacities that have managed to develop through fear and mistrust in an effort to protect you. They are not evil. They were simply a means to survive. Track down each of these rebels and re-educate them to work with you instead of against you.

The opportunity to do this is presented to you in the final part of the Eleventh Hour. This place is a true hell where the transforming flames are stirred up high. Horus is standing here up front to shine a light on all of your sabotaging aspects. These inner saboteurs in turn, do not give up without a fight. They try by any means necessary to prevent the Powerself and the inner Sungod from gaining a place in your world.

Horus represents the heightened vision needed to view your inner saboteurs from an objective and sincere vision. In the Tenth Hour, the Eight Sekhmets together with Thoth have helped you to regain a healthy inner equilibrium. In the present hour this renewed balance is further scrutinised. This is why Horus, "He who is above", is here at your service to provide you with his helicopter view to look upon your inner world. Look through his piercing eyes and observe yourself critically from a distance.

Moreover, five fire-spitting Goddesses are here as well at the fire pits ready to cast their fiery lights on your inner pitfalls. Each pit holds a rebellious aspect of yourself that has enlarged itself in order to try to prevent your ascension into the renewed vision. Lift this negative force up from the depth and be aware of the falsehoods it holds. Do not let yourself be overturned. Instead, take matters into your own hands through the Higher Self. Then you can stir up the transforming fires to melt the destructive power of your saboteurs down and transform it into a constructive power. Horus is standing here by your side to aid you in reshaping your inner division to form a cooperative inner unit.

Then there also are the four desert Goddesses (No. 817 – 820) who offer a helping hand to silence the last of the defiant inner screams and screeches. The desert is a desolate place without shadow and hardly any food. The sun burns, the sand is hot and the life-giving waters have dried up. Within this fiery hell, the intensive purification process takes place. After your saboteurs have transmuted in the transforming flames, this can incite a feeling of loss and emptiness. Up until now, you were accustomed to their existence and old and familiar appearances. Now, all of a sudden, their loudmouthed presence has been silenced. Your inner world has abruptly become deserted and you might feel lonely and abandoned. Although you might experience this as very contradicting and unsettling, it is also a very important phase in your process. Loneliness and seclusion always precede a transitional process. You need inner silence to connect with the profound insights of your inner Sungod. Only then, you are capable of making the transition; from alone to all one.

Once you are ready to leave the desert, you meet the Guardian "He above his kettles". Together with you, he makes a final round to inspect whether all of the rebels, who were present previously in this hour, have been hunted down. During your journey you have made a start in identifying and transforming these defiant capacities within yourself. However, you always need to be aware of the opposite forces and work on them. As you know by now, the forces of duality are essential to enable your consciousness to grow. After this final check, the Guardian opens the gate for you. The time has come to enter the final hour and complete the final stage of your voyage.

THE TWELFTH HOUR
"With emerging darkness and appearing births"

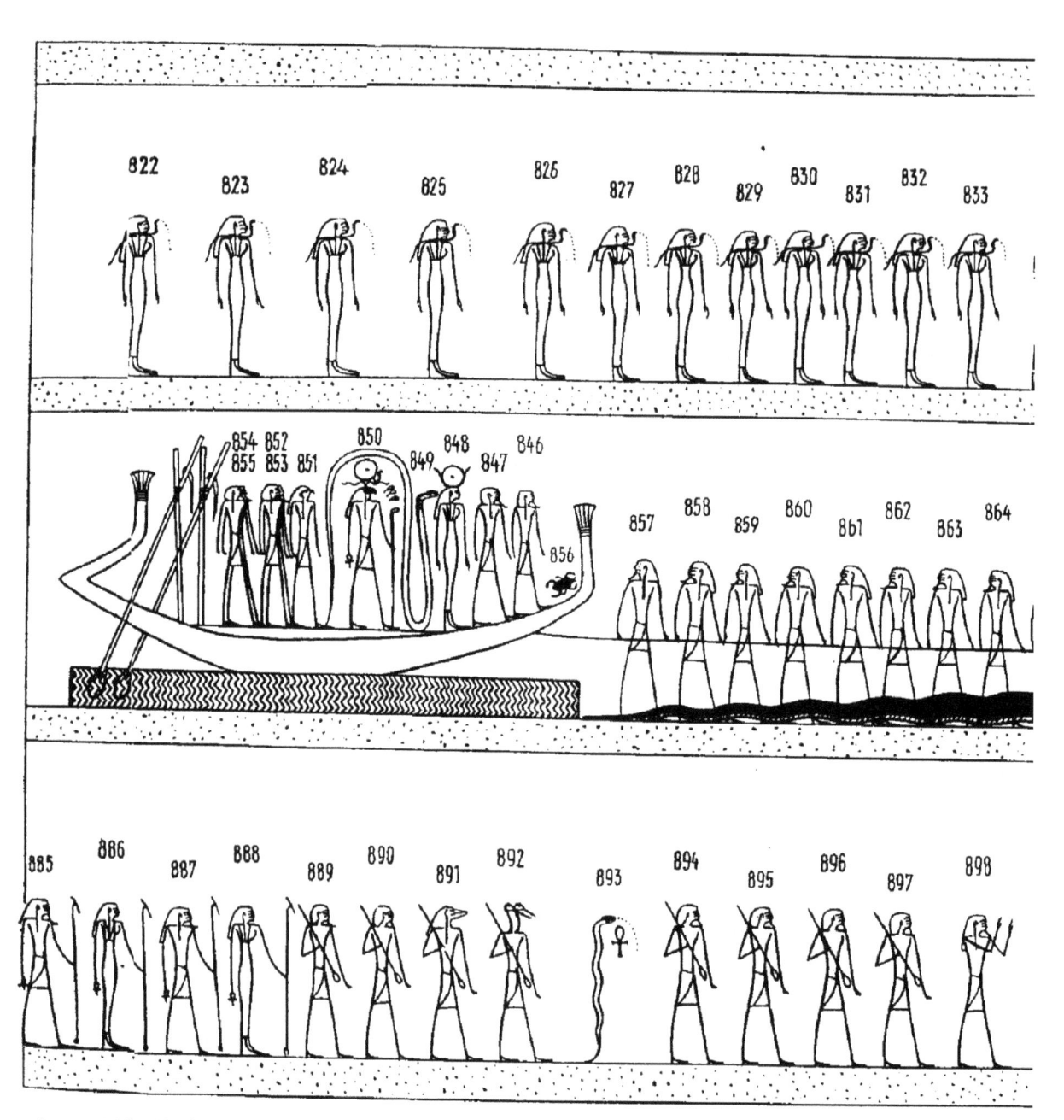

figure 35: The Twelfth Hour

The Gate: "Which raises the Gods"
The Hour Goddess: "Beholding the perfection of Râ"
The Guardian: (no name mentioned)

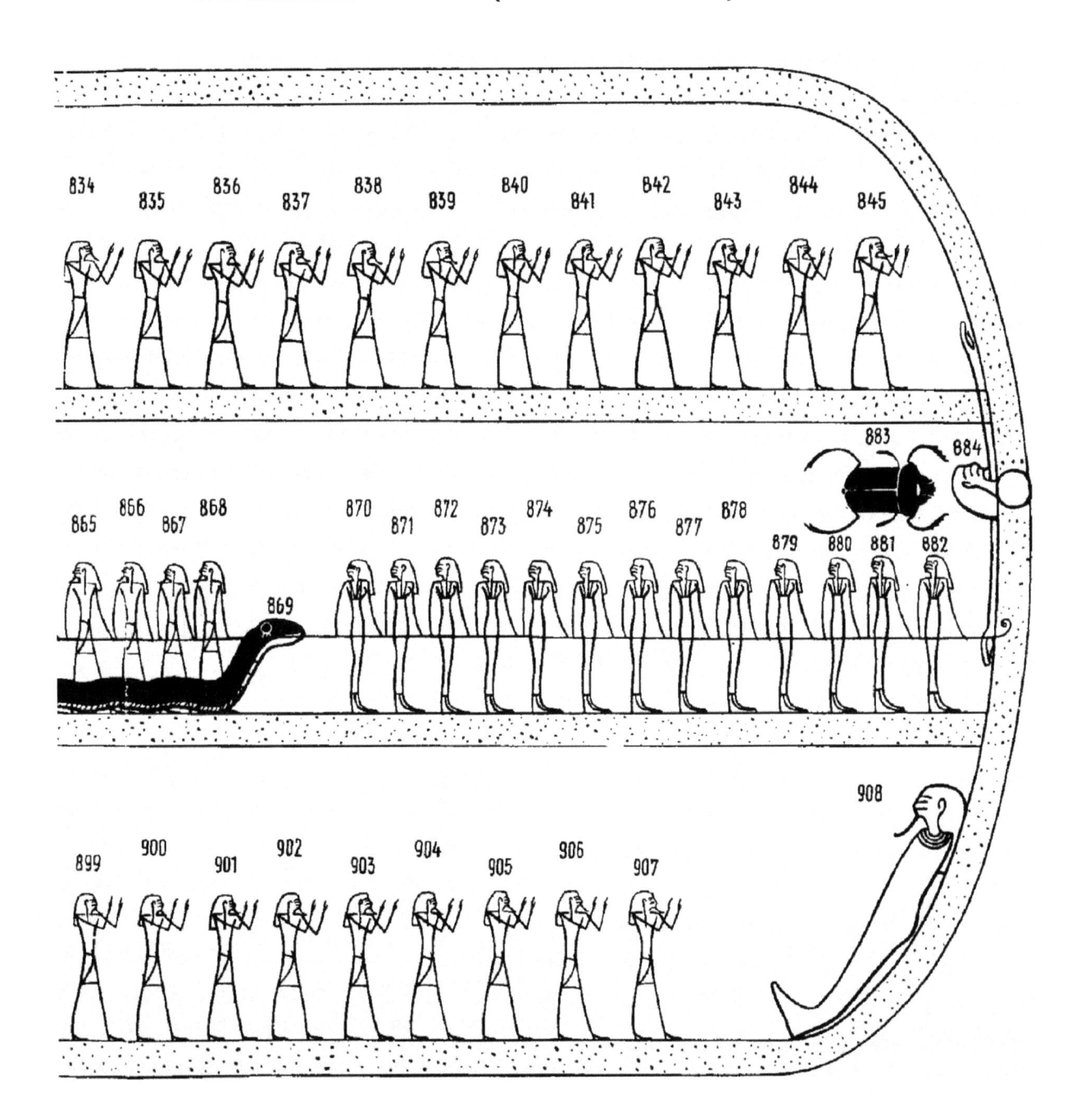

Introduction

Pausing by the person of this Great God
in this cavern of the end
of the Unified Darkness.
This Great God is born in his
manifestations of Khepri at this cavern.
Nun and Nunet, Heh and Hehet,
emerge at this cavern
at the birth of this Great God,
that he goes forth from the Duat,
places himself in the Day barque,
and appears from the thighs of Nut.
The name of the Gate of this place is
"Which raises the Gods".
The name of this Place is
"With emerging darkness
and appearing births".
The name of the Hour of the night
at which this Great God regenerates is,
"Beholding the perfection of Râ".
The mysterious cavern of the Duat
at which this Great God is born,
that he goes forth from the Nun
and sets at the body of Nut.
This is made like this image
which is painted
on the Eastern side of the Hidden Chamber
in the Duat.
It is beneficial for whoever knows it,
on earth, in heaven and in the earth.[1]

The Sungod Râ now enters through the last *seba* gate in this final hour of the nightly journey.

The name of this gate is *Tjenen Netjeru (tnn ntr.w)*, meaning "Which raises the Gods". The verb *tjeni (tni)*, which means "raises", can also be translated as "lift up, promote or distinguish". This is the hour of Truth wherein both Râ and Osiris will rise up. After the long night of being together, they both go their separate ways. The Sungod is now going to make the transition from the Night Sun barque, *Mesketet*, to his Day Sun barque, *Mândjet*, into the world of the living. That is the moment where his shining light pierces through the darkness. Consequently, it is high time to announce the birth of Khepri. All of the Gods in this hour are extending a helping hand to assist during the impending birth. None of the Duatians are standing in a half upraised position anymore. Instead, every Deity is standing tall and up straight to support this upraising process in their own specific way.

The Hour Goddess, "Beholding the perfection of Râ", personally assists during the birthing process. In this hour, she is depicted in the row of towing Goddesses at the final part of the Sacred River. Here, she herself has taken the towrope of the Sun barque into her hands. Together with twelve other Goddesses, she pulls Râ through the birthing canal. Râ no longer has the need to hide in the dark protective womb of Nut nor within the safe coils of Mehen. Now, he may step forward and be gazed upon in all his shining beauty. The final *ârryt* gateway shall open at the Eastern horizon to allow for the miracle, which comes forth from the Secret Mystery, to manifest. Each and everyone who takes part in this miracle will emerge renewed and reborn with Râ.

The Duatians on the left riverbank (upper section)

The first half of the left riverbank consists of a procession of twelve Goddesses. They all wear a fire spitting Uraeus-serpent around their necks that is resting upon their shoulders.

(No. 822) "She who appears in beauty"
(No. 823) "She who prepares the way for Râ"
(No. 824) "Lady of the earth-powers"
(No. 825) "Mistress of cobras"
(No. 826) "She who makes the two banks of the sky prosper"
(No. 827) "She who rejoices in her two lands"
(No. 828) "She who is elevated in her forms"
(No. 829) "She who is powerful of her *Akh*-spirits"
(No. 830) "She who acclaims Râ in his forms"
(No. 831) "She who beholds the corpse when his barque stops"
(No. 832) "She who came forth from the front of Râ"
(No. 833) "Lady of the Uraeus-serpents in the barque of millions"

The Uraeus-Goddesses belong to those who follow the Sungod and their presence here is needed to protect him. Even now Râ is still at risk of being attacked by his biggest enemy, Apophis. This evil serpent has restored himself after the various attacks in the previous hours. Again, he makes a desperate attempt at stopping Râ. However, unlike the Seventh Hour, Apophis is not physically depicted in the present hour. This is done on purpose for the upcoming light is so beautiful that the image should not be tainted by the presence of this monster. Despite the fact that he still poses a threat, the artists who gave shape to the Amduat have deliberately refrained from portraying him. After all, depicting something is one of the steps in magically manifesting it and they did not dare to tempt fate.

The Goddesses are standing here as warriors on the Eastern horizon. They aim the flames that are coming from the mouths of their Uraeus-serpents at Apophis. In doing so they ward off Apophis's attack and ensure the Sungod has a safe passage to his Day Sun barque. No matter how tedious it might be that Apophis appears to be indestructible, he actually plays an essential part once again. His attack is necessary for Râ to raise his resilience and the will to fight. The resistance against Apophis sets the birthing process in motion and promotes the inevitable process of detachment.

Aside from their very important task, the Uraeus-Goddesses also have another responsibility. The flames from the mouths of the Uraeus-serpents are bright enough to function like torches. This breaches the darkness and grants enlightenment. The deceased, who live here in the darkness, are now feeling relieved and released.

> What they have to do in the earth is
> to give release (*sefekh*)
> to those in the darkness
> with the torches of their Uraeus-serpents,
> when they return,
> after they have escorted Râ,
> and after having punished Apophis
> for him in the sky.[2]

The hieroglyphic word *sefekh* (*sfḫ*) means "release", but can also be translated as "lose, remove, let go or lay aside (garment)". Thus, the deceased are released from their restrictive mummy wrappings and able to move and breathe again. Due to the Uraeus-Goddessess, they are permitted to share in the process of the enlightenment of the Sungod.

However, not only the "blessed dead" are grateful for the Uraeus-Goddesses with all their hearts. The hearts of the Gods of the West are filled with delight as well, for these Goddesses enable the light of the Sungod to triumph over the darkness. Then, as Râ emerges from the horizon, not only has he transformed in his new form as Khepri, but he also receives the new name Râ-Horakhty (*ḥrw-ȝḫty*) "Horus of the two horizons".

> He who turns his face to the West of Heaven. How beautiful is Amon-Râ!
> Thou risest anew being young.
> Apophis has fallen, thy knife is in him.
> The hot breath of the Uraeus-Goddess has taken hold of his flesh.
> Râ-Horus (Râ-Horakhty)
> of the Horizon rises!
> This thy barque sails with a good wind,
> the hearts of thy crew are glad (?).[3]
> – Papyrus of Djed-Khonsu-Ius-Ankh

Râ-Horakhty is usually depicted as a hawk-headed man wearing the solar disk surmounted

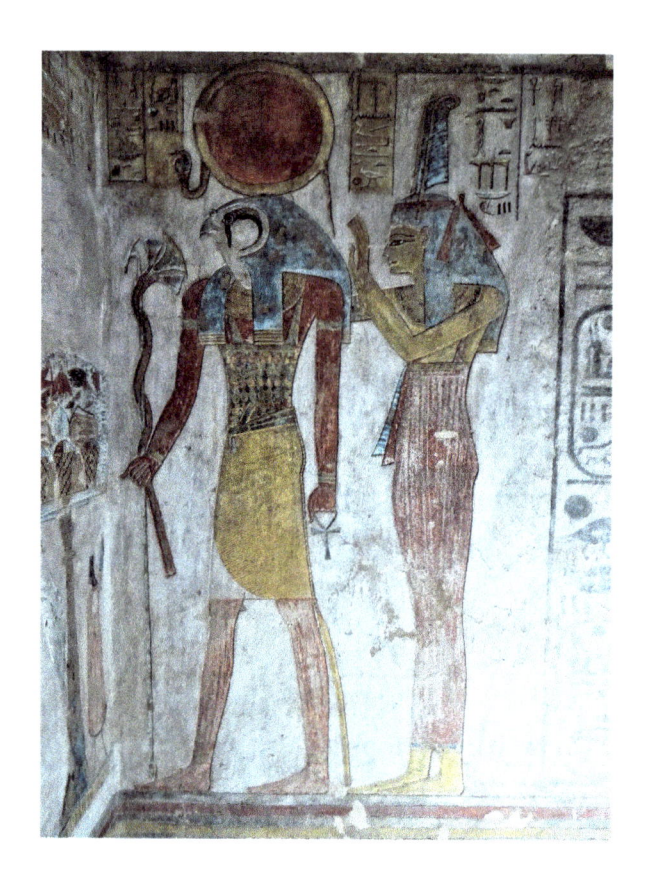

The God Râ-Horakhty supported by the Goddess Maât, KV 14 Tausert/Setnakht

with the Uraeus-serpent. In this form, the Sungod makes his daily journey in the Day Sun barque from the horizon of sunrise to the horizon of sunset.

Technically, Râ-Horakhty is the merged God form of both the Sungod Râ and the God Horus. When death is prevailed in the night, Horus ascends, just like Râ, and takes over the crook and flail of his father Osiris. Therefore, Râ-Horakhty symbolises the Divine lordship that is fully charged with power and might. The presently reigning Pharaoh also takes part in this powerful moment since his own rulership is revitalised as well. This fact does not only apply to the current Pharaoh, but to every deceased Pharaoh who once reigned over Egypt before him as well.

> O King,
> free course is given to you by Horus,
> you flash as the Lone Star
> in the midst of the sky;
> you have grown wings
> as a great-breasted falcon,
> as a hawk seen in the evening
> traversing the sky.
> May you cross the firmament
> by the waterway of Râ-Horakhty,
> may Nut put her hands on you.[4]
> – Pyramid Texts; Utterance 488

The job of the twelve cobra Goddesses is done the moment Râ has crossed the "secret sandbank" and reached the eastern gateway of the horizon. They then resume their positions on their thrones and wait for Râ's return during the next night for he then once again requires their protection.

Following them, there is another procession of twelve Gods who are standing with their hands upraised in a posture of adoration. Their names indicate that they are the embodiment of joyful and happy adoration.

(No. 834) "Lord of Life"
(No. 835) "He who acclaims"
(No. 836) "Lord of Jubilation"
(No. 837) "Lord of Worshippings"
(No. 838) "He with pleasant heart"
(No. 839) "He who rejoices because of Râ"
(No. 840) "He with joyful heart"
(No. 841) "The Child"
(No. 842) "He who praises the East (eye)"
(No. 843) "He who renews the Heads of the Gods"
(No. 844) "He who restores the Heads of the Gods"
(No. 845) "He who praises Khepri"

As the moment of daybreak is drawing near, the worshipping Gods are here to honour Râ. Birth is a very intense process and the Sungod can use all the upraising and supporting powers he can get. Using a jubilant hymn, these Gods praise the Sungod and encourage him at the top of their lungs during his battle to come into being.

> They say to Râ:
> Born is he, who is born,
> who has emerged, has emerged!

Venerated of the earth,
Ba-soul of the Lord of heaven,
the sky belongs to your *Ba*-soul,
that it may rest in it,
the earth belongs to your corpse,
Lord of veneration!
You have seized the horizon,
that you may rest in your shrine,
the two Goddesses raise you
with their body!
Acclamation to you,
Ba-soul which is in heaven!
Your two daughters receive you
in your form. [5]

They show Râ loud and clear that his place is in the sky of the day world as the Lord of heaven. However, his corpse, which is Osiris, belongs in the nightly world within the depth of the earth. Thus, Osiris remains in the Duat while Râ is enthusiastically encouraged by these Gods to take his rightful place in the shrine on the Day Sun barque where he can settle down.

The worshipping Gods are standing here upfront at the gate of the Eastern horizon at the end of the Duat. The heavens are about to be opened and the first colours have returned to the world in the beginning light. The night sky begins to slowly transform into the heavenly blue of the day sky. As the darkness is no longer impenetrable, these Gods are the first to catch the light, which shows they have a turquoise appearance. They hold the Divine title of the "Turquoise Ones" *mefkatyu* (*mfk3tyw*) and associated with rebirth and resurrection. The word *mefkatyu* also means the friendly Gods. They are here to uplift Râ through their acclamations. Although the turquoise Gods are here in human form, they are sometimes depicted as baboons.

The turquoise Gods are not the only ones to confirm that Râ is now truly on the verge of emerging. The presence of the important Sun-folk *henemmet* (*ḥnmmt*) is also an indication of this event. This folk of the Sun consists of a group of beings who are all connected to the Sungod. The Coffin Texts frequently mention them where they are associated with "the Justified". In these texts, they pay homage to all of the deceased who have risen from the dead. These deceased are part of "the Venerated Ones" since their hearts are in balance with the feather of Truth. The Sun-folk welcome these possessors of the True Heart where they worship them and bow before them. Every single time a deceased matches up with the dark enemy that is death, the Sun-folk are filled with joy. No matter how often it happens, every single time it remains a remarkable event when the light, and thus the Divine Law of *Maât*, prevails.

Ho N! I have set your striking power
into the disaffected
and those who are on earth
come to you bowing
as to […] and the Sun-folk [who give] you
worship as to one vindicated;
they see you when you go down
among the spirits,

for you are equipped as the God himself.[6]
– Coffin Texts; Spell 694

Thus, the Sun-folk dedicate themselves to the upraising of the light, which simultaneously makes them the servants of Shu. This is not surprising since Shu is the one who helps lift the solar disk up in the sky. The moment Shu makes his appearance before the Sun-folk, as happens here, the heavens open up and the light appears. The Sun-folk are all present here to share in this joyful moment and to pay their respects to the upraising light, that is their beloved Sungod.

The Duatians of the Sacred River (middle section)

The Sungod Râ is surrounded by his entire crew. His crew has a special position here as they experience the birthing process together with the Sungod. They will emerge rejuvenated and renewed just like Râ at the end of this hour.

(No. 846) "Wepwawet"
(No. 847) "Sia"
(No. 848) "Nebet wia"
(No. 849) "Mehen"
(No. 850) "Iuf"
(No. 851) "Heru Hekenu"
(No. 852) "Ka Maât"
(No. 853) "Nehes"
(No. 854) "Hu"
(No. 855) "Kherep wia"

The crew in this hour has an extra member for the scarab "Khepri" (No. 856) is sitting upfront on the Sun barque. During the previous hour, Râ was guided by the female solar disk, "Shining One of the Duat" (No. 785) that lay on top of the prow of the barque. In the present hour, this has changed. Râ has undergone several transformations, which gave him the power to finally convey his own shining light. This is the ultimate purpose of Râ's voyage. Consequently, "Shining One of the Duat" has been replaced by the scarab that lies in front of Râ as the focal point. Khepri is also known as the "Shining One".

The Sungod is now completely restored and wears the Uraeus-serpent on his solar disk as the sign of his power and might. He is now prepared to fully assume his lordship and to take his rightful place in the day sky after the twelve hours of the dark night. This remains a very special and solemn event despite the fact that it repeats itself every single night. Hence, Râ is silent and completely focussed and does not give out orders to anyone within this hour. The process of being born is a very delicate situation where life struggles to emerge. There will always be the danger of the situation where the vulnerable new life is not viable at the last moment and dies.

Even though Râ is already wearing the Uraeus-serpent on his solar disk, he will not be able to embody his ultimate power before he has left the Twelfth Hour. Only after leaving will he be truly reborn. Furthermore, the Sun barque is once again unable to sail since there is no water.

This is also a sign of the impending birth since the waters of the Goddess Nut have now broken. All of the water, or amniotic fluid, has drained away which is why the Sun barque needs to be towed during this final part. A rope has been attached to the Sun barque and two groups of Deities, twelve Gods (No. 857 – 868) and thirteen Goddesses (No. 870 – 882) have gripped this rope firmly in their hands. With unified forces, they help the solar God emerge from the dark Duat. The length of the rope and the considerable number of towing Deities indicates that the birth of the newborn sun does not come easy.

Due to the absence of the water, a sandbank has emerged directly in front of the Sun barque in the form of an enormous serpent. His name is "Life of the Gods" (No. 869), also known as "The *Ka*-energy of him who makes the Gods live". As opposed to the Seventh Hour, where a sandbank in the form of the evil serpent Apophis blocked the Sun barque, this time the serpent in question is a beneficial one. This is made apparent by the body of "Life of the Gods" that is lying in the right direction with his head pointed towards the Eastern horizon. Contrary to Apophis, who lay with his head and body against the shipping route during the Seventh Hour. Moreover, "Life of the Gods" is a truly enormous serpent with a length of 1300 cubits, whereas Apophis was only 440 cubits long. This emphasises the power of "Life of the Gods" that is also far greater than the destructive powers of Apophis.

The length of "Life of the Gods" is measured with the sacred measurement unit, the cubit. This indicates that Thoth as the "Lord of measurement" used his forearm, which has the exact length of the royal cubit, to measure this sacred creature. Therefore, this serpent was created from the perfect basic measurement that is in accordance with the sacred creation and, thus, the Divine Law of *Maât*. His length needs to be accurate within a millimetre since his body functions as the birth canal for the Sungod. It should not be too long nor too short. It has to be perfect to be able to realise the trans-figuration. As mentioned before in the Sixth Hour, the meaning of the hieroglyphic word cubit, *meh (mh)*, is "make whole, complete or finish". Within the perfectly measured body of 1300 cubits in length of "Life of the Gods", the process of Râ to become whole is completed.

Interestingly, the body of the serpent Apophis is measured with the sacred cubits as well. This should come as no surprise since Apophis is a sacred being similar to "Life of the Gods". He too was created from the perfect basic measurement in accordance with the Divine Law of *Maât*. The destruction, as embodied by Apophis, is just as important for creation as are the life-giving qualities of "Life of the Gods". Together they provide for duality that is required for the renewal of life.

Every night "Life of the Gods" is right here where he loyally awaits Râ's return. He never leaves his place for he knows his body serves as the gate towards redemption from the Duat. Thus, the Sungod cannot go around him. Râ actually needs to pass right through him, through his spinal cord. Râ is most certainly aware of this fact and breaks his concentrated silence to address the serpent. Instead of calling the serpent by his usual name, "Life of the Gods", Râ calls him "Smooth". With this specific name Râ tries to warrant that his journey through the serpent's body will be fluent and smooth. Therefore, at the same time his words are an order for the serpent since this serpent is the one responsible for the birth canal.

Râ needs to travel through the backbone of the serpent. The reason for this is because the serpent is the symbol of the process of transformation and renewal. Secondly because the backbone is the representation of the fundamental support of a body. It is the symbol of the *Djed* that represents stability, power, confidence and steadfastness. The Sungod has to connect with all of these powers on his way through.

The function of the serpent "Life of the Gods" is reflected in his other name "The *Ka*-energy of him who makes the Gods live", which is similar to the role of the serpent God Neheb Kau. Thus, "Life of the Gods" is probably another form of Neheb Kau. As mentioned in the Fourth Hour, Neheb Kau embodies the *Ka* to which every God is connected. He is the bearer of the Vital Life Force and every God is able to live thanks to him. "Life of the Gods", like Neheb Kau, transmits his *Ka*-force to the Sungod the moment Râ connects himself with the body of this serpent. Furthermore, "Life of the Gods" can also be regarded as the serpent Mehen. Râ has outgrown the "skin" of Mehen, which is now actually restricting him in his development. Therefore, Mehen's flexible form, has changed from the protective coils, as shown in the Eleventh Hour, into the horizontal canal of "Life of the Gods" to allow Râ to smoothly come into being.

Contrary to many other Deities in the Duat, "Life of the Gods" does not live off the voice of Râ. Instead, he is nourished by the sounds of the Venerated Ones of Râ (No. 857 – 867) who are all travelling through his spine. Like Râ, they go through the birth canal to be renewed. A birth is an intensive process during which the one being born needs to work hard to emerge. Hence, the "Venerated Ones" produce loud battle shouts during their struggle to move forward. This is not an easy task for the "forward" movement actually proceeds in a reversed order. They enter via the tail of "Life of the Gods" and exit through his mouth. This allows old age to be reversed and to transform in rejuvenation. It is a miraculous process and the secret to realising this remains hidden within the mysterious body of "Life of the Gods". Therefore, he is also known as "secret sandbank".

The reversal of old age into total renewal is reflected in the names of the towing Gods and Goddesses before the Sun barque as well. They have all turned their heads in the opposite direction where they gaze at the Sungod.

The twelve Gods directly in front of the Sun barque are still within the body of "Life of the

Gods" and demonstrate the aging process that has yet to be transformed.

(No. 857) "The Old One"
(No. 858) "The Elder"
(No. 859) "Who is weak from age"
(No. 860) "The Wise"
(No. 861) "Who enters his life"
(No. 862) "Who has passed his years"
(No. 863) "He with immense time"
(No. 864) "The Venerable"
(No. 865) "Lord of the Venerated state"
(No. 866) "The Grey-haired"
(No. 867) "He who belongs to the grey hairs"
(No. 868) "The Living One"

Night after night they enter the spinal cord of "Life of the Gods", like the Sungod, to emerge reborn at the end. After this birthing process they are part of the blessed dead and receive the honorary title of "The Venerated Ones of Râ", *imakhyu ni Râ* (*im3ḫy.w ni rʿ*). Not only are they now worshipped by the ones living on earth, but by the Gods themselves as well. The hieroglyphic word *imakh* (*im3ḫ*) can be translated as "honour, veneration or the blessed state of the dead", but also as "spinal cord". This is why the honorary title of these blessed dead is written with the hieroglyphic sign for the backbone. Hence, it may be clear that every deceased, who undergoes the birthing process, needs to go through the backbone of "Life of the Gods", to be a part of the group of Venerable Ones.

Fig. 36. The honorary title of the blessed dead, "The Venerated or Revered One".

The twelve Gods emerge directly after the birth of Râ and follow him into the sky. However, instead of being filled with joy after the birth, they scream in horror. They have to leave their old appearances behind if they wish to follow the Sungod into the Eastern sky. Like Râ in his form as Khepri, they are cast out of the Duat once the birthing process is complete. As terrible as this is, they do understand they cannot stay behind. They have to resume their journey in the sky. Therefore, they loudly exclaim the name of the Great God. However, what is the name they call when they ascend into the day sky? Is it the name of Râ with the underlying desire to return to the old familiar? Or is it the name of Khepri who serves as the renewed shining role model? After all, the utterance of the Divine name acts like a magical word of power that precedes the manifestation of their own enlightened state of being. Hence, the name being uttered is a choice, a choice between life and death.

At the end of the Sacred River are thirteen Goddesses standing with the end of the rope in their hands. Among them is the Hour Goddess "She who beholds the perfection of Râ"

(No. 870) "She who tows"
(No. 871) "She who beholds the perfection of Râ"

(No. 872) "She who beholds Khepri"
(No. 873) "She who beholds the corpse of her Lord"
(No. 874) "Lady of the Rejuvenated"
(No. 875) "Lady of Eternity"
(No. 876) "The Eternal"
(No. 877) "She with living shoulder"
(No. 878) "She who speaks upon the barque"
(No. 879) "She who jubilates in her horizon"
(No. 880) "She who rests in her horizon"
(No. 881) "She who brings her God"
(No. 882) "She who protects the East"

The towing Goddesses have already completed the journey of rejuvenation through the spine of "Life of the Gods" before. Even before Râ himself. Each of them now embodies the renewed life, the eternal perfection as symbolised by "Khepri" (No. 883). Due to their experience, they are eminently suited to support and guide Râ during this powerful but also fearsome moment. This is the moment what it is all about. The moment the Sungod has worked hard for to reach during every hour of his journey. Now, finally, the perfect time has arrived. He has to let go of his old and trusted form as Râ before he can transform into the newborn sun. No matter how much Râ has anticipated and focused on this moment of enlightenment, though the moment of the event has arrived, he still needs to gather his strength and courage. The Goddesses have complete faith in him and show him that renewal is an absolute blessing. It is, after all, the joyful and triumphant reversal of death into eternal Life. To realise this, Râ has to travel through the narrow body of "Life of the Gods", whether he likes it or not. Râ resigns himself to this fact for he knows "Life of the Gods" is not the only one responsible for a successful birth. The serpent is merely providing for the perfect circumstances since it is up to Râ himself whether he submits himself to it and be pulled along smoothly.

Now that Râ is ready, all thirteen Goddesses grab the rope and pull Râ through the body of "Life of the Gods" from tail to mouth. The Sungod is now inside the birth canal where he is "embraced" by the *Ka*-force of this benevolent serpent. Gradually and smoothly, he is pulled through the spinal cord and the further he gets, the more stable, powerful and steadfast he becomes. The Sungod experiences an amazing transformation that initiates him in the secrets of creation. His light is beginning to get a whole new shine to it and he is conscious of the fact that he is no longer the same. Slowly but surely Râ transforms into Khepri, the "Shining One", or the *Akh*.

Then the Goddesses know the right time has arrived to pull the Sungod through the mouth of "Life of the Gods" and out of the body of Nut through the *ârryt* gate. A beautiful shining light then appears at the dawn of a new creation. The Uraeus-serpent is on the brow of Khepri as a sign of his Divine rulership. The Goddesses are filled with great happiness and triumph and utter loud shouts of great joy. What a beautiful and shining perfectibility!

Simultaneously the God of the sky Shu, "Image of Shu" (No. 884), makes his appearance. He is the Lord of the horizon for he separates the sky from the earth with both hands. The space he creates in between gives access to the West, the realm of the Dead, and the East, the realm of the living. Shu guards both doors, together with his twin sister and consort Tefnut, as "the Double lion". His presence here is needed to open the door to the East. With both of his hands, he creates an opening between the earth and the sky that allows room for Khepri. For just a brief moment the hidden world of the Duat is unsealed. Then Shu "The Great" lifts the newborn sun up in the sky at the Eastern horizon. After the restrictive journey through the narrow body of "Life of the Gods", the Sungod is finally given room again. He is able to breathe and fills his lungs with the life-giving air gifted to him by Shu.

> Open, O sky and earth; open,
> O Western and Eastern horizons;
> Open, you chapels of Upper
> and Lower Egypt;
> Open, you doors; open,
> you Eastern gates of Râ,
> that he may issue from the horizon.
> Open to him,
> you double doors of the Night barque;
> Open to him, you gates of the Day barque,
> that he may kiss Shu,
> that he may create Tefnut.
> Those who are in the Suite will serve him,
> and they will serve me like Râ daily.[7]
> – Coffin Texts; Spell 1065

Subsequently, the thirteen Goddesses show Khepri the way to heaven. Here he is welcomed with open arms by his two daughters, the Maât Goddesses. They too are not depicted here, but they are most definitely present to support the rising light. During the first hour of the night, at the entrance of the Duat, they were already present as they welcomed Râ inside the Duat. Presently, at the exit of the Duat, they are present once more at the beginning of the first hour of the new day. With their presence and as guardians of Order, Truth and Justice, they warrant day and night that the Divine Law is abided by.

In all his shining glory, Khepri now takes his place in the Day Sun barque and begins the next cycle of life, death and rebirth. The day world embraces his life-giving light with great joy. Birds start to whistle and baboons begin to shout and dance. The people wake up fresh and reborn after a night of sleep to start moving again. All of life awakens at this breathtaking morning light. The grey world regains its colours and the turquoise sky is tinted in various shades of red. The red is the result of the blood loss of Nut after the birth of Râ and the blood of the defeated Apophis.

> Raise yourself, Râ; raise yourself,
> you who are in your shrine;
> May you snuff the air,
> swallow the backbones,
> spit out the day, and kiss Maât;

may the Suite go about,
may your barque travel to Nut,
may the Great Ones quake at your voice,
may you count your bones
and gather your members together,
may you turn your face to the beautiful
West and return anew every day,
because you are indeed that
fair image of gold
under the branches of the *itnws*-tree;
sky and earth fall to you,
being possessed with trembling at your travelling around anew every day.
The horizon is joyful and acclamation
is at your tow-rope.[8]

– Coffin Texts; Spell 1029

Aside from the towing of Râ, the thirteen sky Goddesses also have another task. Not only do they ensure the shining sun rises in the sky of the Eastern horizon every day at the right time, they also fill the sky with various weather conditions like wind, calmness, storm and rain. In doing so, Khepri is subjected to numerous confrontations during his journey through the

A pair of arms and a head, probably Shu, emerge from the depths and assume the Ka-posture. On the palms of his hands there are two worshipping Goddesses called "West" and "East". On top of his head stands the Goddess "Annihilator" with her arms stretched out in the Ka-posture to embrace the Sungod. KV 9 Ramses VI, Book of the Earth on the Eastern wall.

twelve hours of the day. These counteracting weather conditions result in him slowly but surely losing his life force and power to shine. As strange as it may sound, this is of vital importance. No matter how perfect Khepri may seem, he too is subjected to the earthly laws and is required to transform. Therefore, he ages during the day, which gives him grounds to return to the Duat at the end of the day. Then he submerges himself once again in the life-giving waters of Nun, in his form as the dying Râ, to start a new and essential cycle of life. This demonstrates that perfection is an illusion on earth. There is only the necessary aim to reach for perfection that keeps evolution in motion.

The Duatians on the right riverbank (lower section)

At the beginning of the right riverbank there are four primeval Deities in human form. Each one of them is holding an *Ankh* in their right hand and a *Was*-sceptre in their left hand.

(No. 885) "Nun"
(No. 886) "Nunet"
(No. 887) "Heh"
(No. 888) "Hehet"

They are part of the Ogdoad of Hermopolis. These primeval Deities, known as the Heh or chaos Gods, precede the creation of the world. One of their tasks is to help the God Shu to lift up the heavenly body of the Goddess Nut during twilight in the early morning. Sometimes the Heh Gods appear in baboon form to welcome and greet the new born Sungod.

The complete Ogdoad is comprised of eight primeval Deities who are referred to as "the Company of Eight". The God Thoth is regarded as the leader of this group. The main cult centre of Thoth was Khemenyu (*ḥmnyw*), "City of Eight", which was later known as Hermopolis Magna. Some of the priesthoods referred to the Ogdoad as the "Souls of Thoth". Thoth, as a self created God, gave birth to every God and man. Hence, he seems to embody the spirit and soul of the primordial waters of the pre-creation that those eight Gods are a part of.[9]

The Deities of the Ogdoad are divided in four pairs. Each of these pairs is comprised of a frog-headed God and a snake-headed Goddess. Although these pairs contain two different genders, they are not simply regarded as female and male Deities. The different genders had not yet taken shape in this state of pre-creation. Therefore, the feminine and masculine forms of the Deities depicted here are simply intended to indicate duality, which is needed to continue creation.

Furthermore, it is no coincidence it are the frog and the snake that give shape to the Ogdoad. The frog is the symbol of fertility and the snake of regeneration. Additionally, both creatures are viewed as a primitive manifestation. They have lived on earth for millions of years in these respective forms and are the embodiment of primordial life forms. Moreover, they are able to live on land as well as in water. Thus, they symbolise the emergence from the primeval waters and the transition from non-existence to becoming manifested in the material world. The Ogdoad is like the inspiration stream that moves in the non-existence, beyond the manifested world. As such, this primordial forcefield of the Ogdoad is needed to express the physical world. It is the link between the non-existence and the existence.

The four pairs of the Ogdoad each represent a specific principle of the pre-creation that is the primeval waters or the abyss. The first pair is the God Nun (*nw*) and his female counterpart Nunet (*nw.t*). They represent the watery Chaos or the Great Deep itself. The God Nun is the personification of the primordial waters and was described as the "Father of the Gods". Nunet is the representation of the heavenly waters that are reflected in the water on earth, the Nile. She is also regarded as the very first sky Goddess who preceded the Goddess Nut.

The second pair is the God Heh (*ḥḥ*) and his female counterpart Hehet (*ḥḥ.t*). The hieroglyphic word *heh* (*ḥḥ*) means "millions or a great number". Hence, this pair symbolises the primeval principal of eternal infinity "millions of millions of years".

The third pair is the God Kek (*kkw*) and his female counterpart Keket (*kkw.t*). Originally, this pair was represented by the God Gereh (*grḥ*) and his female counterpart Gerehet (*grḥ.t*). The hieroglyphic word *Keku* means "darkness" and *Gereh* means "night or eternal night (of the Netherworld)". Both pairs represent the principle of the primordial darkness of pre-creation.

The fourth pair, the God Amun (*imn*) and his female counterpart Amunet (*imn.t*), represents the hidden and the unknowable nature of the pre-creation. They emphasise that the sacred mystery of life is concealed and hidden within the pre-creation and is impossible to comprehend or grasp.

All of these different elemental powers, as symbolised by the four pairs of Deities, form the basic structure upon which the primordial mound is built. The God Atum made this hill and was seen as the original creation himself. After his birth, Atum gave shape to the Deities of the Ennead from this primordial matrix or primal hill. However, the Deities in the Ogdoad are actually the creators of the pre-creation before Atum. Thus, they are technically the "fathers" and the "mothers" of this self-created God. In other words, the beginning of time, or *Zep Tepi*, came into being from the pre-creation by the eight Deities of the Ogdoad.

There are several versions of the Ogdoad. Each version contains variations of the pairs of the Deities wherein they can have different appearances like with jackal or cat heads. In almost every version, the first pair is the God Nun and his female counterpart Nunet. In the Duat this pair is present as well together with the second pair which consists of the God Heh and the Goddesses Hehet. Here they symbolise the two basic principles of the pre-creation; the Great

Deep, or primordial waters, and the everlasting eternity. Following the creation of Atum, the Sungod forms the next layer of the evolution of life and is therefore bound to these basic, or primordial, concepts. Without the Ogdoad Khepri would not be able to be born for he too, like every other life form, is composed of these cosmic basic principles.

Four of the eight Deities of the Ogdoad are standing here to welcome Khepri at the Eastern gate of the horizon. The God Nun is standing at the edge of the abyss with one foot in the Duat and the other in the world of the pre-creation. This is depicted in the image of the Twelfth Hour as well, where he stands at the beginning of the right riverbank. Here the frame is interrupted and he is standing slightly over the edge. Together with the other three Deities he makes a short appearance from behind the veil of non-existence to bind the fundamental principles of the pre-creation to the creation. Furthermore, these four Deities are here to assist the God Shu with upholding of the sky. It goes without saying that the sky is the celestial body of the Goddess Nut. So, now a path is created for Khepri which allows him to rise up in all of his glory. The two pairs of the Ogdoad Deities in human shape; Nun, Nunet, Heh and Hehet, form a reception committee to greet Khepri.

> O Nu in company with the Chaos-Gods
> – and vice versa –
> make for me a way that I may go forth and see men,
> and that the common people may worship me.[10]
> – Coffin Texts; Spell 107

Following the four Deities of the Ogdoad are two groups of four Gods with in between a serpent who is upraised on its tail.

(No. 889) "He who is embellished"
(No. 890) "He with high Authority"
(No. 891) "The Terrible" has the head of a crocodile.
(No. 892) "The Petitioner" has two bird heads.

The God of Eternity "Heh" kneels on the sign for gold and holds a palm branch in both his hands, a symbol of long life, Temple of Hathor, the House of Birth, at Dendera

(No. 893) "He who burns with his Eye" is an upraised fire-spitting serpent.
(No. 894) "Flaming of *Akh*-spirits"
(No. 895) "Foremost of his adoration"
(No. 896) "He with powerful heart"
(No. 897) "He of the Duat"

These Gods are present here to guarantee that the Great Sungod will ascend from the Duat. To do this they use their specific powers, like adoration and authority, as emphasised by their names. To enable the ascension, the Sungod requires a safe environment. Therefore, the eight Gods have unified their powers and joined hands with the twelve Uraeus-Goddesses (No. 822 – 833) who are standing across from them on the opposite riverbank. These Gods and Goddesses each use their own weapons and talents to provide for the best possible protection.

As mentioned before, the twelve Goddesses use the fire from the mouths of the Uraeus-serpents around their necks as a weapon. The Gods, however, use a very different method to fight as they wield the paddles in their hands. With these paddles they ward off Apophis and keep him at a safe distance from the Sun barque. The dangerous Apophis is trying to attack the Sun barque from both sides in his effort to stop the Sungod. Although this may seem very frightening, it is exactly what Râ needs to be stimulated to let go and detach himself from the Duat. Râ is no longer allowed to remain here. The time has come for the Sungod to rise up and to start a new day.

The fact that the fighters aiding Râ here, include both males and females, makes perfect sense. Only through the unification of the opposite forces can the birth be manifested. This is also reflected in the opposite forces of the weapons for there is the fire of the Uraeus-serpents along with the water from the paddles.

In between the two groups of four oarsmen Gods is the serpent "He who burns with his Eye" (No. 893) who is in an upraised position at the tip of his tail. He is spitting his fire in a powerful arch, which makes him a dangerous opponent to the other enemies of Râ, aside from Apophis. No matter how far the Sungod has come, these rebels continue to attempt to prevent the birth of Râ. The serpent "He who burns with his Eye" is here waiting for these enemies, just before sunrise, to boil them with his fire in a most gruesome way. This guarantees the destruction of these final foes as they do not stand a fighting chance. Therefore, this serpent is equally dangerous as is the Uraeus-serpent "The Fiery Eye" that has made an appearance on the brow of Râ.

As we know from one of the myths of the Sungod, "The Fiery Eye" was the eye that Râ ripped out to find his lost children, Shu and Tefnut. When the eye returned, Râ provided it with a new place on his forehead. Here, it transformed in an upraised cobra, the Uraeus-serpent, that spits fire and poison at the enemies of Râ.

Both upraised cobras make short work of anyone who dares to challenge the Divine lordship of Râ. Their goals are similar since they wish to ensure the light of the Sungod, and thus life itself, prevails over darkness at all times. This is pointed out by the sign for eternal Life, the *Ankh* that is visible next to the head of "He who burns with his Eye".

Following the serpent and the eight oarsmen, there is a procession of ten Gods with their hands raised up in a gesture of adoration.

(No. 898) "He who praises the *Akh*-spirits"
(No. 899) "He with brave mouth"
(No. 900) "He who donates"
(No. 901) "He who embraces"
(No. 902) "He who supports"
(No. 903) "He who makes music"
(No. 904) "He with shining arm"
(No. 905) "He with efficient mouth"
(No. 906) "He who is loaded"
(No. 907) "He who is a *Netjer*"

These adoring Gods are the loyal followers of the God Osiris, "Image of flesh" (No. 908). Each night again they are present here to support Osiris, "Foremost of the Unified Darkness", during his ascension. There is nothing more motivating than magical incantations in the form of beautiful prayers. At the top of their lungs, with their hearts filled with love and their hands upraised in a blessing gesture, they sing to Osiris. With this hymn they praise and honour him to fully awaken the powerful life within his being, the Vital Life Force.

Live, Living one, Foremost of his darkness!
Live, Great one, Foremost of his darkness.
Lord of life, Ruler of the West, Osiris,
Foremost of the Westerners, and live,
Living one, Foremost of the Duat!
The breath of Râ belongs to your nose,
the breathing of Khepri is with you,
so that you live and remain alive!
Hail to Osiris, Lord of life! [11]

Osiris is lying here in front of them as a mummy with his back on the semi circular edge of the Duat. His entire being is nourished by the loving and powerful prayers. The adoring Gods stimulate him to regain his full power and to embrace his Great Self. This is also reflected in his enormous stature that is many times greater than that of the other Deities. Now, he has once again truly become the Lord and Master of the Duat and fully embodies his lordship. The ten adoring Gods, in turn, profit from his development as well for their lives are connected to that of Osiris. Not only do they survive through their own prayers, but also through the Breath of Life that they receive through the words of the awakened Osiris.

Together with the twelve worshipping Gods (No. 834 – 845) on the opposite side of the riverbank, these Gods form a worshipping homage. In doing so, the worshipping twelve Gods, at the left riverbank, assist with the ascension of the Sungod, while the ten adoring Gods on the right riverbank assist with the renewal of Osiris. When both of the processions of these Gods begin their adoration, it simultaneously marks the final phase of the process of rejuvenation for both Râ and Osiris. These two are bound together as each other's body and soul. Râ needs Osiris just as much as Osiris needs Râ. Since Osiris is a passive God and unable to travel himself, Râ, as "the Traveller" and "the Wanderer", makes the journey for him as well. When the Sungod travels through the backbone of "Life of the Gods", Osiris travels with him. In addition, Osiris connects himself through the Sungod with the stabilising powers of the spinal cord that enables him to become completely renewed.

With his vibrant and enormous stature, Osiris supports the arms of Shu from the depths of the Duat when the latter begins to open the horizon. When that happens, for a moment a ray of light shines through the gate and illuminates Osiris's body. This enlightens his entire being and fills him with power and dynamics. His Vital Life Force, that carries the potential of every life within, is ensouled and completely restored. Osiris straightens his back and gives Khepri, the "Shining One", via Shu, a final push to support him to disappear through the final *ârryt* gateway into the outside world.

During this particular moment of enlightenment, Osiris too is granted more room to take a deep breath and fill himself with the breath gifted to him by Khepri. To allow this to happen, Shu pauses for a brief moment before he seals the exit of the Duat. At the same time the fresh air of Shu flows inside and provides Osiris with double nourishment together with the breath of Khepri. Aside from his cooperation with Râ, Osiris also has a reciprocal interaction with Shu where they support each other.

> […] I am he (Shu) who provides provisions, who makes fresh the sustenance of Osiris […] [12]
> – Coffin Texts; Spell 75

Then comes the moment where Shu closes the horizon to re-establish the division between the Duat and the sky of the Eastern horizon. This severs the unity between the Sungod and Osiris after twelve hours. Khepri rises above the horizon in all his perfection where he brings the day world with all its colours back to life. Osiris resumes his rightful place with the crook and the flail in his hands. From within his kingdom he gifts the Vital Life Force to enable the transformation of death into new life. Like a great flood, the germinating power flows out of him into the deep earth to make it fertile. Horus confirms the triumph of life when he ascends the throne of his father in earthly life. Then the eternal indestructible life prevails over chaos and non-existence in the world of the living as well as in the Duat. Therefore, it seems clear there is no such thing as true death. Death is simply a state of transformation where life passes into a new form.

Despite the joy and celebration, there is also another side to this special moment. As the Sungod ascends, Osiris is left behind in the dark world of the Duat. Râ, who is also Osiris's soul, leaves him. This is a painful process of detachment. It is heartbreaking and results in quite some grief. However, this is simply the duality, for here too joy and sadness go together. These are the two sides that lie at the heart of the process of rebirth.

The opposing themes of both harmony and imbalance are reflected in the division of the Twelfth Hour. On the left riverbank there are a total of 24 Deities. On the right riverbank there also are 24 Deities including Osiris. These two sides are, therefore, well-balanced and give of a vibe of order that results in them being reliable supports to the process of birth that takes place in between them.

However, the Sacred River itself consists of a procession of twelve Gods and thirteen Goddesses, which totals up to 25 Deities. Hence, the odd number of thirteen towing Goddesses clearly disrupts the harmony within this hour. Though, harmony is beautiful and the ultimate goal, it stops the development, growth and renewal of life. In fact, the imbalance created by the Goddesses is on purpose to trigger the evolution of life. Life itself will always do everything within its power to create a form of equilibrium to protect the life forms. Thus, it is the task of the thirteen Goddesses to stimulate creation and to set the next cycle of life, death and rebirth into motion.

The manifestation of the Twelfth Hour in daily life

The Guardian of the previous hour, "He above his kettles", has opened the final *seba* gate, "Which raises the Gods", for you. You have now gained access to the Twelfth Hour where you are given the chance to realise the final step in your transformation. You are god-like and the perfect moment has arrived for you to truly embody your divinity. Do you have the courage to raise and embody your renewed divine self? Are you

The Pharaoh has just been reborn. This is reflected by his posture where he slightly leans back with his arms upraised. The scarab above his head confirms the resurrection has been completed. KV 6 Ramses IX

subsequently ready to convey the light that is shining through you to the outside world? This final transition you are about to experience determines the amount of light you are capable of carrying after this journey.

The tension is starting to rise now that you have worked hard through all the previous hours to get here. The final distance seems very small since you can already see the *ârryt* gate that marks the exit of the Duat in front of you. This means you have once again arrived in a transitional area just like in the First Hour. However, this time it is a twilight zone that works in a reversed order. Here the dark night is breached by the first light of day. Only the travellers who have ventured through the Duat have access here, in contrast to the open area of the First Hour. In the First Hour anyone may entre as long as they turn their perspective around. Therefore, the Twelfth Hour is a mysterious and forbidden area that lies hidden behind this *ârryt* gate.

Due to the pull towards this redemptive door, it is very tempting to make one last sprint. After an eleven hour journey, you long for the fresh air and enlightenment that lies behind that door. The quicker this thick darkness ends the better. However, despite the magnitude of this temptation, do not give in to it. First, you have to travel through the Twelfth Hour. Especially this final hour needs time and your total and undivided attention. The complete process is necessary to enable the birth of a healthy and renewed self. An unnatural premature birth will destroy everything you have built and worked so hard for. The entire journey will then have been for nothing. Therefore, do not make haste but take all the time you need. As you know, the meaning of "time" within the Duat is quite different from our earthly concept. This is about your own time and your own hour and it takes as long as it needs.

Suddenly you have become aware that the Twelfth Hour is not about the birth of the light into the outside, in the day world. What all of these hours have really been about is the birth within, into your own spiritual world. This is the reversed process, which is reflected in the way Râ travels through the body of the serpent "Life of the Gods" (No. 869). This process starts in the tail, goes through the body and exits through the mouth. In other words, it progresses from the below, or the world of the living, to the above, or the world of the Divine. This is in contrast to the conventional birthing process that advances from the Divine (head) to the material world (tail). Hence, the essence of this birthing process is not only to transform old age and decay into rejuvenation and renewal. It actually is about the birth and the activation of the highest light, the Divine Spark, into your being. And yes, this sparkling vibration gives your soul a renewed and revitalised vibe.

Naturally, it is not intended for the Divine Spark, the *Akh*, to shine directly into your soul. This would burnout your entire physical system and make the continuation of the earthly life impossible. Without the limitations of the body, you melt together with the *Akh*. This also means that you are unable to ascend through the *âryt* gate at the end of this hour since your physical vessel would be no more. Thankfully, this is where the Higher Self steps in and acts as your guardian angel where he absorbs all of the radiation for you. Subsequently, he allows small doses of the shining light to enter into your soul at a rate that your physical vessel is able to handle.

Along your journey, not only have you expanded your consciousness, but your body has joined in the transformation as well. It has become more transparent due to the connection with the Higher Self and the inner cleanup you have experienced. The contact with the Powerself has given it a better foundation and more power. Due to this overall development on the spiritual, emotional, mental and physical level, your spiritual body is given room to develop itself. It has already grown into a vast magical forcefield that is strongly resonating and vibrating with dynamic power. This means that you have become capable of withstanding the higher energetic voltage. Thus, you have transformed in an ideal nutrient medium for the Divine Spark.

> Rise up, stride with thy legs,
> O mighty one of strength!
> Thou sittest at the head of the Gods,
> And thou doest what Osiris did
> in the House of the Prince in Anu.
> Thou hast received thy *Sâhu*.
> Thy foot slips not in heaven,
> Thou art not repulsed on earth.
> Thou are a spirit *(Akh)*.[13]

Consider this hour a very special moment wherein you finish your final development and hone your inner contact with the Higher Self even further. As you turn the focus inwards, you experience intense moments during which your soul is deeply inspired. You are always receiving an outer confirmation of these inner experiences so that you will know that the things you have encountered in your unseen world were absolutely real. You perceive this form of synchronicity within this hour more powerfully and vividly than you have had in any of the previous hours.

Through your connection with the Higher Self over the hours, you have established a firm contact with the Powerself. You have familiarised yourself with this lingering power step by step. Consequently, you are finally truly beginning to comprehend what this inner power entails. It is a mighty and neutral force. You and you alone have the choice how to express this power. You could choose to act upon your self-centred desires in an effort to raise your power and dominion. This will then be achieved via any means necessary. In that case, your power is expressed as the uncontrolled raw power of the roaring lion of the Sixth Hour. In that particular hour, you learned to surrender yourself to the Divine Will of the Higher Self. Through this Higher Will the Powerself has established a completely different impact over the hours. His power expresses itself now in dignity, strength, integrity, self respect, potentiality and creativity. This is the representation of Divine rulership and manifests itself by means of mastery and control over your own life as opposed to having power over the lives of others. The Powerself, who is now at the service of the Divine, takes the role of the guardian of the Divine Law of *Maât*; Truth, Order and Justice. Through his powerful influx, you receive the strength and backbone to act in accordance with this sacred Law.

Thus, the Twelfth Hour is a time during which you gain beautiful realisations that are the result of the inner Wisdom and Knowledge that you have made your own. It is a wonderful time where you are surrounded and embraced by an ambience of clarity, beauty and serenity. It makes you feel like the goal of your journey has finally been realised. However, nothing could be further from the truth. As you know by now, the Duat always makes you see and experience two sides of life in order to stimulate the development of consciousness. This growth process has yet to reach its highest point. To come to this point, you have to complete the most intense and vigorous test of the entire voyage yet.

The profound unity you have experienced with the inner Sungod is now rudely disturbed. The Higher Self takes a step back, which results in the disappearance of his entire presence. There you are, once again, completely alone. No matter how hard you try to re-establish the contact, the inner Voice remains silent. Although you have experienced this loneliness before during previous hours, you are not prepared for the hollow feeling of emptiness that you wound up in now. There is nothing to hold on to, no reassurance, only complete desertion and abandonment that has left you completely on your own. It would almost seem like a cruel joke after everything you have been through. However, this is a test to confirm and validate your unreserved dedication and faith in the inner Sungod.

Therefore, the guiding light of the inner Sungod is temporarily extinguished, resulting in a thick darkness. This deep Dark Night of the Soul is so poignant that it would almost seem as if you have a genuine hole in your soul. Within this emptiness, everything is taken from you that could hinder the upcoming birthing process. It is a process of dying wherein both the heart and soul are cleansed. This is where the actual passing away of the old self takes place, a process that you have to complete.

This is reflected in the moment during which Râ's body is pulled through the body of "Life of the Gods" (No. 869). His old appearance undergoes its final transformation so he can finally change into Khepri. Within the body of the serpent, Râ is shrouded in complete darkness with nothing to hold on to. The twelve towing Gods (No. 857 – 868) are the ones that pull him through the body. They symbolise all of the aspects of the old consciousness that no longer serves a purpose and needs to be let go.

Do not rush this process, but take your time to bid farewell. Like an artist, you must take a step back to gaze upon the work of art you have created during the hours from a distance. Then you can see the bigger picture of the remarkable transformation you have undergone. This is precisely the insight and the awareness you need to free yourself from the darkness. No longer are your old vision and convictions in sync with your renewed knowledge and experience. They are only blocking you from moving forward. If you are prepared to leave the old self to die, you distance yourself from ignorance and your old truth that no longer abides the Law of *Maât*.

This process of dying allows the heart to transform into the True Heart, which is the seat of Wisdom and Knowledge. The inner connection has now become stable due to your persistence and trust, your own True Faith. The Divine Spark has now gained a bigger opening through the Higher Self into your True Heart. That is the moment where the darkness is cracked open to allow the Divine Spark to strike into your heart like a thunderbolt without the risk of an internal shortcut. His radiance gives you the wings to become a Winged One. Your True Heart now begins to beat and pump Love through your veins. After an extensive slumber, you open your Eyes to give rise to the Great Awakening.

The Sun-folk celebrate this special moment and welcome you as a "Justified One". They honour you and bow before you in joy. You have now allowed the shining light into your True Heart and become one of the Sun-folk.

> In the happy night, in secret,
> when non saw me,
> nor I beheld aught,
> without light or guide,
> save that which burned in my heart.[14]
> – Saint John of the Cross

Hence, the road through the Duat is the Way of the True Heart that opens along the way. In the Sixth Hour, Thoth (No. 440) had already mentioned the opening of the True Heart in a subtle way. The Ibis he carried is a reference to the heart since the word "heart" was sometimes written with an ibis. Thus, Thoth symbolically held the True Heart in his hands that has been weighed during your voyage. Now, it has been transformed in the True Heart through your unconditional submission to your inner light. It is this heart you may follow at all times to truly express your purpose in Life.

> Follow thine Heart during thy lifetime;
> do not more than is commanded thee.
> Diminish not the time of following
> the Heart;
> it is abhorred of the Soul,
> that its time (of ease) be taken away.
> Shorten not the daytime more than
> is needful to maintain thine house.
> When riches are gained, follow the Heart;
> for riches are of no avail if one be weary.[15]
> – The instruction of Ptahhotep

It is the True Heart that holds the seat for the heightened consciousness and it overflows with Love. This Divine Love has healed the inner dismemberment and is the building block of life.

It embodies the most powerful force in the world. However, this Love should not be confused with personal sentimental love. It is not about "feeling happy" or "feeling loved". It is not a love that needs to be displayed on the outside. In fact, it is a silent underlying power that you carry around inside your heart. It makes itself known through your actions without the need to prove itself. We are concerned here with the rightful Divine Love expressed through the heightened consciousness in accordance with the Divine Law of *Maât*.

> Now love is not emotion. It is an attitude of the mind and the spirit which can be as cold as ice for the benefit of the loved one. You wouldn't want to be operated on by a surgeon with a blunt scalpel, would you? Yet many people think of love in that way; they're emotionally, not mentally, affected. They say they love a person because they feel emotion. But that's not love; it's simply power going out, emotional power going out from them. It isn't love. It may be selfish power; it may be smother love. It depends entirely upon how our love ideal is balanced.
> – W.E. Butler[16]

This inner birth prepares the ground for the next birth to be expressed into the outside world. You have received your wings that you need to ascend into the day world. However, ideally you would like to remain within this ambience and stay far from the outside world. Somehow, nothing seems more appealing then to become a recluse and start a solitary life somewhere in the middle of nowhere. Still, this is not your purpose. The initiation serves only one goal, which is for you to take responsibility for your own life. This means you have to live in the here and now, both feet on the ground with rolled up sleeves to express your potential. An Initiation means your responsibility will only increase, magnifying the weight on your shoulders. You are now accountable for all of your actions since your insight has increased and you are fully aware of the implications of your actions. You can no longer hide behind others, for you have to stand for who you are. This action actually makes it possible for you to stand in the moment and embrace your potential. These are your gifts and talents that differentiate you from others and enable you to make a difference.

Now you know you have received your wings for a reason. Wings are meant to fly, into the open world, and to emanate the light they contain. Of course, you are allowed to enjoy the beautiful and serene atmosphere before you are ready to fly out. However, when the time comes, do fly out to set your own birth in motion. Go along with the birthing process in a "smooth" fashion without wrangling or resistance. Why would you make it unnecessarily difficult for yourself? After all, the inner connection you have created will resume existing even in the life of everyday. It does not end when you leave the Duat. You will maintain access to both worlds at all times.

The thirteen towing Goddesses (No. 870 –

882) are the escorts of the birthing process into the day world. Each of them represents an aspect of the renewal, which is reflected in their names. Once you have identified yourself properly with each one of them, the moment has arrived to emerge from the nurturing waters of Nun. The final *ârryt* gate is open. Once you go through, you leave the Duat following twelve inspiring hours. After leaving the narrow space within the body of "Life of the Gods", you enter a vast expansion. Both Shu and Osiris support you during your ascend into the day world. Additionally, they gift you the Breath of Life with which you can fill your lungs. The moment you exhale is the moment you truly enter the outside world and become reconnected with the physical and earthly life. The vast turquoise sky above you has absorbed the light of the sparkling stars of the sky Goddess Nut. However, you know through the Knowledge you have gained, though the Divine light might not always be visible, it is always there. Permanently shining down on you.

During the Ninth Hour you took your rightful place as lord and master upon the throne of your inner world. From now on, you are the pharaoh of not only your inner, but also of your outer land. Before you ascend the throne of your outer land, you have to renew your oath and promise to serve and subject yourself to your inner Sungod. You will continue to abide by this oath in your inner world as well as in your actions in real life. You now bear the responsibility for both worlds and are capable of reigning your own life with the crook and the fail. From this day forward, you, and you alone, are the creator of your whole universe and carry the responsibilities in your own two hands. As a worthy pharaoh, you are sitting on the throne that is made of the power of the Powerself. On your head you are wearing the crown of the Higher Self that is now shining with the light of the Divine Spark. In your hands you are balancing the scales of Order, Justice and Truth. From this equilibrium between opposites, you, as a conscious co-creator of the universe, give shape to your own potential in accordance with the Divine Law of *Maât*.

No one but you can tell you how the miracle presents itself within you. It is an occurrence that is reserved for your private experience only. It is your own unique journey, for every human being has to walk their own unique path. This might give you the idea, from an earthly perspective, that it is a lonely path. From time to time you might actually intensely experience it as such. However, from a heightened perspective you are also able to connect indirectly with the Divine Spark through the Higher Self, giving you the feeling of coming Home. These sensations of both loneliness and feeling at Home alternate with each other, for even after the Initiation you will not be continuously aware of the Shining Light of the heightened consciousness. You have to continue to work on it despite the Wisdom and Knowledge you have gained.

Through your renewal, you have been lifted from your small limited world into the infinite eternity that is life. This is emphasised by the presence of the four Deities of the Ogdoad; Nun, Nunet, Heh and Hehet. They give you a sense of the vastness of the cosmos. There are no borders, no limits, only endless space wherein you can grow and develop. It transcends all times while simultaneously bridging them. This voyage you have experienced is only one stage of the eternal journey that never stops. Every soul, including yours, is an essential part of the eternal evolution of creation. Therefore, dare to grow into your greatness, to manifest true Mastery. The Day Sun barque is already here, waiting for you to start the First Hour of the next round. The following cycle in your development.

The beginning is light,
the end is Unified Darkness.
The course of Râ in the West,
the secret plans which this God
brings forth in it,
the excellent guide,
the secret writing of the Duat.
Which is not known by any person
save a few.
This image is done like this in the secrecy
of the Duat,
unseen and unperceived.
Whoever knows this mysterious image will
be a well-provided Akh spirit.
Always will he leave
and enter again the Duat,
and speak to the living.
A true remedy, (proven) a million times.[17]

The Sungod Khepri sits in the Sun barque in between the "Eye of the East" and the "Eye of the West" KV 6 Ramses IX

NOTES

PART ONE: INTRODUCTION

1. Theodor Abt, Erik Hornung, *Knowledge for the Afterlife, The Egyptian Amduat - A Quest for Immortality*, Living Human Heritage, Zurich, 2003, p 17.
2. Sir E.A. Wallis Budge, *The Gods of the Egyptians, Volume 1,* Dover Publications, New York, 1969, p 322.
3. Miriam Lichtheim, *Ancient Egyptian Literature, Volume II: The New Kingdom*, University of California Press, London, 1976, p 87, Hymn of the Sungod, from a Stela of the Brothers Suti and Hor, British Museum 826.
4. R.O. Faulkner, *The Ancient Egyptian Coffin Texts*, Aris & Phillips, Oxford, 2004, Vol. VI, Spell 714, §344, p 270.
5. Miriam Lichtheim, *Ancient Egyptian Literature, Volume II: The New Kingdom*, University of California Press, London, 1976, p 81 - 82, Great Hymn of Osiris, on the Stela of Amenmose, Louvre C 286.
6. Siegfried Morenz, *Egyptian Religion,* Cornell University Press, Ithaca, 1973, p 113.
7. R.O. Faulkner, *The Ancient Egyptian Coffin Texts*, Aris & Phillips, Oxford, 2004, Vol. II, Spell 108, p 105.
8. R.A. Schwaller de Lubicz, *Nature Word, Verbe Nature*, Inner Traditions International, Rochester, Vermont, 1990, p 102.
9. Dr. Heinrich Karl Brugsch, *Religion und Mythologie der alten Aegypter*, Leipzig, 1888, p 93.
10. Plato Epistulae II, 314 b-c.
11. James P. Allen, *Genesis in Egypt, The Philosophy of Ancient Egyptian Creation Accounts*, Yale University, New Haven, Connecticut, 1988, p 1.
12. Isha Schwaller De Lubicz, *The Opening of the Way, A Practical Guide to the Wisdom Teachings of Ancient Egypt*, Inner Traditions International, Rochester, Vermont, 1981, p 201.
13. Ibid., 202.
14. Terence DuQuesne, The Jackal Divinities of Egypt, From the Archaic Period to Dynasty X, Darengo Publications, London, 2005, p 83 and 402.
15. Sir E.A. Wallis Budge, *Osiris & The Egyptian resurrection Volume* II, Dover Publications, Inc., New York, 1973, p 134.
16. R.O. Faulkner, *The Ancient Egyptian Coffin Texts*, Aris & Phillips, Oxford, 2004, Vol. II, Spell 80, §33f - 34d, p 84.
17. Isha Schwaller de Lubicz, *The Opening of the Way, A Practical Guide to the Wisdom Teachings of Ancient Egypt*, Inner Traditions International, Rochester, Vermont, 1981, p 40.
18. Jan Assmann, *Death and Salvation in Ancient*

Egypt, Cornell University Press, Ithaca and London, 2005, p 302.

19. R.O Faulkner, *The Egyptian Book of the Dead, The Book of Going Forth by Day,* Chronicle Books, San Francisco, 1994, Spell 30 B, Plate 3.

20. Sir E.A Wallis Budge, *The Gods of the Egyptians, Volume 1,* Dover Books, New York, 1969, p 402.

21. R.O. Faulkner, *The Ancient Pyramid Texts,* Digireads.com Publishing, Stilwell, 2007, Utterance 217, §157, p 45.

22. R.O Faulkner, *The Egyptian Book of the Dead, The Book of Going Forth by Day,* Chronicle Books, San Francisco, 1994, Spell 30 B, Plate 3.

23. Erik Hornung, Theodor Abt, *The Egyptian Amduat,* Living Human Heritage Publications, Zurich, 2007, p 51.

24. Ibid., p 359.

25. R.A. Schwaller De Lubicz, *The Temple in Man, Sacred Architecture and the Perfect Man,* Inner Traditions International, Rochester, Vermont, 1977, p 32.

26. Erik Hornung, Theodor Abt, *The Egyptian Amduat,* Living Human Heritage Publications, Zurich, 2007, p 11 – 13.

27. R.O. Faulkner, *The Ancient Egyptian Coffin Texts,* Aris & Phillips, Oxford, 2004, Vol. VI, Spell 760, p 293.

28. R.J. Leprohon, *The reign of Amenemhat III,* PhD thesis, University of Toronto 1980, p 308.

29. R.O. Faulkner, *The Ancient Egyptian Coffin Texts,* Aris & Phillips, Oxford, 2004, Vol. VI, Spell 643, p 219.

30. Ibid., Vol. VI, Spell 644, §264a-e, p. 220.

31. Ibid., Vol. VII, Spell 1126, p 166.

32. Terence DuQuesne, *The Jackal Divinities of Egypt, From the Archaic Period to Dynasty X,* Darengo Publications, London, 2005, p 397.

33. Mark Collier, Bill Manley, *How to read Egyptian hieroglyphs* (revised edition), British Museum Press, London, 2003, p 54 - 55.

34. R.O. Faulkner, *The Ancient Pyramid Texts,* Digireads.com Publishing, Stilwell, 2007, Utterance 21, p 3.

35. Ibid., Utterance 210, §127a-b, p 39.

36. Terence DuQuesne, *The Jackal Divinities of Egypt, From the Archaic Period to Dynasty X,* Darengo Publications, London, 2005, p 390 - 391.

37. R.O. Faulkner, *The Ancient Egyptian Coffin Texts,* Aris & Phillips, Oxford, 2004, Vol. I, Spell 24, §74d, p 15.

38. R.O Faulkner, *The Egyptian Book of the Dead, The Book of Going Forth by Day,* Chronicle Books, San Francisco, 1994, Spell 17, Plate 8.

39. M.A. Patrick Boylan, *Thoth, The Hermes of Egypt,* Oxford University Press, London, 1922, p 60.

40. The Book of the Gates describes the journey of the Sungod Râ through the twelve hours of the night in a way similar

to the Amduat. However, there are notable differences in the texts and division of the Book of the Gates. In this book the crew of the Sun barque consists only of Sia, Heka and the Sungod and is towed by four male figures. The hours are inhabited by different Deities. At the end of each hour a gate is depicted that is protected by serpents and guardians. In this book the emphasis lies on the concept of offerings instead of knowledge, contrary to the Amduat.

41. R.O. Faulkner, *The Ancient Egyptian Pyramid Texts*, Digireads.com Publishing, Stilwell, 2007, Utterance 250, p 61.
42. Sir E.A. Wallis Budge, *The Gods of the Egyptians Volume 1*, Dover Publications, New York, 1969, p 40.
43. R.O. Faulkner, The Ancient Egyptian Pyramid Texts, Digireads.com Publishing, Stillwell, 2007, p 17 - 19.
44. Sir E.A. Wallis Budge, *The Egyptian Heaven and Hell; Volume I The book Am-Tuat*, Kegan Paul, Trench, Trüber & Co. Ltd., London, 1905, p 4.
45. Erik Hornung, Theodor Abt, *The Egyptian Amduat*, Living Human Heritage Publications, Zurich, 2007, p 24.
46. R.O. Faulkner, *The Ancient Egyptian Coffin Texts*, Aris & Phillips, Oxford, 2004, Vol. IV, Spell 277, §21a - 22, p 208.
47. M.A. Patrick Boylan, *Thoth, The Hermes of Egypt,* Oxford University Press, London, 1922, p 85.
48. R.O. Faulkner, *The Ancient Egyptian Pyramid Texts*, Digireads.com Publishing, Stilwell, 2007, Utterance 600, p 246.
49. R.O. Faulkner, The Ancient Egyptian Coffin Texts, Aris & Phillips, Oxford, 2004, Vol. VI, Spell 662; § 287j – 288a, p 234.
50. Ibid., Vol VI, Spell 610, §224h-i, p 198.
51. Ibid., Vol. V, Spell 325, §156b - 157, p 252.

PART TWO: THE TWELVE HOURS OF THE NIGHT

The First Hour "Water of Râ"
1. C. Manassa, *The Late Egyptian Underworld: Sarcophagi and Related Texts from the Nectanebid Period*, Harrassowitz Verlag, Wiesbaden, 2007, p 85.
2. Erik Hornung, Theodor Abt, *The Egyptian Amduat*, Living Human Heritage Publications, Zurich, 2007, The Title, p 12.
3. Miriam Lichtheim, *Ancient Egyptian Literature, Volume II: The New Kingdom*, University of California Press, London, 1976, p 108 - 109, Votive Stela of Neferabu with hymn to Meretseger; Turin Museum 102 (= 50058).
4. Erik Hornung, Theodor Abt, *The Egyptian Amduat*, Living Human Heritage

Publications, Zurich, 2007, The Title, p 18.
5. 1 schoenus is 20.000 cubits which is equal to 6,5 miles (10,5 km).
6. Erik Hornung, *Texte zum Amduat*, Éditions de Belles-Lettres, Geneva, 1986, vol. 1, p 114 - 126. Translated by: C. Manassa, *The Late Egyptian Underworld: Sarcophagi and Related Texts from the Nectanebid Period*, Harrassowitz Verlag, Wiesbaden, 2007, p 199.
7. Ibid., p 200.
8. Erik Hornung, Theodor Abt, *The Egyptian Amduat*, Living Human Heritage Publications, Zurich, 2007, p 28.
9. Sir E.A. Wallis Budge, *The Gods of the Egyptians, Volume 1*, Dover Publications, New York, 1969, p 417.
10. Erik Hornung, *Texte zum Amduat*, Éditions de Belles-Lettres, Geneva, 1986, vol. 1, p 126 - 129, 133 - 136. Translated by: C. Manassa, *The Late Egyptian Underworld: Sarcophagi and Related Texts from the Nectanebid Period*, Harrassowitz Verlag, Wiesbaden, 2007, p 202.
11. J.P. Allen, *The Ancient Egyptian Pyramid Texts*, Society of Biblical Literature, Atlanta, 2005, Utterance 228, p 87.
12. R.O. Faulkner, *The Ancient Egyptian Coffin Texts*, Aris & Phillips, Oxford, 2004, Vol. V, Spell 398, §149 b, p 35.
13. Ibid., Vol. VII, Spell 957, §173 e, p 89.
14. Ibid., Vol. VII, Spell 863, p 41.
15. Omm Sety, Hanny El Zeini, *Abydos: Holy City of Ancient Egypt*, L.L. Company, Los Angeles, 1981, p 148.
16. Pinch Geraldine, *Handbook of Egyptian Mythology*, ABC-CLIO Inc., Santa Barbara, 2002, p 170.
17. Sir E.A. Wallis Budge, *The Gods of the Egyptians, Volume 1*, Dover Publications, New York, 1969, p 462.
18. Terence DuQuesne, *The Jackal Divinities of Egypt I, From the Archaic Period to Dynasty X*, Darengo Publications, London, 2005, §201, p 178.
19. R.O. Faulkner, *The Ancient Pyramid Texts*, Digireads.com Publishing, Stilwell, 2007, Utterance 220 and 221, p 49.
20. Erik Hornung, Theodor Abt, *The Egyptian Amduat*, Living Human Heritage Publications, Zurich, 2007, p 40.
21. Sir E.A. Wallis Budge, *Amulets and Superstitions*, Dover Publications, New York, 1978, p 137.
22. R.O. Faulkner, *The Egyptian Book of the Dead, The Book of Going Forth by Day*, Chronicle Books, San Francisco, 1998, plate 32.
23. Sir E.A. Wallis Budge, *The Book of the Dead*, Dover Publications, New York, 1967, p cxii.
24. Sir E.A. Wallis Budge, *The Gods of the Egyptians, Volume 2*, Dover Publications, New York, 1969, p 92.
25. Erik Hornung, Theodor Abt, *The Egyptian*

Amduat, Living Human Heritage Publications, Zurich, 2007, p 34 - 35.

26. The Greatest City is an area of immortality that is located in the Afterlife. The blessed dead enter this City if they are able to successfully pass the weighing of the heart ceremony in the Hall of Judgement. As soon as they arrive in this City, they are released from death and able to live for all eternity.

27. Erik Hornung, Theodor Abt, *The Egyptian Amduat*, Living Human Heritage Publications, Zurich, 2007, p 37.

28. Ibid., p 41 – 42.

The Second Hour "Wernes"

1. The hieroglyphic word *Iaru* means "Reeds or Rushes" and is a reference to the Afterlife.

2. Erik Hornung, Theodor Abt, *The Egyptian Amduat*, Living Human Heritage Publications, Zurich, 2007, p 48 - 51.

3. Ibid., p 50.

4. Ibid., p 57.

5. R.O. Faulkner, *The Ancient Egyptian Pyramid Texts*, Digireads.com Publishing, Stillwell, 2007, Utterance 586; The king is urged to be like Râ, p 238.

6. Ibid., Utterance 478; Invocation of the ladder of the sky, p 165.

7. R.O. Faulkner, *The Ancient Egyptian Coffin Texts*, Aris & Phillips, Oxford, 2004, Vol. VI, Spell 491, p 133.

8. Ibid., Vol. V, Spell 458, §332, p 88.

9. Ibid., Vol. IV, Spell 330, §168 - 170, p 254 - 255.

10. British Museum EA 587; Offering formula from the funerary monument of Amenemhat.

11. Faulkner, The Ancient Egyptian Coffin Texts, Aris & Phillips, Oxford, 1973, Vol. VII, spell 936, P 71-74.

12. R.O. Faulkner, *The Egyptian Book of the Dead, The Book of Going Forth by Day*, Chronicle Books, San Francisco, 1998, Spell 159, p 125.

13. Erik Hornung, Theodor Abt, *The Egyptian Amduat*, Living Human Heritage Publications, Zurich, 2007, p 66.

14. Ibid., p 70.

The Third Hour "Water of the Unique Lord, which brings forth nourishment"

1. Erik Hornung, Theodor Abt, *The Egyptian Amduat*, Living Human Heritage Publications, Zurich, 2007, p 81 - 83.

2. Terence DuQuesne, *The Jackal Divinities of Egypt I, From the Archaic Period to Dynasty X*, Darengo Publications, London, 2005, §235, p 199.

3. Semwet (smwt); persons doomed to an unpleasant fate.

4. R.O. Faulkner, *The Ancient Egyptian Coffin Texts*, Aris & Phillips, Oxford, 2004, Vol. VII, Spell 991, p 99 - 100.

5. Sir E.A. Wallis Budge, *The Gods of the*

Egyptians, Volume 1, Dover Publications, New York, 1969, p 500.

6. Geraldine Pinch, *Handbook of Egyptian Mythology,* ABC-CLIO Inc., Santa Barbara, 2002, p 182.

7. Richard H. Wilkinson, *The Complete Gods and Goddesses of Ancient Egypt,* Thames & Hudson, London, 2017, p 18 - 19.

8. Jan Assmann, *Death and Salvation in Ancient Egypt,* Cornell University Press, Ithaca and London, 2005, p 284.

9. Heidi Jauhiainen, *"Do not celebrate your feast without your neighbours" A study of References to Feasts and Festivals in Non-Literary Documents from Ramesside Period Deir-el-Mediana,* Helsinki University Print, Helsinki, 2009, p 162 - 167.

10. J.C. Goyon, *Le Papyrus d'Lmouthès, fils de Psinthaês,* au Metropolitan Museum of Art de New York (Papyrus MMA 35.9.21) New york, 1999, p. 27 and pl. 1, col. 1. lines 2 - 5. Jan Assmann, *Death and Salvation in Ancient Egypt,* Cornell University Press, Ithaca and London, 2005, p 267.

11. G.A. Gaballa, K.A. Kitchen, *The Festival of Sokar, Orientalia* 38, 1 - 76, Faculty of Ancient Oriental Studies, Pontifical Biblical Institute, Rome, 1969, p 2 - 13, 52 - 53.

12. Jan Assmann, *Death and Salvation in Ancient Egypt,* Cornell University Press, Ithaca and London, 2005, p 318.

13. R.O. Faulkner, *The Ancient Egyptian Coffin Texts,* Aris & Phillips, Oxford, 2004, Vol. VII, Spell 816, p 7.

14. Erik Hornung, Theodor Abt, *The Egyptian Amduat,* Living Human Heritage Publications, Zurich, 2007, p 91.

15. Ibid., p 90.

16. R.O. Faulkner, *Ancient Egyptian Coffin Texts,* Aris & Phillips, Oxford, 2004, Vol. V, Spell 470, §399; Spell for reaching Orion, p 105.

17. The Epigraphic Survey in cooperation with The Department of Antiquities of Egypt, *The Tomb Kheruef, Theban Tomb 192,* The Oriental Institute of the University of Chicago, Chicago, Illinois, 1980, Plate 46.

18. R.O. Faulkner, *The Ancient Egyptian Pyramid Texts,* Digireads.com Publishing, Stillwell, 2007, Utterance 471, §921 - 923, p 160.

19. R.O. Faulkner, *The Ancient Egyptian Coffin Texts,* Aris & Phillips, Oxford, 2004, Vol. I, Spell 24, §74c-d, p 15.

20. James Teackle Dennis, *The burden of Isis, being the laments of Isis and Nephthys,* Forgotten Books, London, 2013, p 20.

21. Erik Hornung, Theodor Abt, *The Egyptian Amduat,* Living Human Heritage Publications, Zurich, 2007, p 94.

22. Ibid., p 94 - 95.

23. Miriam Lichtheim, *Ancient Egyptian Literature, Volume III: The Late Period,* University of California Press, London, 1980, p 112, The Great Hymn to Khnum, Temple of Khnum at Esna.

24. Sir E.A. Wallis Budge, *The Gods of the Egyptians, Volume 2,* Dover Books, New York, 1969, p 50.
25. J.P. Allen, *The Ancient Egyptian Pyramid Texts*, Society of Biblical Literature, Atlanta, 2005, Utterance 38, p 107.
26. J.A.R. Legon, *The Orion Correlation and Air-Shaft Theories, Discussions in Egyptology Vol. 33*, 1995, p 45 - 56.
27. Samuel A.B. Mercer, *The Pyramid Texts,* Pinnacle Press, 2017, Utterance 412, §723a, p 209.
28. R.O. Faulkner, *The Ancient Egyptian Pyramid Texts*, Digireads.com Publishing, Stillwell, 2007, Utterance 477, §959, p 164.
29. Erik Hornung, Theodor Abt, *The Egyptian Amduat,* Living Human Heritage Publications, Zurich, 2007, p 95.
30. Ibid., p 96 - 97.
31. Ibid., p 101.
32. R.O. Faulkner, *The Egyptian Book of the Dead, The Book of Going Forth by Day*, Chronicle Books, San Francisco, 1998, Spell 189, p 134 - 135.
33. *Igeret* is the Hereafter, the realm of the dead, also known as the realm of silence.
34. Erik Hornung, Theodor Abt, *The Egyptian Amduat,* Living Human Heritage Publications, Zurich, 2007, p 103 - 104.
35. Sir E.A. Wallis Budge, *The Book of Opening the Mouth; Volume I*, Kegan Paul, Trench, Trübner & Co. Ltd, London, 1909, p 143.
36. Erik Hornung, Theodor Abt, *The Egyptian Amduat,* Living Human Heritage Publications, Zurich, 2007, p 102.
37. Ibid., p 105.

The Fourth Hour "With Living Manifestations"
1. Erik Hornung, Theodor Abt, *The Egyptian Amduat,* Living Human Heritage Publications, Zurich, 2007, p 113 - 115.
2. Ibid., p 117.
3. R.O. Faulkner, *The Ancient Egyptian Coffin Texts,* Aris & Phillips, Oxford, 2004, Vol. VI, Spell 571, §172c-d, p 173.
4. Sir E.A. Wallis Budge, *The Book of Opening the Mouth; Volume I*, Kegan Paul, Trench, Trübner & Co. Ltd, London, 1909, p 9.
5. Richard H. Wilkinson, *The Complete Gods and Goddesses of Ancient Egypt,* Thames & Hudson, London, 2017, p 233 - 234.
6. R.O. Faulkner, *The Ancient Egyptian Coffin Texts,* Aris & Phillips, Oxford, 2004, Vol. VII, Spell 885, §97 (49), p 49.
7. Richard H. Wilkinson, *The Complete Gods and Goddesses of Ancient Egypt,* Thames & Hudson, London, 2017, p 235.
8. Ibid., p 200 - 201.
9. J. F. Borghouts, *Ancient Egyptian Magical Texts*, E.J. Brill, Leiden, 1978, Spell 123; An adoration of Horus, to glorify Him, p 83.
10. Sir E.A. Wallis Budge, *The Gods of the Egyptians, Volume 1,* Dover Books, New York, 1969, p 466 - 494.
11. R.O. Faulkner, *The Ancient Egyptian Coffin*

Texts, Aris & Phillips, Oxford, 2004, Vol. VI, Spell 762, p 294.
12. Ibid., Vol. VI, Spell 647, §268g-j, p 222.
13. Ibid., Vol. II, Spell 86 - 87, p 90.
14. Ibid., Vol. VII, Spell 822, p 13.
15. Erik Hornung, Theodor Abt, *The Egyptian Amduat,* Living Human Heritage Publications, Zurich, 2007, p 122.
16. Terence DuQuesne, *Spirits of the West,* Darengo Publications, London, 2012, p 10.
17. Ibid., p 14.
18. R.O. Faulkner, *The Ancient Egyptian Coffin Texts,* Aris & Phillips, Oxford, 2004, Vol. III, Spell 249; § 343, p 193.
19. Jan Assmann, *Death and Salvation in Ancient Egypt,* Cornell University Press, Ithaca and London, 2005, p 357.
20. R.O. Faulkner, *The Ancient Egyptian Coffin Texts,* Aris & Phillips, Oxford, 2004, Vol. III, Spell 241, §325g-h, p 190.
21. Erik Hornung, Theodor Abt, *The Egyptian Amduat,* Living Human Heritage Publications, Zurich, 2007, p 129.
22. Ibid., p 133.
23. Sir E.A. Wallis Budge, *The Gods of the Egyptians, Volume 2,* Dover Books, New York, 1969, p 300. I made a few alterations to the transliterations and translations of the list of the fourteen Ka's of Sir Wallis Budge.

The Fifth Hour "West"
1. *Khemyt* is the Goddess "The Demolishing One, who cuts the damned to pieces" (No. 356). She is standing at the end of the left riverbank, while facing the opposite direction.
2. Erik Hornung, Theodor Abt, *The Egyptian Amduat,* Living Human Heritage Publications, Zurich, 2007, p 140 - 142.
3. Ibid., p 144.
4. R.O. Faulkner, *The Ancient Egyptian Coffin Texts,* Aris & Phillips, Oxford, 2004, Vol. II, Spell 111, p 106.
5. Ibid., Vol. VII, Spell 825, §26h-j, p 15.
6. Erik Hornung, Theodor Abt, *The Egyptian Amduat,* Living Human Heritage Publications, Zurich, 2007, p 148.
7. Ibid., p 155 - 156.
8. Ibid., p 157.
9. Ibid., p 159.
10. Erik Hornung, Theodor Abt. *The Egyptian Book of Gates,* Living Human Heritage, Zurich, 2014, p 226 - 227.
11. R.O. Faulkner, *The Ancient Egyptian Coffin Texts,* Aris & Phillips, Oxford, 2004, Vol. III, Spell 242, p 190.
12. Erik Hornung, Theodor Abt, *The Egyptian Amduat,* Living Human Heritage Publications, Zurich, 2007, p 169.
13. R.O. Faulkner, *The Ancient Egyptian Pyramid Texts,* Digireads.com Publishing, Stillwell, 2007, Utterance 519, §1207, p 192.
14. Erik Hornung, Theodor Abt, *The Egyptian*

Amduat, Living Human Heritage Publications, Zurich, 2007, p 169.
15. R.O. Faulkner, The Ancient Egyptian Coffin Texts, Oxbow Books, Oxford, 2015, Vol. IV, Spell 312; Spell for being transformed into a divine Falcon, §81e-g, p 231.

The Sixth Hour "Deep Waters, Lady of the Duatians"
1. Erik Hornung, Theodor Abt, *The Egyptian Amduat,* Living Human Heritage Publications, Zurich, 2007, p 179 - 181.
2. Ibid., p 186.
3. R.O. Faulkner, *The Ancient Egyptian Coffin Texts,* Aris & Phillips, Oxford, 2004, Vol. IV, Spell 345, §369-370 and 375, p 280.
4. Ibid., Vol. VI, Spell 608, p 197.
5. R.O. Faulkner, *The Ancient Egyptian Pyramid Texts,* Digireads.com Publishing, Stillwell, 2007, Utterance 550, p 212.
6. Miriam Lichtheim, *Ancient Egyptian Literature, Volume I: The Old and Middle Kingdom,* University of California Press, London, 1975, p 203, A hymn of Osiris, on the Stela of Sobk-iry, Louvre C 30.
7. Jean-Pierre Corteggiani, *Une stèle Héliopolitaine d'époque Saïte, in Hommages à la mémoire de Serge Sauneron,* vol. I., Institut Francais d' Archeologie Orientale, Cairo, 1979, p 115 - 153.
8. Erik Hornung, Theodor Abt, *The Egyptian Amduat,* Living Human Heritage Publications, Zurich, 2007, p 190 - 191.
9. J. Assmann, *Death and Salvation in Ancient Egypt,* Cornell University Press, Ithaca and London, 2005, p 31.
10. Sir E.A. Wallis Budge, *The Book of Opening the Mouth; Volume I,* Kegan Paul, Trench, Trübner & Co. Ltd, London, 1909, p 16.
11. Samuel A.B. Mercer, *The Pyramid Texts,* Pinnacle Press, 2017, Utterance 373, §654a-d, p 195.
12. R.O. Faulkner, *The Ancient Egyptian Coffin Texts,* Aris & Phillips, Oxford, 2004, Vol. V, Spell 390, p 18.
13. Erik Hornung, Theodor Abt, *The Egyptian Amduat,* Living Human Heritage Publications, Zurich, 2007, p 195.
14. Ibid., p 200.
15. Ibid., p 193.
16. R.O. Faulkner, *The Ancient Egyptian Pyramid Texts,* Digireads.com Publishing, Stilwell, 2007, Utterance 215, §149, p 42.
17. Erik Hornung, Theodor Abt, *The Egyptian Amduat,* Living Human Heritage Publications, Zurich, 2007, p 207.
18. R.O. Faulkner, *The Egyptian Book of the Dead, The Book of Going Forth by Day,* Chronicle Books, San Francisco, 1998, Spell 175, Plate 29.

The Seventh Hour "Mysterious Cavern"
1. Erik Hornung, Theodor Abt, *The Egyptian*

1. *Amduat,* Living Human Heritage Publications, Zurich, 2007, p 217 - 219.
2. Ibid., p 220.
3. Ibid., p 221.
4. Ibid., p 222.
5. Ibid., p 223
6. R.O. Faulkner, *Egyptian Book of the Dead, The Book of Going Forth by Day,* Chronicle Books, San Francisco, 1998, Spell 17, Plate 10.
7. The sacred Ished-tree was the Egyptian Tree of Life located in Heliopolis. It was an evergreen tree and probably similar to the Persea, Tamarisk or Sycomore tree. The fruits contained the Knowledge of the Divine Plan and everyone who ate from these fruits would be granted eternal life. The name of the Pharaoh and the number of the years of his rulership were written on its leaves. The tree was associated with the rising sun. The Sungod Râ, in his form as the Great Cat, was the guardian and protector of this tree.
8. R.O. Faulkner, *The Ancient Egyptian Coffin Texts,* Aris & Phillips, Oxford, 2004, Vol. IV, Spell 335, §283 - 287, p 264.
9. J.P. Allen, *The Ancient Egyptian Pyramid Texts,* Society of Biblical Literature, Atlanta, 2005, Utterance 201, p 54.
10. C. Manassa, *The Late Egyptian Underworld: Sarcophagi and Related Texts from the Nectanebid Period,* Harrassowitz Verlag, Wiesbaden, 2007, p 31.
11. Rosalie David, *Temple Ritual at Abydos,* The Egypt Exploration Society, London, 2018, p 198.
12. Erik Hornung, Theodor Abt, *The Egyptian Amduat,* Living Human Heritage Publications, Zurich, 2007, p. 231.
13. Sir E.A. Wallis Budge, *Legends of the Egyptian Gods,* Dover Publications, Inc., New York, 1994, The legend of Râ and Isis, p 53.
14. J. F. Borghouts, *Ancient Egyptian Magical Texts,* E.J. Brill, Leiden, 1978, Spell 84, p 53.
15. R.O. Faulkner, *The Egyptian Book of the Dead, The Book of Going Forth by Day,* Chronicle Books, San Francisco, 1998, Spell 108, Chapter for knowing the Souls of the Westerners, p 113.
16. Erik Hornung, *Texte zum Amduat,* Éditions de Belles-Lettres, Geneva, 1986, vol. II, p 131.
17. R.O. Faulkner, *The Ancient Egyptian Coffin Texts,* Aris & Phillips, Oxford, 2004, Vol. VI, Spell 752; Spell for entering into the West daily in the retinue of Râ, §381e-g, p 287.
18. Erik Hornung, Theodor Abt, *The Egyptian Amduat,* Living Human Heritage Publications, Zurich, 2007, p. 237 - 238.
19. Ibid., p. 240.
20. R.O Faulkner, *The Egyptian Book of the Dead, The Book of Going Forth by Day,*

Chronicle Books, San Francisco, 1994, Plate 27.
21. Erik Hornung, Theodor Abt, *The Egyptian Amduat*, Living Human Heritage Publications, Zurich, 2007, p 241.
22. Text on the lid of the Coffin of Pa-di-Amun, Cairo Museum item no: 1160.
23. Sir E.A. Wallis Budge, *Egyptian Magic*, Cosimo Classics, New York, 2010, p VIII.
24. Erik Hornung, Theodor Abt, *The Egyptian Amduat*, Living Human Heritage Publications, Zurich, 2007, p. 232.

The Eight Hour "Sarcophagus of her Gods"
1. Erik Hornung, Theodor Abt, *The Egyptian Amduat*, Living Human Heritage Publications, Zurich, 2007, p 249 - 251.
2. Omm Sety, Hanny El Zeini, *Abydos: Holy City of Ancient Egypt*, L.L. Company, Los Angels, 1981, p 95.
3. Erik Hornung, Theodor Abt, *The Egyptian Amduat*, Living Human Heritage Publications, Zurich, 2007, p 254.
4. C. Manassa, *The Late Egyptian Underworld: Sarcophagi and Related Texts from the Nectanebid Period*, Harrassowitz Verlag, Wiesbaden, 2007, p 255.
5. Ibid., p 256.
6. Erik Hornung, Theodor Abt, *The Egyptian Amduat*, Living Human Heritage Publications, Zurich, 2007, p 261.
7. Ibid., 2007, p 263.

The Ninth Hour "Flowing forth of images, with living manifestations"
1. Erik Hornung, Theodor Abt, *The Egyptian Amduat*, Living Human Heritage Publications, Zurich, 2007, p 279 - 281.
2. Ibid., p 283.
3. Ibid., p 284.
4. Ibid., p 285.
5. Ibid., p 293.
6. R.O. Faulkner, *The Ancient Egyptian Coffin Texts*, Aris & Phillips, Oxford, 2004, Vol. VI, Spell 696, §330k - 331b, p 261.
7. Erik Hornung, *Texte zum Amduat*, Éditions de Belles-Lettres, Geneva, 1992, vol. 1, p 78 - 82. Translated by: C. Manassa, *The Late Egyptian Underworld: Sarcophagi and Related Texts from the Nectanebid Period*, Harrassowitz Verlag, Wiesbaden, 2007, p 168.

The Tenth Hour "Deep water and high banks"
1. Erik Hornung, Theodor Abt, *The Egyptian Amduat*, Living Human Heritage Publications, Zurich, 2007, p 301 - 302.
2. R.O. Faulkner, *The Ancient Egyptian Pyramid Texts*, Digireads.com Publishing, Stilwell, 2007, Utterance 670, §1975 - 1976a, p 285.
3. R.O. Faulkner, *The Ancient Egyptian Coffin Texts*, Aris & Phillips, Oxford, 2004, Vol. IV, Spell 307, §62a-b, p 226.
4. Erik Hornung, Theodor Abt, *The Egyptian*

Amduat, Living Human Heritage Publications, Zurich, 2007, p 307.
5. Terence DuQuesne, *The Jackal Divinities of Egypt I, From the Archaic Period to Dynasty X,* Darengo Publications, London, 2005, §340, p 254.
6. Ibid., §200, p 177.
7. Erik Hornung, Theodor Abt, *The Egyptian Amduat,* Living Human Heritage Publications, Zurich, 2007, p 312.
8. Ibid., p 314 - 315.
9. Erik Hornung, *Texte zum Amduat,* Éditions de Belles-Lettres, Geneva, 1994, vol. 3, p 717 - 731. Translated by: C. Manassa, *The Late Egyptian Underworld: Sarcophagi and Related Texts from the Nectanebid Period,* Harrassowitz Verlag, Wiesbaden, 2007, p 348.

The Eleventh Hour "Opening of the Cavern which examines the corpses"
1. Erik Hornung, Theodor Abt, *The Egyptian Amduat,* Living Human Heritage Publications, Zurich, 2007, p 327 - 329.
2. Miriam Lichtheim, *Ancient Egyptian Literature, Volume III: The New Kingdom,* University of California Press, London, 1980, p 112 - 113, The Great Hymn to Khnum, Temple of Khnum at Esna.
3. Erik Hornung, Theodor Abt, *The Egyptian Amduat,* Living Human Heritage Publications, Zurich, 2007, p 341.
4. Sir E.A. Wallis Budge, *The Gods of the Egyptians, Volume 1,* Dover Publications, New York, 1969, P 452 - 453.
5. Erik Hornung, Theodor Abt, *The Egyptian Amduat,* Living Human Heritage Publications, Zurich, 2007, p 343.
6. Ibid., p 345.
7. Jan Assmann, *Death and Salvation in Ancient Egypt,* Cornell University Press, Ithaca and London, 2005, p 28.
8. Erik Hornung, Theodor Abt, *The Egyptian Amduat,* Living Human Heritage Publications, Zurich, 2007, p 345 - 346.
9. R.O. Faulkner, *The Ancient Egyptian Coffin Texts,* Aris & Phillips, Oxford, 2004, Vol. III, Spell 202, p 163.
10. Ibid., Vol. III, Spell 205, §143 - 145c, p 167.
11. Carl G. Jung, *Man and his Symbols,* Bantam Doubleday Dell Publishing Groep Inc., New York, 1969.
12. R.O. Faulkner, *The Ancient Egyptian Coffin Texts,* Aris & Phillips, Oxford, 2004, Vol. VI, Spell 624, §241 f-h, p 207.

The Twelfth Hour "With emerging darkness and appearing births"
1. Erik Hornung, Theodor Abt, *The Egyptian Amduat,* Living Human Heritage Publications, Zurich, 2007, p 357 - 359.
2. Ibid., p 362.
3. Piankoff Alexandre, N. Rambova, *Mythological Papyri, Egyptian Religious Texts and Representations,* Bollingen Series XL - 3,

Pantheon Books Inc., New York, 1957, Papyrus of Djed-Khonsu-Ius-Ankh, Louvre, No. 3276, p 207.

4. R.O. Faulkner, *The Ancient Pyramid Texts*, Utterance 488, Digireads.com Publishing, Stilwell, 2007, p 174.

5. Erik Hornung, Theodor Abt, *The Egyptian Amduat.*, Living Human Heritage Publications, Zurich, 2007, p 364 - 365.

6. R.O. Faulkner, *The Ancient Egyptian Coffin Texts*, Aris & Phillips, Oxford, 2004, Vol. VI, Spell 694, p 259.

7. Ibid., Vol. VII, Spell 1065, p 142.

8. Ibid., Vol. VII, Spell 1029, §253 - 257, p 127.

9. Sir E.A. Wallis Budge, *From fetish to God*, Dover Publications, Inc., New York, 1988, p 153 - 155.

10. R.O. Faulkner, *The Ancient Egyptian Coffin Texts*, Aris & Phillips, Oxford, 2004, Vol. II, Spell 107, §118c - 119a, p 104.

11. Erik Hornung, Theodor Abt, *The Egyptian Amduat*, Living Human Heritage Publications, Zurich, 2007, p 377 - 378.

12. R.O. Faulkner, *The Ancient Egyptian Coffin Texts*, Aris & Phillips, Oxford, 2004, Vol. I, Spell 75, §349 - 350a, p 73.

13. Budge Sir E.A. Wallis, *Osiris & The Egyptian Resurrection Volume I*, Dover Publications, Inc., New York, 1973, p 136 - 137.

14. Saint John of the Cross, *Dark Night of the Soul*, Dover Publications Inc., New York, 2003, p 1 - 2.

15. Battiscombe G. Gunn, *The Wisdom of the East; The Instruction of Ptah-Hotep and the Instruction of Ke'Gemni: The Oldest Books in the World*, Forgotten Books, London, 2016, p 46 - 47.

16. W.E. Butler. *Lords of Light*, Destiny Books, Rochester, Vermont, 1990, p 60.

17. Erik Hornung, Theodor Abt, *The Egyptian Amduat*, Living Human Heritage Publications, Zurich, 2007, p 423 - 424 (closing text).

BIBLIOGRAPHY

Abt Theodor, Hornung Erik, *Knowledge for the Afterlife, The Egyptian Amduat - A Quest for Immortality*, Living Human Heritage Publications, Zurich, 2003

Allen James P., *A New Concordance of the Pyramid Texts*, Brown University, Volume I - VI, 2003

Allen James P., *Genesis in Egypt, The Philosophy of Ancient Egyptian Creation Accounts*, Yale University, New Haven, Connecticut, 1988

Allen James P., *Middle Egyptian, An Introduction to the language and Culture of Hieroglyphs*, Cambridge University Press, Cambridge, 2014

Allen James P., *The Ancient Egyptian Pyramid Texts*, Society of Biblical Literature, Atlanta, 2005

Allen James P., *The Debate between a Man and his Soul*, Brill, Leiden, Boston, 2011

Allen Thomas G., *The Book of the Dead or Going Forth by Day*, The University of Chicago Press, Chicago, 1974

Ashcroft-Nowicki Dolores, *The Sacred Cord Meditations, An Evolutionary Spiritual Journey using the Atlantean Rosary*, Thoth Publications, Loughborough, 2005

Assmann Jan, *Death and Salvation in Ancient Egypt*, Cornell University Press, Ithaca and London, 2005

Bierbrier Morris L., *The Tomb-builders of the Pharaohs*, The American University in Cairo Press, Cairo, 1982

Borghouts J.F., *Ancient Egyptian Magical Texts*, E.J. Brill, Leiden, 1978

Borghouts J.F., *Egyptisch, Een inleiding in taal en geschrift van het Middenrijk I & II*, Ex Oriente Lux, Leiden, Uitgeverij Peeters, Leuven, 1993

Boylan M.A. Patrick, *Thoth, The Hermes of Egypt*, Oxford University Press, London, 1922

Brugsch Heinrich Karl, *Religion und Mythologie der alten Aegypter*, J. C. Hinrichs, Leipzig, 1888.

Buck de Adriaan, *The Egyptian Coffin Texts I-VII, texts of Spells 1–1185*, The University of Chicago Press, Chicago, Illinois, 1935 - 1961

Budge Sir E.A. Wallis, *Amulets and Superstitions*, Dover Publications, Inc., New York, 1978

Budge Sir E.A. Wallis, *Egyptian Magic*, Cosimo Classics, New York, 2010

Budge Sir E.A. Wallis, *From fetish to God in Ancient Egypt*, Dover Publications, Inc., New York, 1988

Budge Sir E.A. Wallis, *Legends of the Egyptian Gods*, Dover Publications, Inc., New York, 1994

Budge Sir E.A. Wallis, *Osiris & The Egyptian Resurrection Volume I and II*, Dover Publications, Inc., New York, 1973

Budge Sir E.A. Wallis, *The Book of the Dead, (The Papyrus of Ani) Egyptian Text Transliteration and Translation,* Dover Publications, Inc., New York, 1967

Budge Sir E.A. Wallis, *The Book of Opening the Mouth; The Egyptian Texts with English translations Volume I & II*, Kegan Paul, Trench, Trübner & Co. Ltd, London, 1909

Budge Sir E.A. Wallis, *The Egyptian Heaven and Hell; Volume I The book Am-Tuat,* Kegan Paul, Trench, Trüber & Co. Ltd., London, 1905

Budge Sir E.A. Wallis, *The Gods of the Egyptians Volume 1 & 2*, Dover Publications, New York, 1969

Butler W.E., *Lords of Light, The Path of Initiation in the Western Mysteries*, Destiny Books, Rochester, Vermont, 1990

Clark R.T. Rundle, *Myth and Symbol in Ancient Egypt,* Thames and Hundson, London, 1978

Collier Mark, Manley Bill, *How to read Egyptian hieroglyphs* (revised edition), British Museum Press, London, 2003

Corteggiani, Jean-Pierre, *Une stèle Héliopolitaine d'époque Saïte, in Hommages à la mémoire de Serge Sauneron*, vol. I., Institut Francais d' Archeologie Orientale, Cairo, 1979

Cross Saint John of the, *Dark Night of the Soul,* Dover Publications Inc., New York, 2003

Darnell John C, Manassa Darnell Colleen, *The Ancient Egyptian Netherworld Books*, SBL press, Atlanta, 2018

Darnell John C., *The Enigmatic Netherworld Books of the Solar-Osirian Unity: Cryptographic Compositions in the Tombs of Tutankhamun, Ramesses VI and Ramesses IX,* University of Chicago, Chicago, 1995

David Rosalie, *Temple Ritual at Abydos*, The Egypt Exploration Society, London, 2018

DuQuesne Terence, *Spirits of the West*, Darengo Publications, London, 2012

DuQuesne Terence, *The Jackal Divinities of Egypt I, From the Archaic Period to

Dynasty X, Darengo Publications, London, 2005

Eaton Katharine, *Ancient Egyptian Temple Ritual*, Taylor & Francis Ltd., 2017

Faulkner Raymond O., *A Concise Dictionary of Middle Egyptian*, Griffith Institute Ashmolean Museum, Oxford, 1996

Faulkner Raymond O., *The Ancient Egyptian Coffin Texts*, Aris & Phillips, Oxford, 2004

Faulkner Raymond O., *The Ancient Pyramid Texts*, Digireads.com Publishing, Stilwell, 2007

Faulkner Raymond O., *The Ancient Pyramid Texts, Supplement of Hieroglyphic Texts*, Oxford University Press, Oxford, 1969

Faulkner Raymond O., *The Egyptian Book of the Dead, The Book of Going Forth by Day*, Chronicle Books, San Francisco, 1998

Flinders Petrie W.M., *Wisdom of the Egyptians*, British School of Archaeology in Egypt and Bernard Quaritch Ltd., London, 1940

Fortune Dion, *The Machinery of the Mind*, SIL Trading Ltd, London, 1995

Fortune Dion, *The Cosmic Doctrine*, The Aquarian Press, Northamptonshire, 1988

Gaballa G. A., Kitchen K.A., *The Festival of Sokar*, Orientalia 38, 1–76, Faculty of Ancient Oriental Studies, Pontifical Biblical Institute, Rome, 1969

Goyon J. C., *Le Papyrus d'Lmouthès, fils de Psinthaês*, au Metropolitan Museum of Art de New York (Papyrus MMA 35.9.21) New york, 1999

Gunn Battiscombe G., *The Wisdom of the East; The Instruction of Ptah-Hotep and the Instruction of Ke'Gemni: The Oldest Books in the World*, Forgotten Books, London, 2016

Hanig Rainer, *Groâes Handwörterbuch Ägyptisch-Deutsch*, Verlag Philipp von Zabern, Mainz, 1995

Hart George, *The Routledge Dictionary of Egyptian Gods and Goddesses, Second Edition*, Routledge, New York, 2005

Hays Harold M., *The Typological Structure of the Pyramid Texts and its continuities with Middle Kingdom Mortuary Literature, Volume I*, The University of Chicago, Chicago, Illinois, 2006

Heerma van Voss M.S.H.G., *Funerary Symbols and Religion*, J.H. Kok, Kampen, 1988

Hornung Erik, *Conceptions of God in Ancient Egypt,* Cornell University Press, Ithaca, 1982

Hornung Erik, *Das Grab Sethos' I, Artemis & Winkler,* Zürich, 1999

Hornung Erik, *Texte zum Amduat, Volume I,* Éditions de Belles-Lettres, Geneva, 1987

Hornung Erik, *Texte zum Amduat, Volume II,* Éditions de Belles-Lettres, Geneva, 1992

Hornung Erik, *Texte zum Amduat, Volume III,* Éditions de Belles-Lettres, Geneva, 1994

Hornung Erik, *The Ancient Egyptian Books of the Afterlife,* Cornell University Press, Ithaca and London, 1999

Hornung Erik, Abt Theodor, *The Egyptian Amduat,* Living Human Heritage Publications, Zurich, 2007

Hornung Erik, Abt Theodor, *The Egyptian Book of Gates,* Living Human Heritage, Zurich, 2014

Hornung Erik, Bryan Betsy M, *The Quest for Immortality, Treasures of Ancient Egypt,* Prestel Publishers, Munich, London and New York, 2002

Jauhiainen Heidi, *"Do not celebrate your feast without your neighbours" A study of References to Feasts and Festivals in Non-Literary Documents from Ramesside Period Deir-el-Mediana,* Helsinki University Print, Helsinki, 2009

Jung Carl G., *Man and his Symbols,* Bantam Doubleday Dell Publishing Groep Inc., New York, 1969

Leprohon Ronald J., *The reign of Amenemhat III, PhD thesis,* University of Toronto, Toronto, 1980

Lichtheim Miriam, *Ancient Egyptian Literature, Volume I: The Old and Middle Kingdoms,* University of California Press, London, 1975

Lichtheim Miriam, *Ancient Egyptian Literature, Volume II: The New Kingdom,* University of California Press, London, 1976

Lichtheim Miriam, *Ancient Egyptian Literature, Volume III: The Late Period,* University of California Press, London, 1980

Manassa C., *The Late Egyptian Underworld: Sarcophagi and Related Texts from the Nectanebid Period,* Harrassowitz Verlag, Wiesbaden, 2007

Mercer Samuel A.B., *The Pyramid Texts,* Pinnacle Press, 2017

Molen Rami van der, *A Hieroglyphic Dictionary of Egyptian Coffin Texts,* Brill, Leiden, Boston, Köln, 2000

Morenz Siegfried, *Egyptian Religion,* Cornell University Press, Ithaca, 1973

Naydler Jeremy, *Temple of the Cosmos; The Ancient Egyptian Experience of the Sacred,* Inner Traditions, Rochester, Vermont, 1996

Piankoff Alexandre, N. Rambova, *Mythological Papyri, Egyptian Religious Texts and Representations,* Bollingen Series XL - 3, Pantheon Books Inc., New York, 1957

Piankoff Alexandre, *The Litany of Re,* Bollingen Series XL - 4, Pantheon Books Inc., New York, 1964

Piankoff Alexandre, *The Pyramid of Unas,* Bollingen Series XL - 5, Princeton University Press, New Princeton, 1968

Piankoff Alexandre, *The Tomb of Ramesses VI, Volume I and II,* Bollingen Series XL - 1, Pantheon Books Inc., New York, 1954

Piankoff Alexandre, *The Wandering of the Soul,* Bollingen Series XL - 6, Princeton University Press, New Jersey, 1972

Pinch Geraldine, *Handbook of Egyptian Mythology,* ABC-CLIO Inc., Santa Barbara, 2002

Plutarch, *Plutarch's Moralia, volume V,* Harvard University Press, Cambridge, Massachusetts, 1984

Schwaller De Lubicz Isha, *The Opening of the Way, A Practical Guide to the Wisdom Teachings of Ancient Egypt,* Inner Traditions International, Rochester, Vermont, 1981

Schwaller De Lubicz R.A., *Esoterism & Symbol, Ancient Egypt, Science, and the Evolution of Consciousness,* Inner Traditions International, Rochester, Vermont, 1985

Schwaller De Lubicz R.A., *Nature Word, Verbe Nature,* Inner Traditions International, Rochester, Vermont, 1990

Schwaller De Lubicz R.A., *Sacred Science, The King of Pharaonic Theocracy,* Inner Traditions International, Rochester, Vermont, 1988

Schwaller De Lubicz R.A., *Symbol and the Symbolic,* Inner Traditions International, Rochester, Vermont, 1978

Schwaller De Lubicz R.A., *The Temple in Man, Sacred Architecture and the Perfect Man,* Inner Traditions International, Rochester, Vermont, 1981

Sety Omm, El Zeini Hanny, *Abydos: Holy City of Ancient Egypt,* L.L. Company, Los Angels, 1981

Teeter Emily, *Religion and Ritual in Ancient Egypt,* Cambridge University Press, New York, 2011

The Epigraphic Survey in cooperation with The Department of Antiquities of Egypt, *The Tomb Kheruef, Theban Tomb 192,* The Oriental Institute of the University of Chicago, Chicago, Illinois, 1980

Tiller William A., Dibble Walter E., Kohane Michael J., *Conscious Acts of Creation; the Emergence of a New Physics,* Pavior Publishing, California, 2001

Turner Philip J., *Seth – A misrepresented God in the Ancient Egyptian Pantheon,* A thesis submitted to the University of Manchester for the degree of Doctor of Philosophy in the Faculty of Life Sciences, 2012

Wilkinson Richard H., *Symbol & Magic in Egyptian Art,* Thames and Hudson, London, 1994

Wilkinson Richard H., *Reading Egyptian Art, A Hieroglyphic Guide to Ancient Egyptian Painting and Sculpture,* Thames and Hudson, New York, 1996

Wilkinson Richard H., *The Complete Gods and Goddesses of Ancient Egypt,* Thames and Hudson, London, 2017

Wilkinson Richard H., *The Complete Temples of Ancient Egypt,* Thames and Hudson, London, 2017

ILLUSTRATION CREDITS

Fig. 1., 3., 4., 6. – 9., 13. – 16., 18., 26., 28. – 30., 32., 34. and 36. From Rosmorduc, Serge. (2014). *JSesh Documentation*. [online]

Fig. 5., 10., 11. and vignette p 1, By Diana Kreikamp.

Fig. 2. and 22., Reproduction by Marly Mosterd, from Theodor Abt, Erik Hornung, *Knowledge for the Afterlife*, Living Human Heritage Publications, Zurich, 2003, p 18; fig. 10. – 11.

Fig. 12., From Theodor Abt, Erik Hornung, *Knowledge for the Afterlife*, Living Human Heritage Publications, Zurich, 2003, p 23.

Fig. 17. Ibid., p 36 – 37.

Fig. 19. Ibid., p 46 – 47.

Fig. 20. Ibid., p 56 – 57.

Fig. 21. Ibid., p 66 – 67.

Fig. 23., Ibid, p 78 – 79.

Fig. 24. Ibid., p 88 – 89.

Fig. 25. Ibid., p 100 – 101.

Fig. 27. Ibid., p 110 – 111.

Fig. 31. Ibid., p 118 – 119.

Fig. 33. Ibid., p 128 – 129.

Fig. 35. Ibid., p 138 – 139.

INDEX

A

Âba-sceptre. *See* Sceptre(s)
Abydos 74, 92, 242
Abyss 24, 85, 232, 243, 391, 392
Adoration 82, 171, 262, 268, 359, 381, 393, 394
Adoring Goddesses 97
Adoring Gods 97, 111, 171, 359, 381, 394
Adze 75, 164, 222. *See also* Seb Ur
Aesculapius 321
Âhâu 173
Air 23, 42, 84, 175, 191, 266, 294, 302, 323, 395
Aker 221, 359
Akeru 221, 226
Akh 22, 31, 32, 37, 38, 40, 44, 52, 140, 247
Akh-spirits 62, 79, 141, 173, 175, 249, 318, 331, 334
Akhet 25. *See also* Season(s)
Amduat
   Book of the Hidden Chamber 16, 21, 32, 35, 43, 53, 54, 62, 68, 69, 71, 91, 210, 285
Amenhotep II 17, 18, **19**
Amenhotep III 167
Âmmut 47, 338
Amniotic fluid 248, 384
Amulet 47, 103, 113, 143, 191
Amun 138, 334
Amunet. *See* Chaos Gods
Ancestors 33, 73, 120, 233, 245, 255, 262, 298, 356, 362
Ankh 20, **99**, 143, 321
Antechamber 91, 94, 100, 109, 114, 117, 120, 128
Anubis 49, 75, 97, 108, 129, 143, 154, 195, 196, 199, 204, 213, 242, 249, 337
Apophis 21, 86, 95, 174, 189, 221, 225, 261, 266, 267, 268, 269, 270, 271, 272, 281, 341, 342, 365, 379, 384, 388, 393
Arrows
   Weapon 106, 215, 301, 339, 342
Ârryt 91, 117, 341, 378, 387, 395
Art 54, 87, 372, 399
Artist 36, 180, 379, 399
Asklepian 321
Atum 42, 63, 85, 87, 103, 106, 224, 236, 239, 251, 267, 270, 274, 282, 294, 355, 362, 371, 391
Authority 29, 77, 87, 100, 113, 116, 132, 174, 202, 216, 235, 263, 265, 295, 300, 311, 393

B

Ba 21, 31, 37, 40, 140, 242
Ba-soul 44, 62, 63, 79, 80, 81, 127, 131, 242, 247, 291, 307, 316
Baboon 96, 110, 119, 154, 249, 336, 382, 390
Baboon-headed 132, 243
Backbone 163, 197, 242, 324, 356, 385, 395, 399
Bandages. *See* Wrappings
Barque of Millions of Years 252. *See also* Night Sun barque
Basket 108, 318
Beheading 242, 264, 320, 330
Big Dipper. *See* Ursa Major
Birth 33, 38, 68, 74, 103, 104, 108, 140, 172, 179, 222, 360, 362, 381, 391, 393, 397
Birth of Khepri 386, 392, 395
Birth of Râ 388
Blessed dead 66, 127, 235, 246, 345, 367, **386**
Body 31, 32, 37, 39, 41, 53, 79, 130, 132, 164, 166, 238, 241, 247, 249, 283, 303, 359, 366
Book of the Dead 48, 51, 77, 113, 143, 176, 252, 265, 271, 278, 283
Book of the Gates 78, 85, 87
Bow
   Weapon 106, 339, 342
Braided ones 124
Bread and beer 134, 149, 233, 318
Breath of Life 38, 99, 100, 169, 189, 192, 205, 266, 273, 292, 336, 339, 344, 360
Bull 83, 235, 296, 318, 360
Bull-headed 144, 215, 296
Burial chamber 17, 35, 155, 181, 187, 196
Butchers 215
Butler W.E. 401

C

Canopic Goddesses 107, 108, 188, 250
Canopic jars 108, 249
Cat
   Great 265
Cavern of Sokar 213, **217**. *See also* Sokar

Cavern(s) 61, 260, 288, 291, 300, 310
Chaos Gods 85, 390. *See also* Ogdoad
Chest 76, 113, 154, 213, 239, 254
Childbirth. *See* Birth
Circumcision 77
Clothing 106, 289, 297, 298, 303, 312, 319
Cobra(s) 92, 103, 110, 113, 116, 128, 133, 188, 263, 360, 361, 363. *See also* Serpent(s)
Cobra-headed 92, 107
Coffin 32, 35, 36, 107, 160, 164, 181, 188, 196, 213, 238
Coffin Texts 31, 43, 66, 70, 73, 74, 77, 84, 85, 86, 87, 102, 131, 134, 157, 164, 167, 169, 173, 186, 192, 198, 199, 213, 222, 238, 239, 242, 265, 273, 323, 332, 367, 371, 382, 388, 389, 392, 395
Consciousness **42**, 47, 49, 59, 81, 127, 237, 247
Coronation 65, 267, 294, 303, 311
Corpse 94, 154, 162, 176, 192, 240, 242, 246, 256, 263, 331, 337, 338, 368, 382
Corpse of Osiris 246. *See also* Osiris, body of
Cow 23, 78, 102, 106, 362
Cow-headed 215, 318
Creative Utterance 77, 87, 157, 180, 200, 201, 292
Crew 17, **72**, 99, 100, 133, 167, 194, 216, 217, 243, 268, 297, 316, 317, 338, 361, 383
Crocodile 47, 104, 106, 136, 190, 193, 212, 247, 257, 278, 283, 301
Crocodile-headed 97, 155, 248, 392
Crown(s) 196, 225, 235, 251, 332, 340, 355, 364
Cubit 244, 268, 384

D

Damned 17, 47, 62, 176, 215, 226
Dancing 78, 110, 119
Dark Night of the soul. *See* Soul
Day consciousness 44, 45, **56**, 59, 62, 119, 127, 373
Day of tying onions. *See* Onions
Day Sun barque 72, 85, 105, 378, 379, 381, 382, 388, 403
Death 16, 20, 25, 29, 38, 40, 47, 52, 61, 68, 74, 79, 94, 102, 108, 112, 127, 128, 134, 139, 154, 158, 170, 179, 189, 196, 204, 213, **241**, 242, 246, 249, 295, 319, 321, 335, 338, 366, 395
Death into life 21, 26, 32, 49, 53, 136, 159, 196, 224, 270, 334, 337, 364
Death of Osiris. *See* Death
Decan 141. *See also* Stars

Decay 25, 39, 52, 81, 108, 139, 145, 154, 187, 238, 337, 338, 344, 354, 366, 397
Deir el-Medina
   Place of Truth **36**, 92
Desert 61, 76, 95, 97, 111, 128, 164, 167, 184, 191, 193, 195, 199, 203, 353, 369, 374
Desert Goddesses 369, 374
Determinative 48, 54
Discernment 146, 172, 228, 280, 306, 325
Dismemberment 236, 242, 289, 334, 368, 372
   Enemies 368
   Osiris 26, 171, 196, 235, 240, 278
   Râ 166, 274
Divine Book 78
Divine Knowledge 47, 54
Divine Pavilion 107, 189, 337
Divine Souls of the West 204. *See also* Anubis
Divine Spark 44, 256. *See also* Akh, Transfigured soul
Djâm-sceptre 321. *See also* Sceptre(s)
Djed 157, 163, 164, 173, 197, 242, 385
Djet 26
   Goddess 357, 370
   Time 26, 354, 357
Donkey 144, 147
Donkey-swallower 124, 126, 144, 147
Double Crown. *See* Crown(s)
Double Lion 222, 228, 388
Dreams 30, 38, **56**, 119, 148, 204, 271, 282, 325, 370
Drinking of urine 366
Drowning 72, 149, 212, 278, 343, 349. *See also* Death
Duality 42, 69, 105, 118, 130, 142, 144, 146, 216, 226, 267, 270, 272, 277, 282, 321, 333, 335, 340, 358, 361, 364, 365, 373, 384, 390, 396
Duamutef 249. *See also* Sons of Horus
Duat 16, 21, 23, 61
Duatians 73, 100, 136, 141, 144, 145, 149, 152, 153, 174, 175, 176, 209, 232, 297, 322, 331, 339, 378

E

East
   Goddess of the 332
Eating faeces 176, 366
Eclipse 224
El-Assasif 167
El-Qurn 91
Eldest Magician 261, 269, 278, 285, 288

Electrum 321
Elephantine 171
Elite priests 30. *See also* Priest(s)
Ellipse 222, 332. *See also* Oval
Embalming 161, 164, 189, 196
Enemies 64, 74, 79, 116, 153, 171, 175, 215, 220, 236, 249, 251, 301, 305, 311, 337, 341, 353
   of Osiris 75, 145, 239, 263, 314, 365, 369. *See also* Osiris
   of Râ 106, 111, 130, 141, 152, 202, 235, 273, 299, 339, 393
Esna 106
Eternal Life 20, 26, 36, 74, 100, 113, 134, 139, 141, 199, 202, 256, 274, 300, 320, 327, 371
Evolution 27, 41, 57, 255, 390, 392, 396, 403
Execration texts 65
Eye 49, 157, 174, 189, 223, 235, 243, 254, 356, 371
   Left 139, 190, 197, 334
   of Atum 116. *See also* Atum
   of Horus 107, **198**, 199, 238, 334
   of Râ 20, 77, 78, 103, 107, 139, 157, 198, 199, 236, 272, 278, 311, 332, 335, 336, 357, 362, 371
   of Sokar 197
   of the East 333, 346, 352, 357
   of the West 331, 346, 352, 356
   of Wadjet. *See* Wadjet

F

Falcon 86, 160, 189, 190, 225, 262, 381
Falcon-headed 105, 138, 193, 219
Feast of Lamps. *See* Neith
Ferryman 318
Festival of Sokar 162. *See also* Sokar
Fields
   Gods of the 320
Fields of Reeds 143
Fiery Eye. *See* Eye of Râ
Fire 39, 72, 103, 110, 113, 116, 132, 141, 144, 175, 201, 210, 212, 215, 218, 225, 226, 241, 264, 267, 302, 320, 345, 353, 364, 368, 369, 373, 393
   pits 61, 368, 369, 374
Flesh of Sokar. *See* Osiris, Sokar
Followers
   of Horus 168
   of Osiris 314
Forbidden Land 49, 76, 88, 196, 199
Forcefield 88, 153, 273, 373, 391, 398
Forecourt 91, 117, 164, 181
Forty-two judges. *See* Judge(s)
   Negative Confession 66
Fourteen Ka's. *See* Ka
Frog 24, 390
Frog-headed 24, 390
Funerary ceremonies 154, 161, 191, 266, 343, 344
Funerary priests. *See* Priest(s)

G

Gate(s) 40, 67, 91, 111, 117, 120, 124, 145, 152, 166, 170, 184, 185, 195, 196, 202, 208, 209, 214, 220, 221, 225, 233, 260, 291, 293, 306, 310, 330, 352, 364, 373, 378
Geb 23, 60, 63, 85, 108, 132, 136, 190, 192, 212, 252, 295
Gereh. *See* Chaos Gods, Ogdoad
Gerehet. *See* Chaos Gods, Ogdoad
Give birth. *See* Birth
Giza 185, 268, 271
Going around the wall. *See* Memphis
Grain 133, 144, 318
   mummies 161. *See also* Grain
Great Awakening 31, 47, 373, 400
Great Ennead 63, 85, 87, 112, 113, 212, 239, 251, 295, 362, 391
Great hacking of the earth 161, 186
Great Pyramid. *See* Giza
Greatest City 115, 117
Guardian(s) 68, 76, 92, 109, 117, 121, 124, 144, 155, 170, 171, 174, 175, 188, 193, 200, 201, 213, 214, 222, 225, 241, 252, 275, 322, 337, 359, 369, 373, 375, 396

H

Hair 125, 159, 266
Hall of Judgement 39, 48, 49, 65, 66, 67, 84, 101, 138, 220, 313, 338
Hall of Maât. *See* Hall of Judgement
Hapy 249. *See also* Sons of Horus
Hathor 78, 98, 103, 138, 139, 190, 248, 361
Hawk 159, 164, 169, 249, 301, 339, 348
Hawk-headed 20, 131, 168, 212, 275, 337, 340, 380
He with living forms 264, 268, 272
Healing 56, 103, 137, 139, 190, 198, 236, 241, 283, 321, 331, 335, 347
Heart 37, 39, 44, 47, 48, 66, 67, 77, 79, 101, 138, 146, 241, 254, 312, 366, 400

of Râ 48, 84, 336
Heh 390. *See also* Chaos Gods; Ogdoad
   Chaos Gods. *See* Ogdoad
Hehet 390
Heka 87, 283. *See also* Magic
   God 78, 85, 87, 270
   sceptre. *See* Sceptre(s)
   Semsu. *See* Eldest Magician
Heliopolis 20, 42
Hell 23, 368, 374, 375
Henu 159, 181
   barque 160. *See also* Sokar
Hermopolis 390
Heru Hekenu **81**, 100, 133, 166, 194, 216, 243, 268, 269, 297, 316, 338, 361, 383
Heru pa khered. *See* Horus
Hidden knowledge 21, 245
Hieroglyphs 54
High Priest 28. *See also* Priest(s)
Higher Self 118, 178, 203, 252, 256, 324. *See also* Ba; Inner Sungod
   Inner Sungod 44
Hippopotamus 47, 86, 104, 297, 343
Holy of Holies. *See* Sanctuary
Honey bee 294, 364, 365
Horn of the West 91, 92, 117
Horrible of face. *See* Apophis
Horus 26, 65, 81, 83, 102, 129, 140, 161, 168, 169, 189, 198, 212, 225, 239, 240, 248, 252, 261, 262, 275, 295, 312, 322, 343, 365, 374, 381
   Khenty-Khety 138
   the Elder 24, 95, 108, 190, 191
Hotep 136, 217, 219
Hour Goddess 67, 98, 116, 117, 126, 152, 184, 208, 233, 261, 291, 311, 330, 353, 378, 386
Hour-watcher 357
Hu 77, 85, 86, 87, 100, 133, 166, 194, 216, 243, 269, 297, 316, 338, 361, 383

I

Iabet 114
Ibis 41, 48, 129, 172, 243, 254, 400
Ibis-headed 132, 172
Ichneumon 297. *See also* Mongoose
Identification 77, 169, 253, 255
Igeret 177, 330, 331
Ihy 248, 257
Image of Horus 189, 292, 302, 314. *See also* Horus
Imentet. *See* Goddess of the West

Imhet 88, 184, 200, 205, 208, 220, 232, 233, 234
Imsety 249. *See also* Sons of horus
In-hert 199, 236
Initiate 31, 35, 55, 136, 320, 364
Initiation 30, 31, 34, 49, 53, 145, 364, 401
Inner Sungod 118, 228, 399. *See also* Higher Self
Inner Wisdom 43, 48, 77, 119, 331, 347
Inpu 154. *See also* Anubis
Intuition 44, 55, 77, 118, 256, 282, 304, 372
Inundation 25, 71, 106, 126, 132, 139, 140, 146, 152, 153, 156, 165, 170, 171, 177, 184, 251, 301, 359
Isis 24, 26, 35, 52, 63, 66, 78, 83, 85, 101, 103, 107, 108, 112, 133, 139, 165, 169, 188, 190, 212, 214, 217, 220, 238, 242, 250, 269, 272, 273, 295, 363, 373
   of Imhet 113, 233
   of the West 219
   Tait 238, 256
Iteru 94, 124, 152
Iuf
   Flesh **79**. *See also* Râ

J

Jackal 40, 49, 74, 76, 97, 158, 175, **195**, 199, 204, 249, 338, 391
Jackal-headed 49, 74, 97, 143, 154, 337
Judge(s) 131, 138, 143, 146, 312, 325, 337
Jung C.G. 370
Justified 50, 67, 196, 245, 255, 311, 312, 313, 358, 382, 400

K

Ka 21, 31, 38, **39**, 40, 46, 64, 140, 164, 172, 192, 193, 235, 251, 359. *See also* Akh
Ka Maât 83, 100, 133, 166, 194, 216, 243, 269, 297, 316, 338, 361, 383
Ka Shu 83, 84
Ka-force 85. *See also* Vital Life Force
Ka-posture 85, 340
Kek
   Chaos Gods. *See* Ogdoad
Keket
   Chaos Gods. *See* Ogdoad
Khaibit. *See* Shadow
Khenty-Imentyu 75, 236, 340
Khenty-Khety 137
Khepri 16, 22, 37, 41, 43, 47, 81, 95, 103, 105, 138, 201, 212, 214, 217, 246, 252, 274,

294, 332, 349, 383
Kher-âha 239
Kherep wia 78, 87, 100, 133, 166, 178, 194, 204, 216, 243, 262, 268, 269, 297, 316, 338, 361, 383
Kherep-sceptre. *See* Sceptre(s)
Kherty 318
Kheruef 167
Khnum 132, 171, 359
King 95, 235. *See also* Pharaoh
Kite 169, 178
Kite-headed 169
Knife 101, 104, 126, 130, 131, 141, 144, 145, 146, 157, 172, 215, 234, 235, 239, 251, 264, 273, 274, 298, 306, 368
 Gate 185, 188, 195, 196, 202, 205, 233, 293, 294, 295, 296, 297, 300, 301, 302, 305, 306, 310
Knives
 Magic 104, 159, 198, 283
Know Thy Self 42, 43, 46, 64
Knowledge 35, 43, 48, 55, 58, 63, 67, 81, 120, 145, 153, 154, 284, 304, 336

L

Lake of Fire 61, 212, 220, 226, 229
Lamentation 159, 169, 170, 178, 214, 295
Land of Sokar. *See* Sokar
Lasso 215, 264, 273
Life of the Gods 384. *See also* Serpent Deity
Light of Râ. *See* Râ
Lightning 322
Lion 47, 129, 221, 227, 235, 254, 318
Lion-headed 114, 131, 201, 236, 262, 335, 347
Lioness 103, 114, 167, 199, 335, 347, 368
Living One of the earth 340. *See also* Khenty-Imentyu
Logogram 54
Lord of Entry. *See* Anubis
Lord of Maât
 Thoth. *See* Ka Maât
Lord of the Duat. *See* Osiris
 Osiris 26, 46
Love 52, 113, 170, 214, 327, 373, 400
Lower Egypt 29, 65, 95, 107, 138, 190, 235, 236, 239, 267, 294, 301, 333, 364
Luxor 17, 92, 102, 117

M

Maâ Kheru

True of Voice **67**, 311
Maât 29, 83, 101, 126, 128, 148, 202, 382
 Cosmic order 29, 32, 39, 47, 49, 78, 82, 83, 84, 101, 131, 138, 140, 157, 235, 311, 325
 Maâty 100, 105, 114, 174, 388
Mafdet 266
Magic 87, 145, 234, 261, 283. *See also* Heka
 Names 66, 67
 Net 88, 100, 167
 Power 26, 36, 112, 192, 202, 234, 261, 267, 269, 288
 Words 106, 215, 218, 270, 314, 327
Maiden 97, 300, 335
Many-faced. *See* Serpent Deity
Master of Secrets 337. *See also* Anubis
Mastery 44, 46, 65, 70, 100, 127, 145, 194, 264, 399, 403
Meditation 30, 32, 58, 117, 127
Mehen 264, 268, 269, 272, 281, 297, 300, 316, 333, 338, 361, 363, 373, 378, 383, 385
Memphis 159, 163, 185
Menit 102, 157, 196, 338
Meretseger 92, 117
Meskhenet 172, 179
Meskhtyu 164, 360
Middle Kingdom 65
Milky Way 41, 68, 72
Mongoose. *See* Ichneumon
Moon 139, 171, 190, 197, 224
 God 84, 139
Morning
 Ritual 163, 289
 star 225
Mourning 113, 159, 266, 295, 360
Mummies 130, 136, 164, 166, 173, 176, 181, 185, 196, 238, 247, 249, 301, 312
Mummification 32, 65, 79, 107, 154, 160, 164, 189, 191, 249, 289, 290, 313, 343
Music 78, 110, 114, 248, 295
Mut 103

N

Name of Râ 66. *See also* Râ
Natron 79, 290
Near death experience. *See* Death
Nebet wia 270, 297, 316, 338, 361, 383
Neferabu 92
Neha-her 261. *See also* Apophis
Neheb Kau 189, 191, 205, 385
Neheh

Time 26, 354
Nehes **86**, 95, 133, 166, 194, 216, 243, 269, 297, 316, 338, 345, 361, 383
Neith **106**, 156, 188, 238, 250, 339, 340, 364, 373
Nekhbet 65, 102
Nekheb 102
Neper 133, 134, 136, 139, 149
Nephthys 24, 52, 63, 101, 107, 108, 112, 133, 165, 169, 188, 212, 214, 238, 242, 250, 364, 373
Neshmet barque. *See* Osiris
Netherworld 23
Netjer
   God 32, 69, 334
Netjeru
   Gods **32**, 69, 82, 87, 99
New Kingdom 16, 17, 19, 36, 92
Nezat 318
Night consciousness
   Subconsciousness 127
Night of the Divine 162
Night Sun barque 21, 60, 72, 85, 95, 105, 167, 378
Nile 19, 71, 94, 124, 128, 139, 142, 156, 171, 196, 343, 391
   Valley 25, 143, 239
Nine
   Bows 342
Non-existence 25, 86, 128, 131, 223, 246, 261, 349, 357, 391, 392
Number Two 101, 105
Number Three 63, 105, 188, 241, 264, 266
Number Four 166, 177, 300
Number Five 246, 293
Number Nine 63, 74, 96, 212, 217, 235, 320, 362
Number Ten 293
Number Thirteen 396
Nun **24**, 42, 71, 72, 80, 83, 85, 91, 118, 140, 153, 156, 170, 192, 213, 224, 232, 251, 252, 261, 266, 301, 339, 365
   God 24, 248, 252, 391. *See also* Chaos Gods, Ogdoad
Nunet 390, 403. *See also* Chaos Gods, Ogdoad
Nut 23, 25, 63, 72, 73, 103, 108, 132, 190, 212, 213, 222, 248, 295, 384, 387, 388, 390

O

Oarsmen 318, 325, 393
Oath 327, 402
Offering(s) 33, 39, 40, 78, 134, 143, 145, 149, 162, 198, 219, 234, 245, 253, 289, 318, 338
   List 134
Ogdoad **390**. *See also* Chaos Gods
Old Kingdom 35, 75, 92, 236, 340
Onions 162
Onuris. *See* In-hert
Opening of the Mouth 75, 82, 158, 161, 163, 175, 180, 181, 185, 222, 360
Orion 145, 173
Osiris 21, 24, **26**, 33, 37, 43, 46, 63, 65, 66, 74, 75, 101, 103, 108, 112, 134, 139, 145, 152, 158, 159, 163, 169, 179, 191, 192, 196, 205, 212, 214, 217, 223, 234, 235, 236, 252, 256, 260, 263, 272, 274, 278, 295, 311, 312, 319, 331, 338, 340, 354, 364, 394
   Body of 169
Ouroboros 246
Oval 222, 236, 246. *See also* Cavern of Sokar

P

Paddles 393
Pakhet 167
Palm branch 141, 219
Papyrus 107, 131, 139, 142, 158. *See also* Sceptre(s)
   Sceptre 142
Paradise 105, 126, 131, 320, 322, 324
Peasants of Wernes 139
Pega-the-Gap 92
Peret. *See* Season(s)
Perfection 139, 166, 223, 354, 387, 390
Personality 44, 56, 57, 72, 77, 146, 325
Petry 356. *See also* Seer
Pharaoh 28, 35, 40, 65, 161, 167, 245
   Name 65
Phonogram 54
Physician 103, 154, 189, 198, 321, 336
Plato 35
Poison 116, 174, 189, 215, 221, 241, 270, 320, 321, 393
Poker 75
Potters wheel 171, 299, 359
Power in my feet 70
Powerself 46, 227, 324, 398. *See also* Ka, Vital Life Force
Prayer 10, 33, 64, 82, 100, 107, 114, 263, 268, 315, 318, 322, 327, 394
Pre-creation 390
Pre-dynastic period 65
Priest(s) 29, 43, 54, 75, 77, 82, 163, 242, 248, 284, 290, 337
Primeval serpent. *See* Serpent(s)

Primeval waters 24, 25, 390. *See also* Nun
Primordial hill 42, 186, 213, 224
Ptah 77, 103, 157, 180
Ptah-Sokar-Osiris 158, 159
Ptah-Tatenen 158
Ptahhotep 400
Punishment 65, 70, 132, 175, 215, 264, 273, 314, 336, 337, 338, 366
Pupil 145
Purification 102, 168, 178, 179, 210, 220, 229, 353, 369, 375
Purity 102, 239, 366
Pyramid Texts 23, 35, 40, 41, 50, 75, 78, 82, 85, 87, 102, 107, 114, 128, 130, 168, 173, 192, 225, 239, 242, 250, 266, 318, 331, 381
Pythagoras 43

Q

Qebehsenuef 249. *See also* Sons of Horus

R

Râ 16, 17, 19, 21, 24, 26, 30, 37, 41, 43, 44, 48, 59, 60, 67, 72, 76, 77, 78, 101, 102, 103, 164, 190, 192, 265, 274, 282, 354, 361, 365, 381, 395
Râ-Horakhty 218, 380
Ram 157, 299, 318
Ram-headed 20, 21, 38, 79, 86, 94, 99, 103, 132, 216, 301, 359
Ramesses VI 137
Rebirth 112, 158. *See also* Birth
Recitation 33, 64
Red Crown 107. *See also* Crown(s)
Regeneration 25, 30, 38, 53, 95, 105, 125, 139, 140, 158, 162, 213, 224, 233, 278, 299, 321, 339, 340, 346, 390
Region of turquoise. *See* Turquoise
Rekhyt-people 301
Ren 37
  Name 64
Renenutet 192
Resurrection 26, 47, 92, 102, 105, 125, 126, 128, 134, 143, 157, 158, 160, 173, 192, 196, 222, 247, 300, 331, 364, 382
Retrograde 54, 56
Reversal/reversed 56, 117, 184, 211, 368, 385, 397
Rigel 173. *See also* Stars
Right Eye 140, 190, 333, 334
Ro-Setjau 163, 165, 184, 191, 193, 195, 213
Robber/robbery 152, 157, 159, 166, 235, 278
Route of the Sungod 18, 210
Rowers 167, 317, 325, 339

S

Sacred oils 82
Sacred River 71, 94, 95, 124, 126, 133, 208, 268, 273, 330, 339, 346, 353
Sah 173, 179
Sâhu 80. *See also* Spiritual body
Saint John of the Cross 400
Saiph 173. *See also* Stars
Sais 364, 365, 373
Sanctuary 20, 29, 81, 92, 233, 255, 290, 365
Sand 71, 113, 154, 184, 185, 187, 208, 232, 291, 310, 332, 369, 374
Sandbank 261, 268, 274, 279, 381, 384, 385
Sarcophagus 17, 19, 31, 65, 181, 187, 196, 250, 274, 275, 281, 288, 298, 303
Scales of Maât 47, 50, 66, 101, 254, 307, 327, 402
Scarab 41, 47, 138, 239, 246, 247, 332, 383
Sceptre(s) 129, 136, 219, 251, 345, 366
Scorpion 83, 112, 188, 190, 192, 204, 273
Scribe 54, 78, 84
Season(s) 25, 84, 126, 139, 140, 141, 160
Seb Ur. *See* Adze
Seba 91, 121, 145
Second death 131. *See also* Death
Secret image(s) 119, 148, 191, 205
Secret Knowledge 64, 214, 269, 270, 304
Secret or Hidden Ones 358, 371
Secret path(s) 185, 200, 208. *See also* Zigzag path(s), Unapproachable path(s)
Sed 40
Sed Festival
  Heb Sed 40, 167
Sedge 294
Seer 356, 371. *See also* Petry
Sekhem-sceptre. *See* Sceptre(s)
Sekhmet 103, 128, 167, **335**, 347
Sepa 240
  Osiris. *See* Osiris
Serket 107, 188, 191, 192, 205, 250, 273
Serpent Deity 167, 188, 200, 215, 218, 236, 246, 249, 261, 264, 267, 268, 272, 281, 300, 339, 357, 363, 384, 393
Serpent(s) 105, 107, 108, 116, 184, 187, 204, 241, 251, 264, 265, 320, 326, 332
Serpent-sceptre. *See* Sceptre(s)
Seth 24, 26, 63, **86**, 94, 108, 112, 118, 129, 140,

144, 191, 196, 198, 235, 239, 240, 242, 267, 270, 271, 278, 282, 336, 345, 349
Seti I 36, 38, 137, 180
Shadow 37, 42, 62, 130, 153, 164, 215, 249, 297, 368
Shedshed 74
Shemes sign 298
Shemsu Hor. *See* Followers of Horus
Shemu. *See* Season(s)
Shepherds crook. *See* Sceptre(s)
Shining One 41, 142, 239, 244, 361, 372, 383
Shroud 238, 256
Shu 23, 42, 63, 83, 84, 114, 116, 132, 212, 222, 252, 294, 340, 383, 388, 390, 392, 395, 402
Sia 77, 85, 87, 99, 133, 166, 194, 216, 243, 265, 269, 297, 316, 338, 361, 383
Sidelock of youth. *See* Hair
Silence 92, 187, 201, 202, 209, 257, 375
Singing 33, 78, 81, 82, 110
Sirius 142
Sistrum 138, 149, 248
Slaughter 172, 320, 330, 365, 368
Slaughtering blocks 215
Sleep 59, 127
Smooth One who shines. *See* Serpent Deity
Snakes. *See* Serpent(s)
Sobek 106, 137, 155, 278
Sokar 158, 159, 180, 185, 195, 197, 204, 214, 218, 223, 224, 236, 237, 247, 339, 355
Sokar-Osiris 211, 219, 223
Son of Râ. *See* Râ
Sons of Horus 249, 256, 300
Soul 32, 39, 64, 79, 85, 130, 159, 295, 303
Soul of Osiris 173. *See also* Osiris
Soul of Sokar. *See* Sokar
Souls of Thoth. *See* Chaos Gods, Ogdoad
Sound 138, 149, 187, 200, 223, 301, 314, 360, 385
Spark of light 21, 154, 223, 228, 246, 355
Spears
   Weapon 342
Spirit 39, 85, 130, 190, 293, 345, 390, 398, 401
Spiritual body 79. *See also* Sâhu
Star Hour Goddesses 277, 278
Star Hour Gods 276, 277
Stars 23, 28, 41, 45, 61, 121, 141, 173, 190, 194, 225, 246, 275, 283, 353, 357, 360
Storm 86, 94, 153, 177, 293, 389
Stretching the Cord 194
Subconscious realm 44. *See also* Subconsciousness

Subconsciousness 55, 58, 59, 71, 73, 148, 373
Sun barque 72, 142, 275, 331
Sun-folk 382, 400
Swallow 144, 147, 272, 278, 298, 357
Swallower of forms. *See* Serpent Deity
Symbolic language 55
Symbolism 55
Synchronicity 370, 398

T

Ta Dehent 91
Tatenen 158, 251, 299, 303, 307, 311
Taweret 104
Tears 113, 116, 159, 178, 294, 295, 331, 334, 360, 361, 372
Tears of Râ 294
Tefnut 23, 42, 63, 85, 114, 116, 132, 212, 222, 295, 388
Temple 29, 33, 39, 43, 64, 65, 75, 78, 81, 91, 106, 108, 141, 160, 162, 194, 241, 289, 364, 373
Ter-sign 141
Thebes 17, 92
Third eye. *See* Eyes
Thoth 26, 48, 51, 78, 83, 85, 96, 154, 197, 204, 243, 252, 254, 270, 336, 348, 384, 390, 400
Three 301
Throne 112, 161, 256, 262, 263, 311, 327, 341, 354, 395, 402
Thunis 236
Tibetan book of the Dead 53
Time 352, 370, 397
Tit
   Knot of Isis 113
Towing Goddesses 217, 386
Towing Gods 194, 217, 298, 385
Transfigured soul. *See* Akh
Tribunal 84, 131, 143, 146, 311, 312
True Heart 47, 51, 254, 275, 311, 331, 382, 400
True inner Voice. *See* Ba, Higher Self
True name 64, 66
True of Voice
   Maâ Kheru 67, 311
Turquoise 125
   Ones 382
Tuthmosis III 17, 18, 71, 137
Tuthmosis IV 271
Twelve 96
Twilight zone 59, 91, 117
Two Feathers Crown. *See* Crown(s)

Two-headed-God 129, 142, 358

U

Unapproachable path(s) 191. *See also* Secret path(s), Zigzag path(s)
Unified Darkness 63, 117, 128, 224, 341, 361, 362, 364, 378
Unified darkness 133
Upper Egypt 65, 95, 101, 190, 235, 236, 239, 267, 294, 333
Upside down 176, 181, 365, 366
Uraeus 20, 74, 103, 114, 116, 144, 216, 275, 343, 345, 361, 365, 379, 383, 387, 393
Uraeus-Goddesses 379, 393
Uraeus-serpent(s)
   Deity 174, 263, 302, 319, 326
Ursa Major. *See* Stars
Useramun 17

V

Valley of the Kings 17, 36, 91
Venerated Ones 385. *See* Blessed dead of Râ 385
Venerated Ones of Râ. *See* Râ
Venus 225
Vital Life Force 26, 236, 314. *See also* Ka of Osiris. *See* Osiris
Vulture 101, 367
Vulture-headed 102

W

Wadj-sceptre. *See* Sceptre(s)
Wadjet 65, 107
Wailing 159, 178, 295
Wamemty 218, 220, 225
Warriors of Râ 341, 348
Was-sceptre. *See* Sceptre(s)
Water 24, 39, 94, 111, 126, 140, 156, 171, 175, 187, 212, 220, 226, 249, 290, 302, 343, 393
Wax 365
Weapon 100, 342, 348, 364, 393
Weariness of the heart 366
Weary 250, 365
Weighing of the heart. *See* Heart
Wenennefer. *See* Osiris
Wepwawet 40, 74, 99, 133, 166, 194, 216, 243, 269, 297, 316, 338, 340, 361, 383
Wernes 61, 124, 136, 138, 144, 149
West
   Goddess of. *See* Imenet
White Crown. *See* Crown(s)
Willow 196
Wind 28, 138, 153, 169, 339, 353, 360, 389
Winged One 31, 37, 51, 64, 255, 400
Winged serpent. *See* Serpent(s)
World-encircler. *See* Mehen
Worship 16, 34, 81, 113, 268, 311, 327, 359, 381, 394
Wrappings 238. *See also* Bandages

Z

Zep Tepi 42, 81, 87, 96, 212, 224, 236, 355, 362
Zigzag path(s) 187. *See also* Unapproachable path(s)

AMDUAT
The Great Awakening

Without any doubt *Amduat: The Great Awakening* is the most accurately defined, well researched and stunningly beautiful book I have ever read on the subject. Diana's grasp of the inner and spiritual nature of the journey is superb. This book is a very different and demanding presentation of an ancient teaching system.
—DOLORES ASHCROFT-NOWICKI founder of the Solar Light Video Club, retired Director of Studies of the Servants of the Light School and the author of over 30 books including *The Shining Paths, Illuminations* and *The Guardians Albion Trilogy*

"This is the most erudite, interesting and beautifully produced commentary upon, and ritual use of, an ancient Egyptian text by a modern occultist that I have yet seen."
—RONALD HUTTON, Professor of History, Bristol University, UK, author of 18 books, including *Britain's Pagan Heritage, The Triumph of the Moon: A History of Modern Pagan Witchcraft; Physical Evidence for Ritual Acts, Sorcery and Witchcraft in Christian Britain: A Feeling for Magic* and *The Stations of the Sun: A history of the Ritual Year in Britain*

"Thanks to years of scholarly research work by the author a secret has been revealed. For the ancient story of the Amduat is not only a cipher for the post mortem journey of Egypt's Pharaohs, but also a sophisticated and deeply complex system of spiritual development. And now, everything you need to practise this extraordinary system is in your hands, backed up by Diana's personal experience. This is your opportunity to walk the path of Egypt's Gods."
—HERBIE BRENNAN is a lecturer, a professional writer and the author of 114 books including *Death; the Great Mystery of life, Nectanebo* and *The Secret History of Ancient Egypt*

"Any student of the western esoteric tradition, theurgy, the work of the ancient Egyptian priesthood, or the process of initiation through the Mysteries would benefit from studying this book which presents a fusion of erudite scholarly research and illuminating interpretation of ancient initiatory lore. Symbols, terminology, and complex concepts are discussed by the author in-depth and with clarity of understanding. Diana Kreikamp has succeeded in bringing ancient, key, teachings to life in a way that will be practically useful to students in modern mystery schools."
—DR STEVEN CRITCHLEY, Director of Studies of the Servants of the Light School, wrote his PhD on Thomas Taylor the Platonist (1758-1835) and enjoys writing and teaching internationally

"Diana Kreikamp has done something very difficult. She has unearthed symbols (and indeed energies) from the very depths of Khem and painted them up onto the walls of our everyday consciousness. *Amduat: The Great Awakening* shows us how to approach the Great Journey we all will have, and how marvellous it will be. The book is beautiful, packed with imagery that lies deeper than any pharaonic tomb. At every Hour of the journey through the Amduat there is a new revelation of the sort that makes the reader cry: This is it! This is what I've been looking for! As a text it is far above anything else written by any modern author. Quite simply it is brilliant."
—ALAN RICHARDSON, author of *Priestess, The Magical Kabbalah, Al-Khemy, Aleister Crowley and Dion Fortune* and numerous novels in his local area, especially *On Winsley Hill* and co-author of *The Inner Guide to Egypt*